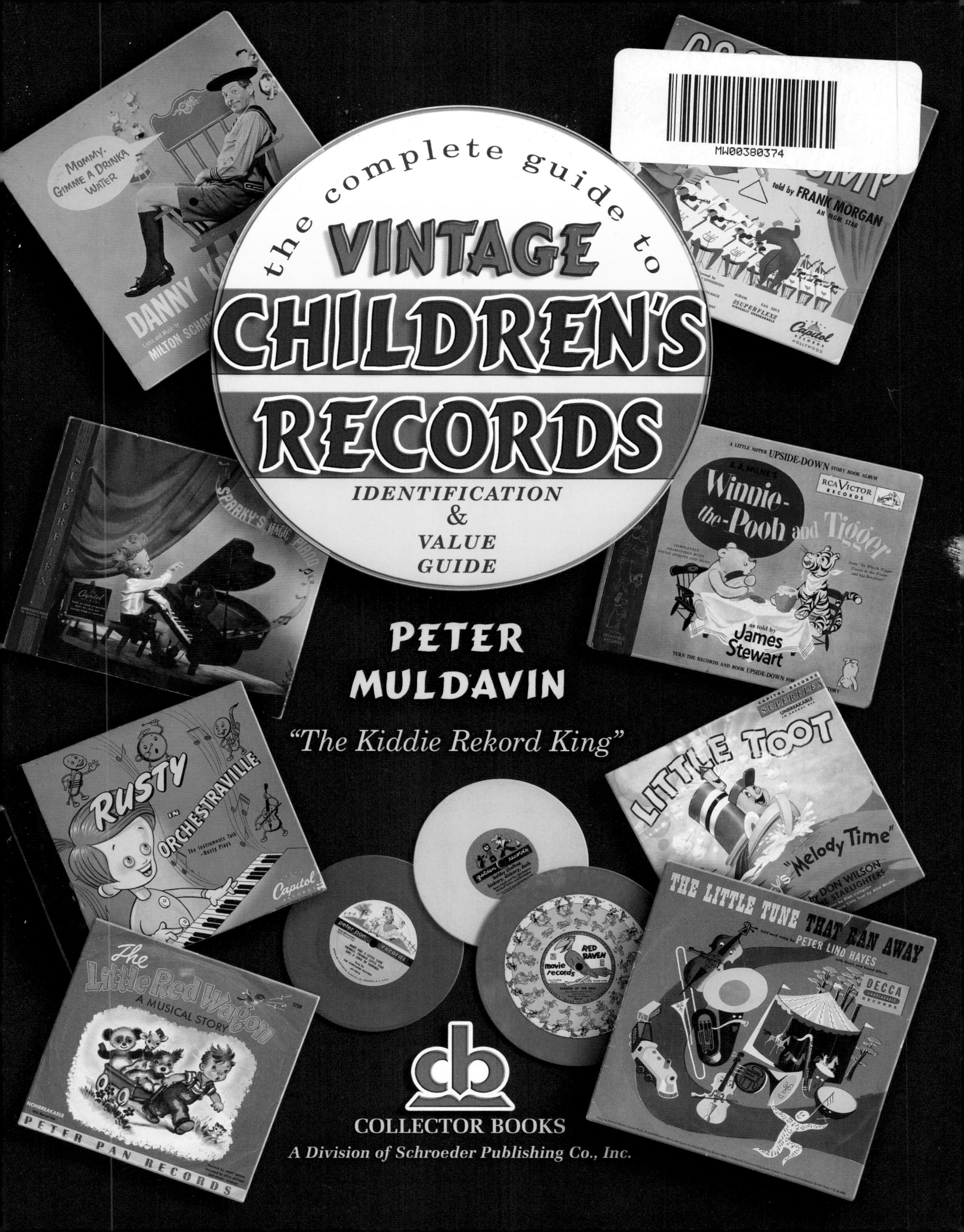


# the complete guide to VINTAGE CHILDREN'S RECORDS

## IDENTIFICATION & VALUE GUIDE

PETER MULDAVIN

*"The Kiddie Rekord King"*

COLLECTOR BOOKS

*A Division of Schroeder Publishing Co., Inc.*

On the front cover:
"Hickory, Dickory, Dock," Bobby Shaftoe, Golden Records; "Genie, the Magic Record," Decca Records; "Mommy, Gimme a Drinka Water," Danny Kaye, Capitol Records; "Mary Had a Little Lamb," Peter Pan Records; "The Churkendoose," Decca Records, Gossamer Wump, Capitol Records; "Rusty in Orchestraville," Capitol Records; "The Little Tune That Ran Away," Decca Records; "The Bear That Wasn't," MGM Records; "The Littlest Angel," Loretta Young, Decca Records; "The Carrot Seed," Children's Record Guild; "Farmer in the Dell," Red Raven Movie Records, Morgan Development Labs Inc.; "Manners Can Be Fun," Decca Records.

On the back cover:
"Tubby the Tuba," Danny Kaye, Decca Records; "Farmer in the Dell," Red Raven Movie Records, Morgan Development Labs Inc.; "Tina the Ballerina," Peter Pan Records; "Little Toot, Disney's 'Melody Time,'" Capitol Records; "Mary Had a Little Lamb," Peter Pan Records; "Sparky's Magic Piano," Capitol Records; "The Little Red Wagon," Peter Pan Records; "Winnie-the Pooh and Tigger," RCA-Victor Records; "Peter, Please, It's Pancakes," Children's Record Guild; "Bozo Sings," Capitol Records; "Hickory, Dickory, Dock," Bobby Shaftoe, Golden Records; "Funniest Song in the World," Groucho Marks, Young People's Records.

Cover design concept by Christine Chagnon
Cover design by Beth Summers
Back cover, author photo by Damon Muldavin
Book design by Barry Buchanan
All records shown in this book are from the collection of Peter Muldavin.
All photos of records are by Peter Muldavin.

COLLECTOR BOOKS
P.O. Box 3009
Paducah, Kentucky 42002-3009

www.collectorbooks.com

The current values in this book should be used only as a guide. They are not intended to set prices, which vary from one section of the country to another. Auction prices as well as dealer prices vary greatly and are affected by condition as well as demand. Neither the author nor the publisher assumes responsibility for any losses that might be incurred as a result of consulting this guide.

Proudly printed and bound in the
United States of America

# CONTENTS

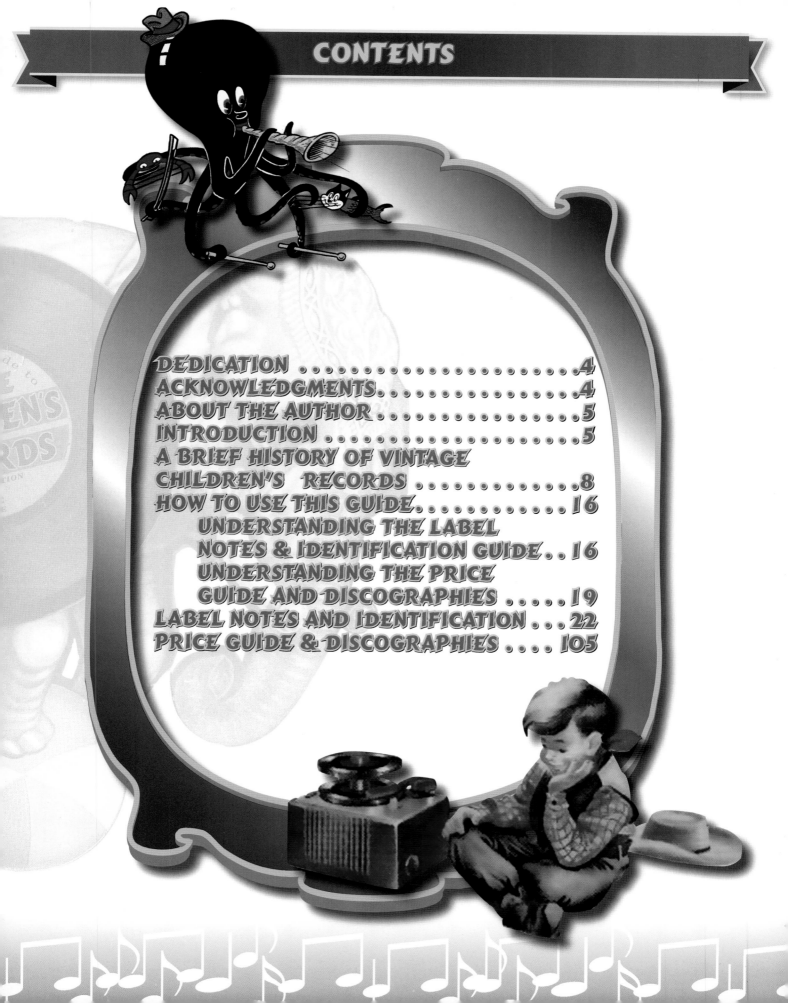

# DEDICATION

To my wife, Helene Krumholz, who in spite of giving up her personal closet space to "the collection" and dealing with untold hours of nonattention from me, has given unwavering support and inspiration for this project. She has always seen the six-year-old inside this sixty-something-year-old.

And to my mother, Beatrice Read, whose purchases of little kiddie records for my early birthdays and holidays surely planted the seeds for this endeavor.

# ACKNOWLEDGMENTS

This work is the fruition of more than 12 years of musing, imagining, hoping, and persevering. This is not to suggest that it has been a struggle. On the contrary, it is extremely gratifying and inspiring and humbling to be in a position to offer a reference book which is a first of its kind in the hobby of record collecting.

Countless contacts with fellow collectors, dealers, buyers, sellers, and assorted other enthusiasts have all contributed in some way to this body of information. I gratefully acknowledge the special input of the people named below. I am really just a custodian of the combined knowledge of all of those who have come before me and will, hopefully, come afterwards. For those whose names I have not included, it is not for lack of appreciation, but is rather an oversight.

Ron Antonelli (Lionel Records)
Peter Bastine (78-rpm picture discs)
John Bolig (Victor records)
Sam Brylawski, Jan McKee, and Mary Bucknum (Library of Congress, Recorded Sound Archives)
Bernadette Peters (RCA-Victor archives)
Don McCormick (Rogers & Hammerstein Archives of Recorded Sound, New York Public Library)
David Bonner (Young People's Records and many other obscure labels)
Christine Chagnon (conceived the design of my book cover — what a great job!)
Paul Charosh (Berliner Records)
Andre DeCerf (The Prince of Picture Discs)
Fred DeHut (Golden records)
Joe Franklin (legendary TV personality and my personal cheerleader)
Rebecca Greason (Golden records)
Marc Grobman (picture discs)
Gertrude Kimble (founder of Kimbo Records)
Judy Gayle Krasnow (daughter of Hecky Krasno, one of the premier children's record producers in the golden age of kiddie records)
David Lennick (Victor and other very old records)
Cy Leslie (founder of VOCO and Cricket Records)
Chuck Miller (the person most responsible for getting the database together for this book)
R. Michael Murray (Disney records, and with the publication of his book, a major inspiration and motivation for me in getting this book done)
Kurt Nauck (general expertise in all vintage discs; major encouragement for this work)
Peter Press (Record Guild of America — son of the founder, and great person)
Joan and Robin Rolfs (phonograph dolls)
Arthur Shimkin (founder of Golden Records)
Merle Sprinzen (Little Wonder records and Bubble Books)
Allan Sutton (record book publisher and inspiration for my book)
Ron Vlach (Talkie Jektor records)
Preston White (my webmaster and search engine optimizer expert)
All the contributors to Wikipedia, the free online encyclopedia
And last but not least, my editor, Gail Ashburn, and all of the great staff at Collector Books and Schroeder Publishing Company

# ABOUT THE AUTHOR

Peter Muldavin has that unique quality that makes a collector of children's ephemera successful: he is "sixty-something going on six." Peter has been a longtime collector of everything from baseball cards, stamps and coins, and antiquarian children's books to his current focus on vintage children's records. As with most of his collections, this one got started as a nostalgic pursuit of some of his most precious childhood memories, when in 1991 he came across one of his favorite records in a used-record store. It was "Said the Piano to the Harpsichord" on Young People's Records. But, when he looked for price guides and checklists to know what the value was, and what else was "out there," he found none. After his collection was well under way, he went to the Library of Congress to research the subject. He discovered, to his surprise, that he had more information on the field than it did. At this point, Peter's hobby became his "mission" — i.e., to list all kiddie 78-rpm records made in the USA. That goal has been realized with the publication of this book.

His current inventory of approximately 11,000 78-rpm children's records (not counting duplicates) is the largest of its kind in the world. He is acknowledged as the country's leading expert in this field.

Peter is always looking to buy, sell, and trade vintage children's records. Additionally, copyright permitting, one can request a custom-burned CD or download directly from his Kiddie Rekord King website. Click on the "Selling" page on his website for pricing and ordering information.

Peter can be contacted at 173 W. 78th St., New York, NY 10024; (212) 362-9606; e-mail: kiddie78s@aol.com or visit http://www.kiddierekordking.com/.

# INTRODUCTION

I am pleased to present this first "almost" complete identification and price guide to American vintage children's records. I use "almost" because collectors are still uncovering heretofore unknown labels and series that will be included in future editions. Just about every area of collectibles from our childhood other than this one has been covered by reference books up until now. For some reason, this important genre, common to the childhoods of most baby boomers, has slipped through the cracks. It has been my goal to end this oversight, a goal that I have been working towards for the past 15 years.

## DEFINITION OF A "VINTAGE" RECORD

The word vintage has some useful synonyms: antiquarian, archaic, classic, obsolete, olden, outdated. But to use these words to describe something to someone who was born in, say, 1945 as compared to someone who was born in 1975 results in totally different connotations. For the purposes of this book, "vintage" refers to records made primarily before 1960 — with a few notable exceptions. The focus here is on 78-rpm records — that is to say, records that play at a speed of 78 revolutions per minute on the turntable (as opposed to 45 or 33$^{1}/_{3}$ rpm, for example). For this first edition, I am limiting the listing to records made and sold in the United States. Future editions will cover records from other countries.

## WHY IS THE FOCUS ONLY ON 78 RPMS? WHAT ABOUT 45S AND LPS?

It is certainly correct to say that the word "vintage" does not apply only to 78 rpms. After all, as just described, "vintage" can and does have a different significance to each person. Also, there are a multitude of children's 45s and 33s out there, some quite "old." My choice to focus on just 78s (with some exceptions described following) is partially personal, and partially to limit the scope of this book to a particular era in our society — the baby-boomers' early childhood years. I was born just before the cutoff date, so my early experience with children's records was only with 78 rpms. The 45s didn't become widespread until the late 50s or early 60s, by which time the 78s were hardly being made. Thus it is for nostalgic reasons that I have chosen 78s as the focus. They helped fill up the kids' leisure time before TV took over.

I have included a few label listings that also show 45s. Without exception, they are series that issued 78s and then switched to 45s midstream, continuing the numbering sequence. Also, some series, such as Golden, mixed 78s and 45s together. As a general rule, any label or series that was wholly 45 rpm or $33^{1/3}$ is not included.

### WHAT THIS BOOK IS INTENDED FOR:

The purpose of this book is to provide relevant information to help identify both the physical appearance of the records as well as to give an overview of the extent of the production of the various record labels: the number of records issued, the year(s) issued, etc. By appearance, I am referring to the size and the color of the records, and the material from which the records are made, and various identifying features on the actual record labels themselves and on the covers, sleeves, boxes, and containers that hold the records. In this sense, I could have named my book a "field guide to the identification of North American vintage children's records."

### WHAT THIS BOOK IS NOT INTENDED FOR:

This book is NOT intended to provide detailed information of recording sessions, background information of artists and performers, or detailed histories of the record companies. For the major record labels, that information has already been made readily available in various books and publications. For the several hundred minor labels listed, there is simply little or no information available, at least from the standpoint of children's records.

### ACCURACY OF THE DESCRIPTIONS AND VALUES

The descriptive information of the physical attributes of the records and covers, as well as the number of different titles issued, is based solely on my verification of the information I have listed, either by direct observation from my own record collection or from records in the possession of a fellow collector or the record company itself.

Values of any collectible are often determined from a subjective, not a scientific, point of view. I have tried to take into account the usual parameters in establishing the values shown for this type of collectible. I rely on such factors as how old the record is, the fame (or lack thereof) of the performers, the subject matter of the recording, and the tracking of transactions by other sellers, eBay, or other auctions, as well as my own extensive experience in buying and selling children's 78 rpms. All prices in the photo captions are for records in EX/nMT (excellent/near mint) condition.

Note: You will notice that none of the photos list any credits or sources. That is because all of them are records from my own collection, with the photos being taken by me.

### WHAT CONSTITUTES A "CHILDREN'S" RECORD?

For the purposes of this book, what first comes to mind is to determine which age groups fall into this category. There would be little or no dispute to include ages 2 – 11. Over age 12 there may be some debate, but I have included young adolescents (12 – 15). Following are some generally accepted age groupings:

Age: up to 2 – 3 (toddlers)
Age: 4 – 12 (children)
Age: 13 – 15 (young adolescents)

All of the above age ranges can be considered appropriate "candidates" for kiddie records. The parenting magazines of the day offered a more detailed breakdown of the type of record content that would appeal to various children's age groups:

Up to 2 years: likes strong rhythm-music with a beat.
2 to 4 years: nursery rhymes, fairy tales, songs mirroring daily routine.
4 to 6 years: fairy tales, records with strong sound effects.
6 to 8 years: more advanced stories; songs about trains, cowboys, and comedy are appreciated.
8 to 12 years: less childish fairy tales, good habits and good manners.

These age ranges are subject to minor variations,

which may be influenced by determinants such as cultural and societal values.

## CATEGORIES OF CHILDREN'S RECORDS

The scope of the listings in this book is confined to children's records. The determination of what is actually a children's record, or a record that is meant to be played by and for children, will always be a source of debate.

The following list of categories is separated into two main sections: "Specifically for Children" and "Suitable for Children and Adults." At the end of the day, who is to definitively say who is a child? And what is to be said of the child within us who will enjoy many of these records at any age?

### SPECIFICALLY FOR CHILDREN

- Nursery rhymes and fairy tales, Mother Goose
- Lullabies, cradle & bedtime stories
- Activity records, rhythm, listening, sing-along, singing games*
- Amusement songs, riddles, and games, e.g., peek-a-boo**
- Fables and folk tales, parables
- Humorous, silly, and nonsense songs for children
- Historical stories, biographies
- Original stories created for and/or by the record company
- Educational, instructional (including counting and alphabet)
- Classical music (interpreted and/or suitable for kids)
- Dance music and instruction (ballet, tap, ballroom, folk, square, and contra)
- Music appreciation (including an introduction to the instruments & orchestra)
- Good manners, etiquette
- Songs of good health, safety, and friendship
- Radio, television, and movie characters and themes
- Characters who appear in comic books and cartoons, both fictional (e.g., Donald Duck) and real (e.g., Roy Rogers).
- Transportation vehicle sounds (trains, planes, fire trucks, etc.)
- Railroad stories and songs
- Farm and zoo stories and songs
- Circus and clown stories and songs
- Foreign language introduction and instruction
- Pop songs (arranged for kids)
- Hit songs from movies
- "Magic" records (a different storyline is possible each time you place the needle down on the record — see more in the Brief History section.)

*An example of an activity record is one with "finger games," or what some refer to as "tickle games." They were used for the amusement of infants and toddlers. Perhaps the two best known are "This Little Piggy Went to Market" and "Pat-a-cake, Pat-a-cake, Baker's Man."

**An example of such a riddle is "As I Went to St. Ives, I met Nine Wives." This riddle was heard near the beginning of the feature film "Die Hard with a Vengeance."

### SUITABLE FOR CHILDREN AND ADULTS

- Broadway musicals
- Opera & operettas (e.g., Gilbert & Sullivan)
- Marches and parade songs (e.g., Sousa)
- Christmas songs and carols
- Cowboy/western songs
- Patriotic songs
- Folklore and myths
- Poetry
- Folk songs, ballads, minstrel songs
- Dance music
- Novelty and comedy songs
- Movie, radio, TV themes
- Religious themes: hymns, Bible stories and songs
- Songs of the Armed Forces

## WHAT IS A VINTAGE "KIDDIE" RECORD?

This book is all about children's 78-rpm records. If you are old enough, you probably remember listening to 78-rpm "kiddie" records when you were growing up. Or maybe your parents did. Being a child of the late 1940s and 1950s, I do. It is the fond memories of warm and fuzzy times and the nostalgia for them that started me off on a collection in uncharted waters — vintage children's records.

A majority of baby boomers reading this article who grew up in the post–World War II years had collections of children's records. It is surprising, therefore, in this current era of nostalgia craze in which anything is collectible that the hobby of collecting old kiddie records has not yet been established. No comprehensive book on the subject has been published — until now!

This book will make a significant contribution to the hobby. The record listings probably will never be completed, as most of the companies that produced the records are long since out of business and left no information behind. In my collection I currently have more than 11,000 vintage children's records on more than 450 labels and label variations. In addition, I show listings of more than 3,000 additional records. And who knows how many more are yet to be discovered? Most of the labels in my discography were marketed exclusively for children, or were from a subsidiary label just for children. As much information as I have gathered so far, there is certainly more to uncover. This is something that I am pursuing with a passion. I have the honor of the Library of Congress acquiring a significant part of my collection for its archives as well as the Smithsonian Institute expressing an interest.

CHILDREN PLAY 'EM, LOVE 'EM, CAN'T BREAK 'EM!


## HOW OLD IS OLD?

The history of sound recording began with Edison's invention of the "talking machine," or phonograph, in 1877. He began his experiments by using paraffin paper tape, and eventually a sheet of tinfoil wrapped around a metal cylinder. His first recording was the nursery rhyme "Mary Had a Little Lamb." The announcement of this invention created an instant sensation — albeit a brief one. The machine was a novelty whose charm quickly wore off. Once the initial public curiosity was satisfied, the technology languished for almost a decade.

In 1886 a patent was granted for a new development in cylinder technology: a cylinder made of cardboard coated with wax on to which the audio track was engraved. The first machines designed to play these types of "records" were called "graphophones." Because wax cylinders provided a sharper, better defined recording than tinfoil cylinders, they became the standard for home entertainment. This lasted for only for a short time, however.

A new development in the late 1880s would prove to cut off the cylinder phonograph at its height of popularity. A German immigrant by the name of Emile Berliner developed a new medium: the record disc. Frank Andrews, in his article on the website of the City of London (UK) Phonograph and Gramophone Society, notes that "the 5-inch Emile Berliner's Gramophone plates (as they were known), made in Germany circa 1890, were the first gramophone records to be offered commercially." Berliner's "records" were offered as alternatives to cylinders. In 1894, 7" discs began to be made in the USA. The formation of the National Gramophone Co. in 1896 promoted the Gramophone and its records and within a few years led to a new international industry, with various companies making 7" and 10" discs. 12" records followed in 1903.

These so-called 78 rpms (some actually played at 80 rpm) were usually pressed in shellac. Diana Tillson, a noted children's music collector, provides more detail on the earliest "flat" records, specifically children's records. In the *Ephemera Journal* (vol. 6, 1993) she states that "the earliest children's recorded discs are 5" celluloid composition discs with nursery rhyme lyrics glued to the back which were included with toy phonographs made in Germany in the early 1890s." It should be noted here that, with a few two-sided experimental exceptions, all the records made for approximately the first 20 years of production were playable on one side only. It was not until early 1908 that Columbia introduced the two-sided record. Victor reluctantly, but quickly, followed suit later in the year.

William Paley, head of Columbia records and CBS-TV, introduced the long-play microgroove 33¹/₃ rpm (LP) in July 1948. NBC's (RCA Victor) David Sarnoff responded with the 45-rpm (EP) record in January 1949. During the late 1950s, the production of 78s phased out in favor of 33s and 45s. By 1955, general adult-market 45s outsold 78s in the US; however, children's 78s remained strong longer than nonchildren's records. The latest American 78-rpm in my collection is dated 1968, although I own some British 78s made in 1984! Most American record companies, in fact, did not make 78s after 1960.

While record sizes (diameters) range from 3½" to 12", most kiddie records are 6", 7", or 10". It is important to note that "78 rpm" refers to the speed at which the record revolves on the turntable — not the diameter (size of the record). This is a common misunderstanding among the noninitiated. If you are not sure of the speed of a particular record you own, find a 78-rpm phonograph and play the record. If it sounds like the Chipmunks, you probably are playing a 45- or $33\frac{1}{3}$-rpm disc. Or alternatively, if you only have access to a long-playing (LP) record turntable, play the record on that machine, and if it sounds way too slow, it is a 78.

## A BRIEF SURVEY OF EARLY KIDDIE RECORD SERIES

For the purpose of this survey, the early years of kiddie record series comprise, more or less, the period from the beginning of WWI to the end of WWII (1914 to 1945). Although the few record companies in existence prior to WWI issued many single children's records, no series or runs of children's titles were made.

The first known exclusively children's series of records (and one of the most well known) was the Bubble Books series produced by Harper-Columbia between 1917 and 1922. Each of the 14 books with records consisted of sleeves for three small ($5\frac{1}{2}$") single-sided records bound into a small book. Each record sleeve included beautiful line drawings in full color, along with several pages devoted to the story and lyrics. These "books with records" are highly collectible by both record and antiquarian book collectors. Other record manufacturers of the era making children's records, either exclusively or as part of their catalogs, included Little Tots, Cameo Kids, Youngster Grey Gull, Lindstrom, Emerson, Talkie-Jektor, Durotone, NIC, LaVelle and Gilbert Bobolink, Little Pal, Talking Books, Kiddie Rekords, and Pictorial Records (the first "picture discs"). Some of these series (e.g., Talkie-Jektor, NIC, and Durotone) came with toy projectors and filmstrips, which were synchronized with the record being played.

A popular series called Little Wonder was founded in 1914 by Henry Waterson and manufactured by Columbia Graphophone Company. The series included over 1,500 small ($5\frac{1}{2}$") one-sided records produced during the next nine years. The records were sold for 10¢ in Woolworth's and other five-and-dime stores, and through Sears, Roebuck catalogs. Despite appearances (as miniature records), Little Wonders were not primarily meant for children. With the exception of about 40 records of nursery rhymes and folk songs, they were intended for adults, as the titles show. This series was the first to place recorded music within reach of most people, and millions upon millions of these records were sold.

Many of the listed series are quite uncommon, but because there is no established collector's market for them, the costs are not high — usually about $4.00 to $6.00 for a single record, and up to $100.00 or more for complete books with matching records in very nice condition. One of the most unusual and beautiful series was the Talking Books series (1918 – 1919). With a few exceptions, they are not actually books, but $4\frac{1}{8}$" records that are riveted to the face of die-cut cards that are several inches larger than the records. The term "phonographic tablet" occasionally appeared in the literature. The backing is a cutout shape, roughly in the form of the subject of the record, usually an animal or generic children's doll theme. Some of the titles are "I Am a Parrot," "The Mocking Bird," and "The Fox." There are also some WWI subjects, a Mother Goose, and a tired baby. Unlike most generic kiddie records, this series commands high prices in sales and at auctions, often reaching $75.00 to $300.00 and more in excellent condition.

The end of this period saw the introduction of extended kiddie series (a.k.a. "youth," "juvenile") by some of the major labels. Columbia's Playtime, a long running series of 6" and 7" records (originally 70 titles, then reissued in a series of 113 titles) began in the late 1930s and continued up to 1954. RCA's budget line, Bluebird, issued its first large kiddie series from 1937 to 1942. It consisted of 119 records in 52 sets. Each set came in an illustrated "envelope" and/or box. Decca (beginning 1939), Columbia's 10" series (1939), and RCA Victor (1944) turned out significant children's series, which continued into the mid-to-late 1950s as 78 rpms. These series continued to be issued as 45s and LPs throughout the 1960s into the 1970s. It should be noted that prior to the launching of the youth series mentioned above, all of the major record companies and many minor ones issued single children's records that were part of their general catalogs. Many were for school music appreciation classes.

### THE "GOLDEN AGE" OF KIDDIE 78-RPM RECORDS: 1946 – 1956

The 1940s brought in a number of major innovations in the production of kiddie records that allowed their sales to soar to astronomical heights as compared with earlier years. The first and most important was the introduction of vinyl ("nonbreakable") records. Earlier produced records were, for the most part, made of brittle shellac. Vinyl records were almost unbreakable. Second, the records themselves were often made of brightly colored materials and were packaged in beautifully designed, vividly colored sleeves and album covers. Third, the availability of small and inexpensive kiddie record players became widespread. Finally, the records themselves were relatively inexpensive. All of these factors combined to encourage parents to buy records for the kids, knowing that they would stand up to the rough handling and abuse that would surely come to pass and that their children would be attracted to them.

Another point of consideration is that the creation and production of the songs and stories were done, in many cases, at great expense and with highly professional and well-known performers. Prior to approximately 1953, record companies did not have to compete with television for the attention of the children with respect to entertainment. Therefore, they competed with one another to get market share. Most major companies hired (sometimes exclusively) the talents of famous actors and singers. Many famous personalities produced some or many kiddie records (Dennis Day, Gene Kelly, Gene Autry, Patti Page, and Bing Crosby, to name a few). Others produced only one or two (e.g., Groucho Marx, Jimmy Stewart, Jack Carson, Ingrid Bergman, and Lionel Barrymore). The end of the 1940s saw a proliferation of companies producing seemingly countless series of kiddie records. Some of the larger producers started releasing the more popular records (e.g., Christmas carols, fairy tales, kiddie best sellers) as parallel issues in both 78- and 45-rpm formats in the early 1950s. The cover artwork was usually identical in both. Eventually, after 78s were phased out entirely, the 45s continued to be released into the 1980s, until they were phased out in favor of cassettes and CDs. Currently, some entrepreneurs are toying with the idea of making vintage kiddie music available on the Internet as MP3 downloads.

One of the most famous children's series from this era was launched in 1948. Golden Records, a division of Simon & Schuster, publisher of the famous Little Golden Books, started issuing small (6"), almost indestructible yellow plastic records. This series was an immediate hit with both parents and kids. They were available at almost any grocery store for 25¢. Most of the first issues were musical story renditions of Little Golden Books. The child could read the book and follow along with the record. The series continued well into the 1960s and to this day remains as the largest of all kiddie record series, with over 700 individual records issued.

RCA Victor's youth series that began in 1944 became known as the famous Little Nipper series in 1950. Many of the popular Disney stories, which were made into movies, as well as the more popular TV shows of the day (e.g., Howdy Doody, Tom Corbett Space Cadet) appeared in this series and today are among the more valuable and popular of all kiddie 78s.

A few companies became known as strictly "children's record" producers. In addition to those mentioned in the previous paragraphs, many readers will remember Peter Pan, Columbia Playtime, Record Guild of America, Voco, Young People's Records/Children's Record Guild (YPR/CRG; CRG was, for a time, distributed by the Book of the Month Club), Mercury Childcraft and Playcraft, Red Raven "movie" records, and Cricket. Contributing to the plethora of products was a host of small companies that came out with a limited quantity of children's records. Following is a small sampling of labels of the post-WWII era: Pied Piper, Rocking Horse, Pilotone, Melodee, Toono, Belda, DeLuxe, Winant, Allegro, Karousel, Twinkle, Color Tunes, Musicraft, Merry-Go-Sound, Mayfair, Musette, Caravan, Wonderland, Adventure, Carnival Toy, Cub, Fox, Star Bright, Jackalee, Kiddie Land, Kiddietoons, Lincoln, Teddy Bear, Little Folks Favorites, Little John, Magic-Tone, Moppet, Playola, Records of Knowledge, Remington Junior, Robin Hood, Small Fry, Hollywood Recording Guild, Spear, Spinner, Superior, Talentoon (came in box with marionette), Tots n' Teens, Treasure, and Willida. In addition, there are dozens of educational, instructional, and religious series. Most of these are not avidly collected, but are, nevertheless, part of the legacy of kiddie 78s.

### THE TOP TEN RECORD COMPANIES IN TERMS OF THE NUMBER OF CHILDREN'S RECORDS LISTED IN THIS BOOK:

1. Golden: 950
2. Victor/RCA Victor: 939
3. Columbia: 932
4. Decca: 797
5. Peter Pan: 610
6. Capitol: 396
7. Mercury: 287
8. Record Guild of America: 286
9. Voco/Tops for Tots: 274
10. Cricket: 217

Note: the preceding list reflects the total number of discs on each label, taking into account that multiple record albums are counted for the number of records in each set.

### SPECIAL AND UNUSUAL RECORDS:

The following four pages of categories refer to records that have special collector interest. Any one of these types can be considered a collectible area in and of itself. Records in this section are included because of unique features that relate to their design and appearance, their physical material, or unusual audio features. Several are not specific to children's records.

### PICTURE DISCS AND QUASI-PICTURE DISCS:

Special note is made here of a whole area of specialized collecting: picture discs. Strictly speaking, picture discs, or pic-discs, are records in which the entire playing surface has graphic illustrations and/or photographic content. They are usually very colorful and certainly more valuable, as collectors prize them. Purists would contend that a true picture disc is a record in which the playing area grooves are cut into the picture itself. There are other variations, however, such as a clear plastic grooved playing area laminated (or in some other way attached) to a picture underneath. For the purpose of this book, I consider these picture discs. Quasi–Picture Discs are records that give the appearance or ambience of being picture discs. Red Raven 8" and Talking Books are examples. While they are not true picture discs in the real sense of the meaning, I nevertheless give special note to them. Some records with large picture labels really do have the appearance of picture discs.

Following is a list of labels for which you can find picture discs. Some of these labels were exclusively picture discs; others had significant series of picture discs. In addition to this list, there are several very small record series, such as those obtained through product purchases as premiums. Related to these types are those records that have ads or messages printed on them — "advertising picture-discs," as it were. They could be acquired through promotions and giveaways, or they may have been inserts or part of the packages themselves. Since most of these are either single records, or a very small amount for any one product, they will be found lumped together in the part of the Miscellaneous section that deals with premiums.

In each individual label notes section for each company, I will indicate if a particular series is a picture-disc series or not.

## COMPANIES INCLUDED IN THIS DISCOGRAPHY THAT PRODUCED PICTURE DISCS:

Bible Storytime
Eckhart
Jack & Jill (Schneider)
Kidisks
Magic Talking Books
Mattel
Menorah
Musette
NIC
Pat
Pictorial
PicturTone
Pix
Playola
Playsong
Record Guild of America
Red Raven (6")
Rhapsody
Sight 'N Sound (H.O. Instant Oatmeal)
Talkie-Jektor
Toy Toons
Victor
Visitone
Voco
Vogue
Wheaties
(Note: many others can be found in the Miscellaneous section.)

## COMPANIES INCLUDED IN THIS DISCOGRAPHY THAT PRODUCED QUASI-PICTURE DISCS:

Emerson
Kiddie Rekord
Red Raven (8")
Talking Books

### RECORDS THAT ARE PART OF PACKAGE DESIGNS:

Besides standard records, you can find a type of record (usually cardboard) that could be cut out of the back of a cereal box, such as a Wheaties box. These kinds of records are usually picture discs. The grooves are either cut right into the picture or on a clear laminate of plastic that is affixed to the picture disc. One places the needle right on the record's picture. As a rule, picture discs are more valuable than standard records. The back of the record is usually unprinted cardboard.

### SHAPE OR DIE-CUT RECORDS:

We normally think of records as being round in shape (discs) and, to be sure, just about all of them are. But in the kiddie record world, especially, is where you will find variants. The most common variations are square shaped (such as "greeting card" types) and rectangular ("postcard" types). But there are any number of other shapes, some in the forms of common objects (heart shapes for Valentine's greetings, e.g.). Many are die-cut and have irregular boundaries in order to allow for graphic displays to be presented as in two-dimensional dioramas. In each case, the playing part (the grooves) is, by necessity, in a round center part of the shape. Included in this category are records mounted onto shaped backgrounds (e.g., Talking Books).

### "FLEXI" RECORDS:

As the word implies, the material from which these records are made can be bent easily with the hands. Examples of this type are very thin and nonbreakable vinyl, plastic, cardboard, heavy paper, etc.

### "MAGIC" RECORDS:

A unique style of recording can be found in a few children's and adults' game records. These are generally referred to as "magic" records. The record is cut with two or more parallel grooves. The stylus is placed on the record and a storyline is played to the end of that groove. The next time the stylus is placed on the record, the listener may or may not hear the same storyline. A second (or third or fourth) variation on the story may be heard. This allows for the possibility of multiple storyline developments and ending scenarios. This style of record generally has more collector value than standard records. I have identified only a small handful of these types. They can be found on the following labels: Golden (44), Atlantic (311 + 313), Peter Pan (356), Belda (105), and Little Folks Favorites (117).

### RECORDS PLAYED IN SYNCHONIZATION WITH FILMSTRIPS:

While the records assigned to this category are not different in appearance or makeup than standard records, I have nevertheless taken special note of them here. Early in the 1920s, various companies (starting with NIC in Spain) started manufacturing record players that were combined with filmstrip projectors. Numerous companies listed in this book (NIC, Talkie-Jektor, Durotone, and Mickey Mouse Newsreel, to name a few) made records that, when played on the turntable, were coordinated with a filmstrip, advanced in synchronization with the record being played. A slide or film frame could be seen projected on the wall or a small screen and synchronized with the verbal story being narrated or sung on the record.

### ANIMATION LABELS:

Another type of record deserving of special note in this section is the "movie" record. Red Raven is the primary example, but Record Guild of America's Picture Play (PP) series is another. The label had a cartoon illustration that was put into motion when spinning on the turntable by use of a special multisided mirror attachment. Companies in at least 12 other countries also produced Red Raven–type Movie Records. See future editions of this guidebook for coverage of foreign children's records.

### PERSONALIZED RECORDINGS AND HOME RECORDINGS:

Personal greeting records could be ordered by mail or purchased at a store (such as one at an amusement park, for example). A recording machine produced a record with a standard greeting, such as "Merry Christmas" or "Happy birthday" or, alternatively, a totally custom personal message. The first name of the intended recipient could be added into the recording itself, thus personalizing it. More likely, there would be a standard generic audio track and a special label on the record, on which the recipient's name could be printed or handwritten. The records were sent or presented in mailers.

### PHONOGRAPH DOLLS:

Dolls with mechanisms to play records inside the dolls themselves have been around literally since day one in the history of the phonograph. When Edison invented the phonograph in 1877, the first test recording he made was "Mary Had a Little Lamb." He intended to produce a talking doll that would produce sounds for children by means of his cylinder phonograph technology. Only a few hundred were actually made, of which very few still exist intact. The popularity of the dolls never took hold, as it was not a very practical toy and was very expensive for its time.

Since this book covers only flat disc 78-rpm records, none of the dolls that play cylinders or 45-rpm or 33⅓-rpm records are mentioned. Because of the scarcity of dolls that play 78-rpm records, I will not list them separately in the main discographical section of this book, but will only mention them here. For more information on this topic the reader is encouraged to read *Phonograph Dolls and Toys* by Joan and Robin Rolfs (Mulholland Press). The Rolfs are the leading experts in this area of collecting. Joan and Robin state that the range of values of records sold separately is between $35.00 and $85.00 (with the exception of the Kammer & Reinhardt doll, which is so rare that no value can be accurately assigned to it). The price of dolls with records ranges from the hundreds to the thousands, depending on the company, condition, etc. The average size of these records is between 3" and 3½".

Following is a list of some of the companies that made dolls that played 78-rpm records:

- Kammer & Reinhardt (ca. 1890)
- Noma (EFFanBEE) (1950)
- Schilling (1950s)
- Winnie (1953)
- Tama (1954)
- Melodie (EFFanBEE, 1953 – 1956)
  - Some Melodie record titles:
    - "One Two, Buckle My Shoe"
    - "Simple Simon"
    - "Eensie Weensie Spider"
    - "Four & Twenty Blackbirds"
    - "Sing a Song of Sixpence"
    - "Twinkle Twinkle Little Star"
    - "Rock a Bye Baby"

## TIPS FOR STARTING A KIDDIE RECORD COLLECTION:

For those of you who have been immersed in more established collecting fields, starting a collection of vintage children's records will be relatively inexpensive. I would estimate that most "generic" kiddie records in at least VG (very good) to EX (excellent) condition (record and original cover combined) could be had for between $2.00 and $10.00, and very often for much less. By generic, I am referring to your basic Mother Goose nursery rhymes, classic tales and stories, fables, folk songs, cowboy songs, etc., which are performed by relatively unknown or anonymous artists. When it comes to the more well-known and collectible characters and performers (e.g., Roy Rogers, Disney characters, Bozo the Clown, etc.), the prices will be about triple the generic value, as a general rule ($6.00 – 30.00).

So, if you are ready to begin your collection of vintage children's records, here are a few pointers to help you get started.

Because most people collect kiddie records for the graphics on the cover, records without original sleeves or album covers have little or no collector value. Generally speaking, you can find loose (sleeveless) records for $.25 – 1.00 at flea markets, garage sales, Goodwill, etc. Having said that, it's not uncommon for someone to pay much more than the current book value to recapture cherished childhood memories with or without the original cover being present. The exception to this rule is, of course, picture discs. The record itself contains the graphics. "Pic-discs" start out in the $3.00 – 4.00 range and go up to $20.00 – 25.00 for the majority. Many, however, are considerably more valuable.

Notwithstanding this price guide, any record is ultimately worth whatever one is willing to pay for it. Supply and demand, along with the subject matter, are the driving forces. Records and their corresponding covers that contain characters from TV shows, cartoons, juvenile series books, movies, comic books, etc., will be more in demand than their generic counterparts. Certain generic subjects, such as black Americana, paper doll cutouts (on the covers), 1950s rocket ships and outer space themes, famous illustrators (of covers), robots, and so forth, will also be more collectible. The crossover collectibility of the previously listed subjects results in greater demand, thus higher values. The dealer knows that these records can usually command his asking price because his customers want anything with these characters on it. Mitigating that situation, however, is the phenomenon of eBay. Many previously scarce records have been surfacing, which helps to bring down prices.

If you are used to collecting items only in mint condition, don't get hung up on this criteria for vintage children's records. Kiddie records haven't survived the decades as well as many other collectible items, because of the wear and tear they received from their young owners. If you see a record you like in less than perfect condition, even if it is only "fair" or "good," you may want to pick it up, especially if the price is low (which it should be). Most of these records, especially those with crossover collectibility or limited production, you may not see again for a very, very long time.

Even though you may be buying the item for the graphic beauty of the cover, the condition of the record is relatively important — in other words, it shouldn't be severely worn, warped, cracked, or otherwise damaged. Just remember, you are not buying CDs here. Ultimately, the record's value is whatever it's worth to you. Just enjoy! Try the Internet (eBay, Google, Craigslist), antique record stores, flea markets, garage sales, antique shows, and record shows — in other words, all the usual suspects. And don't forget the value of word of mouth among your friends and relatives.

### HOW MUCH CAN I EXPECT TO GET IF I WANT TO SELL MY RECORDS?

In this price guide, I have listed the retail value of the records. As with any collectible, the price realized from a sale will vary widely, depending on who the buyer is. The amount that a dealer will pay can range anywhere from 10% to 60% and more, depending on the desirability and condition of the record and cover. On the other hand, if a record is sold directly to a collector, the price realized can be even more than that shown in this book.

To avoid disappointment, figure on the average, a sale to a dealer will get you about 20¢ to 25¢ on the dollar.

In closing, here is a reminder: Don't ever lose sight of the fact that a hobby is generally defined as an activity or interest pursued outside one's regular occupation and engaged in primarily for pleasure. The operative word here is *pleasure*. When the enjoyment of this activity diminishes greatly, it is probably time to move on. So, go out and enjoy!

## HOW TO USE THIS GUIDE

### UNDERSTANDING THE LABEL NOTES & IDENTIFICATION GUIDE

The sections shown below follow the format of perhaps 98% of the record labels and companies covered in this book. A few exceptions have been made for the largest and most complex companies, such as Columbia, Victor, Decca, and perhaps a few others. A more narrative discussion will be used for them.

### FACTS ABOUT THE LABEL:

#### ASSOCIATED/SUBSIDIARY LABELS:

Most of the major record companies and many of the smaller ones, especially those not producing children's records exclusively, issued differently named labels as well as variations of the main company name.

Okeh Records is an example of a subsidiary. Columbia acquired the Okeh label in 1926. Okeh had already been in existence as a stand-alone company since 1918. From 1926 to 1935, and again from 1940 to 1946, and finally in the 1950s, Columbia produced, manufactured, and distributed 78-rpm records under that label. (Note: The scope of this book is limited to 78-rpms. There will be almost no information on LPs and 45s, even though production of those types of records continued by the companies after 78s were discontinued.)

In some cases, a new label was created solely for the purpose of allowing a distributor to have exclusive rights to a series of records or for the purpose of facilitating royalties to a favored artist. An example of this is the Tops for Tots label. This was a spin-off of Voco. The founder of Voco, Cy Leslie, created Tops for Tots so that a certain chain of retail stores could have an exclusive distributorship. The masters used were the exact same as on the Voco label.

Finally, label variations will be shown, to the extent known and appropriate for this book. The most well-known and notable example is the Bluebird label, a variation of Victor and RCA-Victor. Bluebird was considered the budget line. There are dozens of others, as you will discover as you read on.

**DISTRIBUTED, PRODUCED, AND MANUFACTURED BY:**

Most of the information on these three lines is taken from the record labels and record jackets. In some cases, I rely on second- and third-hand sources. If I cannot determine specific information for this section, rather than assume a fact, I will state it as "unknown." I heartily invite readers of this book to contact me with any missing or corrected information.

**OVERALL DESCRIPTION OF CONTENT:**

Rather than automatically classify every listing as simply for children, I have made an attempt to classify the various series in a few main categories. Most will be classified as "general children's entertainment." Others, however, might be shown to be "educational/instructional," "religious," "adult market with some children's material," etc.

Note: Many record labels are not record companies in the usual sense. A label may be a private issue, i.e., a small production run of one or a few records by an organization, a company, or even an individual. These are included in the listings if they are children's records, but the label name may not look like a company in the traditional sense. Most of these listings will be found in the miscellaneous section, in any case, and not come with much detail as to the company.

## PHYSICAL CHARACTERISTICS OF THE RECORDS (FOR IDENTIFICATION PURPOSES):

**RECORD MATERIAL:**

SHELLAC: This refers to hard fragile substances such as shellac, celluloid, hard rubber, Bakelite, or similar. I will lump all of these into generic "shellac" identification.

VINYL: A general term that includes various types of "unbreakable" or "nonbreakable" materials, including but not limited to vinyl, polyvinyl, polystyrene, and the like.

CARDBOARD: All paper-based discs, including thin or thick cardboard, plastic laminated, flexible, etc.

**RECORD SIZE, SHAPE, AND COLOR:**

SIZE: This refers to the diameter, rounded off to the nearest whole inch for the most part. In the case of die-cut or other "shaped" records, the actual size of the playing part of the item is shown. The title of each section will list the size of the records in that particular series. For example: "DECCA CU series 12" singles." For all listings (except in the Miscellaneous section), all records will be the size indicated in the title line unless otherwise indicated next to the record or set number. For example, in this particular series (Decca CU), all the records listed are 12" except CU-110, which is 10" and is so noted next to the record number.

SHAPE: Unless otherwise indicated, all records are round. This would seem obvious on the surface; however, one of the joys of collecting kiddie records is the sub-category known as shaped records. This group includes die-cut records (some Voco), records that form the cover of a book whereby the entire book is placed on the record spindle (Magic Talking Books), and records attached to die-cut backings (Talking Books).

COLOR: As implied, the color of the playing surface is shown here. Variations on solid color are mottled/mixed, translucent, and picture discs.

#### DESCRIPTION OF THE LABEL ON THE RECORD:

The record labels described in this section pertain to the most common examples found. In the case of companies producing records for both the adult and children's markets, there are often labels for the kiddie records that are of different design than the others. I will not attempt to describe the adult varieties, as this would be beyond the scope of this book. The reader who is interested in all the varieties is referred to Kurt Nauck and Allan Sutton's excellent book *American Record Labels and Companies* (Mainspring Press).

The record label is normal size and made of paper unless otherwise noted. Other types of labels, which bear specific descriptions, may be referred to as picture labels (see some Voco series), supersized labels (see Red Raven 8" series), or nonpaper: (i.e., embossed, etched, or stamped directly on the record surface; see Little Wonder).

In the case of a picture disc, the entire record surface is illustrated; therefore, no label is described, since the entire record in effect is the label. There are some series of records that have only one playing side, with the reverse side an illustration (no playing grooves). An example of this type would be one from the Kiddie Rekord Company. I classify these types of records as quasi–picture discs.

#### DESCRIPTION OF THE RECORD HOLDER/COVER:

This is a very important section. It includes the graphics, colors, and designs on the covers, sleeves, and other holders that make these records particularly collectible and desirable for many, if not most, collectors.

The great majority of covers are made of paper or cardboard. Other materials or variations (e.g., cellophane) are noted and described here.

Records usually came in paper or cardboard sleeves or book-style albums. A small percentage appeared in boxed sets of one type or another. Sleeves usually held one record, but various configurations were devised to hold more (such as the "gatefold" type, holding two or more). Such variations will be noted here.

A very popular configuration is records with books. Many of the most popular records from the golden age of children's 78-rpm records (1946 – 1955) had books sewn in (or otherwise attached) to the album covers. Two of the most popular releases were RCA-Victor Storybooks and Capitol Record Readers.

Records were issued with toys (e.g., Talentoon with a marionette), games, and the like. Most of these are very scarce and fall into the higher range of values. Information on which records came in these configurations is found in the label notes section.

### DATES, SERIES, NUMBERING SEQUENCES:

#### DATE RANGE:

To the extent known, the year(s) of issue of a record or series of records is shown. In the case of large series of records that were issued over several years, intervals of years will be listed (e.g., #1 – 30, 1949; #31 – 50, 1950; etc.). If specific dates are not known, I say "ca." (circa).

For those companies producing adult as well as children's records, the dates shown here mainly refer to the years that the children's records were issued.

#### SERIES AND RECORD NUMBERING SEQUENCES:

All of the large major record companies, such as RCA-Victor, Columbia, Decca, etc., had various children's series in their catalogs, along with varying numbers of individual kiddie records sprinkled in their main listings. For nearly all of the smaller record companies that were specifically created to produce children's records, one or more series

with various numbering sequences were issued. I have identified every important series in this book. However, I am sure that, in time, others will surface.

Records are listed in order from the lowest number of the series to the highest. Please note that not all series begin conveniently with the number 1. Whatever is the lowest number shown is the lowest number that I am aware of.

There may be gaps in the sequence (e.g., 25, 26, 30, 31, 35, etc.). The missing numbers indicate that I do not have information (or the record) for that number, the record company never issued a record with that number, or a record or set was issued for numbers not shown in this book because they were not children's records. This last instance would apply, obviously, to the larger labels that did not specialize in children's records. A perfect example is the MGM "L" series. The sequence jumps from L12 to L14. L13 is not a children's set; therefore, it is not listed here.

#### MISCELLANEOUS INFORMATION:

This is a catchall section. Anything particularly relevant about the history of the label, its executives, artists, etc. will be found here. In some cases, there may be little or no information.

## UNDERSTANDING THE PRICE GUIDE AND DISCOGRAPHIES

### SOME ABBREVIATIONS USED IN THIS SECTION AND OTHER PARTS OF THE BOOK:

**s/s:** single-sided, or one-sided play only
**pd:** picture record, picture disc
**ca:** circa, approximately, about (referring to a date)
**sq:** square-shaped record
**mtx:** matrix, the record serial or identification number scratched into playing surface in the "run-off" area — the end of the playing grooves.
**flexi:** flexible, i.e., thin cardboard or plastic that easily bends but does not break.
**":** inch

### NAME OF LABEL (RECORD COMPANY)

Each label or label variation begins with a bold heading, giving the name and possibly some other descriptive information. Some examples of labels:

**Decca (1940s K-series — 10")**
**Voco Picture Discs (7")**
**Capitol Toyland (7")**
**Mercury Miniature Playhouse (7")**

### THE COLUMNS IN THE DISCOGRAPHY (READING LEFT TO RIGHT)

Described below are the primary columns that are displayed for any single label. Since we are not dealing with a homogeneous universe, some labels have fewer columns than those shown. The columns used for each label will be noted at the beginning of each section just below the name of the label header.

#### SET #:

Most of the larger record companies have set or album

numbers in addition to individual record or disc numbers. This is almost always the case for multi-record sets. Set numbers usually have a letter prefix. When both numbers clearly appear on the label and/or cover, a column showing the set numbers will be displayed. Many, if not most, of the smaller labels do not have separate set and disc numbers. In these cases, the identifying number is shown under the "Disc #" column, since set and record numbers are essentially one and the same.

A number appearing in parentheses is one that is arbitrarily listed by the record company in brochures, ads, etc. These numbers don't actually appear on the record cover itself (e.g., No. 1, No. 2, etc.). This designation is also used in the Disc # column when applicable.

#### # REC (NUMBER OF DISCS IN A SET):

This column indicates the number of records (discs) for each set/album/record catalog number.

#### DISC #(S):

Many collectors look for more than one number to identify a particular record, especially in multi-record sets. One or more different numbers may appear on the label. In this column, I include at least one of these numbers, even though some of the larger companies (Victor, Columbia, Decca, etc.) may have as many as three or four different number identifications. This column is in addition to that for the set number.

In cases where no set number or record number is shown on the label or cover, I list the matrix number ("mtx") if any, etched in the run-off area near the label. If no cover came with the record originally, then I just use the number appearing on the record itself.

In the case of multiple record sets (albums, boxed sets, etc.), if they are in a consecutive numerical sequence, I show the first and last numbers of the sequence. For example, the record numbers in a three-record set with numbers 101, 102, and 103 will be shown as 101 – 3. Otherwise, space permitting, I show each number separately.

#### MAIN TITLE:

Titles for each side are separated by a forward slash (/). In those cases where the titles are identical on both sides, the title is shown only once.

#### ARTIST(S):

Artists' (performers') names for each side are separated by a forward slash (/). In those cases where the names are identical on both sides, the names are shown only once. In situations where there are a large number of performers listed, I arbitrarily show only the first one or two so as to save space. In some of the larger labels, such as Peter Pan and Golden, where the same artists appeared on many, many records, I abbreviate the names of some of them to save space. These abbreviations will be explained in each label notes section when relevant.

#### PRICES AND VALUES (IN TWO COLUMNS: G/VG AND EX/NMT):

In this price guide, I have listed the retail value of the records. As with any collectible, the price realized from a sale will vary widely, depending on who the buyer is. The amount that a dealer will pay can range anywhere from 10% to 60% and more, depending on the desirability and condition of the record and cover. On the other hand, if a record is sold directly to a collector, the price realized can be even more than that shown in this book.

I fully expect this guide to stimulate a lot of emotions with respect to the values shown. Some folks may be very upset, others delighted. I have tried my very best to be as accurate as I can in reflecting the median values of the records based on thousands of transactions, auctions, and the like. I generally throw out the highest and lowest amounts and arrive at a happy middle ground. Since the hobby of collecting vintage children's records has not been widely established, there is no scientific way to judge what is a correct value. I am sure future editions will reflect the feedback I receive after publication of this first edition.

The values shown are based on the presence of all of the items that originally came with the record. There are some exceptions to this rule and they are discussed in the label notes section. An example of an exception would be that the record did not come with an original sleeve (other than plain or generic). The "items" being referred to here are anything other than the record and the cover or sleeve. They may include, but are not limited to, outer box, album, mailer, folder, etc.; book or booklet inserted or sewn into the cover; cutout or punch-out paper or cardboard figures; boxed sets with toys (such as plastic or metal figures, puppets, musical instruments); slides and film strips; and jigsaw puzzles.

### UNDERSTANDING THE CONDITION DESIGNATIONS AND RELATIVE VALUES:

The grading parameters described are for the visual appearances of the record and sleeve. Grading of the record itself is visual, not for sound quality. The latter evaluation is relevant more to stereo LPs. Even a new-looking or unplayed old 78-rpm record will not always sound "clean." One can usually get an idea from visual inspection of what grade it should be placed in.

The lists show two columns of values for each record: G/VG and EX/nMT. Values shown are in US dollars and are as a percentage of EX/nMT.

**G/VG** = Good/very good (left column): 50% of EX/nMT; cover will have light to moderate wear at seams and corners; small creases, scratches or light smudges show on surface. Record shows average light use from handling and a few hairline scratches.
**EX/nMT** = Excellent/near mint (right column): would be considered mint, except records in this rating have been played, but still look almost brand new. Cover might show minuscule spots of wear, but nothing that jumps out at you. What most people call mint fits into this category.
**MINT** = Record and cover/sleeve are perfect, like new, pristine and unused. Records, which were sealed originally, are still in this condition. Store-stock with very little or no shelf wear would fit into this category. No flaws of any kind. Very few old records or covers/sleeves will make this rating. (125 – 150% of EX/nMT.)
**Fair/Poor** = Cover shows considerable wear and is marginally presentable; tears at seams, missing pieces, etc. Record has extensive scratches; may have cracks, chips, serious warping, etc. Record many not play through. The lower end of this grade is truly a space filler. 10 – 50% of the value of G/VG (5 – 25% of EX/nMT).

### SPECIAL NOTE ON THE MISCELLANEOUS LABELS SECTION:

This is a section in which all the very small labels of children's records are placed — usually three or fewer for a given company. Some of the companies listed may, in fact, be major labels that simply did not make enough kiddie records to warrant their own sections. Most of the other companies listed in this section, however, will be virtually unknown to most readers.

There are four different lists in this section:

**Large singles + gatefold (10" + 12")**
**Large albums (10" + 12")**
**Small (8" or smaller)**
**Premiums, promotions, package design**

The columns shown in this section are as follows, left to right:

1. **Label:** record company name.
2. **Set and record number**: Combination of both, to the extent that this information is available.
3. **Size:** diameter, rounded to nearest inch. Since this is a heterogeneous listing, it would be impossible to indicate the specific size in the column header.
4. **# Rec:** The same factors pertaining to size apply to this column.
5. **Main title**
6. **Year**: Since there are no label notes for these companies in which this information would be available, I have included it here.

**7&8. Values and prices**

9. **Remarks:** This column appears in certain catagories. Miscellaneous tidbits of information appear here.

**♪A TALKING BOOK**

**Associated/subsidiary labels:** none known

**Distributed and produced by:** Garden City Publishing Co., New York.

**Manufactured by:** Book, same; record, Victor

**Overall description of content:** general children's entertainment

**Record:** 10" black shellac; also, 8" one-sides play flexible cardboard quasi-picture disc.

**Record label:** Shellac records: gold on black; Picture-disc (only one seen): white on red label. Holder/cover: Shellac: hard cover book with DJ and sixteen pages with color prints; Pic-disc in thin cardboard gatefold cover.

**Date range:** 1939 – 1941

**Series and record-numbering sequences:** Two prefixes seen: "GC" and TB". GC = Garden City; TB = Talking Book. Two "TBs" seen; three GCs seen. TB 3 and TB 4 are pic-discs.

**Miscellaneous:** The series is not to be confused with "Talking Books" from the 1918 – 1919 era.

**♪ACTION**

**Associated/subsidiary labels:** none

**Distributed, produced, and manufactured by:** Action Records, Inc., Hollywood, CA

**Overall description of content:** general children's entertainment

**Record:** 10" black vinyl, silver on maroon label, album style, three records per set

**Date range:** 195?

Series and record-numbering sequences: I can only verify that two albums exist (see below). Others may or may not have been produced.

**Miscellaneous:** This is a very scarce label. In addition to the characters "Sunset Carson" and "Monte Hale", it has been reported that a third series, "Wild Bill Hickok & Jingles" exists, but I have never seen one. Readers are invited to contact the author with any additional information for this elusive label.

Only two titles have been seen, even though 17 are listed on the back cover. Action Records, Inc., Hollywood, CA. The following titles are listed on the two known album covers:

"Monte Hale Foils the Colorado Cattle Rustlers"
"Monte Hale Captures the Carson City Kid"
"Monte Hale and the Broken Indian Treaty"
"Monte Hale Saves the Pony Express"
"Monte Hale and the Texas Stampede"
"Monte Hale Finds the Phantom Gold Mine"
"Monte Hale Rounds Up the Montana Bad Men"
"Sunset Carson and the Rustler Gang"
"Sunset Carson with the Texas Rangers"
"Sunset Carson in the Indian Country"
"Sunset Carson and the Payroll Robbery"
"Sunset Carson at Ghost Canyon"
"Sunset Carson and the Apache Raiders"

I doubt that these titles were ever issued, but I hope someone reading this will prove me wrong.

**♪ADMIRAL**

**Associated/subsidiary labels:** none known.

**Distributed, produced, and manufactured by:** Admiral Records, Inc., New York, NY

**Overall description of content:** adult and children's general entertainment

**Record:** 10" black vinyl

**Record label:** black on pink, red on yellow, etc.; floating head photo of artist.

**Holder/cover:** paper sleeves, color graphics

**Date range:** 195?

**Series and record-numbering sequences:** one series of 10 records, consecutively numbered from K-101 to K-110.

**Miscellaneous:** No further information available.

**♪ADVENTURE**

**Associated/subsidiary labels:** none known.

**Distributed, produced, and manufactured by:** Adventure Records, New York, NY

**Overall description of content:** general children's entertainment

**Record:** 10" black vinyl

**Record label:** blue on off-white or pink

**Holder/cover:** paper sleeves for singles; book style holders for albums. Color graphics on covers.

**Date range:** 1946 – 1947; one single record from 1951. Not sure why such a gap is there.

**Series and record-numbering sequences:** Two series: 16 singles (A-1 to A-16) and 7 albums with two records each (ARC 1-7).

**Miscellaneous:** Sol Goodman was president of this company in 1948.

**♪ALLEGRO**

**Associated/subsidiary labels:** none known.

**Distributed, produced, and manufactured by:** Allegro Records, New York, NY

**Overall description of content:** general children's entertainment; also religious for one of the series.

**Record:** 10" black vinyl

**Record label:** white on red (top half); red on yellow (bottom half)

**Holder/cover:** paper sleeves with color graphics.

**Date range:** 1948

**Series and record-numbering sequences:** Three series as follows. Juniors: 26 records numbered AJ-1 to AJ-26,

**Miscellaneous:** This was one of several labels associated with a company called From the Catalog of Music You Enjoy as well as Musette.

Larry Gould was the president of this division in 1949.

## ♪CARNIVAL TOY

**Associated/subsidiary labels:** none
**Distributed, produced, and manufactured by:** Carnival Toy Division of Lorraine Industries, Bridgeport, CT
**Overall description of content:** general children's entertainment
**Record:** 5" black vinyl
**Record label:** silver ink stamped on black vinyl (no paper)
**Holder/cover:** boxed sets of four or five records
**Date range:** 1963 or after (Date does not appear anywhere. I know the approximate year because the company's order form has a Zip Code on it; Zip Codes began July 1963).
**Series and record-numbering sequences:** forty-eight records in eleven boxes sets; not consecutively numbered.
**Miscellaneous:** At 5" in size, this is one of the largest series of records in this size range ever made.
The records were made at least into the mid-1960s, making this label one of the last surviving 78-rpm issues in North America. By virtue of the fact that the company did not start making 78-rpm records until the 1960s makes it one of the last to begin production of kiddie 78s.

The company made a miniature battery-operated record player specifically designed to play Carnival records. The record is inserted into a slot and then plays automatically. The records had a special spindle hole that allowed for this procedure. The record could be played on any manual record player, as well.

## ♪CARTOON

**Associated/subsidiary labels:** none
**Distributed, produced, and manufactured by:** Cartoon Records, Inc., Hollywood, CA
**Overall description of content:** children's general entertainment
**Record:** 10" black shellac
**Record label:** blue on yellow, big smiling cartoon face in center
**Holder/cover:** hard-side book-style album, colorful drawing of cartoon characters
**Date range:** 1946
**Series and record numbering sequences:** six albums issued, numbered Album 1 to 6.
**Miscellaneous:** There are six titles listed on the only album cover in my collection, but I suspect only the first two were actually released. Any readers with information to the contrary are invited to contact me.

On side 1 is the title story. On side 2 is a song, unrelated to the title story.

Notable about this series is the cover cartoon drawings of famous artist Dave Fleischer. David Fleischer (1894 – 1979) was a German-American animator, film director, and film producer, best known as a co-owner of Fleischer Studios with his equally famous older brother Max Fleischer. He was a native of New York City.

Dave Fleischer was notable during the brothers' early days as the rotoscope model for their first character, Koko the Clown. he went on to become director and later producer of the studio's output. Although he is credited as "director" of every film released by the Fleischer studio from 1921 to 1942, the lead animators actually performed directorial duties, and Fleischer served that of a producer. Among the cartoon series Fleischer supervised during this period were Betty Boop and Popeye the Sailor.

In January 1942, Fleischer, no longer able to cooperate with his brother, left the company to become President of Screen Gems at Columbia Pictures. Fleischer Studios ceased on May 24, 1941 when Paramount called in the loan it had given the studio. Now owned wholly by Paramount, it was re-organized as Famous Studios (though the name wasn't offical until May 1943).

In the late 1940s, Fleischer moved over to Universal, where he became a special effects expert and general problem-solver, working on films such as Francis, The Birds, and Thoroughly Modern Millie. He died on June 25, 1979 of a stroke in Woodland Hills, California, having spend over a decade in retirement.

## ♪CHAPEL RECORDS

**Associated/subsidiary labels:** none
**Distributed, produced, and manufactured by:** Chapel Records, a division of Pacific Press Publishing Association, Mountain View, CA (and earlier, Glendale, CA).
**Overall description of content:** children's religious (Christian) and secular
**Record:** 10" black vinyl.
**Record label:** green and brown on beige, cartoon drawing on label matching title
**Holder/cover:** cardboard gatefold (two records), paper sleeves (singles), all in full color
**Date range:** 195?
**Series and record numbering sequences:** at least 42 titles, consecutively numbered from R-701 to R-740, then skipping to R-746. It is possible that 78s only went to the mid-R-730s and then switched to 33$^{1}/_{3}$ rpms.
**Miscellaneous:** This series gives the appearance of being of wholly religious content, but some of the stories are secular in nature, teaching about obedience, manners, friendship, etc.

This is one of several small and obscure labels in my collection that offer religious children's records. Very little is known about these tiny companies, including this one.

## CHILDREN'S RECORD GUILD

**Associated/subsidiary labels:** Young People's Records, Pram
**Distributed by:** primarily the Book of the Month Club
**Produced by:** Children's Record Guild, New York, NY
**Manufactured by:** same
**Overall description of content:** general children's entertainment
**Record:** 10" vinyl
**Record label:** black on blue or orange, black on green or red. Some tiny cartoon drawings, vertical color stripes top half of label.
**Holder/cover:** paper sleeves, two-record sets in gatefold sleeves
**Date range:** 1950 – 1957 (LPs were marketed up to 1977.)
**Series and record numbering sequences:** Known of: 143 titles (159 records: 14 titles issued as two record sets + #206 reissued on #1001 + 1011 double record set and #414 reissued on #9009). Thirteen different series, mainly ascribed to certain age groups: 200s, 300s, 400s, 500s, 600s, 700s, 800s, 1000s, 3400s, 4500s, 5000s, 8000s, 9000s. Numbers within series are not consecutive, as many numbers were reserved for records that were never released.
**Miscellaneous:** This company was an outgrowth of Young People's Records (see separate label notes). Dissatisfied with YPR's ownership, Horace Grenell, its founder, left in 1950 and developed the Children's Record Guild for the publishing house Greystone Press. Greystone also franchised CRG to Book-of-the-Month Club and Encyclopedia Americana, which obtained CRG subscribers from their own mailing lists. In fact, CRG is mostly associated with the Book-Of-The-Month Club. Countless thousands of American families subscribed to this record series.

In 1952, Greystone purchased YPR, while continuing to operate the CRG club throughout the 1950s. Greystone marketed YPR and CRG titles on 78-rpm until the late 1960s.

The CRG label was primarily a mail-order club (75% mail order, 25% stores). (David Bonner)

## CHILDHOOD RHYTHMS (RUTH EVANS)

**Associated/subsidiary labels:** Folk Dances (Ruth Evans)
**Distributed and produced by:** first by Ruth Evans, Springfield, MA; then by Chartwell House, New York, NY
**Manufactured by:** unknown
**Overall description of content:** children's instructional — rhythms
**Record:** 10" black vinyl
**Record Label:** dark blue or black on white or light green; plain text, no design
**Holder/cover:** book style or boxes
**Date range:** 1953 – 1954
**Series and record numbering sequences:** ten albums known, three records each, numbered with Roman numerals. Series 1 to 10.
**Miscellaneous:** This series is sometimes referred to as the "Ruth Evans records." They were prepared for use in the lower grades of elementary schools. They provide accompaniment for simple rhythmic activities for young children.

This is one of several small and obscure labels in my collection that offer school dance and rhythm music and instructions. Very little is known about these tiny companies, including this one.

## CLASSIC

**Associated/subsidiary labels:** none
**Distributed, produced, and manufactured by:** Classic Records, Inc.
**Overall description of content:** general children's entertainment
**Record:** 10" black vinyl
**Record Label:** black on pink
**Holder/cover:** paper gatefold and hard cover albums
**Date range:** 1946
**Series and record numbering sequences:** only four sets identified, no series patterns.
**Miscellaneous:** Dramatized operas with accompaniment by the NY City Center Opera and the NY Philharmonic Orchestra. George Wechsler was an executive with this company.

## CLEF

**Associated/subsidiary labels:** none
**Distributed by:** Educational Recording Co., Houston, TX
**Produced by:** Tony Martin for the Texas State Department of Education, Texas Gulf Sulphur Company
**Manufactured by:** unknown
**Overall description of content:** children's educational (music appreciation)
**Record:** 12" black shellac
**Record label:** silver on blue text; some music notes as graphic, otherwise just text
**Holder/cover:** book-style album, mainly text on the cover, two-color
**Date range:** 1948
**Series and record numbering sequences:** four albums only, consecutively numbered 1 – 4, four records each.
**Miscellaneous:** Ernst Hoffman is the conductor of the Texas Educational Orchestra on these records. He also narrates. These records were not sold in stores, only to schools. I have only seen one album, and therefore cannot verify the existence of the others listed in this book.

This is one of several small and obscure labels in my collection that offer school dance and rhythm music and instructions. Very little is known about these tiny companies, including this one.

## COLOR TUNES

**Associated/subsidiary labels:** none
**Distributed, produced, and manufactured by:** Allied Record

Sales Company, Los Angeles, CA. Sleeve mfg. by Celco Corp, Santa Monica, CA
**Overall description of content:** general children's entertainment
**Record:** 10" color vinyl; translucent blue and black have been seen.
**Record label:** blue and red on beige; small graphics, red and blue circles
**Holder/cover:** paper sleeve, coated with "wipe-off" plastic. Back of cover is for kids to color on and then wipe-off with wet towel. For this reason, it is very difficult to find covers in anything approaching decent shape, as most got destroyed or damaged by water.
**Date range:** 1952
**Series and record numbering sequences:** records numbered consecutively on each side (e.g. 100/101). Lowest number seen is 100/101. Highest number seen is 130/131. I have very few in this set, but if one assumes that all records within this range were issued, then at least 16 titles exist. I only have names for seven titles.
**Miscellaneous:** Very little is known about this label, but famous radio/TV personality Art Linkletter makes an appearance on at least two of the records.

**♪COLOR PHOTO-RECORD**
**Associated/subsidiary labels:** none
**Distributed, produced, and manufactured by:** Roy Gregory, Inc., Bridgeport, CT
**Overall description of content:** adults' and children's general entertainment and instructional
**Record:** 7" picture disc
**Record label:** picture disc; b&w white action photo on one side, color posed shot on reverse
**Holder/cover:** paper sleeve, printing; no graphics
**Date range:** ca. 1948
**Series and record numbering sequences:** unnumbered set of four records
**Miscellaneous:** Action photos of famous Boston Red Sox baseball players are the subject matter. No further information is known about this set.

**♪COLUMBIA**

Due to the size and complexity of Columbia Records and all of its subsidiaries and label variations, I am foregoing the regular template. I am providing the data most relevant for their children's records in a narrative format. The reader interested in greater detail is encouraged to seek out other books and the Internet. I have filtered out all but the most interesting and salient historical points as it relates to the scope of this book.

**A VERY BRIEF HISTORY:**
Columbia Records is the oldest continually-used brand name in recorded sound, dating back to 1888. Columbia was originally the local company distributing and selling Edison phonographs and phonograph cylinders in Washington, D.C., Maryland and Delaware. As was the custom of some of the regional phonograph companies, Columbia produced many commercial cylinder recordings of its own. Columbia severed its ties to Edison and the North American Phonograph Company in 1893, and thereafter sold only records and phonographs of their own manufacture. Columbia began selling disc records and phonographs in addition to the cylinder system in 1901. For a decade Columbia competed with both the Edison Phonograph Company cylinders and the Victor Talking Machine Company disc records as one of the top three names in recorded sound. In 1908 Columbia introduced mass production of double-sided records.

In July of 1912 Columbia decided to concentrate exclusively on disc records, and stopped recording new cylinder records and manufacturing cylinder phonographs, although they continued pressing and selling cylinder records from their back catalog for a year or two more.

In early 1925 Columbia began recording with the new electric recording process licensed from Western Electric. In a secret agreement with Victor, both companies did not make the new recording technology public knowledge for some months, in order not to hurt sales of their existing acoustically recorded catalog while a new electrically recorded catalog was being built. In October 1928, Columbia executive Frank Buckley Walker pioneered some of the first country music or "hillbilly" genre recordings in Johnson City, Tennessee.

In 1931, the English Columbia Graphophone Company merged with the Gramophone Company to form Electric & Musical Industries Ltd. (EMI). EMI was forced to sell its American Columbia operations because of anti-trust concerns to the American Record Corporation (ARC).

ARC, including the Columbia label in the USA, was bought by Columbia Broadcasting System in 1938 for $700,000. CBS was originally co-founded by Columbia Records. The Columbia trademark from this point until the late 1950s was two overlapping circles with the "Magic Notes" in the left circle and a CBS microphone in the right circle.

In 1948 Columbia introduced the Long Playing microgroove (LP) record (sometimes in early advertisements Lp) format, spinning at 33$^{1}/_{3}$ rpm revolutions per minute, which became the standard for the phonograph record for half a century. In 1951, CBS severed its decades long distribution arrangement with EMI and signed a distribution deal with Philips Records outside North America. In 1955, Columbia USA introduced its "Walking Eye" logo which actually depicts a needle (the legs) on a record (the eye). The logo was modified in 1960 to the familiar one still used today and replaced the notes and mike logo. In 1961, CBS ended its arrangement with Philips Records and formed its own international organization, CBS Records which released Columbia recordings outside the USA and Canada on the CBS label.

Columbia became the most successful record company in the 1950s when they hired impressario Mitch Miller away from the Mercury label. Miller quickly signed on Mercury's biggest artist at the time, Frankie Laine, and discovered several of the decade's biggest recording stars including Tony Bennett, Guy Mitchell, Johnnie Ray, The Four Lads, Rosemary Clooney and Johnny Mathis.

In 1988 Columbia/CBS Records was acquired by Sony, who rechristened the parent division Sony Music Entertainment in 1991. As Sony only had a temporary license on the CBS Records name, it then acquired from EMI its former rights to the Columbia trademarks outside the U.S., Canada and Japan (Columbia Graphophone), which generally had not been used by EMI since the 1960s.

Sony merged its music division with Bertelsmann AG's BMG unit in 2004; the combined company, Sony BMG continues to use the Columbia Records name and Walking Eye logo in all markets except Japan (where that division is called Sony Records and is still fully owned by Sony). Sony Music uses a modified version of the Magic Notes trademark for the logo of its Sony Classical label. (Wikipedia and Allan Sutton)

**Associated Labels:** Okeh, Epic, Silver Burdett

**DETAILS ON THE VARIOUS CHILDREN'S SERIES:** Main Series (J, MJ, MJV, JS prefixes): 10" shellac and vinyl. 298 record sets (404 records) issued between 1939 and 1957. Consecutively numbered from J-1 to JS-299. Book style, single and double-record (gatefold) paper and cardboard sleeves. Various label styles, colorful cover art. Many famous characters, performers and personalities permeate this great series.

**Record-a-View (V prefix):** 10" vinyl. Series of 8 records from 1956. Numbered: V-8501 to V-8508. Unique in this series is that two Viewmaster© reels are inserted into a pouch on the cover. They could be viewed with the standard stereo viewers while the record is playing.

**Book-style albums (C, H, MM, MX prefixes):** 10- and 12" shellac and vinyl. I have listed 47 album sets. Some are crossover to adult markets. Some are not on the list because I haven't 'discovered' them as yet. Many famous actors contributed to this series, making it highly collectible.

**Miscellaneous singles:** May include some records that are borderline for children, or have one side which is definitely for adults and others suitable for children.

**Music for living (JS prefix):** 10" vinyl, 1956. Sixty titles numbered consecutively from JS-301 to JS-360. School series. Songbooks accompanied records for teacher and students, which were correlated with the record being played. Six boxed sets of 10 records (albums) each, one box for each grade from one to six. Produced in association with Silver Burdett publishers. Silver Burdett issued the same records without the Columbia label (see separate notes), but their sets had 15 records for each grade.

**Playtime 200 series (No prefix):** 7" shellac. Issued from 1937-41. Previously issued by Plaza and American Record Corp. in 1924. 70 records numbered consecutively from 201 to 270. Two label and sleeve versions. Labels on both black on yellow, 1st version a mother goose with kids drawing; 2nd version a cartoon drawing of the title subject. Generic Playtime paper sleeves, black on green; 1st version silhouettes of kids frolicking; 2nd version is a 'star' pattern of 8 kiddie themes. All sleeves list other titles in the series on the reverse.

**Playtime 300 series (no prefix, but does have suffix):** Each record has a "PV" suffix in the number (e.g. 303-PV). 6- and 7" red or black vinyl. Issued from 1948-54. 114 records nearly consecutively numbered from 303 to 417 (not issued: 324). Three versions were issued. Not all versions had all of the titles.

The first version goes up to at least 332. 7" black vinyl. Labels black on yellow, cartoon drawing of subject. Sleeves generic Playtime paper sleeves, orange on beige. Four cartoon drawings of kiddie characters on front. Lists other titles on back.

The second version goes up to 374 only. Almost all are 7" red or black vinyl. I have seen two 6" size in this version. Labels are four-color except for one or two seen in blue and white only. Sleeves are four-color matte finish, specific to title. Reverse of sleeve has a yellow background with black printing and lists other titles in the series.

The third version spans the entire list, although it is not clear if Columbia issued all the records in this version. They may have selected only the more popular titles, especially from 303 to about 330. Mostly 6", but some 7" red vinyl up to #383; 6" only after #383. Labels are blue on white with cartoon drawing of title subject. Sleeves in four-color artwork, specific to title. They come in both matte and glossy finish. Background color on reverse of sleeves is as follows: up to # 387 blue, yellow, or pink with mainly blue printing (some red); after # 387 blue, white, or pink with blue printing.

**Junior (J prefix):** 7" black vinyl, Issued 1953-55 in both 78 and 45 rpm. 53 titles consecutively numbered from J-701-753. Label is blue on yellow, line drawings of a boy and a girl. Paper sleeve specific to title, four-color, other records in the series listed on back.

**Play Color Record Book (mjv 500 series and 900-pv series):** 6" red vinyl, issued 1952. Series of 12 double-record sets. It was issued with two serial numbered series on the label: 900 and 500. I am not sure of the purpose of this scheme. I have not seen any sleeves, but I assume that at least part of the sleeves were coloring book pages. Labels are red on white, some line drawings of kids at play. Very scarce.

**Baseball (PV 800 series):** 6" red vinyl, 8 records in set, PV-800 to PV-807. The first four were issued in 1952 and the second four were issued in 1953. These are instructional records made by Hall of Fame baseball players. Very scarce set. Labels are blue on white with drawing of baseball theme related to subject on top part of label. Labels of 1st four say "Playtime Baseball Series." Labels on the 2nd four say "Baseball Series." Sleeve on 1st four: drawing of baseball player, head to toe, on solid pastel color background. Labels on 2nd four have four-color photos of player on front. Reverses of 1st four have line drawings showing correct way to play the position; reverse of 2nd four have drawings plus text instructions.

**Harper-Columbia Bubble Books:** This was first true American children's 78-rpm record series, issued between 1917 and 1922. The actual record label is "The Harper-Columbia Book That Sings." There are 14 books in this series, with each book containing three one-sided 5½" records. They were produced by the Columbia Graphophone Company for the Bubble Book Division of Harper & Brothers Publishers (Franklin Square, New York). The first ten in the series are fairly easy to find today, although getting one in top condition is tough. Numbers 11 & 12 are tougher, and 13 & 14 are difficult to find. The records are inserted into sleeves in the book which are beautifully illustrated by Rhoda Chase. The stories are by Ralph Mayhew and Burges Johnson. The illustration on the cover is a drawing of a young boy looking at Mother Goose and fairy tale images that he "sees" in a giant soap bubble he has just blown from a soap-bubble pipe (hence "Bubble Book"). At $1 per set, while relatively expensive for the day, sales were very strong at the beginning, but eventually their popularity wore off and Columbia relinquished the license to Victor Talking Machine Company.

Two Bubble Book ephemera worth mentioning are the ultra-rare "Mother Goose Cut-Out Bubble Book," and the "Mother Goose Paint Book." The "Cut-out Book" contains stand-up cutout figures of characters appearing in some of the earlier Bubble Books. They could be assembled and placed on a cardboard platform that would sit on the record while it was being played and thus "animate" the story to which the child was listening.

**Columbia Bubble Books:** After relinquishing the Bubble Book patent to Victor in 1924 (see separate notes for the Victor Bubble Books), Columbia reacquired it in the late 1920s. In 1930, this time in association with publisher Dodd, Mead & Company, Columbia issued four Bubble Books. While the books themselves are unnumbered, the individual records are. A suffix of "BB" is used, e.g., "1BB." Two books were reissues of Harper-Columbia Bubble Books #13 & 14 and two were new titles, not previously issued by either Columbia or Victor. These were available as a boxed set. Each book has two 5½" records (instead of the original format of three): one record is 2-sided and one is 1-sided. They are electrically recorded (as opposed to the earlier acoustic process). This is a very rare set, especially the box that comes with it.

## ♪CONCORDIA SINGING PICTURE BOOKS

**Associated/subsidiary labels:** none
**Distributed, produced, and manufactured by:** Concordia Publishing House, St. Louis, MO
**Overall description of content:** children's religious (Christian)
**Record:** 7" black vinyl
**Record label:** black on pink, green, or blue; text only
**Holder/cover:** 12-page booklet, 8" x 11". Record is held in the cover. Color drawings and text.
**Date range:** 1959
**Series and record-numbering sequences:** exact name of series is "Concordia Childrens (sic) Singing Picture Book." Six books have been seen. Involved serial number on label (probably an RCA manufactured record).
**Miscellaneous:** This is one of several small and obscure labels in my collection that offer religious children's records. Very little is known about these tiny companies, including this one.

## ♪CONQUEROR

**Associated/subsidiary labels:** none
**Distributed, produced, and manufactured by:** Regal Records and its successor, the American Record Corp., for Sears Roebuck & Co.
**Overall description of content:** general adult entertainment with a few children's records in the catalog
**Record:** 10" black shellac
**Record label:** gold on maroon
**Holder/cover:** none seen
**Date range:** 1926 – 1942
**Series and record-numbering sequences:** catalog for general public with a few children's records sprinkled in
**Miscellaneous:** Produced by Regal Records and its successor, The American Record Corp (ARC), for Sears Roebuck & Co. This was a popular label during the Great Depression. Columbia purchased the masters from ARC in 1938. The record sleeves state that the proper playing speed for Conqueror Records is 80 rpm. (Allan Sutton)

## ♪CONTINENTAL

**Associated/subsidiary labels:** Remington, Remington Junior, Little Chip
**Distributed, produced, and manufactured by:** Continental Record Corp, New York, NY
**Overall description of content:** general children's entertainment

**Record:** 10" black or translucent red vinyl
**Record label:** black on green or blue, name on company in reverse colors (white on black)
**Holder/cover:** paper sleeves, color cartoon drawings specific to title; later releases in cardboard sleeves.
**Date range:** ca. 1948, reissued in 1954 as a Remington subsidiary(?)
**Series and record numbering sequences:** only seven records (six singles and an album) are known of on this label. The singles are numbered 201 to 206.
**Miscellaneous:** Little is known about this label. The main storylines ("Adventures of Edna") show up in related labels. I am not sure which label had the first appearance of this highly collectible character, Continental or Remington Junior. Some of the Continental sleeves list Remington records on the reverse.

## ♪CORAL (DECCA)

**Associated/subsidiary labels:** Decca
**Distributed, produced, and manufactured by:** Decca Records, New York and London
**Overall description of content:** general adult entertainment with a sprinkling of children's records in the mix
**Record:** 10" vinyl and shellac
**Record label:** black on orange; gold on maroon
**Holder/cover:** generic Coral paper sleeves, glossy four-color paper sleeves with artwork and/or photos specific to the record title.
**Date range:** 1952 – 1955 (for children's records)
**Series and record numbering sequences:** no series for children, per se; but a bunch of single kiddie records appeared in the 1300s part of the catalog. I do think it was a separate series, but part of the main catalog. There were also a bunch of single kiddie records in the 60,000 part of the catalogue. I have identified about two-dozen single children's records including some highly collectible discs by Arnold Stang and Gabby Hayes. Three 2-record gatefold sets were produced for children, as well.
**Miscellaneous:** Coral Records was a Decca Records subsidiary based in the USA. Various jazz and swing band recordings were issued on Coral in the 1940s. Coral's A&R manager Bob Thiele would marry Coral artist Teresa Brewer. Coral Records is fondly remembered by early rock & roll fans as the home of the incomparable Buddy Holly and The Crickets. Coral was swallowed up by MCA Records in the late 1960s. In the late 1950s Debbie Reynolds briefly recorded for Coral, with such songs as "Tammy." (Wikipedia)

## ♪CRICKET

**Associated/subsidiary labels:** Kiddie Koncert, Toy Toon
**Distributed, produced, and manufactured by:** Pickwick Sales Corp., Brooklyn, NY
**Overall description of content:** general children's entertainment
**Record:** 6" records, black or yellow vinyl; 7" and 10" records, black and occasional starburst or marbelized colored vinyl (especially UK versions)
**Record label:** 1st version: light brown on yellow, drawing of a cricket; 2nd version: blue on red and yellow; cartoon of a cricket along with kids and animals dancing. Company logo in bull's-eye graphic.
**Holder/cover:** 1st version: three-color; 2nd version: four-color; paper and thin cardboard sleeves; boxed sets sold through the mail. Sleeves have been seen in two versions: an earlier (scarcer) version 1, which appeared in the main series in record numbers C11 to C30 only; there were a few in the Christmas series as well. Version 2 appears on all records released. Values for version 1 covers are about three times higher than second version, as they are very scarce.
**Date range:** 1953 – 1968
**Series and record numbering sequences:**
The main series: consisted of at least 162 records, the first being #11, not #1. The highest number seen is #175. The main series was issued in both 7" and 10" sizes, however the highest number seen in the 10" size is C-89. The series is numbered consecutively with a few missing numbers, either of undiscovered or unreleased records.
The 100 and the 200 series: The main series (C11 to C175 and CX6 to C19) were partially reissued with a different numbering system, the 100 series and 200 series. In the 100 series, 13 titles have been seen, and in the 200 series, 24 titles have been seen. The 100 and 200 series were also issued on a label variation, Kiddie Koncert. See elsewhere in label notes for more details. The 100s are 7" black vinyl; the 200s are 6" black or yellow vinyl.

The Christmas series starts with #CX-6, not #CX-1. Records were issued in both 7" and 10" sizes. The highest number seen in the 10" size is C-89.

Boxed and album sets were issued, usually containing four records, arranged by subjects (e.g. learning, stories, animals, Christmas, TV personalities, Mother Goose, etc.). Following are known boxed and album sets. Add $5 to the combined price of the loose records if the box comes with the records.
**Cricket Record Library (version 1):** six sets seen, four records each, numbered A-4, B-4, C-4, D-4, E-4, X-4. Boxes 7" w x 9" h and are portrait oriented. Records are numbered as in the main series.
Cricket Record Library (version 2): six sets seen, 4 records each, numbered C-4, D-4, E-4, F-4, G-4, X-4. Boxes 9" w x 7" h and are landscape oriented. Records are numbered as in the "200" series.
**Cardboard Gatefold Holders:** four sets known of, four records each, numbered A-4, B-4, C-4, D-4. Boxes are 7" w x 7" h. Records are numbered as in the main series.

**Kiddie 2-Pack:** These are actually just two regular Cricket records packaged together in a cello bag with a cardboard holder at the top. Retail sales lists identify them with a "TP" designation, however this does not appear on the holder. 32 different combinations were produced, numbered from TP1 to TP-28 and TPX 1-4 (Christmas) 1-4.

**Miscellaneous:** Cricket was founded in 1953 by Cy Leslie (who also started VOCO records). The corporate name is Pickwick Sales Corporation.

With a few notable exceptions, most of the titles are generic in nature (e.g. folk songs, mother goose, etc) and the artists are "in-house." Some of the exceptions to the generic titles are the Lassie and Bat Masterson TV personalities, Gerald McBoing Boing, and Walter Lantz characters. Some notable performers include Gisele McKenzie, Kate Smith, Gene Autry, Smiley Burnette and Dennis Day, to name a few.

Cricket records appeared in the UK on the Cricket and Happy Time labels. A series of 45 rpms was issued in Australia on the Cricket label. No Australian 78s have been seen.

Singers and performers often appeared under different names on the different labels, and perhaps within the same label. For example, the Kiddie Koncert series duplicated the same titles as the Cricket series. The label credits show names that are different from the Cricket labels, but when one listens to both versions, the soundtrack is exactly the same. Many Cricket records do not list the credits, but the same titles on the Kiddie Koncert do show credits. I have applied those names to the Cricket listings. Artists' royalty arrangements are the probable reason for this.

## ♪CUB

**Associated/subsidiary labels:** Asch, Stinson, Asch-Stinson, Disc, Folkways.

**Distributed, produced, and manufactured by:** Cub Records, New York, NY

**Overall description of content:** general children's entertainment

**Record:** 10" black vinyl

**Record label:** stylized drawing of a baby animal (a dog?), green on yellow.

**Holder/cover:** two-color paper sleeves, primitive stylized cartoon drawings pertaining to the title

**Date range:** 1948

**Series and record numbering sequences:** 10-record series, numbered consecutively from 1 – 10.

**Miscellaneous:** Moe Asch was the founder of several labels which produced children's records and which are listed in this book. His first label was Asch; then Stinson, Asch-Stinson, Disc, Cub, and Folkways, in that order.

Soon after the bankruptcy of his Disc label in 1948, Moe Asch began issuing some of Disc's children's records, specifically the Young Folksay series, on a new label called Cub. Unlike the Disc issues, the Cub records were vinyl pressings and were packaged singly in illustrated jackets, which by then was industry standard in the children's field. Some of Woody Guthrie's early "songs to grow on" numbers are on Cub, making this a very collectible and high priced series.

When Asch launched his Folkways label in 1950, Cub quickly disappeared.

## ♪DADDY LEW LEHR

**Associated/subsidiary labels:** none

**Distributed, produced, and manufactured by:** Shelley Products, Cold Spring Harbor, NY

**Overall description of content:** children's general entertainment

**Record:** 6" dark blue vinyl

**Record label:** black on yellow

**Holder/cover:** "picture wheel," 11" x 11", square with curved top. A grommeted picture wheel can be turned in synch with the record playing. Illustrated panels show through a cut-out window corresponding with the storyline. Record is held to the cover with a cotter's pin.

**Date range:** 1948

**Series and record-numbering sequences:** 12 records listed on back cover, #1 – 12. The individual numbers do not appear individually on the cover or record label, however. There are individual disc numbers on the label, not in sequence with the order of titles shown on cover.

**Miscellaneous:** This is one of a few children's records (Capitol issued some) with so-called picture wheels. See description above.

## ♪DECCA

Due to the size and complexity of Decca Records and all of its subsidiaries and label variations, I am forgoing the regular template. I am providing the data most relevant for their children's records in a narrative format. The reader interested in greater detail is invited to seek out other books and the Internet. In the following paragraphs, I have filtered out all but the most interesting and salient historical points as it relates to the scope of this book.

Please note that this section refers to American Decca pressings as opposed to English Decca records, which were totally different.

### A VERY BRIEF HISTORY:

Decca started out as a British company in 1929. Within years of its founding in London by former stockbroker Edward Lewis, the Decca Record Company Ltd. was the second largest record label in the world, calling itself "the Supreme Record Company." The term "Decca" was never determined to signify a specific meaning or name, but some theories cite the opening musical notes of a Beethoven symphony: "D-E-C-C-A." A cameo of Beethoven graced the British Decca label for many years.

In 1934 a US branch of Decca was launched, which quickly became a major player in the depressed American record market thanks to its roster of popular artists, particularly Bing Crosby, and the shrewd management of former US Brunswick General Manager Jack Kapp. It was Kapp's intention to go up against popular US budget labels such as RCA-Victor's Bluebird.

Decca, in part through Kapp's entertainment industry contacts at Brunswick, signed an impressive array of popular performers. The focus was on the popular, country, and "race-record" markets. In 1942, Decca released "White Christmas" by Bing Crosby, which became the best-selling single of all time.

The American branch of Decca functioned separately for many years and eventually merged with Music Corporation of America (MCA) in 1962, becoming a subsidiary company under MCA. Because MCA held the rights to the name Decca in the US and Canada, British Decca sold its records in the United States and Canada under the label London Records. In Britain, London Records became a mighty catch-all licensing label for foreign recordings from the nascent post-WW II American independent and semi-major labels such as Cadence, ABC-Paramount, and Liberty. Conversely, US Decca recordings were marketed in Britain by UK Decca on Brunswick Records and Coral Records through 1968 when it began using the MCA Records imprint. The Decca name was dropped by MCA in 1973 in favor of the MCA Records label. The Decca label is currently in use by Universal Music Group worldwide; this is possible because Universal Studios (which officially dropped the MCA name after the Seagram buyout in 1997) acquired PolyGram, British Decca's parent company in 1998, thus consolidating Decca trademark ownership. Today, Decca is a leading label for both classical music and Broadway scores. (Wikipedia and Allan Sutton)

**Associated/subsidiary labels:**
Vocalion, Brunswick, London, Champion, Parlophone, Odeon, Polydor

**DETAILS ON THE VARIOUS CHILDREN'S SERIES:**

**Albums (A, DA, DAU prefixes):** mostly 10" (a few 12") black shellac or vinyl records in book style albums. Most have between 2 and 4 records, but a small handful have more. The DA stands for "drop automatic' (as in record changer). The A stands for 'album'. The U stands for unbreakable, as in vinyl. Most albums had an insert booklet that in and of itself is a collectible item. I have nearly 100 children and children's suitable record sets listed in this category issued between 1938 and 1952. The approximate intervals of dates: Album #4 — 1938; #15 — '39; #93 — '40; #243 — '41; #90 — '42; #350 — '43; #376 — '44; #386 — '45; #401 — '46; #521 — '47; #658 — '48; #724 — '49; #864 — '51; #919 — '52.

Some of the most sought-after children's 78-rpm sets can be found in this monumental series. This series, by the way, was by no means only for children. The album numbers start at 1 and go as high as the 900s — so the great majority are actually not for children.

**CU Series:** 12" vinyl (except for one 10"); 18 titles issued between 1946 and 1949. Many of the titles in this list are on my most requested list—a virtual All-Star team of Baby Boomer favorites. Consecutively numbered from CU-100 to CU-117. Heavy paper sleeves in four-color, many fold out front covers, which allow for extra illustrated panels.

**CUS Series:** 10" vinyl; 26 titles numbered from CUS 1 to 27 (# 24 apparently not issued). 8 titles are single records, 18 are 2-record gatefold cover sets, issued from 1946 to 1951. four-color heavy paper sleeves.

**DU Series:** 10 and 12" vinyl. I show 21 titles with this prefix — more of a grouping than a specific series. Issued in the early 1950s.

**1st K Series (1940s):** 10" shellac. 28 3-record sets in gift envelopes with color illustrated covers. Issued between 1934 and 1942. Numbered consecutively from K-1 to K-29, with no title showing for K-25. This K prefix series is not to be confused with the K series from the 1950s (see next series). There are very many extremely popular titles in this series, one of the most collectible in the genre.

**2nd K Series (1950s):** 10" vinyl. 169 single record sets issued numbered from K-1 to K-177. There are eight numbers for which I have no titles and which may or may not have been issued. Glossy and matte four-color brightly illustrated sleeves. Issued between 1950 and 1954. Dozens of extremely popular, valuable and sought after titles abound in this series. This K series is not to be confused with the 1940s K series (see paragraph above).

**Miscellaneous Singles: 10" shellac.** I have listed about 140 singles issued as part of the general Decca catalog between 1934 and 1955. Many of these were for the adult market, but are suitable for children. There may be quite a few which I have not listed because I have not yet identified them.

A few records have children's songs on one side and nonkiddie songs on the reverse. I have not indicated which ones are non-kiddie because, in many cases, this is a judgment call. I will leave it up to the reader to make the final determination.

**Quaker Cereal Sargeant Preston Send-Away Premiums:** 7" vinyl. I have listed this small 4 record set under Decca, even though the label does not show "Decca." They are mostly reissues of titles from the 2nd K series. Kids could send in cereal box tops to obtain the records in the mail. These are the only 7" Decca 78-rpm children's records that I know of.

♪**DIAMOND**

**Associated/subsidiary labels:** none
**Distributed, produced, and manufactured by:** Diamond Record Corp, New York, NY
**Overall description of content:** general children's entertainment
**Record:** 10" shellac
**Record label:** blue on yellow, diamond drawing in top; Mostly plain text
**Holder/cover:** four-color paper sleeve; full-size front flap opens to provide inside panels of black and white text of script. Reverse illustrates other titles in the series.
**Date range:** 194?
**Series and record-numbering sequences:** only four records seen, consecutively numbered from D-21 to D-24. All titles are standard fairy tales.
**Miscellaneous:** Company slogan: "Diamond: Tones That Sparkle." The same performers appear on two or three other labels, but the other record companies have no known connection with Diamond. No further information is available.

♪**DISC**

**Associated/subsidiary labels:** Asch, Asch-Stinson, Stinson; Cub, Folkways
**Distributed, produced, and manufactured by:** Disc Company of America, New York, NY
**Overall description of content:** general children and adult entertainment
**Record:** 10" black shellac
**Record label:** black and white on gray; distinctive red circle on left side
**Holder/cover:** book-style albums, holding two or three records. Some have photos of kids on the front, simple noncluttered design.
**Date range:** 1947 – 1948
**Series and record-numbering sequences:** I have identified 16 albums which are for children or are suitable for children. This is from the many dozens of albums issued by Disc. There is no children's series in terms of a separate numbering system, however albums of similar content for children were billed as the "Young Folksay Series." It included the Songs To Grow On activity series, School Days, and Youth Builder groups of albums. They were not necessarily in consecutive numerical sequence.
**Miscellaneous:** Moe Asch was the founder of several labels that produced children's records and that are listed in this book. His first label was Asch, then Stinson, Asch-Stinson, Disc, Cub, and Folkways, in that order.

As successor to the Asch label, the Disc label expanded upon the example set by the Asch album of play party songs by Leadbelly. Disc's Young Folksay series (under the direction of childhood educator Beatrice Landeck) consisted mostly of raw, low-budget recordings of folk music, as performed by Woody Guthrie, Charity Bailey, Adelaide Van Wey, Pete Seeger, and Leadbelly himself. Disc is also notable for issuing the children's record debut of Tom Glazer (Funnybone Alley). Low budget or not, many of the albums from Disc, especially those from the Young Folksay Series are extremely rare and super-collectible, especially in nice condition. They are some of the earliest recorded anthologies of the artists listed above.The label went bankrupt in 1948. (See Asch label notes for a more detailed background of Moe Asch.)

♪**DISNEYLAND**

**Associated/subsidiary labels:** Official Mickey Mouse Club, Mattel (Mickey Mouse Club Newsreel + Musical Maps), some Golden records
**Distributed, produced, and manufactured by:** Walt Disney Music Co.; Walt Disney Productions
**Overall description of content:** general children's entertainment

**Original Disneyland Series:**
**Record:** 10" vinyl
**Record label:** Earlier records (#37, #38 only?) had the rare 1st Disneyland label, blue on yellow with the Disneyland logo at the bottom, with 'pixie-dust' drawings surrounding it. Later numbers had the standard Disneyland logo (Sleeping Beauty's Castle), silver on purple.
**Holder/cover:** glossy paper, both color and black and white, depicting photos or drawings from the title subject. Reverse is black and white with sheet music and/or lyrics to songs.

**DBR Series:**
**Record:** 7" standard 45-rpm size with large spindle hole. Black vinyl.
**Record label:** silver on dark green; silver stamped directly on black vinyl, no paper label; standard Disneyland logo.
**Holder/cover:** heavy paper four-color sleeves. Lists other titles in this series appear on the back.
NOTE: this section describes all but DBR #50 to 92. They were issued on the "Official Mickey Mouse Club" label. See that section for details.

**Little Gem Series (LG prefix):**
**Record:** 6" for 78rpms; 7" for 45rpms; black vinyl
**Record label:** black on yellow; silver stamped on the black vinyl of the record itself. Standard Disneyland logo (Sleeping Beauty's castle).
**Holder/cover:** heavy paper four-color sleeves. Lists of titles of other Disney series appear on the back.

**Zorro Series (A prefix):**
**Record:** 10" vinyl

**Record label:** standard Disneyland design, silver on purple
**Holder/cover:** glossy paper sleeve, dramatic 'action' paintings of Zorro scenes. Reverse shows other records in the series.
**Date range:** 1956 – 1958 (45s and 78s)

**Original Disneyland Series:**
**Series and record-numbering sequences:** This is primarily a 45-rpm series of about 65 titles, but because there are some that were also issued as 78rpms, they are included in this book. Following are the 78-rpm numbers: 37, 38, 42, 43, 44, 45, 54, and 63. There is no prefix on the 78-rpm versions; all of the 45s have an "F" prefix.

Note: This was the first Disney produced series of 45-rpm singles.

**DBR Series:**
**Date range:** 1959 – 1964
**Series and record-numbering sequences:** There are a total of 78 DBR titles, divided into two different record labels. This section deals only with the 35 titles issued on the Disneyland label, all 45-rpm EPs. The numbers in this part of the DBR record (Disneyland label) series are DBR 20-49 and DBR 93-97. Previously, the initial release of 43 titles in this series (DBR 50 to DBR 92) was on the "Official Mickey Mouse Club" label, Disneyland's predecessor. They were in both 78 and 45-rpm versions. See label notes and listings for "Official Mickey Mouse Club" elsewhere in this book. "DBR" stand for "Disney Big Record" and refers to the amount of playing time, not to the size.

The DBR series has a convoluted numbering system, one that is very hard to digest, even for the veteran collector/archivist. See R. Michael Murray's book, "The Golden Age Of Walt Disney Records", for a detailed explanation of how this numbering system evolved. To begin with, the first records issued in 1955 started with the number DBR 50. But, the entire DBR series runs from DBR 20 to DBR 97. As you can start to see, the initial DBR series was 'sandwiched' between higher and lower numbered records, all of which came out in later years. Weird, for sure.

The initial run of the first 21 DBRs (DBR 50-70) were issued on the Official Mickey Mouse Club label and were distributed by AM-PAR Record Corporation, a division of ABC Paramount. There was one exception to this: DBR 57, which had a label that said "From Disneyland." This was before "Disneyland" was an official label on it's own merits. ABC, which ran the Mickey Mouse Club TV show, was (along with Golden Records/Simon and Schuster) one of Disney's marketing partners for records. Disney took over distribution and production of the DBR series in 1958 starting with DBR-71 and going to DBR-92, however the label remained "Official Mickey Mouse Club." Not until 1959 did the DBR records bear the Disneyland label. It started with DBR 49 and worked chronologically in reverse number order, more or less, backwards to the lowest number, DBR 20 in 1964. DBR records on the Disneyland label were made as 45s only. These records were also identified as "A Walt Disney Six Big Songs Record." Even though this series is only 45s, it is included in my book as it is really part of the larger DBR set that has 78s in it. See "Official Mickey Mouse Club" listings for the other records in this series.

This DBR series is not to be confused with or relared to another small set of Disney titles with a DBR prefix put out by Golden Records in 1955. The "DBR" in this series stands for "Disney Big Record" — see label notes for Golden Records elsewhere.

**Little Gem Series (LG prefix):**
**Date range:** 1960 – 1971
**Series and record numbering sequences:** 123 titles consecutively numbered from LG-701 to LG-823. Note: All were issued in 78- and 45-rpm, but 78s were issued only up to LG-782. For some reason, 78s are much scarcer than 45s. Not only is this probably the latest starting time (1960) for any major American label to produce records in 78-rpm, it also is among the last to continue to produce them (1964)!

**Zorro Series (A prefix):**
**Date range:** 1958
**Series and record numbering sequences:** four records only, A-501 to A-504. Note: These were also issued on 45-rpm with an "F" prefix.

**Miscellaneous:** The Disneyland Records Company began in 1956. Previously, recordings of Disney music and stories first appeared in 1933, a scant five years after the introduction to the world of Walt Disney's Mickey Mouse in the cartoon *Steamboat Willie*.

From 1933 until 1955, a wealth of Disney material was produced on 78-rpm records, all of it licensed by Walt Disney Enterprises to a large number of different record companies. But with the success of "The Ballad Of Davy Crockett" and "The Mickey Mouse Club" TV show, Disney was persuaded to form his own record production company. Starting in 1956, Disney took over producing and distributing its product on its own labels. All 78-rpms appeared on the "Disneyland" and "Official Mickey Mouse Club" labels (see elsewhere in this book). The Walt Disney Music Company had been formed a few years prior as a way for Disney to consolidate royalties due to it as well as to maintain creative control over the material.

## ♪DUROTONE

**Associated/subsidiary labels:** none
**Distributed, produced, and manufactured by:** Durotone Toy & Novelty Company, New York, NY

**Overall description of content:** general children's entertainment
**Record:** 7" black shellac
**Record label:** blue on white and orange, "Durable Toys Presents" written across top part of label; in middle of label are the words "Durotone Records Synchronized With Duracolor Films." Silhouette depiction of heads of kids watching a movie.
**Holder/cover:** Boxed sets, holding two or three records along with filmstrips.
**Date range:** 1934
**Series and record-numbering sequences:** Nine sets (or series), each with two or three records and two accompanying Duracolor filmstrips for each record. There are 25 records in all, along with over 3,000 pictures in the films.
**Miscellaneous:** Durotone records were made specifically to be played in synchronization with the projection of a filmstrip. This was accomplished with Uncle Sam's movie projector combined with a turntable. The mechanism allowed the filmstrip to advance in sync with the record. In addition, a built-in "movie tracer" set projected images onto a table or desk upon which a paper could be placed. The child would then be able to crayon, paint, or color them exactly like the film. The movie tracer set included a miniature theater box holding tripod, crayons, paints, paper, and full artist's drawing supplies.

**♪ECKART**
**Associated/subsidiary labels:** none
**Distributed, produced, and manufactured by:** The Charles Eckart Company, Hollywood, CA
**Overall description of content:** children's general entertainment
**Record:** 8" laminated cardboard, one sided playing only
**Record label:** picture disc on playing side; black text on nonplaying side
**Holder/cover:** cardboard box
**Date range:** 1941
**Series and record-numbering sequences:** only 4 discs confirmed, numbered consecutively from M-21 to M-24. Series title is "Musical Gems From Mother Goose."
**Miscellaneous:** Continuity, Thomas Glynn; Produced and Directed by: Tibor White. No other information is available.

**♪EDISON**
**Associated/subsidiary labels:** none
**Distributed, produced, and manufactured by:** Thomas A. Edison, Inc., Orange, NJ
**Overall description of content:** general adult entertainment, with small sprinkling of children's records mixed in.
**Record:** phenolic resin laminated over 1/8" fibrous cores. Sleeves say to play at 80 rpm.
**Record label:** etched and paper labels. The paper labels are black and white with a drawing of Thomas Edison.
**Holder/cover:** generic Edison paper sleeves, brown or olive kraft paper
**Date range:** 1912 – 1929
**Series and record-numbering sequences:** Approximately 4,400 disc records were made on this label. I have identified about 35 or so, which are specifically children's material, or at least suited for children. All but one of these is in the 50,000 series (popular); one is in the 80,000 series (classical and opera).
**Miscellaneous:** The Edison Diamond Disc Record was announced to the retail trade in December, 1912. This was a rather long delay for disc records to be introduced, considering the fact that Edison had invented the phonograph 35 years earlier, and that disc records had been around for more than 15 years. Edison had been focused on producing cylinder records.

Edison Laboratories had been experimenting with disc records for some four years, as the general public seemed to prefer them to cylinders. The thick Edison Discs recorded the sound vertically in the groove rather than laterally, and could only be played to their full advantage on Edison Diamond Disc Phonographs. This combination produced audio fidelity superior to any other home record playing system of the time. However, Edison discs and phonographs were more expensive than the competitors. This, together with the incompatability of the Edison system with other discs and machines, had an adverse effect on Edison's market share. Nonetheless, Edison discs for a time became the third best selling brand in the United States, behind Victor and Columbia Records.

With World War I various materials used in Edison Discs came in short supply, and many discs pressed during the war were made in part with such make-shift materials as could be acquired at the time. This resulted in problems with surface noise even on new records, and Edison's market share shrank.

After the war Edison Records started a marketing campaign, hiring prominent singers and Vaudeville performers to perform alongside and alternating with Edison records of their performances played on top-of-the-line "Laboratory Model" Edison Diamond Disc Phonographs. At various stages during these "Edison Tone Tests," all lights in the theater would be darkened and the audience challenged to guess if what they were hearing was live or recorded; accounts often said that much of the audience was astonished when the lights went back up to reveal only the Edison Phonograph on stage.

In 1928 the Edison company began plans for making "needle cut" records, by which they meant standard lateral cut discs like the "78s" marketed by almost every other company of the time. The Edison "Needle Cut" records debuted the following year. The audio fidelity was often comparable to the best of other record companies of the time, but they sold poorly as Edison's market share had declined to the point where it was no longer one of the leading companies and Edison had few distributors compared to leaders like Victor, Columbia, and Brunswick.

Edison Records closed down in 1929. The record plant and many of the employees were transferred to manufacturing radios. The masters for the Edison Records back catalog were purchased by Henry Ford, and became part of the collection of the Henry Ford Museum. Some of the Edison catalog is in the public domain and available for download at the Library of Congress website. (Wikipedia)

### ♪EMERSON

**Associated/subsidiary labels:** Emerson Phone Company, New York, NY
**Distributed, produced, and manufactured by:** Emerson Phone Company, New York, NY
**Overall description of content:** general adult catalog
**Record:** 7" and 10" black shellac (for any of the children's records)
**Record label:** black on red, white, and blue with drawing of the Statue of Liberty; a special three-record children's set of quasi–picture discs were produced (see below for more details).
**Holder/cover:** generic Emerson brown paper sleeve
**Date range:** 1916 – 1928
**Series and record-numbering sequences:** There are a scant few children's records in the catalog of several hundred adult titles. But one three-record set stands out as among the most beautiful of all children's records made. Numbered A100, A101, and A102, it contains Mother Goose rhymes and fairy tales. A standard black shellac 7" record is 'sandwiched' between two 10" circular cardboard slabs and all are affixed in the center spindle hole with a grommet. A facsimile record label is printed in the center of the cardboard cover with beautifully illustrated children's story characters by C.M. Burd (same illustrator of Kiddie Rekords and Pictorial Records). The record is played by placing the stylus on the record in a small slot that is cut out from the cover. The cover stays in place while the record revolves under it. This is unique in the world of not only kiddie records, but also any record.
**Miscellaneous:** Emerson Records was active in the US from 1916 to 1928.

Emerson was founded by Victor H. Emerson, who had worked for Columbia Records since the 1890s. In 1916 he started his namesake company, producing 7" records selling for 25¢ each, and 5 1/2" discs selling for 10¢. Early fare included popular tunes, dance numbers, and patriotic marches, mostly recorded by small groups of unnamed musicians hired in New York City credited as the "Emerson Orchestra" or sometimes grandly "The Emerson Symphony Orchestra." In January of 1918. Emerson added a line of 9" records selling for 75 cents. After World War I Emerson started ambitious expansions of the business, and in 1919 finally introduced a line of 10" discs (the common industry standard) retailing for 85 cents, which went up to $1.00 each the following year. 1919 also saw the debut of a series of 12" Emerson discs, mostly of classical music, retailing for $1.25.

Emerson's expansions turned out to be over-extended to be supported by the economy, and the company went into receivership in 1921, but a group of investors sold the company to the Scranton Button Company of Scranton, Pennsylvania. The Scranton Button Company was a corporation founded in Scranton, Pennsylvania in 1885. In the 1920s it branched out from making buttons into pressing shellac gramophone records. In July of 1929 it merged with Regal Records, Cameo Records, Banner Records and the US branch of Pathé Records to form the American Record Corporation.

The company was acquired in 1946 by Capitol Records. Emerson switched to the electric microphone method of sound recording in 1926. Scranton Button Co. halted production of new records by its Emerson subsidiary in 1928, but continued to use the name for a line of radios.

Emerson Records from the 1910s and early 1920s are generally above average audio fidelity for the era, pressed in high quality shellac. The fidelity of the later 1920s issues compares less favorably. (Wikipedia and Allan Sutton)

### ♪ENCYCLOPEDIA BRITANNICA FILMS

**Associated/subsidiary labels:** Fox; Simmel-Meservey
**Distributed and manufactured by:** Encyclopaedia Britannica Films, Wilmette, IL
**Produced by:** Tuneful Tales sets by Martha Blair Fox; Burl Ives set by?
**Overall description of content:** general children's entertainment
**Record:** 10" and 12" black vinyl
**Record label:** silver on red and reverse
**Holder/cover:** book style albums, three-color front cover
**Date range:** 194?
**Series and record-numbering sequences:** one series of six albums (#1 – 6) by Burl Ives, historical subjects. Other records by Martha Blair Fox, identical to Simmel-Meservey and Fox releases (see separate label notes).
**Miscellaneous:** Some albums are identical to Simmel-Meservey except that the record labels have the Encyclopaedia Britannica logo instead of the S-M logo.

I have no further information at this time.

### ♪ENRICHMENT

**Associated/subsidiary labels:** none

**Distributed and produced by:** Enrichment Materials, Inc., New York, NY
**Manufactured by:** by Columbia Records with the permission of Random House, Inc.
**Overall description of content:** children's educational content
**Record:** 10" black vinyl
**Record label:** silver on purple, text only
**Holder/cover:** three-color paper gatefold sleeve that holds two records. Line drawings of title subject appear on front. Other titles in series are shown on back panel.
**Date range:** 1952 – 1953
**Series and record-numbering sequences:** twenty titles are known, all in two-record gatefold albums. Numbered consecutively from 101 to at least 120. Record sets had two different prefixes: "L" and "ER" (e.g. L-101, ER-101). Same with disc numbers. The "L" prefix had a 1952 copyright; "ER" was copyright 1953. I am not sure how many of the series were issued with "L" and how many were with "ER" prefixes.
**Miscellaneous:** These stories on record are adapted from the well-known Landmark juvenile book series (Random House). This collection consists of 122 titles published between 1950 and 1970. Volumes #1 through 103 were originally published in dust jacket. First printings of volumes #104 through 122, along with later reprints of the earlier 103 titles, were issued in a pictorial or "picture cover" format. *Picture cover* is a collector's term that was coined to describe those titles, which have cover art that is printed directly to the boards of the book, eliminating the need of a dust jacket.

The Landmark Books were available in trade, library, and book club editions. The book club editions, which were issued monthly for $1.50 plus shipping, are identified by the "Young Readers of America Selection" blurb on the dust jacket flap. These editions are often found with facsimile letters from the author. The signatures on these letters often mislead the inexperienced collector to believe it is an authentic letter signed by the author. (Note: Book number does not match up with the record number.)

### ♪ESTAMAE'S DANCES FOR YOUNG FOLK

**Associated/subsidiary labels:** none
**Distributed by:** Estamae, Pueblo, CO
**Produced and manufactured by:** Estamae MacFarlane
**Overall description of content:** children's dance instruction and accompaniment
**Record:** 10" black vinyl
**Record label:** black and white on pink
**Holder/cover:** boxed sets, same colors as label
**Date range:** 1953
**Series and record-numbering sequences:** four boxed sets of three records each, consecutively numbered Album No. 1 to Album No. 4.
**Miscellaneous:** This is one of several small and obscure labels in my collection that offer school dance and rhythm music and instructions. Very little is known about these tiny companies, including this one.

### ♪FAMILY GAMES STORYPLAY

**Associated/subsidiary labels:** none
**Distributed, produced, and manufactured by:** Family Games, Inc., San Francisco, CA
**Overall description of content:** general children's entertainment, records with toys
**Record:** 12" black vinyl
**Record label:** red and black on white; picture label coinciding with title
**Holder/cover:** cardboard box
**Date range:** 1948
**Series and record-numbering sequences:** only three sets seen, numbers on matrix only, not on label or box. Series title: Story Play.
**Miscellaneous:** Box comes with stand-up punch-out figures relating to the story. This series is rare, especially in complete condition with record and punch-outs in box.

### ♪FOLK DANCES (RUTH EVANS)

**Associated/subsidiary labels:** Childhood Rhythms (Ruth Evans)
**Distributed by:** Joseph Burns (Bridgeport, CT) and Ruth Evans (Springfield, MA)
**Produced by:** Joseph Burns, Ruth Evans, Edith Wheeler
**Manufactured by:** ?
**Overall description of content:** children's folk dance instruction
**Record:** 10" black vinyl
**Record label:** brown on white, plain text, no design
**Holder/cover:** book style albums
**Date range:** 1953
**Series and record-numbering sequences:** only two albums seen, Album I and Album II, each with four records.
**Miscellaneous:** Even though there are only two sets, I have created a separate label notes section for them because they are so closely related to the Childhood Rhythms (Ruth Evans) series. The only difference is in the label. The cover designs are almost identical, as is the main producer, Ruth Evans.

This is not a record label in the usual sense. It is almost like a private issue, but it was sold retail to schools.

This is one of several small and obscure labels in my collection that offer school dance and rhythm music and instructions. Very little is known about these tiny companies, including this one.

### ♪FOLKRAFT

**Associated/subsidiary labels:** none

**Distributed, produced, and manufactured by:** Folkraft Records Division, Frank L. Kaltman Enterprises, Newark, NJ
**Overall description of content:** folk, ballroom, party, and square dances; adults' and children's material
**Record:** 10" vinyl
**Record label:** black on green, yellow, orange, etc.; drawing of guitar across label name
**Holder/cover:** plain brown paper sleeves with text and title of songs specific to the record.
**Date range:** 194?
**Series and record-numbering sequences:** one long series of a few hundred records. Many were identified as "children's dances." I have chosen about 80 – 85 as specifically made for children or suitable for children. Thirteen boxed sets for elementary schools were also made, numbered volumes 1 to 13. (Record #s 1000 – 1054, three or four discs each set.)
**Miscellaneous:** Folkraft is well known in the international folk dance world. Anyone who ever took a folk dance class or attended recreational folk dance sessions probably cut their teeth learning basic international folk dances on either this label or those on the Folk Dancer label (not covered in this book, as they did not specifically target children).

Some of the principals of the company are Frank Kaltman, Rickey Holden and Olga Kulbitski. Following is some biographical material on Olga as it relates to this book:

Olga Kulbitsky was born July 16, 1914, in New York to Russian immigrants. Olga is best known for her association with Folkraft Records, Newark, New Jersey. As Folkraft's Educational Dance Consultant, Olga supervised the production and publication of education dance records. The U.S. Information Department has cited these records as examples of American educational recordings and recommended their study as an example of American folk culture. They have been listed for free entry in thirty-one foreign countries where we have an educational exchange program. These recordings are also teaching aids in the school systems of many major cities in the United States. After 35 years of active service, Olga retired in 1972 as Associate Professor in the Department of Physical Education and Department of Education at Hunter College, City University of New York. She died on April 13, 2003, at the age of 89.

## ♪FOLLETT

**Associated/subsidiary labels:** Follett
**Distributed and produced by:** Follett Educational Records, division of Follett Publishing Company, Chicago, IL, and New York, NY
**Manufactured by:** Columbia Records
**Overall description of content:** children's educational/school records
**Record:** 10" vinyl
**Record label:** light blue on white, all text for most records, other variations seen such as black and green on white with drawings pertaining to title.
**Holder/cover:** book-style albums, two- and four-color illustrations, various color spines
**Date range:** 1951 – 1958
**Series and record-numbering sequences:** The entire output of Follett's Educational Records on 78 rpm is approximately 27 albums encompassing 108 records. They are skip-numbered, starting with Album 1, ending with Album 78.

Note on the recordings: All the songs are recorded from the *Together We Sing* basic songbooks for elementary grades. They are also known as the "Fullerton-Wolfe Song Series."

Note on the performers: A large group of artists are involved with this series, variously appearing on different record sides. Only one is listed on individual records for most of the albums (Virginia Speaker or Nancy Carr, e.g.), followed by "et al." Names of all artists are usually found on the liner notes of the album cover.
**Miscellaneous:** Follett is one of a handful of educational publishing companies whose roots go back well over 100 years. Most of these companies produced school songbooks and records to be played in the classroom to go along with the books. Along with Follett, most of the other companies (e.g. Ginn, Silver Burdett, Birchard, and Scott Foresman, to name a few) produced a large amount of 78-rpm educational records.

### A BRIEF HISTORY OF FOLLETT:

Follett Corporation was founded in 1873 when Charles M. Barnes opened a used bookstore in his Wheaton, Illinois home. Three years later, Barnes moved his business, now named C.M. Barnes & Company, to Chicago where he opened a store at 23 LaSalle Street. Here, he sold new and used textbooks, stationary and school supplies.

C.W. Follett joined the company in 1901 as a stock clerk. The following year, Charles Barnes retired and his son William became president. The company had now evolved into a wholesaler, selling used books throughout the Midwest and as far away as the Oklahoma Territory. (www.Follett.com)

According to the company's website, in 1917, "Follett took over management of the company and it was once again renamed, this time as J.W. Wilcox & Follett Company...In 1923 and the following year, C.W. Follett and his wife, Edythe, purchased the company." In 1925, one of Follett's four sons, Dwight, founded the Follett Publishing Company. In 1930 another of Follett's sons, R.D. (Bob), "founded the Follett College Book Company and began wholesaling used textbooks to professors and college bookstores." In 1940, yet another son, Garth, created the Follett Library Book Company. The youngest of the four sons, Laddie Follett:

...ran the company's original business — Wilcox & Follett — from 1952 until 1986."

When C.W. Follett passed away in 1952 at the age of 70, Dwight Follett succeeded his father as chairman. The company continued to grow and was renamed Follett Corporation in 1957. (www.Follett.com)

**In 1997, Follett:**

...joined Internet Systems, Inc., in forming Library Systems & Services, L.L.C., a joint venture that provides library management services to public, academic and corporate libraries across the country. In addition, Follett purchased Book Wholesalers, Inc. (BWI) — a distributor of children's books to public libraries...

In 1998, Follett associates celebrated the company's 125th anniversary. To strengthen the company's ability to meet the needs of its customers, Follett aligned its various business units under three market groups — Higher Education, Elementary and High Schools, and Libraries...

Following a rigorous analysis of the company's portfolio of business units, Follett merged Follett Media Distribution, which provided audio visual products to school and public libraries, into BWI in an effort to provide library customers with one-stop shopping for all of their book and media needs. In addition, in June of 2003, Follett sold its interest in Library Systems & Services, LLC (LSSI).

Today, Follett generates consolidated sales exceeding $2 billion and employs nearly 10,000 associates throughout the United States and Canada. (www.Follett.com)

## ♪FOX

**Associated/subsidiary labels:** Simmel-Meservey; Encyclopaedia Britannica Films
**Distributed, produced, and manufactured by:** Fox Record Company, Hollywood, CA
**Overall description of content:** general children's entertainment
**Record:** 10" black vinyl
**Record label:** silver on maroon and reversed
**Holder/cover:** paper sleeves, both single and gatefold for two records; four-color with drawings specific to record titles
**Date range:** 194?
**Series and record-numbering sequences:** seven known titles consecutively numbered from M-20 to M-26. All but one is a single record, with the remaining a two-record set.
**Miscellaneous:** These same recordings also appeared on the Simmel-Meservey and Encyclopaedia Britannica Films labels.

## ♪FREDA MILLER

**Associated/subsidiary labels:** none
**Distributed, produced, and manufactured by:** Freda Miller Records, New York, NY
**Overall description of content:** children's educational/dance records
**Record:** 10" vinyl
**Record label:** gray on black, very plain text
**Holder/cover:** book-style album, title only on the front, solid color background
**Date range:** 1949
**Series and record-numbering sequences:** only four albums, consecutively numbered 1 to 4, three records each.
**Miscellaneous:** This one of several small and obscure labels in my collection that offer school dance and rhythm music and instructions. Very little is known about these tiny companies, including this one.

## ♪GENEVA

**Associated/subsidiary labels:** none
**Distributed, produced, and manufactured by:** the Westminister Press, Philadelphia, PA
**Overall description of content:** children's religious (Christian)
**Record:** 7" black vinyl
**Record label:** black on blue, plain text, small drawing of subject matter
**Holder/cover:** boxed sets of four records each
**Date range:** 1958
**Series and record-numbering sequences:** A series of four boxed sets, no number on box, only on records. Series is called *For the Children's Hour*.
**Miscellaneous:** This is one of several small and obscure labels in my collection that offer religious children's records. Very little is known about these tiny companies, including this one.

## ♪GINN

**Associated/subsidiary labels:** none
**Distributed and produced by:** Ginn And Company Educational Publishers; Ginn And Company, Boston, MA
**Manufactured by:** Columbia (1920s), RCA Victor (1950s)
**Overall description of content:** children's educational

**Our Singing World (1949 – 1954 for public schools):**
**Record:** 10" black vinyl
**Record label:** black on light pastel background, plain text. Songs reference page numbers in school songbook that the children and teacher sing from while the record is playing.
**Holder/cover:** book-style albums that hold between four and six records each
**Series and record-numbering sequences:** two or three albums (A, B, C) for each grade, K to 8. I have seen at least 23 albums (with 111 records). There is a potential of 4 more albums that I haven't seen. Records are numbered consecutively within each album, but not necessarily from one album to the next. Contact me if you want the exact sequencing. Albums are numbered as to school grade (e.g. 1A, 1B, 1C would be for the

three sets that were issued for the first grade. Each grade has the same color on the front of the albums, matching those of the books issued to go with them.

**We Sing and Praise (1957 – 1962 for Catholic schools):**

**Record:** 10" black vinyl

**Record label:** black on light pastel background, plain text. Songs reference page numbers in school songbook that the children and teacher sing from while the record is playing.

**Holder/cover:** book-style albums that hold between five and six records each.

**Series and record numbering sequences:** two albums for each grade 1 – 8. Only the first "A" album for grades 1 – 6 were on 78 rpm. By the time Ginn got around to producing the records for Grades 7 & 8 as well as the "B" albums for grades 1-6, the days of 78-rpms were pretty much over. Thus, the "B" albums for all grades, as well as the "A" albums for grades 7 & 8 were issued in LP format only. There are 46 records and 16 albums with the records numbered consecutively from 1 to 46.

**Basic Readers (1948 records to accompany the first-grade program):**

**Record:** 7" black vinyl

**Record label:** black on different background colors for each album (red, green, etc.)

**Holder/cover:** cardboard gatefold cover to hold two records. Songs reference page numbers in school songbook that the children and teacher sing from while the record is playing.

**Series and record numbering sequences:** four albums numbered consecutively from Album One to Album Four. The books that went along with these records are highly collectible as they have "Dick and Jane" style pictures. Two of the better-known books are *On Cherry Street* and *The Little White House.*

**Music Education Series (music appreciation course, 1925 – 1930?):**

**Records:** 10" black shellac

**Labels:** gold on blue, pink, green, and beige, et al.; mainly text, some branch and leaves design as well

**Holder/cover:** Records came in a sturdy black carrying case with a lock. Heavy paper brown kraft paper sleeves for individual records; front of sleeve is generic Ginn Music Education Series design. Reverse of sleeve has a lesson plan for the teacher. Price shown is inclusive of records and carrying case

**Series and record numbering sequences:** Ginn contracted first with Starr Piano Company, then Columbia, to produce 120 sides (60 records). It is not known if all 60 records were produced. In addition to most of the sequence from G1 to G15, I also have G40. This is all that I have verified to exist.

**Miscellaneous:** Ginn (pronunciation of "G" is hard, as in "give") is one of a handful of educational publishing companies whose roots go back well over 100 years. Most of these companies produced school songbooks and records to be played in the classroom to go along with the books. Along with Ginn, most of the other companies (e.g. Follett, Silver Burdett, Birchard, and Scott Foresman, to name a few) produced a large amount of 78-rpm educational records.

1883: Ginn & Co. first publishes Classics for Children, *Robinson Crusoe, Plutarch's Lives* and other standard classics studied by children before graduation from grammar school. Valued as models of literary art, their immediate success establishes them as forerunners of the supplementary reading idea.

1985 – 1986: SIMON & SCHUSTER acquires Ginn & Company, a leading elementary and high school publisher, and Silver Burdett Company, an elementary school publisher. The companies are now known as Silver Burdett Ginn, a preeminent publisher of educational materials from pre-school through grade 12.

1998: The newly formed educational publishing company, Pearson Education bought Scott Foresman, Prentice Hall, Ginn, Silver Burdett and other educational imprints such as Simon & Schuster's educational business. The imprints that make up Pearson Education describe a rich educational and literary heritage. They stretch back to 1725 when Thomas Longman published the first book typeset by Benjamin Franklin.

The company is now called Pearson Scott Foresman. Today, Pearson Education has a widely trusted and respected program in educational and professional publishing.

## ♪GOLDEN

**A BRIEF HISTORY OF GOLDEN RECORDS:**

Simon & Schuster Publishing Company (New York) started producing Little Golden Records (LGRs) in 1948. S & S was created in 1924 when two young entrepreneurs, Richard Simon and Max Schuster, pooled their savings to publish a crossword puzzle book that became an instant bestseller and created a nationwide crossword puzzle craze. Simon & Schuster's "sower" logo became a publishing benchmark.

Golden Records was the brainchild of an S & S research associate named Arthur Shimkin. In 1946, he came up with the concept of Golden Records while doing marketing research. The first Little Golden Records were sold at the G. Fox department store in Hartford, CT in August 1948. Less than 8% of LGRs were sold in records stores.

Over the past several years, I have had the great fortune to meet and get to know Arthur, who is still going strong brainstorming sales and distribution plans for the Golden Record library in ways that are compatible with our

**twenty-first century world. Since we both live in New York City, mutual access is easy. Following is the Golden Record story in Arthur's own words, told directly to me:**

Golden Records were inspired by the "information please" postage-paid postcards inserted in each Little Golden Book sold during World War II (note: S & S had been publishing Little Golden Books since 1942.) and faithfully filled out and mailed back to the publisher by interested parents. Among the flattering comments were the reiterated complimentary complaints, expressed in many ways, but all conveying the same message: "if I have to read this story to my child once more, I shall do it with my eyes closed!!"

This inspired the idea to make recordings of the stories, poems, and short tales that were so well received by accomplished actors, musicians, and singers. They were to be packaged with the books. This fact dictated the records six-inch diameter...so that any youngster could listen to the records as many times as they pleased. Parents could stuff their ears with cotton or go out for a stroll. This also inspired the concept of a nonbreakable small record with a picture label, making the title identifiable to a child too young to read.

From the late 1930s to the 1940s there were many sporadic children's albums in the standard 10" size with 78-rpm breakable discs. Most reflected classic stories or popular motion pictures and cartoons — Disney and Warners and Terrytoons, Looney Toons and Popeye and The Wizard of Oz. Some were great originals, like Ray Bolger's "Churkendoose," "Rusty In Orchestraville," and Loretta Young's "Littlest Angel."

These albums were priced like adult record albums and reached a fairly limited market in adult record stores where they were relegated to rear-store display bins. And since radio disc jockies rarely played them, they remained fair and noble attempts to reach children.

The few small companies that attempted to sell low-price small discs did not have the necessary distribution to make feasible large production runs needed for profitability.

So it was with some trepidation that Little Golden Records were marketed by S & S Pocketbooks in the fall of 1948 with a retail price of 29¢ and then 25¢ and a wide distribution of display racks. More than 600,000 records were shipped to distributors who never sold records before.

Displays were set up in drug stores, candy stores, newsstands, and in all the major chain stores as well as bookstores, toy stores, and a small number of record stores.

Disney and Warner Cartoons joined with Golden for a fair royalty share and well-known stars like Jimmy Durante, Hoagy Carmichael, Danny Kaye, and Roy Rogers recorded specially for children. Publishers and writers licensed their songs at special rates, all in consideration of the 25¢ retail price for each record.

**Golden Records represents the largest single series of children's 78-rpm records ever produced. Over the years of production, just about every notable TV personality (fiction and real) was signed to perform on one or more Golden Records — an accomplishment not approached by any other record label for kids. In 1956, Simon & Schuster claimed half of all children's record sales in the US.**

**LITTLE GOLDEN RECORD FACTS AND FIGURES:**
**Golden Records #1 – #12 were test issues. Fifty thousand of each were pressed, hence the 600,000 figure noted prevously. Eventually about one-half were returned by the retailers as unsold. By comparison, the rest of the list had 60,000 – 80,000 pressings for each record. one hundred and twenty three thousand retail outlets were selling LGRs at one point. By March 1965, the rights to market LGRs were sold off. Up to that point, more than 200 million had been sold.**

**Following are the three best-selling LGR records on 78-rpm: "The Ballad of Davy Crockett"** (4 million), **"How Much Is That Doggie in the Window"** (2.5 million), **and "The Night Before Christmas"** (700,000).

**INFORMATION ABOUT GOLDEN RECORDS**
**Associated/subsidiary labels:** Bell, Wonderland
**Distributed by:** first Simon & Schuster, NY (1948 – 1956), then Affiliated Publishers (a joint effort of S&S and Pocketbooks to distribute their products through independent wholesalers).
**Produced by:** first Arthur Shimkin (Hudson Productions) in affiliation with Simon and Schuster (1948 – 1956; note that the Sandpiper Press published the artwork on the sleeves, hence the appearance of its name), then A.A. Records, Inc. (1957 – 1963)
**Manufactured by:** Bestway Products, Inc. (NJ) — financed by Simon & Schuster for the sole purpose of pressing Golden Records
**Overall description of content:** general children's entertainment and educational.

**Except for a test pressing of two 10" discs in 1946, the main series of Little Golden records was launched in the fall of 1948 with the release of the first twelve titles. Most of the Golden 78 rpm records were yellow colored* six-inch polystyrene discs and were practically indestructible in the hands of active children. The Union Carbide-Bakelite Company was contracted to manufacture the material from which the records were made. Polystyrene is a compound with about half the density and weigh of vinyl. Approximately 60 different formulas were tried between 1947 and 1950 to finally arrive at a clean sounding, long lasting record.**

Eventually, a series of 693 records (#1 – 777, skip numbered) was issued between 1948 and 1965. Quite a few of these titles (I don't have a count) were reissues of the same record earlier in the series, so there were not actually 693 different titles—more likely about 500 or so.

In about 1965 The "Golden" name was licensed A.A. Records (a previous distributor), at which time they issued at least 66 records, skip numbered numbered from #1000 to at least #1105. Almost all of the titles in this 'extended' series were reissues of previous titles.

*A few were red or black vinyl. Most of the red vinyls were issued with "Official Mickey Mouse Club" labels (see below), although a few had the regular "Golden" label. The black vinyl had an "S" prefix before the number. They are "extra play" 78s, meaning that the playing time is longer than a normal record. Most "S" records were issued in black, although some appeared in yellow, as well.

**THE NUMBERING & IDENTIFICATION SYSTEM FOR GOLDEN RECORDS:**

I use "skip numbered" to indicate that not every number resulted in an actual record being released. Gaps in the numbering sequence indicate that a record with this number was never issued because it was not acceptable and scrapped. I also use "at least" to indicate that I am still learning of additional records released that I do not have in my discography.

**Prefix Legend:** For the most part, the numbers and prefixes seen on the sleeve or cover match those on the label. Sometimes, a sleeve will show a number without a prefix (e.g., 483), but the record label has a prefix (e.g., R-483). There seems to be no particular pattern to this system, because it changed every few years. Numbers in the discography will always indicate that which is shown on the record label in the case where the sleeve does not match up exactly.

No prefix on #1 – 38; 6" diameter (most of #13 – 38 also issued with "R").

R = record, 6" (note: many sleeves have no prefix before number, but the labels do.

R (Little Golden Record Greeting). Same numbering as regular "R", but different label name.

S = extra play, a 7" record (78 rpm) played as long as a standard play 10" 78 rpm

sR = variety of special extra play

SD = extra play Disney

EP = extended play 45 rpm, 7"

ff = forty-five (45 rpm), 7" (records issued ONLY on 45 rpm are shown in these listings with the 'ff' prefix. Many 78s were also issued as 45s (mainly the better selling records). Those 45s have 'ff' prefixes as well, but are not shown in these listings.

GL = Golden Record library, 78 rpm, 6"

BR = Big Golden Record, 10", 78 rpm

DBR = Big Golden Disney, 10", 78 rpm

D = Disney, 78 rpm

RD = Disney, 78 rpm (occasionally, Disney records did not have a "D" identification, e.g. #483, which is Disney, but label is R-483).

GRC = Golden Record Chest, 45 and 78 rpm

LGRC = Little Golden Record Chest (variation)

LGR = Little Golden Record Albums (between two and four records in a booklet), 78 rpm

DLGR = Disney version of "LGR"

T = A Golden Hi-Fi Extended Play, 45 rpm

C = Little Golden "Books That Read Themselves"—book and record in 45 and 78 rpm

BB = Post Sugar Crisp send away premium of two Roy Rogers records, 78 rpm

WH = *Women's Home Companion* send away premium

**Artists' names:** As with all other listings in this book, wherever artists'/performers' names are given (either on the record label and/or the record cover), the main names will be listed. Wherever listings appear differently on the cover and the record, I will always list what is on the record label.

Golden Records will prove to be one modification to this rule. Certain performers, such as "Mitchell (or Mitch) Miller and Orchestra" (and later "Jimmy Carroll and Orchestra") appear on a large portion of Golden Records. Therefore, to save time and space, I have identified them by their initials in most cases. Following is a list of abbreviations in Golden Records:

MMO = Mitchell (or Mitch) Miller and Orchestra

JCO = Jimmy Carroll and Orchestra

NLO = Norman Leyden Orchestra

MMC = Mickey Mouse Club

OMMC = Official Mickey Mouse Club

WD('s) = Walt Disney('s)

AL = Anne Lloyd (Anne is the lead female singer on most Golden records)

SAND = The Sandpipers (aka the Sandpiper Singers, the Sandpiper Chorus, the Sandpiper Chorus and Orchestra, the Sandpiper Quartet, the Golden Sandpipers). The Sandpipers, along with Anne Lloyd and Gilbert Mack, represented the original "Golden Record sound." They are a male quartet who also appeared with Milton Berle as "The Men of the *Texaco Star Theater*." They are Bob Miller, bottom tenor; Ralph Nyland, top tenor; Dick Byron, baritone; and Mike Stewart, bass.

**DESCRIPTION OF THE VARIOUS SERIES:**

**Main series (1948 – 1964):** The first (main series) consisted of 693 titles, skip-numbered from 1 to 777 (highest number seen). Of this total, according to my latest research,

82 numbers were not assigned titles, 144 were issued as EP (multitrack 45s), 21 were issued as regular 45s (and not issued as 78s), 11 were issued as EPs as part of the Golden Hi-Fi series, and 519 were issued as 78s (many also on 45 rpm). Included in this series were "GL" "C," "T," and "FF" prefix records. The labels for #1 to approximately #245 were very colorful. Beginning at about #245, labels were switched to two colors: silver on purple or silver on blue. Additionally, some records had "stamped ink labels," not paper. This coincided with a change in sleeve size (see below). Records were primarily yellow vinyl, but black and red were also issued.

Sleeve sizes of main series: #1 – 12: 6$^{3/4}$" w x 8" h; #13 – 249: 7$^{1/2}$" w x 6$^{3/4}$" h; #250 and up: 6$^{1/4}$" w x 7$^{1/2}$" h (78 rpm) and 7" w x 7$^{3/4}$" h (45 rpm); note: an occasional smaller format (#13 – 249 size) appears, such as 286, 288.

**Reissues:** Many of the more popular titles were reissued, in most cases with new cover artwork and different size cover format. Often, a colon and "25" would follow the record number on the sleeve (indicating a price of 25¢ (e.g., R35:25).

**Label Variations within main series:**

"From Walt Disney's Official Mickey Mouse Club": These words appear across the top of the label and sleeve. There are about 35 different titles of this variation. These were issued usually on red vinyl with a yellow, black, blue or purple label, but also on yellow vinyl with black label. These do not have the word "Golden" on the label. There are two versions of this variation: 1) "Floating head" picture of Mickey Mouse; #222 and #232 in this subseries were also issued as standard yellow records with Golden Record labels. 2) Version that does not have Mickey Mouse, but a picture of Sleeping Beauty's castle and the word "Disneyland." There are only a small handful of these.

"From Disneyland Official Mickey Mouse Club": Six different of this variation. Same as "From Walt Disney," except the words "From Disneyland" replace them at the top of the label and sleeve. These do not have the word "Golden" on the label. There is a "floating head" picture of Mickey Mouse.

Romper Room (#263 – 268): Six record sub-set. Pink and blue label, yellow vinyl. #263 was issued on a regular Golden Record label as well.

**The 1000 Series:** an extension of the main series, (1965): Skip numbered from 1000 to 1105, totaling 66 known titles.

**Disney Series parallel to main series (1949 – 1954):** 62 numbers, only fourty-four assigned to titles. Skip numbered from RD-1 to RD-62. All of these numbers were duplicates of the main series, differentiated only by the "RD" prefix.

**Record Chests (1954 – 1956):** A total of seven were issued. They are made from sturdy cardboard with slots for eight records. A built-in carrying handle was included. Some had a booklet to go with it (composers and orchestra intros). There were seven in total, GRC 1 – 7, no #5, and LGRC 1 (Mickey Mouse Club). Each set had its own unique prefix (see discography section).

**Record Albums (1949 – 1952):** A total of eight paper sleeve albums holding 6" yellow vinyl records, four for each (except for one which held two). These were re-releases of records from the main series. Numbered consecutively from LGR1 to LGR8.

DLGR-4 ("Mickey Mouse's Christmas Party") comes in three versions. The first version is on Golden Records; the third is on Official Mickey Mouse Club records; the second is a hybrid of both. The audio tracks on all are the same, as are the four-color cartoon illustrations on the covers and record sleeves (eight in total). The reason why there are three versions for this set is because it was issued in a transitional time when Disney was beginning to take control over publishing its own music. See label notes under "Disneyland Records" for more detail.

First Version: yellow vinyl records with the "Golden Records" picture label; text part is black on red; the picture section in the top part is black, red and white. Title on the cover is prefaced with "Walt Disney's". It also states "4 Golden Records." Background color of cover is yellow.

Second Version: yellow vinyl records with later version of Golden Records picture label, silver on black. Title on the cover is prefaced with "songs from Walt Disney's Mickey Mouse Club." Background color of the cover is blue. The cover also feature the "floating head" logo of Mickey Mouse encircled by "Official Mickey Mouse Club" in a black on red band.

Third Version: red vinyl records with "from Walt Disney's Official Mickey Mouse Club" label. Mickey Mouse's floating head drawing in black and white and black text on a blue background for the titles, etc. The cover is the same as the second version.

**Big Golden Records (1951 – 1953):** A series of 10" yellow vinyl records; 27 titles skip-numbered from BR-1 to BR-44. Numbers DBR-16 and DBR-29 are Disney records and are listed under the Disney Big Golden (DBR) series, even though, technically speaking, they are part of the BR series.

**Disney Big Golden Records (1951 – 1953):** A series of ten 10" yellow vinyl records. The first 8 (DBR 1-7 + 13) actually constitute a discrete series of Disney records in that the numbers are unique for the title. In other words, BR 1-7 and BR-13 in the regular Big Golden series are totally different records. #16 and #29 do not exist as other titles in the BR series; so technically speaking these last two listed in the DBR section are part of the BR series.

**Test Issue (1946):** These are the rarest of the rare Golden Records, mainly because they were never offered for sale. There were only two hundred and fifty of each pressed by Simon and Schuster to be distributed within the company and potential customers as demonstration records. If you have them in your collection, count yourself as extremely fortunate.

**Premiums:**

Post Sugar Crisp (1955): set of 2 Roy Rogers records on 6" yellow vinyl; in mailer from "Roy Rogers Records", Brooklyn, NY. Numbers prefixed with "BB."

General Mills (1951): 6" red or black vinyl Alice In Wonderland set of eight records, four mailers from "Wonderland". New York City, two records per mailer; yellow labels. Side numbering system was parallel to the LGR Disney series (RD 18-25). For example, General Mills side #1 = Disney side #RD-18a; General Mills side #2 = #RD-18b, etc.). First issue was on Red Vinyl; Second issue was on black vinyl. The second issue used different numbering pairs on each record. Plain numbers, no prefixes.

*Woman's Home Companion* "Golden Record Of The Month" (195?): set of 11 records. Numbers not prefixed on the label, but "WHC" appears on the matrix. Yellow vinyl, light blue labels. 6" in mailer.

## ♪GRADED PRESS

**Associated/subsidiary labels:** none
**Distributed, produced, and manufactured by:** Graded Press, Nashville, TN
**Overall description of content:** children's religious
**Record:** 7" colored or black vinyl
**Record label:** Gladly Sing: silver printing on green; Sing O Sing: silver printing on varied colors
**Holder/cover:** box
**Date range:** 1956 (Sing O Sing), 1958 (Gladly Sing)
**Series and record-numbering sequences:** only two boxed sets known
**Miscellaneous:** This is one of several small and obscure labels in my collection that offered religious children's records. Very little is known about these tiny companies, including this one.

## ♪GRAPHIC PHONO-BOOKS

**Associated/subsidiary labels:** none
**Distributed, produced, and manufactured by:** Graphic Educational Productions Inc., Hollywood, CA
**Overall description of content:** children's general entertainment and educational
**Record:** 10" black shellac
**Record label:** black on white background with swatches of color patterns, different for each record. Text and line drawings of the title subject.
**Holder/cover:** hardcover spiral-bound book with holder for record on inside of front cover; 12-page book included.
**Date range:** 1946
**Series and record numbering sequences:** single record sets in five categories of subjects: "What" stories, as well as "How," "Why," "Who," and "Where" stories, five titles in each group. The four albums I have seen are numbered consecutively from A-101 to A-104.
**Miscellaneous:** These are records for "children who ask questions." In other words, they are for every kid.

I have seen only four of the twenty-five titles. I suspect, although I have no hard evidence of my suspicion, that only a very few (perhaps the four that I list) were ever produced. I can't prove this — it is just an intuition.

Although the book with the record included is a nice concept, the spiral binding did not hold the pages very securely. Thus, it is hard to find these in VG+ or better condition, with the book pages intact.

## ♪GREETING REC-CARDS

**Associated/subsidiary labels:** none
**Distributed by:** Rec-cards, Inc., Hollywood, CA
**Produced and manufactured by:** Hub Records of Hollywood, Inc.
**Overall description of content:** general children's entertainment + greeting records (holidays, special occasions, etc.)
**Record:** 6" vinyl, different colors; green and light blue seen
**Record label:** black on yellow, silver on red (for Xmas). "A" side of label has "To" and "From" blank lines to fill in names of giver and receiver.
**Holder/cover:** heavy paper gatefold, color drawing on front, greeting card message on inside front cover; record is held in back cover in four slots.
**Date range:** 1955
**Series and record-numbering sequences:** records seen with a "B" (birthday) and "X" (Christmas) prefix. It is unknown how many were produced.
**Miscellaneous:** No other information is available on this company.

## ♪GREY GULL YOUNGSTER

**Associated/subsidiary labels:** Grey Gull; Radiex
**Distributed, produced, and manufactured by:** Grey Gull, Boston, USA
**Overall description of content:** general children's entertainment
**Record:** 6" black or dull orange color shellac
**Record label:** four-color graphics, yellow background
**Holder/cover:** generic "Youngster Grey Gull For Children" paper sleeves
**Date range:** late 1920s
**Series and record-numbering sequences:** one series, #100 – #132 (highest # seen).
**Miscellaneous:** Listings in the book show performers' names as they appear on the label (except where none are shown). Collectors who are more expert than I on

this subject have indicated that the labels are often mislabeled, and that artists other than the ones shown are often the case. Pseudonyms were used as well.

**♪H-O INSTANT OATMEAL**

**Associated/subsidiary labels:** none
**Distributed by:** H-O Instant Oatmeal
**Produced and manufactured by:** Sight 'N Sound
**Overall description of content:** baseball instruction for kids
**Record:** 5" laminated cardboard, photos on both sides
**Record label:** picture disc
**Holder/cover:** mailer (send away premium)
**Date range:** 1952 – 1953
**Series and record-numbering sequences:** no numbered sequence. I believe there were as many as 12 baseball records in this series.
**Miscellaneous:** This series is very scarce for us record collectors, as we are competing against the vast baseball memorabilia hobby. It was offered as a send-away premium from H-O Quaker Oats cereal. The one-sided playing cardboard record measures 4 3/4" in diameter and has a color photo with facsimile autograph on the reverse side, while the grooved recording side has an action pose in black and white. It comes with a cardboard mail-in order form that accompanied the record, which offered three additional records for 25¢ plus two box tops.

**♪HARMONIA**

**Associated/subsidiary labels:** none
**Distributed, produced, and manufactured by:** Harmonia Distributing & Publishing Co., New York, NY
**Overall description of content:** children's general entertainment
**Record:** 10" black shellac
**Record label:** red on blue, drawings of two harps, text
**Holder/cover:** book-style albums holding three records.
**Date range:** 1946
**Series and record-numbering sequences:** short series of three albums known, numbered HR-25 to HR-27. Know of one single, whose disc number places it in sequence between records in albums.
**Miscellaneous:** No further information available. This is one of several small and obscure labels in my collection. Very little is known about these tiny companies, including this one.

**♪HOLLYWOOD RECORDING GUILD**

**Associated/subsidiary labels:** Star-Bright, Superior
**Distributed, produced, and manufactured by:** Hollywood Recording Guild, Inc.; Hollywood, USA
**Overall description of content:** general children's entertainment
**Record:** 6" black vinyl
**Record label:** maroon printing, yellow background; logo graphic
**Holder/cover:** paper sleeves specific for each title; some with cut-out figures on back (1000 series — see below).
**Date range:** 1949 – 1951
**Series and record-numbering sequences:** 7": 1 and 2-digit series, 400 series, 1000 series; 10": 3-digit series, 2000 series
**Miscellaneous:** This is a very difficult series for discographers to get their arms around. Several different numbers appear on sleeve and label in 1- and 2-digit 7" series. In addition to the HRG number, other numbers may refer to Star Bright and/or Superior, two related companies that apparently shared with or sold masters to. Some labels on 1000 series are Star-Bright, even though sleeves are Hollywood Recording Guild. HRG must have inherited stock from Star-Bright. The 1000 series has cut-out figures on back. That makes this series more valuable than those with standard sleeves.

**♪HONOR YOUR PARTNER**

**Associated/subsidiary labels:** none
**Distributed, produced, and manufactured by:** First as Square Dance Associates; now by Educational Activities, Inc., Baldwin, NY (from 1964 to present); formerly in Freeport, NY
**Overall description of content:** adult and children instructional, educational square and ballroom dance.
**Record:** 12" black vinyl
**Record label:** black and red on white, mainly text, minimal graphics
**Holder/cover:** cardboard gatefold covers, black & red printing on white background.
**Date range:** 1948 – 1967
**Series and record-numbering sequences:** 22 sets, three or four records per set, numbered HYP-1 to HYP-25. No # 17,19, or 20. #21 issued on LP only; all of the rest on 78 and 33.
**Miscellaneous:** Because of the continuing existence of Educational Activities, you could say that Honor Your Partner is one of only six companies still in existence that made primarily or exclusively 78-rpm children's records in the 1950s and earlier. The other surviving companies are: Peter Pan, Singspiration, Star-Bright, Stepping Tones and Kimbo. With the exception of Kimbo, none of these companies exist by the name used on the label.

I am not including in this discussion the current "Big Four" mega-music conglomerates (Sony/BMG, EMI, Universal, and Warner) that hold over 75% of the music market share. Each of the aforementioned corporations has acquired the rights to many children's record lines released by the venerable stalwarts of the record industry, going back to the 1890s. I am referring here to the large companies, which were not in the children's record business exclusively. Such familiar labels as Columbia, Capitol, RCA-Victor, Decca, and Mercury fall into this category.

As recently as 1998 Educational Activities annually sold 175,000 educational records, cassettes, videos, CDs and software programs. Annual sales are said to be between $3 million and $6 million, mainly to some of the 52,000 schools in the USA.

The founder and inspirational leader of the company was Ed Durlacher. He traveled around the country with his "Top Hands" back-up accompaniment group for several decades, starting in the 1930s. Ed died in 1964.

## ♪HUMPTY DUMPTY (PETER PAN)

**Associated/subsidiary labels:** Peter Pan, Prom, Rocking Horse
**Distributed, produced, and manufactured by:** Humpty Dumpty Records, New York, NY (cover art and books copyright James & Jonathan Co, Kenosha, WI
**Overall description of content:** general children's entertainment
**Record:** 10" red or orange vinyl
**Record label:** black on pastel green or pink
**Holder/cover:** All but the last in the series are records in "picturebook" albums; gatefold cover holding one record + an additional inside page. The paper in these picturebook covers is very poor and is often found in brittle condition. It is difficult to find them in very nice condition.
**Date range:** 1950
**Series and record-numbering sequences:** a series of eight records (known), consecutively numbered from 500 to 507.
**Miscellaneous:** This label is a subsidiary and/or spin-off of Peter Pan Records. No further information is available.

## ♪IMP

**Associated/subsidiary labels:** none known of
**Distributed and produced by:** Imp Records
**Manufactured by:** Holyoke Plastics Inc., Holyoke, MA
**Overall description of content:** general children's entertainment
**Record:** 6" vinyl
**Record label:** two colors: orange and yellow; background and lettering interchange colors; company logo. No number printed on label; number is only seen in matrix.
**Holder/cover:** none seen
**Date range:** unknown, probably late 1940s
**Series and record-numbering sequences:** unknown
**Miscellaneous:** These are reissues of single records that appeared previously on the Music You Enjoy label variations such as Pied Piper, Little Masters, and Look-Listen.

## ♪IMPERIAL

**Associated/subsidiary labels:** Moppet
**Distributed and produced by:** Commodore Music Corp., Hollywood, CA
**Manufactured by:** Imperial Records, L.A., CA
**Overall description of content:** general children's entertainment
**Record:** 10" black vinyl
**Record label:** silver on red; Imperial "5-star" design
**Holder/cover:** paper sleeves specific to record titles, three-color and two-tone seen. Song lyrics printed on reverse.
**Date range:** 1952 – 1954
**Series and record-numbering sequences:** no specific series for children's records. At least five Sheriff John and one Deputy Dave record has been seen. That's it as far as Imperial's kiddie records that I know of.
**Miscellaneous:** The Imperial Records listed in this book was the third US based label with that name and is unrelated to the two earlier ones. Started in 1947 by Lew Chudd, it was famous for recordings of rhythm & blues and early rock & roll like Fats Domino and Ricky Nelson. Imperial was licensed to London Records in the UK. In 1960 Lew Chudd bought Aladdin Records and Minit Records. In 1963, after Imperial lost Fats Domino and Ricky Nelson to rival labels, Chudd sold the label to Liberty Records. By 1969 the label was phased out with the artists transferred to the parent Liberty label. EMI now owns the Imperial Records catalog.

The Sheriff John records: The main feature of this label as it relates to children's 78-rpms is the Sheriff John records. In nice condition, record and sleeve together can go for well over $100. This puts their value in the top 5% of all records listed in this book.

If you were a So-Cal (L.A., Southern California) kid in the 1950s or 1960s, you likely remember Sheriff John. This friendly, fatherly law enforcement officer (played by John Rovick) hosted the popular kiddie shows *Sheriff John's Lunch Brigade* and (his afternoon show) *Sheriff John's Cartoon Time* beginning in 1952 on KTTV Channel 11. The programs opened with Sheriff John entering his office (a jailhouse like Andy Taylor's in Mayberry) while lip-sinking to the record lyrics: "Laugh and be happy and the world will laugh with you/When people see you smiling, they can't help smiling, too..." Then Sheriff John would go to the checklist, the bulletin board for pictures about safety, and then to the US flag for the Pledge of Allegiance. During the show, Sheriff John showed cartoons like Crusader Rabbit and Porky the Pig. Occasionally, real farm animals visited the set or an artist named Sketchbook Suzie arrived and drew pictures requested by the kids at home. Sheriff John taught lessons about life and appropriate behavior to his viewers. To teach the lessons, the Sheriff used songs like "The Advice Song" ("If you like to scatter your toys, don't do it, don't do it..."); the "Eat your food, wash your hands and face, brush your teeth and take a nap" song that promoted good heath habits ("This is the way we wash our hands...Merrily, we brush our teeth"); and "The Safety Song" that cautioned kids of the "Fun Brigade" not to play with matches, run with sharp objects ("I could fall down and spoil my fun"), and most of all "Safety, safety all the while, safety, safety with a smile; safety on the way to school, safety first our Golden Rule." These shows ran for 18 years! (TVAcres.com)

## ♪INTERNATIONAL

**Associated/subsidiary labels:** none
**Distributed, produced, and manufactured by:** International Record Co., New York, NY
**Overall description of content:** children's general entertainment
**Record:** 10" shellac
**Record label:** brown on beige, scroll-type logo design
**Holder/cover:** book-style album cover, usually holds three records.
**Date range:** 194?
**Series and record-numbering sequences:** a series, of sorts; I am aware of at least seven sets of records, most with three discs, some are singles; all with the album prefix of IRC.
**Miscellaneous:** William Feldstein was an executive of this company in the late 1940s. No other information is available.

## ♪JACKALEE

**Associated/subsidiary labels:** none
**Distributed, produced, and manufactured by:** Jackalee Records, Inc., Chicago, IL
**Overall description of content:** general children's entertainment
**Record:** 10" black or translucent red vinyl
**Record label:** black and red on gray, pink; red border; cute graphic of a kid on a pony (perhaps a carousel pony), waving a flag with the label name on it
**Holder/cover:** paper gatefold sleeves for two records; four-color graphics, quite imaginative
**Date range:** 1947
**Series and record numbering-sequences:** only three children's record sets known on this label, with no uniform numbering system. Each has two records.
**Miscellaneous:** The main feature of the Jackalee records listed in this book is the use of the "Sonovox" on the audio tracks. "Sonovox" is a brand name for a vocoder (name derived from voice coder, formerly also called voder). It is a speech analyser and synthesizer. It was used in a number of songs from the 1940s to the 1960s and is used to create the voice of the Reluctant Dragon, Casey Junior the train in *Dumbo*, the instruments in the "Rusty in Orchestraville" recordings, and the piano in "Sparky's Magic Piano," etc.

"Sonovox" was originally developed as a speech coder for telecommunications applications in the 1930s, the idea being to code speech for transmission. Its primary use in this fashion is for secure radio communication, where voice has to be digitized, encrypted, and then transmitted on a narrow, voice-bandwidth channel. The vocoder has also been used extensively as an electronic musical instrument. As an instrument, it is primarily used with guitars and synthesizers and produces a sound that can be described as a "talking guitar" or "talking keyboard." Vocoders are also often used to create the sound of a robot talking. (Wikipedia)

## ♪JACK & JILL (Joseph Schneider)

**Associated/subsidiary labels:** none known
**Distributed and produced by:** Joseph Schneider, Inc., New York, NY
**Manufactured by:** Siemon Co., Bridgeport, CT
**Overall description of content:** general children's entertainment
**Record:** 6" laminated cardboard; colors seen: blue, orange, red, green; graphic logo of Jack & Jill holding hands.
**Record label:** not a separate label, but part of the laminate, almost like a picture disc, except the groove area has no picture.
**Holder/cover:** unknown; probably cardboard box holder
**Date range:** 193?
**Series and record-numbering sequences:** only one series known, numbered consecutively from 201/2 to 235/6
**Miscellaneous:** Record was meant to be played with a Jack & Jill phonograph, player/projector; synchronized with film strip (?), similar to Talkie Jektor (see separate label notes). In fact, record states "licensed for Movie Jektor only." Movie Jektor was a filmstrip projector combination record player designed to play Talkie Jektor records synchronized with a filmstrip. The Jack and Jill Phonograph played by means of a wind-up key. The base and horn came in various colors.

## ♪JACK & JILL (Sage Music)

**Associated/subsidiary labels:** none known
**Distributed, produced, and manufactured by:** Sage Music, New York, NY
**Overall description of content:** general children's entertainment
**Record:** 6" red or black vinyl
**Record label:** no paper labels, silver ink stamped directly on vinyl
**Holder/cover:** four-color paper sleeve, specific to record title. Same artwork appears on Record Guild of America.
**Date range:** 195?
**Series and record-numbering sequences:**
"J" series: 36 titles, general kiddie subjects such as nursery rhymes, fairy tales.

"X" series: 12 titles, all Christmas related
**Miscellaneous:** Important note: This is not the same company as "Jack & Jill" by Joseph Schneider, Inc., from the 1930s. See separate label notes for that company.

## ♪JIM DANDY (RECORD GUILD OF AMERICA)

**Associated/subsidiary labels:** Record Guild of America, Jim Dandy
**Distributed by:** Cosmo Recording Co., NY
**Produced and manufactured by:** Record Guild of America
**Overall Description of Content:** general children's entertainment
**Record:** 10" black vinyl
**Record label:** black and red on yellow, pink and red. Text only.
**Holder/cover:** cardboard sleeves, four-color illustrations relating to subject and title.
**Date range:** 1953
**Series and record-numbering sequences:** a series of 12 single records consecutively numbered from 801 to 812.
**Miscellaneous:** Jim Dandy records are verified only up to #812. I have seen titles of higher numbers but I have decided not to include them in this edition. It is possible that the titles were in preparation, but never produced. Any readers with definitive information on them are encouraged to contact me.

Jim Dandy records, being a label variation of Record Guild of America, use the same masters. A list of all Record Guild of America/Jim Dandy stable of performers is shown here. I have used this list as a general reference. Some performers appear on almost all of the records. Most records in the series will have one or more of the following performing artists. Vocalists: Christine Johnson, Andy Gainey, Phil Proud, Rue Knapp, Doug Martin, Bob Davis, Dorothy Proud, Jenefer Bunker, Jane Davis, Inez Manier, Esther Metz, Roth Cottingham, Ruth Owen; narration: Staats Cotsworth, James Monks, Hester Sondergaard, Martin Wolfson, Mady Lee, Cliff Carpenter, Darren McGavin, Melanie York, Danny Dee, Lita Darwin.

## ♪KAROUSEL

**Associated/subsidiary labels:** Lyric
**Distributed, produced, and manufactured by:** Karousel Records, New York, NY
**Overall description of content:** children's general entertainment
**Record:** 10" vinyl, black or purple
**Record label:** red on yellow or blue; drawing of a carousel.
**Holder/cover:** paper sleeves, four-color, illustrations match the subject title.
**Date range:** 194?
**Series and record-numbering sequences:** two series, KK (4 titles) and TC (6 titles) prefixes
**Miscellaneous:** All of the "KK" series were issued on the Lyric label as well.

This is one of several small and obscure labels in my collection. Very little is known about these tiny companies, including this one. No other information is known.

## ♪KEYNOTE

**Associated/subsidiary labels:** none
**Distributed, produced, and manufactured by:** Keynote Recordings, Inc., New York
**Overall description of content:** general adult entertainment with some albums suitable for children sprinkled in.
**Record:** 10" black shellac
**Record label:** maroon on gray; drawing of a record disc, stylized to appear like a musical note
**Holder/cover:** book-style album cover
**Date range:** 194?
**Series and record-numbering sequences:** no series or sets specifically for children
**Miscellaneous:** Keynote was founded in 1940. Its initial focus was on materials of folk singers and balladeers with socialist empathies. Some of the artists were the Almanac Singers, Paul Robeson and Josh White. Later, the emphasis was shifted to jazz and this is what Keynote is mainly noted for.

## ♪KIDDIE LAND

**Associated/subsidiary labels:** Willida
**Distributed, produced, and manufactured by:** Kiddie Land Records, New York, NY
**Overall description of content:** general children's entertainment
**Record:** 10" black vinyl
**Record label:** maroon on white cartoon drawing of kids and castle
**Holder/cover:** paper sleeve, four-color specific to title
**Date range:** 194?
**Series and record-numbering sequences:** 22 titles seen, skip numbered from KL-1 to KL-28
**Miscellaneous:** This is a companion label to Willida, albeit with a much larger offering. Several of these titles also appeared on Willida, but Willida had titles of their own.

## ♪KIDDIE RECORD (KIDDIE REKORD)

**Associated/subsidiary labels:** none known
**Distributed by:** Kiddie Rekord Company (1922), Kiddie Record Company (1923), Inc., Plainfield, NJ
**Produced by:** Victor Emerson and Kiddie Rekord Company
**Manufactured by:** Bridgeport Die & Machine Company (CT)
**Overall description of content:** general children's entertainment
**Record:** 6" black shellac, one playing side only; nonplay-

promotional campaign, staff copywriter Robert L. May created the character and illustrated poem of Rudolph, the Red-Nosed Reindeer. Six million copies of the storybook were distributed in 1946. The song was popularized by Gene Autry.

Montgomery Ward is also the name of a new Internet- and catalog-based retailer that was established in late 2004.

♪**MOPPET**

**Associated/subsidiary labels:** Imperial
**Distributed by:** Kid Stuff, Inc., Hollywood, CA
**Produced by:** Commodore Music Corp, Hollywood, CA
**Manufactured by:** Moppet Records
**Overall description of content:** general children's entertainment
**Record:** 10" black vinyl
**Record label:** yellow on black, drawing of a boy and girl (floating heads)
**Holder/cover:** four- and two-color paper sleeves, illustrated specifically for title of the record.
**Date range:** 1954
**Series and record-numbering sequences:** at least 8 titles known, numbered consecutively from 7001 to 7008.
**Miscellaneous:** This series features kids' TV personalities, similar to the related series on Imperial with Sheriff John (see separate label notes). One of the performers in this series is Dick "Two Ton" Baker. A lot of his early recordings appeared on the Mercury label.

Dick "Two Ton" Baker was a giant — literally and figuratively — on the Chicago entertainment scene for nearly four decades, from the late 1930s until his death in 1975. He played piano quite well and sang in a pleasing, infectious baritone voice, but mainly he entertained, in whatever medium. His radio show on WGN went out nationwide over the Mutual network. He was on the first television broadcast on WGN-TV (April 5, 1945), and later had a very popular children's program on that and other Chicago TV stations.

♪**MOUSKETEER T-V**

**Associated/subsidiary labels:** none
**Distributed, produced, and manufactured by:** T. Cohn, Inc., Brooklyn, NY
**Overall description of content:** general children's entertainment
**Record:** 7" black vinyl; have seen with standard regular small 78-rpm spindle hole, and most unusual, there are some with large 45-rpm style spindle holes, but are nevertheless 78 rpms. I have never seen anything like this. It probably has to do with the special record player/projector that these records were meant to be played on (see notes below).
**Record label:** blue on yellow, cartoon drawings of heads of Disney characters
**Holder/cover:** plain brown envelopes
**Date range:** ca. 1956
**Series and record-numbering sequences:** five records in one set, numbered from 300 – 1+2 to 300 – 9+10.
**Miscellaneous:** These records were part of a toy set that included a "Mouseketeer Electric T.V. Storyteller." It played records and displayed film reels in the false TV screen. The "television" is 13" x 9" x 10". It's really a low-tech movie-reel viewer with a built-in record player. The instructions explain how to turn on the electric motor for the movie reel at the same time you place the phonograph needle on the record. This can sell for $100.00 to $175.00.

♪**MUSETTE: JACK AND JILL SINGERS**

**Associated/subsidiary labels:** Superman pictures discs, Zoo-Zoo, Musical Radio Script
**Distributed and produced by:** Musette Publishers, Inc., Steinway Hall, New York (some second issues by McCombs Publications, Inc., NY)
**Manufactured by:** Musette (first issue), Plastic Record Co. (second issue)
**Overall description of content:** general children's entertainment
**Record: First issue, first style (1942):** 7" black shellac (no records seen for second style).
**2nd issue (1946):** 7" black or green vinyl; the green records are flexible, very thin plastic.
**Record label:**
First issue, first style: Black print on red or orange background, or red print on light blue background. No graphics, only text. (No records seen for second style.)
Second issue: Two styles seen, both white and black printing on red background. The black vinyl records have a paper sleeve, with cartoon figures of Jack and Jill. The green vinyl records have a color 'label' that is actually part of the plastic, much like a picture disc. There are two green ink figures of Jack and Jill on the label.
**Holder/cover:**
First issue, first style: record/book combination, record in holder on inside back cover. Twelve page booklet illustrated by Mildred Drusin. The text in the booklet is the actual script of the audio track. Two-color printing. Cover is heavy paper card stock and has the words "Jack And Jill Singers" in large text along top. Record number (without prefix as on record label) is shown. There is a headshot photo of "Announcer Master Ted Donaldson" shown in a circle, along with cartoon drawings of the characters in the songs. Reverse has a list of the other records in the series.
First issue, second style: Generally the same as first style, except cover is lighter weight semi-gloss card stock and there is no photo of Ted Donaldson. Graphics are slightly different, but information is the same.
Second issue: Flexible cardboard cover in four-color that folds together from the top, opening with slot holder on

bottom; left and right flaps fold in. Attached with a grommet to inside front cover is a rotating picture wheel which shows a cartoon illustration through a circular opening near the top edge of the cover when the wheel is manually turned. Illustrations by D.B. Icove. No record number appears on the cover. Other titles in series listed on reverse. Information on records issued.

**Date range:** 1942 (first issue) and 1946 (second issue)

**Series and record-numbering sequences:**
First issue: one series of five records, numbered consecutively from JJ-1 to JJ-5; second issue: one series of six records, numbered consecutively from No. 1 to No. 6.

**Miscellaneous:** The child singer in this series, Ted Donaldson, was in *Life with Father*, the popular radio show of the time. All the performers are children. Each record opens with a musical signature and closes with a radio fade-out.

## ♪MUSETTE — MUSICAL RADIO SCRIPT

**Associated/subsidiary labels:** Superman picture discs, Zoo-Zoo, Jack & Jill Singers, Caravan

**Distributed, produced, and manufactured by:** Musette Publishers, Inc., Steinway Hall, NY

**Overall description of content:** general children's entertainment

**Record:** 10" black shellac

**Record label:** gold on blue or red; stylized "M" in Musette, made to look like a musical note.

**Holder/cover:** hardcover book with 28 – 30 pages and color and b&w illustrations; a simulated radio script is included for children to play at a make-believe radio broadcast; sheet music is also in the book.

Two cover and book versions: first, 1940 – 1943, "Musical Radio Script" on cover; second, 1940 – 1945 "Musical Radio Script and Record." Artwork is sometimes different on different printings. I have seen up to five printings of some titles, although not necessarily five different cover artworks.

**Date range:** 1940 – 1945

**Series and record-numbering sequences:** Series of 10 "books," not specific numerical sequence

**Miscellaneous:** This is one of several children's series on the Musette label. Many of these titles were later released on Caravan records.

## ♪MUSETTE: SUPERMAN

**Associated/subsidiary labels:** Superman picture discs, Zoo-Zoo, Musical Radio Script

**Distributed and produced by:** Musette Publishers, Inc., Steinway Hall, New York, NY

**Manufactured by:** Picturtone Records, Inc., New York, NY

**Overall description of content:** general children's entertainment

**Record:** 7" flexible cardboard, laminated picture disc; striking four-color design.

**Record label:** picture disc

**Holder/cover:** 12-page color booklet; quasi-comic book format; outer cover heavy paper, inner cover regular paper. Designs on both covers are identical.

Values shown in price guide are for records and book complete.

**Date range:** 1947

**Series and record-numbering sequences:** Only two record sets, numbered 1 and 2.

**Miscellaneous:**" This is one of the most striking designs of all the records in the genre, featuring the popular original DC Comics "Superman" artwork. Copyright National Comics Pub. Inc.

## ♪MUSETTE: ZOO-ZOO SONGS

**Associated/subsidiary labels:** Jack & Jill Singers; Superman pic discs; Musical Radio Script

**Distributed and produced by:** Musette, Inc., Steinway Hall, New York, NY

**Manufactured by:** Longacre Press, Inc.

**Overall description of content:** general children's entertainment

**Record:** 5" thin cardboard picture disc integrated into three-fold panel; record is center panel. Entire folded panel is placed on record player. Four-color artwork, fairly crude in style. Cartoon designs refer to song titles. Panel dimensions unfolded are approx 18" long by 5½" high. Each individual record panel is about 6" wide. Record plays on both sides. Story narration printed on outside panels.

**Record label:** see above

**Holder/cover:** no covers or holders seen

**Date range:** 1947

**Series and record-numbering sequences:**
One set of five records/panels numbered from 1 to 5.

**Miscellaneous:** One of the several children's series on the Musette label.

## ♪MUSICAL SOUND BOOKS

**Associated/subsidiary labels:** none

**Distributed, produced, and manufactured by:** Sound Book Press Society, Inc., Scarsdale, NY

**Overall description of content:** children's educational (music appreciation)

**Record:** 10" black vinyl

**Record label:** various combinations of colors, mainly silver or black printing on solid color backgrounds—different colors corresponding to different series (see below). All text, no graphics.

**Holder/cover:** thin cardboard sleeves, semi Musical Sound Book generic front of the sleeves and totally generic MSB sleeves. By "semi-generic," I mean that the front has the same front cover design for each series: a white line drawing of music related themes surrounding a list of title in the series. The reverse is text only, specific to the record in the sleeve.

Sleeves are often found in brittle condition, with the labels falling off the records.
**Date range:** 1953 – 1956
**Series and record-numbering sequences:** all series are consecutively numbered.

At least seven series and 142 titles exist on 78 rpm, as follows:

Edward Mac Dowell series: 8 titles
Tiny Masterpieces for Young Listeners (1954): 7 titles
Green Section: 18 titles
Crimson Section (aka Red Section): 38 titles
Blue Section: 13 titles
Music to Remember: 56 titles
Tiny Masterpieces for Young Listeners (1956): 20 titles

**Miscellaneous:** There is a large gap between 78051 and 78101 for which I do not have information. It is reasonable to expect that records were issued for these numbers, in which case the total would increase by at least 50. Perhaps this will become known by the time the next edition of this book comes out.

MSB records were issued on long playing 33 1/3 rpms that continued the consecutive numbering of these series.

No other information is available about this company.

## ♪MUSICRAFT

**Associated/subsidiary labels:** Masterpiece, Musicraft Red Robin
**Distributed, produced, and manufactured by:** Musicraft Corporation, New York, NY
**Overall description of content:** general adult catalog with several children's albums in the mix and the Red Robin children's series
**Record:** 10" black shellac and red vinyl
**Record label:**
Main label: gold on blue or red (shellac); red on yellow (vinyl); stylized "M" in "Musicraft" in the shape of a lyre.
Red Robin series: Red Robin in a wavy red banner, robin and chicks in nest graphic above the banner, blue text on light yellow
**Holder/cover:** book-style albums, paper gatefold two-record sleeves, envelopes. All have four-color illustrations specific to the record's title.
**Date range:** 1941– 1947
**Series and record-numbering sequences:**
Albums: ten albums are listed, with seven being specifically identified by Musicraft as being for children. I have added three others that are suitable. The prefixes "M" and "N" apply to most of them. They are skip-numbered, as many other albums were not for children, but were part of the same numbering system.
Red Robin series: a total of ten two-record sets with the prefix "RR" consecutively numbered starting with RR 1. These were partially previously issued with an "A" prefix (eight sets: A 6-7 + A 20-25)); the A 20s were combined into three "C" sets (C 1-3).
**Miscellaneous:** Gordon Mercer and Samuel Puner formed this label in 1936. Their partners were a youngish Manhattan lawyer named Milton L. Rein and a music teacher named Henry Cohen. They took in Herman Adler, a musical researcher from Germany, as "digger-in-chief" for recordable works. Musicraft was the biggest independent label in the U.S. during the Depression. In 1948, there was a big shakeout in the record industry, and Musicraft bit the dust, along with many others such as Majestic and Sonora.

In addition to putting out some critically acclaimed albums of esoteric chamber music, it also had a stellar catalog of popular and jazz artists, including Mel Torme, Teddy Wilson, Sarah Vaughn, and Duke Ellington. It also recorded folk music, including Leadbelly's first commercial album (*Negro Sinful Songs*), in 1939.

The label's earliest children's records, starring the well-known Metropolitan Opera announcer Milton Cross, were licensed from Eli Oberstein who had previously issued the recordings on one of his own labels, Varsity.

Soon after WWII, Musicraft began producing original children's records (the Red Robin series), under the direction of Hecky Krasno, who, along with his brother-in-law Philip Eisenberg, wrote all of the material. (Krasno later went to Columbia Records, where he produced Rudolph the Red-Nosed Reindeer, among many others.) Earl Rogers was the primary performer in this series.

The Red Robin series was originally on shellac discs. After World War II, they were reissued in red vinyl called "Toughies." Set numbers (RR-1 to RR-10) remained the same, but the disc numbers became RR T1 to RR T20.

Musiccraft went bankrupt in 1947, but Puner returned in 1948 with a new label: Allegro.

## ♪MUSIKING

**Associated/subsidiary labels:** none known
**Distributed, produced, and manufactured by:** Musiking
**Overall description of content:** general children's entertainment
**Record:** 7" black vinyl
**Record label:** black on pink, company logo
**Holder/cover:** none seen
**Date range:** 1950s?
**Series and record-numbering sequences:** one series seen, six records consecutively numbered from 1 to 6.
**Miscellaneous:** This is one of several small and obscure labels in my collection that offer children's records. Very little is known about these tiny companies, including this one.

## ♪NANETTE GUILFORD

**Associated/subsidiary labels:** Records of Knowledge, Rexford

**Distributed by:** Girl Scouts and Boy Scouts of America, NY
**Produced and manufactured by:** Nanette Guilford Productions
**Overall description of content:** children's general entertainment
**Record:** 10" vinyl
**Record label:** silver on blue, plain text, no graphics
**Holder/cover:** paper gatefold, holding two discs. Black and white photos on cover, some color graphics.
**Date range:** ca. 1954
**Series and record-numbering sequences:** small series of at least four sets of double records for Boy Scouts and Girl Scouts, Cub Scouts, etc.
**Miscellaneous:** Nanette Guilford was a Broadway and Metropolitan Opera performer, going back to the 1930s. Her short series of these records was also issued on the Records of Knowledge label. I have no other information about this, her own, label.

## ♪NIC

**Associated/subsidiary labels:** none known
**Distributed, produced, and manufactured by:** NIC Projector Corp., New York, NY
**Overall description of content:** general children's entertainment
**Record:** 5" black shellac and 5" laminated cardboard picture discs
**Record label:** shellac version: black and white on red with NIC logo (black boy riding white elephant).
**Holder/cover:** shellac: none seen, probably a boxed set; Picture discs: packaged in a box with two filmstrips. Box is 5" square with cutout hole in center to partially view the record. Filmstrips placed on either side of the record in a cardboard container. Back of box lists other titles in the series.
**Date range:** 1934
**Series and record-numbering sequences:**
Picture discs: seven records were made, six double-sided with stories and a seventh with a story on the obverse side and the reverse side containing a text message to parents on the mission of the NIC Projector Talkie records. Thus, there are 13 titles in the series. The numbers on each side refer to a companion filmstrip number. There were 35 (known) filmstrips made but only 13 were put on records. The 13 titles, which also appeared on the records, were randomly chosen, as far as the numbering sequence. The combining of two stories on one record is assigned a letter (A, B, C, D, E, F) when the list is shown on the packaging; but this letter does not appear on the picture discs (although it does on the black shellac version — see next paragraph).
Black shellac discs: Records are 'numbered' with letters, as well as serial numbers. The letter (I have seen A, D, I, K, J) refer to the packaging scheme of NIC to combine two titles on one record. For example, "Combination A" (the letter A is on the record) is two stories: "Jack & the Giant Killer" and "The Owl & The Pussycat.") On the picture discs, this same combination on one record exists, but the numbers on that disc refer to the filmstrip number. The black shellac records do not refer to the filmstrip numbers, even though the combinations on the records are the same.
**Miscellaneous:** The NIC projector/record player is non-electric (except for a light bulb) toy, invented in 1931 in Barcelona, Spain by three brothers of German origin: Tomàs, Ramon, and Josep Nicolau Griñó. The name "NIC" comes from the "Nicolau" surname. The first version was a projector only. The talkie version (slide strip synchronized with record) was not developed until 1934. NIC records were to be played on the talkie version. NIC was the first company to make these types of toy projectors for kids. The company went out of business in 1974, but a museum in Girona (near Barcelona) curated by Tomas Mallol contains much of the original equipment, records, etc. from the factory, which was mostly destroyed in a fire in 1932.

The information in this section refers only to the US made records. NIC records were made initially in Spain, and then licensed in other countries such as Japan and Germany. Records are extremely rare, especially the picture discs.

## ♪OFFICIAL BOY SCOUT

**Associated/subsidiary labels:** none
**Distributed and produced by:** The Boy Scouts of America
**Manufactured by:** American Record Mfg. Co., Framingham, MA
**Overall description of content:** general children's entertainment
**Record:** 10" black shellac
**Record label:** picture label, red and black on olive green; beautiful script used for label name; line drawings of Boy Scouts in the field.
**Holder/cover:** none seen
**Date range:** 1925
**Series and record-numbering sequences:** no known series per se, but according to Kurt Nauck, five of these records were made.
**Miscellaneous:** Jackie Coogan is one of the performers on this label, making it supercollectible.

No further information is available.

## ♪OFFICIAL MICKEY MOUSE CLUB

**Associated/subsidiary labels:** Disneyland, Mattel (Mickey Mouse Club Newsreel and Musical Maps), some Golden Records.
**Distributed by:** initially by AM-PAR Record Corp, then by Disneyland Records (California)
**Produced and manufactured by:** initially Simon & Schuster, then Walt Disney Productions
**Overall description of content:** general children's entertainment

**Record:** 10" orange (first 11 records) or black vinyl (remaining records)
**Record label:** black on yellow, Mickey Mouse floating head logo at top of logo
**Holder/cover:** cardboard sleeves for first 11 records (#50 – 61), then paper sleeves, all richly colored and/or photographed with the famous Mousketeers, Disney characters, et al.
**Date range:** 1955 – 1958 (Official Mickey Mouse Club portion of this series)
**Series and record-numbering sequences:** There are 43 titles in this part of the DBR record series, numbered consecutively from DBR 50 to 92. All were issued in both 78- and 45-rpm speed.
**Miscellaneous:** All told, there are a total of 78 DBR titles, divided into two different record labels. "Official Mickey Mouse Club" is the predecessor to Disneyland Records (see separate label notes). It represents a transition from production and distribution of Disney material from non-Disney companies (e.g., Golden Records) to the Disney company itself. The remaining issues of the series are on the Disneyland label. They are: DBR 20 – 49 and DBR 93 – 97. See label notes for Disneyland.

The DBR series has a convoluted numbering system, one that is very hard to digest even for the veteran collector/archivist. See R. Michael Murray's book, *The Golden Age of Walt Disney Records*, for a detailed explanation of how this numbering system evolved. To begin with, the first records issued in 1955 started with the number DBR 50. But, the entire DBR series runs from DBR 20 to DBR 97. As you can start to see, this initial DBR series was sandwiched between higher and lower numbered records, all of which came out in later years. Weird, for sure.

The initial run of the first 21 DBRs (DBR 50 – 70) were issued on the Official Mickey Mouse Club label and were prepared by Simon and Schuster and distributed by AM-PAR Record Corporation, a division of ABC Paramount. There was one exception to this: DBR 57, which had a label that said "From Disneyland." This was before "Disneyland" was an official label on its own merits. ABC, which ran the Mickey Mouse Club TV show, was (along with Golden Records/Simon and Schuster) one of Disney's marketing partners for records. Disney took over distribution and production of the DBR series in 1958 starting with DBR-71 and going to DBR-92, however the label remained "Official Mickey Mouse Club." Not until 1959 did the DBR records bear the Disneyland label. (See label notes for Disneyland.) This DBR series is not to be confused with another small set of Disney titles with a DBR prefix put out by Golden Records in 1955 — see label notes for Golden Records elsewhere. Not only that, but Golden issued "Disneyland" label variations within their own main series with their own numbering (not DBR). It is a hybrid of Mickey Mouse Club and Disneyland. It says "From Disneyland — Official Mickey Mouse Club." Boy, this is hard work, trying to explain all of this. I should stop now, but I can't!

Nor is this Official Mickey Mouse Club label to be confused with the Golden Record label variation (see label notes for Golden Records). Official Mickey Mouse Club records had previously appeared as part of the main Golden Record series in the mid-1950s. Several of the Golden series were issued with label variations (such as Official Mickey Mouse Club, Disneyland, Romper Room, etc. — see Golden Record label note section for more details on these label variations). There were more than two dozen on Golden with labels very similar to the Disney made records. They both have the Mickey Mouse floating head logo. The only difference is that the Golden Records say "From Walt Disney's Official Mickey Mouse Club." The words "from Walt Disney's" are added.

"DBR" stands for Disney Big Record, but the name refers more to the amount of content on the disc, not the size (e.g., 10" vs. 7").
DBR 50 – 57 + 66 – 70: The content and material was prepared by Simon & Schuster and Walt Disney Productions, and distributed AM-PAR Record Corporation (ABC Paramount).
DBR 71 to end: A Product of Disneyland Records. DBR 71 came out in 1958, the year that Disney took control over production and distribution of their records.

The following abbreviations are used in the listings to save space:

JD = Jimmie Dodd
JC = Jiminy Cricket
MMC = Mickey Mouse Club Chorus and Orchestra

## ♪OKEH (COLUMBIA)

**Associated/subsidiary labels:** Columbia, Epic, Vocalion
**Distributed, produced, and manufactured by:** Okeh, Columbia
**Overall description of content:** general adult catalog with a few children's records sprinkled in the mix.
**Record:** 10" black shellac
**Record label:** gold on maroon; text only
**Holder/cover:** generic Okeh paper sleeves
**Date range:** 1918 – 1950s
**Series and record-numbering sequences:** no children's series. Just randomly issued children's records in their regular catalog.
**Miscellaneous:** Okeh Records began as an independent record label based in the USA in 1918; from the late 1920s it was was a subsidiary of Columbia Records. Okeh was founded by Otto Heinemann (1877 – 1965), a German-American manager for the U.S. branch of German owned Odeon Records. As World War I raged in Europe, Heinemann thought it best to have an American based

company. He incorporated the Otto Heinemann Phonograph Corporation in 1916, set up his own recording studio and gramophone record pressing plant in New York City, and introduced the company's line of records for public sale in September of 1918. Heinemann formed the name of the record label "Okeh," from his initials; early disc labels rendered the name as "OkeH." That same year the name of the label's owning company was changed to the General Phonograph Corporation. The name on the labels was changed to "OKeh."

Okeh began by issuing popular songs, dance numbers, and vaudeville skits similar to the fare of other labels, but Heineman also wished to experiment with music for audiences neglected by the larger record companies. Okeh produced lines of recordings in German, Czech, Polish, Swedish, and Yiddish for the USA's immigrant communities. Some were pressed from masters leased from European labels, others were recorded by Okeh in New York.

Okeh Records pioneered the practice of "location recording" in 1922. Okeh also sent mobile recording trucks to tour parts of the country to record performers not heard in New York or Chicago. Regular return trips were made once or twice a year to New Orleans and other cities, recording a wealth of jazz and early country music artists.

In 1926 Okeh switched to the electric microphone system of audio recording. On November 11 of that year, controlling interest in Okeh was purchased by Columbia Records. The Okeh label was continued until 1935. Columbia again revived the label in 1940 after they lost the rights to the Vocalion name (by dropping the Brunswick label) and pressed it until 1946; it was revived in the 1950s and used sporadically through the 1990s.

## ♪PACKAGED PROGRAMS

**Associated/subsidiary labels:** none
**Distributed, produced, and manufactured by:** Packaged Programs, Inc., Pittsburgh, PA
**Overall description of content:** general children's entertainment
**Record:** 10" red vinyl
**Record label:** multicolor text on yellow background (only one record seen). No graphics.
**Holder/cover:** very thin cardboard, four-color drawing, may be the same for each record; however, I have not seen others. Reverse shows other titles in series (see note below about my feelings as to their existence).
**Date range:** 1948
**Series and record-numbering sequences:** cover lists 33 albums and is called "Mr. Rumple Bumple." I have only seen two in fifteen years and I own only one (album #1); as with Action Records, I have a theory that all of the records listed were not released.
**Miscellaneous:** Nothing more is known about the company. The series referred to a storyteller named "Mr. Rumple Bumple." In fact, this name is the most prominent feature on the record label. He looks and sounds like an "Uncle Remus" type of jovial elderly man. All of the stories take up one side of a 10" record and have alliterative titles (e.g., "Wallie the Walrus," "Annie The Alligator," etc.).

## ♪PAL PICTURE PLAYER

**Associated/subsidiary labels:** Little Pal, Little Tots, Playtime
**Distributed and manufactured by:** Plaza Mfg. Co.
**Produced by:** American Record Corp
**Overall description of content:** general children's entertainment
**Record:** 7" black shellac
**Record label:** blue text on orange background; generic cartoon of kids watching movie or slides, which were to be played in coordination with record. A projector was made to go along with the records. (See also Little Pal Records.)
**Holder/cover:** paper sleeves for each record; generic Pal Picture Player Records design, black printing on blue background; front is cartoon drawings of characters in the stories and songs; reverse show a list of all other titles in the series.

A book-style album may have been issued, as with Little Pal, but I have not seen one.
**Date range:** 1930
**Series and record-numbering sequences:** one series known, ten titles, consecutively numbered from #501 to #510. Each record had a corresponding issue on Little Tots, Little Pal and Playtime.
**Miscellaneous:** These records were meant to be played with synchronized filmstrips (see also Duratone and NIC) on a record player/projector combination. They are extremely rare.

## ♪PAT

**Associated/subsidiary labels:** none
**Distributed, produced, and manufactured by:** Pat Records, Newark, NJ
**Overall description of content: general children's entertainment**
**Record:** 10" cardboard picture-disc, however only 6" of the surface have playing grooves. That makes this quite unique in the kiddie 78-rpm field.
**Record label:** picture disc
**Holder/cover:** none seen
**Date range:** 194?
**Series and record-numbering sequences:** this series has potentially fourteen records, but I only have titles for five, and own only one. The numbering is in sequence with a 6A prefix followed by consecutive numbers from the A-side to the B-side, and onto the next record. For example: 6A-1/2, 6A-3/4. The highest number I show is 6A-27/8. I have not verified if all numbers between 1/2 and 27/28 were issued.

**Miscellaneous:** The performer and writer of this series is Scotty MacGregor. He also appears on the Continental, Remington Junior and Little Chip records. That makes me wonder if there is a connection between those companies and Pat, or if MacGregor just went off on his own with this label. The label does have the words "A Scotty MacGregor Creation."

♪ PETER PAN

**Associated/subsidiary labels:** Humpty Dumpty, Prom, Rocking Horse
**Distributed and produced by:** Peter Pan Records, Newark, NJ
**Manufactured by:** Synthetic Plastics, Newark, NJ
**Overall description of content:** general children's entertainment
**Record:** 7" and 10" red, orange, black vinyl
**Record label:** the first wave of labels were silver on red (A-side) and silver on blue (B-side) with a line drawing of a boy playing the panpipes in a field; these were followed by four-color picture labels, with some of the pictures being generic in nature and others having pictures specific to the title. Some of the illustrations were quite striking. The last version was similar to the second, however four-color gave way to red and black on yellow.
**Holder/cover:** paper sleeves, some semi-generic (same illustrations but just the title different), others quite nice in four-color. Some small cardboard albums were issued with groups of records that were issued singly.
**Date range:** 1948 to ca. 1967 (that makes this just about the latest date that any 78-rpms were produced in the US!)
**Series and record-numbering sequences:**
100 series: (7"): Nine different records issued, skip numbered. Lowest number is 102, highest is 120. Up to 112, numbers every other in most issues, (e.g., 102, 104, etc) but some are consecutive (e.g., 102/103). Records issued with and without letter prefixes and suffixes. Many sleeve variations seen for each record issued. Some are die-cut at the top.

Label numbering systems: 102 A/102 B, PP-102 A/ PP-102 B, PL-A 102/ PL-A 103, PP-102 A/PP-103-A. Sleeve numbering systems: 102, PP 102.
200 series (7"): Fourteen different records issued. Lowest number is 200/201. Highest number is 228/229. Numbering can be either 200/201 or 200-A/200-B. Record #217/218 has not been seen, thus existence is not verified.

Label numbering systems: PP-200/PP-201, PP-200-A/PP-200-B. Sleeve number systems: 200 A/200 B, PP-200. 300 to 700 series (7"): This is the main series of the Peter Pan 7" records, with 367+ titles, many of which are multiple repeats, however. Most were issued on 78 rpm only (see below), although many were issued on both 78 and 45. "L": 36 titles, "P": 14 titles, "X": 33 titles.

If I have two or more versions in my collection, the versions will be indicated by a "v.1, v.2, etc." next to the number (e.g., 498 [v.1]). Titles and artists' names for each side are separated by a forward slash (/). In those cases where the titles and/or titles are identical on both sides, the names and titles are shown only once.

The numbering system is a little strange and as such it can be a collector's dream, but an archivist's nightmare. Many titles were reissued on different record numbers, and flip sides could be various different titles, as new records were issued several times, usually with different artwork on the covers, and often paired with a different song or story on the back.

The lowest number, for whatever reason, is #326. The highest number is #709. The highest number on 78-rpm that I have seen is #659. All the rest are on 45 rpm only. I have listed the 45-rpm only records (660-709), since they are part of the main series, which started out as 78s. (I have also done this with a few other series, notably Golden, Disneyland Little Gem and Cricket. See label notes elsewhere for details on those labels.)

Most records have an A side and a B side (e.g., 326A/ 326B). In most cases the label and sleeve will match, but sometimes the number on the label will be different from the sleeve. This different number may be from another series, such as the 10" series. Many of the 7" records were also issued in 10" format. A surplus of 10" labels for a particular record (e.g., #371) may have prompted the Peter Pan Company to use them on the 7" issues to save money. This is just my theory.
10" series: Up to this point, I have identified 99 single records in this series; many are duplicates within the series. There are 23 titles in the 500 subseries. These 500 numbers are totally different than those in the main 7" series. There are four titles in the 2100s and 68 titles in the 2200s. There are also four other singles with miscellaneous oddball numbers.

**Miscellaneous other information:** The Peter Pan label first appeared in 1948. The original parent company, Synthetic Plastics (Newark, NJ), had been in the plastics business since 1928, producing miscellaneous products such as buttons. In its current incarnation (2007) the company's name is Inspired Corporation (Roseland, NJ). Inspired has multiple product lines including fitness and wellness videos, book, films and CDs. Only a small part of its product line is targeted for children.

Because of the continuing existence of Inspired Corporation, you could say that Peter Pan is one of only six still-existing companies that made primarily or exclusively 78-rpm children's records in the 1950s and earlier. The other surviving companies are: Honor Your Partner, Singspiration, Star-Bright, Stepping Tones and Kimbo. With the exception of Kimbo, none of these companies exist today with the same name.

I am not including in this discussion the large record companies of that era which targeted the adult market. Such familiar labels as Columbia, Capitol, RCA-Victor, Decca, and Mercury fall into this category. All of these companies have been subsumed into the current "Big 4" mega-music conglomerates (Sony/BMG, EMI, Vivendi/Universal and Warner) that hold over 75% of the music market share. Each of the aforementioned corporations has acquired the rights to many children's record lines released by the venerable stalwarts of the record industry, going back to the 1890s.

While Peter Pan records could be found in millions of households starting in the late 1940s, and well into the 1960s, it, nevertheless, existed in the shadow of the kiddie record giant company, Golden Records. In its heyday, Golden had a 50% market share of kiddie record sales in a field that included many hundreds of record labels. Peter Pan tended to reissue copies of the original songs and stories released by Golden, but without its roster of famous personalities. I do not have access to sales figures, but I suspect Peter Pan was greatly outsold by Golden.

One thing that is unique about Peter Pan records with respect to 78-rpm records is that some of the latest issued 78s (at least in the US) were put out by this company. While most record companies discontinued making 78s in favor of 45s and 33s by the end of the 1950s, Peter Pan continued with 78s until at least 1966 – 1967!

General discographical notes: Several personalities appeared on many, or most of the Peter Pan records. To save space and time, the principal names have been abbreviated as follows:

VK = Vicky Kasen, director
JA = Jack Arthur
PM = Peggy Marshall, director
SS = Syl Stewart, director
WD's = Walt Disney's
BW = Billy Williams and his Cowboy Rangers, directed by Don Cope (Note: Billy Williams starred as Kit Carson on TV.)
PPO = The Peter Pan Orchestra (aka the Peter Pan Players, the Peter Pan Orchestra & Chorus, the Peter Pan "March Leaders" Band, the Peter Pan Marching Band)

### ♪PHOEBE JAMES CREATIVE RHYTHMS FOR CHILDREN

**Associated/subsidiary labels:** none
**Distributed and produced by:** Phoebe James Productions-
**Manufactured by:** unknown
**Overall description of content:** children's dance and rhythm content
**Record:** 10" translucent red vinyl
**Record label:** black on white, text only; prefix of "AED" before each number
**Holder/cover:** heavy paper sleeve, black on white text with minimal graphics on the front and back; generic "Creative Rhythms for Children" on the front. Reverse lists other titles in series plus text on the specific record in the sleeve.
**Date range:** 196?
**Series and record-numbering sequences:** a series of 22 single records, consecutively numbered from AED 1 to AED 22.
**Miscellaneous:** This is one of several small and obscure labels in my collection that offer school dance and rhythm music and instructions. Very little is known about these tiny companies, including this one.

### ♪PHONODISC — STORY TIME

**Associated/subsidiary labels:** Phonodisc
**Distributed, produced, and manufactured by:** Phonodiscs, Inc., Woodside, NY
**Overall description of content:** general children's entertainment
**Record:** 5" record as part of a die-cut shaped picture disc; also, 7" red or black vinyl (Storytime series)
**Record label:** picture discs, plus Storytime series red on yellow, drawing of a boy and girl singing.
**Holder/cover:** Picture discs sometimes came in mailer; Storytime has paper sleeves, four-color front, specific to record title.
**Date range:** 1948
**Series and record-numbering sequences:** three known pic-discs for children, all shaped; nine known Storytime series singles, consecutively numbered on the label 7-1 to 7-7 plus a 7-57. The sleeves have the same numbers except there is a prefix of "PH."
**Miscellaneous:** This is one of several small and obscure labels in my collection. Very little is known about these tiny companies, including this one.

### ♪PICTORIAL

**Associated/subsidiary labels:** none
**Distributed by:** New Record Corp, Brooklyn, NY
**Produced and manufactured by:** Pictorial Records, Inc.
**Overall description of content:** general children's entertainment, religious
**Record:** 6" laminated "metallized" shellac picture discs. Illustrations are by Miss. C(lara), M. Burd, and Mr. Helguerd.
**Record label:** picture discs
**Holder/cover:** three-panel gatefold cover
**Date range:** 1928
**Series and record-numbering sequences:** Two series of records.
First series: Nursery Rhymes, six records numbered consecutively from 10,001 to 10,006. Two sets of three records, each in folder.
Second series: A Child's Life of Christ. Two sets of three records, each in folder. Numbers of first set: 20,001/2 to 20,005/6. Second set unknown.
**Miscellaneous:** The Pictorial Records are considered the

very first true picture discs made in the USA. The artwork was previously seen on the Kiddie Rekord Company series from 1922, but those records were not true picture discs (see notes in separate section for Kiddie Rekords). Even though the artwork is the same as the Kiddie Rekord set, the recordings are by different artists.

♪**PICTO TOONS**
**Associated/subsidiary labels:** none known
**Distributed and produced by:** Selchow & Richter, New York, NY
**Manufactured by:** Silvertone Records, New York, NY
**Overall description of content:** general children's entertainment
**Record:** 6", thin cardboard; plays on one side only.
**Record label:** side A has colorful picture label; non-playing reverse side B has SelRight name and copyright information.
**Holder/cover:** box that also contains 4 puzzle and 6 stand-up pieces.
**Date range:** 1958
**Series and record-numbering sequences:** six known boxed records, numbered from 502-A to 502-F.
**Miscellaneous:** Full name of product is Picto Toons: The Singing Picture Puzzles. It is a boxed toy type of item; includes record, cardboard puzzle pieces, and stand-up pieces, illustrating the subject of the record.

♪**PICTURTONE**
**Associated/subsidiary labels:** Playsong
**Distributed, produced, and manufactured by:**Picturtone Records, Brooklyn, N.Y.
**Overall description of content:** general children's entertainment
**Record:** 7" laminated cardboard
**Record label:** picture discs. Illustrated by Frank Bolle
**Holder/cover:** thin cardboard box to hold 3 records. Each box has a title (e.g., Folk Songs) and most have a volume number. Cut-out circular area in front to view top record.
**Date range:** 1948
**Series and record-numbering sequences:** 18 boxed sets of three records plus a single issue of an alphabet record that came with a book — 55 in total. The records are divided into sets by subject matter (e.g., Folk Dances, Marching Songs, etc.). Each set except one has its own letter prefix (one, two, or three letters), which is an abbreviation for the subject matter (e.g., GSS for Gilbert & Sullivan). Some of the subjects (Gilbert & Sullivan, Folk Dances, e.g.) have multiple sets of three.

In addition, there is a "Greetingsong" series of sixteen records. The latter series is meant for the adult market with the exception of #214 and #215. The entire Greetingsong series is included in this book for reference purposes, as they are quite collectible by children's record collectors.
**Miscellaneous:** This is one of the more popular and easily found labels of the late 1940s (although a couple of the small sets are very scarce). Companion label is Playsong, listed separately. The artwork on both sets is by the same artist. Sound quality, even on a new and unplayed record, is generally poor. Leroy Pearlman was an executive at the company.

♪**PIED PIPER (MUSIC YOU ENJOY)**
**Associated/subsidiary labels:** Kiddie Records, Merry-Go-Round, Little Masters, Songs Of The Shmoo, Toytime, Caravan, Pixie
**Distributed, produced, and manufactured by:** Music You Enjoy, Inc, New York, NY
**Overall description of content:** general children's entertainment
**Record:** 7" black shellac or very thin vinyl
**Record label:** three variations, all with same graphic design of the Pied Piper leading the children; yellow on green; green on yellow, gold on blue.
**Holder/cover:** individual sleeves and book-style albums and boxes. Individual sleeves are generic Pied Piper brown sleeves with green printing; reverse lists titles in series. Book-style albums: hard cardboard covers hold four records; front has generic Pied Piper drawing and title of album (no number of album); back lists other titles in albums. Boxed sets: hold four records; box top has same design as album covers. Bottom of box is blank. Boxes are yellow and green; one box seen is red and white.
**Date range:** 194?
**Series and record-numbering sequences:** a single series of twenty-eight records consecutively numbered from PP 1 to PP 29. No PP 13 was issued. Twenty of the twenty-nine records were issued in albums (see above). The nine, which have not been seen in albums, are: 15 and 23 through 29. Five albums or boxes were issued for 20 records (four per album). Albums are not numbered, but are titled as follows with record numbers following:

Dance Records (Album No. 1) 2, 3, 8, 9
Dance Records (Album No. 2); 1, 10, 11, 12
Marches; 4, 5, 6, 7
Nursery Rhymes; 14, 16, 17, 18
Cowboy Songs: 19, 20, 21, 22

**Miscellaneous:** This is one of the group of Music You Enjoy labels. Founder of company was John H. Alderson, Jr.

♪**PIX**
**Associated/subsidiary labels:** none
**Distributed and produced by:** Pix Records, New York, NY
**Manufactured by:** Dupli-Kut Corporation
**Overall description of content:** general children's entertainment
**Record:** 10" cardboard with clear flexi plastic disc with

playing grooves etched in taped to cardboard. Single-side playing.
**Record label:** picture disc on playing side in four-colors. Reverse side is nonplaying, black and white sheet music for part of the design; also a list of other titles in the series.
**Holder/cover:** box holding three records
**Date range:** 1941
**Series and record-numbering sequences:** one series of nine records, numbered consecutively from 101 to 109.
**Miscellaneous:** No further information is available.

### ♪PIXIE (MUSIC YOU ENJOY)

**Associated/subsidiary labels:** Kiddie Records, Merry-Go-Round, Little Masters, Songs Of The Shmoo, Toytime, Caravan, Pied Piper, Pixie
**Distributed, produced, and manufactured by:** Caravan Records, Steinway Hall, NY
**Overall description of content:** general children's entertainment
**Record:** 10" black vinyl
**Record label:** green on yellow, bottom half; reversed, top half; Pixie logo on top.
**Holder/cover:** paper sleeves, four-color; front illustration specific for record; reverse is Pixie generic, list of other titles in series and cartoon drawing around edges.
**Date range:** 194?
**Series and record-numbering sequences:** series of ten single records, consecutively numbered from P-1 to P-10.
**Miscellaneous:** This was one of several labels associated with a company called From the Catalog of Music You Enjoy as well as Musette.

Larry Gould was the president of this division in 1949.

### ♪PLASCO

**Associated/subsidiary labels:** none
**Distributed, produced, and manufactured by:** Plastic Art Toy Corporation of America, Inc. (first E. Rutherford, NJ; then E. Paterson, NJ).
**Overall description of content:** general children's entertainment
**Record:** 7" red vinyl
**Record label:** two series: first series (regular — no prefix): white and black on red, white & blue; second series (C.P.C. prefix): black on red, yellow & white. Graphic of a drum majorette, which is the company logo.
**Holder/cover:** They came in boxes of miniature dollhouse furniture manufactured by this company.
**Date range:** 1949
**Series and record-numbering sequences:** two series of single records.
First series ("regular" series, no prefix to number): at least eight records, numbered consecutively from: 1/2 to 15/16.
Second series ("C.P.C." prefix): possibly nine records. I have only three, so I cannot verify total amount. Numbering seems random. My three records are numbered as follows: 1/5, 2/6, 17/18.
**Miscellaneous:** As mentioned above, the Plasco records were inserted into boxes with dollhouse furniture made by this company.

For the longest time dollhouses have been known as a product that only the wealthy and well to do could afford. But as America began to flourish, the dollhouse became available to even the middle class, who by all means, could afford as much as most upper class individuals in other countries.

Beginning in 1947, Plasco issued an extensive line of tiny dollhouse accessories under the name Little Homemaker. They were immediately popular with consumers because of the large number of different pieces they offered, and their low retail prices, which were 15% to 25% cheaper than similar toys from major brand names such as Mattel, F.A.O. Schwartz, Marx, and Duracraft. Some of the furniture included plastic records. Plasco's product was marketed as a "Plasco Toy." The company even made a small toy phonograph. (Andy Hooper, collectingchannel.com)

### ♪PLASTIC

**Associated/subsidiary labels:** none
**Distributed, produced, and manufactured by:** Plastic Record Corporation, Long Island City, NY
**Overall description of content:** general children's entertainment
**Record:** 7" flexi colored vinyl: have seen red, green blue
**Record label:** four-color picture label, specific to title. The artwork seems to be rather juvenile in style, but that may be on purpose.
**Holder/cover:** none seen
**Date range:** 195?
**Series and record-numbering sequences:** series of at least eight records (most likely), prefix of "K" before the number.

Records numbered consecutively as follows: K 500/K 501; K 502/K 503, etc. I have only five records, not in consecutive order. So, my estimate of at least eight records in the series is hypothetical.
**Miscellaneous:** This is one of several small and obscure labels in my collection that offer children's records. Very little is known about these tiny companies, including this one.

No further information is available.

### ♪PLAYOLA

**Associated/subsidiary labels:** none
**Distributed, produced, and manufactured by:** Atlas Toy Company, Chicago, IL (picture discs), Norton-Honer Company, Chicago, IL (standard records)
**Overall description of content:** general children's entertainment

**Record:** 4" laminated cardboard picture discs — one of the smallest kiddie 78s seen! Also issued as a regular vinyl record (red, 4").
**Record label:** picture discs (four-color) or white stamped right on the red vinyl; text and graphics. No record number printed; it is etched into the vinyl in the runoff area.
**Holder/cover:** thin cardboard sleeves, three stapled together to form a book-style album. Illustrations on cover and inside sleeves specific to record title; the back lists other records in the series.
**Date range:** 1948
**Series and record-numbering sequences:** five album sets (three records each). Both the albums and the individual records are numbered. The albums are numbered consecutively from 101 to 105. The records within each set are numbered consecutively as well, but not from one set to the next.
**Miscellaneous:** These are among the most striking designs of children's records on 78 rpm, being that they are richly illustrated picture discs only 4" in diameter. A plastic mechanical record player was packaged in a box with the records. The records can be played on any standard phonograph, however.

## ♪PLAYSONG

**Associated/subsidiary labels:** PicturTone
**Distributed, produced, and manufactured by:** Playsong Record Company, New York
**Overall description of content:** general children's entertainment
**Record:** 7" laminated cardboard
**Record label:** picture discs. Illustrated by Frank Bolle
**Holder/cover:** thin cardboard box to hold three records. Each box has a title (e.g., Mother Goose Songs) and most have a volume number. Cut-out circular area in front to view top record.
**Date range:** ca. 1948
**Series and record-numbering sequences:** eight sets, 24 records. The records are divided into four subject-related sets (six records, two sets each). Wild West and Mother Goose are examples of the subject themes. Each set except one has its own two-letter prefix.
**Miscellaneous:** This is one of the more popular and easily found labels of the late 1940s. Companion label is PicturTone, listed separately. The artist is the same as on PicturTone. Sound quality, even on a new and unplayed record, is generally poor. Leroy Pearlman was an executive at the company.

## ♪PLAYTIME (PLAZA)

**Associated/subsidiary labels:** none
**Distributed by:** Plaza
**Produced and manufactured by:** Regal, American Record Corporation
**Overall description of content:** children's entertainment
**Record:** black shellac, 7"
**Record label:** first version: four-color, Mother Goose surrounded by children
**second version:** two-color, black line drawings on yellow background
Labels at the bottom will indicate either Plaza, American Record Corp, or have nothing. Most of the second version were Columbia Playtime (see separate label notes under Columbia.
**Holder/cover:** generic Playtime sleeves; generic Playtime book-style holder, holding six records.
**Date range:** 1924 – 1937 (Company was taken over by Columbia in 1938; continued as Columbia Playtime into the 1950s.)
**Series and record-numbering sequences:** seventy records numbered from 201 to 270.
**Miscellaneous:** Playtime series, originally published by Plaza

## ♪POST'S RAISIN BRAN

**Associated/subsidiary labels:** Toy Time Record & Picture Books, Kiddie Records, Merry-Go-Round, Little Masters, Songs of the Shmoo, Pied Piper, Toytime, Caravan
**Distributed, produced, and manufactured by:** Music You Enjoy, Inc., New York, NY
**Overall description of content:** general children's entertainment
**Record:** 7" black shellac
**Record label:** red, white, and blue
**Holder/cover:** This series utilizes the *Toy Time Record and Picture Book*. Holder for record as part of front cover; 24-page book, four-color on every other page; story text black ink on facing pages.
**Date range:** 1941?
**Series and record-numbering sequences:** set of six book and record sets, numbered TT-100, TT-105, TT-110, TT-115, TT-120, TT-124.
**Miscellaneous:** Two versions of this series were released: Toytime label and this one: Post's Raisin Bran Presents label, the latter probably a send-away premium. No box seen, but it probably exists.

## ♪PRAM (YOUNG PEOPLE'S RECORDS)

**Associated/subsidiary labels:** Young People's Records, Children's Record Guild
**Distributed, produced, and manufactured by:** Young People's Records, New York, NY
**Overall description of content:** general children's entertainment, especially for one- and two-year olds.
**Record:** 10" vinyl
**Record label:** black on blue and white/black on red and white. Cartoon drawing of baby carriage.
**Holder/cover:** paper sleeve
**Date range:** 1949 – 1951
**Series and record-numbering sequences:** one series of six

records, numbered 1 to 6. The first three records were issued in 1949. The complete set of six was issued in 1951 with different cover art.
**Miscellaneous:** Pram, begun in 1949, was a Young People's Records sublabel designed especially for babies. It was the brainchild of YPR and CRG writer Raymond Abrashkin.

### ♪PROM (PETER PAN)

**Associated/subsidiary labels:** Peter Pan
**Name of corporation/manufactured by/location:** Prom Record Co., Newark, NJ
**Primary target market:** adult
**Record:** 7" and 10", black vinyl
**Record label:** black print, yellow background; label logo
**Holder/cover:** paper sleeves, two-color
**Date range:** unknown
**Series and record-numbering sequences:** miscellaneous singles within main listings — no specific kiddie groups.
**Miscellaneous:** No further information on Prom. See Peter Pan for more details on main company.

### ♪PUNCH AND JUDY

**Associated/subsidiary labels:** none
**Distributed, produced, and manufactured by:** Ar. Tex Mfg. Corp., Brooklyn, NY
**Overall description of content:** general children's content
**Record:** 6" laminated cardboard, yellow.
**Record label:** black on yellow lower half; reversed on upper half. Technically speaking, this is a picture disc, but only the center label area has any graphics or printing (cartoon of Punch & Judy puppets). The rest of the disc is solid yellow, giving it the appearance of a vinyl record,
**Holder/cover:** none seen
**Date range:** 194?
**Series and record-numbering sequences:** not enough information for a definitive statement; however, I have four records numbered 2, 3, 7, and 10. It is reasonable to expect that a consecutively numbered series of at least 10 records was produced. The numbers on each record are, for example, 3A/3B.
**Miscellaneous:** This is one of several small and obscure labels in my collection that offer children's records. Very little is known about these tiny companies, including this one. No other information is available on this rare and obscure label.

### ♪RECORD GUILD OF AMERICA

**Associated/subsidiary labels:** Jim Dandy, Simon Says, Picture Play
**Distributed, produced, and manufactured by:** The Record Guild of America, Inc. first in Brooklyn, then in New York City, NY
**Overall description of content:** general children's entertainment
**Records:** 6", 7", and 10" vinyl, various colors; mostly black and red, but also yellow, green, and blue as well; 7" laminated cardboard picture discs.
**Record labels:** picture discs, picture labels, standard Record Guild of America (RGA) black and red on yellow, pink and red with spiral line drawing around the outside edge of the label. An oddball series of 7" black vinyl records (quantity unknown) with RGA numbers was issued (by RGA?) with totally plain labels, black on gray, with only the words "Children's Records," along with a title and record number.
**Holders/covers:** paper sleeves, cardboard boxed sets, cello clear holders with cardboard header stapled to top; all covers in four-color; most have lists of other records in the series on the back. The 7" vinyl set had two sleeve versions: matte and glossy; different lists of other titles on the back; the first version has a company logo of a court jester juggling two records. The 7" picture disc records had individual picture sleeves for the "P" series only. There were two versions of these sleeves. Version 1 is glossy and lists only other pic-discs on the back. The 2nd version is glossy or matte finish and can be identified with the number "2525" on the back (presumably a code for the price?). The back lists pic and non-pic disc records. The P series also came in boxed sets like all the rest of the pic-discs.
**Date range:** 1948 (7" and 10") + 1953 – 1954 (10")
**Series and record-numbering sequences** 7" picture discs, RGA: 81 records divided into nine subsets, each with its own prefix or suffix. There are at least 18 boxed sets of four records each with known subset titles. They are identified with the words "4 Picture Records" on the cover, which has a cut-out hole for viewing the top record of the four. The first twelve titles (Album 1-12) also appear in the non–picture disc boxed sets (see below). The last six titles (Album 13-18) were used exclusively for picture discs (referred to as "Sealed Edge picture records" by RGA). Each box has white or black text and two-colors, which are different from one set to the next. The box refers to these records as "Trade-A-Records," encouraging children to trade amongst themselves as with baseball cards. Additionally, a six 3-record paper-folder set was issued ("3 unbreakable picture records"). All 18 records in this series are from the "G," "S," and "T" subsets.
6" picture discs, Picture Play: two series of 12 records each, consecutively numbered C-1 to C-12 and PP-1 to PP-12 respectively. The PP series is super-rare. It is an 'animation' picture disc similar to Red Raven records (see separate notes); a special 8-sided "Action Viewer" mirror attachment that is placed on the phonograph spindle allows the cartoon drawings on the record label to go into animation. Records were available individually packed in cellophane with a cardboard header identifying the title. A record was also packed with the Action Viewer in a box. Records in this series were also sold as sets in a carrying case, chest, or album.

There is one other 6" series of six pic-discs that is a

**Overall description of content:** children's religious (Christian)
**Records:** 7" black and various colors of vinyl ("Sunday School" series); 10" black vinyl and shellac ("Bible Storyman" series)
**Record label:** 7": Two designs, various colors (all two-color) — green on white, black on yellow, red on yellow, maroon on white. First version has photo of little girl's head; Second version has "Sunday School" on a banner with kids in a Sunday School class. 10": Silver on red; a cross is placed over the word "Sacred."
**Holder/cover:** book-style albums. 7" books hold ten records; albums hold three records; small albums have generic front ("Children's Library — Bible Stories and Songs"), but spine has information specific to the volume. 7" records were also issued in individual two-color paper sleeves with the record's number on the front and other titles on the back.
**Date range:** 1952 – 1953
**Series and record-numbering sequences:**
7": "Sunday School" series by the "Radio Kids Bible Club." This is a division of Sacred Records; three 10-record volumes referred to as the Red volume (Old Testament); Blue volume (New Testament) and White volume (songs). Note: the color designations are mine, not the record company's. They happen to be the colors of the album covers. The Red and Blue volume each contain 10 records. I am not sure about the White volume, as I do not have it. Each album (volume) contains records from the two different series of 7" records produced: the 700 series of songs and the 800 series of stories. The 700 series consists of 11 records numbered consecutively from 701 to 711. The 800 series has one set of five records on the Old Testament (801 to 805) and another set of eight records on the New Testament (851 to 858). Each of the Red and Blue volumes has five records from each group (700s and 800s). I am not sure of the content of the White volume.
10": known as the "Bible Storyman Series"; I know of only two sets from this series: BS-1 (album of 3 records) and BS-2, a single record.
**Miscellaneous:** This is one of several small and obscure labels in my collection that offer religious children's records. Very little is known about these tiny companies, including this one.

## ♪SCOTT FORESMAN

**Associated/subsidiary labels:** none
**Distributed and produced by:** Scott, Foresman and Company (currently Pearson Scott Foresman, Upper Saddle River, NJ)
**Manufactured by:** RCA Victor
**Overall description of content:** children's educational (music & poetry)
**Record:** 10" black vinyl
**Record label:** beige on maroon
**Holder/cover:** hardcover book-style album; text only, pastel background.
**Date range:** 1951
**Series and record-numbering sequences:** no series or sequence — just two albums
**Miscellaneous:** The two record albums listed in this book are songs to accompany the New Basic Readers book series and are to be played by teachers in elementary grades. They go along with school texts with cross references to the pages in the book and the track playing on the record. The record albums do not feature any artwork, but nevertheless, they are highly collectible due to their tie-in with the "Dick and Jane" readers (see below.)

Following is some historical background on the company: Scott Foresman and Company is the venerable publisher of school books (including music) dating back to its founding in 1894 by Erastus Scott and Hugh Foresman. The Scott Foresman imprint first appeared in 1889. The company entered the elementary school market with the Elson Grammar School Readers in 1909.

The Scott Foresman imprint, dating back to 1889, taught generations of Americans to read with the first Dick, Jane, and Spot stories. The characters were created by William Elson and William Gray. They first appeared in the Elson-Gray Basic Reader primers in 1930, and became famous in the 1950s. Nowadays, Scott Foresman is most known for its Basic Readers curriculum featuring the oft-imitated and Dick and Jane characters. The books are quite costly. These two "average middle-class white kids" are American icons. The name was even borrowed for the recent Columbia feature film *Fun with Dick and Jane* (2005), starring Jim Carrey and Tea Leoni (a reworking of the 1977 flick with the same title starring Jane Fonda and George Segal).

In the 1980s, after almost 90 years of being a stand-alone independent company, Scott Foresman and Company was sold to Time, Inc. and then to Harper & Row. In 1998 the newly formed educational publishing company, Pearson Education bought Scott Foresman, Prentice Hall, Ginn, Silver Burdett and other educational imprints such as Simon & Schuster's educational business. The imprints that make up Pearson Education describe a rich educational and literary heritage. They stretch back to 1725 when Thomas Longman published the first book typeset by Benjamin Franklin.

The company is now called Pearson Scott Foresman, but publishes under the Scott Foresman imprint. Today, Pearson Education has a widely trusted and respected program in educational and professional publishing.

## ♪SIGNATURE

**Associated/subsidiary labels:** none

**Distributed, produced, and manufactured by:** Signature Recording Corporation, New York, NY
**Overall description of content:** children's general entertainment
**Record:** 10" shellac and vinyl ("Signaflex")
**Record label:** Shellac: standard Signature red on silver and reversed (top half and bottom half), C-Clef graphic. Vinyl: I have seen black on yellow or blue, tiny cartoon drawing across the middle of label.
**Holder/cover:** gatefold and book-style albums, two-records each; four-color illustrations specific to title.
**Date range:** 1946 – 1948
**Series and record-numbering sequences:** very few children's records seen: 3 albums numbered C1 to C3 and two gatefold sets, numbered CF1 & CF2.
**Miscellaneous:** George Jaycox was vice president in 1948. The original recording of "Celeste" by Victor Jory is on this label. In fact, all but one of the records in this series in my collection is narrated by Victor Jory.

No further information is available.

**♪ SILVER BURDETT**
**Associated/subsidiary labels:** Columbia
**Distributed by:** Currently Pearson Scott Foresman, Upper Saddle River, NJ. At the time of the records listed here, by Time, Inc.
**Produced by:** The Silver Burdett Company (at the time in Morristown, NJ)
**Manufactured by:** Columbia Records
**Overall description of content:** children's educational content
**Record:** 10" black vinyl
**Record label:** Music for Living series: black on white, text only. What you might expect from an educational record.
**Holder/cover:** Music for Living series: cardboard sleeves, two-color, mainly text. Individual records came in larger boxed sets of ten records or five records.
**Date range:** Music for Living series: 1960; there is also a "New Music Horizons series from the 1950s. For more information on these records, see notes under Miscellaneous section on next page.
**Series and record-numbering sequences:** initial set of 60 records consecutively numbered from 8241 to 8300. Every 10 records are in a single box, six boxes in all, one for each school grade, first through sixth grade. So, for example, numbers 8241 to 8250 are in one box for first grade. Silver Burdett had another way to number each record. Each boxed set is called a book and each individual record is called an album. For example, the eighth record for fourth grade would be referred to as Album 8, Book 4.

In addition to the initial run of 60 records, another 30 records were issued in boxes of five records each, one for each of the six grades. Each box was sort of an extension of the first 10 records. Unlike the first 60, these 30 records did not have a convenient four-digit number, but rather a longer, more complicated number issued by the Columbia Records pressing plant. For example, the first record in the second box for first grade is FR – 947/5. The alternate identification continues with the same system as the first run. In this example, the record is Book 1, Album 11 (first grade, eleventh record).
**Miscellaneous:** "The Music for Living" series on Silver Burdett was issued in 1960, four years after the original series came out on the Columbia label. Whereas the Columbia series only had the first 60 records, this one had 90 (30 new ones). Slogan on the record covers: "Records That Teach."

"New Music Horizons" is a schoolroom music curriculum for ages 4 to 16. Songbooks for grade schools with this series title were first issued in 1944 – 1946. In 1950 and 1952, Columbia Records made records to specifically go along with these books. A series of 15 albums (36) records was produced as part of the main series (J, MJ, MJV) of 10" singles and albums. See Columbia discography for details. These same records were also issued (or at least announced) as being available on the Silver Burdett label; however, I have not seen any of them. I do have all of the Columbia records in this series.

Historical timeline for the Silver Burdett Company: Silver-Burdett is one of a handful of educational publishing companies whose roots go back well over 100 years. Most of these companies produced school songbooks and records to be played in the classroom to go along with the books. In addition to Silver-Burdett, most of the other companies (e.g., Follett, Ginn, Birchard, and Scott Foresman, to name a few) produced a large amount of 78-rpm educational records.

Late 1880s:
SILVER & CO.'s Summer Music Workshops are first introduced. The workshops for music teachers sponsored by Silver Burdett Company began in 1885 and have continued every summer without interruption.

1886:
SILVER & CO. enters the general textbook field with its series Normal Course in Reading.

1888:
SILVER & CO.: M.Thatcher Rogers sells his interests in the company to Frank W. Burdett. The firm becomes known as Silver, Burdett & Co.

1962:
SILVER, BURDETT & CO. is acquired by Time, Inc. Silver, Burdett distributes Time-Life books to schools and libraries.

1965:
SILVER, BURDETT & CO. — Time, Inc., Silver Burdett, and General Electric put up $18 million to jointly form General Learning Corporation. Silver Burdett is the first division in this new alliance.

1985 – 1986:
SIMON & SCHUSTER acquires Ginn & Company, a leading elementary and high school publisher, and Silver Burdett Company, an elementary school publisher. The companies are now known as Silver Burdett Ginn, a preeminent publisher of educational materials from pre-school through grade twelve.
1998:
The newly formed educational publishing company, Pearson Education bought Scott Foresman, Prentice Hall, Ginn, Silver Burdett and other educational imprints such as Simon & Schuster's educational business. The imprints that make up Pearson Education describe a rich educational and literary heritage. They stretch back to 1725 when Thomas Longman published the first book typeset by Benjamin Franklin.

## ♪SILVERTONE RECORD CLUB

**Associated/subsidiary labels:** none
**Distributed and manufactured by:** Sears Roebuck & Co., Chicago, IL
**Produced by:** Mercury Records
**Overall description of content:** general adult entertainment with a couple of single and one multiple record album children's records in the catalog
**Record:** 12" red vinyl
**Record label:** black on silver
**Holder/cover: singles:** generic Silvertone cover with mailer; brown Kraft heavy paper. Album: four-color artwork specific to title (Hansel & Gretel).
**Date range:** 1950
**Series and record-numbering sequences:** no series as far as the children's records are concerned. Approximately 100 records issued for the Club, mostly 12", and some 10."
**Miscellaneous:** The Silvertone Record Club existed in 1950 only. It represented a last revival of the Silvertone (Sears Roebuck) label, which originally existed from 1916 to 1928, and again briefly in 1940 and 1941.

## ♪SIMMEL-MESERVEY

**Associated/subsidiary labels:** Fox, Encyclopaedia Britannica Films
**Distributed and manufactured by:** Simmel-Meservey, Beverly Hills, CA; also Encyclopaedia Britannica, Wilmette, IL
**Produced by:** Martha Blair Fox, Simmel-Meservey
**Overall description of content:** general children's entertainment
**Record:** 10" and 12" black vinyl
**Record label:** silver on blue, drawing of globe at top; large logotype letters "S-M" in center
**Holder/cover:** book-style albums and paper sleeves, both in three-color and specific to the titles of the records
**Date range:** 194?
**Series and record-numbering sequences:** various single albums and one set of seven records called Tuneful Tales, not consecutively numbered. The set appeared as single 12" records and were combined together in one seven-record album as well.
**Miscellaneous:** Edward Simmel was one of the founders. He was a low budget producer who shot 16mm films in a rented industrial cartoon studio on Sunset Blvd. in Hollywood, CA. Some of the recordings were distributed by S-M (Simmel Meservey), others by Encyclopaedia Britannica.

I saw one Simmel Meservey picture disc on eBay quite some time ago. I have never seen another one. Unfortunately, I do not have any discographical information about it other than the picture was of a little boy in a cowboy outfit practicing lassoing. The drawing was a cartoon type of figure, mainly red clothes on a yellow background.

## ♪SIMON SAYS (RECORD OF AMERICA)

**Associated/subsidiary labels:** Record Guild of America; Jim Dandy
**Distributed by:** Cosmo Recording Co., NY
**Produced and manufactured by:** Record Guild of America
**Overall description of content:** general children's entertainment
**Record:** 6", black vinyl
**Record label:** black printing, solid orange or light green background, company logo
**Holder/cover:** heavy paper, approx. 6" w x 8" h
**Date range:** 195?
**Series and record-numbering sequences:** series of 32 single records, numbered consecutively from A-1 to A-32. A parallel 45-rpm set was issued without the "A" prefix.
**Miscellaneous:** Simon Says is a subsidiary of Record Guild of America and as such, uses some of its masters. Most of the records with the same titles in both lists will be the same recording. However, some will be totally different (e.g., Goosey Goosey Gander), so it is difficult to say with any certainty who the performers might be on the Simon Says version.

A list of the Record Guild of America (and hence Simon Says) stable of performers will be found under label notes for Record Guild of America. I have used this list as a general reference. Most records in the series will have one or more of the performing artists listed.

Some performers appear on almost all of the records.

## ♪SINGSPIRATION

**Associated/subsidiary labels:** Sunny Songs, Songtime, Happy-Time
**Distributed and produced by:** Singspiration Recording Division (Wheaton, IL) of Zondervan Publishing House (Grand Rapids, MI), for Songtime Series; also distributed by Back to the Bible Broadcast, Lincoln, NE.

**Manufactured by:** RCA Custom Record Division, Camden, NJ
**Overall description of content:** children's religious content (Christian)
**Record:** 7" black vinyl, red (both opaque and translucent) vinyl, 10" black vinyl
**Record label:**
Albums and singles (10"): silver on maroon; church steeple, music notes, text.
Happy-Time series (7"): black on white (A side), red on white (B side), photo of four children top half. Place of issue: Wheaton, IL.
Songtime series (7"): black on yellow; photos of two floating heads of children. Place of issue Grand Rapids, MI
Sunny Songs series (7"): almost exactly the same as Songtime label; place of issue Wheaton, IL
**Holder/cover:**
Albums and singles (10"): book-style (three records) and single generic Singspiration paper sleeves.
Happy-Time series (7"): paper gatefold (two-records) sleeves, blue and red on white or yellow; yellow versions have large red circle in center; Bible figure drawings on front. Ad for other albums on reverse; slogan on cover: "The Little Record with the Big Message."
Songtime series (7"): paper gatefold (two-records) sleeves, first version: blue and red on white, photo of a group of children with kneeling adult on front cover; inside pages have lyrics to songs. Second version: purple on white and green;
Sunny Songs series (7"): generic Sunny Songs single record paper sleeves, orange on white, drawings of children's heads on front; reverse is blank; slogan on front says "A Singspiration Sunny Song Record For Happy Listening." The songs were performed on a *Back to the Bible Hour* radio show. *A Songs For Christmas* cardboard album holding three records with green and red on white was issued. The three records do not have their own individual sleeves.
**Date range:** Happy-Time, 1948; other series, 195?
**Series and record-numbering sequences:**
Albums and singles (10"): four children's albums: two are Bible Story Adventures (alb #s 1B and 2B); two are Missionary Adventures (alb #s 1M and 2M); three records each; some singles are suitable for children, but there is no kiddie series, per se.
Happy-Time series (7"): at least twelve two-record sets numbered consecutively from 1H to 12H. Records are numbered consecutively from H-2500 to H-2509 (two per set for sets 1H to 5H); then H-2515 to H-2528 (two per set for sets 6H to 12H). An oddball #H-2514 is in my collection, but just as a loose record.
Songtime series (7"): at least twelve two-record sets numbered consecutively from ST-1 to ST-12; records numbered (two per set) with an "S prefix and a four-digit number in the 2600s.
Sunny Songs series (7"): at least fourteen single records, numbered SS-1 to SS-14.
**Miscellaneous:** Singspiration was originally one of the imprints of Benson Music, the first music publishing company in Nashville, TN. It was started in 1902. Benson produced hymnals and other Christian literature. The distribution company for Benson, as far as the records went, initially was Zondervan Publishing House (now just "Zondervan") of Wheaton, IL. Zondervan has been around for almost 75 years. It is an international Christian communications company. At some point in the 1940s or 1950s, when Singspiration records were made, Zondervan became not just the distributor, but the owner of the Singspiration label. Zondervan is no longer in the music business, and returned Singspiration to its original owner, Benson. In the late 1990s, Benson merged with another Nashville music house, Brentwood Music, and is now known as Brentwood-Benson Music Publishing, of Franklin, TN.

Brentwood-Benson Music Publishing owns close to 60,000 copyrights and is the world's largest Christian music publishing catalog, and the second largest evangelically styled choral music catalog.

Because of the continuing existence of Brentwood-Benson Music Publishing, you could say that Singspiration is one of only six companies still in existence that made primarily or exclusively 78-rpm children's records in the 1950s and earlier. The other surviving companies are Honor Your Partner, Peter Pan, Star-Bright, Stepping Tones, and Kimbo. With the exception of Kimbo, none of these companies exist by the name used on the label.

## ♪SMALL FRY

**Associated/subsidiary labels:** none
**Distributed, produced, and manufactured by:** Small Fry Records, USA
**Overall description of content:** general children's entertainment
**Record:** 6" blue vinyl
**Record label:** picture-label, four-color, drawing corresponds to title
**Holder/cover:** plain clear plasticene with the words "Small Fry Records" printed in yellow block letters; no other text or graphics
**Date range:** 194?
**Series and record-numbering sequences:** series of at least eight single records, consecutively numbered SF-1 to SF-8.
**Miscellaneous:** This is one of several small and obscure labels in my collection that offer children's records. Very little is known about these small companies, including this one.

## ♪SONGS OF THE SHMOO (MUSIC YOU ENJOY)

**Associated/subsidiary labels:** Kiddie Records, Merry-Go-Round, Little Masters, Pied Piper, Toytime, Caravan, Pixie

of the record sets have three or four discs, but some have two, five, or even six. Some are not specifically for children, but are nevertheless suitable. The albums are designated by the letter prefix as to which category RCA places them in. For example: "M" (AM, DM) Series is the Musical Masterpiece Sets; "P" series is for "Popular Album Sets"; etc.

**RCA Victor "Y" series: (10" and 12" black shellac and vinyl):** This is the most extensive of all of the Victor and RCA-Victor children's series, with 231 titles issued between 1944 and 1955. Within the series are sub-series: Youth, Showpiece, Little Nipper, and Little Nipper Junior. The main group is the Y-300-400s (175 records between Y-301 and Y-492). There are other groups: Y-1 to Y-35, Y-600s (mostly 12"), Y-2000s, and Y-4000s. Several dozen are repeats. RCA converted from shellac to vinyl and reissued earlier titles with new numbers. This series is packed with highly collectible and desirable records, probably more so than any other series in this book.

**RCA Victor educational, 1947 – 1950; folk & square dance albums, 1952 – 1955 (10" black vinyl):** This company was always big on educational records. An extensive catalog of albums and singles was produced, the great bulk as miscellaneous singles on the Victor label (see next paragraph). This section deals with four specific series produced on the RCA-Victor label. They are as follows:

1. "Record Library for Elementary Schools" (1947): 83 records plus a demo record for teachers in 21 albums or boxed sets. Sets are numbered from E-71 to E-91. Records are numbered from 45-5000 to 45-5082.
2. "A Singing School" (1949): 50 records plus a demo record for teachers in 10 albums. Sets are numbered from E-94 to E-103. Records are numbered from 45-6000 to 45-6049. This series of records was designed to go with a series of school songbooks published by C.C. Birchard with the same title. These books were initially published from 1939 to 1949. The record labels show the page numbers on which the songs are found in the corresponding book. The series of volumes and books are sequential from grades 1 to 8.
3. "Folk Dance Series" (1952): a series of 16 single records in generic paper sleeves, specific for this series; numbered sequentially from 45-6169 to 45-6184.
4. "Let's Square Dance" (1956): a series of five albums designated, collectively, as EC-3. The individual albums are numbered E-3000 to E-3004 (Album #1 to #5) with four discs in each set. The records are consecutively numbered from 45-6203 to 45-6222. Each album comes with fully illustrated instructions. The instruction level starts with ages 8 – 10 (grades 3 – 4) and progresses up to ages 16 – 18 (grades 11 – 12).

**Miscellaneous Bluebird, Victor, and RCA-Victor singles:** There are between 1000 and 1500 records suitable for children from among the tens of thousands of Victor/RCA records produced between 1901 and the mid-1950s. This book lists about 425. I haven't attempted to catalog every single one, due to space limitations. Furthermore, a large portion is of classical recordings that were not made specifically for children. Victor tried to get school districts to purchase them for use in music appreciation classes. For the reader interested in acquiring a more complete listing of these educational records, I suggest obtaining any of the RCA-Victor catalogs from the 1920s or 1930s.

Among the more interesting records in this section are the single-sided releases from 1900 to 1908. Victor started making two-sided records in 1908, but continued to press one-sided recordings into the 1920s. The company pressed single sided Red Seal classical records such as 88640 until 1927, but most were deleted from their catalogs in 1924.

**VOCALION (COLUMBIA, DECCA)**
**Associated/subsidiary labels:** Columbia, Decca, Brunswick, Aeolian Vocalion
**Distributed, produced, and manufactured by:** first The Aeolian Company, NY (1918), then Brunswick Records, NY (1924), then American Record Corp, NY (1931), and finally Columbia Records, Bridgeport, CT (1938)
**Overall description of content:** general adult catalog with a sprinkling of kiddie records in the mix.
**Record:** 10" shellac, originally reddish-brown (identified with Vocalion), then black.
**Record label:** originally the well-known gold on black scroll design; later under Brunswick, gold on blue, no scroll. A special series of Roy Rogers picture labels was produced in the later 1930s.
**Holder/cover:** generic Vocalion paper sleeves
**Date range:** 1920 – 1940
**Series and record-numbering sequences:** no series specific for children's records — just a random mix in its overall catalog.
**Miscellaneous:** Vocalion Records was a record label historically active in the USA and in the UK. Vocalion was founded in 1916 by the Aeolian Piano Company (NY), which also introduced a line of phonographs at the same time. The label first issued single sided vertical cut disc records, soon switching to double sided, then switching to the more common lateral cut system in 1920.

Vocalion pressed its discs in a good quality reddish brown shellac, which set the product apart from the usual black shellac used by other labels. Advertisements stated "Vocalion Red Records are best," "Red Records last longer." However the shellac was no more durable than good quality black shellac. Vocalion red surfaces are less hardy than contemporary Victor Records. Audio fidelity of Vocalion records are well above average for the era.

In 1925 the label was acquired by Brunswick Records.

In 1931 Vocalion was acquired by the American Record Corporation.

Vocalion then became a subsidiary of Columbia Records in 1938.

Due to poor sales, Columbia discontinued the Vocalion label in 1940, replacing its catalog with a revived Okeh label. The Vocalion brand was revived in 1958 by Decca Records (USA) as a budget LP label.

**VOCO**

**Associated/subsidiary labels:** Cricket, Kiddie Koncert, Tops for Tots, Tops

**Distributed by:** Voco Distributing Corporation, Inc., New York, NY

**Distributed and manufactured by:** Voco, Inc., New York, NY

**Overall description of content:** general children's entertainment

**Record:** 6" and 7" cardboard laminated picture discs; a very few of these cardboard records were sealed in clear plastic ("plastic-sealed"), but they were too expensive to produce en masse; 7" vinyl, various colors, including a few marbelized-style; 10" vinyl, black mostly, but some red seen.

**Record label:** many varieties including picture labels (generic kiddie pictures and illustrations specific to the titles. Most labels are four-color, but many are three-color. There is one issue of Christmas record with plain silver on maroon, all text, no graphics.

**Holder/cover:** 1) Paper sleeves, four-color, generic and specific; reverse is usually a song-sheet; one color, orange on white Kiddie Hit Parade generic sleeves with cutout hole to view label. 2) Hard cover book-style albums holding four records, either specific to a theme (e.g., Western Favorites) or generic "Kiddie Hit Parade" albums with space for any nine Voco records. 3) Boxed set of the eight Christmas records; song sheets are included with this set. 4) Envelope sets; three were issued (P-101 to P-103). Each holds four pic-discs.

**Date range:** 1948 – 1952

**Series and record-numbering sequences (Voco "Kiddie Hit Parade" Records):**

7" and 6" picture discs: 52 different pic-discs issued. The first 10 were issued in a small (6") size and a larger (7") size. The smaller ones are much scarcer and hence are more valuable. The numbering is consecutive but also a little unusual. Each record (with two exceptions) has a 500s number on the A side and 600s number on the B side. EX: 501/601. The series goes from 501/601 to 539/639 (no # 532/632). There is a Christmas series embedded in this sequence with an "X" prefix. It is an eight record subset, issued in two versions, each version with different artwork (X524/X624 to X531/X631 and X524-2/X624-2 to X531-2/X631-2). The exceptions to the numbering system, as noted above, are die cut (shaped records). There is a two-record sub-set for Christmas and Easter (SC1/1A and EB1/2 respectively). Each came with a mailer. There is also a four-record "Cutout Circus", a boxed set numbered 701/801 to 704/804. These are among the most striking of all kiddie picture discs. Illustrations are of circus performers and animals, on die-cut "shaped" discs.

7" vinyl two-digit and three-digit number regular records (non pic-disc): at least 77 different singles were issued between 1949 and 1952. Two-digit: An initial run of 16 records consecutively numbered from V-11 to V-27 (no #13) was issued in 1949. This two-digit series continued in 1951 from V-28 to V-41 (highest two-digit number seen). The numbering system from side A to side B took various forms. EX: V-11/11A; V-11A/11B; V-11T/11B. The 1949 sleeves featured a front cover with illustrations of both songs — one on the top half and one on the bottom half. The 1951 sleeves have only one illustration, for one of the songs, although titles of both songs are printed on front. A wavy solid color border distinguishes these sleeves: red, green or blue. All two-digit records have four-color picture labels. (Note: I have seen a totally plain label with just the word "VOCO" and a title and number.) This style continued to at least V-34.

The series continued in 1952 with V-35 or V-36. The label became two-color generic: blue on yellow, drawing of a girl with a goose (standard on most Tops for Tots records that continued where VOCO left off. Perhaps this was a transition label from Voco to Tops for Tots. This style label was retroactively issued for the lower V numbers, in some cases with a red and blue generic design. It should be mentioned that there is an overlap of titles between the earlier VOCO series and the later issued Tops For Tots list. This overlap consists of only 9 records (#s 14, 16, 25, 27B, 28A, 31A, 32A, 33 and 41.). The "girl with goose" design, more or less, is found on the overlap records.

Three-digit: issued in 1950, and 1951. These are Vinylite picture label versions of the cardboard picture discs. Some of the pictures are the same; some are similar. A second issue that came in albums (see above) had two color semi-generic pictures, not the same as the pic-discs. The front sleeve illustrations have the same format as the earlier two-digit series, i.e., both sides had their own illustration, one on the top half, the second on the bottom half. The reverse is sheet music. A Christmas set (524 to 531) was issued with plain text labels, silver on maroon. Numbering variations on label: EX 514-A/B and 514/614.

10" vinyl: A total of 12 titles have been seen in this format (quite a few more on the continuation and/or extension of this series on the Tops For Tots label. In addition to one with an "R" prefix (train sounds), there are eight in consecutive order with a TC prefix (TC-11 to TC-18) and three Christmas titles TX 102/202 to TX 104/204.

**Miscellaneous:** Cy Leslie and George Fishman started Voco in 1946 with a line of 18 "record greeting cards" aimed at the general adult market. He was inspired to make this kind of product after serving in Europe in World War 2 during which portable recording devices were brought to the troops who could cut a record of their voice to send back to their families and loved ones.

Leslie's Brooklyn-based company started distributing these cards in racks at five-and-dime stores, such as S.S. Kresge's and F.W. Woolworth. At the suggestion of the Kresge's, Leslie started a line of children's picture discs, and the rest is history.

Credit is not always given to specific artists. Credits on the labels will often state "Voco list." This terminology refers to an ensemble of performers, some of who would be the recording artists for a given record. Some of the featured artists are: Kay Armen, Toby Deane, Clark Dennis, Bob Kennedy, and the Swantones.

**VOGUE**

**Associated/subsidiary labels:** none

**Distributed, produced, and manufactured by:** Sav-Way Industries, Detroit, MI

**Overall description of content:** essentially an adult line with a few children's records

**Record:** 10" aluminum and paper in hard plastic laminate

**Record label:** picture disc

**Holder/cover:** several hard cardboard two-record holders (for the "album" sets); no covers seen for singles.

**Date range:** 1947

**Series and record-numbering sequences:** For the children there is only one 10" set, album V-106 with two records (R-745 and R-746). There are also three 12" singles that are extremely rare and valuable. At least two are probably just promotional pieces with very limited productions runs.

**Miscellaneous:** Although the name Vogue Picture Records is frequently given to only those records manufactured by Tom Saffady's Vogue Record Company, some early picture records were pressed and sold by his Sav-Way Company. These were the first records to be called "vogue records," a term he coined when referring to their stylish appearance. It was only after some prototype and limited edition records were successfully pressed that Saffady founded the Vogue Record Company.

The idea for producing a record that prominently displayed an illustration across the entire surface probably came to Tom Saffady sometime in 1945. Although Saffady was new to the phonograph record manufacturing business, he had already made a fortune from the plastic products he manufactured and sold through one of his original companies, Sav-Way Industries.

The first Vogue Picture Record was pressed in early 1946, featuring Clyde McCoy and his orchestra playing the "Sugar Blues" on the A side and the "Basin Street Blues" on the flip side. This record was meant to show the public what to expect from the newly formed company, and it was a tremendous success. Literally millions of this record were pressed and sold, and even to this day it is easily recognizable and available for most Vogue Picture Record collectors.

It's commonly accepted that at least 65 different Vogue Picture Records were produced and released, with music that ranged from blues songs to country crooners. Saffady seemed to have little trouble employing well-known artists, and soon artists like Frankie Laine, Ted Weems, and Vic Damone were recording for Vogue records.

His record company, which had begun so meteorically and brought such great innovations to the record industry, failed. In April 1947, a mere 11 months after the company was founded, the Vogue Record Company went into receivership, leaving a few unsold phonograph records and no written records to document their existence.

Vogue picture records were of a very high quality, with little surface noise. The records were produced using a complicated process whereby a central core aluminum disc was sandwiched between the paper illustrations and vinyl. Perfecting this process took quite a while; Tom Saffady and his engineers spent several months working out the bugs that often resulted in torn or dislodged paper illustrations.

When Sav-Way entered into receivership all remaining stock was liquidated through distributors. This is the source of all those Factory Reject and Vogue second records that are seen. It is reported that many of the leftover records were melted down to recycle the aluminum used in the core of the record. (Wikipedia)

**VOX**

**Associated/subsidiary labels:** none

**Distributed, produced, and manufactured by:** Vox, New York(?)

**Overall description of content:** general entertainment, some children's albums.

**Record:** 10" shellac and "plastic" (as it says on the record — probably vinyl).

**Record label:** various background colors seen (e.g., blue, black, gray); printing could be black, gold, white, etc.

**Holder/cover:** book style albums, color graphics

**Date range:** 1946 – 1947

**Series and record-numbering sequences:** Two series identified: Spotlight Series (two known) and Music Master

series (six known). No particular sequence of numbering. Album numbers of Music Masters is in the 200s, Spotlight is in the 600s.
**Miscellaneous:** Originally introduced in Germany in the 1920s, the Vox 78s appeared in limited release in the US in 1945.

**WALDORF MUSIC HALL**
**Associated/subsidiary labels:** none
**Distributed by:** F.W. Woolworth, New York
**Produced and manufactured by:** Waldorf Record Corp., Harrison, NJ
**Overall description of content:** general children's entertainment
**Record:** 10" black vinyl
**Record label:** Regular series: various combinations of two colors such as red on pink, blue on yellow, or silver on maroon. Plain text, little or no graphics. Music Hall series: silver on blue, essentially all text; an "FDR" (full dynamic range) logographic near center of label.
**Holder/cover:** Regular series: none seen. Music Hall series: four-color illustrations, specific to contents. Reverse side is either blank or text of script.
**Date range:** ca. 1953 – 1954
**Series and record-numbering sequences:**
Regular series: not enough examples known to give a full accounting; however, there are subseries of themes as follows: Pops for Tots (KD prefix), Happy Children Songs(D prefix); Christmas (H prefix). I don't know how many records were issued in each subseries, or what other themes may exist.
Music Hall series: MH prefix. Unknown as to the extent of this series.
**Miscellaneous:** Waldorf Music Hall Records was a budget record label, which made records exclusively sold in Woolworth stores. It was started in 1953 by Enoch Light and sold in October 1959 to ABC-Paramount Records.

**WHEATIES RED RECORDS & WHEATIES MOUSEKETEER RECORDS**
**Associated/subsidiary labels:** none
**Distributed by:** General Mills, Inc., Minneapolis, MN
**Produced by:** General Mills; Disney (for Mouseketeer series)
**Manufactured by:** Rainbo Record, Lawndale, CA
**Overall description of content:** general children's entertainment

**Non-Disney cereal box and send-away records:**
**Record:** Cereal box: 5" red and blue on white, one-side playing only; send away: 7" red vinyl or (strangely) green vinyl
**Record label:** Cereal Box: picture disc; send away: black on yellow, small cartoon
**Holder/cover:** Cereal box: cardboard, cutout from back of box; send away: two records per envelope; paper 3-color graphics mailer

**Walt Disney's Mouseketeer cereal box and send-away records:**
**Record:** Cereal box: 5" blue on white, one-side playing only; send away: 7" red vinyl.
**Record label:** Cereal Box: picture disc; send away: black on yellow
**Holder/cover:** Cereal box: cardboard, cutout from back of box; send away: one record per envelope; paper three-color graphics mailer

**Non-Disney records:**
**Date range:** 1954
**Series and record-numbering sequences:** Cereal box: eight cutout records, no numbers. "Red Records" send-away: four sets of two records each, consecutively numbered from GM1 to GM8.

**Walt Disney's Mouseketeer records:**
**Date range:** 1956
**Series and record numbering sequences:** Cereal box: eight cutout records, no numbers; send-away: series of four records numbered GM-101 to GM-104.
**Miscellaneous:** Send away records: Red Records were sold in sets of two. Mouseketeer records were sold singly. Values shown for send-away records are for record with mailer. Loose records are about 25% of that value. Values for cereal box records are for records cut out from the box. Records still intact in a Wheaties box back are very valuable: $75.00 – 100.00 for non-Disney and $150.00 – 200.00 for Disney. If the entire box is present (not just the back panel), these values increase by at least 50%.

**WILLIDA**
**Associated/subsidiary labels:** Kiddie Land
**Distributed, produced, and manufactured by:** Willida-Kiddie Land Records, New York, NY
**Overall description of content:** general children's entertainment
**Record:** 10" vinyl, mostly black, but some translucent red; one 12" black vinyl exists.
**Record label:** mostly red on white, but some green on red; graphic of a pixie with wings and magic wand coming out of a phonograph in front of which are two children in silhouette listening.
**Holder/cover:** four-color cartoon artwork in the late 1940s comic-book style on front; reverse lists other records on Willida, with some covers listing Kiddie Land records. All but three are single record sleeves; one is a gatefold two-

record cover; and two are book-style albums. No record numbers are seen on the paper sleeves.
**Date range:** 1946
**Series and record-numbering sequences:** eleven titles have been identified; the first ten all have a "WR" prefix and are numbered from WR1 to WR-11 (WR-4 has not been seen). WR-1 is a 12" disc; WR-2 is a two-record album; the last of the eleven is not numbered with a "WR" prefix. It is simply called Album #1.
**Miscellaneous:** This is a companion Willida label to Kiddie Land (see separate label notes). Some of the sleeves actually say "Kiddie Land," even though the label on the records is Willida.

Irving Bizman, Julie Marvin, and W.F. Martens were executives of this company (and Kiddie Land) in 1949.

### WINANT

**Associated/subsidiary labels:** none
**Distributed, produced, and manufactured by:** Winant Productions, New York, NY
**Overall description of content:** general children's entertainment; instructional
**Record:** 10" black vinyl
**Record label:** blue, red, or black on yellow, pink, green, blue
**Holder/cover:** paper sleeves with extra fold-out page; book-style album
**Date range:** 1946 – 1947
**Series and record-numbering sequences:** a tiny series of three record sets, G-1 (three records), G-2, and G-3 (single records).
**Miscellaneous:** While recuperating at Camp Shelby (Mississippi) in 1946, Army Lieutenant Murray Winant and his wife Sylvia got the idea for a trio of cartoonish record albums designed to teach children how to eat, how to be neat, and how to put away their toys. For the project, they hired a Disney animator (James Tyer) and a composer of popular cartoon music (Winston Sharples). The Winants then launched a huge publicity campaign and got write-ups in such major media outlets as *Newsweek*. But the records didn't sell very well, and they were not well received by children's specialists. According to *Consumer Reports*, they were "sadly lacking in the understanding of children."

Now this little set is highly prized and collectible by kiddie 78-rpm collectors.

### WINDSOR HAPPY HOUR

**Associated/subsidiary labels:** none
**Distributed, produced, and manufactured by:** Windsor Records, Temple City, CA
**Overall description of content:** children's basic dances
**Record:** 10" black vinyl
**Record label:** silver on green and reversed, line drawing of a couple dancing (very small), all text otherwise
**Holder/cover:** thin cardboard two-color single record holder; pattern of repeating dancing figures on cover, same illustration but different combinations of colors (brown on white; black on orange, etc.). Cover design is generic except for album number in top left corner. Reverse has dance instructions.
**Date range:** 195? or 196?
**Series and record-numbering sequences:** a series of at least five single records (referred to on the cover as both School Series/Happy Hour Records). The records have two numbering systems: I have seen set numbers with Roman numerals III to VIII with corresponding disc numbers A-7S1 to A-7S5.
**Miscellaneous:** This is one of several small and obscure labels in my collection that offer school dance and rhythm music and instructions. Very little is known about these tiny companies, including this one.

Slogan on cover says: "Windsor Records — Just for Dancing."

### WING RADIO (DAYTON, OH)

**Associated/subsidiary labels:** none
**Distributed and produced by:** WING Radio, Dayton, OH
**Manufactured by:** unknown
**Overall description of content:** chorus of children singing for both adult and children's market
**Record:** 12" translucent red vinyl
**Record label:** blue or black on white, beige or green background; very plain label
**Holder/cover:** none seen
**Date range:** 194?
**Series and record-numbering sequences:** unknown. Record numbers on matrix only, not on label
**Miscellaneous:** No further information about this label other than it is produced by radio station WING, Dayton, OH. This type of material falls into a gray area as far as being considered for children. The fact that the material is performed by a children's chorus helped me to decide to include it.

### WONDERLAND (PYRO PLASTICS)

**Associated/subsidiary labels:** none known
**Distributed, produced, and manufactured by:** Pyro Plastics Corp.
**Overall description of content:** general children's entertainment
**Record:** 6"; vinyl, black, red, green seen
**Record label:** red printing on white background, company logo
**Holder/cover:** none seen
**Date range:** 195?
**Series and record-numbering sequences:** unknown. I have only three records, numbered 144, 145, 150. Additional information welcomed.

**Miscellaneous:** This is one of several small and obscure labels in my collection that offer children's records. Very little is known about these tiny companies, including this one. No other information available. Titles of songs are unique and not seen on other labels.

**WONDERLAND JUNIOR**
**Associated/subsidiary labels:** none known
**Distributed by:** Junior Record Guild; Junior Records
**Produced and manufactured by:** Junior Records, Inc., New York, NY
**Overall description of content:** general children's entertainment
**Record:** 7" and 10" versions; black, red, green vinyl seen.
**Record label:** yellow background, red printing; company logo
**Holder/cover:** four-color paper, specific to record title
**Date range:** 1951
**Series and record-numbering sequences:** 7" series: #1601 to #1648 (48 titles numbered consecutively); first 10" series: #1501 to #1524 (24 titles numbered consecutively); second 10" issued series: #1501 to #1548 (48 titles numbered consecutively).
**Miscellaneous:** The first issued 10" series states, "Junior Record Guild presents Wonderland Records for children."

The second 10" series and the only 7" series states "Junior Records, Inc. presents Wonderland Records for children." Note: This label is not to be confused with and is unrelated to another "Wonderland" label, which was distributed by Pyro Plastics (sell separate label notes).

The 7" Wonderland Junior series is seemingly a carbon copy of the Treasure 7" issue, right down to the cover illustrations on front and back. The exact same list of titles and record numbers is on both labels. That's where the similarities partially end. In a rather strange twist (just short of inexplicable to me) the audio-tracks of the corresponding title on each label are not the same. In the first place, many of the records have totally different performers. Even when the performers are the same, the recording sessions were different. In other words, there was no sharing of the masters. On the other hand, every sleeve has the inscription in the lower left-hand corner "Original Songs and Adaptations by Marion Rosette."

**THE WORLD OF FUN**
**Associated/subsidiary labels:** none
**Distributed by:** The Methodist Publishing House, Nashville, TN
**Produced by:** The Methodist Radio And Film Commission, Nashville, TN
**Manufactured by:** RCA Victor
**Overall description of content:** children's "folk games and dances'" suitable for adults.
**Record:** 12" black vinyl
**Record label:** two-color, plain text, minimal graphics
**Holder/cover:** none seen
**Date range:** 1951 – 1959
**Series and record-numbering sequences:** 21 single records, consecutively numbered from M-101 to M-121
**Miscellaneous:** This is one of several small and obscure labels in my collection that offer school dance and rhythm music and instructions. Very little is known about these tiny companies, including this one.

Michael Herman, whose orchestra plays on all of the records, is a legendary figure in the world of International Folk Dance, especially on the East Coast. He recorded several hundred dances on his own label, Folkdancer, as well. It would be difficult to find an international folk dance aficionado who has not danced to many, many of his records.

**YOUNG PEOPLE'S RECORDS/YOUNG PEOPLE'S RECORD CLUB**
**Associated/subsidiary labels:** Young People's Record Club, Pram, Children's Record Guild
**Distributed, produced, and manufactured by:** Young People's Records (YPR), New York, NY
**Overall description of content:** general children's entertainment
**Record:** 10" black vinyl
**Record label:** YPR: pastel blue and yellow or pink and green background, blue printing, cartoon drawing of child in front of small record player. YPR Club: printing on beige background; spiral design with kids toys in center of label.
**Holder/cover:** paper sleeve with flap on back; cartoon/stylized drawings on front; company name along left border, top to bottom. YPR and YPR Club are the same except for the word "CLUB" appearing. Two record sets in gatefold sleeves.
**Date range:** YPR: 1946 – 1957; YPR Club style cover: 1946 – 1947
**Series and record numbering sequences:**
YPR: 133 titles, totaling 140 records (seven titles are two record sets); 13 different series, mainly ascribed to certain age groups: 200s, 300s, 400s, 500s, 600s, 700s, 800s, 1000s, 2000s (only one in this series); 3400s, 4500s, 8000s, 9000s. Numbers within series are not consecutive, as many numbers were reserved for records that were never released.
YPR Club: 33 single records issued in the following series only: 300s through 700s and 1000s. Four did not appear on YPR: YPR 303/4, 305/6, 315/6, 319/20.
**Miscellaneous:** Young People's Records was founded in 1946 by Horace Grenell. Managed by Grenell and his associate, Lester Troob, it functioned primarily as a mail-order subscription club (Young People's Record Club), though the records were also available to the retail trade beginning in 1947. The musician most closely as-

sociated with the label was Tom Glazer, who became the most popular children's music specialist of the era. All the records at first had a YPR Club label and sleeve designation.

From 1946 to 1952, the YPR label (regardless of label style or jacket) was primarily a mail-order club. Club members were divided into two groups: pre-school age and elementary school age. Records were issued monthly (except July and August). Probably 90% of the records were sold through the club (i.e. mail). According to Lester Troob, about 35,000 of each title was pressed. In the transition from YPR Club to just regular YPR, some records were sold with YPR Club jackets, but regular YPR labels. I mention this so the collector is not confused if he or she stumbles upon one. This is not a mismatch, but intentionally done by YPR. They were probably using up old stock of old YPR Club jackets before totally converting to just YPR covers.

After 1952, the YPR label was retail only, except those titles that were reissued on Children's Record Guild (CRG). (See separate label notes section.)

Were any YPRs with Club label and/or jacket sold in stores instead of directly through the Club? I don't know. When they entered the retail market, that's when they removed the word "club" from the labels and jackets — so they wouldn't have to have two sets of labels/jackets for every record. But there might have been some overlap during the transition.

Dissatisfied with YPR's ownership, Grenell left in 1950 and developed the Children's Record Guild for the publishing house Greystone Press. Greystone also franchised CRG to Book-of-the-Month Club and Encyclopedia Americana, which obtained CRG subscribers from their own mailing lists. In 1952, Greystone purchased YPR, while continuing to operate the CRG club throughout the 1950s. Greystone marketed YPR and CRG titles on 78 rpm until the late 1960s. (David Bonner)

**MISCELLANEOUS**

This category is generally reserved for record labels for which I have two or fewer records or record sets. This is an arbitrary decision, but is pretty consistent throughout the book.

Unlike the other lists, in this section I am including the record company name along with each individual record listing. Otherwise, you would have no way to know the label. Specific notes are not given for each label due to space limitations and paucity of information about them.

Most records listed in this section will fall into the general children's entertainment category; however, many are: educational or instructional; religious; or adult targeted, but suitable for children. If you want to categorize any of these records as to content, you will have to use your best judgment as to which category it fits into.

When indicating the record sizes, I round off to the nearest whole inch — just in case anybody is measuring and finds his or her copy slightly different in size than that which is shown in this book.

Most of the records in this section are from established record companies, but there are a significant number of one-of-a-kind issues. These are sometimes referred to as private labels, or individual company issues. They will be indicated as such when such information is known. This designation will be given based on limited knowledge, so if any readers find incorrect information, he or she is urged to contact me.

The overwhelming majority of children's records were issued in paper or cardboard sleeves (covers) or book-style albums. Some records were issued in a box with toys or other ephemera. To the extent that space in the book and my knowledge allow, I will indicated these exceptions. Of course, in the main label listings by company, records that fall into this oddball category will be properly documented.

The miscellaneous section is divided into several lists, as follows:

**Miscellaneous small records (8" or less in diameter):** This section is for "normal" commercially issued discs. Actual size is given.

**Miscellaneous large records — singles and gatefolds (9" or more in diameter):** This section lists one and two-record sets in paper or light cardboard covers — if in fact they were issued with covers. All entries are for records 10" in diameter unless otherwise indicated. The great majority will be 10", with a smattering of 12" and even fewer 9".

**Miscellaneous large records — albums (9" or more in diameter):** An album style cover refers to the physical characteristics of the record holder or cover or case. In most listings, it will be a book-style heavy cardboard cover with sleeves for individual records attached inside. Various other terms (e.g., folio) may be used by collectors for this type of record holder. What I want to emphasize here is that "album" in this context does not refer to the record itself, as it would in describing a vinyl LP. I have albums holding anywhere from two to twelve records in my collection. Some records in this category may have been issued as boxed sets or various other configurations. I will try to make note of any of particular interest. All entries in this section are for records 10" in size unless otherwise indicated.

**Miscellaneous premiums, promotions, inserts, and package design ("PD"):** This is a catchall category. It refers to records that are given away or sold as premiums, promotions, inserts, or package design (PD). In the last case, the record is actually integrated into the package itself. For me to assign a record into this category (such as with private labels — see previous) often requires a best guess. The great majority of these records are in the small category (8" or less). Actual size is given. There are many sets of these records that were issued by the major record labels, and they are included in the respective listings for each company — not in this section.

A TALKING BOOK
DAN BEARD TALKS TO SCOUTS
$20.00

ACTION RECORDS
SUNSET CARSON AND THE BLACK BANDIT
$90.00

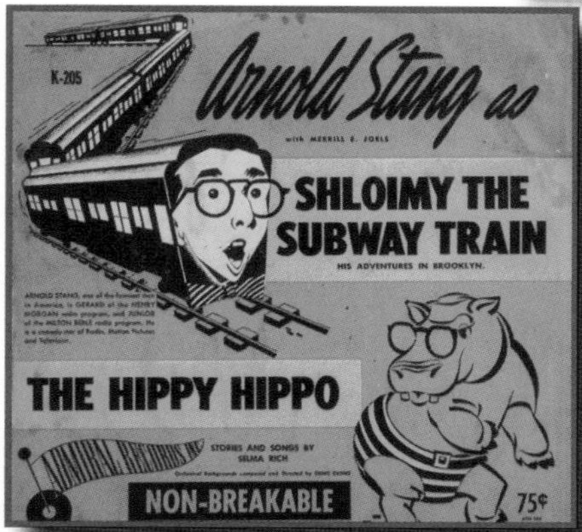


ADMIRAL RECORDS
SHLOIMY THE SUBWAY TRAIN
$30.00

## A

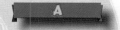

### A TALKING BOOK SINGLES — 10" REGULAR, 8" AND 10" SINGLE PICTURE DISCS IN BOOK

| # REC | DISC # | MAIN TITLE | ARTIST | YEAR | G/VG | EX/NMT | REMARKS |
|---|---|---|---|---|---|---|---|
| 3 | CF-146-8 | SNOW WHITE & THE SEVEN DWARFS | GEORGE KEAN | 1938 | $75.00 | $150.00 | ONE SIDE OF EACH RECORD IS BRAILLE! |
| 1 | GC-1 | MOTHER GOOSE PARADE: PIED PIPER, ETC. | ALICE REMSEN | 1939 | $8.00 | $15.00 | |
| 1 | GC-2 | DAN BEARD TALKS TO SCOUTS | DANIEL CARTER BEARD | 1940 | $10.00 | $20.00 | |
| 1 | TB-1 (8") | BIRTHDAY GREETINGS (PIC-DISC—ONE-SIDED) | MILTON CROSS; TED DONALDSON | | $8.00 | $15.00 | 8-INCH |
| 1 | TR-4 | A CHILD'S GARDEN OF VERSES | HELEN MYERS; JOSEPHINE THERESE | | $15.00 | $30.00 | |
| 1 | TP-3 | THE STORY OF LITTLE BLACK SAMBO | HELEN HAYES | | $50.00 | $100.00 | |
| 1 | 67866/7 | HIAWATHA'S CHILDHOOD (PICTURE DISC) | NOT LISTED | 1941 | $50.00 | $100.00 | 8" IN BOOK |
| 1 | ? | NOAH'S ARK (PICTURE DISC) | ? | | $50.00 | $100.00 | 8" IN BOOK |

### ACTION SINGLES — 10" ALBUMS

| # REC | DISC # | MAIN TITLE | ARTIST | YEAR | G/VG | EX/NMT |
|---|---|---|---|---|---|---|
| 3 | 101/6-2/5-3/4 | MONTE HALE AND THE FLAMING ARROW | SANFORD DICKINSON, DIRECTOR | 194? | $45.00 | $90.00 |
| | | MONTE HALE FOILS THE COLORADO CATTLE RUSTLERS | | | $45.00 | $90.00 |
| | | MONTE HALE CAPTURES THE CARSON CITY KID | | | $45.00 | $90.00 |
| | | MONTE HALE AND THE BROKEN INDIAN TREATY | | | $45.00 | $90.00 |
| | | MONTE HALE SAVES THE PONY EXPRESS | | | $45.00 | $90.00 |
| | | MONTE HALE AND THE TEXAS STAMPEDE | | | $45.00 | $90.00 |
| | | MONTE HALE FINDS THE PHANTOM GOLD MINE | | | $45.00 | $90.00 |
| | | MONTE HALE ROUNDS UP THE MONTANA BAD MEN | | | $45.00 | $90.00 |
| | | MONTE HALE AND THE DODGE CITY DOUBLE CROSS | | | $45.00 | $90.00 |
| 3 | 201/6-2/5-3/4 | SUNSET CARSON AND THE BLACK BANDIT | SANFORD DICKINSON, DIRECTOR | | $45.00 | $90.00 |
| | | SUNSET CARSON AND THE RUSTLER GANG | | | $45.00 | $90.00 |
| | | SUNSET CARSON WITH THE TEXAS RANGERS | | | $45.00 | $90.00 |
| | | SUNSET CARSON IN THE INDIAN COUNTRY | | | $45.00 | $90.00 |
| | | SUNSET CARSON AND THE PAYROLL ROBBERY | | | $45.00 | $90.00 |
| | | SUNSET CARSON AT GHOST CANYON | | | $45.00 | $90.00 |
| | | SUNSET CARSON AND THE APACHE RAIDERS | | | $45.00 | $90.00 |

ADMIRAL RECORDS
AN ADVENTURE OF THE ZEBRA DUN
$50.00

ADVENTURE RECORDS
HI DIDDLE DIDDLE
$10.00

ADVENTURE RECORDS
LITTLE BRAVE SAMBO
$50.00

## ADMIRAL 10" SINGLES

| SET # | # REC | DISC # | ARTIST | A TITLE | B TITLE | YEAR | G/VG | EX/NMT |
|---|---|---|---|---|---|---|---|---|
| K-201 | 1 | K1-50-501/2 | ARNOLD STANG | THE ADVENTURES OF HARRY THE HORSE (PT. 1) | THE ADVENTURES OF HARRY THE HORSE (PT. 2) | 195? | $15.00 | $30.00 |
| K-202 | 1 | K1-50-503/4 | ARNOLD STANG | THE ELEPHANT WHO FORGOT | PERCY THE POLITE SEAL | | $15.00 | $30.00 |
| K-203 | 1 | K1-50-505/6 | SHERIFF BOB DIXON | THE ADVENTURE OF THE ZEBRA DUN | NIGHT-HERDING SONG | | $25.00 | $50.00 |
| K-204 | 1 | K1-50-507/8 | SHERIFF BOB DIXON | THE COWBOY | THE RAILROAD CORRAL | | $25.00 | $50.00 |
| K-205 | 1 | K1-50-509/10 | ARNOLD STANG | THE HAPPY HIPPO | SHLOIMY THE SUBWAY TRAIN | | $15.00 | $30.00 |
| K-206 | 1 | K1-50-511/2 | ARNOLD STANG | THE CLOCK THAT WENT TOCK-TICK | BEEZY THE SNEEZY BEE | | $15.00 | $30.00 |
| K-207 | 1 | K1-50-513/4 | DENNY DIMWIT | YOUSE IS A GOOD BOY | THE MILLIONAIRE | | $10.00 | $20.00 |
| K-208 | 1 | K1-50-515/6 | DENNY DIMWIT | THE RINKEYDINKS | BE OBEDIENT | | $10.00 | $20.00 |
| K-209 | 1 | K1-50-517/8 | FREDDIE BARTHOLOMEW | ANDROCLES AND THE LION | WHAT FATHER DOES IS ALWAYS RIGHT | | $10.00 | $20.00 |
| K-210 | 1 | K1-50-519/20 | FREDDIE BARTHOLOMEW | THE GREEDY DOG; THE HONEST LUMBERJACK | THE DONKEY'S SALT STORY; THE MILKMAID AND HER PAIL | | $10.00 | $20.00 |

## ADVENTURE SINGLES — 10" SERIES

| # REC | DISC # | MAIN TITLE | ARTIST | YEAR | G/VG | EX/NMT |
|---|---|---|---|---|---|---|
| 1 | A-1 | PINOCCHIO | UNCLE HENRY | 1946 | $5.00 | $10.00 |
| 1 | A-6 | GINGERBREAD BOY | UNCLE HENRY | | $5.00 | $10.00 |
| 1 | A-3 | LITTLE BRAVE SAMBO | UNCLE HENRY | | $25.00 | $50.00 |
| 1 | A-4 | SNOW WHITE AND THE SEVEN DWARFS | UNCLE HENRY | 1947 | $5.00 | $10.00 |
| 1 | A-5 | ALICE IN WONDERLAND | UNCLE HENRY | | $5.00 | $10.00 |
| 1 | A-6 | HI DIDDLE DIDDLE AND OTHER RHYMES | LANNY & GINGER | | $5.00 | $10.00 |
| 1 | A-7 | PETER RABBIT AND OTHER STORIES | THORNTON BURGESS | | $50.00 | $100.00 |
| 1 | A-8 | JACK AND THE BEANSTALK | UNCLE HENRY | | $5.00 | $10.00 |
| 1 | A-9 | THREE LITTLE PIGS | UNCLE HENRY | | $5.00 | $10.00 |
| 1 | A-10 | GOLDILOCKS AND THE THREE BEARS | UNCLE HENRY | | $5.00 | $10.00 |
| 1 | A-11 | HANSEL AND GRETEL | UNCLE HENRY | | $5.00 | $10.00 |
| 1 | A-12 | LITTLE RED RIDING HOOD | UNCLE HENRY | | $5.00 | $10.00 |
| 1 | A-13 | TEDDY BEARS' PICNIC/OLD MACDONALD HAD A FARM | DICK MANNING | | $5.00 | $10.00 |
| 1 | A-14 | BALLADS FOR LITTLE BUCKAROOS (VOL. 1) | STEVE BARRY | | $5.00 | $10.00 |
| 1 | A-15 | BALLADS FOR LITTLE BUCKAROOS (VOL. 2) | STEVE BARRY | | $5.00 | $10.00 |
| 1 | A-16 | HOP SCOTCH POLKA/I'M A LITTLE TEAPOT | VERA BARTON; JACK EMERSON | 1951 | $5.00 | $10.00 |

ALLEGRO (BANTAM)
PICKING UP PAW PAWS
$6.00

ALLEGRO JUNIORS
UNCLE REMUS' WONDERFUL TAR BABY
$10.00

ALLEGRO JUNIORS
THE SHMOO SINGS
$75.00

## ADVENTURE ALBUMS — 10" SERIES

| ALBUM # | DISC # | MAIN TITLE | ARTIST | YEAR | G/VG | EX/NMT |
|---|---|---|---|---|---|---|
| ARC-1* | ADV99/103 - 101/2 | PINOCCHIO | UNCLE HENRY | 1946 | $7.00 | $15.00 |
| ARC-2* | GINI/2 - SAMI/2 | GINGER BREAD BOY/LITTLE BLACK SAMBO | UNCLE HENRY | | $25.00 | $50.00 |
| ARC-3* | SNOW WHITE 1/4-2/3 | SNOW WHITE AND THE SEVEN DWARFS | UNCLE HENRY | 1947 | $7.00 | $15.00 |
| ARC-4* | AW 1/2 - 3/4 | ALICE IN WONDERLAND | UNCLE HENRY | | $7.00 | $15.00 |
| ARC-5* | ARC 5-1/4 - 2/3 | HI DIDDLE DIDDLE AND OTHER RHYMES | LANNY & GINGER | | $7.00 | $15.00 |
| ARC-6* | ARC 6-1/4 - 2/3 | SING A SONG OF SAFETY | DICK GILBERT & THE BLUEBIRDS | | $7.00 | $15.00 |
| ARC-7** | ARC 7-1/4 - 2/3 | PETER RABBIT AND OTHER STORIES | THORNTON BURGESS | | $100.00 | $200.00 |

*2 RECORDS PER SET **3 DISCS

## ALLEGRO JUNIORS — 10" SINGLES

| SET # | # REC | DISC # | MAIN TITLE | ARTIST | YEAR | G/VG | EX/NMT |
|---|---|---|---|---|---|---|---|
| AJ-1 | 1 | 301 | SINGING TIME WITH MOTHER GOOSE | FLORENCE CALDER | 1948 | $3.00 | $6.00 |
| AJ-2 | 1 | 302 | SIMPLE SIMON & OTHER NURSERY SONGS | CRANE CALDER | | $3.00 | $6.00 |
| AJ-3 | 1 | 303 | RING-A-ROUND THE ROSY & OTHER SINGING GAMES | FLORENCE CALDER | | $3.00 | $6.00 |
| AJ-4 | 1 | 304 | THE ELEPHANT AND THE FLEA | CRANE CALDER | | $3.00 | $6.00 |
| AJ-5 | 1 | 305 | SKIP TO MY LOU | CRANE CALDER | | $3.00 | $6.00 |
| AJ-6 | 1 | 306 | ALL AROUND THE MULBERRY BUSH | FLORENCE CALDER | | $3.00 | $6.00 |
| AJ-7 | 1 | 307 | THE BIRTHDAY RECORD | CRANE CALDER | | $3.00 | $6.00 |
| AJ-8 | 1 | 308 | LET'S PLAY ANIMALS | CRANE CALDER | | $3.00 | $6.00 |
| AJ-9 | 1 | 309 | PETER AND THE WOLF | CRANE CALDER | | $3.00 | $6.00 |
| AJ-10 | 1 | 310 | SICK IN BED: CHEERIE SONGS FOR CHILDREN | CRANE CALDER | | $3.00 | $6.00 |
| AJ-11 | 1 | 311 | THE PARTY RECORD | CRANE CALDER | | $3.00 | $6.00 |
| AJ-12 | 1 | 312 | GOING TO SLEEP | CRANE & FLORENCE CALDER | | $3.00 | $6.00 |
| AJ-13 | 1 | 313 | THE NUTCRACKER SUITE FOR DANCING | CRANE & FLORENCE CALDER | | $3.00 | $6.00 |
| AJ-14 | 1 | 314 | COWBOYS & INDIANS: THEIR SONGS & DANCES | CRANE CALDER | | $3.00 | $6.00 |
| AJ-15 | 1 | 315 | THE BATHTUB SAILOR: SEA SHANTIES | CRANE CALDER | | $3.00 | $6.00 |
| AJ-16 | 1 | 316 | UNCLE REMUS' "WONDERFUL TAR BABY" | CRANE CALDER | | $5.00 | $10.00 |
| AJ-17 | 1 | 317 | WILLIAM TELL | CRANE CALDER | | $3.00 | $6.00 |
| AJ-18 | 1 | 318 | THE SITTER WHO SAT | CRANE & FLORENCE CALDER | | $3.00 | $6.00 |
| AJ-19 | 1 | 319 | SONGS FROM BABES IN TOYLAND | CRANE CALDER | | $3.00 | $6.00 |
| AJ-20 | 1 | 320 | STICKS AND STONES | CRANE CALDER | | $3.00 | $6.00 |
| AJ-21 | 1 | 321 | THE PEER GYNT SUITE FOR DANCING | CRANE CALDER | | $3.00 | $6.00 |
| AJ-22 | 1 | 322 | THE OWL AND THE PUSSYCAT (& OTHER FUNNY SEA SONGS) | CRANE CALDER | | $3.00 | $6.00 |
| AJ-23 | 1 | 323 | THE LAUGHING RECORD/THE HORSE NAMED BILL, JENNIE JENKINS | SANDY WALKER & ROSLYN DICK/CRANE CALDER | | $3.00 | $6.00 |
| AJ-24 | 1 | 324 | THE COWBOY RIDES THE RANGE | CRANE CALDER | | $3.00 | $6.00 |
| AJ-25 | 1 | 325 | THE GREAT BIG PARADE | CRANE CALDER | | $3.00 | $6.00 |
| AJ-26 | 1 | 326 | THE SHMOO SINGS | EARL ROGERS | | $35.00 | $75.00 |

ALLEGRO JEWISH HOLIDAYS
HANUKKAH THE FEAST OF LIGHTS
$8.00

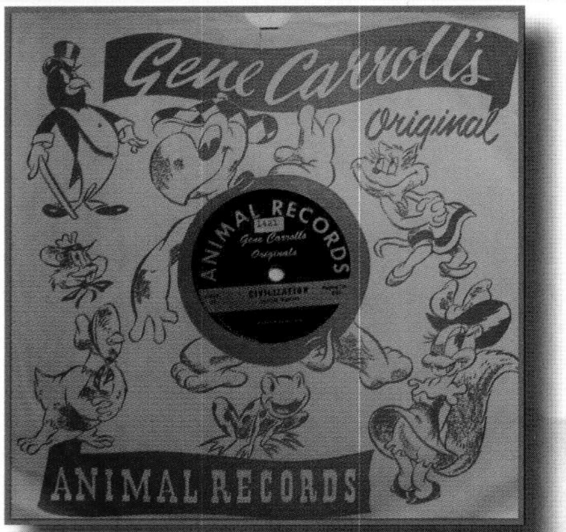


ANIMAL RECORDS
CIVILIZATION
$4.00

ASCH RECORDS
THE WAYFARING STRANGERS
$25.00

## ALLEGRO INTERMEDIATES (BANTAM) 10" SINGLES

| SET # | # REC | DISC # | MAIN TITLE | ARTIST | YEAR | G/VG | EX/NMT |
|---|---|---|---|---|---|---|---|
| AK-51 | 1 | 101 | THE MIKADO | THE LITTLE OPERA GROUP | 1948 | $3.00 | $6.00 |
| AK-52 | 1 | 102 | BEETHOVEN PIANO MUSIC | JACOBO DUJOVNE | | $3.00 | $6.00 |
| AK-53 | 1 | 103 | PIRATES OF PENZANCE | THE LITTLE OPERA GROUP | | $3.00 | $6.00 |
| AK-54 | 1 | 104 | SQUARE DANCES | DICK KRAUS | | $3.00 | $6.00 |
| AK-55 | 1 | 105 | H.M.S. PINAFORE | THE LITTLE OPERA GROUP | | $3.00 | $6.00 |
| AK-56 | 1 | 106 | FROM "ALICE IN WONDERLAND": JABBERWOCKY/THE SOUP SONG | CRANE CALDER | | $3.00 | $6.00 |
| AK-57 | 1 | 107 | IOLANTHE | THE LITTLE OPERA GROUP | | $3.00 | $6.00 |
| AK-58 | 1 | 108 | PICKING UP PAW PAWS/TAKE A LITTLE PEEK | DICK KRAUS | | $3.00 | $6.00 |

## ALLEGRO JEWISH HOLIDAYS 10" SINGLES

| SET # | # REC | DISC # | MAIN TITLE | ARTIST | ALSO ISSUED ON | G/VG | EX/NMT |
|---|---|---|---|---|---|---|---|
| AY-102 | 1 | 3196/7 | HANUKKAH (THE FEAST OF LIGHTS) | EMANUEL ROSENBERG | 1948 | $4.00 | $8.00 |
| AY-103 | 2 | 3214/7 - 3215/6 | ZEMIROT SHABBAT (JEWISH SABBATH AT HOME) | EMANUEL ROSENBERG | | $6.00 | $12.00 |
| AY-104 | 1 | 3212/3 | TU B'SHVAT (ARBOR DAY) | EMANUEL ROSENBERG | | $4.00 | $8.00 |
| AY-106 | 1 | 3224/5 | PURIM | EMANUEL ROSENBERG | | $4.00 | $8.00 |
| AY-107 | 2 | 3231/4 - 3232/3 | PASSOVER | EMANUEL ROSENBERG | | $6.00 | $12.00 |

## ANIMAL SINGLES - 10" SERIES

| SET # | # REC | DISC # | MAIN TITLE | ARTIST | A TITLE | B TITLE | DATE | G/VG | EX/MT |
|---|---|---|---|---|---|---|---|---|---|
| | 1 | 162 - 3 | CIVILIZATION/HAWAIIAN WAR CHANT* | GENE CARROLL | CIVILIZATION | HAWAIIAN WAR CHANT | 195? | $2.00 | $4.00 |
| | 1 | 164 - 5 | BEG YOUR PARDON/YOU WERE MEANT FOR ME* | GENE CARROLL | BEG YOUR PARDON | YOU WERE MEANT FOR ME | | $2.00 | $4.00 |
| | 1 | 166 | FOUR LEAF CLOVER/ FEUDIN 'N FIGHTIN'* | GENE CARROLL | FOUR LEAF CLOVER | FEUDIN 'N FIGHTIN' | | $2.00 | $4.00 |
| | 1 | 168 | ANIMAL POLKA/LITTLE SIR ECHO | GENE CARROLL | ANIMAL POLKA | LITTLE SIR ECHO | | $2.00 | $4.00 |
| | 1 | 170 | WOODY WOODPECKER/ AIN'T SHE SWEET | GENE CARROLL | WOODY WOODPECKER | AIN'T SHE SWEET | | $3.00 | $6.00 |
| | 1 | 172 | DID YOU EVER SEE A DREAM WALKING?/ CIMMANON CAKE | GENE CARROLL | DID YOU EVER SEE A DREAM WALKING? | CIMMANON CAKE | | $2.00 | $4.00 |
| | 1 | 174 | ? | GENE CARROLL | ? | ? | | $2.00 | $4.00 |
| | 1 | 176 | THE ICE CREAM SONG/ PICCOLO PETE | GENE CARROLL | THE ICE CREAM SONG | PICCOLO PETE | | $2.00 | $4.00 |
| | 1 | 178 | EASTER PARADE/ SNOWFLAKE JAMBOREE | GENE CARROLL | EASTER PARADE | SNOWFLAKE JAMBOREE | | $2.00 | $4.00 |
| 200 | 2 | 200 A/B - C/D | ORIGINAL CHRISTMAS ALBUM | GENE CARROLL | | | | $4.00 | $8.00 |
| 550 | 3 | 550 1/2, 3/4, 5/6 | JERRY BARTELL'S PLAYTIME | JERRY BARTELL | | | | | |

*NOT SPECIFICALLY FOR CHILDREN

AUDIO EDUCATION
CALYPSO FOR CHILDREN
$8.00

AUDIO EDUCATION
PANDA BALLOON
$8.00

AUNT THERESA'S
KYB CLUB RECORDS
$55.00

## ASCH 10" ALBUMS

| SET # | # REC | DISC # | MAIN TITLE | ARTIST | YEAR | G/VG | EX/NMT |
|---|---|---|---|---|---|---|---|
| 101 | 3 | SC4/3, 12/11, 13/9 | IN THE BEGINNING: ADAM, EVE, ETC. | DAVID NILES, SHOLEM ASCH | 1941 | $50.00 | $100.00 |
| A-345 | 3 | 523/20, 518/25, 522/4 | THE WAYFARING STRANGER | BURL IVES | | $12.00 | $25.00 |
| A-358 | 3 | 170/149, 171/4, 175/3 | FOLK SONGS SUNG BY JOSH WHITE | JOSH WHITE | | $10.00 | $20.00 |
| ? | ? | ? | PLAY PARTIES IN SONG & DANCE | HUDDIE LEDBETTER ("LEADBELLY") | | $25.00 | $50.00 |

## AUDIO EDUCATION LISTEN AND DO SERIES 10" ALBUMS

| SET # | # REC | DISC # | MAIN TITLE | ARTIST | YEAR | G/VG | EX/NMT | REMARKS |
|---|---|---|---|---|---|---|---|---|
| ABC-1 | 2 | 13044 – 5 | LISTEN & DO SERIES: VOL. 1: GINGER & JOSH/THE FRIENDLY TRAIN | NOT LISTED | 1951 | $4.00 | $8.00 | GATEFOLD |
| ABC-2 | 2 | 13046 – 7 | LISTEN & DO SERIES: VOL. 2: THE HANDSOME SCARECROW/LITTLE CLOWN | NOT LISTED | | $4.00 | $8.00 | GATEFOLD |
| ABC-3 | 2 | 13116 – 7 | LISTEN & DO SERIES: VOL. 3: PANDA BALOON/JOCKO | LEE SWEETLAND | | $4.00 | $8.00 | GATEFOLD |
| ABC-4 | 2 | 13118 – 9 | LISTEN & DO SERIES: VOL. 4: WORK & SING, PLAY & SING/MY SHADOW | LEE SWEETLAND | | $4.00 | $8.00 | GATEFOLD |

## AUDIO EDUCATION THE AMERICAN SINGER SERIES 10" ALBUMS

| SET # | # REC | DISC # | MAIN TITLE | ARTIST | YEAR | G/VG | EX/NMT |
|---|---|---|---|---|---|---|---|
| AS-1 | 6 | 13026 – 31 | THE AMERICAN SINGER: BOOK 1: HOME, SCHOOL-TRANSPORTATION, ETC. | JOHN BEATTIE, ETC. | 1950 | $6.00 | $12.00 |
| AS-2 | 4 | 13000 – 03 | THE AMERICAN SINGER: BOOK 2: LULLABY & FANCY, SONG STORIES, ETC. | JOHN BEATTIE, ETC. | | $4.00 | $8.00 |
| AS-3 | 4 | 13004 – 7 | THE AMERICAN SINGER: BOOK 3: NATURE & FANCY, LULLABIES, ETC. | JOHN BEATTIE, ETC. | | $4.00 | $8.00 |
| AS-4 | 5 | 13008 – 12 | THE AMERICAN SINGER: BOOK 4: EARLY AMERICAN SONGS & CHANTEYS, ETC. | JOHN BEATTIE, ETC. | | $5.00 | $10.00 |
| AS-5 | 5 | 13013 – 17 | THE AMERICAN SINGER: BOOK 5: MUSIC OF GREAT COMPOSERS, AROUND THE CALENDAR, ETC. | JOHN BEATTIE, ETC. | | $5.00 | $10.00 |
| AS-6 | 6 | ? | THE AMERICAN SINGER: BOOK 6 | JOHN BEATTIE, ETC. | | $6.00 | $12.00 |
| AS-7 | 6 | ? | THE AMERICAN SINGER: BOOK 7 | JOHN BEATTIE, ETC. | | $6.00 | $12.00 |
| AS-8 | 6 | ? | THE AMERICAN SINGER: BOOK 8 | JOHN BEATTIE, ETC. | | $6.00 | $12.00 |

## AUDIO EDUCATION PRIMARY MUSIC SERIES 10" ALBUMS

| SET # | # REC | DISC # | MAIN TITLE | ARTIST | YEAR | G/VG | EX/NMT |
|---|---|---|---|---|---|---|---|
| AS-30 | 4 | 13155 – 8 | MUSIC APPRECIATION SERIES: DANCE FORMS IN MUSIC: GAVOTTE, ETC. | HENRI TAMIANKA | 1955 | $4.00 | $8.00 |
| AS-31 | 4 | 13159 – 62 | MUSIC APPRECIATION SERIES: MUSICAL FORMS: VARIATIONS ON A THEME BY CORELLI, ETC. | HENRI TAMIANKA | | $4.00 | $8.00 |
| AS-32 | 4 | 13163 – 6 | MUSIC APPRECIATION SERIES: DANCES OF MANY COUNTRIES: NORWEGIAN DANCE, ETC. | HENRI TAMIANKA | | $4.00 | $8.00 |
| AS-33 | 4 | 13167 – 70 | MUSIC APPRECIATION SERIES: INTRODUCTION TO GREAT COMPOSERS OF OUR TIME: SCARAMOUCHE, ETC. | HENRI TAMIANKA | | $4.00 | $8.00 |

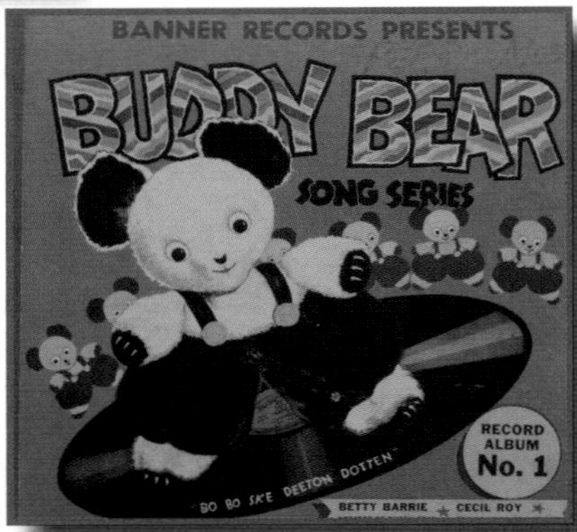


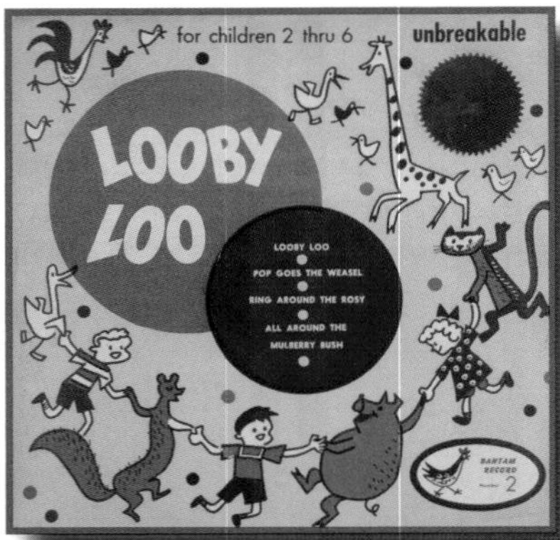


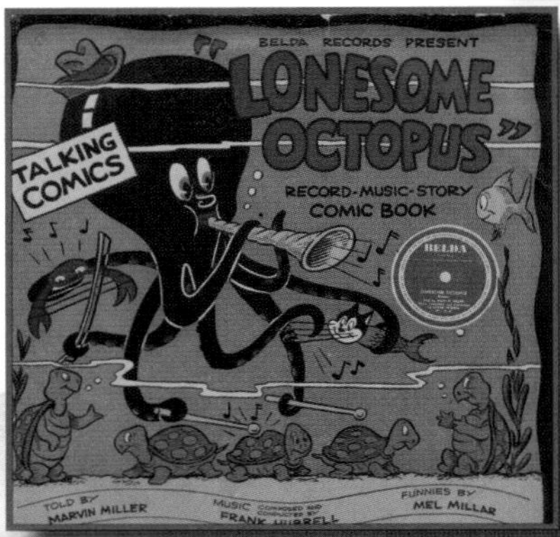


BANNER RECORDS
BUDDY BEAR
$20.00

BANTAM RECORDS
LOOBY LOO
$3.00

BELDA RECORDS
LONESOME OCTOPUS
$30.00

## AUDIO EDUCATION MUSIC APPRECIATION 10" ALBUMS

| SET # | # REC | DISC # | MAIN TITLE | ARTIST | YEAR | G/VG | EX/NMT |
|---|---|---|---|---|---|---|---|
| AS-30 | 4 | 13155 – 8 | MUSIC APPRECIATION SERIES: DANCE FORMS IN MUSIC: GAVOTTE, ETC. | HENRI TAMIANKA | 1955 | $4.00 | $8.00 |
| AS-31 | 4 | 13159 – 62 | MUSIC APPRECIATION SERIES: MUSICAL FORMS: VARIATIONS ON A THEME BY CORELLI, ETC. | HENRI TAMIANKA | | $4.00 | $8.00 |
| AS-32 | 4 | 13163 – 6 | MUSIC APPRECIATION SERIES: DANCES OF MANY COUNTRIES: NORWEGIAN DANCE, ETC. | HENRI TAMIANKA | | $4.00 | $8.00 |
| AS-33 | 4 | 13167 – 70 | MUSIC APPRECIATION SERIES: INTRODUCTION TO GREAT COMPOSERS OF OUR TIME: SCARAMOUCHE, ETC. | HENRI TAMIANKA | | $4.00 | $8.00 |

## AUDIO EDUCATION MISCELLANEOUS 10" ALBUMS

| SET # | # REC | DISC # | MAIN TITLE | ARTIST | YEAR | G/VG | EX/NMT |
|---|---|---|---|---|---|---|---|
| ABC-10 | 4 | 13098 – 101 | HOW YOU TALK!: STORIES THAT BUILD ORAL LANGUAGE FACILITY: BOBTAIL BUNNY, ETC. | MABEL COLE | 1953 | $4.00 | $8.00 |
| AS-25 | 4 | 13120 – 3 | CALYPSO FOR CHILDREN: LET'S GO; MEET THE INSTRUMENTS, ETC. | LEE SWEETLAND | 1954 | $4.00 | $8.00 |
| AS-26 | 2 | 13133 – 4 | DANCE SUITE: GARDEN FESTIVAL; EXCURSIONS | CAMERON MCGRAW | | $2.00 | $4.00 |
| AS-? | 4 | ? | TALL TALES OF AMERICA: PAUL BUNYAN, ETC. | ? | 1953 | $4.00 | $8.00 |
| SD 1 | 3 | 13082 – 4 | LET'S DANCE THE SQUARE DANCE: ADD TWO MORE INDIAN STYLE, ETC. | MARGOT MAYO, JOHNNY O'LEARY | | $2.00 | $4.00 |
| ? | ? | 13092 | WORLDS OF LITERATURE: POETRY VI (TO BE OR NOT TO BE), ETC. | ALEXANDER SCOURBY | | $1.00 | $2.00 |

## AUNT THERESA'S 4" AND 7" BOXED SETS AND ALBUMS SERIES

| SET # | # REC | DISC # | MAIN TITLE | ARTIST | YEAR | G/VG | EX/NMT |
|---|---|---|---|---|---|---|---|
| 1 | 5 (4") | KYB-A/A1 – E/E-1 | AUNT THERESA'S KYB CLUB SINGS: BEHOLD! BEHOLD!, ETC. | KYB CLUB | 195? | $3.00 | $6.00 |
| 2 | 5 (4") | KYB-F/F1 – J/J1 | AUNT THERESA'S KYB CLUB SINGS: EVERY STEP WITH JESUS, ETC. | KYB CLUB | | $3.00 | $6.00 |
| NO # | 8 (7") | AT 1 A/B – 8 A/B | AUNT THERESA'S BIBLE STORIES": ABRAHAM, ETC. | AUNT THERESA | | $3.00 | $6.00 |

# B

## BANNER 10" SINGLES

| SET # | # REC | DISC # | ARTIST | A TITLE | B TITLE | YEAR | G/VG | EX/NMT |
|---|---|---|---|---|---|---|---|---|
| | 1 | 2064 | VICTOR FLETCHER | A VISIT FROM ST. NICHOLAS | SANTA CLAUS HIDES IN THE TALKING MACHINE | 1927 | $8.00 | $15.00 |
| | 1 | 33247 | JACK PARKER | DICKORY DICKORY DOCK/ DING DONG BELL | HARK! HARK! THE DOGS DO BARK/10 LITTLE INDIANS | 1934 | $2.00 | $4.00 |
| | 1 | 33248 | JACK PARKER | THE KING OF FRANCE | THE THREE LITTLE PIGS | | $2.00 | $4.00 |
| | 1 | FF1 | LOUIS NEISTAT | HOW TO DRAW 1000 FUNNY FACES | HOW TO DRAW 1000 FUNNY FACES | | $4.00 | $8.00 |
| B 101 | 3 | A 101 – 3 | BETTY BARRIE, CECIL ROY | BUDDY BEAR | BUDDY BEAR | 193? | $10.00 | $20.00 |

BELDA RECORDS
LONESOME OCTOPUS
$30.00

BELDA RECORDS
LONESOME OCTOPUS
$30.00

BELDA RECORDS
MYSTO MAGIC
$30.00

## BANTAM 10" SINGLES

| SET # | # REC | DISC # | MAIN TITLE | ARTIST | YEAR | G/VG | EX/NMT |
|---|---|---|---|---|---|---|---|
| BR-1 | 1 | PW 101-2 | THREE LITTLE PIGS/LITTLE RED RIDING HOOD | SANDY WALKER | 195? | $1.50 | $3.00 |
| BR-2 | 1 | PW 103-4 | LOOBY LOO; ET AL/RING AROUND THE ROSY, ETC. | RAY FRANCIS | | $1.50 | $3.00 |
| BR-3 | 1 | PW 105-6 | PLAY PARTY GAMES: ROUND & ROUND THE VILLAGE, ETC. | RAY FRANCIS | | $1.50 | $3.00 |
| BR-4 | 1 | PW 107-8 | FIRST NURSERY SONGS: LITTLE BO PEEP, ETC. | VIRGINIA BOYER | | $1.50 | $3.00 |
| BR-5 | 1 | PW 109-10 | ABC/COUNT TO 10 | ? | | $1.50 | $3.00 |
| BR-6 | 1 | PW 111-2 | JACK AND THE BEANSTALK/CINDERELLA | SANDY WALKER | | $1.50 | $3.00 |

## BELDA TALKING KOMICS 10" SINGLES

| # REC | DISC # | MAIN TITLE | ARTIST | YEAR | G/VG | EX/NMT |
|---|---|---|---|---|---|---|
| 1 | 101 | LONESOME OCTOPUS | MARVIN MILLAR | 1946 | $15.00 | $30.00 |
| 1 | 102 | GRUMPY SHARK | MARVIN MILLAR | | $15.00 | $30.00 |
| 1 | 103 | CHIRPY CRICKET | DAWS BUTLER & TIP CORNING | 1947 | $20.00 | $40.00 |
| 1 | 104 | HAPPY GRASSHOPPER | DAWS BUTLER &TIP CORNING | | $20.00 | $40.00 |
| 1 | 105 | MYSTO MAGIC: THE WIZARD RECORD | THE SPARKETTES | 1948 | $25.00 | $50.00 |
| 1 | 106 | FLYING TURTLE | DAWS BUTLER & MARIAN RICHMAN | 1949 | $20.00 | $40.00 |
| 1 | 107 | SLEEPY SANTA | DAWS BUTLER & MARIAN RICHMAN | | $20.00 | $40.00 |
| 1 | 108 | 3 BLIND MICE | DAWS BUTLER & MARIAN RICHMAN | 1950 | $20.00 | $40.00 |
| 1 | 109 | ENCHANTED TOYMAKER | DAWS BUTLER & MARIAN RICHMAN | | $20.00 | $40.00 |

## BELL 7" SINGLES

| # REC | DISC # | ARTIST | A TITLE | B TITLE | YEAR | G/VG | EX/NMT |
|---|---|---|---|---|---|---|---|
| 1 | 102 | THE MILLER SISTERS/THE PLAYMAKERS | LITTLE DRUMMER BOY | THE CHIPMUNK SONG | 195? | $3.00 | $6.00 |
| 1 | 1050 | ROY ROGERS AND DALE EVANS | FRIENDS AND NEIGHBORS | THE LITTLE SHOEMAKER | | $5.00 | $10.00 |
| 1 | ? | ? | SANTA DISTRIBUTES HIS TOYS | SANTA CLAUS' ARRIVAL | | $1.00 | $2.00 |
| 1 | 1091 | TEX STEWART & SONS OF THE ALAMO/ BUDDY & HIS PALS | THE BALLAD OF DAVY CROCKETT | THE CRAZY OTTO | | $4.00 | $8.00 |

## BEL-TONE* 7" SINGLES

| SET # | # REC | DISC # | MAIN TITLE | ARTIST | YEAR | ALSO ISSUED ON | G/VG | EX/NMT |
|---|---|---|---|---|---|---|---|---|
| BT-AL-1 | 2 | BT 4001 - 2 | JUMP JUMP AND THE UGLY DUCKLING | MARY MCCONNELL | 194? | MERCURY MINIATURE PLAYHOUSE | $4.00 | $8.00 |
| BT-AL-2 | 2 | BT 4003 - 4 | JUMP JUMP AND SLEEPY SLIM, THE TIRED LION | MARY MCCONNELL | | MERCURY MINIATURE PLAYHOUSE | $4.00 | $8.00 |
| BT-AL-3 | 3 | BT 4005- 7 | KING THRUSHBEARD | UNCLE BOB | | MERCURY MINIATURE PLAYHOUSE | $4.00 | $8.00 |
| BT-AL-4 | 3 | BT 4008 - 10 | THE FISHERMAN AND THE FLOUNDER/THE ELVES AND THE SHOEMAKER | UNCLE BOB | | MERCURY MINIATURE PLAYHOUSE | $4.00 | $8.00 |
| BT-AL-5 | 1 | BT - 4011 | THE PRINCESS AND THE PEA | UNCLE BOB | | MERCURY MINIATURE PLAYHOUSE | $2.00 | $4.00 |
| BT-AL-6 | 3 | BT 4012 - 4 | JUMP JUMP & THE LITTLE LITTLE LOST STAR | MARY MCCONNELL | | MERCURY MINIATURE PLAYHOUSE | $4.00 | $8.00 |

*LABEL VARIANT: PLAYHOUSE SERIES

BELL RECORDS
THE CHIPMUNK SONG
$6.00

BEL-TONE RECORDS
JUMP JUMP & THE LOST LITTLE STAR
$8.00

BIBLE STORYTIME RECORDS
JESUS LOVES ME
$10.00

## BIBLE STORYTIME 7" SINGLES

| # REC | DISC # | ARTIST | A TITLE | B TITLE | YEAR | G/VG | EX/NMT |
|---|---|---|---|---|---|---|---|
| 1 | RN 701/702 | NOT LISTED | NOAH'S ARK | BABY MOSES | 194? | $5.00 | $10.00 |
| 1 | RN 703/704 | NOT LISTED | BOY WHO LISTENED | SHEPHERD BOY | | $5.00 | $10.00 |
| 1 | RN 705/706 | NOT LISTED | POKY CATERPILLAR | LITTLE BROWN SEED | | $5.00 | $10.00 |
| 1 | RN 711/712 | NOT LISTED | SHEPHERDS OF BETHLEHEM | THE SHEPHERDS WORSHIP BABY JESUS | | $5.00 | $10.00 |
| 1 | RN 713/714 | NOT LISTED | GOOD SAMARITAN | A GIFT FOR JESUS | | $5.00 | $10.00 |
| 1 | RN 715/716 | NOT LISTED | JESUS LOVES ME | PRAISE HIM | | $5.00 | $10.00 |
| 1 | RN 751/752 | NOT LISTED | WHEN JESUS WAS BORN | THE WISE MEN | | $5.00 | $10.00 |
| 1 | RN 753/754 | NOT LISTED | JESUS AND THE CHILDREN | RUNAWAY BOY | | $5.00 | $10.00 |
| 1 | RN 755/756 | NOT LISTED | GOOD MORNING | GOOD NIGHT | | $5.00 | $10.00 |
| 1 | RO 771/772 | NOT LISTED | JACOB'S DREAM | JOSEPH AND HIS BROTHERS | | $5.00 | $10.00 |
| 1 | RO 773/774 | NOT LISTED | DANIEL IN THE LION'S DEN (PT. 1) | DANIEL IN THE LION'S DEN (PT. 2) | | $5.00 | $10.00 |
| 1 | RO 775/776 | NOT LISTED | RUTH | GOOD NIGHT SONG | | $5.00 | $10.00 |
| N/A | BOX CONTAINER | N/A | N/A | N/A | | $8.00 | $15.00 |

## BIBLETONE 10" ALBUMS

| SET # | # REC | DISC # | MAIN TITLE | ARTIST | YEAR | G/VG | EX/NMT |
|---|---|---|---|---|---|---|---|
| A | 5 | ? | THE TEN BEST LOVED HYMNS (ORGAN) | NOT LISTED | 194? | $2.00 | $4.00 |
| AV | 5 | ? | THE TEN BEST LOVED HYMNS (VOCAL) | NOT LISTED | | $2.00 | $4.00 |
| B | 6 | ? | THE BIBLE SPEAKS | NOT LISTED | | $2.00 | $4.00 |
| C | 4 | 601-4 | CHRISTMAS AT THE ORGAN | NOT LISTED | | $2.00 | $4.00 |
| CH 50 | 2 | CH50/1 - 52/3 | ADVENTURES IN BIBLELAND: DANIEL IN THE LION'S DEN/DAVID & GOLIATH | NOT LISTED | | $2.00 | $4.00 |
| CS | 4 | ? | CHRISTIAN SCIENCE HYMNS | NOT LISTED | | $2.00 | $4.00 |
| CV | 4 | ? | CHRISTMAS CAROLS | NATIONAL VESPERS CHOIR | | $2.00 | $4.00 |
| D | 3 | ? | HYMNS OF INSPIRATION | NOT LISTED | | $2.00 | $4.00 |
| DC | 4 | ? | CHIMES OF DEVOTION | NOT LISTED | | $2.00 | $4.00 |
| EE | 4 | ? | HYMNS OF GLADNESS | NOT LISTED | | $2.00 | $4.00 |
| F | 4 | ? | MELODIES THAT LIVE FOREVER | NOT LISTED | | $2.00 | $4.00 |
| G | 4 | ? | BELOVED GOSPEL HYMNS | NOT LISTED | | $2.00 | $4.00 |
| HV | 3 | 301 - 3 | HYMNS CHILDREN LOVE (ORGAN) | MURIEL WILSON | | $2.00 | $4.00 |
| HV | 3 | 1801 - 3 | HYMNS CHILDREN LOVE (VOCAL) | PAULA HEMINGHOUSE; MURIEL WILSON | | $2.00 | $4.00 |
| J | 5 | ? | HYMNS OF COMFORT & JOY | NOT LISTED | | $2.00 | $4.00 |
| K | 4 | ? | HYMNS OF FAITH | NOT LISTED | | $2.00 | $4.00 |
| L | 4 | ? | THE LORDS PRAYER/THANKSGIVING HYMN | NOT LISTED | | $2.00 | $4.00 |

BIBLETONE RECORDS
ADVENTURES IN BIBLELAND
$4.00

BINGOLA RECORDS
AMERICA
$15.00

BIRTHSTONE RECORDS
SONGS FOR JANUARY
$6.00

## BIBLETONE 10" ALBUMS

| SET # | # REC | DISC # | MAIN TITLE | ARTIST | G/VG | EX/NMT |
|---|---|---|---|---|---|---|
| LF | 3 | ? | LE FEVRE TRIO & BIG JIM WAITS | NOT LISTED | $2.00 | $4.00 |
| M | 4 | ? | HYMNS OF CHRISTIAN GLORY | NOT LISTED | $2.00 | $4.00 |
| P | 4 | ? | CHIMES AT CHRISTMAS TIME | NOT LISTED | $2.00 | $4.00 |
| R | 4 | ? | CATHEDRAL CHIMES OF GOSPEL HYMNS | NOT LISTED | $2.00 | $4.00 |
| SP | 3 | ? | JUBILEE SPIRITUALS | NOT LISTED | $2.00 | $4.00 |
| SW | 3 | ? | THE STAMPS QUARTET | NOT LISTED | $2.00 | $4.00 |
| Y | 4 | ? | ONWARD CHRISTIAN SOLDIERS | NOT LISTED | $2.00 | $4.00 |

## BIBLETONE 10" SINGLES

| # REC | DISC # | ARTIST | A TITLE | B TITLE | YEAR | G/VG | EX/NMT |
|---|---|---|---|---|---|---|---|
| 1 | CH 52/53 | NOT LISTED | DANIEL IN THE LION'S DEN | THE STORY OF DANIEL IN THE LION'S DEN | 194? | $1.00 | $2.00 |
| 1 | SRK-200 | HILDOR JANZ, THE CHILDREN'S CHOIR | ADAM AND EVE IN THE GARDEN | DARE TO BE A DANIEL, DANIEL WAS A MAN OF PRAYER | | $1.00 | $2.00 |

## BILLY GRAHAM 8" SQUARE PICTURE DISCS

| # REC | DISC # | MAIN TITLE | ARTIST | YEAR | G/VG | EX/NMT |
|---|---|---|---|---|---|---|
| 1 | NO # | BILLY GRAHAM...ON THE STEPS OF THE CAPITOL | BILLY GRAHAM | 1952 | $15.00 | $30.00 |
| 1 | NO # | THE HOME | BILLY GRAHAM | | $15.00 | $30.00 |
| 1 | NO # | SEASON'S GREETINGS/WONDERFUL PEACE | BILLY GRAHAM | | $15.00 | $30.00 |
| 1 | NO # | THE LONELINESS OF DESPAIR | BILLY GRAHAM | 1953 | $25.00 | $50.00 |
| 1 | NO # | LET FREEDOM RING/HOUR OF DECISION IN HISTORY | BILLY GRAHAM | | $25.00 | $50.00 |
| 1 | NO # | CHRISTMAS '54 | BILLY GRAHAM | 1954 | $15.00 | $30.00 |
| 1 | NO # | THE RESPONSIBILITY OF THE AMERICAN HOME | BILLY GRAHAM | | $15.00 | $30.00 |
| 1 | NO # | THE NINETY AND NINE | GEORGE BEVERLY SHEA | 1955 | $15.00 | $30.00 |
| 1 | NO # | ALL-SCOTLAND CRUSADE | SCOTTISH MALE CHOIR | | $15.00 | $30.00 |
| 1 | NO # | TORONTO CRUSADE | GEORGE BEVERLY SHEA | | $15.00 | $30.00 |
| 1 | NO # | SWITZERLAND | GEORGE BEVERLY SHEA, CLIFF BARROWS | | $15.00 | $30.00 |
| 1 | NO # | CHRISTMAS GREETINGS | BILLY GRAHAM, CLIFF BARROWS/GEO. BEV. SHEA | | $15.00 | $30.00 |
| 1 | NO # | HOW GREAT THOU ART (THE NEW YORK CRUSADE SOUVENIR) | GEORGE BEVERLY SHEA/BILLY GRAHAM | 1957 | $25.00 | $50.00 |
| 1 | NO # (LP) | BILLY GRAHAM ANSWERS TEEN-AGERS QUESTIONS | BILLY GRAHAM | 1962 | $15.00 | $30.00 |
| 1 | NO # (LP) | BILLY GRAHAM IN DEUTSCHLAND | BILLY GRAHAM | | $15.00 | $30.00 |
| 1 | NO # (LP) | DANIEL IN THE LION'S DEN | CLIFF BARROWS | | $15.00 | $30.00 |
| 1 | NO # (LP) | THE PEACE WE SEEK | BILLY GRAHAM | | $15.00 | $30.00 |

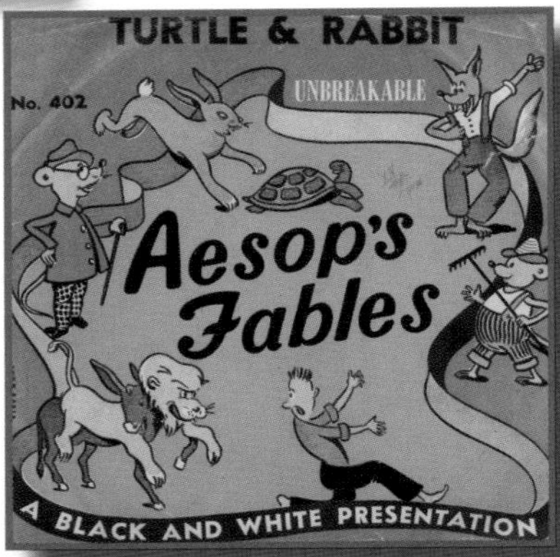


BLACK & WHITE
AESOP'S FABLES
$4.00

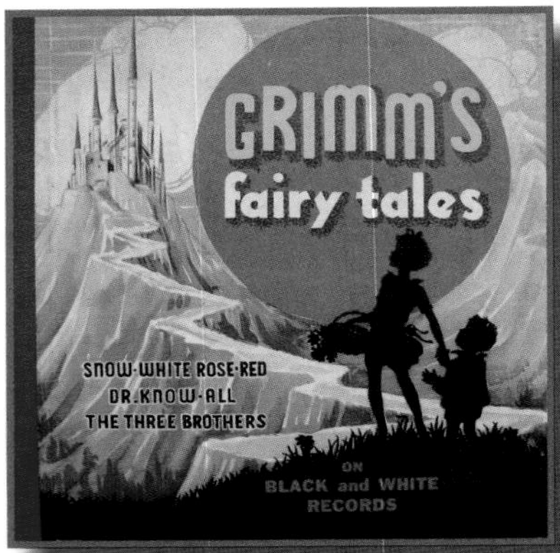


BLACK & WHITE
GRIMM'S FAIRY TALES
$4.00

BILLY GRAHAM
THE BILLY GRAHAM FAMILY AT HOME
$30.00

## BINGOLA 6" SINGLES

| # REC | DISC # | ARTIST | A TITLE | B TITLE | G/VG | EX/NMT |
|---|---|---|---|---|---|---|
| 1 | 500 | ? | STAR SPANGLED BANNER | YANKEE DOODLE | $8.00 | $15.00 |
| 1 | 501 | ? | COLUMBIA | DIXIE | $8.00 | $15.00 |
| 1 | 502 | ? | SWANEE RIVER | OLD KENTUCKY HOME | $8.00 | $15.00 |
| 1 | 503 | ? | OLD BLACK JOE | CARRY ME BACK TO OLD VIRGINNIE | $8.00 | $15.00 |
| 1 | 504 | ? | BEN BOLT | SANTA LUCIA | $8.00 | $15.00 |
| 1 | 505 | ? | HOME SWEET HOME | SWEET GENEVIEVE | $8.00 | $15.00 |
| 1 | 506 | ? | SLEEP BABY SLEEP | ROLL ON SILVERY MOON | $8.00 | $15.00 |
| 1 | 507 | ? | MOCKING BIRD | TURKEY IN THE STRAW | $8.00 | $15.00 |
| 1 | 508 | ? | SEEING NELLIE HOME | FAREWELL | $8.00 | $15.00 |
| 1 | 509 | ? | OLD OAKEN BUCKET | CAPTAIN JINKS | $8.00 | $15.00 |
| 1 | 510 | ? | NOEL | O COME ALL YE FAITHFUL | $8.00 | $15.00 |
| 1 | 511 | ? | WHEN THE ROLL IS CALLED | WHAT A FRIEND IS JESUS | $8.00 | $15.00 |
| 1 | 512 | ? | KAWAHA | LA PALOMA (HAWAIIAN) | $8.00 | $15.00 |
| 1 | 513 | ? | KAWAIHAN | ALOHA OE (HAWAIIAN) | $8.00 | $15.00 |
| 1 | 514 | ? | SILENT NIGHT | MY MARYLAND | $8.00 | $15.00 |
| 1 | 515 | JOHN RYAN/MR. X | NEARER MY GOD TO THEE | MY COUNTRY 'TIS OF THEE | $8.00 | $15.00 |
| 1 | 516 | ? | MARCHING THROUGH GEORGIA | STARS AND STRIPES | $8.00 | $15.00 |
| 1 | 517 | ? | BLUE DANUBE | SKATERS WALTZ | $8.00 | $15.00 |
| 1 | 518 | ? | O SOLO MIO | OVER THE WAVES | $8.00 | $15.00 |
| 1 | 519 | ? | ARKANSAS TRAVELER | THE WATERS OF MINNETONKA | $8.00 | $15.00 |
| 1 | 520 | ? | COME BACK TO ERIN | MY WILD IRISH ROSE | $8.00 | $15.00 |
| 1 | 521 | ? | OH SUSANNA | LAST ROSE OF SUMMER | $8.00 | $15.00 |
| 1 | 522 | NOT LISTED | AMERICA | ANVIL CHORUS | $8.00 | $15.00 |
| 1 | 523 | ? | BONNIE | LOVE'S OLD SWEET SONG | $8.00 | $15.00 |
| 1 | 601 | ? | STAR SPANGLED BANNER | YANKEE DOODLE | $8.00 | $15.00 |
| 1 | 602 | ? | KAWAIHAN | ALOHA OE (HAWAIIAN) | $8.00 | $15.00 |
| 1 | 603 | ? | WASHINGTON POST (MARCH) | BABES IN TOYLAND | $8.00 | $15.00 |
| 1 | 604 | ? | MARCHING THROUGH GEORGIA | STARS AND STRIPES | $8.00 | $15.00 |
| 1 | 605 | ? | SWANEE RIVER | OLD KENTUCKY HOME | $8.00 | $15.00 |
| 1 | 606 | ? | LA PALOMA | KAWAHA | $8.00 | $15.00 |
| 1 | 607 | ? | LITTLE BO PEEP | THREE LITTLE KITTENS | $8.00 | $15.00 |
| 1 | 608 | JERRY WHITE/ERNEST HARE | OLD KING COLE | TOM TOM THE PIPER'S SON | $8.00 | $15.00 |
| 1 | 609 | ? | THREE BLIND MICE | LONDON BRIDGE IS FALLING DOWN | $8.00 | $15.00 |
| 1 | 610 | ? | LITTLE MISS MUFFETT | WHERE ARE YOU GOING MY PRETTY MAID | $8.00 | $15.00 |
| 1 | 611 | ? | I LOVE LITTLE PUSSY | I HAD A LITTLE DOGGIE | $8.00 | $15.00 |
| 1 | 612 | ? | RING AROUND A ROSY | ROCK-A-BYE BABY | $8.00 | $15.00 |

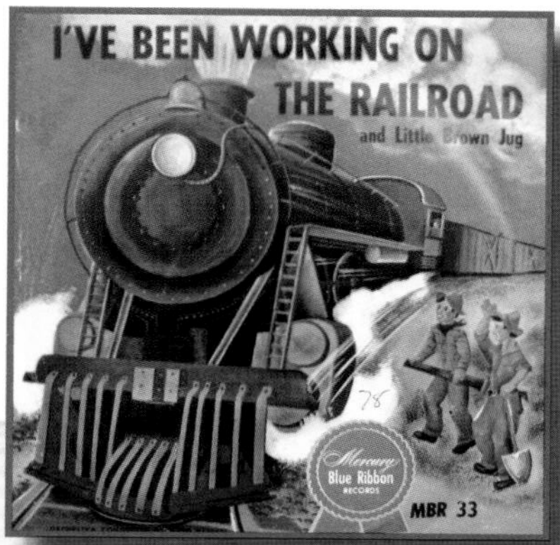

BLUE RIBBON RECORDS
TRIP TO THE MOON
$10.00

BLUE RIBBON RECORDS
I'VE BEEN WORKING ON THE RAILROAD
$3.00

BLUE RIBBON RECORDS
THE LITTLE RED FIRE ENGINE
$6.00

## BINGOLA 6" SINGLES

| # REC | DISC # | ARTIST | A TITLE | B TITLE | G/VG | EX/NMT |
|---|---|---|---|---|---|---|
| 1 | 613 | ? | SIMPLE SIMON | FARMER IN THE DELL | $8.00 | $15.00 |
| 1 | 614 | ? | THREE LITTLE PIGS | MULBERRY BUSH | $8.00 | $15.00 |
| 1 | 615 | ? | HEY DIDDLE DIDDLE | DING DONG BELL | $8.00 | $15.00 |
| 1 | 616 | ? | SING A SONG OF SIXPENCE | JACK AND JILL | $8.00 | $15.00 |
| 1 | 617 | ? | MARY HAD A LITTLE LAMB | LITTLE BOY BLUE | $8.00 | $15.00 |
| 1 | 618 | ? | LISTEN TO THE MOCKING BIRD | SKATERS WALTZ | $8.00 | $15.00 |
| 1 | 619 | ? | WHAT ARE LITTLE BOYS MADE OF | THE OLD WOMAN AND THE PEDDLER | $8.00 | $15.00 |
| 1 | 620 | ? | ONE TWO BUCKLE MY SHOE | THE LITTLE GIRL WITH A CURL | $8.00 | $15.00 |
| 1 | 621 | ? | THE OLD WOMAN WHO LIVED IN A SHOE | I SAW A SHIP | $8.00 | $15.00 |
| 1 | 622 | ? | OH SUSANNA | IF ALL THE SEAS WERE ONE SEA | $8.00 | $15.00 |
| 1 | 623 | ? | LAZY MARY WILL YOU GET UP | BAA BAA BLACK SHEEP | $8.00 | $15.00 |
| 1 | 624 | ? | THERE WAS A CROOKED MAN | THREE CHILDREN ON THE ICE | $8.00 | $15.00 |

## BIRTHSTONE 6" SINGLES

| # REC | DISC # | MAIN TITLE | ARTIST | YEAR | G/VG | EX/NMT |
|---|---|---|---|---|---|---|
| 1 | 201 | SONGS FOR JANUARY (GARNET BIRTHSTONE) | TOM GLAZER | 1956 | $3.00 | $6.00 |
| 1 | 202 | SONGS FOR FEBRUARY (AMETHYST BIRTHSTONE) | TOM GLAZER | | $3.00 | $6.00 |
| 1 | 203 | SONGS FOR MARCH (AQUAMARINE BIRTHSTONE) | TOM GLAZER | | $3.00 | $6.00 |
| 1 | 204 | SONGS FOR APRIL (DIAMOND BIRTHSTONE) | TOM GLAZER | | $3.00 | $6.00 |
| 1 | 205 | SONGS FOR MAY (EMERALD BIRTHSTONE) | TOM GLAZER | | $3.00 | $6.00 |
| 1 | 206 | SONGS FOR JUNE (PEARL BIRTHSTONE) | TOM GLAZER | | $3.00 | $6.00 |
| 1 | 207 | SONGS FOR JULY (RUBY BIRTHSTONE) | TOM GLAZER | | $3.00 | $6.00 |
| 1 | 208 | SONGS FOR AUGUST (PERIDOT BIRTHSTONE) | TOM GLAZER | | $3.00 | $6.00 |
| 1 | 209 | SONGS FOR SEPTEMBER (SAPPHIRE BIRTHSTONE) | TOM GLAZER | | $3.00 | $6.00 |
| 1 | 210 | SONGS FOR OCTOBER (OPAL BIRTHSTONE) | TOM GLAZER | | $3.00 | $6.00 |
| 1 | 211 | SONGS FOR NOVEMBER (TOPAZ BIRTHSTONE) | TOM GLAZER | | $3.00 | $6.00 |
| 1 | 212 | SONGS FOR DECEMBER (TURQUOISE BIRTHSTONE) | TOM GLAZER | | $3.00 | $6.00 |

## BLACK & WHITE 10" ALBUMS

| SET # | # REC | DISC # | MAIN TITLE | ARTIST | G/VG | EX/NMT |
|---|---|---|---|---|---|---|
| BW 50 | 3 | 5000 - 2 | GRIMM'S FAIRY TALES: SNOW WHITE ROSE RED, DR. KNOW-ALL, THE THREE BROTHERS | EARLE ROSS | $8.00 | $15.00 |
| BW 51 | 3 | 5003 - 5 | GRIMM'S FAIRY TALES: THE DRAGON & HIS GRANDMOTHER, THE THREE FEATHERS, THE TOWN MUSICIANS OF BREMEN | EARLE ROSS | $8.00 | $15.00 |
| BW 57 | 3 | 5006 - 8 | AESOP'S FABLES — VOL. I: SILLY DONKEY, TURTLE & RABBIT | JERRY MARLOWE | $8.00 | $15.00 |
| BW 59 | 3 | 5009 - 11 | ANDERSON'S FAIRY TALES: THE STEADFAST TIN SOLDIER, THE TINDER BOX | EARLE ROSS | $8.00 | $15.00 |
| BW 67 | 3 | 5012 - 4 | AESOP'S FABLES — VOL. II: THE TOWN MOUSE & THE COUNTRY MOUSE, THE LION & THE MOUSE | JERRY MARLOWE | $8.00 | $15.00 |

BOWMAR RECORDS
SONGS FROM "SINGING FUN"
$10.00

BOWMAR RECORDS
LITTLE FAVORITES
$10.00

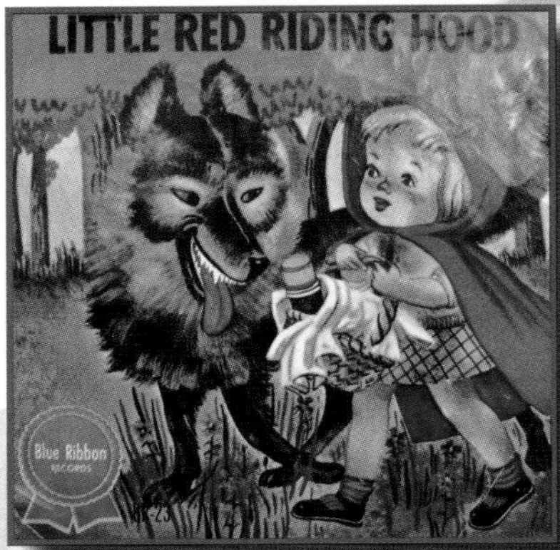


BLUE RIBBON RECORDS
LITTLE RED RIDING HOOD
$3.00

## BLACK & WHITE 6" SINGLES

| SET # | # REC | DISC # | MAIN TITLE | ARTIST | YEAR | G/VG | EX/NMT |
|---|---|---|---|---|---|---|---|
| 401 | 2 | BW 289/90 - 91/2 | AESOP'S FABLES NO. 1: THE SILLY DONKEY | JERRY MARLOWE | 195? | $2.00 | $4.00 |
| 402 | 2 | BW 285/6 - 87/8 | AESOP'S FABLES NO. 1: TURTLE & RABBIT | JERRY MARLOWE | | $2.00 | $4.00 |
| 411 | 2 | BW 408/9 - 10/11 | AESOP'S FABLES NO. 2: THE LION & THE MOUSE | JERRY MARLOWE | | $2.00 | $4.00 |
| 412 | 2 | BW 404/5 - 6/7 | AESOP'S FABLES NO. 2: THE CITY MOUSE & THE COUNTRY MOUSE | JERRY MARLOWE | | $2.00 | $4.00 |
| 421 | 1 | BW 135/6 | GRIMMS FAIRY TALES: DOCTOR KNOW ALL | EARLE ROSS | | $2.00 | $4.00 |
| 431 | 1 | ? | GRIMMS FAIRY TALES: DRAGON & HIS GRANDMOTHER | EARLE ROSS | | $2.00 | $4.00 |
| ? | ? | ? | ANDERSON'S FAIRY TALES: STEADFAST TIN SOLDIER | EARLE ROSS | | $2.00 | $4.00 |
| ? | ? | ? | ANDERSON'S FAIRY TALES: THE TINDER BOX | EARLE ROSS | | $2.00 | $4.00 |
| ? | ? | ? | GRIMMS FAIRY TALES: MUSICIANS OF BREMEN | EARLE ROSS | | $2.00 | $4.00 |
| ? | ? | ? | GRIMMS FAIRY TALES: SNOW WHITE & ROSE WHITE | EARLE ROSS | | $2.00 | $4.00 |
| ? | ? | ? | GRIMMS FAIRY TALES: THREE BROTHERS | EARLE ROSS | | $2.00 | $4.00 |
| ? | ? | ? | GRIMMS FAIRY TALES: THREE FEATHERS | EARLE ROSS | | $2.00 | $4.00 |

## BLUE RIBBON* 7" SINGLES

| # REC | DISC # | MAIN TITLE | ARTIST | A TITLE | B TITLE | ALSO ISSUED ON | G/VG | EX/NMT |
|---|---|---|---|---|---|---|---|---|
| 1 | BR-1 | LITTLE BO PEEP, ETC. | HUGO PERETTI, COND. | LITTLE BO PEEP | | 195? | $1.50 | $3.00 |
| 1 | BR-2 | MARY HAD A LITTLE LAMB, ETC. | HUGO PERETTI, COND. | MARY HAD A LITTLE LAMB | LAZY MARY, ET AL. | | $1.50 | $3.00 |
| 1 | BR-3 | A TISKET, A TASKET, ETC. | HUGO PERETTI, COND. | A TISKET, A TASKET | | | $1.50 | $3.00 |
| 1 | BR-4 | HERE WE GO ROUND THE MULBERRY BUSH, ET AL. | HUGO PERETTI, COND. | HERE WE GO ROUND THE MULBERRY BUSH | | | $1.50 | $3.00 |
| 1 | BR-5 | OLD MCDONALD HAD A FARM, ETC. | HUGO PERETTI, COND. | OLD MCDONALD HAD A FARM | | | $1.50 | $3.00 |
| 1 | BR-6 | 10 LITTLE INDIANS, ETC. | HUGO PERETTI, COND. | LONDON BRIDGE | 10 LITTLE INDIANS/ DID YOU EVER SEE A LASSIE? | | $1.50 | $3.00 |
| 1 | BR-7 | SILENT NIGHT HOLY NIGHT/COME ALL YE FAITHFUL | HUGO PERETTI, COND. | SILENT NIGHT HOLY NIGHT | | | $1.50 | $3.00 |
| 1 | BR-8 | HARK THE HERALD ANGELS SING/OH LITTLE TOWN OF BETHLEHEM | HUGO PERETTI, COND. | HARK THE HERALD ANGELS SING | OH LITTLE TOWN OF BETHLEHEM | | $1.50 | $3.00 |
| 1 | BR-9 | HAPPY BIRTHDAY SONG | HUGO PERETTI, COND. | HAPPY BIRTHDAY SONG | | | $1.50 | $3.00 |
| 1 | BR-10 | PLAY PARTY SONGS: THIS IS THE WAY GENTLEMEN RIDE, ETC. | HUGO PERETTI, COND. | PLAY PARTY SONGS | | | $1.50 | $3.00 |
| 1 | BR-11 | POP GOES THE WEASEL, ETC. | HUGO PERETTI, COND. | GOOSEY GANDER | | | $1.50 | $3.00 |
| 1 | BR-12 | BIG ROCK CANDY MOUNTAIN/WHERE HAVE YOU GONE BILLY BOY | HUGO PERETTI, COND. | BIG ROCK CANDY MOUNTAIN | | | $1.50 | $3.00 |
| 1 | BR-13 | YANKEE DOODLE, ETC. DIXIE, OH SUSANNAH | HUGO PERETTI, COND. | YANKEE DOODLE, DIXIE, OH SUSANNAH | SKIP TO MY LOU | | $1.50 | $3.00 |

*LABEL: MERCURY

BRUNSWICK RECORDS
LITTLE RED RIDING HOOD
$12.00

BURNS RECORDS
VISIT TO THE FARM
$4.00

BOBOLINK RECORDS
WHERE HAS MY LITTLE
DOG GONE? $3.00

## BLUE RIBBON* 7" SINGLES

| # REC | DISC # | MAIN TITLE | ARTIST | A TITLE | B TITLE | G/VG | EX/NMT |
|---|---|---|---|---|---|---|---|
| 1 | BR-14 | SAILOR'S HORNPIPE, ETC. | HUGO PERETTI, COND. | SAILOR'S HORNPIPE | | $1.50 | $3.00 |
| 1 | BR-15 | SONGS OF THE SADDLE: HOME ON THE RANGE, ETC. | HUGO PERETTI, COND. | SONGS OF THE SADDLE | | $1.50 | $3.00 |
| 1 | BR-16 | COWBOY SONGS: GET ALONG LITTLE DOGGIE, ETC. | HUGO PERETTI, COND. | GET ALONG LITTLE DOGGIE | RED RIVER VALLEY | $1.50 | $3.00 |
| 1 | BR-17 | CINDERELLA | HUGO PERETTI, COND. | CINDERELLA | | $1.50 | $3.00 |
| 1 | BR-18 | PETER RABBIT | HUGO PERETTI, COND. | PETER RABBIT | | $1.50 | $3.00 |
| 1 | BR-19 | PINOCCHIO | HUGO PERETTI, COND. | PINOCCHIO | PINOCCHIO | $1.50 | $3.00 |
| 1 | BR-20 | THREE LITTLE PIGS | HUGO PERETTI, COND. | THREE LITTLE PIGS | | $1.50 | $3.00 |
| 1 | BR-21 | SNOW WHITE | HUGO PERETTI, COND. | SNOW WHITE | | $1.50 | $3.00 |
| 1 | BR-22 | LITTLE RED HEN | HUGO PERETTI, COND. | LITTLE RED HEN | | $1.50 | $3.00 |
| 1 | BR-23 | LITTLE RED RIDING HOOD | HUGO PERETTI, COND. | LITTLE RED RIDING HOOD | | $1.50 | $3.00 |
| 1 | BR-24 | GOLDILOCKS AND THE THREE BEARS | HUGO PERETTI, COND. | GOLDILOCKS AND THE THREE BEARS | | $1.50 | $3.00 |
| 1 | BR-25 | BRAHMS' LULLABY | HUGO PERETTI, COND. | BRAHMS' LULLABY | | $1.50 | $3.00 |
| 1 | BR-26 | LITTLE BRAVE SAMBO | HUGO PERETTI, COND. | LITTLE BRAVE SAMBO | | $5.00 | $10.00 |
| 1 | BR-27 | HENNY PENNY | HUGO PERETTI, COND. | HENNY PENNY | | $1.50 | $3.00 |
| 1 | BR-28 | THE LORD'S PRAYER | HUGO PERETTI, COND. | THE LORD'S PRAYER | | $1.50 | $3.00 |
| 1 | BR-29 | TREASURE ISLAND | HUGO PERETTI, COND. | TREASURE ISLAND | | $1.50 | $3.00 |
| 1 | BR-30 | ALPHABET SONG | HUGO PERETTI, COND. | ALPHABET SONG | | $1.50 | $3.00 |
| 1 | BR-31 | BUFFALO GALS | HUGO PERETTI, COND. | BUFFALO GALS | | $1.50 | $3.00 |
| 1 | BR-32 | ALOUETTE | HUGO PERETTI, COND. | ALOUETTE | | 1.50 | $3.00 |
| 1 | BR-33 | I'VE BEEN WORKING ON THE RAILROAD | HUGO PERETTI, COND. | I'VE BEEN WORKING ON THE RAILROAD | LITTLE BROWN JUG | $1.50 | $3.00 |
| 1 | BR-34 | PETER COTTONTAIL | HUGO PERETTI, COND. | PETER COTTONTAIL (PT. 1) | PETER COTTONTAIL (PT. 2) | $1.50 | $3.00 |
| 1 | BR-35 | MEXICAN HAT DANCE | HUGO PERETTI, COND. | MEXICAN HAT DANCE | | $1.50 | $3.00 |
| 1 | BR-36 | THE ARKANSAS TRAVELER | HUGO PERETTI, COND. | THE ARKANSAS TRAVELER | | $1.50 | $3.00 |
| 1 | BR-37 | BIRTHDAY PARTY | HUGO PERETTI, COND. | BIRTHDAY PARTY | | $1.50 | $3.00 |
| 1 | BR-38 | RUDOLPH THE RED-NOSED REINDEER | HUGO PERETTI, COND. | RUDOLPH THE RED-NOSED REINDEER | | $1.50 | $3.00 |
| 1 | BR-39 | GAME SONGS | HUGO PERETTI, COND. | GAME SONGS | | $1.50 | $3.00 |
| 1 | BR-40 | SONGS FOR PLAY | HUGO PERETTI, COND. | SONGS FOR PLAY (PT. 1) | SONGS FOR PLAY (PT. 2) | $1.50 | $3.00 |
| 1 | BR-41 | PETER PAN | HUGO PERETTI, COND. | PETER PAN | | $1.50 | $3.00 |
| 1 | BR-42 | RUMPLESTILTSKIN | HUGO PERETTI, COND. | RUMPLESTILTSKIN | | $1.50 | $3.00 |
| 1 | BR-43 | THE LITTLE RED FIRE ENGINE | HUGO PERETTI, COND. | THE LITTLE RED FIRE ENGINE | | $3.00 | $6.00 |
| 1 | BR-44 | THE STORY OF NOAH'S ARK | HUGO PERETTI, COND. | THE STORY OF NOAH'S ARK | | $1.50 | $3.00 |

*LABEL: MERCURY

## BLUE RIBBON* 7" SINGLES

| # REC | DISC # | MAIN TITLE | ARTIST | A TITLE | B TITLE | G/VG | EX/NMT |
|---|---|---|---|---|---|---|---|
| 1 | BR-45 | DAVID AND GOLIATH | HUGO PERETTI, COND. | DAVID AND GOLIATH | | $1.50 | $3.00 |
| 1 | BR-46 | TRIP TO THE MOON | HUGO PERETTI, COND. | TRIP TO THE MOON | | $5.00 | $10.00 |
| 1 | BR-47 | LITTLE TIN SOLDIER | HUGO PERETTI, COND. | LITTLE TIN SOLDIER | | $1.50 | $3.00 |
| 1 | BR-48 | QUACKY THE DUCK | HUGO PERETTI, COND. | QUACKY THE DUCK | | $1.50 | $3.00 |
| 1 | BR-49 | SUPER CIRCUS BAND | HUGO PERETTI, COND. | SUPER CIRCUS BAND | | $5.00 | $10.00 |
| 1 | BR-50 | SUPER CIRCUS CLOWN ALLEY | HUGO PERETTI, COND. | SUPER CIRCUS CLOWN ALLEY | | $5.00 | $10.00 |
| 1 | BR-51 | SUPER CIRCUS MENAGERIE | HUGO PERETTI, COND. | SUPER CIRCUS MENAGERIE | | $5.00 | $10.00 |
| 1 | BR-52 | SUPER CIRCUS SIDESHOW | HUGO PERETTI, COND. | SUPER CIRCUS SIDESHOW | | $5.00 | $10.00 |
| 1 | BR-53 | SANTA IS COMING TO TOWN | HUGO PERETTI, COND. | SANTA IS COMING TO TOWN | | $1.50 | $3.00 |
| 1 | BR-54 | CHRISTMAS CAROLS | HUGO PERETTI, COND. | CHRISTMAS CAROLS | | $1.50 | $3.00 |
| 1 | BR-55 | WHITE CHRISTMAS | HUGO PERETTI, COND. | WHITE CHRISTMAS | | $1.50 | $3.00 |
| 1 | BR-56 | FIRST NOEL; ET AL | HUGO PERETTI, COND. | FIRST NOEL; CAROL OF BELLS | JINGLE BELLS, WE WISH YOU A MERRY CHRISTMAS | $1.50 | $3.00 |
| 1 | BR-57 | FROSTY THE SNOWMAN | HUGO PERETTI, COND. | FROSTY THE SNOWMAN | CHRISTMAS STOCKINGS | $1.50 | $3.00 |

*LABEL: MERCURY

## BLUE RIBBON* 10" SINGLES

| # REC | DISC # | MAIN TITLE | ARTIST | A-TITLE | B-TITLE | YEAR | G/VG | EX/NMT |
|---|---|---|---|---|---|---|---|---|
| 1 | BR-1001 | LITTLE BO PEEP, ETC./ MARY HAD A LITTLE LAMB, ETC. | NOT LISTED | LITTLE BO PEEP/DING DONG BELL/THE MUFFIN MAN/ PETER PIPER/THERE WAS A CROOKED MAN | MARY HAD A LITTLE LAMB/ GEORGY PORGY/COCK-A-DOODLE-DOO/POLLY PUT THE KETTLE ON/ LAZY MARY | 195? | $1.50 | $3.00 |
| 1 | BR-1002 | TRIP TO THE MOON | ? | TRIP TO THE MOON | TREASURE ISLAND | | $8.00 | $15.0015 |
| 1 | BR-1003 | PETER PAN | ? | PETER PAN | PINOCCHIO | | $1.50 | $3.00 |
| 1 | BR-1004 | HERE WE GO ROUND THE MULBERRY BUSH, ETC./A TISKET, A TASKET, ETC. | NOT LISTED | HERE WE GO ROUND THE MULBERRY BUSH/A FROG HE WOULD A WOOING GO | A TISKET, A TASKET/RING AROUND A ROSIE/DANCE THE LOBBY LOO | | $1.50 | $3.00 |
| 1 | BR-1005 | OLD MACDONALD HAD A FARM, ETC./THE BIG ROCK CANDY MOUNTAIN, ETC. | NOT LISTED | OLD MACDONALD HAD A FARM/THE BEAR THAT WENT OVER THE MOUNTAIN/THE FARMER IN THE DELL | THE BIG ROCK CANDY MOUNTAIN/ WHERE HAVE YOU BEEN BILLY BOY? | | $1.50 | $3.00 |
| 1 | BR-1006 | 10 LITTLE INDIANS, ETC./ BUFFALO GALS, ETC. | NOT LISTED | 10 LITTLE INDIANS/LONDON BRIDGE/DID YOU EVER SEE A LASSIE | BUFFALO GALS/POLLY WOLLY DOODLE | | $1.50 | $3.00 |
| 1 | BR-1007 | PETER COTTONTAIL/PETER RABBIT | NOT LISTED | PETER COTTONTAIL | PETER RABBIT | | $1.50 | $3.00 |
| 1 | BR-1008 | HARK! THE HERALD ANGELS SING, ETC./SILENT NIGHT, HOLY NIGHT | NOT LISTED | HARK THE HERALD ANGELS SING/OH LITTLE TOWN OF BETHLEHEM | SILENT NIGHT HOLY NIGHT/O COME ALL YE FAITHFUL | | $1.50 | $3.00 |
| 1 | BR-1009 | HAPPY BIRTHDAY SONG/ BIRTHDAY PARTY | NOT LISTED | HAPPY BIRTHDAY SONG | BIRTHDAY PARTY | | $1.50 | $3.00 |
| 1 | BR-1010 | ALPHABET SONG/COUNTING SONG; GAME SONGS | HUGO PERETTI ORCH. | ALPHABET SONG | COUNTING SONG, GAME SONGS | | $1.50 | $3.00 |
| 1 | BR-1011 | GOOSEY GANDER, ETC./ FIDDLE-DEE-DEE QUACKY THE DUCK, ETC. | NOT LISTED/ GILBERT MACK, TOBY DEANE, HUGO PERETTI ORCH. | GOOSEY GANDER/POP GOES THE WEASEL/FRERE JACQUES | FIDDLE-DEE-DEE/QUACKY THE DUCK | | $1.50 | $3.00 |
| 1 | BR-1012 | PLAY PARTY SONGS: HAIL HAIL THE GANG'S ALL HERE, ETC./OH DEAR WHAT CAN THE MATTER BE, ETC. | HUGO PERETTI, BLUE RIBBON CHORUS | PLAY PARTY SONGS | | | $1.50 | $3.00 |
| 1 | BR-1013 | BEDTIME PRAYERS; THE LORD'S PRAYER, ETC./ NOW I LAY ME DOWN TO SLEEP, ETC. | THE BLUE RIBBON CAROLEERS | BEDTIME PRAYERS/THE LORD'S PRAYER | NOW I LAY ME DOWN TO SLEEP; BRAHMS' LULLABY | | $1.50 | $3.00 |
| 1 | BR-1014 | SAILOR'S HORNPIPE; ETC./ MY BONNIE LIES OVER THE OCEAN, ETC. | NOT LISTED | SAILOR'S HORNPIPE/ SAILING, SAILING/ROW, ROW, ROW YOUR BOAT/BLOW THE MAN DOWN/COMIN' THRU THE RYE | MY BONNIE LIES OVER THE OCEAN/ YANKEE DOODLE/OH SUSANNA/ SKIP TO MY LOU/ DIXIE | | $1.50 | $3.00 |
| 1 | BR-1015 | SONGS OF THE SADDLE: HOME ON THE RANGE; ETC./GET ALONG LITTLE DOGIES, ETC. | NOT LISTED | SONGS OF THE SADDLE/ HOME ON THE RANGE/ CHISHOLM TRAIL | GET ALONG LITTLE DOGIES/RED RIVER VALLEY | | $1.50 | $3.00 |

*LABEL: MERCURY

CADENCE RECORDS
ELOISE
$25.00

CARTOON RECORDS
YONDERLAND
$50.00

CAMEO KID
LITTLE BO-PEEP
$25.00

### BURNS 10" AND 12" SINGLES

| SET # | # REC | DISCS # | MAIN TITLE | ARTIST | YEAR | G/VG | EX/NOT |
|---|---|---|---|---|---|---|---|
| A | 4 | 331/2 - 7/8 | FOLK DANCES: MINUET, ETC. | JOSEPH BURNS, EDITH WHEELER | 195? | $2.00 | $4.00 |
| B | 4 | 341/2 - 7/8 | FOLK DANCES: HIGHLAND SCHOTTISCHE, ETC. | JOSEPH BURNS, EDITH WHEELER | | $2.00 | $4.00 |
| C | 5 | 881/2 - 9/90 | SQUARE DANCES: ARKANSAS TRAVELER, ETC. | JOSEPH BURNS, EDITH WHEELER | | $2.00 | $4.00 |
| D | 5 | 891/2 - 9/900 | SQUARE DANCES: RED RIVER VALLEY, ETC. | JOSEPH BURNS, EDITH WHEELER | | $2.00 | $4.00 |
| E | 4 | 761/2 - 7/8 | FOLK DANCES: LITTLE DUTCH GIRL, ETC. | JOSEPH BURNS, EDITH WHEELER | | $2.00 | $4.00 |
| F | 4 | 771/2 - 7/8 | FOLK DANCES: MEXICAN WALTZ; KALVELIS, ETC. | JOSEPH BURNS, EDITH WHEELER | | $2.00 | $4.00 |
| G | 4 | 511/2 - 7/8 | FOLK DANCES: HANSEL & GRETEL | JOSEPH BURNS, EDITH WHEELER | | $2.00 | $4.00 |
| H | 4 | 521/2 - 7/8 | FOLK DANCES: DONKEY DANCE, ETC. | JOSEPH BURNS, EDITH WHEELER | | $2.00 | $4.00 |
| J | 4 | 551/2 - 7/8 | FOLK DANCES: MEXICAN WALTZ, HIGHLAND SCHOTTISCHE, ETC. | JOSEPH BURNS, EDITH WHEELER | | $2.00 | $4.00 |
| K | 5 | 1001/2 - 9/10 | BALLROOM DANCES: FOXTROT, ETC. | JOSEPH BURNS, EDITH WHEELER | | $2.00 | $4.00 |
| M | 5 | 1021/2 - 9/30 | BALLROOM DANCES: TANGO, ETC. | JOSEPH BURNS, EDITH WHEELER | | $2.00 | $4.00 |
| O | 4 (10") | 1031/2 - 7/8 | THE CIRCUS | JOSEPH BURNS, EDITH WHEELER | | $2.00 | $4.00 |
| R | 4 (10") | 1041/2 - 7/8 | VISIT TO THE FARM | JOSEPH BURNS, EDITH WHEELER | | $2.00 | $4.00 |
| S | 4 (10") | 1051/2 - 7/8 | THE SEASONS | JOSEPH BURNS, EDITH WHEELER | | $2.00 | $4.00 |
| T | 4 (10") | 1061/2 - 7/8 | A VISIT TO THE PARK | JOSEPH BURNS, EDITH WHEELER | | $2.00 | $4.00 |

## C

### CADENCE 10" SINGLES

| SET # | # REC | DISC # | ARTIST | A TITLE | B TITLE | YEAR | G/VG | EX/NMT |
|---|---|---|---|---|---|---|---|---|
| CCS-1 | 1 | 0458-9 | BILL HAYES | THE BALLAD OF DAVY CROCKETT | FAREWELL | 1955 | $12.00 | $25.00 |
| CCS-2 | 1 | 8323-63 | BILL HAYES | THE WHITE BUFFALO | THE LEGEND OF WYATT EARP | | $12.00 | $25.00 |
| CCS-3 | 1 | 0251-1609 | KAY THOMPSON | ELOISE | JUST ONE OF THOSE THINGS | 1956 | $15.00 | $30.00 |
| 1256 | 1 | 1256 | BILL HAYES | THE BALLAD OF DAVY CROCKETT | FAREWELL | 1955 | $10.00 | $20.00 |
| 1610 | 1 | 8205-6 | THE STORY PRINCESS | FLUFFY AND BLUFFY MEETS FATHER TIME (PT. 1) | FLUFFY AND BLUFFY MEETS FATHER TIME (PT. 2) | | $2.00 | $4.00 |

### CAMEO JACKIE COOGAN SERIES 7" SINGLES

| # REC | DISC # | ARTIST | A TITLE | B TITLE | YEAR | PRICE G/VG | PRICE EX/NMT |
|---|---|---|---|---|---|---|---|
| 1 | 110 | JACKIE COOGAN | LITTLE AH SID | CIRCUS | 1925 | $40.00 | $80.00 |
| 1 | 111 | JACKIE COOGAN | A BEAR OF A STORY | ADVICE TO KIDS | | $40.00 | $80.00 |
| 1 | 112 | JACKIE COOGAN | THE MAN WITHOUT A COUNTRY | THE DIRECTOR | | $40.00 | $80.00 |

### CAMEO CAMEO SERIES 10" SINGLES

| # REC | DISC # | ARTIST | A TITLE | B TITLE | YEAR | G/VG | EX/NMT |
|---|---|---|---|---|---|---|---|
| 1 | 807 | GLORIA GEER & CO | SANTA CLAUS AT THE PARTY | THE SPIRIT OF CHRISTMAS | 1925 | $2.00 | $4.00 |
| 1 | 913 | ? | CHRISTMAS EVE AT GRANDPA'S | YULE TIDE ECHOES | 1926 | $2.00 | $4.00 |

CAPITOL RECORDS
BOZO AND HIS ROCKET SHIP
$80.00

CAPITOL RECORDS
STORIES FOR CHILDREN VOL. I
$10.00

CAPITOL RECORDS
GERALD MCBOING BOING
$50.00

## CAMEO-KID 7" SINGLES

| # REC | DISC # | ARTIST | A TITLE | B TITLE | YEAR | G/VG | EX/NMT |
|---|---|---|---|---|---|---|---|
| 1 | 10 | ERNEST HARE | JACK AND JILL | OLD KING COLE | 1924 | $3.00 | $6.00 |
| 1 | 11 | ERNEST HARE, MAUREEN ENGLIN | JACK AND THE BEANSTALK | TOM THUMB | | $3.00 | $6.00 |
| 1 | 12 | MAUREEN ENGLIN | THE THREE BEARS | CINDERELLA | | $3.00 | $6.00 |
| 1 | 13 | BILLY JONES, ERNEST HARE | LONDON BRIDGE | FARMER IN THE DELL | | $3.00 | $6.00 |
| 1 | 14 | BILLY JONES | HERE WE GO ROUND THE MULBERRY BUSH | OATS, PEAS AND BEANS | | $3.00 | $6.00 |
| 1 | 15 | ERNEST HARE | TOM TOM THE PIPER'S SON | SIMPLE SIMON | | $3.00 | $6.00 |
| 1 | 16 | LEROY MONTESANTO | LITTLE BO-PEEP | MARY HAD A LITTLE LAMB | | $3.00 | $6.00 |
| 1 | 17 | ? | YANKEE DOODLE | HAIL COLUMBIA | | $3.00 | $6.00 |
| 1 | 18 | ERNEST HARE, BILLY JONES | DIXIE | AMERICA | | $3.00 | $6.00 |
| 1 | 19 | ERNEST HARE, BILLY JONES | STAR SPANGLED BANNER | COLUMBIA, THE GEM OF THE OCEAN | | $3.00 | $6.00 |
| 1 | 20 | BILLY JONES, ERNEST HARE | LAZY MARY WILL YOU GET UP? | TEN LITTLE INDIANS | | $3.00 | $6.00 |
| 1 | 21 | HARRY SMITH | THREE LITTLE KITTENS | WHERE ARE YOU GOING MY PRETTY MAID | | $3.00 | $6.00 |
| 1 | 22 | MAUREEN ENGLIN | ROCK-A-BYE BABY | SING A SONG OF SIXPENCE | | $3.00 | $6.00 |
| 1 | 23 | HARRY SMITH | COCK-A-DOODLE DOO | OLD MOTHER HUBBARD | | $3.00 | $6.00 |
| 1 | 24 | MAUREEN ENGLIN | SWEET AND LOW | DOLL SONG | | $3.00 | $6.00 |
| 1 | 25 | MAUREEN ENGLIN | THE SANDMAN | SLUMBER BOAT | | $3.00 | $6.00 |
| 1 | 26 | MAUREEN ENGLIN | GO TO SLEEP MY LITTLE PICKANINNY | THE DREAM MAN | | $8.00 | $16.00 |
| 1 | 27 | MAUREEN ENGLIN | LITTLE RED RIDING HOOD | THE FROG PRINCE | | $3.00 | $6.00 |
| 1 | 28 | IRVING FISHER | THUMBKIN SAYS "I'LL DANCE" | FIVE LITTLE CHICKADEES | | $3.00 | $6.00 |
| 1 | 29 | IRVING FISHER | LAZY MOON | TWINKLE, TWINKLE LITTLE STAR | | $3.00 | $6.00 |
| 1 | 30 | IRVING FISHER | NURSERY MEDLEY | NURSERY MEDLEY | | $3.00 | $6.00 |
| 1 | 31 | ERNEST HARE & COMPANY | SANTA CLAUS' TOY SHOP | SANTA CLAUS' GREETINGS | | $4.00 | $8.00 |
| 1 | 32 | ? | HOW THE BIRDS TALK | THE LION IS KING | | $3.00 | $6.00 |
| 1 | 33 | IRVING FISHER | JENNY JONES | ROUND AND ROUND THE VILLAGE | | $3.00 | $6.00 |
| 1 | 34 | HARRY SMITH | I HAD A LITTLE DOGGY | PUSSY CAT, PUSSY CAT | | $3.00 | $6.00 |
| 1 | 35 | NOT LISTED | GOOD MORNING MERRY SUNSHINE | THE GOLDEN RULE | | $3.00 | $6.00 |
| 1 | 36 | MARY EARL | WATER WATER WILDFLOWER | LITTLE DROPS OF WATER | | $3.00 | $6.00 |
| 1 | 37 | NOT LISTED | THE SNOW MAN | THE BLACKSMITH | | $3.00 | $6.00 |
| 1 | 38 | MARY EARL | PETER PETER PUMPKIN EATER | MUSICAL ALPHABET | | $3.00 | $6.00 |
| 1 | 39 | NOT LISTED | LITTLE BOY BLUE/SEE SAW MARJORIE DAW | LITTLE GIRLS GOOD-NIGHT | | $3.00 | $6.00 |
| 1 | 40 | NOT LISTED | RING AROUND A ROSY — MEDLEY | GOOSEY, GOOSEY GANDER — MEDLEY | | $3.00 | $6.00 |
| 1 | 41 | NOT LISTED | WELCOME, SWEET SPRINGTIME | LULLABY | | $3.00 | $6.00 |
| 1 | 42 | HARRY SMITH | PUSS IN BOOTS | THE SLEEPING BEAUTY | | $3.00 | $6.00 |
| 1 | 43 | HARRY SMITH | ALICE IN WONDERLAND | GRANDFATHER'S CLOCK | | $3.00 | $6.00 |

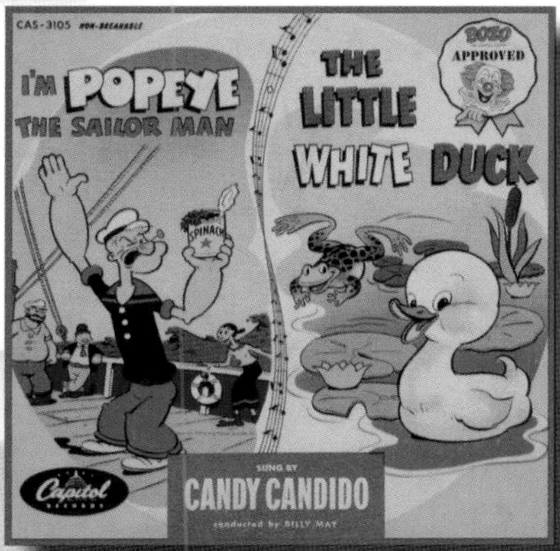


CAPITOL RECORDS
I'M POPEYE THE SAILOR MAN
$15.00

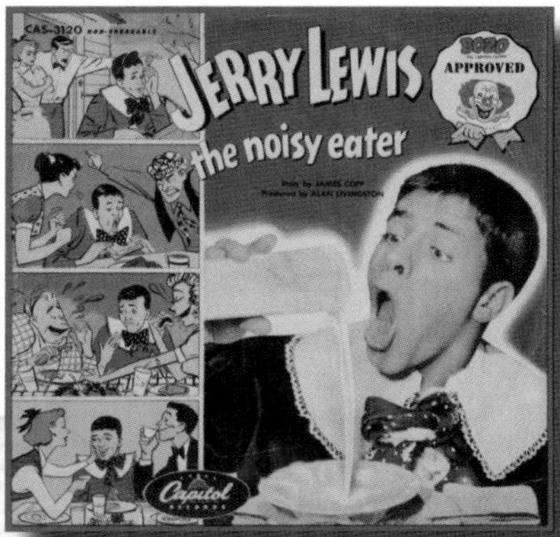


CAPITOL RECORDS
THE NOISY EATER
$20.00

CAPITOL RECORDS
BUGS BUNNY AND ALADDIN'S LAMP $15.00

## CAMEO-KID 7" SINGLES

| # REC | DISC # | ARTIST | A TITLE | B TITLE | G/VG | EX/NMT |
|---|---|---|---|---|---|---|
| 1 | 44 | GLORIA GEER | INKY MOUSE | HANSEL & GRETEL | $3.00 | $6.00 |
| 1 | 45 | GLORIA GEER | THE BOOGY MAN | THE SQUIRREL | $3.00 | $6.00 |
| 1 | 46 | ? | THE SUNBEAM'S JOKE | MOTHER GOOSE'S PARTY | $3.00 | $6.00 |
| 1 | 47 | GLORIA GEER | THE ELEPHANT GLORIA GEER | A LITTLE BROWN DOG | $3.00 | $6.00 |
| 1 | 48 | GLORIA GEER | LITTLE ONE'S GOOD NIGHT PRAYER | NOW I LAY ME DOWN TO SLEEP | $3.00 | $6.00 |
| 1 | 49 | ? | RAMBLE ROUND THE CHRISTMAS TREE | SANTA CLAUS IS A JOLLY OLD FELLOW | $3.00 | $6.00 |
| 1 | 50 | ? | I'VE WRITTEN A LETTER TO SANTA CLAUS | A NICE GAME (CLAP, CLAP, CLAP) | $3.00 | $6.00 |

## CAMEO-KID UNCLE WIGGLY SERIES 7" SINGLES

| # REC | DISC # | ARTIST | A TITLE | B TITLE | YEAR | G/VG | EX/NMT |
|---|---|---|---|---|---|---|---|
| 1 | 51 | NOT LISTED | UNCLE WIGGLY AND THE DARK | UNCLE WIGGLY'S ALPHABET SONG | 1925 | $25.00 | $50.00 |
| 1 | 52 | NOT LISTED | UNCLE WIGGLY'S SLEEPING SONG | UNCLE WIGGLY & OLD MOTHER HUBBARD | | $25.00 | $50.00 |
| 1 | 53 | NOT LISTED | UNCLE WIGGLY AND THE WIND | UNCLE WIGGLY'S PINK NOSE | | $25.00 | $50.00 |
| 1 | 54 | NOT LISTED | UNCLE WIGGLY AND THE PHOEBE BIRDS | AT THE CIRCUS | | $25.00 | $50.00 |
| 1 | 55 | NOT LISTED | UNCLE WIGGLY'S SWIMMING LESSON | UNCLE WIGGLY IN THE WOODS | | $25.00 | $50.00 |

## CAPITOL MAIN SERIES 10" ALBUMS AND SINGLES

| SET # | # REC | DISC # | MAIN TITLE | ARTIST | YEAR | ALSO ISSUED ON | G/VG | EX/NMT |
|---|---|---|---|---|---|---|---|---|
| CD-11 (ALSO J-1) | 4 | 10017 - 20 | STORIES FOR CHILDREN, VOL. 1: PUSS IN BOOTS, RUMPLESTILTSKIN, JACK & THE BEANSTALK | THE GREAT GILDERSLEEVE | 1946 | J-1, DBS-132 | $5.00 | $10.00 |
| BD-14 | 4 | 20037 - 40 | CHILDREN'S SONGS AND STORIES: BILLY THE KID, THE PONY EXPRESS,ETC. | TEX RITTER | | DBS-134 | $8.00 | $15.00 |
| CC-20 | 3 | 10041 - 3 | ON THE NIGHT BEFORE CHRISTMAS | FIBBER MCGEE AND MOLLY | | | $5.00 | $10.00 |
| CC-21 | 3 | 10044 - 6 | STORIES FOR CHILDREN: TOWN MUSICIANS, 3 BILLY-GOATS GRUFF | MARGARET O'BRIEN | | DC-123 | $6.00 | $12.00 |

## CAPITOL MAIN SERIES 10" ALBUMS AND SINGLES

| SET # | # REC | DISC # | MAIN TITLE | ARTIST | YEAR | ALSO ISSUED ON | G/VG | EX/NMT |
|---|---|---|---|---|---|---|---|---|
| BD-27 | 4 | 20065 - 8 | COWBOY FAVORITES: CHISHOLM TRAIL, SAN ANTONIO ROSE, ETC. | TEX RITTER | | | $8.00 | $15.00 |
| CD-33 | 4 | 10058 - 61 | STORIES FOR CHILDREN, VOL. II: THE BRAVE LITTLE TAILOR, HANSEL & GRETEL | THE GREAT GILDERSLEEVE | | DBS-128 | $5.00 | $10.00 |
| BBX-34 | 2 | 20077 - 8 | BOZO AT THE CIRCUS | PINTO COLVIG | | DBX-114 | $30.00 | $60.00 |
| BC-35 | 3 | 20079 - 81 | RUSTY IN ORCHESTRAVILLE | HENRY BLAIR: BILLY BLETCHER | | DCN-115 | $25.00 | $50.00 |
| CC-40 | 3 | 10069 - 71 | TALES OF UNCLE REMUS | JOHNNY MERCER | 1947 | DC-116 | $30.00 | $60.00 |
| CC-50 | 4 | 48000 - 3 | FOLK SONGS OF THE HILLS | MERLE TRAVIS | | | $5.00 | $10.00 |
| DAS-60 | 1 | 25000 | COLONNA'S TROLLEY | JERRY COLONNA | | | $5.00 | $10.00 |
| CC-64 | 3 | 10089 - 91 | BUGS BUNNY STORIES FOR CHILDREN: BUGS BUNNY MEETS ELMER FUDD, DAFFY DUCK FLIES SOUTH, PORKY PIG IN AFRICA | MEL BLANC | | DC-117 | $15.00 | $30.00 |
| BBX-65 | 2 | 20122 - 3 | BOZO AND HIS ROCKET SHIP | PINTO COLVIG | | DBX-118 | $40.00 | $80.00 |
| BC-66 | 3 | 20132 - 4 | SPARKY AND THE TALKING TRAIN | HENRY BLAIR; VERNE SMITH | | DC-119 | $25.00 | $50.00 |
| CCX-67 | 3 | 10098 - 100 | MICKEY AND THE BEANSTALK | JOHNNY MERCER | | DCX-120 | $35.00 | $75.00 |
| CD-69 | 4 | 10094 - 7 | STORIES FOR CHILDREN, VOL. III: CINDERELLA, SNOW WHITE & ROSE RED | THE GREAT GILDERSLEEVE | | DBS-130, DBS-131 | $5.00 | $10.00 |
| CC-71 | 3 | 10115 - 6 - 7 | LET'S FLY TO MEXICO | MARGARET O'BRIEN | | DC-122 | $5.00 | $10.00 |
| BC-73 | 3 | 20139 - 41 | SPARKY'S MAGIC PIANO* | HENRY BLAIR, VERNE SMITH | | DC-78 | $25.00 | $50.00 |
| DC-78 | 3 | 25001 - 3 | SPARKY'S MAGIC PIANO | HENRY BLAIR, VERNE SMITH | | BC-73 | $25.00 | $50.00 |
| DAS-80 | 1 | 25004 | LITTLE TOOT | DON WILSON, THE STARLIGHTERS | | | $10.00 | $20.00 |
| DBS-84 | 1 | 25005 - 6 | BOZO SINGS: BOZO'S SONG, FILBERT THE FROG/ HONKETY HANK, MY MULE CHARLIE | PINTO COLVIG | 1948 | | $8.00 | $15.00 |
| DC-89 | 3 | 25009 - 11 | KING COLE FOR KIDS | KING COLE TRIO | | | $12.00 | $25.00 |
| DBS-90 | 2 | 25007 - 8 | NURSERY RHYMES | KEN CARSON | | | $4.00 | $8.00 |
| DC-91 | 3 | 25012 - 4 | SONGS FOR CHILDREN: ANIMAL FAIR, I WAS BORN A HUNDRED YEARS AGO, ETC. | TEX RITTER | | | $8.00 | $15.00 |
| DBS-92 | 2 | 25015 - 6 | BIBLE STORIES FOR CHILDREN: DAVID & GOLIATH; JOSEPH & HIS COAT OF MANY COLORS | CLAUDE RAINS | | | $6.00 | $12.00 |
| DBX-93 | 2 | 25017 - 8 | BUGS BUNNY AND THE TORTOISE | MEL BLANC | | | $15.00 | $30.00 |
| DB-94 | 2 | 25019 - 20 | BIBLE STORIES FOR CHILDREN: NOAH & THE ARK, MOSES IN THE BULRUSHES | CLAUDE RAINS | | | $6.00 | $12.00 |
| DBX-99 | 2 | 25021 - 2 | BOZO UNDER THE SEA | PINTO COLVIG | | | $35.00 | $75.00 |
| DD-109 | 4 | 25050 - 3 | SO DEAR TO MY HEART | JOHN BEAL | | BD-124 | $15.00 | $30.00 |
| DBX-114 | 2 | 25023 - 4 | BOZO AT THE CIRCUS | PINTO COLVIG | | BBX-34 | $15.00 | $30.00 |
| DC-115 | 3 | 25025 - 7 | RUSTY IN ORCHESTRAVILLE** | HENRY BLAIR; BILLY BLETCHER | | BC-35 | $25.00 | $50.00 |
| DC-116 | 3 | 25028 - 30 | TALES OF UNCLE REMUS | JOHNNY MERCER | | CC-40 | $30.00 | $60.00 |
| DC-117 | 3 | 25031 - 3 | BUGS BUNNY STORIES FOR CHILDREN: BUGS BUNNY MEETS ELMER FUDD, DAFFY DUCK FLIES SOUTH, PORKY PIG IN AFRICA | MEL BLANC | | CC-64 | $15.00 | $30.00 |
| DBX-118 | 2 | 25034 - 5 | BOZO AND HIS ROCKET SHIP | PINTO COLVIG | | BBX-65 | $40.00 | $80.00 |
| DC-119 | 3 | 25036 - 8 | SPARKY AND THE TALKING TRAIN*** | HENRY BLAIR, VERNE SMITH | | BC-66 | $25.00 | $50.00 |
| DCX-120 | 3 | 25039 - 41 | MICKEY AND THE BEANSTALK | JOHNNY MERCER | | CCX-67 | $35.00 | $75.00 |
| DB-121 | 2 | 25042 - 3 | GOLDILOCKS AND THE THREE BEARS | MARGARET O'BRIEN | | CB-32 | $6.00 | $12.00 |
| DC-122 | 3 | 25044 - 6 | LET'S FLY TO MEXICO | MARGARET O'BRIEN | | CC-71 | $6.00 | $12.00 |
| DC-123 | 3 | 25047 - 9 | STORIES FOR CHILDREN: TOWN MUSICIANS, 3 BILLY-GOATS GRUFF | MARGARET O'BRIEN | | CC-21 | $6.00 | $12.00 |
| BD-124 | 4 | 20157 - 60 | SO DEAR TO MY HEART | JOHN BEAL | | DD-109 | $15.00 | $30.00 |
| DC-127 | 3 | 25057 - 9 | STORIES FOR CHILDREN, VOL. I: PUSS IN BOOTS, RUMPLESTILTSKIN, JACK & THE BEANSTALK | THE GREAT GILDERSLEEVE | | CD-11 | $5.00 | $10.00 |
| DBS-128 | 2 | 25060 - 1 | THE BRAVE LITTLE TAILOR | THE GREAT GILDERSLEEVE | | CD-33 | $5.00 | $10.00 |
| DBS-129 | 2 | 25062 - 3 | HANSEL AND GRETEL | THE GREAT GILDERSLEEVE | | CD-33 | $5.00 | $10.00 |
| DBS-130 | 2 | 25064 - 5 | CINDERELLA | THE GREAT GILDERSLEEVE | | CD-69 | $5.00 | $10.00 |
| DBS-131 | 2 | 25066 - 7 | SNOW WHITE AND ROSE RED | THE GREAT GILDERSLEEVE | | CD-69 | $5.00 | $10.00 |

*ISSUED AS BOX SET: DCN-78 **ISSUED AS BOX SET: DCN-115 ***ISSUED AS BOX SET: DCN-119

## CAPITOL MAIN SERIES 10" ALBUMS AND SINGLES

| SET # | # REC | DISC # | MAIN TITLE | ARTIST | YEAR | ALSO ISSUED ON | G/VG | EX/NMT |
|---|---|---|---|---|---|---|---|---|
| DAS-132 | 1 | 25068 | RUMPLESTILTSKIN | THE GREAT GILDERSLEEVE | | CD-11 | $5.00 | $10.00 |
| DBS-133 | 2 | 25069 - 70 | SONGS FOR CHILDREN | TEX RITTER | | | $8.00 | $15.00 |
| DBS-134 | 2 | 25071 - 2 | CHILDREN'S SONGS AND STORIES | TEX RITTER | | BD-14 | $8.00 | $15.00 |
| DAS-138 | 1 | 25073 | FAVORITE FAIRY TALES, V. 1: SLEEPING BEAUTY/THE PRINCESS WHO COULD NOT LAUGH | MARGARET O'BRIEN | | | $5.00 | $10.00 |
| DAS-143 | 1 | 30040 | FAVORITE FAIRY TALES, V. 2: THE FROG PRINCE/ LITTLE RED RIDING HOOD | MARGARET O'BRIEN | | | $5.00 | $10.00 |
| DC-253 | 3 | 15660 - 2 | BOZO'S CIRCUS BAND | BOZO'S CIRCUS BAND | | | $10.00 | $20.00 |
| DAS-3011 | 1 | 30038 | IN JINGLE JUNGLE LAND/THE LAUGHING HYENA SONG | PINTO COLVIG | 1949 | | $4.00 | $8.00 |
| EAS-3012 (12") | 1 | 30039 | GOSSAMER WUMP | FRANK MORGAN | | | $25.00 | $50.00 |
| DBX-3013 | 2 | 30041 - 2 | THE THREE LITTLE PIGS | DON WILSON | | | $5.00 | $10.00 |
| EAS-3016 (12") | 1 | 30045 | TICKETY TOCK | KNOX MANNING & ARTHUR Q. BRYAN | | | $5.00 | $10.00 |
| CCN-3019 | 3 | 30050 - 2 | SPARKY'S MUSIC MIX-UP | HENRY BLAIR | | | $12.00 | $25.00 |
| DBX-3021 | 2 | 30056 - 7 | BUGS BUNNY IN STORYLAND | MEL BLANC | | | $5.00 | $10.00 |
| DBX-3023 | 2 | 32150 - 1 | BOZO AT THE DOG SHOW | PINTO COLVIG | | | $10.00 | $20.00 |
| DAS-3028 | 1 | 30069 | FAVORITE FAIRY TALES, V. 3: BEAUTY & THE BEAST/ THE PRINCESS & THE PEA | MARGARET O'BRIEN | | | $4.00 | $8.00 |
| DBX-3032 | 2 | 30075 - 6 | WOODY WOODPECKER AND HIS TALENT SHOW | MEL BLANC | | | $12.00 | $25.00 |
| DBX-3033 | 2 | 30077 - 8 | BOZO AND THE BIRDS | PINTO COLVIG | | | $10.00 | $20.00 |
| DBX-3034 | 2 | 30079 - 80 | THE GRASSHOPPER AND THE ANTS | DON WILSON | | | $12.00 | $25.00 |
| DAS-3046 | 1 | 30110 | BOZO'S LAUGHING SONG/GOONEY GOOSE | PINTO COLVIG | | | $4.00 | $8.00 |
| ECD-3047 (12") | 3 | 30111 - 3 | DOROTHY AND THE WIZARD OF OZ | ROSEMARY RICE | | | $20.00 | $40.00 |
| EAS-3048 (12") | 1 | 30114 | MISTER TOAD | BASIL RATHBONE | | | $25.00 | $50.00 |
| DC-3049 | 3 | 30115 - 7 | THE STORY OF JESUS | CLAUDE RAINS | | | $40.00 | $80.00 |
| DBS-3051 | 2 | 30126 - 7 | LITTLE JOHNNY STRIKEOUT | JOE DIMAGGIO | | | $50.00 | $100.00 |
| CAS-3054 | 1 | 32001 | GERALD MCBOING-BOING | THE GREAT GILDERSLEEVE | 1950 | | $25.00 | $50.00 |
| DBX-3056 | 2 | 32153 - 4 | THE LADY AND THE TRAMP | ORIGINAL CAST OF THE MOVIE | | | $12.00 | $25.00 |
| DC-3057 | 3 | 32002 - 4 | WALT DISNEY SONGS | HAPPY JACK SMITH | | | $12.00 | $25.00 |
| CBX-3058 | 2 | 32005 - 6 | HOPALONG CASSIDY & THE SINGING BANDIT | WILLIAM BOYD | | | $12.00 | $25.00 |
| CAS-3071 | 1 | 32010 | FRANCIS THE TALKING MULE/A MULE IS A FOOL | CHILL WILLS | | | $10.00 | $20.00 |
| CAS-3072 | 1 | 32011 | BUGS BUNNY MEETS HIAWATHA | MEL BLANC | | | $8.00 | $15.00 |
| CAS-3073 | 1 | 32012 | DAFFY DUCK MEETS YOSEMITE SAM | MEL BLANC | | | $8.00 | $15.00 |
| CAS-3074 | 1 | 32013 | TWEETIE PIE | MEL BLANC | | | $8.00 | $15.00 |
| CBX-3075 | 2 | 32014 - 5 | HOPALONG CASSIDY & THE SQUARE-DANCE HOLD-UP | WILLIAM BOYD | | | $12.00 | $25.00 |
| DBX-3076 | 2 | 32016 - 7 | BOZO ON THE FARM | PINTO COLVIG | | | $10.00 | $20.00 |
| DBS-3077 | 2 | 32018 - 9 | BUGS BUNNY SINGS: DAFFY DUCK'S RHAPSODY, I'M SO GLAD THAT I'M BUGS BUNNY/I TAUT I TAW A PUDDY TAT, YOSEMITE SAM | MEL BLANC | | | $8.00 | $15.00 |
| DBS-3078 | 2 | 32020 - 1 | SUNDAY SCHOOL SONGS FOR CHILDREN | TEX RITTER | | | $5.00 | $10.00 |
| CAS-3079 | 1 | 32026 | FROSTY THE SNOWMAN/THE TUBBY THE TUBA SONG | JERRY MARLOWE | | | $4.00 | $8.00 |
| CAS-3080 | 1 | 32022 | DESTINATION MOON | TOM REDDY | | | $37.00 | $75.00 |
| DC-3081 | 3 | 32023 - 5 | BABY SNOOKS LEARNS: TO TELL THE TRUTH, ETC. | FANNY BRICE | | | $15.00 | $30.00 |
| CAS-3082 | 1 | 32027 | GABBY THE GOBBLER/THE LITTLE RED HEN | KEN CARSON | | | $3.00 | $6.00 |
| CAS-3083 | 1 | 32028 | THE TEDDY BEARS' PICNIC/I'M A LITTLE TEA POT | FRANK DEVOL | | | $3.00 | $6.00 |

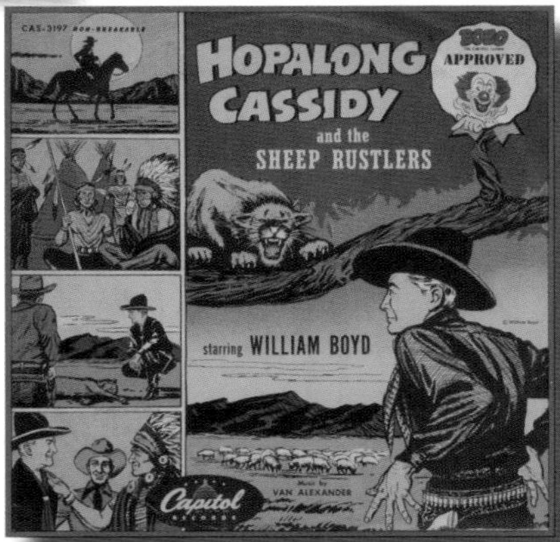


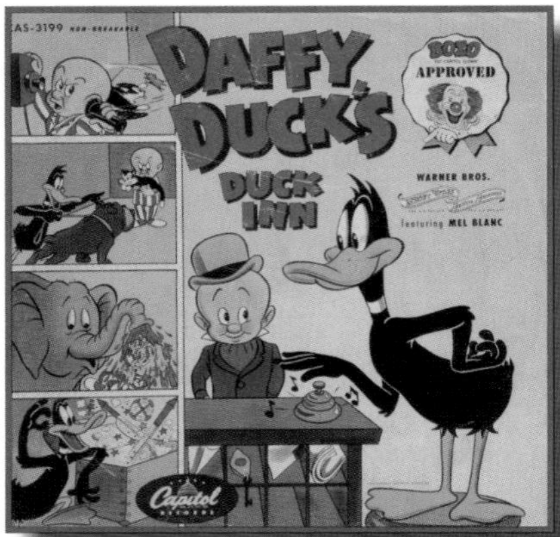


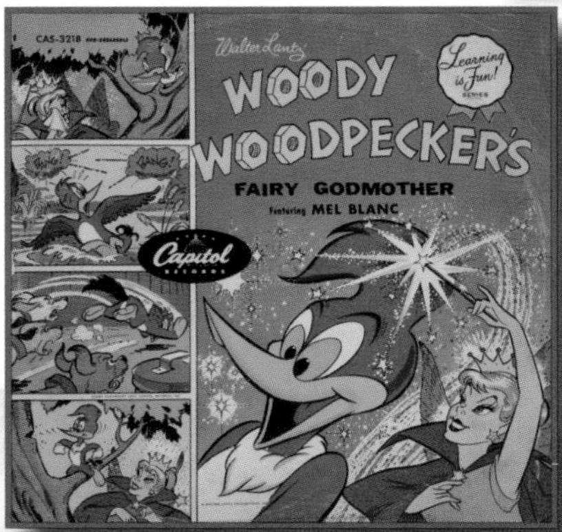


CAPITOL RECORDS
HOPALONG CASSIDY AND THE SHEEP RUSTLERS $25.00

CAPITOL RECORDS
DAFFY DUCK'S DUCK INN
$15.00

CAPITOL RECORDS
WOODY WOODPECKER'S FAIRY GODMOTHER $15.00

## CAPITOL MAIN SERIES 10" ALBUMS AND SINGLES

| SET # | # REC | DISC # | MAIN TITLE | ARTIST | YEAR | G/VG | EX/NMT |
|---|---|---|---|---|---|---|---|
| CAS-3084 | 1 | 32029 | DO YOU BELIEVE IN SANTA CLAUS?/I DON'T WANT A LOT FOR CHRISTMAS | SANTA CLAUS & SPARKY | | $5.00 | $10.00 |
| CAS-3085 | 1 | 32030 | RUDOLPH THE RED-NOSED REINDEER/CHRISTMAS BOOGIE | SUGAR CHILE ROBINSON | | $3.00 | $6.00 |
| DAT-3086 | 1 | 32031 | TEENA, THE LAUGHING HYENA | PINTO COLVIG | 1951 | $8.00 | $15.00 |
| DAT-3087 | 1 | 32032 | PANCHITO, THE LITTLE DONKEY WHO COULD NOT BRAY | LARRY MOREY | | $8.00 | $15.00 |
| CAS-3088 | 1 | 32033 | I'M GLAD I'M NOT A RUBBER BALL | ARTHUR Q. BRYAN | | $5.00 | $10.00 |
| CAS-3089 | 1 | 32034 | THE WHISTLE AND HIS DOG | JERRY MARLOWE | | $3.00 | $6.00 |
| CAS-3090 | 1 | 32035 | PETER COTTONTAIL | JIMMY WAKELY | | $3.00 | $6.00 |
| DBS-3091 | 2 | 32036 - 7 | WOODY WOODPECKER'S PICNIC | MEL BLANC | | $12.00 | $25.00 |
| CAS-3092 | 1 | 32038 | THE FLYING MOUSE | DON WILSON | | $4.00 | $8.00 |
| DAT-3093 | 1 | 32039 | CASPER, THE CURIOUS KITTEN | STANLEY MYERS | | $3.00 | $6.00 |
| DBS-3094 | 2 | 32040 - 1 | THE SORCERER'S APPRENTICE | DON WILSON | | $5.00 | $10.00 |
| CAS-3095 | 1 | 32042 | FERDINAND THE BULL | DON WILSON | | $5.00 | $10.00 |
| CAS-3096 | 1 | 32043 | THREE ORPHAN KITTENS | DON WILSON | | $5.00 | $10.00 |
| CAS-3098 | 1 | 32045 | HENRY HAWK | MEL BLANC | | $8.00 | $15.00 |
| CAS-3099 | 1 | 32046 | ELMER THE ELEPHANT | DON WILSON | | $4.00 | $8.00 |
| CAS-3100 | 1 | 32047 | BLUETAIL, THE RED FOX/THE NOISE SONG | TEX RITTER | | $3.00 | $6.00 |
| DBX-3102 | 2 | 32049 - 50 | TWEETY'S PUDDY TAT TWOUBLE | MEL BLANC | | $10.00 | $20.00 |
| CAS-3103 | 1 | 32051 | CARBON, THE COPY CAT/MR. BUZZARD | TEX RITTER | 1952 | $3.00 | $6.00 |
| CAS-3104 | 1 | 32052 | I TAUT I TAW A PUDDY TAT/YOSEMITE SAM | MEL BLANC | | $8.00 | $15.00 |
| CAS-3105 | 1 | 32053 | I'M POPEYE THE SAILOR MAN/LITTLE WHITE DUCK | CANDY CANDIDO | | $8.00 | $15.00 |
| CAS-3106 | 1 | 32054 | BR'ER RABBIT AND THE TAR BABY | JAMES BASKETT | | $10.00 | $20.00 |
| CAS-3107 | 1 | 32055 | BR'ER RABBIT'S LAUGHING PLACE | JAMES BASKETT | | $8.00 | $15.00 |
| CAS-3108 | 1 | 32056 | BR'ER RABBIT RUNS AWAY | JAMES BASKETT | | $8.00 | $15.00 |
| CAS-3109 | 1 | 32062 | HOPALONG CASSIDY AND THE TWO-LEGGED WOLF | WILLIAM BOYD | | $12.00 | $25.00 |
| CAS-3110 | 1 | 32058 | HOPALONG CASSIDY AND THE STORY OF TOPPER | WILLIAM BOYD | | $12.00 | $25.00 |
| CAS-3111 | 1 | 32059 | BUGS BUNNY MEETS ELMER FUDD | MEL BLANC | | $10.00 | $20.00 |
| CAS-3112 | 1 | 32060 | DAFFY DUCK FLIES SOUTH | MEL BLANC | | $10.00 | $20.00 |
| CAS-3113 | 1 | 32061 | PORKY PIG IN AFRICA | MEL BLANC | | $10.00 | $20.00 |
| CAS-3114 | 1 | 32057 | HOPPY'S HAPPY BIRTHDAY | WILLIAM BOYD | | $12.00 | $25.00 |
| CAS-3115 | 1 | 32063 | TABLE MANNERS/TRUTHFULNESS | FANNY BRICE (BABY SNOOKS) | | $8.00 | $15.00 |
| CAS-3116 | 1 | 32064 | CLEANLINESS/GOOD AND BAD | FANNY BRICE (BABY SNOOKS) | | $8.00 | $15.00 |
| CAS-3117 | 1 | 32065 | CROSSING STREETS/KINDNESS TO ANIMALS | FANNY BRICE (BABY SNOOKS) | | $8.00 | $15.00 |
| CAS-3118 | 1 | 32066 | TWEET, TWEET, TWEET | MEL BLANC | | $8.00 | $15.00 |
| CAS-3119 | 1 | 32067 | BUGS BUNNY AND THE GROW-SMALL JUICE | MEL BLANC | | $8.00 | $15.00 |
| CAS-3120 | 1 | 32068 | THE NOISY EATER | JERRY LEWIS | | $10.00 | $20.00 |

## CAPITOL MAIN SERIES 10" ALBUMS AND SINGLES

| SET # | # REC | DISC # | MAIN TITLE | ARTIST | YEAR | G/VG | EX/NMT |
|---|---|---|---|---|---|---|---|
| CAS-3121 | 1 | 32069 | TWAS THE NIGHT BEFORE CHRISTMAS | THE MELLOMEN | | $3.00 | $6.00 |
| CAS-3122 | 1 | 32070 | JOSEPH AND THE COAT OF MANY COLORS | CLAUDE RAINS | | $4.00 | $8.00 |
| CAS-3123 | 1 | 32071 | DAVID AND GOLIATH | CLAUDE RAINS | | $4.00 | $8.00 |
| CAS-3124 | 1 | 32072 | THE LAUGHING HYENA SONG/IN JINGLE JUNGLE LAND | PINTO COLVIG | | $4.00 | $8.00 |
| CAS-3125 | 1 | 32073 | FILBERT THE FROG/MY MULE CHARLIE | PINTO COLVIG | | $4.00 | $8.00 |
| CAS-3126 | 1 | 32074 | BOZO'S SONG/HONKETY HANK | PINTO COLVIG | | $4.00 | $8.00 |
| CAS-3127 | 1 | 32075 | BOZO'S LAUGHING SONG/GOONEY GOOSE | PINTO COLVIG | | $4.00 | $8.00 |
| CAS-3128 | 1 | 32076 | NURSERY RHYMES | KEN CARSON | | $3.00 | $6.00 |
| CAS-3129 | 1 | 32077 | NURSERY SONGS | KEN CARSON | | $3.00 | $6.00 |
| CAS-3130 | 1 | 32078 | NOAH AND THE ARK | CLAUDE RAINS | | $3.00 | $6.00 |
| DBX-3133 | 2 | 32081 – 2 | BOZO HAS A PARTY | PINTO COLVIG | | $10.00 | $20.00 |
| CAS-3134 | 1 | 32083 | SPARKY'S MAGIC ECHO | LEE LEDOUX | | $10.00 | $20.00 |
| CAS-3135 | 1 | 32084 | COUNTRY COUSIN | DON WILSON | | $8.00 | $15.00 |
| CAS-3136 | 1 | 32085 | LITTLE HIAWATHA | DON WILSON | | $8.00 | $15.00 |
| CAS-3137 | 1 | 32086 | HENRY HAWK'S CHICKEN HUNT | MEL BLANC | | $8.00 | $15.00 |
| DBX-3138 | 2 | 32087 – 8 | ROBIN HOOD | NESTOR PALVA | | $12.00 | $25.00 |
| CAS-3139 | 1 | 32089 | BUGS BUNNY AND ALADDIN'S LAMP | MEL BLANC | | $8.00 | $15.00 |
| CAS-3140 | 1 | 32090 | WOODY WOODPECKER AND THE SCARECROW | MEL BLANC | | $8.00 | $15.00 |
| CAS-3141 | 1 | 32091 | OLD MACDONALD HAD A FARM/SWINGIN' ON A STAR | RUFE DAVIS | 1953 | $3.00 | $6.00 |
| CAS-3142 | 1 | 32092 | THE LITTLE ENGINE THAT COULD/THE OLD SOW SONG | RUFE DAVIS | | $3.00 | $6.00 |
| CAS-3143 | 1 | 32093 | TEENA THE LAUGHING HYENA | PINTO COLVIG | | $4.00 | $8.00 |
| CAS-3144 | 1 | 32094 | ANIMAL FAIR/I WAS BORN A HUNDRED YEARS AGO | TEX RITTER | | $4.00 | $8.00 |
| CAS-3145 | 1 | 32095 | THANK YOU/THE BIG ROCK CANDY MOUNTAIN* | TEX RITTER | | $4.00 | $8.00 |
| CAS-3146 | 1 | 32096 | CACTUS JACK HAD A RANCH/THE GREEN GRASS GROWS ALL AROUND | TEX RITTER | | $4.00 | $8.00 |
| CAS-3147 | 1 | 32097 | DAFFY DUCK'S FEATHERED FRIEND | MEL BLANC | | $8.00 | $15.00 |
| CAS-3148 | 1 | 32098 | SYLVESTER AND HIPPETY HOPPER | MEL BLANC | | $8.00 | $15.00 |
| CAS-3149 | 1 | 32099 | WOODY WOODPECKER AND THE ANIMAL CRACKERS | MEL BLANC | | $8.00 | $15.00 |
| CAS-3151 | 1 | 32101 | LITTLE SONGS FOR LITTLE PEOPLE | DON WILSON | | $4.00 | $8.00 |
| CAS-3153 | 1 | 32103 | THE UGLY DUCKLING | STAN FREBERG & DON WILSON | | $4.00 | $8.00 |
| CAS-3154 | 1 | 32104 | BOZO'S NURSERY SONGS | PINTO COLVIG | | $4.00 | $8.00 |
| CAS-3155 | 1 | 32105 | THE E. I. O. SONG/THE TWEET AND TOOT | MEL BLANC | | $8.00 | $15.00 |
| CAS-3156 | 1 | 32106 | YOU'RE NOTHING BUT A NOTHIN'/BARNACLE BILL THE SAILOR | CANDY CANDIDO | | $3.00 | $6.00 |
| CAS-3157 | 1 | 32107 | BLUE BOTTLE FLY/SMART ALEC CROW | SMILEY BURNETT | | $8.00 | $15.00 |
| CAS-3158 | 1 | 32108 | THE GRANDADDY FROG/THE COURTIN' CRICKET | SMILEY BURNETT | | $8.00 | $15.00 |
| CAS-3159 | 1 | 32109 | THE DONKEY ENGINE/I WISH THAT I'D SAID THAT | SMILEY BURNETT | | $8.00 | $15.00 |
| CAS-3160 | 1 | 32110 | RUDOLPH THE RED-NOSED REINDEER/THE SWISS BOY | SMILEY BURNETT | | $8.00 | $15.00 |
| CAS-3161 | 1 | 32111 | WOODY WOODPECKER AND THE LOST MONKEY | MEL BLANC | | $4.00 | $8.00 |
| CAS-3162 | 1 | 32112 | DINKY PINKY | STAN FREBERG | | $6.00 | $12.00 |
| CAS-3163 | 1 | 32113 | FOLLOWING THE LEADER/NEVER SMILE AT A CROCODILE | JERRY LEWIS | | $6.00 | $12.00 |
| CAS-3164 | 1 | 32114 | HOPALONG CASSIDY AND THE MAIL TRAIN ROBBERY | WILLIAM BOYD | | $12.00 | $25.00 |
| DBX-3165 | 2 | 32115 – 6 | MICKEY MOUSE'S BIRTHDAY PARTY | STAN FREBERG | | $15.00 | $30.00 |
| CAS-3166 | 1 | 32117 | HOPALONG CASSIDY AND THE HAUNTED GOLDMINE | WILLIAM BOYD | | $12.00 | $25.00 |
| CAS-3167 | 1 | 32118 | ONE MISTY, MOISTY MORNING/MUSKRAT | TEX RITTER | | $3.00 | $6.00 |
| CAS-3168 | 1 | 32119 | BUGS BUNNY AND RABBIT SEASONING | MEL BLANC | | $8.00 | $15.00 |
| CAS-3169 | 1 | 32120 | SNOWBOUND TWEETY | MEL BLANC | | $8.00 | $15.00 |
| CAS-3170 | 1 | 32121 | LITTLE RED MONKEY/PUSSY CAT PARADE | MEL BLANC | | $8.00 | $15.00 |
| CAS-3171 | 1 | 32122 | WOODY WOODPECKER AND HIS SPACE SHIP | MEL BLANC | | $8.00 | $15.00 |
| CAS-3172 | 1 | 32123 | WILD WEST HENRY HAWK | MEL BLANC | 1954 | $8.00 | $15.00 |
| CAS-3173 | 1 | 32124 | BOZO'S MERRY GO ROUND MUSIC, RIDE 1 | PINTO COLVIG | | $4.00 | $8.00 |
| CAS-3174 | 1 | 32125 | BOZO'S MERRY GO ROUND MUSIC, RIDE 2 | PINTO COLVIG | | $4.00 | $8.00 |
| CAS-3188 | 1 | 32127 | PIED PIPER PUSSYCAT | MEL BLANC | | $4.00 | $8.00 |
| CAS-3189 | 1 | 32128 | PEPPY POSSUM | DAWS BUTLER | | $12.00 | $25.00 |
| CAS-3190 | 1 | 32129 | THE NAGGER | JERRY LEWIS | | $12.00 | $25.00 |

*EXISTENCE NOT VERIFIED.

## CAPITOL MAIN SERIES 10" ALBUMS AND SINGLES

| SET # | # REC | DISC # | MAIN TITLE | ARTIST | YEAR | G/VG | EX/NMT |
|---|---|---|---|---|---|---|---|
| CAS-3191 | 1 | 32130 | I TAN'T WAIT TIL QUITHMUTH DAY/YAH, DAS IST EIN CHRISTMAS TREE | MEL BLANC | | $12.00 | $25.00 |
| CAS-3192 | 1 | 32131 | I SAW MOMMY KISSING SANTA CLAUS/WHERE DID MY SNOWMAN GO | MOLLY BEE | | $3.00 | $6.00 |
| CAS-3193 | 1 | 32132 | CHIN CHOW AND THE GOLDEN BIRD/LITTLE ABOU, THE CAMEL* | DON WILSON | | $3.00 | $6.00 |
| DAS-3194 | 1 | 32133 | EL TORITO, THE LITTLE BULL* | DON WILSON | | $3.00 | $6.00 |
| DAS-3195 | 1 | 32134 | THE SEASONS* | DON WILSON | | $3.00 | $6.00 |
| CAS-3196 | 1 | 32135 | THE LITTLE ENGINE THAT LAUGHED | DON WILSON | | $3.00 | $6.00 |
| CAS-3197 | 1 | 32126 | HOPALONG CASSIDY AND THE SHEEP RUSTLERS | WILLIAM BOYD | | $12.00 | $25.00 |
| CAS-3198 | 1 | 32137 | ROB ROY (THE HIGHLAND ROGUE) | ART GILMORE | | $3.00 | $6.00 |
| CAS-3199 | 1 | 32128 | DAFFY DUCK'S DUCK INN | MEL BLANC | | $8.00 | $15.00 |
| CAS-3200 | 1 | 32129 | BUGS BUNNY AND THE PIRATE | MEL BLANC | | $8.00 | $15.00 |
| CAS-3202 | 1 | 32141 | HAPPY HANDS/LITTLE WENDY WHY WHY | TEX RITTER | | $4.00 | $8.00 |
| CAS-3203 | 1 | 32142 | PINOCCHIO | ART GILMORE & TOM CONWAY | | $5.00 | $10.00 |
| DAS-3204 | 1 | 32143 | WALTZ OF THE FLOWERS | ART GILMORE | | $2.00 | $4.00 |
| CAS-3205 | 1 | 32144 | THE LITTLE ENGINE THAT COULD | ART GILMORE | | $3.00 | $6.00 |
| DBX-3206 | 2 | 32145 - 6 | SPARKY'S MAGIC BATON | LEE LEDOUX | | $4.00 | $20.00 |
| DAS-3207 | 1 | 32147 | THE TROJAN HORSE* | ART GILMORE | | $2.00 | $4.00 |
| CAS-3208 | 1 | 32148 | TWO LITTLE MAGIC WORDS/HAS ANYBODY SEEN MY KITTY** | TEX RITTER | | $3.00 | $6.00 |
| DAS-3209 | 1 | 32149 | DIANA AND THE GOLDEN APPLES* | ART GILMORE | | $2.00 | $4.00 |
| CAS-3210 | 1 | 32155 | BOZO'S SONGS ABOUT GOOD MANNERS** | PINTO COLVIG | | $4.00 | $8.00 |
| CAS-3211 | 1 | 32156 | WOODY WOODPECKER AND THE TRUTH TONIC** | MEL BLANC | | $8.00 | $15.00 |
| CAS-3212 | 1 | 32157 | TWEETY'S GOOD DEED** | MEL BLANC | | $8.00 | $15.00 |
| CAS-3213 | 1 | 32158 | LOTS OF FUN TO SHARE/PARTY SONG** | MEL BLANC | | $5.00 | $10.00 |
| CAS-3214 | 1 | 32159 | MAXIE THE TAXI | EDDIE CANTOR | | $4.00 | $20.00 |
| CAS-3216 | 1 | 32161 | THE PUPPY DOG DREAM** | JERRY LEWIS | 1955 | $8.00 | $15.00 |
| CAS-3217 | 1 | 32162 | LITTLE TOOT LOST IN THE FOG | ART GILMORE | | $3.00 | $6.00 |
| CAS-3218 | 1 | 32163 | WOODY WOODPECKER'S FAIRY GODMOTHER** | MEL BLANC | | $8.00 | $15.00 |
| CAS-3219 | 1 | 32164 | D-O-G SPELLS DOG, D-O-G | MEL BLANC | | $8.00 | $15.00 |
| DAS-3220 | 1 | 32165 | PEER GYNT'S ADVENTURES ON THE STORMY SEA* | ART GILMORE | | $2.00 | $4.00 |
| DAS-3221 | 1 | 32166 | ANITRA'S DANCE/ARABIAN DANCE* | ART GILMORE | | $2.00 | $4.00 |
| DAS-3222 | 1 | 32167 | PEER GYNT'S ADVENTURES IN THE HALL OF THE MOUNTAIN KING* | ART GILMORE | | $2.00 | $4.00 |
| CAS-3224 | 1 | 32168 | CHILDREN'S SONGS FROM FRANCE** | GISELE MACKENZIE | | $2.00 | $4.00 |
| CAS-3225 | 1 | 32169 | IT'S FUN TO BE GENEROUS/WHEEZY, WOOZY WHATMOBILE** | MEL BLANC | | $8.00 | $15.00 |
| CAS-3227 | 1 | 32171 | MRS. HAZARD'S HOUSE** | MEL BLANC | | $8.00 | $15.00 |
| CAS-3228 | 1 | 32172 | IT DOESN'T HURT A BIT TO BE POLITE/PICK UP AFTER YOU** | TEX RITTER | | $3.00 | $6.00 |
| CAS-3229 | 1 | 32173 | BALLAD OF DAVY CROCKETT/FAREWELL** | TENNESSEE ERNIE FORD | | $4.00 | $20.00 |
| CAS-3230 | 1 | 32174 | WOODY WOODPECKER IN MIXED-UP LAND** | MEL BLANC | | $8.00 | $15.00 |
| CAS-3231 | 1 | 32175 | HOPALONG CASSIDY AND A BOY'S BEST FRIEND | WILLIAM BOYD | | $12.00 | $25.00 |
| DAS-3232 | 1 | 32176 | SWAN LAKE/FREDERIC & THE DANCING LEAF* | ART GILMORE | | $2.00 | $4.00 |
| DAS-3233 | 1 | 32177 | THE SLEEPING BEAUTY/THE STORY OF SUZETTE* | ART GILMORE | | $2.00 | $4.00 |
| DAS-3234 | 1 | 32178 | THE THREE-CORNERED HAT/INVITATION TO THE DANCE* | ART GILMORE | | $2.00 | $4.00 |
| CAS-3235 | 1 | 32179 | TALES OF DAVY CROCKETT | TENNESSEE ERNIE FORD | | $8.00 | $15.00 |
| CAS-3236 | 1 | 32180 | WOODY WOODPECKER AND DAVY CROCKETT | MEL BLANC | | $8.00 | $15.00 |
| CAS-3240 | 1 | 32184 | SAVE UP YOUR PENNIES/DAY DREAMING DADDY | MEL BLANC | | $8.00 | $15.00 |
| CAS-3242 | 1 | 32185 | TOY TIGER/THE THREE FISHERMEN | FRANK DEVOL | | $2.00 | $4.00 |
| CAS-3243 | 1 | 32186 | THE OLD CHISHOLM TRAIL/NIGHT HERDING SONG | ROGER WAGNER CHORALE | 1956 | $2.00 | $4.00 |
| CAS-3244 | 1 | 32187 | HOME ON THE RANGE/BLUE TAIL FLY, OH DEAR | ROGER WAGNER CHORALE | | $2.00 | $4.00 |
| CAS-3245 | 1 | 32188 | WORKING ON THE RAILROAD/SKIP TO MY LOU, CINDY | ROGER WAGNER CHORALE | | $2.00 | $4.00 |
| CAS-3247 | 1 | 32189 | THE MARCH OF THE SIAMESE CHILDREN/GETTING TO KNOW YOU | DEBORAH KERR, ALFRED NEWMAN | | $4.00 | $8.00 |
| DBS-4010 | 2 | 45007 - 8 | SQUARE DANCE PARTY FOR YOUNG FOLKS | LES GOTCHER | | $2.00 | $4.00 |

*MUSIC APPRECIATION SERIES **LEARNING IS FUN SERIES

CAPITOL RECORDS
BALLAD OF DAVY CROCKETT
$20.00

CAPITOL RECORDS
BLUE BOTTLE FLY
$10.00

CAPITOL RECORDS
SONGS ABOUT DOGS
$2.00

## CAPITOL TINY TUNE SERIES 10" SINGLES

| SET # | # REC | DISC # | ARTIST | A TITLE | B TITLE | ALSO ISSUED ON | G/VG | EX/NMT |
|---|---|---|---|---|---|---|---|---|
| 30000 | 1 | 3367/8 | NANCY MARTIN | THE STRANGE KANGAROO* | THE HUGE ELEPHANT | J-11 | $1.00 | $2.00 |
| 30001 | 1 | 3365/6 | NANCY MARTIN | THE BIG LION | THE FUNNY MONKEY | J-4 | $1.00 | $2.00 |
| 30002 | 1 | 3369/70 | NANCY MARTIN | THE FUZZY DANCING BEARS | THE SHINY SEAL | | $1.00 | $2.00 |
| 30003 | 1 | 3371/2 | NANCY MARTIN | THE FAT HIPPOPOTAMUS | THE STRIPED ZEBRAS | | $1.00 | $2.00 |
| 30004 | 1 | 3433/4 | JACK SMITH | TWO UNUSUAL MEN: MICHAEL FINNEGAN, ROBINSON CRUSOE | SONGS ABOUT THE SEA: BLOW THE MAN DOWN, I'VE BEEN TO FRANCE | (B) J-11 | $1.00 | $2.00 |
| 30005 | 1 | 3435/6 | JACK SMITH | ANIMAL SONGS: THE BEAR WENT OVER THE MOUNTAIN, ETC. | CALENDAR SONG | | $1.00 | $2.00 |
| 30006 | 1 | 3437-8 | JACK SMITH | HOLIDAYS: JINGLE BELLS, ETC. | FOUR FUNNY PEOPLE: SIMPLE SIMON, ETC. | | $1.00 | $2.00 |
| 30007 | 1 | 3439/40 | JACK SMITH | TEN LITTLE "INJUNS" | THE GIGGELY PIG | (B) J-22 | $1.00 | $2.00 |
| 30008 | 1 | 3481/2 | THE THREE PIXIES | SONGS ABOUT BIRDS: THE CUCKOO, SING A SONG OF SIXPENCE | RIG-A-JIG-JIG | J-7 | $1.00 | $2.00 |
| 30009 | 1 | 3483/4 | THE THREE PIXIES | SONGS ABOUT DOGS: BINGO (JOHNNY HAD A LITTLE DOG), THE DOG AND CAT | A FROG HE WOULD A-WOOING GO | | $1.00 | $2.00 |
| 30010 | 1 | 3485/6 | THE THREE PIXIES | THREE OLD MEN: OLD KING COLE, ETC. | SONGS ABOUT CHILDREN: JACK HORNER, ETC. | | $1.00 | $2.00 |
| 30011 | 1 | 3487/8 | THE THREE PIXIES | SONGS ABOUT FOOD: PEASE PORRIDGE HOT, ETC. | MOTHER GOOSE SOUNDS: DING DONG BELL, ETC. | | $1.00 | $2.00 |
| 05-30081 | 1 | 4226/7 | JACK SMITH | A CAPITOL SHIP FOR AN OCEAN TRIP* | ABDUL, THE BULBUL AMEER | | $1.00 | $2.00 |
| 05-30082 | 1 | ? | JACK SMITH | THE ALPHABET SONG | ONE TWO BUCKLE MY SHOE | | $1.00 | $2.00 |
| 05-30083 | 1 | ? | JACK SMITH | FRERE JACQUES | MARY HAD A LITTLE LAMB | | $1.00 | $2.00 |
| 05-30084 | 1 | ? | TEX RITTER | SHE'LL BE COMING 'ROUND THE MOUNTAIN WHEN SHE COMES | YANKEE DOODLE | | $2.00 | $4.00 |
| 05-30085 | 1 | 4715/6 | TEX RITTER | JESUS LOVES ME | I'LL BE A SUNBEAM (JESUS WANTS ME FOR A SUNBEAM) | | $2.00 | $4.00 |
| 05-30086 | 1 | ? | THE LOUIS CASTELLUCCI MILITARY BAND | STARS AND STRIPES FOREVER | ? | | $1.00 | $2.00 |
| 05-30087 | 1 | 1687A/B | THE LOUIS CASTELLUCCI MILITARY BAND | SEMPER FIDELIS | ? | | $1.00 | $2.00 |
| 05-30118 | 1 | ? | THE SPORTSMEN QUARTET | AWAY IN A MANGER | UP ON THE HOUSE-TOP | | $1.00 | $2.00 |
| 05-30119 | 1 | 4481/65 | THE SPORTSMEN QUARTET | DECK THE HALLS | PATAPAN | | $1.00 | $2.00 |
| 05-30120 | 1 | 4480/4 | HAL DERWIN WITH ORCHESTRA | JINGLE BELLS | I SAW THREE SHIPS | | $1.00 | $2.00 |
| 05-30121 | 1 | 3697/4845 | HAL DERWIN WITH ORCHESTRA | GOOD KING WENCESLAS | JOLLY OLD ST. NICHOLAS | | $1.00 | $2.00 |

*YEAR: 1949

## CAPITOL TOYLAND SERIES 6" SINGLES

| SET # | # REC | DISC # | ARTIST | A TITLE | B TITLE | YEAR | ALSO ISSUED ON | G/VG | EX/NMT |
|---|---|---|---|---|---|---|---|---|---|
| J-1 | 1 | 11514-5 | TEX RITTER | SHE'LL BE COMING 'ROUND THE MOUNTAIN WHEN SHE COMES | YANKEE DOODLE | 1953 | TINY TUNES 3008$4.00 | $2.00 | $4.00 |
| J-2 | 1 | 11516-7 | TEX RITTER | I'LL BE A SUNBEAM (JESUS WANTS ME FOR A SUNBEAM) | JESUS LOVES ME | | TINY TUNES 30085 | $2.00 | $4.00 |
| J-3 | 1 | 11492-3 | THE LOUIS CASTELLUCCI MILITARY BAND | STARS AND STRIPES FOREVER | STARS AND STRIPES FOREVER | | TINY TUNES 30086 | $1.00 | $2.00 |
| J-4 | 1 | 11505-6 | NANCY MARTIN | THE BIG LION | THE FUNNY MONKEY | | TINY TUNES 30001 | $1.00 | $2.00 |
| J-5 | 1 | ? | HAL DERWIN WITH ORCHESTRA | JINGLE BELLS | JOLLY OLD ST. NICHOLAS | | A) TINY TUNES 30084, B) 30121 | $1.00 | $2.00 |
| J-6 | 1 | 11486-7 | SMILIN' JACK SMITH | A CAPITOL SHIP FOR AN OCEAN TRIP | FRERE JACQUES | | A) TINY TUNES 30081; B) 30083 | $1.00 | $2.00 |
| J-7 | 1 | 11480-1 | THE THREE PIXIES | SONGS ABOUT BIRDS: THE CUCKOO, SING A SONG OF SIXPENCE | RIG-A-JIG-JIG | | TINY TUNES 30008 | $1.00 | $2.00 |
| J-8 | 1 | 11484-5 | JACK SMITH | THE ALPHABET SONG | ONE TWO BUCKLE MY SHOE | | TINY TUNES 30082 | $1.00 | $2.00 |
| J-9 | 1 | 11482-3 | THE THREE PIXIES | SONGS ABOUT CHILDREN: JACK HORNER, ETC. | SONGS ABOUT FOOD: PEASE PORRIDGE HOT, ETC. | | A) TINY TUNES 30011, B)30010 | $1.00 | $2.00 |
| J-10 | 1 | 11488-9 | JACK SMITH | MARY HAD A LITTLE LAMB | ABDUL, THE BULBUL AMEER | | A) TINY TUNES 30083, B) 30081 | $1.00 | $2.00 |
| J-11 | 1 | 11507-8 | NANCY MARTIN | THE STRANGE KANGAROO | THE STRIPED ZEBRAS | | A) TINY TUNES 30000, B) 30003 | $1.00 | $2.00 |
| J-12 | 1 | 11509-10 | PINTO COLVIG | BOZO AND HIS FRIENDS (PT. 1) | BOZO AND HIS FRIENDS (PT. 2) | | | $3.00 | $6.00 |
| J-13 | 1 | 3697-4844 | HAL DERWIN WITH ORCHESTRA | GOOD KING WENCESLAS | I SAW THREE SHIPS | 1955 | A) TINY TUNES 30121, B) 30120 | $1.00 | $2.00 |
| J-14 | 1 | 4631-65 | THE SPORTSMEN QUARTET | AWAY IN A MANGER | PATAPAN | | A) TINY TUNES 30018, B) 30119 | $1.00 | $2.00 |
| J-15 | 1 | ? | THE SPORTSMEN QUARTET | DECK THE HALLS | UP ON THE HOUSE-TOP | | A) TINY TUNES 30119, B) 30119 | $1.00 | $2.00 |
| J-17 | 1 | 11486-13488 | JACK SMITH | SONGS ABOUT THE SEA: A CAPITOL SHIP FOR AN OCEAN TRIP | SONGS ABOUT THE SEA: BLOW THE MAN DOWN; I'VE BEEN TO FRANCE | | A) TINY TUNES 30081, B) 30004 | $1.00 | $2.00 |
| J-22 | 1 | 13582-4 | THE THREE PIXIES AND JACK SMITH | SEVEN FUNNY PEOPLE: SIMPLE SIMON, ETC. | SEVEN FUNNY PEOPLE: OLD KING COLE, ETC. | | A) TINY TUNES 30006, B) 30010 | $1.00 | $2.00 |

## CAPITOL MISCELLANEOUS 10" SINGLES

| DISC # | ARTIST | A TITLE | B TITLE | YEAR | G/VG | EX/NMT |
|---|---|---|---|---|---|---|
| B-385 | SMILIN' ED MCCONNELL AND HIS BUSTER BROWN GANG | THE DOCTOR SONG | FUNNY THINGS | 1946 | $10.00 | $20.00 |
| 3353/4 | VOICES OF BOZO THE CLOWN & BUGS BUNNY | BOZO & BUGS TALK BIG BUSINESS | BOZO & BUGS TALK BIG BUSINESS | 1948 | $10.00 | $20.00 |
| NO # (7") | VOICE OF BOZO THE CLOWN | FEDDERS FAMILY ALBUM (PROMOTIONAL SAMPLER RECORD) | [ONE-SIDED PLAY ONLY] | | $12.00 | $25.00 |
| PR 17-8 (7") | VOICE OF BOZO THE CLOWN | BOZO & HIS FRIENDS (PROMOTIONAL SAMPLER RECORD) | | | $3.00 | $6.00 |
| PRO 162-3 | MEL BLANC | THE WOODY WOODPECKER SHOW | THE WOODY WOODPECKER SHOW | | $50.00 | $100.00 |
| 323 | JOHNNY MERCER AND THE PIED PIPERS | ZIP-A-DEE DOO DAH | EV'RYBODY HAS A LAUGHING PLACE | | $4.00 | $8.00 |
| B-447 | SMILIN' ED MCCONNELL AND HIS BUSTER BROWN GANG | THE TEACHER SONG | I'M A KITTY KATTY WAMPUS SUPERDOO | | $10.00 | $20.00 |
| B-464 | SMILIN' ED MCCONNELL AND HIS BUSTER BROWN GANG | THE BACKWARDS SONG | ME AND I | | $10.00 | $20.00 |
| 1360 | MEL BLANC | I TAWT I TAW A PUDDY TAT | YOSEMITE SAM | | $4.00 | $8.00 |
| 1560 | FRANK DEVOL | HOPALONG CASSIDY MARCH | CIRCUS DAYS | | $5.00 | $10.00 |
| 1830 | TENNESSEE ERNIE FORD | A ROOTIN' TOOTIN' SANTA CLAUS | CHRISTMAS DINNER | | $4.00 | $8.00 |
| 1997 | GISELLE MCKENZIE | EGGBERT THE EASTER EGG | BENNY, THE BOB-TAILED BUNNY | | $3.00 | $6.00 |
| 2567 | MOLLY BEE | THIS IS MY DOG | GOD BLESS US ALL | | $1.00 | $2.00 |
| 6170-1 | MEL BLANC | I TAWT I TAW A PUDDY TAT | YOSEMITE SAM | | $4.00 | $8.00 |
| 27000 | SMILIN' ED MCCONNELL AND HIS BUSTER BROWN GANG | THE DOCTOR SONG | FUNNY THINGS | | $10.00 | $20.00 |
| 27001 | SMILIN' ED MCCONNELL AND HIS BUSTER BROWN GANG | THE TEACHER SONG | I'M A KITTY KATTY WAMPUS SUPERDOO | | $10.00 | $20.00 |

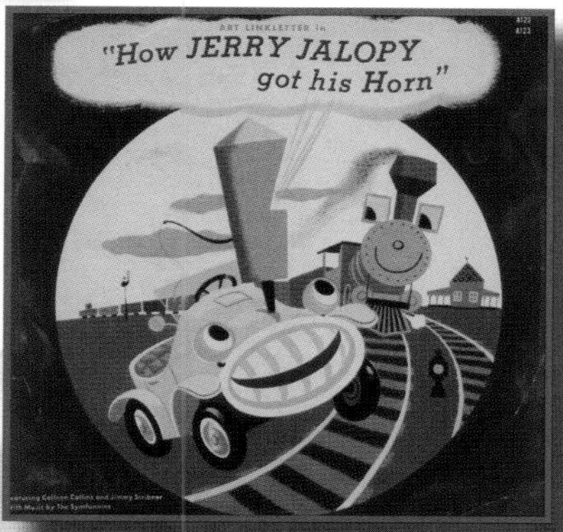

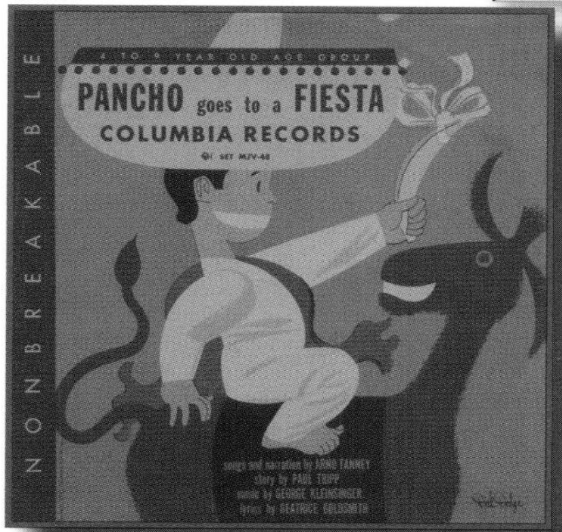


COLOR TUNES
HOW JERRY JALOPY GOT HIS HORN
$15.00

COLUMBIA RECORDS
JACK AND THE BEANSTALK
$8.00

COLUMBIA RECORDS
PANCHO GOES TO A FIESTA
$12.00

## COLUMBIA RECORD-A-VIEW 10" ALBUMS

| SET # | # REC | DISC # | MAIN TITLE | ARTIST | A TITLE | B TITLE | G/VG | EX/NMT |
|---|---|---|---|---|---|---|---|---|
| V-8506 | 1 | 54385-6 | LET'S TAKE A TRIP TO WASHINGTON, D.C.* | SONNY FOX, GINGER MACMANUS, PUD FLANAGAN | LET'S TAKE A TRIP TO WASHINGTON, D.C. (PT. 1) | LET'S TAKE A TRIP TO WASHINGTON, D.C. (PT. 2) | $5.00 | $10.00 |
| V-8507 | 1 | 54387-8 | LET'S TAKE A TRIP TO THE ZOO* | SONNY FOX, GINGER MACMANUS, PUD FLANAGAN | LET'S TAKE A TRIP TO THE ZOO (PT. 1) | LET'S TAKE A TRIP TO THE ZOO (PT. 2) | $5.00 | $10.00 |
| V-8508 | 1 | 54359-60 | SOME OF MY FRIENDS ARE BIRDS* | EDDIE BRACKEN WITH RAY CARTER ORCHESTRA | SOME OF MY FRIENDS ARE BIRDS (PT. 1) | SOME OF MY FRIENDS ARE BIRDS (PT. 2) | $5.00 | $10.00 |

*PRICES SHOWN ARE WITH VIEW-MASTER REEL: SUBTRACT $3.00 IF REEL IS MISSING.

## COLUMBIA 10" AND 12" ALBUMS

| SET # | # REC | DISC # | MAIN TITLE | ARTIST | A TITLE | YEAR | ALSO ISSUED ON | G/VG | EX/NMT |
|---|---|---|---|---|---|---|---|---|---|
| C-47 | 4 | 36018 - 21 | SQUARE DANCES | CARSON ROBINSON & HIS OLD TIMERS | | | | $2.00 | $4.00 |
| C-48 | 4 | 36035 - 8 | MARCHES | THE GOLDMAN BAND | | | | $2.00 | $4.00 |
| C-58 | 4 | 36166 - 9 | CIRCUS* | RINGLING BROS & BARNUM BAILEY BAND | | 1946 | | $5.00 | $10.00 |
| C-94 | 4 | 36653 - 6 | CHRISTMAS CAROLS | THE LYNN MURRAY SINGERS | | | | $2.00 | $4.00 |
| C-103 | 4 | 36733 - 6 | THE WAYFARING STRANGER | BURL IVES | | | | $5.00 | $10.00 |
| C-120 | 4 | 37183 - 6 | GENE AUTRY'S WESTERN CLASSICS | GENE AUTRY | | | H-1 | $5.00 | $10.00 |
| C-191 | 4 | 38650 - 3 | SOUSA-GOLDMAN MARCHES | THE GOLDMAN BAND | | | | $2.00 | $4.00 |
| C-213 | 4 | 38935 - 8 | MORE FOLKSONGS BY BURL IVES* | BURL IVES | | 1950 | | $5.00 | $10.00 |
| C-343 | 4 | 40070 - 3 | CHRISTMAS WITH JIMMY BOYD | JIMMY BOYD | | CVRFT | | $5.00 | $10.00 |
| C-348 | 3 | 40109 - 12 | CHRISTMAS WITH ARTHUR GODFREY | ARTHUR GODFREY | | | | $5.00 | $10.00 |
| C-516 | 2 | 40476 - 7 | DAVY CROCKETT: INDIAN FIGHTER** | FESS PARKER & BUDDY EBSEN | INDIAN FIGHTER | 1955 | | $25.00 | $50.00 |
| C-517 | 2 | 40478 - 9 | DAVY CROCKETT: GOES TO CONGRESS** | FESS PARKER & BUDDY EBSEN | GOES TO CONGRESS | | | $25.00 | $50.00 |
| C-518 | 2 | 40480 - 1 | DAVY CROCKETT: AT THE ALAMO** | FESS PARKER & BUDDY EBSEN | AT THE ALAMO | | | $25.00 | $50.00 |
| H-1 | 4 | 20084 - 7 | GENE AUTRY'S WESTERN CLASSICS* | GENE AUTRY | | 1947 | C-120 | $5.00 | $10.00 |
| H-3 | 4 | 20195 - 8 | SONGS OF THE SMOKY MOUNTAINS | ROY ACUFF & SMOKEY MTN. BOYS | | | | $5.00 | $10.00 |
| H-5 | 4 | 20414 - 7 | SWING YOUR PARTNER | ARKANSAS (ARKIE) WOODCHOPPER & HIS SQUARE DANCE BAND | | | | $2.00 | $4.00 |
| H-6 | 4 | 20481 - 4 | EARLY AMERICAN FOLK SONGS | BOB ATSCHER | | | | $3.00 | $6.00 |
| MX-212 | 2 | 11673 - 4 | THE SORCERER'S APPRENTICE | MPLS ORCH. | | | | $10.00 | $20.00 |
| MX-239 | ? | ? | CINDERELLA | ? | | | | $5.00 | $10.00 |
| MX-315 | ? | ? | STRAUSS WALTZES | THE PHILADELPHIA ORCH; EUGENE ORMANDY, COND | | | | $2.00 | $4.00 |
| MX-320 | ? | ? | MOTHER GOOSE SUITE | RAVEL | | 1947 | | $5.00 | $10.00 |

*NOT SPECIFICALLY FOR CHILDREN **BOX AND GATEFOLD ISSUES

## COLUMBIA 10" AND 12" ALBUMS

| SET # | # REC | DISC # | MAIN TITLE | ARTIST | YEAR | G/VG | EX/NMT |
|---|---|---|---|---|---|---|---|
| MM-350 (12") | ? | ? | THROUGH THE LOOKING GLASS | HOWARD BARLOW, CBS SYMPHONY ORCH | | $4.00 | $8.00 |
| MM-395 (12") | 3 | 70067 - 9-D | THE NUTCRACKER SUITE | FREDERICK STOCK, COND. | | $10.00 | $20.00 |
| MM-477 (12") | 3 | 11650 - 2-D | PETER AND THE WOLF | BASIL RATHBONE | 1941 | $10.00 | $20.00 |
| MM-506 (12") | 5 | 11795 - 9 | DON QUIXOTE | FRITZ REINER, PGH SYMPH. | | $8.00 | $15.00 |
| MM-521 (12") | 3 | 11883 - 5-D | A CHRISTMAS CAROL | BASIL RATHBONE | 1942 | $10.00 | $20.00 |
| MM-553 (12") | 3 | 7413 - 5-M | TREASURE ISLAND | BASIL RATHBONE | 1944 | $10.00 | $20.00 |
| MM-583 (12") | 4 | 7436 - 9 | ROBIN HOOD | BASIL RATHBONE | 1945 | $10.00 | $20.00 |
| MM-627 (12") | 3 | 12386 - 8-D | NUTCRACKER SUITE | ARTUR RODZINSKI, COND. | | $10.00 | $20.00 |
| MM-632 (12") | 4 | 74689 - 91-M | HANSEL AND GRETEL | BASIL RATHBONE, JANE POWELL | 1946 | $10.00 | $20.00 |
| MM-640 (10") | 3 | 4345 - 7-M | THE WHALE WHO WANTED TO SING AT THE MET | NELSON EDDY | | $25.00 | $50.00 |
| MM-659 (12") | 4 | 7488 - 91-M | THE THREE MUSKETEERS | ERROL FLYNN | 1947 | $15.00 | $30.00 |
| MM-700 (12") | 3 | 7574 - 6-M | THE ADVENTURES OF OLIVER TWIST AND FAGIN | BASIL RATHBONE | | $10.00 | $20.00 |
| MM-703 (12") | ? | ? | YOUNG PEOPLE'S GUIDE TO THE ORCHESTRA | ? | | $5.00 | $10.00 |
| MM-713 (12") | 4 | 7581 - 4-M | ALICE IN WONDERLAND | JANE POWELL | | $10.00 | $20.00 |
| MM-714 (12") | 3 | 7585 - 7-M | NUTCRACKER SUITE | ANDRE KOSTELANETZ, COND. | | $10.00 | $20.00 |
| MM-767 (12") | 3 | 7613 - 5-M | SINBAD THE SAILOR | BASIL RATHBONE | 1948 | $10.00 | $20.00 |
| MM-848 (12") | 4 | 7640 - 3-M | CHRISTMAS MUSIC FOR ORCHESTRA | MORTON GOULD & HIS ORCH. | | $3.00 | $3.00 |
| MM-856 (12") | 3 | 7248 - 50-M | CHRISTMAS CAROLS | MT. HOLYOKE COLLEGE GLEE CLUB | | $3.00 | $3.00 |
| MM-857 (12") | 3 | 17594 - 6-D | CHRISTMAS CAROLS | CELEBRITY QUARTETTE | | $3.00 | $3.00 |
| M-905 (12") | 3 | 11-8353 - 5 | KIPLING'S JUNGLE BOOK | SABU | | $15.00 | $30.00 |
| MM-931 (12") | 6 | 7657 - 62-M | PETER PAN | LEONARD BERNSTEIN; BORIS KARLOFF | 1950 | $15.00 | $30.00 |
| MM-1034 (12") | 2 | 7746 - 7-M | PETER AND THE WOLF | ? | 1953 | $10.00 | $20.00 |
| MOP-26 (12") | 12 | 12646 - 57-D | HANSEL AND GRETEL | METROPOLITAN OPERA ASSN, MAX RUDOLPH, COND. | 1947 | $15.00 | $30.00 |
| X-180 (12") | 2 | 70370 - 1-D | PEER GYNT SUITE NO. 1 | SIR THOMAS BEECHAM, COND. | | $5.00 | $10.00 |

## COLUMBIA MISCELLANEOUS SINGLES, 10" AND 12"

| REC # | DISC # | ARTIST | A TITLE | B TITLE | YEAR | G/VG | EX/NMT |
|---|---|---|---|---|---|---|---|
| 1 | A-1691 | BILLY WILLIAMS | WHERE DOES DADDY GO WHEN HE GOES OUT? | WHEN FATHER PAPERED THE PARLOR | 1914 | $2.00 | $4.00 |
| 1 | A-2101 | ADELINE FRANCIS | THE SHOEMAKER AND THE BROWNIES | THE MOUSE AND THE THOMAS CAT | 1916 | $2.00 | $4.00 |
| 1 | A-2133 | PRINCE'S ORCHESTRA | CHILDREN'S SONGS AND GAMES | ? | | $2.00 | $4.00 |
| 1 | A-2369 | COLUMBIA STELLAR QUARTET | MEDLEY OF CHILDREN'S SONGS (PT. 1) | MEDLEY OF CHILDREN'S SONGS (PT. 2) | 1917 | $2.00 | $4.00 |
| 1 | A-2377 | ADELINE FRANCIS | JOHNNY'S CHRISTMAS DREAM OF OLD MOTHER GOOSE (PT. 1) | JOHNNY'S CHRISTMAS DREAM OF OLD MOTHER GOOSE (PT. 2) | | $2.00 | $4.00 |
| 1 | A-2380 | ADELINE FRANCIS | CINDERELLA, OR THE GLASS SLIPPER (PT. 1) | CINDERELLA, OR THE GLASS SLIPPER (PT. 2) | | $2.00 | $4.00 |
| 1 | A-2490 | HENRY BURR | A BABY'S PRAYER AT TWILIGHT | LORRAINE | | $2.00 | $4.00 |
| 1 | A-2605 | SIGNOR HURDI-GURDI | SONGS OF YOUR CHILDHOOD DAYS | ? | 1918 | $2.00 | $4.00 |
| 1 | A-2800 | COLUMBIA ORCHESTRA | THE KIDDIES CHRISTMAS FROLIC (PT. 1 — MORNING) | THE KIDDIES CHRISTMAS FROLIC (PT. 2 — EVENING) | 1919 | $2.00 | $4.00 |
| 1 | A-2996 | ? | CHILDREN'S TOY MARCH | CHILDREN'S TOY SYMPHONY | 1920 | $2.00 | $4.00 |
| 1 | A-3014 | EDUCATIONAL DEPARTMENT | FORGE IN THE FOREST | JOLLY COPPERSMITH | | $2.00 | $4.00 |
| 1 | A-3042 | PRINCE'S BAND | THE ASSEMBLY MARCH | BATTLESHIP CT. MARCH | | $2.00 | $4.00 |
| 1 | A-3124 | ? | RIDER'S STORY/CHILDREN'S DANCE | HALLOWEEN/ON THE TRAIN | | $2.00 | $4.00 |
| 1 | A-3130 | COLUMBIA MINIATURE ORCHESTRA | RATALPAN, SERENATA, WALTZ NO. 5 | GYPSY RONDO, SHADOWS | | $2.00 | $4.00 |
| 1 | A-3146 | BESSIE CALKINS SHIPMAN | PUSSY WILLOW, MY LITTLE YELLOW DUCK | APRIL BLOSSOMS, APRIL SHOWS | | $2.00 | $4.00 |
| 1 | A-3148 | BESSIE CALKINS SHIPMAN | SINGING GAMES: LOOBY LOO, ETC. | SINGING GAMES: LONDON BRIDGE, ETC. | | $2.00 | $4.00 |
| 1 | A-3151 | EDMUND VANCE COOKE | THE MONKEY MAN, THE SHAVE STORE | THE MOW-COW-MOO, THE HIGH GIRAFFE | | $2.00 | $4.00 |
| 1 | A-7515 (12") | EDUCATIONAL DEPARTMENT | WASHINGTON POST MARCH | PETITS PIERROTS MARCH | 1918 | $2.00 | $4.00 |

## COLUMBIA MISCELLANEOUS SINGLES — ALL SIZES

| REC # | DISC # | ARTIST | A TITLE | B TITLE | ALSO ISSUED AS | G/VG | EX/NMT |
|---|---|---|---|---|---|---|---|
| 1 | A-7524 (12") | THORNTON BURGESS | JOHNNY CHUCK FINDS THE BEST THINGS IN THE WORLD | THE JOY OF THE BEAUTIFUL PINE | | $12.00 | $25.00 |
| 1 | A-7525 (12") | THORNTON BURGESS | PETER RABBIT PLAYS A JOKE | LITTLE JOE OTTER'S SLIPPERY SLIDE | | $12.00 | $25.00 |
| 1 | A-7526 (12") | THORNTON BURGESS | HOW OLD MR. TOAD WON A RACE | HOW OLD MR. TOAD HAPPENED TO DINE WITH BUSTER BEAR | | $12.00 | $25.00 |
| 1 | A-7527 (12") | THORNTON BURGESS | BUSTER BEAR GETS A GOOD BREAKFAST | WHEN OLD MR. TOAD WAS PUFFED UP | | $12.00 | $25.00 |
| 1 | A-7528 (12") | THORNTON BURGESS | THE TEACHING OF REDDY FOX | LITTLE JOE OTTER TRIES TO GET EVEN | | $12.00 | $25.00 |
| 1 | S-3022 | ? | DIXIE | STAR-SPANGLED BANNER | | $1.50 | $3.00 |
| 1 | S-3041 | PRINCE'S BAND | I SEE YOU | NORWEGIAN MOUNTAIN DANCE | | $1.50 | $3.00 |
| 1 | 1478-D | PAUL WHITEMAN | FELIX THE CAT | MOTHER GOOSE PARADE | | $5.00 | $10.00 |
| 1 | 1698-D | ETHEL & DOROTHEA PONCE | I FAW DOWN AN' GO BOOM! | DOWN WHERE THE LOLLY-POPS GROW | | $2.00 | $4.00 |
| 1 | 2319-D | GUY LOMBARDO | BABY'S BIRTHDAY PARTY | ? | | $2.00 | $4.00 |
| 1 | 17088-D | WALTER GIESEKING | THE CHILDREN'S CORNER SUITE (PT. 1) | THE CHILDREN'S CORNER SUITE (PT. 2) | | $2.00 | $4.00 |
| 1 | 319-M | HAROLD WILLIAMS & THE BBC MALE VOICE CHOIR | GRANDFATHER'S CLOCK | LITTLE BROWN JUG | | $2.00 | $4.00 |
| 1 | 340-M | RAWICZ & LANDAUER | NOLA | PARADE OF THE WOODEN SOLDIERS | | $2.00 | $4.00 |
| 1 | 4552-M | CHRISTOPHER LYNCH | SING A SONG OF SIXPENCE | LITTLE BOY BLUE | | $2.00 | $4.00 |
| 1 | 20377 | GENE AUTRY | AN OLD-FASHIONED TREE | HERE COMES SANTA CLAUS | | $3.00 | $6.00 |
| 1 | 20604 | GENE AUTRY | JOLLY OLD ST. NICK | ? | | $3.00 | $6.00 |
| 1 | 20616 | GENE AUTRY | SANTA, SANTA, SANTA | HE'S A CHUBBY LITTLE FELLOW | | $3.00 | $6.00 |
| 1 | 35766 | ? | MARCH OF THE TOYS | DOWN IN TOYLAND VILLAGE | | $3.00 | $6.00 |
| 1 | 37942 | GENE AUTRY | HERE COMES SANTA CLAUS | AN OLD-FASHIONED TREE | | $3.00 | $6.00 |
| 1 | 38170 | BUDDY CLARK | BLUE SHADOWS ON THE TRAIL (MELODY TIME: PECOS BILL) | BLUE | | $2.00 | $4.00 |
| 1 | 38197 | KAY KYSER'S CAMPUS COWBOYS | WOODY WOODPECKER | WHEN VERONICA PLAYS THE HARMONICA | | $3.00 | $6.00 |
| 1 | 38610 | GENE AUTRY | RUDOLPH THE RED-NOSED REINDEER | IF IT DOESN'T SNOW ON CHRISTMAS | | $3.00 | $6.00 |
| 1 | 38744 | MARY MARTIN & ARTHUR GODFREY | GO TO SLEEP, GO TO SLEEP, GO TO SLEEP | NON-KIDDIE | | $3.00 | $6.00 |
| 1 | 38750 | GENE AUTRY | PETER COTTONTAIL | THE FUNNY LITTLE BUNNY | | $3.00 | $6.00 |
| 1 | 38766 | ROSEMARY CLOONEY | I FOUND MY MAMMA | ME AND MY TEDDY BEAR | MJ-70 | $3.00 | $6.00 |
| 1 | 38907 | GENE AUTRY | FROSTY THE SNOWMAN | ? | | $3.00 | $6.00 |
| 1 | 38591 | BURL IVES | MR. FROGGIE WENT A-COURTIN' | THE WORRIED MAN BLUES | J-227 | $3.00 | $6.00 |
| 1 | 39068 | ARTHUR GODFREY | THE THING | YEA-BOO | | $3.00 | $6.00 |
| 1 | 39328 | PERCY FAITH, BURL IVES | ON TOP OF OLD SMOKEY | SYNCOPATED CLOCK | | $3.00 | $6.00 |
| 1 | 39542 | GENE AUTRY | POPPY THE PUPPY | HE'LL BE COMING DOWN THE CHIMNEY | MJV-122 | $3.00 | $6.00 |
| 1 | 39543 | GENE AUTRY | THE THREE LITTLE DWARFS | ? | J-121 | $3.00 | $6.00 |
| 1 | 39612 | ROSEMARY CLOONEY | SUZY SNOWFLAKE | LITTLE RED RIDING HOOD'S CHRISTMAS TREE | MJV-123 | $2.00 | $4.00 |
| 1 | 39696 | JIMMY BOYD | GOD'S LITTLE CANDLES | OWL LULLABY | | $3.00 | $6.00 |
| 1 | 39871 | JIMMY BOYD | I SAW MOMMY KISSING SANTA | THUMBELINA | MJV-152 | $3.00 | $6.00 |
| 1 | 39906 | DORIS DAY | YOUR MOTHER AND MINE | ? | | $3.00 | $6.00 |
| 1 | 39945 | JIMMY BOYD | THE LITTLE BOY AND THE OLD MAN | TELL ME A STORY | MJV-161 | $3.00 | $6.00 |
| 1 | 39951 | CHRISTOPHER LYNCH | LITTLE BOY BLUE | SING A SONG OF SIXPENCE | | $3.00 | $6.00 |
| 1 | 39988 | JIMMY BOYD & ROSEMARY CLOONEY | DENNIS THE MENACE | LITTLE JOSEY | MJV-182 | $3.00 | $6.00 |
| 1 | 40007 | JIMMY BOYD | SHOO-FLY PIE AND APPLE PAN DOWDY | PLAYMATES | (B) J-202 | $3.00 | $6.00 |
| 1 | 40049 | JIMMY BOYD | MARCO, THE POLO PONY | GOD BLESS US ALL | J-181 | $3.00 | $6.00 |
| 1 | 40056 | ROSEMARY CLOONEY | SHOO, TURKEY SHOO | LONELY AM I (NON-KIDDIE) | | $3.00 | $6.00 |
| 1 | 40080 | JIMMY BOYD | SANTA GOT STUCK IN THE CHIMNEY | I SAID A PRAYER FOR SANTA | MJV-183 | $3.00 | $6.00 |
| 1 | 40092 | GENE AUTRY | FREDDIE, THE LITTLE FIR TREE | WHERE DID MY SNOWMAN GO | MJV-172 | $3.00 | $6.00 |
| 1 | 40106 | GAYLA PEEVEY | I WANT A HIPPOPOTAMUS FOR CHRISTMAS | ARE MY EARS ON STRAIGHT | MJV-186 | $3.00 | $6.00 |
| 1 | 40138 | JIMMY BOYD | BLUES | JELLY ON MY HEAD | MJV-172 | $3.00 | $6.00 |

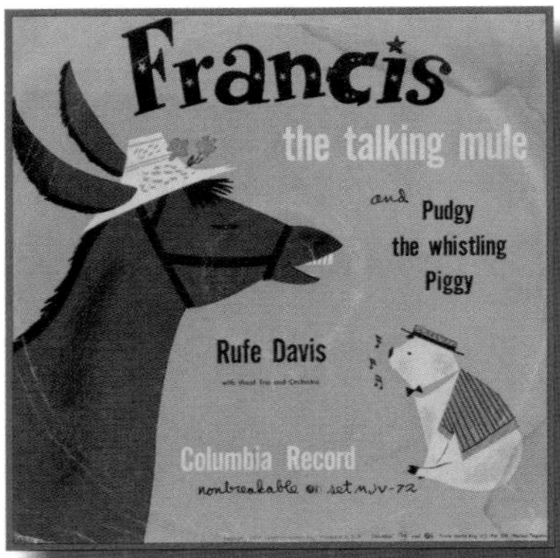


COLUMBIA RECORDS
FRANCIS THE TALKING MULE
$40.00

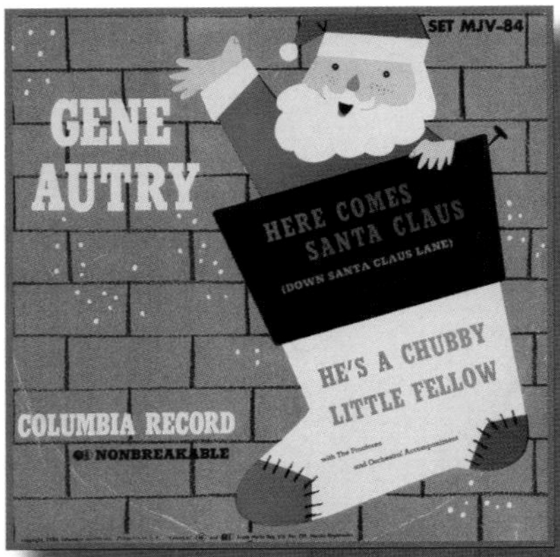


COLUMBIA RECORDS
HERE COMES SANTA CLAUSE
$8.00

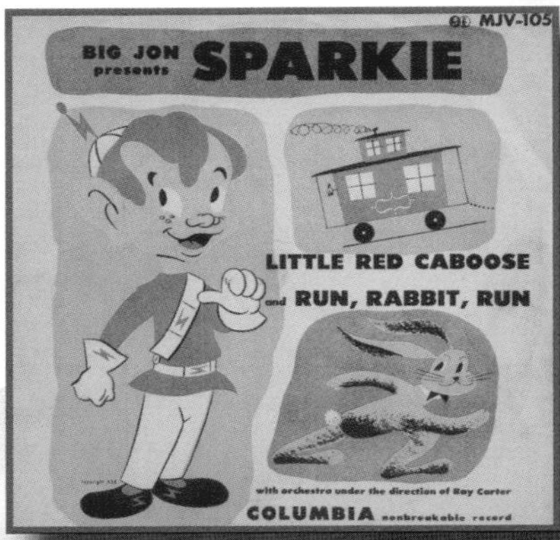


COLUMBIA RECORDS
LITTLE RED CABOOSE
$10.00

## COLUMBIA MISCELLANEOUS SINGLES — ALL SIZES

| REC # | DISC # | ARTIST | A TITLE | B TITLE | ALSO ISSUED AS | G/VG | EX/NMT |
|---|---|---|---|---|---|---|---|
| 1 | 40167 | GENE AUTRY | THE HORSE WITH THE EASTER BONNET | EASTER MORNIN' | MJV-194 | $3.00 | $6.00 |
| 1 | 40181 | JIMMY BOYD | LITTLE BONNIE BUNNY | JIMMY ROLL ME GENTLY | MJV-199 | $3.00 | $6.00 |
| 1 | 40182 | GAYLA PEEVEY | THREE LITTLE BUNNIES | WISH I WUZ A WHISKER | MJV-198 | $3.00 | $6.00 |
| 1 | 40218 | JIMMY BOYD AND GAYLA PEEVEY | I'M SO GLAD | KITTY IN THE BASKET | | $3.00 | $6.00 |
| 1 | 40253 | JIMMY BOYD & GAYLA PEEVEY | MA, I MISS YOUR APPLE PIE | SHEPHERD BOY | | $3.00 | $6.00 |
| 1 | 40264 | GAYLA PEEVEY | A DOG NAMED JOE | UPSY DOWN TOWN | | $3.00 | $6.00 |
| 1 | 40364 | GAYLA PEEVEY | GOT A CODE IN THE NODE | ANGEL IN CHRISTMAS PLAY | | $3.00 | $6.00 |
| 1 | 40365 | JIMMY BOYD | SANTA CLAUS BLUES | I SAW MOMMY DOING THE MAMBO | MJV-225 | $3.00 | $6.00 |
| 1 | 40384 | ? | BOW-WOW WANTS A BOY FOR CHRISTMAS | LITTLE RED RIDING HOOD | | $3.00 | $6.00 |
| 1 | 40400 | ART CARNEY | SANTA AND THE DOODLE-LI-BOOP | TWAS THE NIGHT BEFORE CHRIST-MAS | MJV-255 | $3.00 | $6.00 |
| 1 | 40425 | GAYLA PEEVEY | DADDY'S REPORT CARD | NIGHT I RAN AWAY | | $3.00 | $6.00 |
| 1 | 40449 | FESS PARKER | BALLAD OF DAVY CROCKETT | I GAVE MY LOVE | MJV-242 | $3.00 | $6.00 |
| 1 | 40602 | GAYLA PEEVEY | 77 SANTAS | RUBBER LEGS | | $3.00 | $6.00 |
| 1 | 40932 | GAYLA PEEVEY | ? | ? | | $3.00 | $6.00 |
| 1 | 44271/2 | ROSEMARY CLOONEY | FUZZY WUZZY | MY CHOC'LATE RABBIT | MJ-95 | $3.00 | $6.00 |
| 1 | 48003 | RICHIE ANDRUSCO | THE LITTLE FUGITIVE (PT. 1) | THE LITTLE FUGITIVE (PT. 2) | | $4.00 | $8.00 |
| 1 | 48921/3 | ROSEMARY CLOONEY | LITTLE RED MONKEY | LITTLE JOE WORM | MJV-164 | $3.00 | $6.00 |
| 1 | 18820-1 (7") | ROSEMARY CLOONEY/ROY ROGERS | DANDY, HANDY AND CANDY* | A MESSAGE FROM ROY ROGERS | | $5.00 | $10.00 |
| 1 | ZP 49870 (7") | NOT LISTED | FAMILY RECORD CLUB: STOP WORRYING... START LISTENING** | STOP WORRYING...START LISTENING | | $1.50 | $3.00 |
| 1 | NN1 | NORMAN LUBOFF CHOIR | NITEY NITE LULLABIES, SIDE 1 | NIGHTY NIGHT LULLABIES, SIDE 2 | | $2.00 | $4.00 |

*SPECIAL RECORD NOT FOR SALE. B SIDE PROMOTES ROY ROGERS TV SHOW. **PROMOTION RECORD

## COLUMBIA MUSIC FOR LIVING SERIES 10" SINGLES

| SET # | # REC | DISC # | MAIN TITLE | ARTIST | YEAR | G/VG | EX/NMT | REMARKS |
|---|---|---|---|---|---|---|---|---|
| JS-301 | 1 | 54058-9 | THROUGH THE DAY — ALBUM 1, BOOK 1 | NOT LISTED | 1956 | $1.00 | $2.00 | GRADE 1 |
| JS-302 | 1 | 54060-1 | THROUGH THE DAY — ALBUM 2, BOOK 1 | NOT LISTED | | $1.00 | $2.00 | |
| JS-303 | 1 | 54062-3 | THROUGH THE DAY — ALBUM 3, BOOK 1 | NOT LISTED | | $1.00 | $2.00 | |
| JS-304 | 1 | 54064-5 | THROUGH THE DAY — ALBUM 4, BOOK 1 | NOT LISTED | | $1.00 | $2.00 | |
| JS-305 | 1 | 54066-7 | THROUGH THE DAY — ALBUM 5, BOOK 1 | NOT LISTED | | $1.00 | $2.00 | |
| JS-306 | 1 | 54068-9 | THROUGH THE DAY — ALBUM 6, BOOK 1 | NOT LISTED | | $1.00 | $2.00 | |
| JS-307 | 1 | 54070-1 | THROUGH THE DAY — ALBUM 7, BOOK 1 | NOT LISTED | | $1.00 | $2.00 | |
| JS-308 | 1 | 54072-3 | THROUGH THE DAY — ALBUM 8, BOOK 1 | NOT LISTED | | $1.00 | $2.00 | |

## COLUMBIA MUSIC FOR LIVING SERIES 10" SINGLES

| SET # | # REC | DISC # | MAIN TITLE | ARTIST | G/VG | EX/NMT | REMARKS |
|---|---|---|---|---|---|---|---|
| JS-309 | 1 | 54074-5 | THROUGH THE DAY — ALBUM 9, BOOK 1 | NOT LISTED | $1.00 | $2.00 | |
| JS-310 | 1 | 54076-7 | THROUGH THE DAY — ALBUM 10, BOOK 1 | NOT LISTED | $1.00 | $2.00 | |
| JS-311 | 1 | 54251-2 | IN OUR TOWN — ALBUM 1, BOOK 2 | NOT LISTED | $1.00 | $2.00 | GRADE 2 |
| JS-312 | 1 | 54253-4 | IN OUR TOWN — ALBUM 2, BOOK 2 | NOT LISTED | $1.00 | $2.00 | |
| JS-313 | 1 | 54255-6 | IN OUR TOWN — ALBUM 3, BOOK 2 | NOT LISTED | $1.00 | $2.00 | |
| JS-314 | 1 | 54257-8 | IN OUR TOWN — ALBUM 4, BOOK 2 | NOT LISTED | $1.00 | $2.00 | |
| JS-315 | 1 | 54259-60 | IN OUR TOWN — ALBUM 5, BOOK 2 | NOT LISTED | $1.00 | $2.00 | |
| JS-316 | 1 | 54261-2 | IN OUR TOWN — ALBUM 6, BOOK 2 | NOT LISTED | $1.00 | $2.00 | |
| JS-317 | 1 | 54263-4 | IN OUR TOWN — ALBUM 7, BOOK 2 | NOT LISTED | $1.00 | $2.00 | |
| JS-318 | 1 | 54265-6 | IN OUR TOWN — ALBUM 8, BOOK 2 | NOT LISTED | $1.00 | $2.00 | |
| JS-319 | 1 | 54267-8 | IN OUR TOWN — ALBUM 9, BOOK 2 | NOT LISTED | $1.00 | $2.00 | |
| JS-320 | 1 | 54269-70 | IN OUR TOWN — ALBUM 10, BOOK 2 | NOT LISTED | $1.00 | $2.00 | |
| JS-321 | 1 | 56421-2 | NOW AND LONG AGO — ALBUM 1, BOOK 3 | NOT LISTED | $1.00 | $2.00 | GRADE 3 |
| JS-322 | 1 | 56423-4 | NOW AND LONG AGO — ALBUM 2, BOOK 3 | NOT LISTED | $1.00 | $2.00 | |
| JS-323 | 1 | 56425-6 | NOW AND LONG AGO — ALBUM 3, BOOK 3 | NOT LISTED | $1.00 | $2.00 | |
| JS-324 | 1 | 56427-8 | NOW AND LONG AGO — ALBUM 4, BOOK 3 | NOT LISTED | $1.00 | $2.00 | |
| JS-325 | 1 | 56429-30 | NOW AND LONG AGO — ALBUM 5, BOOK 3 | NOT LISTED | $1.00 | $2.00 | |
| JS-326 | 1 | 56431-2 | NOW AND LONG AGO — ALBUM 6, BOOK 3 | NOT LISTED | $1.00 | $2.00 | |
| JS-327 | 1 | 56433-4 | NOW AND LONG AGO — ALBUM 7, BOOK 3 | NOT LISTED | $1.00 | $2.00 | |
| JS-328 | 1 | 56435-6 | NOW AND LONG AGO — ALBUM 8, BOOK 3 | NOT LISTED | $1.00 | $2.00 | |
| JS-329 | 1 | 56437-8 | NOW AND LONG AGO — ALBUM 9, BOOK 3 | NOT LISTED | $1.00 | $2.00 | |
| JS-330 | 1 | 56439-40 | NOW AND LONG AGO — ALBUM 10, BOOK 3 | NOT LISTED | $1.00 | $2.00 | |
| JS-331 | 1 | 54094-5 | NEAR AND FAR — ALBUM 1, BOOK 4 | NOT LISTED | $1.00 | $2.00 | GRADE 4 |
| JS-332 | 1 | 54096-7 | NEAR AND FAR — ALBUM 2, BOOK 4 | NOT LISTED | $1.00 | $2.00 | |
| JS-333 | 1 | 54098-9 | NEAR AND FAR — ALBUM 3, BOOK 4 | NOT LISTED | $1.00 | $2.00 | |
| JS-334 | 1 | 54100-1 | NEAR AND FAR — ALBUM 4, BOOK 4 | NOT LISTED | $1.00 | $2.00 | |
| JS-335 | 1 | 54102-3 | NEAR AND FAR — ALBUM 5, BOOK 4 | NOT LISTED | $1.00 | $2.00 | |
| JS-336 | 1 | 54104-5 | NEAR AND FAR — ALBUM 6, BOOK 4 | NOT LISTED | $1.00 | $2.00 | |
| JS-337 | 1 | 54106-7 | NEAR AND FAR — ALBUM 7, BOOK 4 | NOT LISTED | $1.00 | $2.00 | |
| JS-338 | 1 | 54108-9 | NEAR AND FAR — ALBUM 8, BOOK 4 | NOT LISTED | $1.00 | $2.00 | |
| JS-339 | 1 | 54110-1 | NEAR AND FAR — ALBUM 9, BOOK 4 | NOT LISTED | $1.00 | $2.00 | |
| JS-340 | 1 | 54112-3 | NEAR AND FAR — ALBUM 10, BOOK 4 | NOT LISTED | $1.00 | $2.00 | |
| JS-341 | 1 | 56877-8 | IN OUR COUNTRY — ALBUM 1, BOOK 5 | NOT LISTED | $1.00 | $2.00 | GRADE 5 |
| JS-342 | 1 | 56879-80 | IN OUR COUNTRY — ALBUM 2, BOOK 5 | NOT LISTED | $1.00 | $2.00 | |
| JS-343 | 1 | 56881-2 | IN OUR COUNTRY — ALBUM 3, BOOK 5 | NOT LISTED | $1.00 | $2.00 | |
| JS-344 | 1 | 56883-4 | IN OUR COUNTRY — ALBUM 4, BOOK 5 | NOT LISTED | $1.00 | $2.00 | |
| JS-345 | 1 | 56885-6 | IN OUR COUNTRY — ALBUM 5, BOOK 5 | NOT LISTED | $1.00 | $2.00 | |
| JS-346 | 1 | 56887-8 | IN OUR COUNTRY — ALBUM 6, BOOK 5 | NOT LISTED | $1.00 | $2.00 | |
| JS-347 | 1 | 56889-90 | IN OUR COUNTRY — ALBUM 7, BOOK 5 | NOT LISTED | $1.00 | $2.00 | |
| JS-348 | 1 | 56891-2 | IN OUR COUNTRY — ALBUM 8, BOOK 5 | NOT LISTED | $1.00 | $2.00 | |
| JS-349 | 1 | 56893-4 | IN OUR COUNTRY — ALBUM 9, BOOK 5 | NOT LISTED | $1.00 | $2.00 | |
| JS-350 | 1 | 56895-6 | IN OUR COUNTRY — ALBUM 10, BOOK 5 | NOT LISTED | $1.00 | $2.00 | |
| JS-351 | 1 | 55960-1 | AROUND THE WORLD — ALBUM 1, BOOK 6 | NOT LISTED | $1.00 | $2.00 | GRADE 6 |
| JS-352 | 1 | 55962-3 | AROUND THE WORLD — ALBUM 2, BOOK 6 | NOT LISTED | $1.00 | $2.00 | |
| JS-353 | 1 | 55964-5 | AROUND THE WORLD — ALBUM 3, BOOK 6 | NOT LISTED | $1.00 | $2.00 | |
| JS-354 | 1 | 55966-7 | AROUND THE WORLD — ALBUM 4, BOOK 6 | NOT LISTED | $1.00 | $2.00 | |
| JS-355 | 1 | 55968-9 | AROUND THE WORLD — ALBUM 5, BOOK 6 | NOT LISTED | $1.00 | $2.00 | |
| JS-356 | 1 | 55970-1 | AROUND THE WORLD — ALBUM 6, BOOK 6 | NOT LISTED | $1.00 | $2.00 | |
| JS-357 | 1 | 55972-3 | AROUND THE WORLD — ALBUM 7, BOOK 6 | NOT LISTED | $1.00 | $2.00 | |
| JS-358 | 1 | 55974-5 | AROUND THE WORLD — ALBUM 8, BOOK 6 | NOT LISTED | $1.00 | $2.00 | |
| JS-359 | 1 | 55976-7 | AROUND THE WORLD — ALBUM 9, BOOK 6 | NOT LISTED | $1.00 | $2.00 | |
| JS-360 | 1 | 55978-9 | AROUND THE WORLD — ALBUM 10, BOOK 6 | NOT LISTED | $1.00 | $2.00 | |

## COLUMBIA PLAYTIME 200 SERIES 7" SINGLES

| # REC | DISC # | ARTIST | A TITLE | B TITLE | YEAR | G/VG | EX/NMT |
|---|---|---|---|---|---|---|---|
| 1 | 201 | IRVING KAUFMAN/ERNEST HARE | JACK AND JILL | OLD KING COLE | 1937 | $2.00 | $4.00 |
| 1 | 202 | VERNON DALHART/IRVING KAUFMAN | LITTLE BO-PEEP | MARY HAD A LITTLE LAMB | | $3.00 | $6.00 |
| 1 | 203 | JANE BARTLETT/IRVING KAUFMAN | ROCK-A-BYE BABY | SING A SONG OF SIXPENCE | | $2.00 | $4.00 |
| 1 | 204 | ERNEST HARE/ARTHUR HALL | TOM, TOM, THE PIPER'S SON | SIMPLE SIMON | | $2.00 | $4.00 |
| 1 | 205 | ARTHUR HALL/VERNON DALHART | THE THREE LITTLE KITTENS | WHERE ARE YOU GOING, MY PRETTY MAID? | | $3.00 | $6.00 |
| 1 | 206 | ERNEST HARE/VERNON DALHART | COCK-A-DOODLE DOO | OLD MOTHER HUBBARD | | $3.00 | $6.00 |
| 1 | 207 | ARTHUR HALL | GO ROUND THE MULBERRY BUSH | OATS, PEAS, AND BEANS | | $2.00 | $4.00 |
| 1 | 208 | ARTHUR HALL | LONDON BRIDGE IS FALLING DOWN | THE FARMER IN THE DELL | | $2.00 | $4.00 |
| 1 | 209 | ARTHUR HALL | LAZY MARY WILL YOU GET UP | TEN LITTLE DARKIES | | $8.00 | $15.00 |
| 1 | 210 | JEAN ALEXANDER | LITTLE RED RIDING HOOD | THE FROG PRINCE | | $2.00 | $4.00 |
| 1 | 211 | JEAN ALEXANDER | CINDERELLA | THE THREE BEARS | | $2.00 | $4.00 |
| 1 | 212 | ERNEST HARE | JACK AND THE BEANSTALK | TOM THUMB | | $2.00 | $4.00 |
| 1 | 213 | BILLY JONES/ARTHUR HALL | THE NIGHT BEFORE CHRISTMAS | TOMORROW WILL BE CHRISTMAS | | $2.00 | $4.00 |
| 1 | 214 | SANTA CLAUS & HIS BAND/MOTHER & LITTLE TOTS | THE COMING OF SANTA CLAUS | CHRISTMAS MORNING | | $5.00 | $10.00 |
| 1 | 215 | ERNEST HARE/ARTHUR HALL | SANTA CLAUS HIDES IN THE PHONOGRAPH | SANTA CLAUS WILL SOON BE HERE | | $6.00 | $12.00 |
| 1 | 216 | JANE BARTLETT | THE SANDMAN | SLUMBER BOAT | | $2.00 | $4.00 |
| 1 | 217 | JANE BARTLETT | GO TO SLEEP MY LITTLE PICKANINNY | THE DREAM MAN | | $8.00 | $15.00 |
| 1 | 218 | JANE BARTLETT | SWEET AND LOW | DOLL SONG | | $2.00 | $4.00 |
| 1 | 219 | ERNEST HARE/CHAS. HARRISON | STAR SPANGLED BANNER | COLUMBIA THE GEM OF THE OCEAN | | $2.00 | $4.00 |
| 1 | 220 | CHAS. HARRISON/VERNON DALHART | AMERICA | DIXIE | | $3.00 | $6.00 |
| 1 | 221 | ERNEST HARE/VERNON DALHART | YANKEE DOODLE | HAIL COLUMBIA | | $3.00 | $6.00 |
| 1 | 222 | ARTHUR FIELDS/ARTHUR HALL | I HAD A LITTLE DOGGY | MOTHER TABBYSKINS | | $2.00 | $4.00 |
| 1 | 223 | ARTHUR HALL | I LOVE LITTLE PUSSY | THREE LITTLE PIGS | | $2.00 | $4.00 |
| 1 | 224 | ARTHUR HALL | MISS JENIA JONES | WATER, WATER, WILDFLOWER; GO ROUND THE VALLEY | | $2.00 | $4.00 |
| 1 | 225 | ARTHUR HALL & ARTHUR FIELDS/ ARTHUR HALL & CO. | PUSS IN BOOTS | SLEEPING BEAUTY | | $2.00 | $4.00 |
| 1 | 226 | ARTHUR HALL/ARTHUR FIELDS | THE TOYMAN'S SHOP | A CHRISTMAS CAROL | | $2.00 | $4.00 |
| 1 | 227 | JANE BARTLETT | LULLABY (ERMINE) | BIRDIES' LULLABY | | $2.00 | $4.00 |
| 1 | 228 | ARTHUR FIELDS/VERNON DALHART | AMERICA, THE BEAUTIFUL | BATTLE HYMN OF THE REPUBLIC | | $3.00 | $6.00 |
| 1 | 229 | NOT LISTED | HEY, DIDDLE DIDDLE, ETC. | SEE SAW, ETC. | | $2.00 | $4.00 |
| 1 | 230 | NOT LISTED | LITTLE JACK HORNER, ETC. | THREE BLIND MICE, ETC. | | $2.00 | $4.00 |
| 1 | 231 | NOT LISTED | HUMPTY DUMPTY, ETC. | DING DONG DELL, ETC. | | $2.00 | $4.00 |
| 1 | 232 | NOT LISTED | LITTLE BOY BLUE, ETC. | BAA BAA BLACK SHEEP, ETC. | | $2.00 | $4.00 |
| 1 | 233 | ARTHUR HALL/ARTHUR FIELDS | OH DEAR! WHAT CAN THE MATTER BE | THE JOLLY MILLER | | $2.00 | $4.00 |
| 1 | 234 | ARTHUR FIELDS/ARTHUR HALL | TWINKLE, TWINKLE, LITTLE STAR | GOOD MORNING, MERRY SUNSHINE | | $2.00 | $4.00 |
| 1 | 235 | ARTHUR HALL | THE HOUSE THAT JACK BUILT | THE PLOUGH BOY IN LUCK | | $2.00 | $4.00 |
| 1 | 236 | ARTHUR HALL | A FROG HE WOULD A WOOING GO | THE DOG AND CAT | | $2.00 | $4.00 |
| 1 | 237 | ARTHUR HALL | THERE WAS AN OLD MAN WHO LIVED IN A SHOE | LITTLE ROBIN REDBREAST | | $2.00 | $4.00 |
| 1 | 238 | ? | SEE-SAW | OLD MOTHER GOOSE | | $2.00 | $4.00 |
| 1 | 239 | IRVING KAUFMAN/ARTHUR HALL | CALENDAR SONG | TRY AGAIN | | $2.00 | $4.00 |
| 1 | 240 | IRVING KAUFMAN/ARTHUR HALL | LITTLE DROPS OF WATER | THE BIRD BAND | | $2.00 | $4.00 |
| 1 | 241 | IRVING KAUFMAN | TEN LITTLE DARKIES | JINGLE BELLS | | $8.00 | $15.00 |
| 1 | 242 | VERNON DALHART | JESUS LOVES ME | ONWARD CHRISTIAN SOLDIERS | | $5.00 | $10.00 |
| 1 | 243 | VERNON DALHART | CHRIST WAS ONCE A LITTLE BABY | CHRISTMAS (MERRY MERRY CHRISTMAS BELLS) | | $5.00 | $10.00 |
| 1 | 244 | PLAYTIME DANCE ORCHESTRA | TAP DANCE | WALTZ CLOG | | $2.00 | $4.00 |
| 1 | 245 | PLAYTIME DANCE ORCHESTRA | MINUET | POLKA | | $2.00 | $4.00 |
| 1 | 246 | PLAYTIME DANCE ORCHESTRA | HIGHLAND FLING | SAILOR'S HORNPIPE | | $2.00 | $4.00 |

COLUMBIA RECORDS
ALL ABOARD SHOWBOAT W/MR.I. MAGINATION $20.00

COLUMBIA RECORDS
SKYLINER FLIGHT 35
$10.00

COLUMBIA RECORDS
ROCKY JONES AND THE SPACE PIRATES $50.00

## COLUMBIA PLAYTIME 200 SERIES 7" SINGLES

| # REC | DISC # | ARTIST | A TITLE | B TITLE | G/VG | EX/NMT |
|---|---|---|---|---|---|---|
| 1 | 247 | PLAYTIME DANCE ORCHESTRA | JIG | CHILDREN'S MARCH | $2.00 | $4.00 |
| 1 | 248 | UNCLE DON | MICKEY MOUSE SONG | THE ELEPHANT | $10.00 | $20.00 |
| 1 | 249 | ? | MOTHER GOOSE'S PARTY | THUMBKIN SAYS, I'LL DANCE | $2.00 | $4.00 |
| 1 | 250 | FRANK LUTHER | GAMES | SCHOOL STUDIES | $2.00 | $4.00 |
| 1 | 251 | FRANK LUTHER | FARMYARD SONGS | BIRDS | $2.00 | $4.00 |
| 1 | 252 | FRANK LUTHER | LITTLE FRIENDS | BABIES | $2.00 | $4.00 |
| 1 | 253 | FRANK LUTHER | DOLLS | WINTER | $2.00 | $4.00 |
| 1 | 254 | JOE GREEN'S ORCHESTRA | PARADE OF THE DUCKS | THE WOMAN IN THE SHOE | $2.00 | $4.00 |
| 1 | 255 | JOE GREEN'S ORCHESTRA | DOLL DANCE | THE WEDDING OF THE PAINTED DOLL | $2.00 | $4.00 |
| 1 | 256 | JOE GREEN'S ORCHESTRA | TIN PAN PARADE | BABY'S BIRTHDAY PARTY | $2.00 | $4.00 |
| 1 | 257 | JOE GREEN'S ORCHESTRA | PARADE OF THE WOODEN SOLDIERS | TOM THUMB'S DREAM | $2.00 | $4.00 |
| 1 | 258 | UNCLE DON | THE GREEN GRASS GROWS ALL AROUND (PT. 1) | THE GREEN GRASS GROWS ALL AROUND (PT. 2) | $2.00 | $4.00 |
| 1 | 259 | UNCLE DON | A FROG WENT A COURTIN' (PT. 1) | A FROG WENT A COURTIN' (PT. 2) | $2.00 | $4.00 |
| 1 | 260 | NOT LISTED | AESOP'S FABLES: THE GOOSE THAT LAID THE GOLDEN EGG | TWO FELLOWS AND A BEAR; THE TRAVELERS AND THE AX | $2.00 | $4.00 |
| 1 | 261 | NOT LISTED | AESOP'S FABLES: THE TOWN MOUSE AND THE COUNTRY MOUSE | THE BOY WHO CRIED WOLF | $2.00 | $4.00 |
| 1 | 262 | NOT LISTED | AESOP'S FABLES: THE DOG AND HIS SHADOW, THE ANTS AND THE GRASS-HOPPERS | THE FOX AND THE CROW | $2.00 | $4.00 |
| 1 | 263 | NOT LISTED | AESOP'S FABLES: THE FOX AND THE GRAPES | THE MILKMAID AND HER PAIL | $2.00 | $4.00 |
| 1 | 264 | MARGARET DAUM/DONALD DAME | PAT A CAKE, ETC. | PETER PETER PUMPKIN EATER, ETC. | $2.00 | $4.00 |
| 1 | 265 | DONALD DAME | WHO KILLED COCK ROBIN, THE ROBIN SONG | LITTLE POLLY FLINDERS, THE SPIDER AND THE FLY | $2.00 | $4.00 |
| 1 | 266 | ? | HAPPY BIRTHDAY TO YOU | FOR HE'S A JOLLY GOOD FELLOW; AULD LANG SYNE | $2.00 | $4.00 |
| 1 | 267 | ? | THE OWL AND THE PUSSY CAT | WYNKEN, BLYNKEN AND NOD | $2.00 | $4.00 |
| 1 | 268 | VERNON CRANE | THE LITTLE RED HEN AND THE ONE GRAIN OF WHEAT | LITTLE ORPHAN ANNIE | $4.00 | $8.00 |
| 1 | 269 | MARGARET DAUM/DONALD DAME | SILENT NIGHT, HOLY NIGHT | HARK, THE HERALD ANGELS SING | $2.00 | $4.00 |
| 1 | 270 | MARGARET DAUM/DONALD DAME | O LITTLE TOWN OF BETHLEHEM | IT CAME UPON A MIDNIGHT CLEAR | $2.00 | $4.00 |
| N/A | N/A | GENERIC PLAYTIME BOX FOR RECORDS | | | $10.00 | $20.00 |

## COLUMBIA PLAYTIME 300 SERIES 6" AND 7" SINGLES

| # REC | DISC # | ARTIST | A TITLE | B TITLE | YEAR | ALSO ISSUED ON | G/VG | EX/NMT |
|---|---|---|---|---|---|---|---|---|
| 1 | 303 | MARGARET DAUM | ROCK-A-BYE BABY | SING A SONG OF SIXPENCE | 1948 | 203 | $2.00 | $4.00 |
| 1 | 304 | DONALD DAME | LITTLE BO-PEEP | MARY HAD A LITTLE LAMB | | 202 | $2.00 | $4.00 |

## COLUMBIA PLAYTIME 300 SERIES 6" AND 7" SINGLES

| # REC | DISC # | ARTIST | A TITLE | B TITLE | YEAR | ALSO ISSUED ON | G/VG | EX/NMT |
|---|---|---|---|---|---|---|---|---|
| 1 | 305 | PLAYTIME MALE QUARTET | OLD MACDONALD HAD A FARM (PT. 1) | OLD MAC DONALD HAD A FARM (PT. 2) | | | $2.00 | $4.00 |
| 1 | 306 | PLAYTIME MALE QUARTET | O' COME ALL YE FAITHFUL | THE FIRST NOWELL | | | $2.00 | $4.00 |
| 1 | 307 | PLAYTIME MALE QUARTET | GOD REST YE MERRY GENTLEMEN | WE THREE KINGS OF ORIENT ARE | | | $2.00 | $4.00 |
| 1 | 308 | PLAYTIME BAND | THE STARS AND STRIPES FOREVER | WASHINGTON POST MARCH | | | $2.00 | $4.00 |
| 1 | 309 | PLAYTIME BAND | EL CAPITAN | SEMPER FIDELIS | | | $2.00 | $4.00 |
| 1 | 310 | PLAYTIME DANCE ORCH. | SAILOR'S HORNPIPE | THE THUNDERER | | 246 | $2.00 | $4.00 |
| 1 | 311 | (A) DONALD DAME, (B) STANLEY CARLSON | TOM, TOM THE PIPER'S SON | BAA BAA BLACK SHEEP | | | $2.00 | $4.00 |
| 1 | 312 | DONALD DAME | COCK-A-DOODLE DOO | OLD MOTHER HUBBARD | | | $2.00 | $4.00 |
| 1 | 313 | EARL ROGERS | ALPHABET SONG, ETC. | TO BED, TO BED, ETC. | | | $3.00 | $6.00 |
| 1 | 314 | STANLEY CARLSON | GEORGIE PORGIE, ETC. | LAVENDER BLUE, ETC. | | | $2.00 | $4.00 |
| 1 | 315 | STANLEY CARLSON | BABY BUNTING, ETC. | TO BABYLAND, ETC. | | | $2.00 | $4.00 |
| 1 | 316 | DONALD DAME | HARK, HARK, THE DOGS DO BARK; I HAD A LITTLE DOGGIE | RING AROUND THE ROSEY, ETC. | | | $2.00 | $4.00 |
| 1 | 317 | DONALD DAME | WHO KILLED COCK ROBIN | THE ROBIN SONG, ETC. | | | $2.00 | $4.00 |
| 1 | 318 | DONALD DAME | HARK, THE HERALD ANGELS SING | IT CAME UPON A MIDNIGHT CLEAR | | | $2.00 | $4.00 |
| 1 | 319 | MARGARET DAUM | THE SANDMAN | SLUMBER BOAT | | | $2.00 | $4.00 |
| 1 | 320 | MARGARET DAUM | THE DOLL SONG | SWEET AND LOW | | | $2.00 | $4.00 |
| 1 | 321 | MARGARET DAUM | SILENT NIGHT, HOLY NIGHT | O LITTLE TOWN OF BETHLEHEM | | | $2.00 | $4.00 |
| 1 | 322 | EARL ROGERS | CHRISTMAS (MERRY, MERRY, CHIMING BELLS) | CHRIST WAS ONCE A LITTLE BABY | | | $3.00 | $6.00 |
| 1 | 323 | EARL ROGERS | MY OLD KENTUCKY HOME | OLD FOLKS AT HOME | | | $3.00 | $6.00 |
| 1 | 325 | DONALD DAME | THE FROG PRINCE | LITTLE RED RIDING HOOD | | | $2.00 | $4.00 |
| 1 | 326 | STANLEY CARLSON | CINDERELLA | THE THREE BEARS | | | $2.00 | $4.00 |
| 1 | 327 | VERNON CRANE | WYNKEN, BLYNKEN, AND NOD | THE OWL AND THE PUSSY-CAT | | | $3.00 | $6.00 |
| 1 | 328 | VERNON CRANE | LITTLE ORPHAN ANNIE | THE LITTLE RED HEN AND THE ONE GRAIN OF WHEAT | | | $3.00 | $6.00 |
| 1 | 329 | EARL ROGERS | AMERICA | DIXIE | | | $3.00 | $6.00 |
| 1 | 330 | MARGARET DAUM | AULD LANG SYNE | HAPPY BIRTHDAY TO YOU; JOLLY GOOD FELLOW | | | $2.00 | $4.00 |
| 1 | 331 | JERRY WAYNE | JINGLE BELLS | GOOD KING WENCESLAS | 1949 | | $2.00 | $4.00 |
| 1 | 332 | HARRY BABBITT | MY A.B.C. SONG (PT. 1) | MY A.B.C. SONG (PT. 2) | | | $2.00 | $4.00 |
| 1 | 333 | STANLEY CARLSON | THE THREE BEARS | PARADE OF THE DUCKS | | | $2.00 | $4.00 |
| 1 | 334 | STANLEY CARLSON | CINDERELLA | DANCE OF THE SUGAR-PLUM FAIRY | | | $2.00 | $4.00 |
| 1 | 335 | STANLEY CARLSON | LITTLE RED RIDING HOOD | MEXICAN "CLAP HANDS" | | | $2.00 | $4.00 |
| 1 | 336 | EARL ROGERS | DING DONG BELL, ETC. | HEY DIDDLE DIDDLE, ETC. | | | $3.00 | $6.00 |
| 1 | 337 | JERRY WAYNE | LITTLE BO-PEEP | TOM, TOM THE PIPER'S SON | | | $2.00 | $4.00 |
| 1 | 338 | DONALD DAME | THREE BLIND MICE, ETC. | PETER, PETER PUMPKIN EATER, ETC. | | | $2.00 | $4.00 |
| 1 | 339 | GENE KELLY | FARMER IN THE DELL | MULBERRY BUSH | | | $3.00 | $6.00 |
| 1 | 340 | GENE KELLY | POP! GOES THE WEASEL | LONDON BRIDGE | | | $3.00 | $6.00 |
| 1 | 341 | GENE KELLY | JACK AND JILL | LITTLE BOY BLUE, SEE SAW MARGERY DAW | | | $3.00 | $6.00 |
| 1 | 342 | GENE KELLY | SING A SONG OF SIXPENCE, TEN LITTLE INDIANS | MARY HAD A LITTLE LAMB, PUSSY CAT | | | $3.00 | $6.00 |
| 1 | 343 | JERRY WAYNE | OLD KING COLE | FIDDLE-DE-DEE, SIMPLE SIMON | | | $2.00 | $4.00 |
| 1 | 344 | JERRY WAYNE | DID YOU EVER SEE A LASSIE? | LOOBY LOO | | | $2.00 | $4.00 |
| 1 | 345 | JIMMY BLAINE | GIT ALONG LITTLE DOGIES | BIG ROCK CANDY MOUNTAIN | | | $2.00 | $4.00 |
| 1 | 346 | JIMMY BLAINE | HOME ON THE RANGE | DONEY GAL | | | $2.00 | $4.00 |
| 1 | 347 | JIMMY BLAINE | BLUE TAIL FLY | BILLY BOY | | | $2.00 | $4.00 |
| 1 | 348 | JIMMY BLAINE | TURKEY IN THE STRAW | ARKANSAS TRAVELER | | | $2.00 | $4.00 |
| 1 | 349 | JIMMY BLAINE | SKIP TO MY LOU | BUFFALO GALS | | | $2.00 | $4.00 |
| 1 | 350 | JERRY WAYNE | TODAY IS MONDAY | THE BEAR WENT OVER THE MOUNTAIN, A HUNTING WE WILL GO | | | $2.00 | $4.00 |
| 1 | 351 | FLOYD SHERMAN | JESUS LOVES ME | CHILDREN OF THE HEAVENLY KING | | | $2.00 | $4.00 |
| 1 | 352 | FLOYD SHERMAN | SAVIOR TEACH ME DAY BY DAY | JESUS TENDER SHEPHERD HEAR ME | | | $2.00 | $4.00 |

## COLUMBIA PLAYTIME 300 SERIES 6" AND 7" SINGLES

| # REC | DISC # | ARTIST | A TITLE | B TITLE | YEAR | G/VG | EX/NMT |
|---|---|---|---|---|---|---|---|
| 1 | 353 | FLOYD SHERMAN | AWAY IN A MANGER | STAND UP FOR JESUS | 1950 | $2.00 | $4.00 |
| 1 | 354 | FLOYD SHERMAN | NOW THE DAY IS OVER | JESUS CALLS US | | $2.00 | $4.00 |
| 1 | 355 | RAY HEATHERTON | THREE LITTLE PIGS (PT. 1) | THREE LITTLE PIGS (PT. 2) | | $2.00 | $4.00 |
| 1 | 356 | RAY HEATHERTON | HANSEL AND GRETEL (PT. 1) | HANSEL AND GRETEL (PT. 2) | | $2.00 | $4.00 |
| 1 | 357 | RAY HEATHERTON | THE HAPPY BIRTHDAY RECORD | HOW OLD ARE YOU? | | $2.00 | $4.00 |
| 1 | 358 | RAY HEATHERTON | SCHOOL DAYS | DAISY BELL | | $2.00 | $4.00 |
| 1 | 359 | RAY HEATHERTON | TWAS THE NIGHT BEFORE CHRISTMAS (PT. 1) | TWAS THE NIGHT BEFORE CHRISTMAS (PT. 2) | | $2.00 | $4.00 |
| 1 | 360 | RAY HEATHERTON | SNOW WHITE AND THE SEVEN DWARFS (PT. 1) | SNOW WHITE AND THE SEVEN DWARFS (PT. 2) | | $2.00 | $4.00 |
| 1 | 361 | RAY HEATHERTON | A-TISKET A-TASKET | LAZY MARY | | $2.00 | $4.00 |
| 1 | 362 | RAY HEATHERTON | DADDY WOULDN'T BUY ME A BOW-WOW | I DON'T WANT TO PLAY IN YOUR YARD | | $2.00 | $4.00 |
| 1 | 363 | JERRY WAYNE | JACK AND THE BEANSTALK (PT. 1) | JACK AND THE BEANSTALK (PT. 2) | | $2.00 | $4.00 |
| 1 | 364 | JERRY WAYNE | THE LITTLE RED HEN | CHICKEN LICKEN | | $2.00 | $4.00 |
| 1 | 365 | JERRY WAYNE | THE THREE BILLY GOATS GRUFF (PT. 1) | THE THREE BILLY GOATS GRUFF (PT. 2) | | $2.00 | $4.00 |
| 1 | 366 | JERRY WAYNE | RUMPLESTILTSKIN (PT. 1) | RUMPLESTILTSKIN (PT. 2) | | $2.00 | $4.00 |
| 1 | 367 | RAY HEATHERTON | PARADE OF THE WOODEN SOLDIERS (PT. 1) | PARADE OF THE WOODEN SOLDIERS (PT. 2) | | $2.00 | $4.00 |
| 1 | 368 | RAY HEATHERTON | I'M A LITTLE TEAPOT (PT. 1) | I'M A LITTLE TEAPOT (PT. 2) | | $2.00 | $4.00 |
| 1 | 369 | RAY HEATHERTON | IF I KNEW YOU WERE COMIN' I'D'VE BAKED A CAKE | WEEVILY WHEAT | | $2.00 | $4.00 |
| 1 | 370 | COLUMBIA PLAYTIME ORCH. | SWANEE RIVER | EAST SIDE, WEST SIDE | 1951 | $2.00 | $4.00 |
| 1 | 371 | GLENN ROWELL | JONAH AND THE WHALE (PT. 1) | JONAH AND THE WHALE (PT. 2) | | $2.00 | $4.00 |
| 1 | 372 | GLENN ROWELL | NOAH'S ARK (PT. 1) | NOAH'S ARK (PT. 2) | | $2.00 | $4.00 |
| 1 | 373 | GLENN ROWELL | DAVID AND GOLIATH (PT. 1) | DAVID AND GOLIATH (PT. 2) | | $2.00 | $4.00 |
| 1 | 374 | GLENN ROWELL | DANIEL IN THE LION'S DEN (PT. 1) | DANIEL IN THE LION'S DEN (PT. 2) | | $2.00 | $4.00 |
| 1 | 375 | ARTHUR GODFREY | I'VE BEEN WORKING ON THE RAILROAD | OH SUSANNA | | $3.00 | $6.00 |
| 1 | 376 | RAY CARTER | ANCHORS AWEIGH | FROM THE HALLS OF MONTEZUMA | | $2.00 | $4.00 |
| 1 | 377 | RAY CARTER | THE CAISSONS GO ROLLING ALONG | WHEN JOHNNY COMES MARCHING HOME | | $2.00 | $4.00 |
| 1 | 378 | ARTHUR GODFREY | ANIMAL FAIR | BULL FROG ON THE BANK | | $3.00 | $6.00 |
| 1 | 379 | RAY HEATHERTON | ALICE IN WONDERLAND (PT. 1) | ALICE IN WONDERLAND (PT. 2) | | $2.00 | $4.00 |
| 1 | 380 | RAY HEATHERTON | RUDOLPH THE RED-NOSED REINDEER | JOLLY OLD SAINT NICHOLAS | | $2.00 | $4.00 |
| 1 | 381 | RAY HEATHERTON | FROSTY THE SNOWMAN | PUNKINHEAD (THE LITTLE BEAR) | | $2.00 | $4.00 |
| 1 | 382 | BISHOP FULTON J. SHEEN | OUR FATHER | HAIL MARY | 1952 | $4.00 | $8.00 |
| 1 | 383 | RAY HEATHERTON | PETER COTTONTAIL | EGGBERT THE EASTER EGG | | $2.00 | $4.00 |
| 1 | 384 | GENE AUTRY | OLD CHISHOLM TRAIL | THE BIG CORRAL | | $3.00 | $6.00 |
| 1 | 385 | MEN OF SONG | THE STAR-SPANGLED BANNER | AMERICA | | $2.00 | $4.00 |
| 1 | 386 | GENE AUTRY | ON TOP OF OLD SMOKY | CLEMENTINE | | $3.00 | $6.00 |
| 1 | 387 | SALLY SWEETLAND | THAT DOGGIE IN THE WINDOW | OH, WHERE HAS MY LITTLE DOG GONE! | 1953 | $4.00 | $8.00 |
| 1 | 388 | ARTHUR MELVIN | SILENT NIGHT, HOLY NIGHT | AULD LANG SYNE | | $2.00 | $4.00 |
| 1 | 389 | ARTHUR MELVIN | WHITE CHRISTMAS | ? | | $2.00 | $4.00 |
| 1 | 390 | ARTHUR MELVIN | SANTA CLAUS IS COMING TO TOWN | UP ON THE HOUSE TOP | | $2.00 | $4.00 |
| 1 | 391 | ARTHUR MELVIN | PEEWEE, THE KIWI BIRD | THE MOCKING BIRD | | $2.00 | $4.00 |
| 1 | 392 | ARTHUR MELVIN | THE LITTLE WHITE DUCK | OVER IN THE MEADOW | | $2.00 | $4.00 |
| 1 | 393 | SALLY SWEETLAND | I SAW MOMMY KISSING SANTA CLAUS | CHRISTMAS CHOPSTICKS | | $2.00 | $4.00 |
| 1 | 394 | SALLY SWEETLAND | ROCK-A-BYE BABY | BRAHMS' LULLABY | | $2.00 | $4.00 |
| 1 | 395 | SALLY SWEETLAND | ME AND MY TEDDY BEAR | LITTLE KITTY | | $2.00 | $4.00 |
| 1 | 396 | BOB HANNON | GOLDILOCKS AND THE THREE BEARS (PT. 1) | GOLDILOCKS AND THE THREE BEARS (PT. 2) | | $2.00 | $4.00 |
| 1 | 397 | BOB HANNON | PETER RABBIT (PT. 1) | PETER RABBIT (PT. 2) | | $2.00 | $4.00 |
| 1 | 398 | BOB HANNON | PINOCCHIO, THE WOODEN PUPPET (PT. 1) | PINOCCHIO, THE WOODEN PUPPET (PT. 2) | | $2.00 | $4.00 |
| 1 | 399 | BOB HANNON | THE UGLY DUCKLING (PT. 1) | THE UGLY DUCKLING (PT. 2) | | $2.00 | $4.00 |
| 1 | 400 | ARNOLD AMARU | NOW THE DAY IS OVER | GOD BLESS US ALL | | $2.00 | $4.00 |
| 1 | 401 | PATTY MAC | THREE LITTLE FISHES (PT. 1) | THREE LITTLE FISHES (PT. 2) | 1954 | $2.00 | $4.00 |
| 1 | 402 | PATTY MAC | I'M A LONELY LITTLE PETUNIA (IN AN ONION PATCH) | I'M CALLED LITTLE BUTTERCUP | | $2.00 | $4.00 |
| 1 | 403 | JEFFREY CLAY AND CLAIRE SEGRAVE | DENNIS THE MENACE (PT. 1) | DENNIS THE MENACE (PT. 2) | | $8.00 | $15.00 |
| 1 | 404 | JEFFREY CLAY AND CLAIRE SEGRAVE | TELL ME A STORY (PT. 1) | TELL ME A STORY (PT. 2) | | $2.00 | $4.00 |

## COLUMBIA PLAYTIME 300 SERIES 6" AND 7" SINGLES

| # REC | DISC # | ARTIST | A TITLE | B TITLE | G/VG | EX/NMT |
|---|---|---|---|---|---|---|
| 1 | 405 | JEFFREY CLAY AND CLAIRE SEGRAVE | PLAYMATES | JIM ALONG JOSIE | $2.00 | $4.00 |
| 1 | 406 | (A) CLIFF ROBERTSON — ROCKET RANGERS (B) COLUMBIA PLAYTIME ORCH. | ROCKET RANGER SONG | ROCKET RANGER MARCH | $12.00 | $25.00 |
| 1 | 407 | ROD MORRIS AND BURT TAYLOR | BIMBO | BOBBY SHAFTO | $2.00 | $4.00 |
| 1 | 408 | ROD MORRIS AND BURT TAYLOR | THE JONES BOY (PT. 1) | THE JONES BOY (PT. 2) | $2.00 | $4.00 |
| 1 | 409 | ROD MORRIS AND BURT TAYLOR | ROO ROO (KANGAROO) (PT. 1) | ROO ROO (KANGAROO) (PT. 2) | $2.00 | $4.00 |
| 1 | 410 | DOTTY EVANS | THE SYNCOPATED CLOCK (PT. 1) | THE SYNCOPATED CLOCK (PT. 2) | $2.00 | $4.00 |
| 1 | 411 | THE PLAYTIMES | SMOKEY THE BEAR (PT. 1) | SMOKEY THE BEAR (PT. 2) | $4.00 | $8.00 |
| 1 | 412 | NOT LISTED | SPOOKY MUSIC FOR SPOOKY OCCASIONS (PT. 1) | SPOOKY MUSIC FOR SPOOKY OCCASIONS (PT. 2) | $3.00 | $6.00 |
| 1 | 413 | COLUMBIA PLAYTIME ORCH. | DANCE OF THE SUGAR-PLUM FAIRY | CHINESE DANCE | $2.00 | $4.00 |
| 1 | 414 | DOTTY EVANS | THE LITTLE SHOEMAKER | PRETTY LITTLE SUSIE | $2.00 | $4.00 |
| 1 | 415 | DOTTY EVANS | SKINNIE MINNIE (FISH TAIL) | BRING BACK MY BONNIE TO ME | $2.00 | $4.00 |
| 1 | 416 | DOTTY EVANS | SUZY SNOWFLAKE | JINGLE AT THE WINDOWS | $2.00 | $4.00 |
| 1 | 417 | GENE AUTRY | HERE COMES SANTA CLAUS | CHRISTMAS GIFTS | $3.00 | $6.00 |

## COLUMBIA PLAY-COLOR RECORD BOOK 6" MJV-500/900-PV SERIES

| SET # | # REC | DISC # | MAIN TITLE | ARTIST | A TITLE | B TITLE | YEAR | G/VG | EX/NMT |
|---|---|---|---|---|---|---|---|---|---|
| MJV-501 | 2 | 901 – 2 PV | LITTLE RED RIDING HOOD | DAVID ALLEN | LITTLE RED RIDING HOOD (PT. 1) | LITTLE RED RIDING HOOD (PT. 2) | 1952 | $2.00 | $4.00 |
| MJV-502 | 2 | 903 – 4 PV | THREE LITTLE PIGS, CHICKEN LICKEN, THE LITTLE RED HEN | RAY HEATHERTON, JERRY WAYNE | THREE LITTLE PIGS (PT. 1) | THREE LITTLE PIGS (PT. 2) | | $2.00 | $4.00 |
| MJV-503 | 2 | 905 – 6 PV | ALICE IN WONDERLAND, SNOW WHITE & THE SEVEN DWARFS | RAY HEATHERTON | | | | $2.00 | $4.00 |
| MJV-504 | 2 | 907 – 8 PV | RUMPELSTILTSKIN, THE THREE BILLY GOATS GRUFF | JERRY WAYNE WITH ORCHESTRA | | | | $2.00 | $4.00 |
| MJV-505 | 2 | 909 – 10 PV | JACK AND THE BEANSTALK, HANSEL AND GRETEL | JERRY WAYNE, RAY HEATHERTON | | | | $2.00 | $4.00 |
| MJV-506 | 2 | 911 – 2 PV | DAVID AND GOLIATH, DANIEL IN THE LIONS' DEN | GLENN ROWELL ORCHESTRA, RAY CARTER, COND | | | | $2.00 | $4.00 |
| MJV-507 | 2 | 913 – 4 PV | JONAH AND THE WHALE, NOAH'S ARK | GLENN ROWELL ORCHESTRA, RAY CARTER, COND | | | | $2.00 | $4.00 |
| MJV-508 | 2 | 915 – 6 PV | THE FIRST DAY OF SCHOOL | DINAH SHORE | | | | $3.00 | $6.00 |
| MJV-509 | 2 | 917 – 8 PV | THE ADVENTURES OF PETER COTTONTAIL | WILLIAM KEENE, JOELS, P. MONSEN | WILLIAM KEENE, JOELS, P. MONSEN | WILLIAM KEENE, JOELS, P. MONSEN | | $2.00 | $4.00 |
| MJV-510 | 2 | 919 – 20 PV | RUDOLPH THE RED-NOSED REINDEER, ETC. | RAY HEATHERTON, S. SHULMAN | RAY HEATHERTON, S. SHULMAN | RAY HEATHERTON, S. SHULMAN | | $2.00 | $4.00 |
| MJV-511 | 2 | 921 – 2 PV | FROSTY THE SNOWMAN, ETC./ PUNKINHEAD (THE LITTLE BEAR) | RAY HEATHERTON, JERRY WAYNE | RAY HEATHERTON, JERRY WAYNE | RAY HEATHERTON, JERRY WAYNE | | $2.00 | $4.00 |
| MJV-512 | 2 | 923 – 4 PV | CINDERELLA, A TISKET, A TASKET, PARADE OF THE WOODEN SOLDIERS | STANLEY CARLSON, RAY HEATHERTON | STANLEY CARLSON, RAY HEATHERTON | STANLEY CARLSON, RAY HEATHERTON | | $2.00 | $4.00 |

## COLUMBIA PLAY-COLOR RECORD BOOK 6" 900-PV SERIES

| SET # | # REC | ARTIST | A TITLE | B TITLE | YEAR | G/VG | EX/NMT |
|---|---|---|---|---|---|---|---|
| 901-PV | 1 | DAVID ALLEN | LITTLE RED RIDING HOOD (PT. 1) | LITTLE RED RIDING HOOD (PT. 2) | 1952 | $1.00 | $2.00 |
| 902-PV | 1 | DAVID ALLEN | LITTLE RED RIDING HOOD (PT. 3) | LITTLE RED RIDING HOOD (PT. 4) | | $1.00 | $2.00 |
| 903-PV | 1 | RAY HEATHERTON | THREE LITTLE PIGS (PT. 1) | THREE LITTLE PIGS (PT. 2) | | $1.00 | $2.00 |
| 904-PV | 1 | JERRY WAYNE | CHICKEN LICKEN | THE LITTLE RED HEN | | $1.00 | $2.00 |
| 905-PV | 1 | RAY HEATHERTON | ALICE IN WONDERLAND (PT. 1) | ALICE IN WONDERLAND (PT. 2) | | $1.00 | $2.00 |
| 906-PV | 1 | RAY HEATHERTON | SNOW WHITE AND THE SEVEN DWARFS (PT. 1) | SNOW WHITE AND THE SEVEN DWARFS (PT. 2) | | $1.00 | $2.00 |
| 907-PV | 1 | JERRY WAYNE | RUMPELSTILTSKIN (PT. 1) | RUMPELSTILTSKIN (PT. 2) | | $1.00 | $2.00 |
| 908-PV | 1 | JERRY WAYNE | THE THREE BILLY GOATS GRUFF (PT. 1) | THE THREE BILLY GOATS GRUFF (PT. 2) | | $1.00 | $2.00 |
| 909-PV | 1 | JERRY WAYNE | JACK AND THE BEANSTALK (PT. 1) | JACK AND THE BEANSTALK (PT. 2) | | $1.00 | $2.00 |
| 910-PV | 1 | RAY HEATHERTON | HANSEL AND GRETEL (PT. 1) | HANSEL AND GRETEL (PT. 2) | | $1.00 | $2.00 |

## COLUMBIA PLAY-COLOR RECORD BOOK 6" 900-PV SERIES

| SET # | # REC | ARTIST | A TITLE | B TITLE | G/VG | EX/NMT |
|---|---|---|---|---|---|---|
| 911-PV | 1 | GLENN ROWELL ORCH, RAY CARTER, COND. | DAVID AND GOLIATH (PT. 1) | DAVID AND GOLIATH (PT. 2) | $1.00 | $2.00 |
| 912-PV | 1 | GLENN ROWELL ORCH, RAY CARTER, COND. | DANIEL IN THE LIONS' DEN (PT. 1) | DANIEL IN THE LIONS' DEN (PT. 2) | $1.00 | $2.00 |
| 913-PV | 1 | GLENN ROWELL ORCH, RAY CARTER, COND. | JONAH AND THE WHALE (PT. 1) | JONAH AND THE WHALE (PT. 2) | $1.00 | $2.00 |
| 914-PV | 1 | GLENN ROWELL ORCH, RAY CARTER, COND. | NOAH'S ARK (PT. 1) | NOAH'S ARK (PT. 2) | $1.00 | $2.00 |
| 915-PV | 1 | DINAH SHORE | THE FIRST DAY OF SCHOOL (PT. 1) | THE FIRST DAY OF SCHOOL (PT. 2) | $1.00 | $2.00 |
| 916-PV | 1 | DINAH SHORE | THE FIRST DAY OF SCHOOL (PT. 3) | THE FIRST DAY OF SCHOOL (PT. 4) | $1.00 | $2.00 |
| 917-PV | 1 | WILLIAM KEENE, P. MONSEN. | THE ADVENTURES OF PETER COTTON-TAIL (PT. 1) | THE ADVENTURES OF PETER COT-TONTAIL (PT. 2) | $1.00 | $2.00 |
| 918-PV | 1 | WILLIAM KEENE, P. MONSEN. | THE ADVENTURES OF PETER COTTON-TAIL (PT. 3) | THE ADVENTURES OF PETER COT-TONTAIL (PT. 4) | $1.00 | $2.00 |
| 919-PV | 1 | RAY HEATHERTON/S. SHULMAN | RUDOLPH THE RED-NOSED REINDEER | DANCE OF THE SUGAR-PLUM FAIRY | $1.00 | $2.00 |
| 920-PV | 1 | RAY HEATHERTON | TWAS THE NIGHT BEFORE CHRISTMAS (PT. 1) | TWAS THE NIGHT BEFORE CHRIST-MAS (PT. 2) | 1 | 2 |
| 921-PV | 1 | RAY HEATHERTON | FROSTY THE SNOWMAN | JOLLY OLD SAINT NICHOLAS | 1 | 2 |
| 922-PV | 1 | JERRY WAYNE | PUNKINHEAD (THE LITTLE BEAR) (PT. 1) | PUNKINHEAD (THE LITTLE BEAR) (PT. 2) | 1 | 2 |
| 923-PV | 1 | STANLEY CARLSON/RAY HEATHERTON | CINDERELLA | A-TISKET, A-TASKET | 1 | 2 |
| 924-PV | 1 | RAY HEATHERTON | PARADE OF THE WOODEN SOLDIERS (PT. 1) | PARADE OF THE WOODEN SOL-DIERS (PT. 2) | 1 | 2 |

## COLUMBIA JUNIOR SERIES 7" SINGLES

| SET # | # REC | ARTIST | A TITLE | B TITLE | YEAR | G/VG | EX/NMT |
|---|---|---|---|---|---|---|---|
| J-701 | 1 | BOB HANNON | THE LITTLE WHITE DUCK | PEEWEE THE KIWI BIRD | 1953 | $1.50 | $3.00 |
| J-702 | 1 | BOB HANNON | LITTLE RED CABOOSE | DANIEL THE SPANIEL | | $1.50 | $3.00 |
| J-703 | 1 | BOB HANNON | I'M A BIG RED FIRE ENGINE | I'VE GOT TO HAVE A PONY | | $1.50 | $3.00 |
| J-704 | 1 | JIMMY BLAINE | GIT ALONG LITTLE DOGIES | DONEY GAL | | $1.50 | $3.00 |
| J-705 | 1 | RAY HEATHERTON | SNOW WHITE AND THE SEVEN DWARFS | ALICE IN WONDERLAND | | $1.50 | $3.00 |
| J-706 | 1 | RAY HEATHERTON | THREE LITTLE PIGS | THE THREE BILLY GOATS GRUFF | | $1.50 | $3.00 |
| J-707 | 1 | JIMMY BLAINE | SKIP TO MY LOU, BUFFALO GALS | TURKEY IN THE STRAW, ARKANSAS TRAVELER | | $1.50 | $3.00 |
| J-708 | 1 | JERRY WAYNE | LOOBY LOU, FIDDLE-DE-DEE | OLD KING COLE, SIMPLE SIMON | 1954 | $1.50 | $3.00 |
| J-709 | 1 | RAY HEATHERTON | PARADE OF THE WOODEN SOLDIERS | DANCE OF THE SUGAR-PLUM FAIRY | | $1.50 | $3.00 |
| J-710 | 1 | RAY HEATHERTON/ HARRY BABBITT | SCHOOL DAYS | MY A.B.C. SONG | | $1.50 | $3.00 |
| J-711 | 1 | BOB HANNON | FROSTY THE SNOWMAN | JINGLE BELLS | | $1.50 | $3.00 |
| J-712 | 1 | BOB HANNON | SANTA CLAUS IS COMING TO TOWN | JOLLY OLD SAINT NICHOLAS | | $1.50 | $3.00 |
| J-713 | 1 | BOB HANNON | RUDOLPH THE RED-NOSED REINDEER | UP ON THE HOUSE TOP | | $1.50 | $3.00 |
| J-714 | 1 | BOB HANNON | PETER RABBIT | THE UGLY DUCKLING | | $1.50 | $3.00 |
| J-715 | 1 | BOB HANNON | GOLDILOCKS AND THE THREE BEARS | PINOCCHIO, THE WOODEN PUPPET | | $1.50 | $3.00 |
| J-716 | 1 | SINGING PRINCESSES | THE SYNCOPATED CLOCK | WILLIE THE WHISTLING GIRAFFE | | $1.50 | $3.00 |
| J-717 | 1 | SINGING PRINCESSES | WE'RE ON OUR WAY | TOY TOWN CHOO CHOO | | $1.50 | $3.00 |
| J-718 | 1 | PETER PIPER | OLD MACDONALD HAD A FARM | THE BLUETAIL FLY | | $1.50 | $3.00 |
| J-719 | 1 | BERT TAYLOR | PETER COTTONTAIL | SONNY, THE BUNNY | | $1.50 | $3.00 |
| J-720 | 1 | BERT TAYLOR | FUZZY WUZZY | WHAT KIND OF ANIMAL ARE YOU? | | $1.50 | $3.00 |
| J-721 | 1 | SINGING PRINCESSES | ON THE GOOD SHIP LOLLIPOP | THE WEDDING OF THE KNIFE AND FORK | | $1.50 | $3.00 |
| J-722 | 1 | SINGING PRINCESSES | ME AND MY TEDDY BEAR | HAPPY LITTLE TEDDY BEAR | | $1.50 | $3.00 |
| J-723 | 1 | HARRY BABBITT | PARADE OF THE WOODEN SOLDIERS | THE TEDDY BEARS' PICNIC | | $1.50 | $3.00 |
| J-710 | 1 | RAY HEATHERTON/HARRY BABBITT | SCHOOL DAYS | MY A.B.C. SONG | | $1.50 | $3.00 |
| J-711 | 1 | BOB HANNON | FROSTY THE SNOWMAN | JINGLE BELLS | | $1.50 | $3.00 |
| J-712 | 1 | BOB HANNON | SANTA CLAUS IS COMING TO TOWN | JOLLY OLD SAINT NICHOLAS | | $1.50 | $3.00 |
| J-713 | 1 | BOB HANNON | RUDOLPH THE RED-NOSED REINDEER | UP ON THE HOUSE TOP | | $1.50 | $3.00 |
| J-714 | 1 | BOB HANNON | PETER RABBIT | THE UGLY DUCKLING | | $1.50 | $3.00 |
| J-715 | 1 | BOB HANNON | GOLDILOCKS AND THE THREE BEARS | PINOCCHIO, THE WOODEN PUPPET | | $1.50 | $3.00 |
| J-716 | 1 | SINGING PRINCESSES | THE SYNCOPATED CLOCK | WILLIE THE WHISTLING GIRAFFE | | $1.50 | $3.00 |
| J-717 | 1 | SINGING PRINCESSES | WE'RE ON OUR WAY | TOY TOWN CHOO CHOO | | $1.50 | $3.00 |
| J-718 | 1 | PETER PIPER | OLD MAC DONALD HAD A FARM | THE BLUETAIL FLY | | $1.50 | $3.00 |

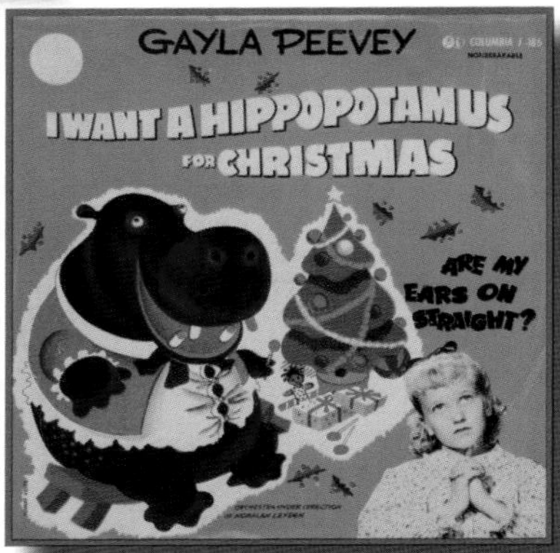

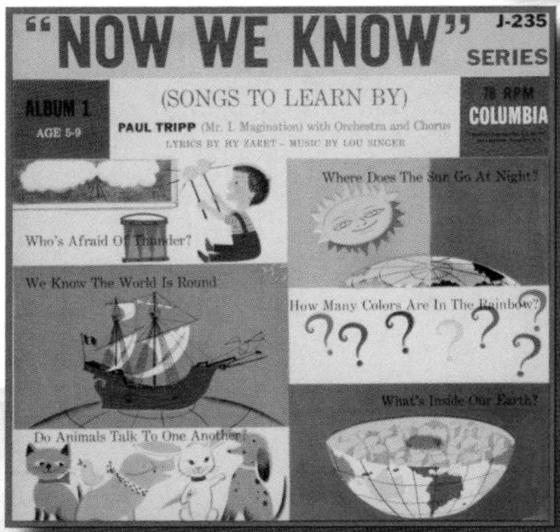


COLUMBIA RECORDS
I WANT A HIPPOPOTAMUS FOR CHRISTMAS $20.00

COLUMBIA RECORDS
DR. SNIFFLESWIPER
$8.00

COLUMBIA RECORDS
NOW WE KNOW, ALB I
$15.00

## COLUMBIA JUNIOR SERIES 7" SINGLES

| SET # | # REC | ARTIST | A TITLE | B TITLE | G/VG | EX/NMT |
|---|---|---|---|---|---|---|
| J-719 | 1 | BERT TAYLOR | PETER COTTONTAIL | SONNY, THE BUNNY | $1.50 | $3.00 |
| J-720 | 1 | BERT TAYLOR | FUZZY WUZZY | WHAT KIND OF ANIMAL ARE YOU? | $1.50 | $3.00 |
| J-721 | 1 | SINGING PRINCESSES | ON THE GOOD SHIP LOLLIPOP | THE WEDDING OF THE KNIFE AND FORK | $1.50 | $3.00 |
| J-722 | 1 | SINGING PRINCESSES | ME AND MY TEDDY BEAR | HAPPY LITTLE TEDDY BEAR | $1.50 | $3.00 |
| J-723 | 1 | HARRY BABBITT | PARADE OF THE WOODEN SOLDIERS | THE TEDDY BEARS' PICNIC | $1.50 | $3.00 |
| J-724 | 1 | GENE AUTRY | RUDOLPH THE RED-NOSED REINDEER | IF IT DOESN'T SNOW ON CHRISTMAS | $3.00 | $6.00 |
| J-725 | 1 | FLOYD SHERMAN | JESUS LOVES ME; CHILDREN OF THE HEAVENLY KING | SAVIOR,TEACH ME DAY BY DAY; JESUS, TENDER SHEPHERD, HEAR ME | $1.50 | $3.00 |
| J-726 | 1 | BURL IVES | MOTHER GOOSE SONGS (PT. 1) | MOTHER GOOSE SONGS (PT. 2) | $2.00 | $4.00 |
| J-727 | 1 | PATTY MCGOVERN | I'M A LONELY LITTLE PETUNIA (IN AN ONION PATCH) | I'M A LITTLE TEAPOT | $1.50 | $3.00 |
| J-728 | 1 | ROSEMARY CLOONEY | ME AND MY TEDDY BEAR | I FOUND MY MAMMA | $2.00 | $4.00 |
| J-729 | 1 | JEFFREY CLAY, CLAIRE SEGRAVE | TELL ME A STORY | WHY, DADDY? | $1.50 | $3.00 |
| J-730 | 1 | CLAIRE SEGRAVE | MOTHER GOOSE PARADE (PT. 1) | MOTHER GOOSE PARADE (PT. 2) | $1.50 | $3.00 |
| J-731 | 1 | BOB HANNON | PINOCCHIO, THE WOODEN PUPPET | JACK AND THE BEANSTALK | $1.50 | $3.00 |
| J-732 | 1 | JERRY WAYNE | SMOKEY THE BEAR | THE BEAR WENT OVER THE MOUNTAIN; TODAY IS MONDAY | $2.00 | $4.00 |
| J-733 | 1 | FORTY-NINERS | ALEXANDER'S RAGTIME BAND | THE STARS AND STRIPES FOREVER | $1.50 | $3.00 |
| J-734 | 1 | COLUMBIA SYMPHONETTE | DANCE OF THE SUGAR-PLUM FAIRY | TREPAK; DANCE OF THE REDD-PIPES | $1.50 | $3.00 |
| J-735 | 1 | FORTY-NINERS | PECOS BILL (PT. 1) | PECOS BILL (PT. 2) | $2.00 | $4.00 |
| J-736 | 1 | COLUMBIA SYMPHONETTE | IN THE HALL OF THE MOUNTAIN KING | ANITRA'S DANCE | $1.50 | $3.00 |
| J-737 | 1 | FORTY-NINERS | THE BULLDOG ON THE BANK | DUCKS ON PARADE | $1.50 | $3.00 |
| J-738 | 1 | FORTY-NINERS/BOB HANNON | LITTLE TOOT | WILLY THE SPIDER | $1.50 | $3.00 |
| J-739 | 1 | BOB HANNON | THE LITTLE ENGINE THAT COULD | I'VE BEEN WORKING ON THE RAILROAD | $1.50 | $3.00 |
| J-740 | 1 | BOB HANNON | BIMBO | GOING TO BOSTON | $1.50 | $3.00 |
| J-741 | 1 | BURT TAYLOR | THE JONES BOY | WILBUR THE WIGGILY WORM | $1.50 | $3.00 |
| J-742 | 1 | BOB HANNON | CRAZY QUILT FARM | THE BARNYARD SONG | $1.50 | $3.00 |
| J-743 | 1 | SINGING PRINCESSES | THE LITTLE SHOEMAKER | PRETTY LITTLE SUSIE | $1.50 | $3.00 |
| J-744 | 1 | SINGING PRINCESSES | SKINNIE MINNIE | SODA POP PARADE | $1.50 | $3.00 |
| J-745 | 1 | SINGING PRINCESSES | SUZY SNOWFLAKE | OVER THE RIVER (AND THROUGH THE WOOD) | $1.50 | $3.00 |
| J-746 | 1 | SINGING PRINCESSES | HERE COMES SANTA CLAUS | I SAW THREE SHIPS | $1.50 | $3.00 |
| J-747 | 1 | SINGING PRINCESSES | THE MAMA DOLL SONG | COCKLES AND MUSSELS | $1.50 | $3.00 |
| J-748 | 1 | SINGING PRINCESSES | (DON'T LET THE) KIDDYGEDDIN | I HAD A LITTLE MULE | $1.50 | $3.00 |
| J-749 | 1 | MACK EDWARD | THE HORSE WITH THE EASTER BONNET | GIT ALONG LITTLE DOGIES | $1.50 | $3.00 |
| J-750 | 1 | SINGING PRINCESSES | EGGBERT, THE EASTER EGG | MR. EASTER BUNNY | $1.50 | $3.00 |
| J-751 | 1 | SINGING PRINCESSES | NEVER-NEVER LAND | IMTY-MIMTY | $1.50 | $3.00 |
| J-752 | 1 | FORTY-NINERS | BALLAD OF DAVY CROCKETT | WINDY BILL | $2.00 | $4.00 |
| J-753 | 1 | FORTY-NINERS | HEY, MR. BANJO | THREE LITTLE PUPPIES | $1.50 | $3.00 |

CONTINENTAL RECORDS
EDNA AND THE THUNDER MAN
$10.00

CRICKET RECORDS
THE MIKADO
$3.00

CRICKET RECORDS
THE ANDY PANDA POLKA
$10.00

## CRICKET MAIN SERIES 7" AND 10" SINGLES

| # REC | DISC # | MAIN TITLE | ARTIST | YEAR | G/VG | EX/NMT |
|---|---|---|---|---|---|---|
| 1 | C-113 | CLEMENTINE/BOSS OF THE TOWN | SMILEY BURNETTE | | $5.00 | $10.00 |
| 1 | C-114 | NICK, NACK, PADDY WHACK/THE LITTLE DUTCH GIRL | CRICKETONE CHORUS | | $1.50 | $3.00 |
| 1 | C-115 | TOM THUMB'S TUNE/FUNICULI, FUNICULA | CRICKETONE PLAYERS | | $4.00 | $8.00 |
| 1 | C-116 | THE LITTLE ENGINE THAT COULD/I'VE BEEN WORKING ON THE RAILROAD | CRICKETONE PLAYERS | | $1.50 | $3.00 |
| 1 | C-117 | SEBASTIAN, THE MERRY-GO-ROUND HORSE/I WENT TO THE ANIMAL FAIR | CRICKETONE PLAYERS | | $1.50 | $3.00 |
| 1 | C-118 | PAUL BUNYAN/LOGGING, NORTH DAKOTA | DENNIS DAY | | $3.00 | $6.00 |
| 1 | C-119 | SMART ALEC CROW/GRAN'PA FROG | SMILEY BURNETTE | | $5.00 | $10.00 |
| 1 | C-120 | ROMPER ROOM: "PUNCH-A-BALL SONG"/"BOUNCING BALL SONG" | CHILDREN'S CHOIR & CRICKETONE ORCH. | 1959 | $5.00 | $10.00 |
| 1 | C-121 | RINGLING BROS. BARNUM & BAILEY CIRCUS: CHILDREN OF ALL AGES/BILLBOARD | CIRCUS BAND; I. CERVONE, COND. | | $3.00 | $6.00 |
| 1 | C-122 | SING ALONG — RAY HEATHERTON: BE KIND TO YOUR WEB-FOOTED FRIENDS, ETC | RAY HEATHERTON | | $2.00 | $4.00 |
| 1 | C-123 | MARCHING ALONG TOGETHER: STARS & STRIPES FOREVER/THE DIPLOMAT | CRICKETEER MARCHING BAND | | $1.50 | $3.00 |
| 1 | C-124 | I'M POPEYE THE SAILOR MAN/I WANNA BE A LIFE GUARD | CAPTAIN PAUL & THE SEAFARING BAND | | $5.00 | $10.00 |
| 1 | C-125 | FELIX THE CAT SONG/THE CAT MARCH | CRICKETONE CHORUS/CRICKETEER MARCHING BAND | | $5.00 | $10.00 |
| 1 | C-126 | LULLABIES: ROCK-A-BYE BABY/BRAHM'S LULLABY | VAN TALBERT | | $1.50 | $3.00 |
| 1 | C-127 | KIDDIE POLKA PARTY: JOLLY CLARINET POLKA/HAPPY HELENA POLKA | CRICKET POLKA-TONE ORCH. | | $1.50 | $3.00 |
| 1 | C-128 | HAWAIIAN KIDDIE LUAU: ALOHA OE/HAWAIIAN DRUMS | JOHNNY POI & HIS OAHU ISLANDERS | | $3.00 | $6.00 |
| 1 | C-129 | SING ALONG — RAY HEATHERTON: THE SOW TOOK THE MEASLES, ETC | RAY HEATHERTON | | $2.00 | $4.00 |
| 1 | C-130 | DO-RE-MI/WALTZING MATILDA | CRICKETONE CHILDREN'S CHORUS & ORCH. | | $1.50 | $3.00 |
| 1 | C-131 | BAT MASTERSON/MARCH TO THE WEST | CRICKETONE ORCH. | | $4.00 | $8.00 |
| 1 | C-132 | THE STORY OF SLEEPING BEAUTY | NORMAN ROSE | | $2.00 | $4.00 |
| 1 | C-133 | HOBBLE-DE-HOY/WHOOPEE TI YI YO, GET ALONG LITTLE DOGIE | EDDIE DEAN | | $1.50 | $3.00 |
| 1 | C-134 | DAVID AND GOLIATH/DANIEL IN THE LION'S DEN | EDMOND BLAKEMAN | | $1.50 | $3.00 |
| 1 | C-135 | SONGS OF THE SEA: BLOW THE MAN DOWN/SAILING, SAILING | CAPTAIN PAUL & HIS CREWMAN | | $1.50 | $3.00 |
| 1 | C-137 | PEPE/MEXICAN HAT DANCE | CRICKETONE CHORUS & ORCH | 1960 | $3.00 | $6.00 |
| 1 | C-138 | DOGGIE IN THE WINDOW/BINGO | CRICKETONE CHORUS & ORCH | | $2.50 | $5.00 |
| 1 | C-139 | I'M A LITTLE TEAPOT/REUBEN, REUBEN | DOROTHY SEASON & CRICKETONE CHORUS & ORCH | | $1.50 | $3.00 |
| 1 | C-140 | YELLOW ROSE OF TEXAS/DOWN IN THE VALLEY | CRICKETONE CHORUS & ORCH | | $1.50 | $3.00 |
| 1 | C-141 | SCHOOL DAYS/DAISY, DAISY | CRICKETONE CHORUS & ORCH | | $1.50 | $3.00 |
| 1 | C-142 | OLD MACDONALD/I TISKET, I TASKET | CRICKETONE CHORUS & ORCH | | $1.50 | $3.00 |
| 1 | C-143 | TOYLAND/MARCH OF THE TOYS | HANKY PANK PLAYERS | 1961 | $2.00 | $4.00 |

*A "ROMPER ROOM RECORD"

## CRICKET MAIN SERIES 7" AND 10" SINGLES

| # REC | DISC # | MAIN TITLE | ARTIST | YEAR | G/VG | EX/NMT |
|---|---|---|---|---|---|---|
| 1 | C-144 | THE WORK SONG/YOU'LL GO TO THE BALL | GISELE MACKENZIE | | $2.00 | $4.00 |
| 1 | C-145 | WE'RE OFF TO SEE THE WIZARD/THE THANK YOU SONG | HANKY PANK PLAYERS | | $4.00 | $8.00 |
| 1 | C-146 | HE'S GOT THE WHOLE WORLD IN HIS HANDS/ABIDE WITH ME | CRICKETONE CHORUS & ORCH. (CCO) | | $2.00 | $4.00 |
| 1 | C-147 | THE BOLL-WEEVIL SONG/THE RIDDLE SONG (I GAVE MY LOVE A CHERRY) | THE CHARLESTON TRIO | | $1.50 | $3.00 |
| 1 | C-148 | WHEN JOHNNY COMES MARCHING HOME/GOOBER PEAS | JEFF SMITH & THE SMITH BROTHERS | | $1.50 | $3.00 |
| 1 | C-149 | LITTLE TOOT/TUGGLY | CANDY ANDERSON/CCO | | $1.50 | $3.00 |
| 1 | C-150 | TEDDY BEARS PICNIC/CANDY CAROUSEL | CCO | | $1.50 | $3.00 |
| 1 | C-151 | PUFF THE MAGIC DRAGON/THE MONKEY WHO WANTED TO FLY | CCO | 1963 | $2.00 | $4.00 |
| 1 | C-152 | THE THREE LITTLE FISHES/SILLY SONG | CANDY ANDERSON/CCO | | $1.50 | $3.00 |
| 1 | C-153 | PLAYMATES/THE FROG AND THE OX | CANDY ANDERSON/CCO | | $1.50 | $3.00 |
| 1 | C-154 | ON THE GOOD SHIP LOLLIPOP/FIDDLE DEE DEE | CANDY ANDERSON/CCO | | $1.50 | $3.00 |
| 1 | C-155 | ON TOP OF SPAGHETTI/SKIP TO MY LOU | CCO | | $2.00 | $4.00 |
| 1 | C-157 | GOD BLESS AMERICA/MY OLD KENTUCKY HOME | KATE SMITH | | $5.00 | $10.00 |
| 1 | C-158 | MARIZY DOATS/SILLY SONG, GREEN GRASS GREW ALL AROUND | CRICKETONE CHORUS & ORCH. | | $2.00 | $4.00 |
| 1 | C-159 | SONGS OF BABAR: "DID YOU EVER LOSE AN ELEPHANT"/"THE BIG GREY ELEPHANT" | GISELE MACKENZIE | | $4.00 | $8.00 |
| 1 | C-160 | POPEYE ON PARADE/STRIKE ME PINK DO I SEE RED | CAPTAIN PAUL & THE SEAFARING BAND | | $5.00 | $10.00 |
| 1 | C-161 | THE CAMPTOWN RACES/OH SUZANNAH | CCO | | $1.50 | $3.00 |
| 1 | C-162 | DEEP IN THE HEART OF TEXAS/BUFFALO GALS | CCO | | $1.50 | $3.00 |
| 1 | C-163 | CHIM CHIM CHER-EE/THE FOX | THE CRICKET CHILDREN'S CHORUS/ MICHAEL STRANGE | 1964 | $2.00 | $4.00 |
| 1 | C-164 | WHISTLE A HAPPY TUNE/KEEPER OF THE EDDYSTONE LIGHT | THE CRICKET CHILDREN'S CHORUS/ MICHAEL STRANGE | | $2.00 | $4.00 |
| 1 | C-165 | GREENSLEEVES/BLUE TAIL FLY | KATE SMITH/CHARLESTON TRIO | | $4.00 | $8.00 |
| 1 | C-166 | SUPERCALIFRAGILISTICEXPIALIDOCIOUS/SCARLET RIBBONS | CCO | | $4.00 | $8.00 |
| 1 | C-167 | BIG ROCK CANDY MOUNTAIN/BILLY MCGHEE MCGRAW | THE CITY SINGERS | | $1.50 | $3.00 |
| 1 | C-168 | THE GREEN HORNET/THE BLUE MIRAGE | THE SUPER DUPERS | | $3.00 | $6.00 |
| 1 | C-169 | MARCH OF TARZAN | ? | | $5.00 | $10.00 |
| 1 | C-170 | THE YELLOW SUBMARINE | THE THREE PIRATES | 1968 | $4.00 | $8.00 |
| 1 | C-171 | DR. DOLITTLE: TALK TO THE ANIMALS/MONKEY SHINES | CCO | | $10.00 | $20.00 |
| 1 | C-172 | RUNNING FREE/FOR A FRIEND | CCO | | $3.00 | $6.00 |
| 1 | C-173 | HAPPINESS/THE HAPPY POLKA | CCO, RON MARSHALL | | $2.00 | $4.00 |
| 1 | C-174 | ALLEY CAT DANCE/LA CUCARACHA | THE PLAYMATES | | $1.50 | $3.00 |
| 1 | C-175 | BORN FREE/NEVERLAND | THE CRICKETONES | | $4.00 | $8.00 |

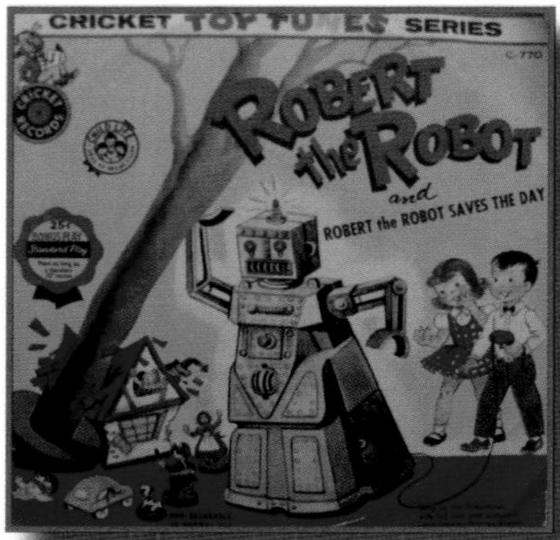


CRICKET RECORDS
ROBERT THE ROBOT
$30.00

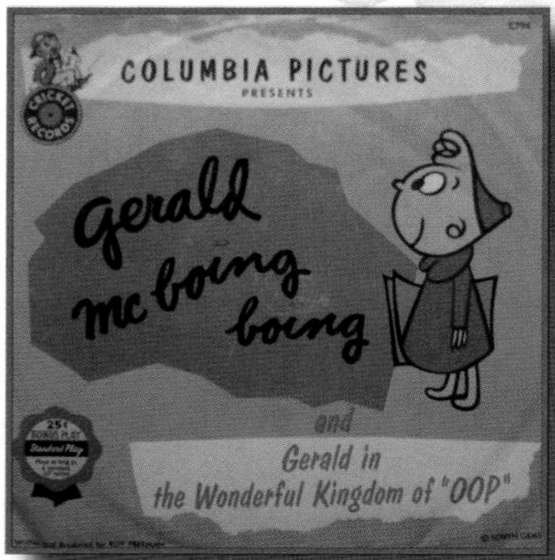


CRICKET RECORDS
GERALD MCBOING-BOING
$30.00

CRICKET RECORDS
KIDDY ROCK 'N ROLL PARTY
$10.00

## DECCA MISCELLANEOUS (10" SINGLES)

| # REC | DISC # | MAIN TITLE | ARTIST | YEAR | G/VG | EX/NMT |
|---|---|---|---|---|---|---|
| 1 | 1960 | SMALL FRY | BING CROSBY | | $1.00 | $2.00 |
| 1 | 2238 | FERDINAND THE BULL/I GOT RINGS ON MY FINGERS | MERRY MACS | | $3.00 | $6.00 |
| 1 | 2257 | JUST A KID NAMED JOE | BING CROSBY | | $1.00 | $2.00 |
| 1 | 2306 | LITTLE SIR ECHO /I CAN'T GET YOU OUT OF MY MIND | GUY LOMBARDO ORCHESTRA | 1939 | $1.00 | $2.00 |
| 1 | 2318 | MARCH OF THE TOYS | VICTOR YOUNG ORCHESTRA | | $1.00 | $2.00 |
| 1 | 2385 | LITTLE SIR ECHO | BING CROSBY | | $1.00 | $2.00 |
| 1 | 2408 | POOR PINOCCHIO'S NOSE | TED WEEMS ORCHESTRA | | $1.00 | $2.00 |
| 1 | 2445 | GAY PARADE/MARCH OF THE GNOMES | FRANK LUTHER AND QUARTET | | $2.00 | $4.00 |
| 1 | 2446 | HI DIDDLE DIDDLE/THREE LITTLE FISHIES | GUY LOMBARDO ORCHESTRA | | $1.00 | $2.00 |
| 1 | 2505 | JUNE BUGS DANCE | PAUL WHITEMAN ORCHESTRA | | $1.00 | $2.00 |
| 1 | 2604 | GOLDILOCKS AND THE THREE BEARS | ARTHUR TRACY | | $1.00 | $2.00 |
| 1 | 2640 | APPLE FOR THE TEACHER | BING CROSBY | | $1.00 | $2.00 |
| 1 | 2700 | SCHOOL DAYS (MEDLEY) | BING CROSBY | | $1.00 | $2.00 |
| 1 | 2739 | JIMINY CRICKET/MONSTRO THE WHALE | TED WEEMS ORCHESTRA | | $3.00 | $6.00 |
| 1 | 2782 | NIGHT BEFORE CHRISTMAS/THAT'S WHAT I WANT FOR CHRISTMAS | ROBERTSON ORCHESTRA | | $1.00 | $2.00 |
| 1 | 2793 | JIMINY CRICKET | TED WEEMS ORCHESTRA | | $2.00 | $4.00 |
| 1 | 2793 | MONSTRO THE WHALE/JIMINY CRICKET | TED WEEMS ORCHESTRA | | $2.00 | $4.00 |
| 1 | 2801 | PARADE OF THE LITTLE WHITE MICE | GUY LOMBARDO ORCHESTRA | | $1.00 | $2.00 |
| 1 | 2823 | GIRL WITH THE PIGTAILS IN HER HAIR/WEDDING OF THE WOODEN SOLDIER | RUSS MORGAN ORCHESTRA | | $1.00 | $2.00 |
| 1 | 2828 | HELLO, MISTER KRINGLE | ROBERTSON ORCHESTRA | | $1.00 | $2.00 |
| 1 | 2834 | BLUEBIRDS IN THE MOONLIGHT/IT'S A HAP-HAP-HAPPY DAY | GUY LOMBARDO ORCHESTRA | | $1.00 | $2.00 |
| 1 | 2835 | FAITHFUL FOREVER | GUY LOMBARDO ORCHESTRA | | $1.00 | $2.00 |
| 1 | 2906 | MARCH OF THE TOYS | TEDDY POWELL ORCHESTRA | | $1.00 | $2.00 |
| 1 | 2969 | TURN ON THE OLD MUSIC BOX/WHEN YOU WISH UPON A STAR | GUY LOMBARDO ORCHESTRA | 1940 | $1.00 | $2.00 |
| 1 | 2994 | SOMEDAY YOU'LL FIND YOUR BLUEBIRD | H. KING ORCHESTRA | | $1.00 | $2.00 |
| 1 | 3008 | GIVE A LITTLE WHISTLE | WOODY HERMAN ORCHESTRA | | $1.00 | $2.00 |
| 1 | 3035 | WHEN YOU WISH UPON A STAR | ROY SMECK ORCHESTRA | | $1.00 | $2.00 |
| 1 | 3041 | PARADE OF THE WOODEN SOLDIERS | SAVITT ORCHESTRA | | $1.00 | $2.00 |
| 1 | 3050 | WHEN YOU WISH UPON A STAR | FRANCES LANGFORD | | $1.00 | $2.00 |
| 1 | 3065 | WOODPECKER SONG | THE ANDREWS SISTERS | | $6.00 | $12.00 |
| 1 | 3098 | GIRL WITH THE PIGTAILS IN HER HAIR | BING CROSBY | | $1.00 | $2.00 |
| 1 | 3126 | WAR DANCE FOR WOODEN INDIANS | AMBROSE ORCHESTRA | | $1.00 | $2.00 |
| 1 | 3130 | WOODPECKER SONG | HARDEN ORCHESTRA | | $4.00 | $8.00 |
| 1 | 3281 | LION AND THE MOUSE | LOU HOLDEN ORCHESTRA | | $1.00 | $2.00 |
| 1 | 3301 | LAZY LACK-A-DAISY MELODY/LITTLE SWEETHEART OF THE VALLEY | MOYLAN SISTERS | | $5.00 | $10.00 |
| 1 | 3464 | DOWN IN TOYLAND VILLAGE IN THE LAND OF BLOCKS) | GUY LOMBARDO ORCHESTRA | | $1.00 | $2.00 |
| 1 | 3716 | THE FARMER IN THE DELL/MARY HAD A LITTLE LAMB | DICK ROBERTSON | 1941 | $1.00 | $2.00 |
| 1 | 3740 | TOY PIANO MINUET | MILT HERTH TRIO | | $1.00 | $2.00 |
| 1 | 3777 | ALEXANDER THE SWOOSE/TOY PIANO MINUET | JOHNNY MESSNER ORCHESTRA | | $1.00 | $2.00 |
| 1 | 3895 | THE RELUCTANT DRAGON | RICHARD HIMBER ORCHESTRA | | $1.00 | $2.00 |
| 1 | 3935 | THE RELUCTANT DRAGON | THE KING'S MEN | | $3.00 | $6.00 |
| 1 | 4061 | FROM "DUMBO": BABY MINE/WHEN I SEE AN ELEPHANT FLY | JOHNNY MESSNER ORCHESTRA | | $2.00 | $4.00 |
| 1 | 4109 | SUPERMAN/THE NADOCKY | FREDDIE "SCHNICKELFRITZ" FISCHER | | $5.00 | $10.00 |
| 1 | 4208 | THE TALE OF PETER AND THE WOLF | GUY LOMBARDO ORCHESTRA | 1942 | $2.00 | $4.00 |
| 1 | 5037 | I'M POPEYE THE SAILOR MAN/PEG LEG JACK | FRANK LUTHER | | $5.00 | $10.00 |
| 1 | 18134 | FROM "SALUDOS AMIGOS": BRAZIL | FERNANDO ALVAREZ | | $3.00 | $6.00 |
| 1 | 18387 | THE BIG BAD WOLF IS BACK AGAIN, ETC./THE PIED PIPER, ETC. | NAT BRANDWYNNE ORCHESTRA | | $3.00 | $6.00 |
| 1 | 18388 | FROM "FLYING MOUSE": YOU'RE NOTHIN' BUT A NOTHIN', ETC. | NAT BRANDWYNNE ORCHESTRA | | $3.00 | $6.00 |
| 1 | 18389 | FROM "GRASSHOPPER & THE ANTS": FUNNY LITTLE BUNNIES, ETC. | NAT BRANDWYNNE ORCHESTRA | | $3.00 | $6.00 |
| 1 | 18390 | FROM "DUMBO": LOOK OUT FOR MISTER STORK, ETC. | NAT BRANDWYNNE ORCHESTRA | | $3.00 | $6.00 |
| 1 | 18412 | FROM "SALUDOS AMIGOS": BRAZIL | FRED WARING ORCHESTRA | 1943 | $3.00 | $6.00 |
| 1 | 18445 | FROM "BAMBI": LOVE IS A SONG | GUY LOMBARDO ORCHESTRA | | $3.00 | $6.00 |

DECCA RECORDS
BOBBY BENSON'S B-BAR-B RIDERS
$8.00

DECCA RECORDS
MAX MAINSPRING: THE MECHANICAL MAN
$30.00

DECCA RECORDS
THE LONE RANGER: HE FINDS SILVER$20.00

## DECCA MISCELLANEOUS 10" SINGLES

| # REC | DISC # | MAIN TITLE | ARTIST | YEAR | G/VG | EX/NMT |
|---|---|---|---|---|---|---|
| 1 | 18460 | FROM "SALUDOS AMIGOS": BRAZIL | JIMMY DORSEY ORCHESTRA | | $3.00 | $6.00 |
| 1 | 18606 | FROM "SALUDOS AMIGOS": TICO-TICO | THE ANDREWS SISTERS | 1944 | $4.00 | $8.00 |
| 1 | 18607 | SPRING WILL BE A LITTLE LATE THIS YEAR/CHRISTOPHER ROBIN IS SAYING HIS PRAYERS | MORTON DOWNEY | | $4.00 | $8.00 |
| 1 | 18874 | WITHOUT YOU | RANDY BROOKS | | $2.00 | $4.00 |
| 1 | 23126 | HAPPY FARMER | DECCA LITTLE SYMPHONY ORCHESTRA | | $1.00 | $2.00 |
| 1 | 23190 | CHILDREN'S CHRISTMAS | GRANADOS TRIO | | $1.00 | $2.00 |
| 1 | 23318 | FROM "SALUDOS AMIGOS": PEDRO FROM CHILE/TICO-TICO | CHARLES WOLCOTT ORCHESTRA | | $3.00 | $6.00 |
| 1 | 23353 | TICO-TICO/LERO LERO; BEM TE VI ATREVIDO (FROM "SALUDOS AMIGOS") | ETHEL SMITH | | $3.00 | $6.00 |
| 1 | 23364 | SONGS FROM "THREE CABALLEROS" | BING CROSBY, THE ANDREWS SISTERS | | $3.00 | $6.00 |
| 1 | 23413 | YOU BELONG TO MY HEART/BAIA (FROM "THE THREE CABALLEROS") | BING CROSBY | 1945 | $2.00 | $4.00 |
| 1 | 23474 | JOHNNY FEDORA (AND ALICE BLUE BONNET) | GUY LOMBARDO ORCH, ANDREWS SISTERS | | $1.00 | $2.00 |
| 1 | 23532 | SONGS FROM "MAKE MINE MUSIC" | ROY ELDRIDGE ORCH | | $2.00 | $4.00 |
| 1 | 23748 | SONGS FROM "SONG OF THE SOUTH" | CONNIE BOSWELL, BOB CROSBY, BOB-O-LINKS | 1946 | $2.00 | $4.00 |
| 1 | 23768 | DOLL DANCE | GUY LOMBARDO ORCHESTRA | | $1.00 | $2.00 |
| 1 | 23799 | UNCLE REMUS SAID/ANNIVERSARY SONG | GUY LOMBARDO ORCHESTRA | | $3.00 | $6.00 |
| 1 | 23819 | BLUE SHADOWS ON THE TRAIL/EASTER PARADE | BING CROSBY | | $3.00 | $6.00 |
| 1 | 24174 | LAZY COUNTRYSIDE | JOE MOONEY | | $2.00 | $4.00 |
| 1 | 24511 | THE CHOCOLATE CHOO-CHOO | GUY LOMBARDO ORCHESTRA | 1948 | $1.00 | $2.00 |
| 1 | 24547 | SONGS FROM "SO DEAR TO MY HEART": LAVENDER BLUE/BILLY BOY | BURL IVES, CAPT' STUBBY & BUCCANEERS | 1949 | $3.00 | $6.00 |
| 1 | 24555 | DOWN BY THE STATION /SWEET GEORGIA BROWN | GUY LOMBARDO ORCHESTRA | | $3.00 | $6.00 |
| 1 | 24702 | ADVENTURES OF ICHABOD & MR. TOAD/THE HEADLESS HORSEMAN | BING CROSBY | | $4.00 | $8.00 |
| 1 | 24704 | HOP-SCOTCH POLKA (SCOTCH HOT) | GUY LOMBARDO ORCHESTRA | | $1.00 | $2.00 |
| 1 | 24951 | PETER COTTONTAIL | GUY LOMBARDO ORCHESTRA | 1950 | $1.00 | $2.00 |
| 1 | 25493 | YOU MADE ME LOVE YOU/OVER THE RAINBOW | JUDY GARLAND | | $10.00 | $20.00 |
| 1 | 27032 | BIBBIDI BOBBIDI BOO/RAG MOP SAMBA | BANDO DA LUA | | $2.00 | $4.00 |
| 1 | 27242 | JING-A-LING, JING-A-LING (FROM "BEAVER VALLEY")/PARADE OF THE WOODEN SOLDIERS | ANDREW SISTERS | | $5.00 | $10.00 |
| 1 | 27257 | FROSTY THE SNOWMAN/IF I WERE SANTA CLAUS | GUY LOMBARDO ORCHESTRA | | $1.00 | $2.00 |
| 1 | 27314 | JING-A-LING, JING-A-LING (FROM "BEAVER VALLEY")/MAMBO #5 | SONNY BURKE ORCH | | $2.00 | $4.00 |
| 1 | 27462 | LITTLE WHITE DUCK/THE UNBIRTHDAY SONG | GUY LOMBARDO ORCHESTRA | 1951 | $1.00 | $2.00 |
| 1 | 27482 | BUNNY ROUND-UP TIME/SONNY THE BUNNY | MERVIN SHINER | | $1.00 | $2.00 |
| 1 | 27564 | I'M LATE/THE WALRUS & THE CARPENTER | DANNY KAYE | | $5.00 | $10.00 |

FOLLETT RECORDS
OUR FIRST SONGS
$6.00

FOX RECORDS
THE LITTLE GRAY PONY
$6.00

FREDA MILLER RECORDS
MUSIC FOR RYTHM AND DANCE
$4.00

## FOLKRAFT 10" AND 12" SINGLES, 10" ALBUMS

| # REC | DISC # | ARTIST | A TITLE | B TITLE | G/VG | EX/NMT |
|---|---|---|---|---|---|---|
| 1 | 1184 | THE FOLKRAFTERS | HERE WE GO LOOBIE LOO | FIVE LITTLE CHICADEES, LET YOUR FEET GO TAP | $1.00 | $2.00 |
| 1 | 1185 | THE FOLKRAFTERS | SHOO FLY | GAY MUSICIAN | $1.00 | $2.00 |
| 1 | 1186 | THE FOLKRAFTERS | BROWN EYED ROCKER | OH SUSANNAH | $1.00 | $2.00 |
| 1 | 1187 | THE FOLKRAFTERS | SHOEMAKER'S DANCE | DANISH DANCE OF GREETING, CHIL-DREN'S POLKA | $1.00 | $2.00 |
| 1 | 1188 | THE FOLKRAFTERS | THE MUFFIN MAN | CHIMES OF DUNKIRK, BLEKING | $1.00 | $2.00 |
| 1 | 1189 | THE FOLKRAFTERS | BINGO | BOW BELINDA | $1.00 | $2.00 |
| 1 | 1190 | THE FOLKRAFTERS | HOW DO YOU DO MY PARTNER | I SHOULD LIKE TO GO TO SHET-LAND, PEASE PORRIDGE HOT | $1.00 | $2.00 |
| 1 | 1191 | THE FOLKRAFTERS | A-HUNTING WE WILL GO | BRIDGE OF AVIGNON; ROUND AND ROUND THE VILLAGE | $1.00 | $2.00 |
| 1 | 1192 | THE FOLKRAFTERS | SKIP TO MY LOU | INDIAN DANCE, JOLLY IS THE MILLER | $1.00 | $2.00 |
| 1 | 1193 | THE FOLKRAFTERS | HANSEL AND GRETEL | SKIP ANNIKA | $1.00 | $2.00 |
| 1 | 1194 | THE FOLKRAFTERS | DANISH DANCE OF GREETING | OLD DUTCH DANCE, CRESTED HEN | $1.00 | $2.00 |
| 1 | 1195 | THE FOLKRAFTERS | COME LET US BE JOYFUL | SKATING AWAY | $1.00 | $2.00 |
| 1 | 1196 | THE FOLKRAFTERS | CSARDAS | CSHEBOGAR | $1.00 | $2.00 |
| 1 | 1197 | THE FOLKRAFTERS | TEN LITTLE INDIANS, I SEE YOU | LITTLE SALLY WALTER | $1.00 | $2.00 |
| 1 | 1198 | THE FOLKRAFTERS | SALLY GO ROUND THE MOON | THE SNAIL | $1.00 | $2.00 |
| 1 | 1199 | THE FOLKRAFTERS | RING AROUND THE ROSIE | PUSSY CAT, PUSSY CAT; RIG-A-JIG JIG | $1.00 | $2.00 |
| 1 | 1203 (12") | TOM DICKEY'S ORCH. | SAN ANTONIO ROSE | GRAY EAGLE | $1.00 | $2.00 |
| 1 | 1209 (12") | THE PINEWOODS PLAYERS | LA RUSSE QUADRILLE | CUMBERLAND SQUARE DANCE, YORKSHIRE SQUARE DANCE | $1.00 | $2.00 |
| 1 | 1241 | ? | CUMBERLAND SQUARE (WITH CALLS) | CUMBERLAND SQUARE (INSTRU-MENTAL) | $1.00 | $2.00 |
| 1 | 1242 | FRANK KALTMAN/FOLKRAFT AMERICANA ORCH. | SICILIAN CIRCLE (WITH CALLS) | SICILIAN CIRCLE (INSTRUMENTAL) | $1.00 | $2.00 |
| 1 | 1243 | FRANK KALTMAN/FOLKRAFT AMERICANA ORCH. | PORTLAND FANCY (WITH CALLS) | PORTLAND FANCY (INSTRUMENTAL) | $1.00 | $2.00 |
| 1 | 1247 | FRANK KALTMAN/FOLKRAFT AMERICANA ORCH. | CIRCASSIAN CIRCLE (WITH CALLS) | CIRCASSIAN CIRCLE (INSTRUMEN-TAL) | $1.00 | $2.00 |
| 1 | 1248 | FRANK KALTMAN/FOLKRAFT AMERICANA ORCH. | RUSTIC REEL (WITH CALLS) | RUSTIC REEL (INSTRUMENTAL) | $1.00 | $2.00 |
| 1 | 1249 | FRANK KALTMAN | VIRGINIA REEL (SIMPLFIED) | VIRGINIA REEL | $1.00 | $2.00 |
| 1 | 1250 | FRANK KALTMAN/FOLKRAFT AMERICANA ORCH. | BRIGHTON MIXER (TUNE: GIRL I LEFT BEHIND ME) | GIRL I LEFT BEHIND ME (INSTRU-MENTAL) | $1.00 | $2.00 |
| 1 | 1251 | BOB BRUNDAGE/FOLKRAFT AMERICANA ORCH. | LIFE ON THE OCEAN WAVE (WITH CALLS) | LIFE ON THE OCEAN WAVE (INSTRU-MENTAL) | $1.00 | $2.00 |
| 1 | 1252 | ? | SISTERS FORM A RING (WITH CALLS) | SISTERS FORM A RING (INSTRU-MENTAL) | $1.00 | $2.00 |

## FOLKRAFT 10" AND 12" SINGLES, 10" ALBUMS

| # REC | DISC # | ARTIST | A TITLE | B TITLE | G/VG | EX/NMT |
|---|---|---|---|---|---|---|
| 1 | 1253 | ? | TAKE A PEEK (WITH CALLS) | TAKE A PEEK (INSTRUMENTAL) | $1.00 | $2.00 |
| 1 | 1254 | ? | GRAPEVINE TWIST (WITH CALLS) | GRAPEVINE TWIST (INSTRUMENTAL) | $1.00 | $2.00 |
| 1 | 1255 | ? | COTTON EYED JOE MIXER (WITH CALLS) | COTTON EYED JOE MIXER (INSTRUMENTAL) | $1.00 | $2.00 |
| 1 | 1256 | ? | TEXAS STAR (WITH CALLS) | TEXAS STAR (INSTRUMENTAL) | $1.00 | $2.00 |
| 1 | 1257 | BOB BRUNDAGE/FOLKRAFT AMERICANA ORCH. | HAYMAKER'S JIG (WITH CALLS) | HAYMAKER'S JIG (TUNE: LADY IN THE BOAT) | $1.00 | $2.00 |
| 1 | 1259 | BOB BRUNDAGE/SLEEPY MARTIN, FOLKRAFT AMERICAN ORCH. | FAIRFIELD FANCY | FAIRFIELD FANCY (TUNE: PADDY ON THE TURNPIKE) | $1.00 | $2.00 |
| 3 | F-1440 – 3 | ? | BOXED SET: RHYTHM RECORDS FOR ELEMENTARY GRADES: WALK, ETC. | BOXED SET: RHYTHM RECORDS FOR ELEMENTARY GRADES: WALK, ETC. | $3.00 | $6.00 |
| 4 | F-1444 – 7 | NOT LISTED | BOXED SET: DANCE STEPS FOR ELEMENTARY SCHOOL: TWO STEP, ETC. | BOXED SET: DANCE STEPS FOR ELEMENTARY SCHOOL: TWO STEP, ETC. | $4.00 | $8.00 |

## FOLLETT TOGETHER WE SING SERIES 10" ALBUMS

| SET # | # REC | DISC # | MAIN TITLE | ARTIST | YEAR | G/VG | EX/NMT |
|---|---|---|---|---|---|---|---|
| ALBUM 1 | 4 | 101 – 4 | TOGETHER WE SING — ALBUM 1 | VIRGINIA SPEAKER, ET AL. | 1949 | $3.00 | $6.00 |
| ALBUM 2 | 4 | 201 – 4 | TOGETHER WE SING — ALBUM 2 | VIRGINIA SPEAKER, ET AL. | | $3.00 | $6.00 |
| ALBUM 3 | 4 | 301 – 4 | TOGETHER WE SING — ALBUM 3* | VIRGINIA SPEAKER, ET AL. | | $3.00 | $6.00 |
| ALBUM 4 | 4 | 401 – 4 | TOGETHER WE SING — ALBUM 4 | VIRGINIA SPEAKER, ET AL. | | $3.00 | $6.00 |
| ALBUM 10 | 4 | 1001 – 4 | OUR FIRST SONGS (FOR KINDERGARTEN & FIRST GRADE) | VIRGINIA SPEAKER, ET AL. | 1953 | $3.00 | $6.00 |
| ALBUM 11 | 4 | 1101 – 4 | OUR FIRST SONGS (LOWER GRADES) | VIRGINIA SPEAKER, ET AL. | | $3.00 | $6.00 |
| ALBUM 12 | 4 | 1201 – 4 | OUR FIRST SONGS (LOWER GRADES) | VIRGINIA SPEAKER, ET AL. | | $3.00 | $6.00 |
| ALBUM 13 | 4 | 1301 – 4 | OUR FIRST SONGS (UPPER GRADES, 5 – 8) | VIRGINIA SPEAKER, ET AL. | | $3.00 | $6.00 |
| ALBUM 14 | 4 | 1401 – 4 | OUR FIRST SONGS (UPPER GRADES, 5 – 8) | VIRGINIA SPEAKER, ET AL. | | $3.00 | $6.00 |
| ALBUM 20 | 5 | 2001 – 5 | ALBUMS FOR SPECIAL OCCASIONS: CHRISTMAS CAROLS | VIRGINIA SPEAKER, ET AL. | | $3.00 | $6.00 |
| ALBUM 21 | 5 | 2101 – 5 | ALBUMS FOR SPECIAL OCCASIONS: PATRIOTIC SONGS | VIRGINIA SPEAKER, ET AL. | | $3.00 | $6.00 |
| ALBUM 22 | 4 | 2201 – 4 | ALBUMS FOR SPECIAL OCCASIONS: AMERICAN FOLK SONGS | VIRGINIA SPEAKER, ET AL. | | $3.00 | $6.00 |
| ALBUM 23 | 4 | 2301 – 4 | ALBUMS FOR SPECIAL OCCASIONS: RHYTHM IN MUSIC | VIRGINIA SPEAKER, ET AL. | | $3.00 | $6.00 |
| ALBUM 31 | 3 | 3101 – 3 | MUSIC 'ROUND THE CLOCK (KINDERGARTEN) | NANCY CARR, ET AL. | 1955 | $3.00 | $6.00 |
| ALBUM 32 | 3 | 3201 – 3 | MUSIC 'ROUND THE CLOCK (GRADE 1) | NANCY CARR, ET AL. | | $3.00 | $6.00 |
| ALBUM 35 | 4 | 3501 – 4 | MUSIC 'ROUND THE TOWN (GRADE 2) | NANCY CARR, ET AL. | | $3.00 | $6.00 |
| ALBUM 36 | 4 | 3601 – 4 | MUSIC 'ROUND THE TOWN (GRADE 3) | NANCY CARR, ET AL. | | $3.00 | $6.00 |
| ALBUM 41 | 4 | 4101 – 4 | MUSIC THROUGH THE YEAR (GRADE 3) | NANCY CARR, ET AL. | 1956 | $3.00 | $6.00 |
| ALBUM 42 | 4 | 4201 – 4 | MUSIC THROUGH THE YEAR (GRADE 3) | NANCY CARR, ET AL. | | $3.00 | $6.00 |
| ALBUM 45 | 4 | 4501 – 4 | MUSIC ACROSS OUR COUNTRY (GRADE 4) | NANCY CARR, ET AL. | | $3.00 | $6.00 |
| ALBUM 46 | 4 | 4601 – 4 | MUSIC ACROSS OUR COUNTRY (GRADE 4) | NANCY CARR, ET AL. | | $3.00 | $6.00 |
| ALBUM 51 | 4 | 5101 – 4 | VOICES OF AMERICA (GRADE 5) | NANCY CARR, ET AL. | 1957 | $3.00 | $6.00 |
| ALBUM 52 | 4 | 5210 – 4 | VOICES OF AMERICA (GRADE 5) | NANCY CARR, ET AL. | | $3.00 | $6.00 |
| ALBUM 53 | 4 | 5301 – 4 | VOICES OF THE WORLD (GRADE 6) | NANCY CARR, ET AL. | | $3.00 | $6.00 |
| ALBUM 54 | 4 | 5401 – 4 | VOICES OF THE WORLD (GRADE 6) | NANCY CARR, ET AL. | | $3.00 | $6.00 |
| ALBUM 56 | 4 | 5601 – 4 | TOGETHER WE SING (FOR JUNIOR HIGH SCHOOL) | NANCY CARR, ET AL. | 1958 | $3.00 | $6.00 |
| ALBUM 78 | 4 | 7801 – 4 | TOGETHER WE SING (FOR JUNIOR HIGH SCHOOL) | NANCY CARR, ET AL. | | $3.00 | $6.00 |

*THE CHARLES FULLERTON MEMORIAL ALBUM

## FOX 10" SINGLES AND DOUBLES

| SET # | # REC | DISC # | MAIN TITLE | ARTIST | YEAR | G/VG | EX/NMT |
|---|---|---|---|---|---|---|---|
| M-20 | 1 | FR-101/2 | GEORGE WASHINGTON RABBIT AND HIS GRANNY | MARTHA BLAIR FOX | 194? | $3.00 | $6.00 |
| M-21 | 2 | FR-103/6 – 4/5 | THE LITTLE TUG THAT TRIED | MARTHA BLAIR FOX | | $3.00 | $6.00 |
| M-22 | 1 | FR-107/8 | HENNY PENNY | MARTHA BLAIR FOX | | $3.00 | $6.00 |
| M-23 | 1 | FR-109/10 | THE LITTLE GRAY PONY | MARTHA BLAIR FOX | | $3.00 | $6.00 |
| M-24 | 1 | FR-111/2 | THE OLD WOMAN AND HER PIG | MARTHA BLAIR FOX | | $3.00 | $6.00 |
| M-25 | 1 | FR-113/4 | TWENTY FROGGIES WENT TO SCHOOL | MARTHA BLAIR FOX | | $3.00 | $6.00 |
| M-26 | 1 | FR-115/6 | LITTLE JO-JO (THE ORGAN GRINDER'S MONKEY) | MARTHA BLAIR FOX | | $3.00 | $6.00 |

## FREDA MILLER 10" ALBUMS

| SET # | # REC | DISC # | MAIN TITLE | ARTIST | YEAR | G/VG | EX/NMT |
|---|---|---|---|---|---|---|---|
| ALBUM 1 | 3 | NO #S | ACCOMPANIMENT FOR DANCE TECHNIQUE | FREDA MILLER | 1949 | $2.00 | $4.00 |
| ALBUM 2 | 3 | NO #S | ACCOMPANIMENT FOR DANCE TECHNIQUE | FREDA MILLER | | $2.00 | $4.00 |
| ALBUM 3 | 3 | NO #S | THIRD ALBUM FOR DANCE | FREDA MILLER | | $2.00 | $4.00 |
| ALBUM 4 | 3 | NO #S | MUSIC FOR RHYTHM AND DANCE | FREDA MILLER | | $2.00 | $4.00 |

## GENEVA 7" BOXED SETS

| SET # | # REC | DISC # | MAIN TITLE | ARTIST | YEAR | G/VG | EX/NMT | REMARKS |
|---|---|---|---|---|---|---|---|---|
| NO # | 4 | 69-0011 - 4 | HOLIDAYS: CHRISTMAS, ETC. | NOT LISTED | 1958 | $5.00 | $10.00 | PRICE IS FOR BOXED SET OF 4 RECORDS |
| NO # | 4 | 69-0021 - 4 | MY FAMILY: MY HOUSE, ETC. | NOT LISTED | | $5.00 | $10.00 | |
| NO # | 4 | MTX: MA 9 - 12 | THE WORLD I LIVE IN: CREATION, ETC. | NOT LISTED | | $5.00 | $10.00 | |
| NO # | 4 | 69-0211 - 4 | THROUGH THE YEAR: SPRING, ETC. | NOT LISTED | | $5.00 | $10.00 | |

## GINN & CO. OUR SINGING WORLD SERIES 10" ALBUMS

| SET # | # REC | DISC # | MAIN TITLE | ARTIST | YEAR | G/VG | EX/NMT |
|---|---|---|---|---|---|---|---|
| KA | 5 | 1K - 5K | THE KINDERGARTEN BOOK - ALBUM K-A | NOT LISTED | 1949 | $3.00 | $6.00 |
| KB | 5 | 85 - 89 | THE KINDERGARTEN BOOK - ALBUM K-B | NOT LISTED | | $3.00 | $6.00 |
| 1A | 4 | 1 - 4 | THE FIRST GRADE BOOK - ALBUM 1-A | NOT LISTED | | $3.00 | $6.00 |
| 1B | 4 | 5 - 8 | THE FIRST GRADE BOOK - ALBUM 1-B | NOT LISTED | | $3.00 | $6.00 |
| 1C | 4 | 90 - 93 | THE FIRST GRADE BOOK - ALBUM 1-C | NOT LISTED | | $4.00 | $8.00 |
| 2A | 4 | 9 - 12 | SINGING ON OUR WAY (2ND GRADE) - ALBUM 2-A | NOT LISTED | | $3.00 | $6.00 |
| 2B | 4 | 34 - 37 | SINGING ON OUR WAY (2ND GRADE) - ALBUM 2-B | NOT LISTED | | $3.00 | $6.00 |
| 2C | 4 | 94 - 97 | SINGING ON OUR WAY (2ND GRADE) - ALBUM 2-C | NOT LISTED | | $4.00 | $8.00 |
| 3A | 4 | 13 - 16 | SINGING AND RHYMING (3RD GRADE) - ALBUM 3-A | NOT LISTED | 1950 | $3.00 | $6.00 |
| 3B | 4 | 38 - 41 | SINGING AND RHYMING (3RD GRADE) - ALBUM 3-B | NOT LISTED | | $3.00 | $6.00 |
| 3C | 4 | 98 - 101 | SINGING AND RHYMING (3RD GRADE) - ALBUM 3-C | NOT LISTED | | $4.00 | $8.00 |
| 4A | 5 | 17 - 21 | SINGING EVERY DAY (4TH GRADE) - ALBUM 4-A | NOT LISTED | | $3.00 | $6.00 |
| 4B | 5 | 42 - 46 | SINGING EVERY DAY (4TH GRADE) - ALBUM 4-B | NOT LISTED | | $3.00 | $6.00 |
| 4C | 4 | 102 - 105 | SINGING EVERY DAY (4TH GRADE) - ALBUM 4-C | NOT LISTED | | $4.00 | $8.00 |
| 5A | 6 | 22 - 27 | SINGING TOGETHER (5TH GRADE) - ALBUM 5-A | NOT LISTED | 1951 | $3.00 | $6.00 |
| 5B | 5 | 47 - 51 | SINGING TOGETHER (5TH GRADE) - ALBUM 5-B | NOT LISTED | | $3.00 | $6.00 |
| 5C | 4 | 106 - 109 | SINGING TOGETHER (5TH GRADE) - ALBUM 5-C | NOT LISTED | | $4.00 | $8.00 |
| 6A | 6 | 28 - 33 | SINGING IN HARMONY (6TH GRADE) ALBUM 6-A | NOT LISTED | | $3.00 | $6.00 |
| 6B | 6 | 52 - 57 | SINGING IN HARMONY (6TH GRADE) ALBUM 6-B | NOT LISTED | | $3.00 | $6.00 |
| 7A | 6 | 58 - 63 | SINGING JUNIORS (7TH GRADE) - ALBUM 7-A | NOT LISTED | 1953 | $5.00 | $10.00 |
| 7B | 6 | 70 - 75 | SINGING JUNIORS (7TH GRADE) - ALBUM 7-B | NOT LISTED | | $5.00 | $10.00 |
| 8A | 6 | 64 - 69 | SINGING TEENAGERS (8TH GRADE) - ALBUM 8-A | NOT LISTED | 1954 | $6.00 | $12.00 |
| 8B | 6 | 76 - 81 | SINGING TEENAGERS (8TH GRADE) - ALBUM 8-B | NOT LISTED | | $6.00 | $12.00 |

## GINN & CO. WE SING AND PRAISE SERIES 10" ALBUMS

| SET # | # REC | DISC # | MAIN TITLE | ARTIST | YEAR | G/VG | EX/NMT |
|---|---|---|---|---|---|---|---|
| 1 | 6 | 1 - 6 | WE SING AND PLAY (1ST GRADE) | NOT LISTED | 1957 | $5.00 | $10.00 |
| 2 | 5 | 7 - 11 | WE SING AND LISTEN (2ND GRADE) | NOT LISTED | | $5.00 | $10.00 |
| 3 | 5 | 12 - 16 | WE SING AND DANCE (3RD GRADE) | NOT LISTED | | $5.00 | $10.00 |
| 4 | 6 | 17 - 22 | WE SING AND CHANT (4TH GRADE) | NOT LISTED | 1958 | $5.00 | $10.00 |
| 5 | 6 | 23 - 28 | WE SING AND BLEND (5TH GRADE) | NOT LISTED | | $5.00 | $10.00 |
| 6 | 6 | 29 - 34 | WE SING AND HARMONIZE (6TH GRADE) | NOT LISTED | 1959 | $5.00 | $10.00 |
| 7 | 2 (LPS) | 35 - 36 | WE SING OF OUR LAND (7TH GRADE) | NOT LISTED | 1960 | $5.00 | $10.00 |
| 8 | 2 (LPS) | 37 - 38 | WE SING OF OUR WORLD (8TH GRADE) | NOT LISTED | 1962 | $5.00 | $10.00 |
| 1B | 1 (LP) | 39 | WE SING AND PLAY (1ST GRADE) | NOT LISTED | | $5.00 | $10.00 |
| 2B | 1 (LP) | 40 | WE SING AND LISTEN (2ND GRADE) | NOT LISTED | | $5.00 | $10.00 |
| 3B | 1 (LP) | 41 | WE SING AND DANCE (3RD GRADE) | NOT LISTED | | $5.00 | $10.00 |
| 4B | 1 (LP) | 42 | WE SING AND CHANT (4TH GRADE) | NOT LISTED | | $5.00 | $10.00 |
| 5B | 1 (LP) | 43 | WE SING AND BLEND (5TH GRADE) | NOT LISTED | | $5.00 | $10.00 |
| 6B | 1 (LP) | 44 | WE SING AND HARMONIZE (6TH GRADE) | NOT LISTED | | $5.00 | $10.00 |
| 7B | 1 (LP) | 45 | WE SING OF OUR LAND (7TH GRADE) | NOT LISTED | | $5.00 | $10.00 |
| 8B | 1 (LP) | 46 | WE SING OF OUR WORLD (8TH GRADE) | NOT LISTED | | $5.00 | $10.00 |

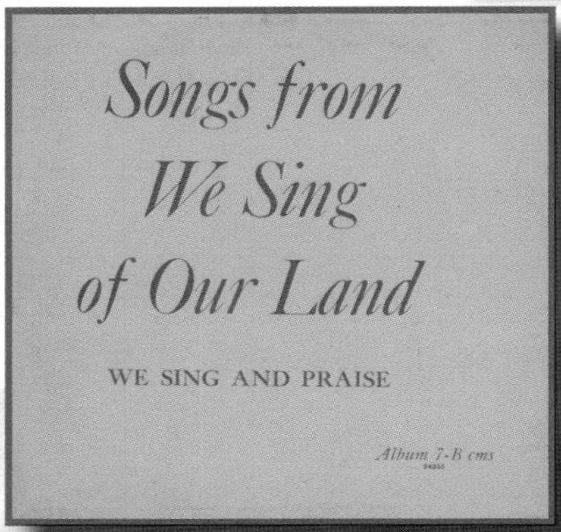


GENEVA RECORDS
HOLIDAYS
$10.00

GINN & CO. RECORDS
THE KINDERGATEN BOOK
$6.00

GINN & CO. RECORDS
SINGING JUNIORS
$10.00

## GINN & CO. BASIC READER SERIES 7" ALBUMS

| SET # | # REC | MAIN TITLE |
|---|---|---|
| ALBUM 1 | 2 | THE READING READINESS PROGRAM |
| ALBUM 2 | 2 | THE PRE-PRIMER PROGRAM |
| ALBUM 3 | 2 | THE LITTLE WHITE HOUSE |
| ALBUM 4 | 2 | ON CHERRY STREET |

## GINN & CO. MUSIC EDUCATION SERIES 10" SINGLES (MUSIC APPRECIATION COURSE)

| # REC | DISC # | MAIN TITLE | ARTIST | YEAR | G/VG | EX/NMT |
|---|---|---|---|---|---|---|
| 1 | G 1- A/B | INITIAL SONGS FROM "SONGS OF CHILDHOOD": SINGING, ETC. | NY PHILHARMONIC; HENRY HADLEY, COND. | 1925 | $4.00 | $8.00 |
| 1 | G 2 A/B | RHYTHMIC INSTRUMENTAL FOLK CLASSICS: HARVEST DANCE, ETC. | NY PHILHARMONIC; HENRY HADLEY, COND. | | $4.00 | $8.00 |
| 1 | G 3 A/B | INITIAL SONGS FROM "INTRODUCTORY MUSIC": LITTLE MISS MUFFET, ETC. | NY PHILHARMONIC; HENRY HADLEY, COND. | | $4.00 | $8.00 |
| 1 | G 4 A/B | RHYTHMIC INSTRUMENTAL FOLK CLASSICS: OXDANSEN, ETC. | NY PHILHARMONIC; HENRY HADLEY, COND. | | $4.00 | $8.00 |
| 1 | G 5 A/B | INSTRUMENTAL CLASSICS — RHYTHMIC & PROGRAM: MINUET, ETC. | NY PHILHARMONIC; HENRY HADLEY, COND. | | $4.00 | $8.00 |
| 1 | G 6 A/B | INITIAL SONGS FROM "ELEMENTARY MUSIC," PT. 1 | NY PHILHARMONIC; HENRY HADLEY, COND. | | $4.00 | $8.00 |
| 1 | G 6 C/D | INITIAL SONGS FROM "JUVENILE MUSIC": FAIRY SIGNALS, ETC. | NY PHILHARMONIC; HENRY HADLEY, COND. | | $4.00 | $8.00 |
| 1 | G 7 A/B | RHYTHMIC INSTRUMENTAL CLASSICS: THEME FROM SYMP. 20, HAYDN, ETC. | NY PHILHARMONIC; HENRY HADLEY, COND. | | $4.00 | $8.00 |
| 1 | G 8 A/B | INSTRUMENTAL CLASSICS--RHYTHMIC & PROGRAM: MARCH, ETC. | NY PHILHARMONIC; HENRY HADLEY, COND. | | $4.00 | $8.00 |
| 1 | G 10 A/B | PROGRAM INSTRUMENTAL CLASSICS: THE MOUSE TRAP SCHERZO, ETC. | NY PHILHARMONIC; HENRY HADLEY, COND. | | $4.00 | $8.00 |
| 1 | G 12 A/B | RHYTHMIC INSTRUMENTAL CLASSICS: MARGUERITES, ETC. | NY PHILHARMONIC; HENRY HADLEY, COND. | | $4.00 | $8.00 |
| 1 | G 14 A/B | RHYTHMIC INSTRUMENTAL CLASSIC: PRAELUDIUM/SPINNING SONG | NY PHILHARMONIC; HENRY HADLEY, COND. | | $4.00 | $8.00 |
| 1 | G 15 A/B | PROGRAM INSTRUMENTAL CLASSIC: SERENATA/AT THE BROOK | NY PHILHARMONIC; HENRY HADLEY, COND. | | $4.00 | $8.00 |
| 1 | G 40 A/B | RHYTHMIC MUSIC | NY PHILHARMONIC; HENRY HADLEY, COND. | | $4.00 | $8.00 |
| N/A | CASE FOR RECORDS | MUSIC APPRECIATION COURSE | NY PHILHARMONIC; HENRY HADLEY, COND. | | $5.00 | $10.00 |

## GOLDEN MAIN SERIES 6" AND 7" SINGLES

| REC # | MAIN TITLE | ARTIST | YEAR | G/VG | EX/NMT |
|---|---|---|---|---|---|
| 1 | SCUFFY THE TUGBOAT/GOOD MORNING | ALEC WILDER, GILBERT MACK/IREENE WICKER, GILBERT MACK | 1948 | $5.00 | $10.00 |
| 2 | THE LIVELY LITTLE RABBIT/FARANDOLE | IREENE WICKER, GILBERT MACK/MITCHELL MILLER & ORCHESTRA (MMO) | | $5.00 | $10.00 |
| 3 | THE SHY LITTLE KITTEN/HUMORESQUE | IREENE WICKER, GILBERT MACK/MMO | | $5.00 | $10.00 |
| 4 | TOOTLE/NORWEGIAN DANCE | IREENE WICKER, ALEC WILDER/MMO | | $5.00 | $10.00 |
| 5 | THE POKY LITTLE PUPPY/THE NAUGHTY DUCK | IREENE WICKER, GILBERT MACK, MMO | | $5.00 | $10.00 |
| 6 | CIRCUS TIME: BIG TOP/SIDESHOWS | IREENE WICKER, GILBERT MACK, MMO/GILBERT MACK, IREENE WICKER | | $5.00 | $10.00 |
| 7 | THE FUNNY LITTLE MOUSE/THE TALL GIRAFFE | IREENE WICKER, MMO/IREENE WICKER, GILBERT MACK | | $5.00 | $10.00 |
| 8 | WYNKEN, BLYNKEN AND NOD/STORM IN THE BATHTUB | IREENE WICKER, MMO/IREENE WICKER | | $5.00 | $10.00 |

## GOLDEN MAIN SERIES 6" AND 7" SINGLES

| REC # | MAIN TITLE | ARTIST | YEAR | G/VG | EX/NMT |
|---|---|---|---|---|---|
| 9 | LITTLE PEEWEE/TURKISH MARCH | MMO/IREENE WICKER, GILBERT MACK | | $5.00 | $10.00 |
| 10 | THE GOLDEN EGG/BEETHOVEN'S COUNTRY DANCE | MMO/IREENE WICKER | | $5.00 | $10.00 |
| 11 | THE BIG BROWN BEAR/SCHUBERT'S MERRY MUSIC | MMO/IREENE WICKER, GILBERT MACK | | $5.00 | $10.00 |
| 12 | OUT OF THE WINDOW/THE BUSY ELEVATOR | IREENE WICKER, ALEC WILDER, MMO/IREENE WICKER | | $5.00 | $10.00 |
| 13 | ANIMALS OF FARMER JONES/SCHUMANN'S HAPPY FARMER | IREENE WICKER, GILBERT MACK, MMO/MMO | 1949 | $2.00 | $4.00 |
| 14 | FIVE LITTLE FIREMEN/FLUTE DANCE | IREENE WICKER, GILBERT MACK, MMO/MMO | | $2.00 | $4.00 |
| 15 | TAXI THAT HURRIED/CHILDREN'S DANCE (FROM HANSEL & GRETEL) | IREENE WICKER & GILBERT MACK, MMO/MMO | | $2.00 | $4.00 |
| 16 | FAVORITE SONGS FROM MOTHER GOOSE: THREE LITTLE KITTENS, ETC. | ANNE LLOYD (AL), GILBERT MACK, THE SANDPIPERS (SAND), MMO/AL, BOB MILLER | | $2.00 | $4.00 |
| 17 | FOLK SONGS: OH SUSANNA/TURKEY IN THE STRAW | MICHAEL STEWART, SAND/SAND, MMO | | $2.00 | $4.00 |
| 18 | FAVORITE SONGS FROM MOTHER GOOSE: THE FARMER IN THE DELL, ETC. | AL, SAND, MMO | | $2.00 | $4.00 |
| 19 | DIXIE/YANKEE DOODLE | SAND, MMO | | $2.00 | $4.00 |
| 20 | FAVORITE SONGS FROM MOTHER GOOSE: THE MUFFIN MAN, ETC. | AL, SAND, MMO | | $2.00 | $4.00 |
| 21 | FOLK SONGS: DE CAMPTOWN RACES/CLEMENTINE | DICK BYRON, SAND, MMO/AL, SAND, MMO | | $2.00 | $4.00 |
| 22 | FAVORITE SONGS FROM MOTHER GOOSE: LONDON BRIDGE, ETC. | SAND, MMO/AL, RALPH NYLAND, MMO | | $2.00 | $4.00 |
| 23 | MOTHER GOOSE & OTHER FAVORITES: HUMPTY DUMPTY, ETC. | SAND, MMO/AL, SAND, MMO | | $2.00 | $4.00 |
| 24 | FAVORITE SONGS FROM MOTHER GOOSE: OLD KING COLE, ETC. | MICHAEL STEWART, SAND, MMO/AL, SAND, MMO | | $2.00 | $4.00 |
| 25 | OLD MAC DONALD HAD A FARM/THE OWL AND THE PUSSYCAT | GILBERT MACK, SAND, MMO/AL, MMO | | $2.00 | $4.00 |
| 26 | FAVORITE SONGS FROM MOTHER GOOSE: THREE BLIND MICE/LITTLE BO PEEP, LITTLE JACK HORNER | SAND, MMO/AL, SAND; MMO | | $2.00 | $4.00 |
| 27 | FOLK SONGS: THE BARNYARD/ROUND AND ROUND THE VILLAGE | DICK BYRON, GILBERT MACK, MMO/SAND, MMO | | $2.00 | $4.00 |
| 28 | MOTHER GOOSE & OTHER FAVORITES: BRAHMS' LULLABY/TWINKLE TWINKLE LITTLE STAR, ROCKABYE BABY | AL, SAND/AL, SAND, MMO | | $2.00 | $4.00 |
| 29 | FAVORITE SONGS FROM MOTHER GOOSE: A FROG HE WOULD A-WOOING GO/BOBBY SHAFTOE, HICKROY DICKORY DOCK | GILBERT MACK, SAND, MMO/AL, SAND, MMO | | $2.00 | $4.00 |
| 31 | THE BLUE-TAIL FLY/ROCK CANDY MOUNTAIN | DICK BYRON, SAND, MMO/MICHAEL STEWART, SAND, MMO | | $2.00 | $4.00 |
| 33 | THE NIGHT BEFORE CHRISTMAS | PETER DONALD, MMO | | $2.00 | $4.00 |
| 34 | SILENT NIGHT/IT CAME UPON A MIDNIGHT CLEAR | SAND | | $2.00 | $4.00 |
| 35 | FAVORITE CHRISTMAS SONGS: JINGLE BELLS/DECK THE HALLS, UP ON THE HOUSETOP | DICK BYRON, SAND/MICHAEL STEWART, SAND | | $2.00 | $4.00 |
| 36 | FAVORITE CHRISTMAS CAROLS: GOD REST YE MERRY GENTLEMEN/HARK! THE HERALD ANGELS SING | RALPH NYLAND, SAND/SAND | | $2.00 | $4.00 |
| 37 | FAVORITE CHRISTMAS CAROLS: O LITTLE TOWN OF BETHLEHEM/O CHRISTMAS TREE, JOY TO THE WORLD | BOB MILLER, SAND/SAND | | $2.00 | $4.00 |
| 38 | FAVORITE CHRISTMAS CAROLS: O COME ALL YE FAITHFUL/AWAY IN A MANGER | SAND | | $2.00 | $4.00 |
| R-40 | A LITTLE GOLDEN SLEEPY RECORD: SLEEPING CHILD/CLOSE YOUR EYES | SAND, AL, MMO | 1950 | $2.00 | $4.00 |
| R-41 | THE WHITE BUNNY AND HIS MAGIC NOSE/BUNNY HOP | SAND, AL, GIL MACK, MMO/MMO | | $2.00 | $4.00 |
| R-42 | THE SAGGY BAGGY ELEPHANT/ELEPHANT'S WALK | SAND, AL, GIL MACK, DANNY OCKO, MMO/MMO | | $8.00 | $15.00 |
| R-43 | THE SEVEN SNEEZES/MY TOOTHBRUSH SONG | SAND, AL, GIL MACK, MMO/AL, SAND, MMO | | $8.00 | $15.00 |
| R-44 | THE MAGIC GOLDEN RECORD: THE MAGIC RECORD/THE DANCING RECORD | AL, MICHAEL STEWART, SAND, MMO/SAND, MMO | | $12.00 | $25.00 |
| R-45 | LITTLE FAT POLICEMAN/SAFETY SONG | SAND, MMO | | $8.00 | $15.00 |

## GOLDEN MAIN SERIES 6" AND 7" SINGLES

| # REC | DISC # | MAIN TITLE | ARTIST | YEAR | G/VG | EX/NMT |
|---|---|---|---|---|---|---|
| 1 | R-46 | BRAVE COWBOY BILL | SAND, GILBERT MACK, MMO/GILBERT MACK, MMO | | $8.00 | $15.00 |
| 1 | R-47 | SANTA CLAUS IS COMING TO TOWN/GOLDEN CHRISTMAS SONG | SAND, AL, MMO | | $2.00 | $4.00 |
| 1 | R-48 | PIRATES & SAILOR SONGS: SEA CHANTY/SAILING SAILING, SAILOR'S HORNPIPE | MICHAEL STEWART, SAND, MMO/DICK BYRON, SAND, MMO | | $2.00 | $4.00 |
| 1 | R-49 | THE WIZARD OF OZ: OVER THE RAINBOW/EXPLOSION POLKA | AL, THE SAND, MMO/MMO | | $5.00 | $10.00 |
| 1 | R-50 | THE WIZARD OF OZ: WE'RE OFF TO SEE THE WIZARD/SWAN'S DANCE | SAND, MMO/MMO | | $5.00 | $10.00 |
| 1 | R-51 | DOCTOR DAN, THE BANDAGE MAN/BILLY BOY | AL, DICK BYRON, MMO/AL, SAND, MMO | | $8.00 | $15.00 |
| 1 | R-52 | TIMMY IS A BIG BOY NOW/THE THREE BEARS | AL, DICK BYRON, MMO/ SAND, MMO | | $10.00 | $20.00 |
| 1 | R-53 | POOR MR. FLIBBERTY-JIB/THE NOISE SONG | AL, GILBERT MACK, DICK BYRON, SAND, MMO/AUDREY MARSH, GILBERT MACK, SAND, MMO | | $8.00 | $15.00 |
| 1 | R-54 | THE HAPPY MAN AND HIS DUMP TRUCK/THE HAPPY MAN'S DANCE | AL, DICK BYRON, MMO/MMO | | $8.00 | $15.00 |
| 1 | R-55 | SCUFFY THE TUGBOAT/MY BONNIE LIES OVER THE OCEAN | MIKE STEWART, GILBERT MACK, SAND, MMO/SAND, MMO | | $8.00 | $15.00 |
| 1 | R-56 | TOOTLE/THE CHOO-CHOO TRAIN | PAT O'MALLEY, MMO/SAND, AL, MMO | | $8.00 | $15.00 |
| 1 | R-57 | PETER COTTONTAIL (EASTER VERSION)/PETER COTTONTAIL (YEAR-ROUND VERSION) | AL, SAND, MMO | 1951 | $2.00 | $4.00 |
| 1 | R-58 | WOODY WOODPECKER SONG/WOODPECKER'S DANCE | SAND, MMO/MMO | | $10.00 | $20.00 |
| 1 | R-59 | LITTLE LULU/LAVENDER'S BLUE | AL, SAND, MMO/AUDREY MARSH, MMO | | $10.00 | $20.00 |
| 1 | R-60 | POPEYE, THE SAILOR MAN/BLOW THE MAN DOWN | VOICE OF POPEYE: JACK MERCER, SAND, MMO/SAND, MMO | | $10.00 | $20.00 |
| 1 | R-61 | CASPER THE FRIENDLY GHOST/BARTOK'S LITTLE GHOST DANCE | AL, SAND, MMO/MMO | | $10.00 | $20.00 |
| 1 | R-62 | WINNIE THE POOH: SING HO FOR THE LIFE OF A BEAR/COTTLESTON PIE | SAND, MMO/AL, SAND, MMO | | $8.00 | $15.00 |
| 1 | S-64 | SONGS FROM CAROUSEL AND OKLAHOMA: OH! WHAT A BEAUTIFUL MORNING/JUNE IS BUSTIN' OUT ALL OVER | DICK BYRON, SALLY SWEETLAND, AL, SAND, MMO | | $2.00 | $4.00 |
| 1 | R-65 | MARCH FROM PETER AND THE WOLF/JING-A-LING JING-A-LING | MMO/SAND, AL, MMO | | $2.00 | $4.00 |
| 1 | R-66 | ICKA-BACKA-SODA-CRACKER/COME TO THE BARN DANCE | AL, DICK BYRON, MMO/RALPH NYLAND, GILBERT MACK, SAND, MMO | | $2.00 | $4.00 |
| 1 | R-67 | TARZAN SONG/JUNGLE DANCE | SAND, MMO/MMO | | $5.00 | $10.00 |
| 1 | R-68 | RUDOLPH THE RED-NOSED REINDEER/THE REINDEER'S DANCE | MIKE STEWART, SAND, MMO/MMO | | $2.00 | $4.00 |
| 1 | R-69 | FROSTY THE SNOWMAN | SAND, MMO/PAT O'MALLEY, SAND, MMO | | $2.00 | $4.00 |
| 1 | R-70 | LITTLE AUDREY SAYS/LET'S GO SHOPPING | MAE QUESTAL, SAND, MMO/AL, MMO | | $10.00 | $20.00 |
| 1 | R-71 | PARADE OF THE WOODEN SOLDIERS/SPARROW IN THE TREETOP | SAND, AL, MMO | | $2.00 | $4.00 |
| 1 | R-72 | ALEXANDER'S RAGTIME BAND | AL, SAND, MMO/MMO | | $2.00 | $4.00 |
| 1 | SD-73 | WALT DISNEY'S (WD'S) LITTLE FRIENDS: L'IL BAD WOLF, TINKER BELL (SD73AB)/DOPEY'S WHISTLE; HUEY, LOUIE AND DEWEY (SD73CD) | BRUCE MARSHALL, AL, SAND, MMO/SAND, MMO | | $10.00 | $20.00 |
| 1 | R-74 | DADDY'S WHISTLE/CHOCOLATE COWBOY | SALLY SWEETLAND, MMO/DICK BYRON, MMO | | $2.00 | $4.00 |
| 1 | SR + R-75 | EASTER PARADE | PETER HANLEY, MMO/SAND, MMO | | $2.00 | $4.00 |
| 1 | R-76 | UKELELE AND HER NEW DOLL | AL, SAND, MMO/PAT O'MALLEY, AL, SAND, MMO | 1952 | $5.00 | $10.00 |
| 1 | R-77 | TAWNY SCRAWNY LION SONG & STORY | AL, MICHAEL STEWART, SAND, MMO | | $3.00 | $6.00 |
| 1 | SD-78 | WD'S SONGS OF THE CITY: MICKEY MOUSE TRAFFIC COP, GOOFY STREET CLEANER (SD78AB)/DONALD DUCK FIRE CHIEF, LITTLE POSTMENV (SD78CD) | AL, SAND, MMO | | $10.00 | $20.00 |
| 1 | R-79 | MY COUNTRY, 'TIS OF THEE/STAR-SPANGLED BANNER | SAND, MMO | | $2.00 | $4.00 |
| 1 | R-80 | EGBERT THE EASTER EGG/BUNNY, BUNNY, BUNNY | BETTY CLOONEY, SAND, MMO/SAND, MMO | | $2.00 | $4.00 |
| 1 | S-81 | SONGS ABOUT WOODWINDS: ANTOINETTE THE CLARINET, BOBO THE OBOE (S81AB)/KNUTE THE FLUTE, MULDOON THE OLD BASSOON (SD81CD) | AL, SAND, MMO | | $2.00 | $4.00 |
| 1 | S-82 | JIMMY DURANTE SINGS: RUDOLPH THE RED-NOSED REINDEER/SANTA CLAUS IS COMING TO TOWN | JIMMY DURANTE, SAND, MMO | | $5.00 | $10.00 |
| 1 | S-83 | IRVING BERLIN'S: OH! HOW I HATE TO GET UP IN THE MORNING/I DON'T WANNA GO TO BED | DICK BYRON, MICHAEL STEWART, ROBERT MILLER, RALPH NYLAND, MMO/AL, MICHAEL STEWART, MMO | | $2.00 | $4.00 |
| 1 | R-84 | GOD BLESS AMERICA | PETER HANLEY, SAND, MMO/SAND, MMO | | $2.00 | $4.00 |
| 1 | R-85 | MR. SHORTSLEEVES SUPERMARKET/STOP LOOK AND LISTEN | SAND, MMO | | $4.00 | $8.00 |
| 1 | R-86 | WILLIE THE WHISTLING GIRAFFE/THE POKY LITTLE PUPPY | AL, SAND, MMO | | $4.00 | $8.00 |
| 1 | R-87 | DOWN BY THE STATION/THE LITTLE TRAIN WHO SAID "AH CHOO" | AL, SAND, MMO | | $2.00 | $4.00 |

GOLDEN RECORDS
TOOTLE
$10.00

GOLDEN RECORDS
POOR MR. FLIBBERTY-JIB
$15.00

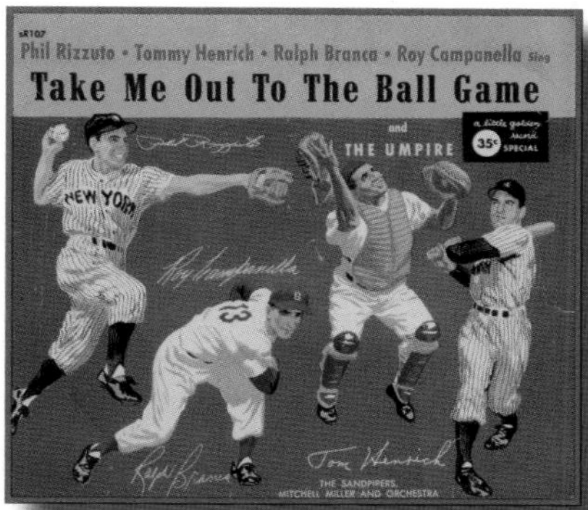


GOLDEN RECORDS
TAKE ME OUT TO THE BALLGAME
$25.00

## GOLDEN MAIN SERIES 6" AND 7" SINGLES

| # REC | DISC # | MAIN TITLE | ARTIST | YEAR | G/VG | EX/NMT |
|---|---|---|---|---|---|---|
| 1 | R-88 | WHEN SANTA CLAUS GETS YOUR LETTER | AL, MICHAEL STEWART, SAND, MMO/PAT O'MALLEY, AL, SAND, MMO | | $2.00 | $4.00 |
| 1 | R-89 | TOM CORBETT SPACE CADET: SPACE ACADEMY SONG/ SPACE CADET MARCH | THE CADET CHORUS & ORCH./SPACE CADET MARCHING BAND | | $20.00 | $40.00 |
| 1 | R-90 | FUZZY WUZZY/THE SLEEPY BEAR'S DANCE | BETTY CLOONEY, MMO/MMO | | $3.00 | $6.00 |
| 1 | R-91 | DENNIS THE MENACE | BOBBY NICK, SAND, MMO | | $10.00 | $20.00 |
| 1 | R-92 | H.M.S. PINAFORE: LITTLE BUTTERCUP/WE SAIL THE OCEAN BLUE | AL, MMO/SAND, MMO | | $3.00 | $6.00 |
| 1 | SR + S-94 | YANKEE DOODLE DANDY/YOU'RE A GRAND OLD FLAG | BERT PARKS, MMO/SAND | | $2.00 | $4.00 |
| 1 | R-95 | GANDY DANCER'S BALL/HAMBONE | SAND, AL, MMO | | $2.00 | $4.00 |
| 1 | R-96 | SHRIMP BOATS/ON TOP OF OLD SMOKY | SAND, SALLY SWEETLAND, MMO/SAND, AL, MMO | | $2.00 | $4.00 |
| 1 | R-97 | PULL TOGETHER/SANTA'S OTHER REINDEER | SAND, MMO | | $2.00 | $4.00 |
| 1 | R-98 | INTRODUCING ROOTIE KAZOOTIE/THE POLKA DOTTIE POLKA | ORIGINAL VOICES FROM ROOTIE KAZOOTIE TV SHOW, NAOMI LEWIS, MMO | | $2.00 | $4.00 |
| 1 | SR-99 | JIMMY DURANTE SINGS: YANKEE DOODLE BUNNY (THE HOLIDAY BUNNY)/I LIKE PEOPLE (THE FRIENDLY SONG) | JIMMY DURANTE, SAND, MMO/JIMMY DURANTE, MMO | | $5.00 | $10.00 |
| 1 | S-100 | SONGS FROM THE KING AND I: I WHISTLE A HAPPY TUNE/ GETTING TO KNOW YOU | AL, ROBERT MILLER, SAND, MMO/SALLY SWEETLAND, SAND, MMO | | $3.00 | $6.00 |
| 1 | R-101 | ON THE GOOD SHIP LOLLIPOP/THE RIDDLE SONG | AL, SAND, MMO/AL, PAT O'MALLEY, MMO | | $2.00 | $4.00 |
| 1 | R-102 | BUMBLE BEE BUMBLE BYE/I'M GONNA GET WELL TODAY | AL, SAND, MMO | | $2.00 | $4.00 |
| 1 | R-103 | WHITE CHRISTMAS | PETER HANLEY, SAND, MMO/BARBARA GUSSOW, DAVID ANDERSON, SAND, MMO | | $2.00 | $4.00 |
| 1 | SR-104 | WHEN THE RED RED ROBIN COMES BOB-BOB-BOBBIN' ALONG/WALKIN' TO MISSOURI | AL, SAND, MMO | | $2.00 | $4.00 |
| 1 | R-105 | PAPER DOLL/PAPER FAMILY | AL, MMO/AL, MICHAEL STEWART, SAND, MMO | | $8.00 | $15.00 |
| 1 | S-106 | SONGS FROM SOUTH PACIFIC: HAPPY TALK/DITES MOI | AL, SAND, MMO | | $2.00 | $4.00 |
| 1 | S-107 | TAKE ME OUT TO THE BALLGAME, THE UMPIRE/CASEY AT THE BAT | PHIL RIZZUTO, TOMMY HENRICH, RALPH BRANCA, ROY CAMPANELLA, SAND, MMO/MEL ALLEN | | $15.00 | $30.00 |
| 1 | SR-107* | TAKE ME OUT TO THE BALLGAME/THE UMPIRE | PHIL RIZZUTO, TOMMY HENRICH, RALPH BRANCA, ROY CAMPANELLA, SAND, MMO | | $12.00 | $25.00 |
| 1 | SR-108 | BERT PARK SINGS: ME AND MY SHADOW/SKI-DA-ME RINK-A-DOO | BERT PARKS, SAND, MMO/BERT PARKS, AL, SAND, MMO | | $2.00 | $4.00 |
| 1 | R-109 | ROOTIE KAZOOTIE IN POLKA DOTTIE'S GARDEN: STORY/ SONG | NAOMI LEWIS, FRANK MILANO, MMO | 1953 | $10.00 | $20.00 |
| 1 | R-110 | I SAW MOMMY KISSING SANTA CLAUS/CHRISTMAS CHOP-STICKS | AL, SAND, MMO | | $2.00 | $4.00 |
| 1 | S-111 | SONGS ABOUT OUR ARMY, NAVY, MARINES AND AIR CORPS | SAND, MMO | | $2.00 | $4.00 |
| 1 | R-112 | THE NIGHT BEFORE CHRISTMAS/CRACKERJACK CHRIST-MAS | JACK ARTHUR, AL, SAND, MMO/AL, SAND, MMO | | $2.00 | $4.00 |
| 1 | R-113 | TEDDY BEARS ON PARADE/ME AND MY TEDDY BEAR | JACK ARTHUR, SAND, MMO | | $2.00 | $4.00 |
| 1 | R-115 | CIRCUS DAY: THE MAN ON THE FLYING TRAPEZE | DICK BYRON, RALPH NYLAND, MICHAEL STEWART, BOB MILLER, MMO | | $2.00 | $4.00 |

*VARIATION

## GOLDEN MAIN SERIES 6" AND 7" SINGLES

| # REC | DISC # | MAIN TITLE | ARTIST | YEAR | G/VG | EX/NMT |
|---|---|---|---|---|---|---|
| 1 | R-116 | TWEET AND TOOT | AL, MICHAEL STEWART, MMO/MMO | | $2.00 | $4.00 |
| 1 | R-117 | TA-RA-RA-BOOM-DER-E/PONY BOY | AL, SALLY SWEETLAND, RALPH NYLAND, SAND, MMO/AL, SAND, MMO | | $2.00 | $4.00 |
| 1 | R-118 | MACNAMARA'S BAND SONG AND MARCH | RALPH NYLAND, SAND, AL, SALLY SWEETLAND, MMO/MMO | | $2.00 | $4.00 |
| 1 | R-119 | SINGING IN THE RAIN/LET'S ALL SING LIKE THE BIRDIES SING | AL, SAND, MMO | | $2.00 | $4.00 |
| 1 | R-120 | THERE'S A RAINBOW 'ROUND MY SHOULDER/INKY DINKY BOB-O-LINKI | AL, MMO | | $2.00 | $4.00 |
| 1 | SD-121 | FROM WD'S "THE GRASSHOPPER AND THE ANTS": THE WORLD OWES ME A LIVING | AL, SAND, MMO/AL, GILBERT MACK, MMO | | $5.00 | $10.00 |
| 1 | R-124 | THE RAG DOLL WITH THE SHOE BUTTON EYES/THE LOLLIPOP TREE | AL, SAND, MMO | | $2.00 | $4.00 |
| 1 | R-125 | SLEIGH RIDE/I JUST CAN'T WAIT 'TILL CHRISTMAS | SAND, MMO/AL, SAND, MMO | | $2.00 | $4.00 |
| 1 | R-126 | SYNCOPATED CLOCK/THE CLOCK SYMPHONY | AL, MIKE STEWART, SAND, MMO/MMO | | $2.00 | $4.00 |
| 1 | R-127 | HOP SCOTCH POLKA/MUSIC, MUSIC, MUSIC | AL, SAND, MMO | | $2.00 | $4.00 |
| 1 | S-128 | SONGS ABOUT THE BRASS: MONSIEUR FORLORN, THE FRENCH HORN; CRUMPET THE TRUMPET/MC-MALONE, THE SLIDE TROMBONE; POOBAH, THE TUBA | SAND, MMO | | $2.00 | $4.00 |
| 1 | R-130 | THUMBELINA/WONDERFUL COPENHAGEN | AL, SAND, MMO | | $2.00 | $4.00 |
| 1 | R-131 | MR. DEETLE DOOTLE SONG/ROOTIE KAZOOTIE & MR. DEETLE DOODLE | NAOMI LEWIS, SAND, MMO | | $8.00 | $15.00 |
| 1 | R-132 | PLAYMATES ("COME OUT AND PLAY WITH ME")/ TATTLE TALE DUCK | AL, SAND, MMO | | $2.00 | $4.00 |
| 1 | R-133 | THREE LITTLE FISHES/THE MUSIC GOES 'ROUND AND AROUND | AL, SAND, MMO | | $2.00 | $4.00 |
| 1 | R-134 | DADDY'S REPORT CARD/DADDIES ("WHAT DOES YOUR DADDY DO?") | MARY JANE SUTHERLAND, SAND, MMO/AL, RALPH NYLAND, JIMMY LEYDEN, SAND, MMO | | $2.00 | $4.00 |
| 1 | R-135 | PIG POLKA/CRAZY QUILT FARM | AL, MICHAEL STEWART, SAND, MMO | | $3.00 | $6.00 |
| 1 | R-137 | MY BUNNY (AND MY SISTER SUE)/POLLY-WOLLY-DOODLE | AL, JIMMY CARROLL & ORCH., SAND (JCO) | | $2.00 | $4.00 |
| 1 | R-138 | (LITTLE JOE WORM, SON OF) THE GLOW-WORM/ MR. TAP-TOE | SAND, JCO/AL, JCO | | $2.00 | $4.00 |
| 1 | S-139 | ANIMAL PLAY TIME: BLING BLANG BUILD A HOUSE FOR BABY, PICK IT UP/MAILMAN, DON'T YOU PUSH ME DOWN | UNCLE WIN STRACKE, AL, SAND, MMO | | $2.00 | $4.00 |
| 1 | S-141 | FOUR HYMNS: JESUS WANTS ME FOR A SUNBEAM, ET AL. | GOLDEN CHOIR, MITCHELL MILLER, DIRECTOR. | | $2.00 | $4.00 |
| 1 | R-142 | FINDER'S KEEPERS ALLEE IN FREE/THE WOOD-CHUCK SONG,; KICK THE CAN WILLIE! | AL, SAND, MMO | | $4.00 | $8.00 |
| 1 | S-143 | JELLY ON MY HEAD, I WISH I WAS A WHISKER/FLIP-PETY FLOPPETY BUNNY, PEE WEE THE BUNNY WITH THE BIG BLUE EYES | MARY JANE SUTHERLAND, SAND, MMO | 1954 | $2.00 | $4.00 |
| 1 | R-144 | THE LITTLE ENGINE THAT COULD | AL, SAND, MMO | | $2.00 | $4.00 |
| 1 | R-145 | HOW MUCH IS THAT DOGGIE IN THE WINDOW/ THREE LITTLE PUPPIES | AL, SAND, MMO/AL, MICHAEL STEWART, SAND, MMO | | $3.00 | $6.00 |
| 1 | R-146 | EUSTIS THE USELESS RABBIT/THE ANIMALS DANCE | AL, MIKE STEWART, MMO/AL, SAND, MMO | | $2.00 | $4.00 |
| 1 | R-147 | ARFY, THE DOGGIE IN THE WINDOW/MAIRZY DOATS | AL, SAND, MMO | | $3.00 | $6.00 |
| 1 | R-149 | ROOTIE KAZOOTIE AND GALA POOCHIE PUP/ROO-TIE KAZOOTIE'S GALA POOCHIE MARCH | BETTY JANE TYLER, FRANK MILANO, ORIGINAL VOICES OF ROOTIE KAZOOTIE TV SHOW, MMO/MMO | | $8.00 | $15.00 |
| 1 | D-150 | WD'S "THE TORTOISE AND THE HARE " | GIL MACK, SAND, MMO | | $4.00 | $8.00 |
| 1 | D-151 | WD'S "GOOFY THE TOREADOR" | GIL MACK, SAND, MMO/SAND, MMO | | $4.00 | $8.00 |
| 1 | R-152 | GASTON AND JOSEPHINE/THE COBBLER ON COB-BLESTONE ROAD | AL, SAND, MMO | | $3.00 | $6.00 |
| 1 | S-154 | GOD BLESS US ALL/NOW I LAY ME DOWN TO SLEEP | MARY JANE SUTHERLAND, THE GOLDEN CHOIR, JCO | | $4.00 | $8.00 |
| 1 | R-155 | I WANT A HIPPOPOTAMUS FOR CHRISTMAS/I DREAMT THAT I WAS SANTA CLAUS | AL, SAND, MMO | | $3.00 | $6.00 |
| 1 | S-157 | SONGS ABOUT STRINGS: LUCY LYNN THE VIOLIN, MELLOW FELLOW THE CELLO/NOLA THE VIOLA, LOVELACE THE BASS | AL, MIKE STEWART, MMO/RALPH NYLAND, MIKE STEWART, MMO | | $2.00 | $4.00 |
| 1 | R-159 | I TAWT I TAW A PUDDY-TAT | ORIGINAL VOICES OF BUGS BUNNY & TWEETIE PIE, MMO | | $4.00 | $8.00 |
| 1 | S-160 | LITTLE WHITE DUCK/LITTLE SIR ECHO | AL, SAND, MMO | | $2.00 | $4.00 |
| 1 | S-161 | LITTLE LULU AND HER MAGIC TRICKS | MARY JANE SUTHERLAND, SAND, MMO | | $8.00 | $15.00 |

## GOLDEN MAIN SERIES 6" AND 7" SINGLES

| # REC | DISC # | MAIN TITLE | ARTIST | YEAR | G/VG | EX/NMT |
|---|---|---|---|---|---|---|
| 1 | D-162 (FROM WD'S OMMC) | FROM WD'S "ADVENTURES IN MUSIC": A TOOT AND A WHISTLE, A PLUNK AND A BOOM | AL, MICHAEL STEWART, MMO/MMO | | $5.00 | $10.00 |
| 1 | S-163 | THE BIG BELL AND THE LITTLE BELL/EASTER MORNIN' | TEX STEWART, BILLY & THE WESTERNERS, MMO | | $2.00 | $4.00 |
| 1 | D-164 | FROM WD'S "BAMBI": THUMPER SONG/LITTLE APRIL SHOWERS | JIMMY LEYDEN, SAND, MMO/MIKE STEWART, JIMMY LEYDEN, BOB MILLER, MMO | | $4.00 | $8.00 |
| 1 | R-166 | LITTLE FIR TREE/WHERE DID MY SNOW MAN GO? | AL, MIKE STEWART, SAND, MMO/MARY JANE SUTHERLAND, SAND, MMO | | $2.00 | $4.00 |
| 1 | R-167 | THE LITTLE STOWAWAY ON SANTA'S SLEIGH/THAT'S WHAT I WANT FOR CHRISTMAS | AL, MIKE STEWART, SAND, MMO/MARY JANE SUTHERLAND, SAND, MMO | | $2.00 | $4.00 |
| 1 | D-168 (FROM WD'S OMMC) | FROM WD'S "MELODY TIME": JOHNNY APPLESEED: PIONEER SONG/APPLE SONG | MIKE STEWART, SAND, MMO/AL, SAND, MMO | | $3.00 | $6.00 |
| 1 | D-169 | SONGS FROM WD'S "DUMBO": WHEN I SEE AN ELEPHANT FLY/IT'S CIRCUS DAY AGAIN | AL, MIKE STEWART, JIMMY LEYDEN, SAND, MMO/SAND, MMO | | $4.00 | $8.00 |
| 1 | SD-172 | FROM WD'S "MELODY TIME": PECOS BILL | MIKE STEWART, JIMMY LEYDEN, RALPH NYLAND, MMO & CHORUS | | $4.00 | $8.00 |
| 1 | D-174 | SONGS FROM WD'S "20,000 LEAGUES UNDER THE SEA": SNOOPY THE SEAL/WHALE OF A TAIL | DICK BYRON, BOB MILLER, MIKE STEWART, RALPH NYLAND, MMO | | $4.00 | $8.00 |
| 1 | SD-175 | WD'S "THE RELUCTANT DRAGON" | AL, MICHAEL STEWART, GIL MACK, MMO | | | |
| 1 | R-176 | HAPPY TRAILS TO YOU/A COWBOY NEEDS A HORSE | ROY ROGERS & DALE EVANS/ROY ROGERS & CHORUS | | $5.00 | $10.00 |
| 1 | R-179 | LORD IS COUNTING ON YOU/OPEN UP YOUR HEART | ROY ROGERS & DALE EVANS WITH CHORUS | | $5.00 | $10.00 |
| 1 | R-180 | BUGS BUNNY "WHAT'S UP DOC?" | SAND, MMO, VOICE OF BUGS BUNNY | 1955 | $5.00 | $10.00 |
| 1 | R-183 | THE NIGHT BEFORE CHRISTMAS | ROY ROGERS & DALE EVANS, MMO | | $5.00 | $10.00 |
| 1 | R-184 | ANNIE OAKLEY SINGS: THE ANNIE OAKLEY SONG/BRIGHT EYED AND BUSHY TAILED | SAND, MMO | | $3.00 | $6.00 |
| 1 | R-185 | SWEDISH RHAPSODY/BAMBOO BOAT | ROY ROGERS, THE RANCH HANDS, MMO | | $5.00 | $10.00 |
| 1 | R-186 | DAFFY DUCK | SAND, MMO | | $5.00 | $10.00 |
| 1 | R-187 | DANIEL THE COCKER SPANIEL/CHICKI WICKI CHOCTAW | ROY ROGERS, SAND, MMO/DALE EVANS, THE RANCH HANDS, MMO | | $5.00 | $10.00 |
| 1 | D-188 | FROM WD'S "AT THE COUNTRY FAIR" | SAND, MMO | | $5.00 | $10.00 |
| 1 | R-189 | ELMER FUDD | SAND, MMO | | $5.00 | $10.00 |
| 1 | D-190 | SONGS FROM WD'S "LADY AND THE TRAMP": LADY/HE'S A TRAMP | MICHAEL MILLER, SALLY SWEETLAND, AL, SAND, MMO/AL, SAND, MMO | | $4.00 | $8.00 |
| 1 | R-191 | BUGS BUNNY EASTER SONG/MR. EASTER RABBIT | SAND, MMO/BUGS BUNNY, SAND, MMO | | $5.00 | $10.00 |
| 1 | R-192 | EASTER IS A LOVING TIME/CANDY KANE CAKEWALK | ROY ROGERS, DALE EVANS, SAND, MMO | | $2.00 | $4.00 |
| 1 | D-194 | THEME SONG FROM WD'S TV SHOW "DISNEYLAND": WHEN YOU WISH UPON A STAR | SAND, MMO | | $4.00 | $8.00 |
| 1 | D-195 | SONGS FROM WD'S "LADY AND THE TRAMP": WHAT IS A BABY?, LA LA LU/SIAMESE CAT SONG | AL, SALLY SWEETLAND, SAND, MMO, AL, SALLY SWEETLAND, MMO | | $3.00 | $6.00 |
| 1 | R-196 | THE LITTLE SHOEMAKER/THE HAPPY WANDERER | ROY ROGERS & DALE EVANS, MMO/SAND, MMO | | $5.00 | $10.00 |
| 1 | D-197 | WD'S "THE BALLAD OF DAVY CROCKETT" | SAND, MMO | | $5.00 | $10.00 |
| 1 | R-198 | THE LITTLE BOY WHO COULDN'T FIND CHRISTMAS/THE STORY OF CHRISTMAS | ROY ROGERS & DALE EVANS, THE RANCH HANDS, MMO | | $5.00 | $10.00 |
| 1 | R-199 | THE CHUCK WAGON SONG/ROY ROGERS HAD A RANCH | ROY ROGERS & DALE EVANS, THE RANCH HANDS, MMO/PAT BRADY, THE RANCH HANDS, MMO | | $5.00 | $10.00 |
| 1 | R-200 | MISTER SANDMAN/THE MAMA DOLL SONG | AL, SAND & ORCHESTRA | | $2.00 | $4.00 |
| 1 | R-202 | I SAW MOMMY DO THE MAMBO (WITH YOU KNOW WHO)/DON'T LET THE KIDDYGEDDIN | AL, SAND & ORCHESTRA | | $2.00 | $4.00 |
| 1 | R-203 | SYLVESTER THE CAT/SYLVESTER THE CAT'S NINE LIVES | SAND, MMO | | $5.00 | $10.00 |
| 1 | R-204 | TWEEDLE DEE/KO KO MO | AL, SAND, MMO | | $2.00 | $4.00 |
| 1 | R-205 | A GOODNIGHT PRAYER/KEEP IN TOUCH | ROY ROGERS, THE RANCH HANDS, MMO/DALE EVANS, THE RANCH HANDS, MMO | | $5.00 | $10.00 |
| 1 | R-206 | PORKY PIG | SAND, MMO | | $5.00 | $10.00 |
| 1 | R-209 | FOGHORN LEGHORN/HENERY HAWK | SAND, MMO | | $5.00 | $10.00 |
| 1 | R-212 | LOOK FOR THE BRIGHT SIDE/LITTLE ONE, LEAN ONE, LONG ONE, LICKPOT, THUMBO | HOWDY DOODY & THE GANG, MMO/BUFFALO BOB, MMO | | $10.00 | $20.00 |
| 1 | D-213 | SONGS FROM WD'S "DAVY CROCKETT": BE SURE YOU'RE RIGHT/OLD BETSY | JIMMY DODD, THE FRONTIER MEN | | $5.00 | $10.00 |
| 1 | D-214 | SONGS FROM WD'S "LADY & THE TRAMP": THE SIAMESE CAT SONG/BELLA NOTTE | AL, SALLY SWEETLAND, MMO/THE PAESANOS, MMO | | $4.00 | $8.00 |
| 1 | R-215 | YOSEMITE SAM/BUGS BUNNY WAY OUT WEST | SAND, MMO | | $5.00 | $10.00 |

## GOLDEN MAIN SERIES 6" AND 7" SINGLES

| # REC | DISC # | MAIN TITLE | ARTIST | YEAR | G/VG | EX/NMT |
|---|---|---|---|---|---|---|
| 1 | R-216 | THE BERRY TREE/HEY MR. BANJO | SAND, MMO | | $2.00 | $4.00 |
| 1 | R-217 | FARMER AL FALFA/MIGHTY MOUSE THEME SONG | THE TERRYTOONERS, MMO | | $8.00 | $15.00 |
| 1 | R-218 | BARKER BILL/STEP RIGHT UP | THE TERRYTOONERS, MMO | | $5.00 | $10.00 |
| 1 | R-219 | LOOK LOOK!/WILL MY DOG BE PROUD OF ME | BUFFALO BOB & THE GANG, MMO/HOWDY DOODY, BUFFALO BOB, CAPT. SCUTTLEBUTT & THE GANG, MMO | | $10.00 | $20.00 |
| 1 | R-220 | THE LAUGHING SONG/JOHN J. FEDOOZLE | BUFFALO BOB, THE PRINCESS & THE GANG, MMO/ JOHN J. FEDOOZLE & THE GANG, MMO | | $10.00 | $20.00 |
| 1 | R-221 | COWABONGA/BIG CHIEF | CHIEF THUNDERTHUD, MMO/THE PRINCESS, MMO | | $10.00 | $20.00 |
| 1 | D-222 (GOLDEN + FROM WD'S OMMC) | OFFICIAL MICKEY MOUSE CLUB (MMC) SONG/OFFICIAL MMC MARCH | JIMMY DODD, THE MERRY MOUSEKETEERS/MICKY MOUSE, DONALD DUCK, JIMINY CRICKET, THE MERRY MOUSEKETEERS | | $8.00 | $15.00 |
| 1 | D-223 (FROM WD'S OMMC) | OFFICIAL MMC PLEDGE/SHO-JO-JI (A JAPANESE PLAY SONG) | MICKEY MOUSE, THE MERRY MOUSEKETEERS, FRANCES ARCHER, BEVERLY GILE, THE OFFICIAL MMC CHORUS | | $8.00 | $15.00 |
| 1 | D-224 (FROM WD'S OMMC) | YOU, THE HUMAN ANIMAL/THE MMC BOOK SONG | JIMINY CRICKET (CLIFF EDWARDS), THE OFFICIAL MMC CHORUS | | $8.00 | $5.00 |
| 1 | D-225 (FROM WD'S OMMC) | THE MICKEY MOUSE PICTURE HOUSE SONG/WHEN I GROW UP | MICKEY MOUSE, THE MERRY MOUSEKETEERS/JIM-MIE DODD, THE OFFICIAL MMC CHORUS | | $8.00 | $15.00 |
| 1 | R-226 | CHAMPION THE WONDER HORSE/BRIDLE AND SADDLE | SAND, MMO | | $8.00 | $5.00 |
| 1 | R-227 | ANNIE OAKLEY SINGS: TEN GALLON HAT/I GOTTA CROW (FROM PETER PAN) | SAND, MMO | | $3.00 | $6.00 |
| 1 | R-231 | BUFFALO BILL JR. | SAND, MMO | | $4.00 | $8.00 |
| 1 | D-232 (GOLDEN + FROM WD'S OMMC) | I'M NO FOOL/FRERE JACQUES | JIMINY CRICKET (CLIFF EDWARDS), MERRY MOUSEKETEERS CHORUS & ORCH./FRANCES AR-CHER, BEVERLY GILE, MERRY MOUSEKETEERS CHORUS & ORCH. | | $8.00 | $5.00 |
| 1 | D-233 (FROM WD'S OMMC) | THE ANIMALS AND CLOWNS SONG/WHO AM I? | MMC CHORUS & ORCH./JIMMIE DODD, MMC CHO-RUS & ORCH. | | $8.00 | $15.00 |
| 1 | D-234 (FROM WD'S OMMC) | THE MICKEY MOUSE NEWSREEL MUSIC/ANYONE FOR EXPLORING? | MMC CHORUS & ORCH./JIMMIE DODD, MMC CHO-RUS & ORCH. | | $8.00 | $15.00 |
| 1 | D-235 (FROM WD'S OMMC) | THE MERRY MOUSKETEERS/TALENT ROUND-UP | JIMMIE DODD, THE MERRY MOUSEKETEERS, MMC CHORUS & ORCH./JIMMIE DODD, MMC CHORUS & ORCH. | | $8.00 | $15.00 |
| 1 | D-238 (FROM DISNEYLAND OMMC) | SONGS FROM DAVY CROCKETT AND THE RIVER PIRATES: KING OF THE RIVER (MIKE FINK'S SONG)/YALLER, YALLER GOLD | THE FRONTIER MEN CHORUS & ORCH. | | $6.00 | $12.00 |
| 1 | R-239 | OKLAHOMA! | SAND, MMO | | $2.00 | $4.00 |
| 1 | R-240 | THE LORD'S PRAYER/AVE MARIA | ROY ROGERS, THE RANCH HANDS, MMO/DALE EVANS, MMO | | $5.00 | $10.00 |
| 1 | R-241 | THE BIBLE TELLS ME SO/HAVE YOU READ THE BIBLE TODAY? | ROY ROGERS, DALE EVAN, THE RANCH HANDS, MMO | | $5.00 | $10.00 |
| 1 | R-242 | THE YELLOW ROSE OF TEXAS/(MY HEART GOES) PID-DILY PATTER PATTER | SAND CHORUS AND ORCHESTRA | | $2.00 | $4.00 |
| 1 | R-243 | ALPHABET SONG/COUNTING SONG | SAND, MMO | | $2.00 | $4.00 |
| 1 | R-244 | SONGS FROM OKLAHOMA: THE SURREY WITH THE FRINGE ON TOP: VOCAL/INSTRUMENTAL | SAND, MMO/MMO | | $2.00 | $4.00 |
| 1 | R-246 | JESUS LOVES THE LITTLE CHILDREN/THE LORD IS GONNA TAKE CARE OF YOU | ROY ROGERS, DALE EVANS, MMO | | $5.00 | $10.00 |
| 1 | R-247 (FROM DISNEYLAND OMMC) | FROM THE STORY OF ROBIN HOOD: ROBIN HOOD BAL-LAD/RIDDLE-DE-DIDDLE-DE-DAY | SAND, MMO | | $3.00 | $6.00 |
| 1 | R-248 | ANNIE OAKLEY SAFETY SONGS: THE TRAFFIC LIGHT SONG/I LOVE TO RIDE MY BIKE | ANNIE OAKLEY, SAND, MMO | | $3.00 | $6.00 |
| 1 | R-249 | BUGS BUNNY, RAILROAD ENGINEER/YOSEMITE SAM, HOLD-UP MAN | THE ORIGINAL VOICES, THE SAND, MMO | | $5.00 | $10.00 |
| 1 | R-250 | COWBOY DAFFY DUCK/KANGAROO HOP | SAND, MMO | | $5.00 | $10.00 |
| 1 | D-251 | DONALD DUCK: QUACK QUACK/DONALD SINGS THROUGHOUT THE WORLD | SAND, MMO | | $5.00 | $10.00 |
| 1 | D-253 (FROM WD'S OMMC) | HI TO YOU (HEJ FORDIG)/DO-ME-SO | JIMMIE DODD, FRANCES ARCHER, BEVERLY GILE, THE MOUSEKETEERS/JIMMIE DODD, THE MOUSEKETEERS CHORUS & ORCH. | | $8.00 | $15.00 |
| 1 | D-254 (FROM WD'S OMMC) | MOUSEKEDANCES: THE PUSSY CAT POLKA, THE MICKEY MOUSE MAMBO/THE MOUSEKEDANCE, THE MOUSEKETAP | JIMMY DODD, THE MOUSEKETEERS, RUTH CAR-RELL, CHORUS & ORCH. | | $8.00 | $15.00 |
| 1 | R-255 | COWBOYS NEVER CRY/I LOVE THE OUTDOORS | ROY ROGERS, THE RANCH HANDS & ORCH./DALE EVANS, THE RANCH HANDS & ORCH. | | $5.00 | $10.00 |
| 1 | R-257 | TUBBY THE TUBA | WILLIAM BELL, MMO/PAUL TRIPP, SAND, MMO | 1956 | $4.00 | $8.00 |

## GOLDEN MAIN SERIES 6" AND 7" SINGLES

| # REC | DISC # | MAIN TITLE | ARTIST | G/VG | EX/NMT |
|---|---|---|---|---|---|
| 1 | R-261 | A CHRISTMAS CAROL | BOB SMITH, HOWDY DOODY, DILLY DALLY, CAPTAIN SCUTTLEBUTT | $10.00 | $20.00 |
| 1 | R-262 | 16 TONS/BONNIE BLUE GAL | SAND, MMO | $2.00 | $4.00 |
| 1 | R-263 (GOLDEN + ROMPER ROOM) | WELCOME TO ROMPER ROOM: POP GOES THE WEASEL/ THUMBKIN, ALL ABOUT ME | SAND, MMO | $5.00 | $10.00 |
| 1 | R-264 (ROMPER ROOM) | ROMPER ROOM: THE DO BEE SONG | SAND, MMO | $5.00 | $10.00 |
| 1 | R-265 (ROMPER ROOM) | ROMPER ROOM SINGING GAMES: SKIP TO MY LOU, RING AROUND THE ROSY/FARMER IN THE DELL | SAND, MMO | $5.00 | $10.00 |
| 1 | R-266 (ROMPER ROOM) | ROMPER ROOM NURSERY RHYMES: JACK & JILL, BAA, BAA, BLACK SHEEP/SING A SONG OF SIXPENCE, LITTLE MISS MUFFET | SAND, MMO | $5.00 | $10.00 |
| 1 | R-267 (ROMPER ROOM) | ROMPER ROOM LEARN ABOUT THE FARM SONGS: OLD MACDONALD HAD A FARM/THE BARNYARD SONG | SAND, MMO | $5.00 | $10.00 |
| 1 | R-268 (ROMPER ROOM) | ROMPER ROOM SING ALONG SONGS | SAND, MMO | $5.00 | $10.00 |
| 1 | GL-269 | HANSEL AND GRETEL | MIKE STEWART, BOB MILLER, RALPH NYLAND, DICK BYRON, AL, MMO | $2.00 | $4.00 |
| 1 | R-270 | BABY'S FIRST RECORD: LOOK AT OUR NEW BABY, BABY'S BELLS/BABY IN THE TUB, TICKLE TOES | MIKE STEWART | $8.00 | $15.00 |
| 1 | GL-272 | LULLABY TIME: TWINKLE TWINKLE LITTLE STAR, ROCK A BYE, BABY/NOW I LAY ME DOWN TO SLEEP | SAND, MMO/AL, SAND, MMO | $2.00 | $4.00 |
| 1 | R-273 | NURSERY SONGS: RING AROUND THE ROSY, SKIP TO MY LOU/ROUND & ROUND THE VILLAGE | THE SAND, MMO | $2.00 | $4.00 |
| 1 | R + GL-274 | THE THREE BEARS: SONG & STORY | MIKE STEWART, AL, MMO/SAND, MMO | $2.00 | $4.00 |
| 1 | R-276 | GET WELL: I'M GONNA GET WELL TODAY/ DR. SNIFFLESWIPER | SAND, MMO | $4.00 | $8.00 |
| 1 | R-277 | PONY BOY/ON TOP OF OLD SMOKEY | AL, SAND, MMO | $2.00 | $4.00 |
| 1 | R-279 | SCHOOL DAYS | SAND, MMO | $2.00 | $4.00 |
| 1 | D-280 (FROM WD'S OMMC) | FROM WD'S "CINDERELLA": BIBBIDI-BOBBIDI-BOO (THE MAGIC SONG) | AL, SAND, MMO/MMO | $8.00 | $15.00 |
| 1 | D-281 (FROM WD'S OMMC) | FROM WD'S "CINDERELLA": CINDERELLA WORK SONG/ WORK SONG | AL, SAND, MMO/MMO | $8.00 | $15.00 |
| 1 | D-282 (FROM WD'S OMMC) | FROM WD'S "CINDERELLA": A DREAM IS A WISH (YOUR HEART MAKES) | CINDERELLA'S MICE, MMO/AL, SAND, MMO | $8.00 | $15.00 |
| 1 | GL-284 | PETER AND THE WOLF: MARCH/STORY | MMO/MIKE STEWART, GIL MACK, SAND, MMO | $2.00 | $4.00 |
| 1 | R-285 | HAPPY BIRTHDAY TO YOU | SAND, MMO | $4.00 | $8.00 |
| 1 | R-286 | DUNGAREE DOLL/MY FRIEND THE GHOST | SAND, MMO/TOMMY & JIMMY DORSEY, VOCAL: GORDON POLK | $10.00 | $20.00 |
| 1 | R-287 | THE MOST HAPPY FELLA/THE HAPPY WHISTLER | SAND, MMO | $2.00 | $4.00 |
| 1 | R-288 | LITTLE CHILD (THE LITTLE BOY & THE OLD MAN)/WILL YOU COME FOR A WALK WITH ME? | AL, MIKE STEWART, MMO/AL, MMO | $2.00 | $4.00 |
| 1 | R-290 | I'M GETTIN' NUTTIN' FOR CHRISTMAS/WISHY WASHY WISH | BILLY QUINN, SAND, MMO/DICKIE BEALS, SAND, MMO | $2.00 | $4.00 |
| 1 | D-291 (FROM WD'S OMMC) | FROM WD'S "HUCKLEBERRY FINN": HUCKLEBERRY FINN/ TOM SAWYER (PAINTING AUNT POLLY'S FENCE) | SAND, MMO | $15.00 | $30.00 |
| 1 | D-292 (FROM WD'S OMMC) | FROM WD'S "SPIN & MARTY": GOOD NIGHT LITTLE WRANGLER/TRIPLE R (YIPP-A YIPP-O) | MIKE STEWART, SAND, MMO/AL, SAND, MMO | $8.00 | $15.00 |
| 1 | D-293 (FROM WD'S OMMC) | FROM WD'S "THE GREAT LOCOMOTIVE CHASE": RAILROADIN' MAN/SONS OF OLD AUNT DINAH | MIKE STEWART, SAND, MMO/SAND, MMO | $8.00 | $15.00 |
| 1 | R-294 | WHOEVER HEARD OF A COWARDLY COWBOY/HOORAY FOR COWBOYS | ARTHUR NORMAN SINGERS | $2.00 | $4.00 |
| 1 | R-295 | CIRCUS BOY (THEME SONG FROM THE TV SHOW) | SAND, MMO | $10.00 | $20.00 |
| 1 | R-297 | JACK AND THE BEANSTALK/MARCH OF THE ILL ASSORTED GUARDS | SAND, MMO | $2.00 | $4.00 |
| 1 | GL-298 | TRAIN SONGS: I'VE BEEN WORKING ON THE RAILROAD/ DOWN BY THE STATION | AL, SAND, MMO | $2.00 | $4.00 |
| 1 | D-300 | WD'S SONG OF FANTASYLAND | NORMAN LUBOFF CHORUS & ORCH. | $8.00 | $15.00 |
| 1 | D-301 | WD'S SONG OF FRONTIERLAND | NORMAN LUBOFF CHORUS & ORCH. | $8.00 | $15.00 |
| 1 | D-302 | WD'S SONG OF TOMORROWLAND | NORMAN LUBOFF CHORUS & ORCH. | $8.00 | $15.00 |
| 1 | D-303 | WD'S SONG OF ADVENTURELAND | NORMAN LUBOFF CHORUS & ORCH. | $8.00 | $18.00 |
| 1 | R-304 | THE STORY OF THE MAGI/THE GIFT OF THE MAGI | AL, SAND, MMO/MIKE STEWART, SAND, MMO | $4.00 | $8.00 |
| 1 | R-305 | A MERRY, MERRY, MERRY, MERRY CHRISTMAS/A HAPPY LITTLE NEW YEAR | AL, SAND, MMO | $2.00 | $4.00 |

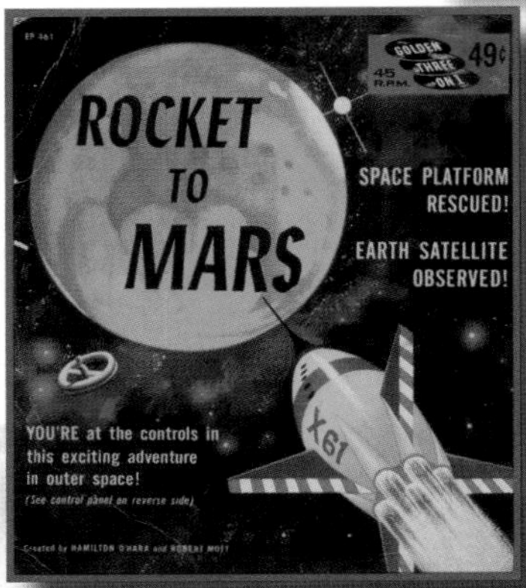


GOLDEN RECORDS
PIG POLKA
$6.00

GOLDEN RECORDS
JESUS LOVES LITTLE CHILDREN
$10.00

GOLDEN RECORDS
ROCKET TO MARS!
$25.00

## GOLDEN MAIN SERIES 6" AND 7" SINGLES

| # REC | DISC # | MAIN TITLE | ARTIST | YEAR | G/VG | EX/NMT |
|---|---|---|---|---|---|---|
| 1 | D-306 (FROM WD'S OMMC) | WD'S PLAY A POLKA/THE DRUM SONG (BUMME, LUMME, LUMME) | SAND, MMO | | $10.00 | $20.00 |
| 1 | R-307 | FOUR HYMNS | THE GOLDEN CHOIR; MITCHELL MILLER, DIR. | | $2.00 | $4.00 |
| 1 | D-308 (FROM WD'S DISNEYLAND) | FROM WD'S "WESTWARD HO THE WAGONS!": THEME SONG | SAND, MMO | | $8.00 | $15.00 |
| 1 | R-309 | O CHRISTMAS TREE, JOY TO THE WORLD/O COME ALL YE FAITHFUL | BOYS' CHOIR, SAND, MMO | | $2.00 | $4.00 |
| 1 | D-310 (FROM WD'S DISNEYLAND) | FROM WD'S "WESTWARD HO, THE WAGONS!": WRINGLE WRANGLE/(I'M LONELY, MY DARLING) GREEN GROW THE LILACS | SAND, MMO | | $8.00 | $15.00 |
| 1 | D-311 (FROM WD'S DISNEYLAND) | FROM WD'S "WESTWARD HO, THE WAGONS!": THE BALLAD OF JOHN COLTER/PIONEER'S PRAYER | SAND, MMO | | $8.00 | $15.00 |
| 1 | R-312 | LET THERE BE PEACE ON EARTH/THANK YOU GOD | ROY ROGERS & DALE EVANS, THE RANCH HANDS, MMO | | $8.00 | $15.00 |
| 1 | R-314 | MERRIE MELODIES | BUGS BUNNY, SYLVESTER, HENRY HAWK & THE OTHERS, SAND, MMO | | $6.00 | $12.00 |
| 1 | R-316 | HOT DIGGITY (DOG ZIGGITY BOOM)/ROCK ISLAND LINE | SAND, JCO/JIMMY LEYDEN, SAND, JCO | | $2.00 | $4.00 |
| 1 | EP-317 | GOLDEN MOTHER GOOSE: 3 LITTLE KITTENS, ETC. | AL, BOB MILLER, SAND, MMO/AL, MIKE STEWART, SAND, MMO | | $2.00 | $4.00 |
| 1 | EP-318 | TRAIN SONGS: TOOTLE, ETC. | AL, SAND, MMO/AL, PAT O'MALLEY, SAND, MMO | | $3.00 | $6.00 |
| 1 | EP-319 | SONGS ABOUT ANIMALS: TAWNY SCRAWNY LION, SAGGY BAGGY ELEPHANT, POKY LITTLE PUPPY, WILLIE THE WHISTLING GIRAFFE, ELEPHANT WALK | AL, MICHAEL STEWART, SAND, MMO/ AL, GIL MACK, DANNY OCKO, SAND, MMO | | $2.00 | $4.00 |
| 1 | EP-320 | GOLDEN TOY PARADE: FUZZY WUZZY, ETC. | BETTY CLOONEY, AL, SAND, MMO/AL, SAND, MMO | | $2.00 | $4.00 |
| 1 | EP-321 | TV WILD WEST FAVORITES: ANNIE OAKLEY SONG, ETC. | ANNIE OAKLEY, SAND, MMO/SAND, MMO | | $2.00 | $4.00 |
| 1 | EP-322 | GOLDEN CHRISTMAS FAVORITES: JINGLE BELLS, ETC. | SAND, MMO/PAT O'MALLEY, SAND, MMO | | $2.00 | $4.00 |
| 1 | EP-323 | LOONEY TUNES: BUGS BUNNY, ETC. | ORIGINAL VOICES OF BUGS BUNNY, SYLVESTER, TWEETIE PIE, SAND, MMO | | $5.00 | $10.00 |
| 1 | EP-324 | ROY ROGERS' COWBOY STORIES: HAPPY TRAILS TO YOU, ETC. | ROY ROGERS, PAT BRADY, THE RANCH HANDS, MMO/ROY ROGERS, THE RANCH HANDS, MMO | | $5.00 | $10.00 |
| 1 | EP-325 | DALE EVANS' SONGS OF FAITH: AVE MARIA, ETC. | DALE EVANS, ROY ROGERS, THE RANCH HANDS, MMO | | $5.00 | $10.00 |
| 1 | EP-326 | GOLDEN SONGS ABOUT AMERICA: THE CAISSONS GO ROLLING ALONG | SAND, MMO | | $2.00 | $4.00 |
| 1 | EP-327 | HOWDY DOODY AND BUFFALO BOB SONGS: LITTLE ONE, LEAN ONE | HOWDY DOODY, BOB SMITH & THE GANG, MMO | | $8.00 | $15.00 |
| 1 | EP-328 | GOLDEN NURSERY SONGS: HUMPTY DUMPTY, ETC. | AL, SAND, MMO | | $2.00 | $4.00 |
| 1 | C-329 | THE NIGHT BEFORE CHRISTMAS | ? | | $2.00 | $4.00 |
| 1 | C-330 | HANSEL & GRETEL | SUSAN DOUGLAS; MITCH MILLER, DIR. | 1957 | $4.00 | $8.00 |

## GOLDEN MAIN SERIES 6" AND 7" SINGLES

| # REC | DISC # | MAIN TITLE | ARTIST | YEAR | G/VG | EX/NMT |
|---|---|---|---|---|---|---|
| 1 | C-331 | HEIDI | SUSAN DOUGLAS; MITCH MILLER, DIR. | | $2.00 | $4.00 |
| 1 | C-332 | THE SAGGY BAGGY ELEPHANT | ? | | $3.00 | $6.00 |
| 1 | C-333 | ROY ROGERS & COWBOY TOBY | DALE EVANS, BOBBY DIAMOND | | $8.00 | $15.00 |
| 1 | CD-334 | WD'S "LITTLE MAN OF DISNEYLAND" | ? | | $5.00 | $10.00 |
| 1 | D-335 (FROM WD'S OMMC) | FROM WD'S "HARDY BOYS": GOLD DOUBLOONS & PIECES OF EIGHT | MIKE STEWART, SAND, MMO | | $8.00 | $15.00 |
| 1 | R-337 | I WISH I HAD A DOG LIKE RIN TIN TIN/I LOVE DOGS | SAND, MMO | | $5.00 | $10.00 |
| 1 | R-338 | OVER THE RAINBOW/WE'RE OFF TO SEE THE WIZARD | AL, SAND, MMO/SAND, MMO | | $3.00 | $6.00 |
| 1 | R-339 | FROM BING CROSBY'S: ALI BABA & THE 40 THIEVES 40 (THE STORY)/THEY ALL LIVED HAPPILY EVER AFTER | BING CROSBY/BING CROSBY, CHORUS & ORCH. | | $2.00 | $4.00 |
| 1 | D-340 | FROM WD'S "JOHNNY TREMAIN": TITLE SONG | SAND, MMO | | $5.00 | $10.00 |
| 1 | R-341 | LITTLE DOG/A DOG IS A MAN'S BEST FRIEND | SAND, MMO | | $2.00 | $4.00 |
| 1 | D-342 | FROM WD'S "SNOW WHITE": SOME DAY MY PRINCE WILL COME | SAND, MMO | | $5.00 | $10.00 |
| 1 | R-343 | O THE TRAIN GOES IN THE MIDDLE OF THE HOUSE/ SONG OF THE SPARROW | MARY LOU BELL, SAND, JCO/PETER MARSHALL, TOMMY FARRELL, JCO | | $2.00 | $4.00 |
| 1 | D-344 | FROM WD'S "JOHNNY TREMAIN": THE LIBERTY TREE | SAND, MMO | | $5.00 | $10.00 |
| 1 | D-345 (FROM WD'S OMMC) | PROVERBS/DO WHAT THE GOOD BOOK SAYS | SAND, MMO | | $10.00 | $20.00 |
| 1 | R-346 | I'M POPEYE THE SAILOR MAN/SCUFFY THE TUGBOAT | VOICE OF POPEYE: JACK MERCER, SAND, MMO/ MIKE STEWART, GILBERT MACK, SAND, MMO | | $5.00 | $10.00 |
| 1 | D-347 | FROM WD'S "PERRI": TITLE SONG/BREAK OF DAY | SAND, MMO | | $8.00 | $15.00 |
| 1 | D-348 (FROM WD'S OMMC) | THOUGHTS FOR THE DAY: A MOUSEKATHOUGHT/SMILE & FACE THE MUSIC | SAND, MMO | | $10.00 | $20.00 |
| 1 | R-349 | RIN TIN TIN SONGS: RINNY, RUSTY AND RIP/1OIST CAVALRY GALLOP (SONG OF THE FIGHTING BLUE DEVILS) | AL, SAND, MMO/SAND, MMO | | $10.00 | $20.00 |
| 1 | R-350 | BING CROSBY SINGS DANIEL BOONE'S SONG STORY: INDIAN ADVENTURE (AN INCIDENT AT ROGER'S CREEK) | BING CROSBY, CHORUS & ORCH. | | $2.00 | $4.00 |
| 1 | EP-351 | RIN TIN TIN SONGS: I WISH I HAD A DOG LIKE RIN TIN TIN | AL, DENNIS BALLABIA, SAND, MMO/AL, SAND, MMO | | $8.00 | $15.00 |
| 1 | EP-352 | COWBOY SONGS: BRAVE COWBOY BILL, ETC. | SAND, MMO/ROY ROGERS, SAND, MMO | | $10.00 | $20.00 |
| 1 | EP-353 | GOLDEN FOLK SONGS: OLD CHISHOLM TRAIL, ETC. | ROY ROGERS, DICK BYRON, MIKE STEWART, AL, SAND, MMO/SAND, MMO | | $2.00 | $4.00 |
| 1 | EP-354 | LET'S DANCE SONGS: HOP SCOTCH POLKA, ETC. | SAND, MMO | | $2.00 | $4.00 |
| 1 | R-355 | FROM BING CROSBY'S "EMPEROR'S NEW CLOTHES": NEVER BE AFRAID (STORY/SONG) | BING CROSBY, CHORUS & ORCH. | | $2.00 | $4.00 |
| 1 | EP-356 | NAVY LOG SONGS: MIGHTY NAVY WINGS, ETC. | THE VOICES OF THE NAVAL CADET CHOIR | | $3.00 | $6.00 |
| 1 | R-357 | WYATT EARP/SAGA OF BILLY THE KID | SAND, MMO | | $5.00 | $10.00 |
| 1 | T-3580 | WIZARD OF OZ | ART CARNEY | | $5.00 | $10.00 |
| 1 | T-3590 | THE STORY OF MOSES: MOSES LITTLE MOSES, ETC. | TERRY GILKYSON, THE ARTHUR NORMAN CHORUS, MMO | | $2.00 | $4.00 |
| 1 | T-3600 | A CHILD'S INTRODUCTION TO THE ORCHESTRA: ANTOINETTE THE CLARINET, ETC. | SAND CHORUS AND ORCHESTRA; MITCH MILLER, DIR. | | $2.00 | $4.00 |
| 1 | EP-361 | ROMPER ROOM PLAY SONGS: WELCOME TO ROMPER ROOM, ETC. | AL, SAND, MMO | | $5.00 | $10.00 |
| 1 | R-362 | CINDY, OH! CINDY/MAMA FROM THE TRAIN (A KISS, A KISS) | SAND, MMO | | $2.00 | $4.00 |
| 1 | R-363 | LONDON BRIDGE/THREE BLIND MICE | RALPH NYLAND, AL, SAND, MMO/AL, SAND, MMO | | $2.00 | $4.00 |
| 1 | R-364 | BING CROSBY SINGS MOTHER GOOSE: HUMPTY DUMPTY/MISTRESS MARY | BING CROSBY, CHORUS & ORCH. | | $2.00 | $4.00 |
| 1 | R-365 | LITTLE WHITE DUCK/WHEN THE RED RED ROBIN COMES BOB BOB BOBBIN' ALONG | AL, SAND, MMO | | $2.00 | $4.00 |
| 1 | R-366 | HAPPY BIRTHDAY: OLLIE OWL — APRIL/DAFFY DUCK — MARCH | MEL BLANC, SAND, MMO | | $5.00 | $10.00 |
| 1 | R-370 | RIN TIN TIN SONGS: A DOG'S BEST FRIEND/COLD NOSE, WARM HEART | DENNIS BALLABIA, AL, SAND, MMO | | $5.00 | $10.00 |
| 1 | R-371 | BING CROSBY SINGS: HOW LOVELY IS CHRISTMAS | BING CROSBY/CHORUS | | $2.00 | $4.00 |
| 1 | R-372 | MOSES LITTLE MOSES/MOSES AND HIS PEOPLE | ARTHUR NORMAN CHORUS, MMO | | $2.00 | $4.00 |
| 1 | R-374 | HAPPY BIRTHDAY TO YOU! | SAND, MMO | | $2.00 | $4.00 |
| 1 | R-375 | JUST WALKING IN THE RAIN/BANANA BOAT SONG | SAND, JCO | | $2.00 | $4.00 |
| 1 | R-376 | MARIANNE/JAMAICA FAREWELL | JIMMY LEYDEN, SAND, MMO/BARRY FRANK, SAND, JCO | | $2.00 | $4.00 |

## GOLDEN MAIN SERIES 6" AND 7" SINGLES

| # REC | DISC # | MAIN TITLE | ARTIST | G/VG | EX/NMT |
|---|---|---|---|---|---|
| 1 | R-377 | ROUND AND ROUND/THE MUSIC GOES 'ROUND AND 'ROUND | RUSS VINCENT, SAND, MMO/PAT O'MALLEY, AL, MMO | $2.00 | $4.00 |
| 1 | EP-378 | SONGS FROM WESTWARD HO THE WAGONS!: WRINGLE WRANGLE, ETC. | SAND, MMO | $5.00 | $10.00 |
| 1 | EP-379 | SONGS FROM WD'S "CINDERELLA": BIBBIDI-BOBBIDI-BOO, ETC. | AL, SAND, MMO | $5.00 | $10.00 |
| 1 | R-380 | THE OLD CHISHOLM TRAIL/THE RED RIVER VALLEY | ROY ROGERS, THE RANCH HANDS, MMO/ DALE EVANS, THE RANCH HANDS, MMO | $5.00 | $10.00 |
| 1 | R-381 | ROY ROGERS HAD A RANCH/HOME ON THE RANGE | PAT BRADY, THE RANCH HANDS, MMO/ DALE EVANS, THE RANCH HANDS, MMO | $5.00 | $10.00 |
| 1 | R-382 | O LITTLE TOWN OF BETHLEHEM/HARK! THE HERALD ANGELS SING | CHORUS AND BOYS CHOIR, MITCH MILLER, DIR. | $2.00 | $4.00 |
| 1 | EP-383 | CALYPSO! — 6 FOR CHILDREN: MARIANNE, ETC. | THE GOLDEN CALYPSO SINGERS | $2.00 | $4.00 |
| 1 | EP-384 | SONGS FROM WD'S "SNOW WHITE": HI-HO-HI-HO! ETC. | SAND, MMO | $5.00 | $10.00 |
| 1 | R-385 | CAPTAIN KANGAROO: CAPTAIN KANGAROO THEME SONG/LITTLE KANGAROO DANCE | BOB KEESHAN, SAND, MMO/SAND, MMO | $4.00 | $8.00 |
| 1 | R-386 | BOY AT THE WINDOW/AN AXE, AN APPLE AND A BUCKSKIN JACKET | BING CROSBY/BING CROSBY, BETTY MULLINER | $2.00 | $4.00 |
| 1 | D-390 | WD'S "OLD YELLER": TITLE SONG | SAND | $5.00 | $10.00 |
| 1 | R-391 | PLAY SONGS FROM MOTHER GOOSE: SING A SONG OF SIXPENCE/LITTLE BO PEEP, HUMPTY DUMPTY | SAND, MMO | $2.00 | $4.00 |
| 1 | EP-392 | 4 SONGS FROM MY FAIR LADY: ON THE STREET WHERE YOU LIVE, ETC. | ELISE RHODES, MIKE STEWART, MMO | $2.00 | $4.00 |
| 1 | D-394 | FROM WD'S "PERRI": TOGETHER TIME/NOW TO SLEEP | SAND, MMO | $5.00 | $10.00 |
| 1 | R-395 | OLD KING COLE/SING A SONG OF SIXPENCE | BING CROSBY AND CHORUS | $2.00 | $4.00 |
| 1 | R-396 | STAR LIGHT, STAR BRIGHT/LITTLE BOY BLUE | BING CROSBY AND CHORUS | $2.00 | $4.00 |
| 1 | R-397 | SONGS WE SING IN NURSERY SCHOOL: ALL WORK TOGETHER, ETC. | UNCLE WIN STRACKE, MMO | $2.00 | $4.00 |
| 1 | EP-400 | DOG SONGS: HOW MUCH IS THAT DOGGIE IN THE WINDOW, ETC. | SAND, MMO/ROY ROGERS, SAND, MMO | $3.00 | $6.00 |
| 1 | EP-401 | FAVORITE LULLABIES: GOODNIGHT PRAYER, ETC. | DALE EVANS, SAND, MMO/SAND, MMO | $2.00 | $4.00 |
| 1 | EP-402 | CHRISTMAS SONGS: I'M DREAMING OF A WHITE CHRISTMAS | SAND, MMO | $3.00 | $6.00 |
| 1 | EP-403 | SILLY SONGS: PIDDILY PATTER PATTER | SAND, MMO | $2.00 | $4.00 |
| 1 | EP-404 | SCHOOL DAYS: SCHOOL DAYS, I LIKE TO GO TO SCHOOL, ETC. | SAND, MMO | $2.00 | $4.00 |
| 1 | EP-405 | BEAR SONGS: ME AND MY TEDDY BEAR | SAND, MMO | $2.00 | $4.00 |
| 1 | EP-406 | SONGS THE CUB SCOUTS SING: AMERICA THE BEAUTIFUL, ETC. | SAND, MMO | $3.00 | $6.00 |
| 1 | EP-407 | BING CROSBY SINGS NEW CHRISTMAS SONGS: HOW LOVELY IS CHRISTMAS/BOY AT A WINDOW | BING CROSBY AND CHORUS | $2.00 | $4.00 |
| 1 | EP-408 | BING CROSBY SINGS MOTHER GOOSE: OLD KING COLE, ETC. | BING CROSBY AND CHORUS | $2.00 | $4.00 |
| 1 | T-4110 | PETER & THE WOLF | FRANK MILANO, STATE SYMPHONIC ORCHESTRA | $5.00 | $10.00 |
| 1 | T-4120 | GREAT MUSICAL FAIRY TALES: HANSEL & GRETEL, ETC. | ? | $2.00 | $4.00 |
| 1 | T-4130 | THE MOST LOVED CHRISTMAS SONGS: WHITE CHRISTMAS, ETC. | SAND, MMO | $2.00 | $4.00 |
| 1 | T-4140 | GREAT SONGS FROM WD'S MOTION PICTURES: HI-HO, HI-HO, ETC. | SAND, MMO | $5.00 | $10.00 |
| 1 | T-4150 | 25 FAVORITES FROM MOTHER GOOSE: LONDON BRIDGE, ETC. | SAND, MMO | $2.00 | $4.00 |
| 1 | FF-416 | DOWN BY THE STATION/I'VE BEEN WORKING ON THE RAILROAD | AL, MIKE STEWART, SAND, MMO | $2.00 | $4.00 |
| 1 | FF-417 | DIXIE/THE YELLOW ROSE OF TEXAS | SAND, MMO | $2.00 | $4.00 |
| 1 | FF-418 | ON TOP OF OLD SMOKY/ROCK CANDY MOUNTAIN | AL, DICK BYRON, MIKE STEWART, SAND, MMO | $2.00 | $4.00 |
| 1 | FF-419 | BATTLE HYMN OF THE REPUBLIC/ONWARD CHRISTIAN SOLDIERS | GOLDEN CHOIR; MITCHELL MILLER, DIRECTOR | $2.00 | $4.00 |
| 1 | FF-420 | POP GOES THE WEASEL | GOLDEN CHOIR; MITCHELL MILLER, DIRECTOR | $2.00 | $4.00 |
| 1 | FF-421 | THE FARMER IN THE DELL/OLD MACDONALD HAD A FARM | AL, SAND, MMO/GILBERT MACK, AL, SAND, MMO | $2.00 | $4.00 |
| 1 | FF-422 | OLD KING COLE, LITTLE BO PEEP/SING A SONG OF SIXPENCE, JACK AND JILL | MICHAEL STEWART, AL, SAND, MMO/AL, SAND, MMO | $2.00 | $4.00 |
| 1 | FF-423 | THREE BLIND MICE | AL, SAND, MMO/SAND, MMO | $2.00 | $4.00 |
| 1 | FF-424 | PETER AND THE WOLF/HANSEL AND GRETEL | GILBERT MACK, MICHAEL STEWART, MMO | $2.00 | $4.00 |
| 1 | FF-425 | SKIP TO MY LOU, ROUND AND ROUND THE VILLAGE/DID YOU EVER SEE A LASSIE? | AL, SAND, MMO/AN, RALPH NYLAND, MMO | $2.00 | $4.00 |
| 1 | FF-426 | THE NIGHT BEFORE CHRISTMAS | PETER DONALD, MMO | $2.00 | $4.00 |
| 1 | FF-427 | JINGLE BELLS, DECK THE HALLS/UP ON THE HOUSETOP | DICK BYRON, SAND, MMO/MICHAEL STEWART, SAND, MMO | $2.00 | $4.00 |
| 1 | C-428 | THE POKY LITTLE PUPPY | AL, MMO | $3.00 | $6.00 |

## GOLDEN MAIN SERIES 6" AND 7" SINGLES

| # REC | DISC # | MAIN TITLE | ARTIST | G/VG | EX/NMT |
|---|---|---|---|---|---|
| 1 | CD-429 | WD'S "THE SEVEN DWARFS FIND A HOUSE" | AL, MMO | $5.00 | $10.00 |
| 1 | C-430 | THE THREE BEARS | AL, MMO | $2.00 | $4.00 |
| 1 | C-431 | LITTLE RED RIDING HOOD | ? | $2.00 | $4.00 |
| 1 | C-432 | JACK & THE BEANSTALK | AL, JACK LAZARE, MMO | $2.00 | $4.00 |
| 1 | CD-433 | WD'S "BAMBI" | ? | $5.00 | $10.00 |
| 1 | R-438 | HECKLE AND JECKLE | ROY HALEE, SAND, MMO | $5.00 | $10.00 |
| 1 | R-439 | BRAHMS' LULLABY/ROCKABYE BABY, TWINKLE, TWINKLE LITTLE STAR | AL, SAND, MMO | $2.00 | $4.00 |
| 1 | R-440 | FURY THEME SONG/WHAT DID YOU DO BEFORE YOU HAD TV? | SAND, MMO | $4.00 | $8.00 |
| 1 | R-441 | DE CAMPTOWN RACES/CLEMENTINE | DICK BYRON, SAND, MMO/AL, SAND, MMO | $2.00 | $4.00 |
| 1 | EP-442 | TV FAVORITES: POPEYE, MIGHTY MOUSE AND BUGS BUNNY | ORIGINAL VOICES OF POPEYE, BUGS BUNNY, THE TERRYTOONERS, SAND, MMO | $5.00 | $10.00 |
| 1 | EP-443 | LET'S ALL SING LIKE THE BIRDIES SING, ETC./LITTLE SWAN'S DANCE, ETC. | AL, SAND, MMO | $2.00 | $4.00 |
| 1 | EP-444 | FROM BING CROSBY'S "ALI BABA AND THE 40 THIEVES": 40 THIEVES 40, ETC. | BING CROSBY, CHORUS & ORCH | $2.00 | $4.00 |
| 1 | EP-445 | SAILOR SONGS: SHRIMP BOATS, ETC. | SAND, MMO | $2.00 | $4.00 |
| 1 | EP-446 | FAVORITE MOTHER GOOSE AND NURSERY SONGS: LONDON BRIDGE, ETC. | SAND, MMO | $2.00 | $4.00 |
| 1 | EP-447 | EASTER PARADE: IRVING BERLIN'S EASTER PARADE, ETC. | AL, PETER HANLEY, SAND, MMO/ROY ROGERS JIMMY DURANTE, BETTY CLOONEY, SAND, MMO | $2.00 | $4.00 |
| 1 | D-448 | FROM WD'S "ADVENTURES OF ZORRO" | SAND, MMO | $5.00 | $10.00 |
| 1 | D-449 | FROM WD'S "THE SAGA OF ANDY BURNETT" | SAND, MMO | $5.00 | $10.00 |
| 1 | R-450 | LASSIE THEME SONG/LASSIE MY FOUR FOOTED FRIEND | SAND, MMO | $5.00 | $10.00 |
| 1 | R-451 | GANDY DANCER'S BALL/SHRIMP BOATS | SAND, AL, MMO/SAND, SALLY SWEETLAND, MMO | $2.00 | $4.00 |
| 1 | FF-452 | FROM WD'S "SNOW WHITE": SOME DAY MY PRINCE WILL COME | SAND, MMO | $4.00 | $8.00 |
| 1 | FF-453 | FROM BING CROSBY'S "THE EMPEROR'S NEW CLOTHES": NEVER BE AFRAID STORY/SONG | BING CROSBY, CHORUS & ORCH | $2.00 | $4.00 |
| 1 | FF-454 | FROM WD'S "THE ADVENTURES OF ZORRO" | SAND, MMO | $5.00 | $10.00 |
| 1 | FF-455 | WYATT EARP (THEME SONG)/SAGA OF BILLY THE KID | SAND, MMO | $5.00 | $10.00 |
| 1 | FF-456 | LASSIE THEME SONG/LASSIE MY FOUR FOOTED FRIEND | SAND, MMO | $5.00 | $10.00 |
| 1 | FF-457 | POLLY WOLLY DOODLE/LAVENDER'S BLUE | SAND, JCO/SAND, MMO | $2.00 | $4.00 |
| 1 | FF-458 | BRAHMS' LULLABY/ROCKABYE BABY, TWINKLE TWINKLE LITTLE STAR | AL, SAND, MMO | $2.00 | $4.00 |
| 1 | FF-459 | CLEMENTINE/DE CAMPTOWN RACES | AL, SAND, MMO/DICK BYRON, SAND, MMO | $2.00 | $4.00 |
| 1 | EP-460 | WD MOVIE FAVORITES: THREE LITTLE PIGS, PINOCCHIO, PETER PAN | AL, DANNY OCKO, DAVID ANDERSON, SAND: MMO | $5.00 | $10.00 |
| 1 | EP-461 | ROCKET TO MARS! | HAMILTON O'HARA, ROBERT MOTT | 1$2.00 | $25.00 |
| 1 | EP-462 | CAPTAIN KANGAROO TREASURE HOUSE OF SONGS WITH MR. GREEN JEANS: THEME SONG, ETC. | BOB KEESHAN (CAPTAIN KANGAROO), LUMPY BRANNUM (MR. GREENJEANS), SAND | $5.00 | $10.00 |
| 1 | R-463 | AROUND THE WORLD/TEDDY BEAR | SAND, JCO/BARRY FRANK, JCO | $2.00 | $4.00 |
| 1 | EP-464 | BING CROSBY SINGS ABOUT THREE WESTERN HEROES: DANIEL BOONE, JOHNNY APPLESEED, PAUL BUNYAN | BING CROSBY, ARTHUR NORMAN CHORUS & ORCH. | $3.00 | $6.00 |
| 1 | EP-466 | WAGON TRAIN — WELLS FARGO — RESTLESS GUN | SAND, MMO | $5.00 | $10.00 |
| 1 | EP-467 | TV FAVORITES: WYATT EARP, LASSIE, JIM BOWIE | SAND, MMO | $5.00 | $10.00 |
| 1 | EP-468 | 6 BEST LOVED CHRISTMAS CAROLS: JOY TO THE WORLD, ETC. | SAND, MMO | $2.00 | $4.00 |
| 1 | EP-469 | THE GOLDEN TREASURY OF POPULAR SONGS: MR. SANDMAN, ETC. | SAND, MMO | $2.00 | $4.00 |
| 1 | R-470 | SONGS ABOUT LASSIE: I LOVE LASSIE, LASSIE IS MY BEST FRIEND | THE ARTHUR NORMAN CHORUS | $5.00 | $10.00 |
| 1 | R-471 | TOYLAND/MARCH OF THE TOYS | BOB KEESHAN (CAPTAIN KANGAROO), LUMPY BRANNUM (MR. GREENJEANS), SAND | $4.00 | $8.00 |
| 1 | R-472 | I TAWT I TAW A PUDDY-TAT MERRIE MELODIES | BUGS BUNNY, SYLVESTER, HENRY HAWK & THE OTHERS, SAND, MMO/BUGS, TWEETIE PIE, MMO | $6.00 | $12.00 |
| 1 | R-473 | I LOVE A PARADE/I WENT TO THE ANIMAL FAIR | BOB KEESHAN (CAPTAIN KANGAROO), LUMPY BRANNUM (MR. GREENJEANS), SAND | $5.00 | $10.00 |
| 1 | EP-474 | TV FAVORITES: LASSIE/RUFF & REDDY | THE ARTHUR NORMAN CHORUS/GIL MACK, SAND, MMO | $5.00 | $10.00 |
| 1 | EP-475 | AMERICAN FOLK SONGS | ? | $2.00 | $4.00 |
| 1 | EP-476 | CHILD'S INTRODUCTION TO THE ORCHESTRA: LUCY LYNN THE VIOLIN | SAND CHORUS AND ORCHESTRA, MITCH MILLER, DIR. | $2.00 | $4.00 |
| 1 | EP-478 | KITTENS AND CATS: I TAUT I SAW A PUTTY CAT, ETC. | SAND, MMO | $5.00 | $10.00 |
| 1 | D-479 | FROM WD'S SLEEPING BEAUTY: I WONDER | DARLENE GILLESPIE, FULL CHORUS & ORCH. | $4.00 | $8.00 |
| 1 | D-480 | FROM WD'S SLEEPING BEAUTY: ONCE UPON A DREAM | DARLENE GILLESPIE, FULL CHORUS & ORCH. | $4.00 | $8.00 |

## GOLDEN MAIN SERIES 6" AND 7" SINGLES

| # REC | DISC # | MAIN TITLE | ARTIST | G/VG | EX/NMT |
|---|---|---|---|---|---|
| 1 | D-481 | FROM WD'S SLEEPING BEAUTY: HAIL TO PRINCESS AURORA | FULL CHORUS & ORCH. | $4.00 | $8.00 |
| 1 | D-482 | FROM WD'S SLEEPING BEAUTY: SING A SMILING SONG | FULL CHORUS & ORCH. | $4.00 | $8.00 |
| 1 | R-483 | FROM WD'S SLEEPING BEAUTY: SKUMPS/THE STORY OF THE TWO KINGS | DARLENE GILLESPIE, FULL CHORUS & ORCH. | $4.00 | $8.00 |
| 1 | EP-484 | EIGHT SONGS FOR PARTIES: HAPPY BIRTHDAY, ETC. | SAND, MMO | $2.00 | $4.00 |
| 1 | EP-485 | DISNEY HEROES: ZORRO, OLD YELLER/OLD YELLER, ANDY BURNETT | SAND, MMO | $5.00 | $10.00 |
| 1 | RD-486 | FROM WD'S SLEEPING BEAUTY: STORY/SONG | DARLENE GILLESPIE, FULL CHORUS & ORCH. | $4.00 | $8.00 |
| 1 | EP-487 | SIX FAVORITE AMERICAN FOLK SONGS: CASEY JONES, ETC. | SAND, MMO | $2.00 | $4.00 |
| 1 | EP-488 | WD'S DONALD DUCK: DONALD'S SONG, ETC. | ORIGINAL VOICE OF DONALD DUCK | $6.00 | $12.00 |
| 1 | EP-489 | PARADE SONGS AND MARCHES BY JOHN PHILLIP SOUSA: STARS & STRIPES, ETC. | ? | $2.00 | $4.00 |
| 1 | EP-490 | THREE LITTLE...: 3 LITTLE KITTENS, ETC. | AL, SAND, MMO | $2.00 | $4.00 |
| 1 | EP-491 | FAIRY TALES: JACK & THE BEANSTALK, HANSEL & GRETEL, ETC. | GIL MACK, SAND, MMO | $2.00 | $4.00 |
| 1 | EP-492 | MORE TV FAVORITES!: WOODY WOODPECKER, MAVERICK/MAVERICK, LEAVE IT TO BEAVER | SAND & ORCH. | $5.00 | $10.00 |
| 1 | R-493 | THE WOODY WOODPECKER SONG/WOODPECKER'S DANCE | SAND, MMO/MMO | $6.00 | $12.00 |
| 1 | R-494 | VOLARE/LITTLE STAR | DOROTHY, ED CEE & ORCH. | $3.00 | $6.00 |
| 1 | R-495 | WAGON TRAIN/SQUARE DANCE | SAND, MMO | $5.00 | $10.00 |
| 1 | RD-496 | WD'S "JOHN SLAUGHTER": THEME SONG | SAND, JCO | $5.00 | $10.00 |
| 1 | R-497 | SMOKEY THE BEAR | SAND, MMO | $5.00 | $10.00 |
| 1 | R-498 | MAVERICK | SAND, JCO | $5.00 | $10.00 |
| 1 | R-499 | CASEY JONES/JOHN HENRY | WIN STRACKE & ARTHUR NORMAN ORCH & CHORUS | $2.00 | $4.00 |
| 1 | R-500 | BUTTON UP YOUR OVERCOAT/THE BEAR WENT OVER THE MOUNTAIN | BOB KEESHAN (CAPTAIN KANGAROO), LUMPY BRANNUM (MR. GREENJEANS), JCO | $4.00 | $8.00 |
| 1 | R-501 | LAZY BONES/SMALL FRY | HOAGY CARMICHAEL, ARTHUR NORMAN CHORUS & ORCH. | $5.00 | $10.00 |
| 1 | R-502 | THE LONE RANGER INTRODUCES, I RIDE AN OLD PAINT/RAILROAD CORRAL | ARTHUR NORMAN CHORUS & ORCH. | $6.00 | $12.00 |
| 1 | R-503 | FROM WD'S "THE NINE LIVES OF ELFEGO BACA": ELFEGO BACA | SAND, JCO | $5.00 | $10.00 |
| 1 | T-5040 | THE GOLDEN TREASURY OF FOLK SONGS: TURKEY IN THE STRAW, ETC. | SAND, MMO | $2.00 | $4.00 |
| 1 | T-5050 | CAPTAIN KANGAROO'S TREASURE HOUSE OF BEST-LOVED SONGS: SAY "SI SI", ETC. | BOB KEESHAN (CAPTAIN KANGAROO), LUMPY BRANNUM (MR. GREENJEANS), SAND, MMO | $2.00 | $4.00 |
| 1 | T-5070 | A CHILD'S INTRODUCTION TO THE GREAT COMPOSERS: MOZART'S TURKISH MARCH, ETC. | MMO | $2.00 | $4.00 |
| 1 | R-509 | TALES OF WELLS FARGO/LONELY RIDER | SAND, MMO | $5.00 | $10.00 |
| 1 | R-511 | GOD BLESS AMERICA | PETER HANLEY, SAND, MMO/SAND, MMO | $2.00 | $4.00 |
| 1 | R-516 | CATCH A FALLING STAR/STRAUSS EXPLOSION POLKA | SAND, MMO | $2.00 | $4.00 |
| 1 | R-518 | LEAVE IT TO BEAVER THEME MUSIC: TOY PARADE | THE ARTHUR NORMAN CHORUS & ORCH. | $5.00 | $10.00 |
| 1 | R-519 | MIGHTY MOUSE (THEME SONG)/FARMER AL FALFA | THE TERRYTOONERS, MMO | $10.00 | $20.00 |
| 1 | EP-520 | CAPTAIN KANGAROO AND MR. GREENJEANS! JOHNNY ONE NOTE, ETC. | BOB KEESHAN (CAPTAIN KANGAROO), LUMPY BRANNUM (MR. GREENJEANS), SAND, MMO | $10.00 | $20.00 |
| 1 | R-521 | THE LONE RANGER THEME MUSIC AND THE SONG/HI-YO, SILVER | THE ARTHUR NORMAN SINGERS | 1$2.00 | $15.00 |
| 1 | EP-522 | THE LONE RANGER! THE LONE RANGER THEME (HI YO SILVER), ETC. | THE ARTHUR NORMAN SINGERS | 1$2.00 | $15.00 |
| 1 | EP-523 | FROM WD'S PETER PAN: THE SECOND STAR TO THE RIGHT, ETC. | ? | $5.00 | $10.00 |
| 1 | EP-524 | 6 SONGS AMERICA SINGS: JOHN HENRY, ETC. | WIN STRACKE & THE ARTHUR NORMAN SINGERS | $2.00 | $4.00 |
| 1 | EP-525 | MICKEY MOUSE CLUB FAVORITES | ? | $8.00 | $15.00 |
| 1 | R-526 | LOLLIPOP/DANCE OF THE CLOWNS | MMO | $2.00 | $4.00 |
| 1 | EP-527 | WD'S THEMES: SLEEPING BEAUTY, MMC/MMC, DISNEYLAND THEME (WHEN YOU WISH UPON A STAR) | THE ARTHUR NORMAN CHORUS & ORCH. | $8.00 | $15.00 |
| 1 | EP-528 | WD'S WESTERN FAVORITES: TEXAS JOHN SLAUGHTER, ELFEGO BACA/ELFEGO BACA, PECOS BILL | SAND, MMO | $5.00 | $10.00 |
| 1 | EP-529 | 6 GREAT GOLDEN BOOK SONG STORIES: SCUFFY THE TUGBOAT, ETC. | AL, SAND, MMO | $2.00 | $4.00 |
| 1 | EP-530 | WD'S HEROINES: SLEEPING BEAUTY, CINDERELLA/SNOW WHITE | SAND, MMO | $5.00 | $10.00 |
| 1 | RD-531 | FROM WD'S "TONKA": THEME SONG/TOMAHAWK WAR DANCE | WAYNE SHERWOOD, SAND, JCO/JCO | $5.00 | $10.00 |
| 1 | R-532 | FROM THE MGM PICTURE "TOM THUMB'S": TOM THUMB'S TUNE/THE STORY OF TOM THUMB | ARTIE MALVIN, SAND, JCO/FRANK MILANO, JCO | $4.00 | $8.00 |
| 1 | R-533 | APRIL SHOWERS/IN THE GOOD OLD SUMMERTIME | BOB KEESHAN (CAPTAIN KANGAROO), SAND, JCO | $2.00 | $4.00 |
| 1 | R-534 | DENNIS THE MENACE | BOBBY NICK, SAND, MMO | $10.00 | $20.00 |

## GRADED PRESS 7" BOXED SETS

| SET # | # REC | DISC # | MAIN TITLE | ARTIST | A TITLE | B TITLE | YEAR | G/VG | EX/NMT |
|---|---|---|---|---|---|---|---|---|---|
| | | 504 | | NOT LISTED | GAME SONGS: BIG JUMBO SWINGS HIS TRUNK, ETC. | ACTIVITIES: SKIP IN "C," ETC. | | $1.00 | $2.00 |
| | | 505 | | NOT LISTED | LISTENING MUSIC: BRAHMS' LULLABY, ALL THROUGH THE NIGHT | LISTENING MUSIC: TO A WILD ROSE, LARGO | | $1.00 | $2.00 |
| NO # | 4 | 1 A/B – 4 A/B | GLADLY SING | NOT LISTED | (BOXED SET WITH 4 RECORDS FOR PRIMARY GRADES) | | 1958 | $4.00 | $8.00 |
| | | SIDE 1 A/B | | NOT LISTED | HE IS SLEEPING IN A MANGER | COME SOFTLY, TREAD GENTLY | | $1.00 | $2.00 |
| | | SIDE 2 A/B | | NOT LISTED | COME WITH HEARTS REJOICING | GOD IS NEAR | | $1.00 | $2.00 |
| | | SIDE 3 A/B | | NOT LISTED | THE CHURCH IT ALWAYS SINGS TO ME | OUR DEAR CHURCH, OUR BEAUTIFUL EARTH | | $1.00 | $2.00 |
| | | SIDE 4 A/B | | NOT LISTED | JESUS, THE FRIEND | FRIENDS OF ALL, FRIENDLY TO EACH OTHER | | $1.00 | $2.00 |

## GRAPHIC-PHOTO BOOKS 10" SINGLES IN BOOK

| SET # | # REC | MAIN TITLE | ARTIST | YEAR | G/VG | EX/NMT |
|---|---|---|---|---|---|---|
| A-101 | 1 | WHAT MAKES RAIN? | NOT LISTED | 1946 | $5.00 | $10.00 |
| A-102 | 1 | WHY ARE BEES SO BUSY? | NOT LISTED | | $5.00 | $10.00 |
| A-103 | 1 | WHO WAS AESOP? | NOT LISTED | | $5.00 | $10.00 |
| A-104 | 1 | WHY DO I HAVE TO GO TO SLEEP? | NOT LISTED | | $5.00 | $10.00 |
| ? | 1 | HOW DID WE LEARN TO COUNT? | NOT LISTED | | $5.00 | $10.00 |
| ? | 1 | HOW DO ANTS LIVE? | NOT LISTED | | $5.00 | $10.00 |
| ? | 1 | HOW DO WE GET OUR MAIL? | NOT LISTED | | $5.00 | $10.00 |
| ? | 1 | HOW DOES A FLOWER GROW? | NOT LISTED | | $5.00 | $10.00 |
| ? | 1 | HOW IS A BUTTERFLY BORN? | NOT LISTED | | $5.00 | $10.00 |
| ? | 1 | WHAT ARE MANNERS? | NOT LISTED | | $5.00 | $10.00 |
| ? | 1 | WHAT ARE STARS? | NOT LISTED | | $5.00 | $10.00 |
| ? | 1 | WHAT IS FIRE? | NOT LISTED | | $5.00 | $10.00 |
| ? | 1 | WHAT IS RHYTHM? | NOT LISTED | | $5.00 | $10.00 |
| ? | 1 | WHERE DO BIRDS GO IN THE WINTER? | NOT LISTED | | $5.00 | $10.00 |
| ? | 1 | WHERE DO BOATS GO? | NOT LISTED | | $5.00 | $10.00 |
| ? | 1 | WHERE DO WE COME FROM? | NOT LISTED | | $5.00 | $10.00 |
| ? | 1 | WHERE DOES MY BREAKFAST GO? | NOT LISTED | | $5.00 | $10.00 |
| ? | 1 | WHERE DOES THE ALPHABET COME FROM? | NOT LISTED | | $5.00 | $10.00 |
| ? | 1 | WHO WAS DANIEL BOONE? | NOT LISTED | | $5.00 | $10.00 |
| ? | 1 | WHO WAS HIAWATHA? | NOT LISTED | | $5.00 | $10.00 |
| ? | 1 | WHO WAS PAUL BUNYAN? | NOT LISTED | | $5.00 | $10.00 |
| ? | 1 | WHO WERE THE PILGRIMS? | NOT LISTED | | $5.00 | $10.00 |
| ? | 1 | WHY DO ANIMALS CHANGE COLOR? | NOT LISTED | | $5.00 | $10.00 |
| ? | 1 | WHY IS THERE NIGHT AND DAY? | NOT LISTED | | $5.00 | $10.00 |
| ? | 1 | WHY SHOULD WE WASH OUR HANDS? | NOT LISTED | | $5.00 | $10.00 |

## GREETING REC-CARDS 6" SINGLES IN GREETING CARD FOLDER

| # REC | DISC # | MAIN TITLE | ARTIST | YEAR | G/VG | EX/NMT |
|---|---|---|---|---|---|---|
| 1 | B-105 | THE HAPPY BIRTHDAY BOAT | NOT LISTED | 1955 | $5.00 | $10.00 |
| 1 | B-106 | HAPPY BIRTHDAY RANCH | NOT LISTED | | $5.00 | $10.00 |
| 1 | X-2002 | TWINKLE, THE CHRISTMAS ANGEL | NOT LISTED | | $5.00 | $10.00 |

## GREY GULL YOUNGSTERS 6" SINGLES

| # REC | DISC # | ARTIST | A TITLE | B TITLE | YEAR | G/VG | EX/NMT |
|---|---|---|---|---|---|---|---|
| 1 | 100 | AUNT SARAH/MISS PRICE | LITTLE BO PEEP | THREE LITTLE KITTENS | 192? | $4.00 | $8.00 |
| 1 | 101 | ARTHUR FIELDS/ERNEST HARE | OLD KING COLE | TOM TOM THE PIPER'S SON | | $4.00 | $8.00 |
| 1 | 102 | AUNT SARAH/UNCLE LEWIS | MARY HAD A LITTLE LAMB | LITTLE BOY BLUE | | $4.00 | $8.00 |
| 1 | 103 | UNCLE LEWIS/MISS PRICE, MR. KENNEDY | MOTHER HUBBARD | JACK AND JILL | | $4.00 | $8.00 |
| 1 | 104 | MR. KENNEDY/UNCLE LEWIS | OLD MOTHER GOOSE | SING A SONG OF SIXPENCE | | $4.00 | $8.00 |

GREETING REC-CARDS
THE HAPPY BIRTHDAY BOAT
$10.00

HARMONIA RECORDS
BUSTER BAGS THE BANDIT
$10.00

HOLLYWOOD RECORDING GUILD
RUMPLESTILTSKIN
$10.00

## GREY GULL YOUNGSTERS 6" SINGLES

| # REC | DISC # | ARTIST | A TITLE | B TITLE | G/VG | EX/NMT |
|---|---|---|---|---|---|---|
| 1 | 105 | MR. KENNEDY/MR KENNEDY, UNCLE LEWIS | HEY DIDDLE DIDDLE | DING DONG BELL | $4.00 | $8.00 |
| 1 | 106 | ARTHUR HALL | RING AROUND A ROSY | WATER WATER WILD FLOWER | $4.00 | $8.00 |
| 1 | 107 | ROB ROY | LITTLE RED RIDING HOOD | ALICE IN WONDERLAND | $4.00 | $8.00 |
| 1 | 108 | ARTHUR FIELDS | THE MULBERRY BUSH | SIMPLE SIMON | $4.00 | $8.00 |
| 1 | 109 | ARTHUR FIELDS | FARMER IN THE DELL | ROCK-A-BYE BABY | $4.00 | $8.00 |
| 1 | 110 | JACK KAUFMAN | I HAD A LITTLE DOGGIE | THREE LITTLE PIGS | $4.00 | $8.00 |
| 1 | 111 | JACK KAUFMAN | I LOVE LITTLE PUSSY | WHERE ARE YOU GOING TO MY PRETTY MAID | $4.00 | $8.00 |
| 1 | 112 | ARTHUR FIELDS | LONDON BRIDGE IS FALLING DOWN | LITTLE MISS MUFFET | $4.00 | $8.00 |
| 1 | 113 | JACK KAUFMAN/ARTHUR FIELDS | THE HOUSE THAT JACK BUILT | THREE BLIND MICE | $4.00 | $8.00 |
| 1 | 114 | UNCLE JOE | THE GIRL WHO DANCED WITH THE FAIRIES | OWNSELF | $4.00 | $8.00 |
| 1 | 115 | UNCLE JOE | DIAMONDS AND TOADS | THE BOGGART | $4.00 | $8.00 |
| 1 | 116 | UNCLE JOE | THE MAGIC OINTMENT | THE TOMTS | $4.00 | $8.00 |
| 1 | 117 | KEY BAND/SOUSA BAND | STAR SPANGLED BANNER | STARS AND STRIPES | $4.00 | $8.00 |
| 1 | 120 | JIG ORCHESTRA | TURKEY IN THE STRAW | ARKANSAS TRAVELER | $4.00 | $8.00 |
| 1 | 122 | BAND | YANKEE DOODLE | DIXIE | $4.00 | $8.00 |
| 1 | 125 | JACK KAUFMAN/MILDRED GRIZZELLE | THE OLD WOMAN & THE PEDLAR | THE JACK OF HEARTS | $4.00 | $8.00 |
| 1 | 126 | ? | LITTLE GIRL WITH A CURL | WHAT ARE LITTLE BOYS MADE OF | $4.00 | $8.00 |
| 1 | 128 | ? | THE OLD WOMAN THAT LIVED IN A SHOE | IF ALL THE SEAS WERE ONE SEA | $4.00 | $8.00 |
| 1 | 129 | JACK KAUFMAN | LAZY MARY WILL YOU GET UP | THREE CHILDREN ON THE ICE | $4.00 | $8.00 |
| 1 | 130 | MILDRED GRIZZELLE/JACK KAUFMAN | THERE WAS A CROOKED MAN | BAA BAA BLACK SHEEP | $4.00 | $8.00 |
| 1 | 132 | JACK KAUFMAN | OH DEAR WHAT CAN THE MATTER BE | TEN LITTLE INDIANS | $4.00 | $8.00 |

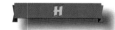

# H

## HARMONIA 10" ALBUMS AND SINGLES

| SET # | # REC | DISC # | MAIN TITLE | ARTIST | YEAR | G/VG | EX/NMT |
|---|---|---|---|---|---|---|---|
| HR-25 | 3 | 5001 - 3 | SLEEPING BEAUTY | HAAKON BERGH, LESLIE BIEBL | 1946 | $5.00 | $10.00 |
| HR-26 | 2 | 5006 - 7 | BUSTER BAGS THE BANDIT | LON CLARK | | $5.00 | $10.00 |
| HR-27 | 2 | 5008 - 9 | THE GOBBLE FAIR | LON CLARK | | $5.00 | $10.00 |
| ? | ? | ? | CINDERELLA | ? | | $5.00 | $10.00 |
| H-5004 | 1 | ? | TIGI THE BEAUTIFUL BUTTERFLY | LESLIE BIEBL | | $5.00 | $10.00 |

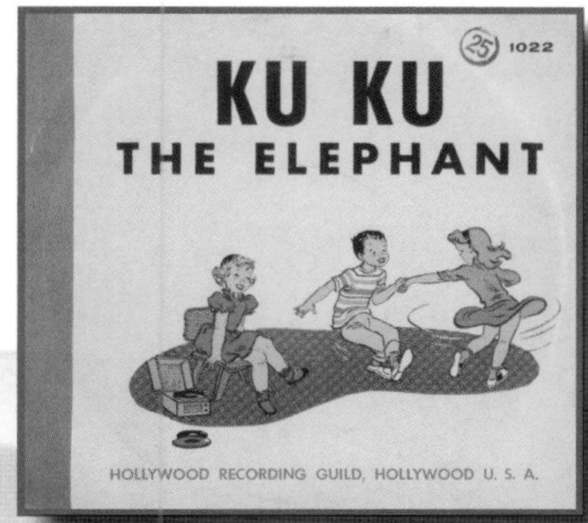

HOLLYWOOD RECORDING GUILD
KU-KU THE ELEPHANT
$2.00

HONOR YOUR PARNTER
COUPLE DANCES AND MIXES
$12.00

HUMPTY DUMPTY
HENRY'S WAGON
$15.00

## H-O INSTANT OATMEAL 5" ROUND AND SQUARE SINGLE-SIDE PICTURE DISC PREMIUMS

| # REC | DISC # | MAIN TITLE | ARTIST | YEAR | G/VG | EX/NMT |
|---|---|---|---|---|---|---|
| 1 | NO # (S/S) | HOW TO CATCH | ROY CAMPANELLA | 1952 | $35.00 | $70.00 |
| 1 | NO # (S/S) | HOW TO PITCH | ALLIE REYNOLDS | | $35.00 | $70.00 |
| 1 | NO # (S/S) | HOW TO PLAY FIRST BASE | WHITEY LOCKMAN | | $30.00 | $60.00 |
| 1 | NO # (S/S) | TIPS ON BATTING | DUKE SNIDER | | $40.00 | $80.00 |
| 1 | NO # (S/S) SQUARE | BROOKLYN DODGERS | ROY CAMPANELLA | 1953 | $35.00 | $70.00 |
| 1 | NO # (S/S) SQUARE | BROOKLYN DODGERS | GIL HODGES | | $35.00 | $70.00 |
| 1 | NO # (S/S) SQUARE | BROOKLYN DODGERS | PREACHER ROE | | $30.00 | $60.00 |
| 1 | NO # (S/S) SQUARE | BROOKLYN DODGERS | DUKE SNIDER | | $40.00 | $80.00 |
| 1 | NO # (S/S) SQUARE | PHILADELPHIA PHILLIES | EDDIE SAWYER | | $30.00 | $60.00 |
| 1 | NO # (S/S) SQUARE | BOSTON RED SOX | MEL PARNELL | | $30.00 | $60.00 |
| 1 | NO # (S/S) SQUARE | BOSTON RED SOX | BIRDIE TIBBETTS | | $30.00 | $60.00 |
| 1 | NO # (S/S) SQUARE | BOSTON RED SOX | TED WILLIAMS | | $40.00 | $80.00 |

## HOLLYWOOD RECORDING GUILD 7" SINGLES

| # REC | DISC # | MAIN TITLE | ARTIST | YEAR | G/VG | EX/NMT |
|---|---|---|---|---|---|---|
| 1 | 1 | THE THREE LITTLE PIGS | ? | 194? | $1.00 | $2.00 |
| 1 | 2 | OLD MOTHER GOOSE | ? | | $1.00 | $2.00 |
| 1 | 3 | OLD MACDONALD HAD A FARM | ? | | $1.00 | $2.00 |
| 1 | 4 | LITTLE BO PEEP | ? | | $1.00 | $2.00 |
| 1 | 5 | LONDON BRIDGE | ? | | $1.00 | $2.00 |
| 1 | 6 | SIMPLE SIMON | ? | | $1.00 | $2.00 |
| 1 | 7 | TISKET A TASKET | ? | | $1.00 | $2.00 |
| 1 | 8 | HI DIDDLE DIDDLE | ? | | $1.00 | $2.00 |
| 1 | 9 | HUMPTY DUMPTY | ? | | $1.00 | $2.00 |
| 1 | 10 | MARY HAD A LITTLE LAMB | ? | | $1.00 | $2.00 |
| 1 | 11 | LITTLE MISS MUFFET | ? | | $1.00 | $2.00 |
| 1 | 12 | HAPPY BIRTHDAY | ? | | $1.00 | $2.00 |
| 1 | 13 | A B C'S AT THE ZOO | ? | | $1.00 | $2.00 |
| 1 | 14 | OLD MOTHER HUBBARD | ? | | $1.00 | $2.00 |
| 1 | 15 | OLD KING COLE/SING A SONG OF SIXPENCE | BUELL THOMAS/MADELEINE & HANS COLLIN | | $1.00 | $2.00 |
| 1 | 16 | THREE LITTLE KITTENS | ? | | $1.00 | $2.00 |
| 1 | 17 | THE HOUSE THAT JACK BUILT | ? | | $1.00 | $2.00 |

## HOLLYWOOD RECORDING GUILD 7" SINGLES

| # REC | DISC # | MAIN TITLE | ARTIST | G/VG | EX/NMT |
|---|---|---|---|---|---|
| 1 | 18 | POP GOES THE WEASEL | ? | $1.00 | $2.00 |
| 1 | 19 | THE PIGGY BANK SONG | ? | $1.00 | $2.00 |
| 1 | 21 | THE BALLAD OF DAVY CROCKETT/THE TENDERFOOT | JACK ANDREWS & THE RHYTHM BOYS | $1.00 | $2.00 |
| 1 | 15 (SUP 31/23) | OLD KING COLE/SING A SONG OF SIXPENCE | ? | $1.00 | $2.00 |
| 1 | 21 (2001) | THE BALLAD OF DAVY CROCKETT/THE TENDERFOOT | ? | $4.00 | $8.00 |
| 1 | R-400 | THE THREE PIGS | JACK & JILL PLAYERS, JIM ANDELIN, JOAN SIMPSON | $5.00 | $10.00 |
| 1 | R-401 | THE THREE BEARS | JACK & JILL PLAYERS, JIM ANDELIN, JOAN SIMPSON | $5.00 | $10.00 |
| 1 | R-402 | THE SHOEMAKER AND THE ELVES | JACK & JILL PLAYERS, JIM ANDELIN, JOAN SIMPSON | $5.00 | $10.00 |
| 1 | R-403 | SNOW WHITE AND THE SEVEN DWARFS | JACK & JILL PLAYERS, JIM ANDELIN, JOAN SIMPSON | $5.00 | $10.00 |
| 1 | R-404 | THE GINGERBREAD BOY | CLAUDE KIRCHNER | $5.00 | $10.00 |
| 1 | R-405 | OLD MACDONALD | CLAUDE KIRCHNER AND ELMIRA ROESSLER | $5.00 | $10.00 |
| 1 | R-406 | HANSEL AND GRETEL | CLAUDE KIRCHNER | $5.00 | $10.00 |
| 1 | R-407 | PINOCCHIO | CLAUDE KIRCHNER | $5.00 | $10.00 |
| 1 | R-408 | LITTLE RED RIDING HOOD | CLAUDE KIRCHNER | $5.00 | $10.00 |
| 1 | R-409 | CINDERELLA | CLAUDE KIRCHNER | $5.00 | $10.00 |
| 1 | R-410 | LITTLE RED HEN | CLAUDE KIRCHNER | $5.00 | $10.00 |
| 1 | R-411 | THE THREE LITTLE KITTENS | CLAUDE KIRCHNER | $5.00 | $10.00 |
| 1 | R-412 | ALICE IN WONDERLAND | JIM AMECHE | $5.00 | $10.00 |
| 1 | R-413 | PETER RABBIT | JIM AMECHE | $5.00 | $10.00 |
| 1 | R-414 | RUMPLESTILTSKIN | JIM AMECHE | $5.00 | $10.00 |
| 1 | R-415 | PETER RABBIT | JIM AMECHE | $5.00 | $10.00 |
| 1 | R-416 | THE UGLY DUCKLING | NOT LISTED | $5.00 | $10.00 |
| 1 | R-417 | THE LITTLE OLD WOMAN AND HER PIG | NOT LISTED | $5.00 | $10.00 |
| 1 | R-418 | THREE BILLY GOATS GRUFF/RAR-A-TAT GOES THE LITTLE DRUM | NOT LISTED | $5.00 | $10.00 |
| 1 | R-419 | CHICKEN LITTLE AND HENNY PENNY | NOT LISTED | $5.00 | $10.00 |
| 1 | R-422 | WEE WILLY THE WHALE/BLOW YE WINDS WESTERLY, WEIGH, HAUL AWAY | NOT LISTED | $5.00 | $10.00 |
| 1 | R-1000 | NURSERY RHYMES | NOT LISTED | $1.00 | $2.00 |
| 1 | R-1001 | NURSERY GAMES | NOT LISTED | $1.00 | $2.00 |
| 1 | R-1002 | NURSERY LULLABIES | NOT LISTED | $1.00 | $2.00 |
| 1 | R-1003 | COWBOY ROUNDUP | NOT LISTED | $1.00 | $2.00 |
| 1 | R-1004 | FARMYARD FUN: CLEMENTINE, ETC. | NOT LISTED | $1.00 | $2.00 |
| 1 | R-1005 | OH, SUSANNA!, CAMPTOWN RACES, ETC. | NOT LISTED | $1.00 | $2.00 |
| 1 | R-1006 | TOY PARADE | NOT LISTED | $1.00 | $2.00 |
| 1 | R-1007 | SLEIGH BELLS RING, JINGLE BELLS, ETC. | NOT LISTED | $1.00 | $2.00 |
| 1 | R-1008 | THE STORY OF CHRISTMAS: SILENT NIGHT, ETC. | NOT LISTED | $1.00 | $2.00 |
| 1 | R-1009 | HAPPY BIRTHDAY, ETC. | ? | $1.00 | $2.00 |
| 1 | R-1009 | HAPPY BIRTHDAY, ETC. (WITH JIGSAW PUZZLE) | ? | $5.00 | $10.00 |
| 1 | R-1010 | HURDY GURDY TUNES: SKATERS WALTZ, ETC. | ? | $1.00 | $2.00 |
| 1 | R-1011 | LET'S PLAY SCHOOL | ? | $1.00 | $2.00 |
| 1 | R-1012 | PLAY BOAT | ? | $1.00 | $2.00 |
| 1 | R-1013 | PLAY TRAIN | ? | $1.00 | $2.00 |
| 1 | R-1014 | PLAY AIRPLANE | ? | $1.00 | $2.00 |
| 1 | R-1015 | LITTLE ENGINE THAT COULD/DOWN BY THE STATION | FRANN WEIGLE | $1.00 | $2.00 |
| 1 | R-1016 | NIGHT BEFORE CHRISTMAS | ? | $1.00 | $2.00 |
| 1 | R-1017 | WHOPPER THE WHALE | ? | $1.00 | $2.00 |
| 1 | R-1018 | WHO'S IN THE ZOO/MONKEYS ARE FUNNY, WHEN AN ELEPHANT WALKS | ? | $1.00 | $2.00 |
| 1 | R-1020 | THE WESTERN PONY/YIPPI-TI-YI-YO, RED RIVER VAL-LEY | FRANN WEIGLE | $1.00 | $2.00 |
| 1 | R-1021 | ZEBBY THE ZEBRA/WHO'S IN THE ZOO | HRG ORCHESTRA | $1.00 | $2.00 |
| 1 | R-1022 | KU-KU THE ELEPHANT/WHEN AN ELEPHANT WALKS, MONKEYS ARE FUNNY | HRG ORCHESTRA | $1.00 | $2.00 |
| 1 | R-1026 | JOLLY OLE FELLA/CHRISTMAS STORIES | THE DUNCAN SISTERS | $1.00 | $2.00 |

## HOLLYWOOD RECORDING GUILD 10" SINGLES

| # REC | DISC # | ARTIST | A-TITLE | B-TITLE | YEAR | ALSO ISSUED ON | G/VG | EX/NMT |
|---|---|---|---|---|---|---|---|---|
| 1 | 104 | DAVE ROMAINE & ORCH. | WEE WILLIE THE WHALE | HOKEY POKEY POLKA | 195? | TOPS FOR TOTS V-37 | $2.00 | $4.00 |
| 1 | 601 | ? | ROCKY THE ROCKIN' HORSE | HIPPO POLKA | | | $1.00 | $2.00 |
| 1 | 602 | ? | LITTLE BETTY BLUE | RAG DOLL POLKA | | | $1.00 | $2.00 |
| 1 | 603 | ? | THE ROCKET SHIP | UNCLE BERNIE'S POLKA | | | $8.00 | $15.00 |
| 1 | 604 | DAVE ROMAINE & ORCH. | WEE WILLIE THE WHALE | HOKEY POKEY POLKA | | TOPS FOR TOTS V-37 | $2.00 | $4.00 |
| 1 | 606 | ? | HANSEL & GRETEL, SIDE 1 | HANSEL & GRETEL, SIDE 2 | | | $1.00 | $2.00 |
| 1 | 619 | ? | THE PIGGY BANK SONG | | | | $1.00 | $2.00 |
| 1 | 2001 | JACK ANDREWS & THE RHYTHM BOYS | THE BALLAD OF DAVY CROCKETT | THE TENDERFOOT | | | $4.00 | $8.00 |
| 1 | 2002 | DORIS PAULY, HRG ORCH./DAD & JUNIOR, HRG ORCH. | DISNEY'S "LADY & THE TRAMP": THE SIAMESE CAT SONG | A DAY AT THE ZOO | | | $4.00 | $8.00 |
| 1 | 2005 | ? | THE MOUSKETEERS MARCH | THE PIGGY BANK SONG | | | $4.00 | $8.00 |
| 1 | 2006 | ? | THE TRIPLE R SONG | ? | | | $1.00 | $2.00 |

## HONOR YOUR PARTNER 12" ALBUMS

| SET # | # REC | MAIN TITLE | ARTIST | YEAR | G/VG | EX/NMT |
|---|---|---|---|---|---|---|
| HYP-1 | 3 | SQUARE DANCES | ED DURLACHER, THE TOP HANDS | 1948 | $5.00 | $10.00 |
| HYP-2 | 3 | SQUARE DANCES | ED DURLACHER, THE TOP HANDS | | $5.00 | $10.00 |
| HYP-3 | 3 | SQUARE DANCES | ED DURLACHER, THE TOP HANDS | | $5.00 | $10.00 |
| HYP-4 | 3 | SQUARE DANCES | ED DURLACHER, THE TOP HANDS | 1949 | $5.00 | $10.00 |
| HYP-5 | 3 | RHYTHMIC MUSIC | ED DURLACHER, THE TOP HANDS | 1950 | $5.00 | $10.00 |
| HYP-6 | 4 | COUPLE DANCES AND MIXERS | ED DURLACHER, THE TOP HANDS | 1953 | $6.00 | $12.00 |
| HYP-7 | 3 | RHYTHMS (BASIC) | ED DURLACHER, THE TOP HANDS | 1955 | $5.00 | $10.00 |
| HYP-8 | 4 | SQUARE DANCES — MUSIC AND CALLS | ED DURLACHER, THE TOP HANDS | 1956 | $6.00 | $12.00 |
| HYP-9 | 4 | COUPLE DANCES AND MIXERS | ED DURLACHER, THE TOP HANDS | 1957 | $6.00 | $12.00 |
| HYP-10 | 4 | PLAY PARTY GAMES, SINGING GAMES, FOLK DANCES | ED DURLACHER, THE TOP HANDS | | $6.00 | $12.00 |
| HYP-11 | 4 | MARCHES | ED DURLACHER, THE TOP HANDS | | $6.00 | $12.00 |
| HYP-12 | 4 | ROPE SKIPPING | ED DURLACHER, THE TOP HANDS | 1958 | $6.00 | $12.00 |
| HYP-13 | 4 | MIXERS | ED DURLACHER, THE TOP HANDS | | $6.00 | $12.00 |
| HYP-14 | 4 | MODERN DYNAMIC PHYSICAL FITNESS ACTIVITIES (PRIMARY GAMES) | ED DURLACHER, THE TOP HANDS | 1959 | $6.00 | $12.00 |
| HYP-15 | 4 | MODERN DYNAMIC PHYSICAL FITNESS ACTIVITIES (ELEMENTARY AND HIGH SCHOOL) | ED DURLACHER, THE TOP HANDS | | $6.00 | $12.00 |
| HYP-16 | 4 | ADVANCED MODERN DYNAMIC PHYSICAL FITNESS ACTIVITIES (FOR GIRLS & WOMEN) | ED DURLACHER, THE TOP HANDS | 1960 | $6.00 | $12.00 |
| HYP-18 | 4 | SQUARE DANCES (VARIATIONS OF FIGURES IN V. 1, 2) | ED DURLACHER, THE TOP HANDS | 1961 | $6.00 | $12.00 |
| HYP-21 | 1 (LP) | MODERN ACTIVITIES & SKILLS | ED DURLACHER, THE TOP HANDS | 1962 | $6.00 | $12.00 |
| HYP-22 | 4 | INTERNATIONAL FOLK DANCES | ED DURLACHER, THE TOP HANDS | 1963 | $6.00 | $12.00 |
| HYP-23 | 4 | PRIMARY MUSICAL GAMES | ED DURLACHER, THE TOP HANDS | 1964 | $6.00 | $12.00 |
| HYP-24 | 4 | FITNESS FUN FOR EVERYONE (GRADES K – 3) | ED DURLACHER, THE TOP HANDS | 1966 | $6.00 | $12.00 |
| HYP-25 | 4 | POSTURAL IMPROVEMENT ACTIVITIES | ED DURLACHER, THE TOP HANDS | 1967 | $6.00 | $12.00 |

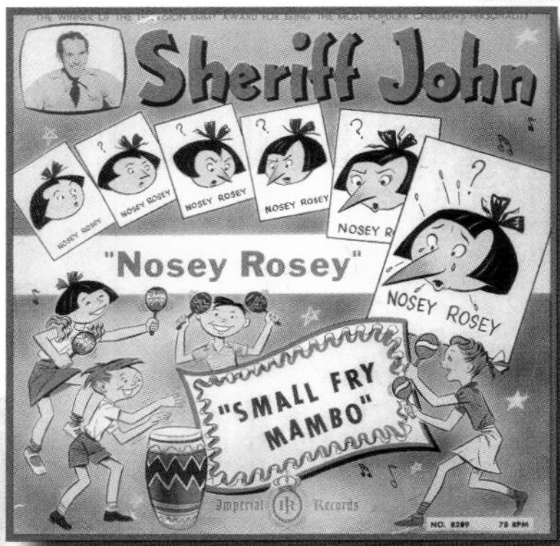


INTERNATIONAL RECORDS WIGGELY WORM AND OTHER SONGS $25.00

IMP RECORDS CIVILIZATION $2.00

IMPERIAL RECORDS NOSEY ROSEY $150.00

## HUMPTY DUMPTY 10" SINGLES IN PICTUREBOOK ALBUM

| # REC | DISC # | ARTIST | A TITLE | B TITLE | YEAR | ALSO ISSUED ON | G/VG | EX/NMT |
|---|---|---|---|---|---|---|---|---|
| 1 | 500 | HUMPTY DUMPTY PLAYERS | SONGS FROM MOTHER GOOSE: TWINKLE TWINKLE LITTLE STAR, ETC. | SONGS FROM MOTHER GOOSE: DID YOU EVER SEE A LASSIE, ETC. | 1950 | | $2.00 | $4.00 |
| 1 | 501 | JACK ARTHUR; VICKY KASEN, DIR. | MR. GALLAGHER'S DONKEY (AKA PANCHO THE CIRCUS DONKEY) | MR. GALLAGHER'S DONKEY (AKA "PANCHO THE CIRCUS DONKEY") | | PANCHO THE CIRCUS DONKEY (ON PETER PAN) | $5.00 | $10.00 |
| 1 | 502 | THE PETER PAN PLAYERS; VICKY KASEN, DIR. | HAPPY BIRTHDAY TO YOU | HAPPY BIRTHDAY TO YOU | | | $2.00 | $4.00 |
| 1 | 503 | JACK ARTHUR; BERNARD HAAS, DIR. | TEDDY BEARS PICNIC | TEDDY BEARS POLKA | | | $2.00 | $4.00 |
| 1 | 504 | JACK ARTHUR, BOBBY HOOKEY, PPO, VK | HENRY'S WAGON (AKA THE LITTLE RED WAGON) | HENRY'S WAGON (AKA "THE LITTLE RED WAGON") | | THE LITTLE RED WAGON (ON PETER PAN) | $8.00 | $15.00 |
| 1 | 505 | BILLY WILLIAMS & HIS COWBOY RANGERS; DON COPE, DIR. | OLD MACDONALD HAD A FARM | OH, SUSANNA! | | | $2.00 | $4.00 |
| 1 | 506 | HUMPTY DUMPTY PLAYERS | FAVORITE NURSERY RHYMES: FRERE JACQUES, ETC. | FAVORITE NURSERY RHYMES: LONDON BRIDGE, ETC. | | | $2.00 | $4.00 |
| 1 | 507 | JACK ARTHUR; BERNARD HAAS, DIR./ VICKY WHITE; BERNARD HAAS, DIR. | BUFFALO BILLY | I FOUND MY MOMMA | | | $2.00 | $4.00 |

*PICTUREBOOK ALBUM

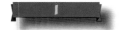

## IMP 7" SINGLES

| # REC | DISC # | ARTIST | A TITLE | B TITLE | YEAR | ALSO ISSUED ON | G/VG | EX/NMT |
|---|---|---|---|---|---|---|---|---|
| 1 | LL 5 | NOT LISTED | MYRTLE THE TURTLE (PT. 1) | MYRTLE THE TURTLE (PT. 2) | 194? | LOOK-LISTEN LL-5 | $1.00 | $2.00 |
| 1 | LL-6 | NOT LISTED | CINDERELLA (PT. 1) | CINDERELLA (PT. 2) | | LOOK-LISTEN LL-6 | $1.00 | $2.00 |
| 1 | LM-19 | NOT LISTED | CORONATION MARCH | MINUET IN G | | LITTLE MASTERS LM-19 | $1.00 | $2.00 |
| 1 | PP-1 | NOT LISTED | CARRY ME BACK TO OLD VIRGINIA | OH SUSANNA | | PIED PIPER PP-1 | $1.00 | $2.00 |
| 1 | PP-14 | NOT LISTED | FARMER IN THE DELL | A TISKET, A TASKET | | PIED PIPER PP-14 | $1.00 | $2.00 |
| 1 | PP-9 | NOT LISTED | COMIN' THRU' THE RYE | OLD FOLKS AT HOME | | PIED PIPER PP-9 | $1.00 | $2.00 |

## IMPERIAL 10" SINGLES

| SET # | # REC | DISC # | ARTIST | A TITLE | B TITLE | YEAR | G/VG | EX/NMT |
|---|---|---|---|---|---|---|---|---|
| 8221 | 1 | ? | SHERIFF JOHN | LAUGH AND BE HAPPY | GRUMBLE BEE, CARELESS CROW, SOURPUSS | | $75.00 | $150.00 |
| 8248 | 1 | IF-596-7 | DEPUTY DAVE | COME ALONG | SAFETY FIRST | 1954 | $35.00 | $75.00 |
| 8254 | 1 | ? | SHERIFF JOHN | GRIZZLY GRUMP | MOM KNOWS BEST | | $75.00 | $150.00 |
| 8270 | 1 | IF-644-3 | SHERIFF JOHN | BIRTHDAY CAKE POLKA | LITTLE TV COWBOY | | $75.00 | $150.00 |
| 8289 | 1 | IF-689-90 | SHERIFF JOHN | NOSEY ROSEY | SMALL FRY MAMBO | 1953 | $75.00 | $150.00 |
| ? | 1 | ? | SHERIFF JOHN | DON'T BE AFRAID OF THE DOCTOR | DON'T BE AFRAID OF THE DENTIST | | $75.00 | $150.00 |

## KIMBO 10" SINGLES

| # REC | DISC # | MAIN TITLE | ARTIST | YEAR | G/VG | EX/NMT |
|---|---|---|---|---|---|---|
| 1 | 174 | A PENNY A KISS | NOT LISTED | 1961 | $1.00 | $2.00 |
| 1 | 175 | WE COME FROM MARS | NOT LISTED | | $5.00 | $10.00 |
| 1 | 176 | FANCY DANCE PARADE | NOT LISTED | | $1.00 | $2.00 |
| 1 | 177 | THE COWGIRL BALLET | NOT LISTED | | $1.00 | $2.00 |
| 1 | 178 | HOW DO YOU DO — I'M A BAT | NOT LISTED | | $1.00 | $2.00 |
| 1 | 179 | SQUEAKY, THE MOUSE | NOT LISTED | | $1.00 | $2.00 |
| 1 | 180 | THE POWDER PUFF MOB'S IN TOWN | NOT LISTED | | $1.00 | $2.00 |
| 1 | 181 | FIREMAN CHA CHA | NOT LISTED | | $1.00 | $2.00 |
| 1 | 182 | THE KIMBO POLKA | NOT LISTED | | $1.00 | $2.00 |
| 1 | 183 | THE ARISTO-CATS | NOT LISTED | | $2.00 | $4.00 |
| 1 | 184 | WEDDING OF THE KIMBO KIDS | NOT LISTED | | $1.00 | $2.00 |
| 1 | 185 | LET'S GO BACK TO 1892 | NOT LISTED | | $1.00 | $2.00 |
| 1 | 186 | ELLIE THE ELF | NOT LISTED | | $1.00 | $2.00 |
| 1 | 187 | ELEGANT ELEPHANTS | NOT LISTED | | $1.00 | $2.00 |
| 1 | 188 | CHILDREN'S SONGS FOR SELF-EXPRESSION | NOT LISTED | | $1.00 | $2.00 |
| 1 | 500 | WHY DO I LOVE YOU/OH LEO | NOT LISTED | | $1.00 | $2.00 |
| 1 | 502 | BOOGIE ROCK | NOT LISTED | | $1.00 | $2.00 |
| 1 | KI 2 | DANCING ON THE CEILING | NOT LISTED | | $1.00 | $2.00 |
| 1 | KI 4 | LULLABY OF THE LEAVES | NOT LISTED | | $1.00 | $2.00 |
| 1 | KI 6 | WALTZ FANTASY | NOT LISTED | | $1.00 | $2.00 |
| 1 | KI 8 | FROM THIS MOMENT ON | NOT LISTED | | $1.00 | $2.00 |

## KTAV 7" SINGLES AND DOUBLES

| # REC | DISC # | MAIN TITLE | ARTIST | YEAR | G/VG | EX/NMT | REMARKS |
|---|---|---|---|---|---|---|---|
| 1 | STORY # 1 | THE STORY OF CHANUKAH | EDWARD GOLD | 1951 | $3.00 | $6.00 | |
| 2 | NO NUMBER | HAPPY CHANUKAH: MOTHER GOOSE RHYMES/ LITTLE YOMO | FRED VOGEL | | $5.00 | $10.00 | GATEFOLD SLEEVE |
| 1 | ? | MOTHER GOOSE RHYMES FOR SABBATH | ? | | $3.00 | $6.00 | |
| 1 | ? | MOTHER GOOSE RHYMES FOR PASSOVER | ? | | $3.00 | $6.00 | |
| 1 | ? | MOTHER GOOSE RHYMES FOR ISRAEL | ? | | $3.00 | $6.00 | |
| 1 | ? | ISRAELI MELODIES | ? | | $3.00 | $6.00 | |
| 1 | ? | SABBATH MELODIES | ? | | $3.00 | $6.00 | |
| 1 | ? | CHANUKAH MELODIES | ? | | $3.00 | $6.00 | |
| 1 | ? | PASSOVER MELODIES | ? | | $3.00 | $6.00 | |
| 1 | ? | BAR MITZVAH BLESSINGS | ? | | $3.00 | $6.00 | |
| 1 | ? | HATIKVAH/STAR SPANGLED BANNER | ? | | $3.00 | $6.00 | |

## KTAV 10" SINGLES

| # REC | DISC # | MAIN TITLE | ARTIST | YEAR | ALSO ISSUED ON | G/VG | EX/NMT |
|---|---|---|---|---|---|---|---|
| 1 | 102 | HANUKKAH | EMANUEL ROSENBERG | 1954 | ALLEGRO | $2.00 | $4.00 |
| 1 | 109 | MORE SONGS FOR HANUKKAH | EMANUEL ROSENBERG | | ALLEGRO | $2.00 | $4.00 |
| 1 | 501 | PURIM | SHIRLEY COHEN, ELI GAMLIEL | | ALEPH | $2.00 | $4.00 |
| 1 | CP 1/2 | THE CHANUKAH PARTY | FRED VOGEL | 1955 | | $2.00 | $4.00 |

# L

## LA VELLE BOB O LINK 6" AND 7" IN BOOKS

| SET # | # REC | DISC # | MAIN TITLE | ARTIST | A TITLE | B TITLE | YEAR | G/VG | EX/NMT |
|---|---|---|---|---|---|---|---|---|---|
| SONG BOOK NO. 1 | 2 | | SONGS, GAMES AND STORIES | | | | 1922 | $50.00 | $100.00 |
| | | 550 (2200) | | CHARLES HARRISON | OLD KING COLE | CHOOSING THE QUEEN | | | |
| | | 551 (2201) | | CHARLES HARRISON | RIG-A-JIG-JIG | THE POSTILION | | | |
| SONG BOOK NO. 2 | 2 | | SONGS, GAMES AND STORIES | | | | | $50.00 | $100.00 |

LA VELLE BOB O LINK
A VISIT WITH MOTHER GOOSE
$100.00

LINCOLN
WYNKEN, BLYNKEN AND NOD
$4.00

LINDSTROM
THERE WAS A CROOKED MAN
$8.00

## LA VELLE BOB O LINK 6" AND 7" IN BOOKS

| SET # | # REC | DISC # | MAIN TITLE | ARTIST | A TITLE | B TITLE | YEAR | G/VG | EX/NMT |
|---|---|---|---|---|---|---|---|---|---|
| | | 552 (2202) | | NEVADA VANDERVEER/ CHARLES HARRISON | UNDER THE DREAMLAND TREE | THE SUNNY SOUTH | | | |
| | | 553 (2203) | | CHARLES HARRISON | JINGLE BELLS | THE TUNE OF THE FORGE | | | |
| SONG BOOK NO. 3 | 2 | | A VISIT WITH MOTHER GOOSE | | | | | $50.00 | $100.00 |
| | | 560 (2210) | | VICTOR VALENTI | MARY HAD A LITTLE LAMB | O DEAR WHAT CAN THE MATTER BE | | | |
| | | 561 (2212) | | VICTOR VALENTI | MISS JENNIA JONES | HUSH-A-BYE BABY | | | |
| SONG BOOK NO. 4 | 2 | | MOTHER GOOSE & HER FAIRYLAND FRIENDS | | | | | $50.00 | $100.00 |
| | | 558 (2208) | | VICTOR VALENTI | SING A SONG OF SIX-PENCE | JACK AND JILL | | | |
| | | 559 (2209) | | VICTOR VALENTI | PAT-A-CAKE | HICKORY, DICKORY, DOCK | | | |
| READING BOOK NO. 1 | 2 | | THE STORY OF BETTY AND BOB AND THEIR FRIENDS | | | | | $50.00 | $100.00 |
| | | 554 (2204) | | CHARLES HARRISON | PRETTY BOBOLINK | OUR OLD DOG & LITTLE PUSSY | | | |
| | | 555 (2205) | | CHARLES HARRISON | HEEL AND TOE | SWEET GOOD NIGHT | | | |
| READING BOOK NO. 2 | 2 | | THE STORY OF BETTY AND BOB AND THEIR FRIENDS | | | | | $50.00 | $100.00 |
| | | 556 (2206) | | GILBERT GIRARD/ CHARLES HARRISON | IN THE BARNYARD | GOOD MORNING | | | |
| | | 557 (2207) | | CHARLES HARRISON/ NOT LISTED | THE GYPSY CAMP | THE PARTY (MEDLEY) | | | |
| TALKING GAMES | 2 | | TALKING GAMES | | | | 1920 | $50.00 | $100.00 |
| | | 809/813 | | NOT LISTED | HERE WE GO ROUND THE MULBERRY BUSH | THE FARMER IN THE DELL | | | |
| | | 810/811 | | NOT LISTED | LONDON BRIDGE IS FALLING DOWN | JOHN BROWN HAD A LITTLE INDIAN | | | |

## LIBRARY OF CONGRESS 10" AND 12" ALBUMS

| SET # | # REC | DISC # | MAIN TITLE | ARTIST | YEAR | G/VG | EX/NMT | REMARKS |
|---|---|---|---|---|---|---|---|---|
| NO # (10") | 2 | FM 1 - 2 | FRIENDS OF MUSIC ALBUM | ALAN LOMAX, EDITOR | 1940 | $75.00 | $150.00 | WOODY GUTHRIE |
| 1 (10") | 5 | AAFS 1 - 5 | ANGLO-AMERICAN BALLADS | ALAN LOMAX, EDITOR | 1942 | $35.00 | $75.00 | |

LINDSTROM RECORDS
THE WEDDING OF THE PAINTED DOLL
$8.00

LIONEL RECORDS
JINGLE BELLS
$10.00

LIONEL RECORDS
LIONEL TRAIN SOUND EFFECTS
$50.00

## LIBRARY OF CONGRESS 10" AND 12" ALBUMS

| SET # | # REC | DISC # | MAIN TITLE | ARTIST | YEAR | G/VG | EX/NMT | REMARKS |
|---|---|---|---|---|---|---|---|---|
| 2 | 5 | AAFS 6 - 10 | ANGLO-AMERICAN SHANTIES, LYRIC SONGS, DANCE TUNES AND SPIRITUAL | ALAN LOMAX, EDITOR | | $35.00 | $75.00 | |
| 3 | 5 | AAFS 11 - 15 | AFRO-AMERICAN SPIRITUALS, WORK SONGS, AND BALLADS | ALAN LOMAX, EDITOR | | $50.00 | $100.00 | BLACK AMERICANA |
| 4 (10") | 5 | AAFS 16 - 20 | AFRO-AMERICAN BLUES AND GAME SONGS | ALAN LOMAX, EDITOR | | $35.00 | $75.00 | |
| 5 (10") | 5 | AAFS 21 - 25 | BAHAMAN SONGS, FRENCH BALLADS AND DANCE TUNES, SPANISH RELIGIOUS SONGS AND GAMES | ALAN LOMAX, EDITOR | | $35.00 | $75.00 | |
| 6 | 5 | AAFS 26 - 30 | SONGS FROM THE IROQUOIS LONGHOUSE | WILLIAM FENTON, EDITOR | | $35.00 | $75.00 | |
| 7 | 5 | AAFS 31 - 35 | ANGLO-AMERICAN BALLADS | B.A. BOTKIN, EDITOR | | $35.00 | $75.00 | |
| 8 (10") | 5 | AAFS 36 - 40 | NEGRO WORK SONGS AND CALLS | B.A. BOTKIN, EDITOR | | $40.00 | $80.00 | BLACK AMERICANA |
| 9 | 5 | AAFS 41 - 45 | PLAY AND DANCE SONGS AND TUNES | B.A. BOTKIN, EDITOR | | $35.00 | $75.00 | |
| 10 | 5 | AAFS 46 - 50 | NEGRO RELIGIOUS SONGS AND SERVICES | B.A. BOTKIN, EDITOR | | $35.00 | $75.00 | |
| 11 | 5 | AAFS 51 - 55 | SACRED HARP SINGING | GEORGE P. JACKSON, EDITOR | | $35.00 | $75.00 | |
| 12 | 5 | AAFS 56 - 60 | ANGLO-AMERICAN SONGS AND BALLADS | DUNCAN EMRICH, EDITOR | | $35.00 | $75.00 | |
| 13 | 5 | AAFS 61 - 65 | AFRO-BAHIAN RELIGIOUS SONGS FROM BRAZIL | MELVILLE & FRANCES HERSKOVITS, EDITORS | | $35.00 | $75.00 | |
| 14 | 5 | AAFS 66 - 70 | ANGLO-AMERICAN SONGS AND BALLADS | DUNCAN EMRICH, EDITOR | | $50.00 | $100.00 | EARLY JEAN RITCHIE |
| 15 | 5 | AAFS 71 - 75 | FOLK MUSIC OF VENEZUELA | JUAN LISCANO, EDITOR | | $35.00 | $75.00 | |
| 16 | 5 | AAFS 76 - 80 | SONGS AND BALLAD OF THE ANTHRACITE MINERS | GEORGE KORSON, EDITOR | 1947 | $35.00 | $75.00 | |
| 17 | 5 | AAFS 81 - 85 | SENECA SONGS FROM THE COLDSPRING LONG-HOUSE | WILLIAM FENTON, EDITOR | | $35.00 | $75.00 | |
| 18 (10") | 5 | AAFS 86 - 90 | FOLK MUSIC OF PUERTO RICO | RICHARD WATERMAN, EDITOR | | $35.00 | $75.00 | |
| 19 | 5 | AAFS 91 - 95 | FOLK MUSIC OF MEXICO | HENRIETTA YURCHENCO, EDITOR | | $35.00 | $75.00 | |
| 20 | 5 | AAFS 96 - 100 | ANGLO-AMERICAN SONGS AND BALLADS | DUNCAN EMRICH, EDITOR | | $35.00 | $75.00 | |
| 21 | 5 | AAFS 101 - 105 | ANGLO-AMERICAN SONGS AND BALLADS | DUNCAN EMRICH, EDITOR | | $40.00 | $80.00 | EARLY SAM HINTON |
| 22 | 5 | AAFS 106 - 110 | SONGS OF THE CHIPPEWA | FRANCES DENSMORE, EDITOR | | $35.00 | $75.00 | |

## L'IL PODNER LIPTON SOUP PREMIUM 4" SQUARE PICTURE DISCS

| # REC | DISC # | MAIN TITLE | ARTIST | YEAR | G/VG | EX/NMT |
|---|---|---|---|---|---|---|
| 1 | NO # | HONESTY | A LI'L PODNER SPECIAL | 1957 | $5.00 | $10.00 |
| 1 | NO # | NAUGHTY WORDS | A LI'L PODNER SPECIAL | | $5.00 | $10.00 |
| 1 | NO # | CLEANLINESS AND NEATNESS | A LI'L PODNER SPECIAL | | $5.00 | $10.00 |
| 1 | NO # | MANNERS | A LI'L PODNER SPECIAL | | $5.00 | $10.00 |

## LINCOLN 10" SINGLES AND ALBUMS

| # REC | DISC # | ARTIST | A TITLE | B TITLE | YEAR | G/VG | EX/NMT |
|---|---|---|---|---|---|---|---|
| 1 | 501 | MARIE GERARD, BARBARA TOUCHETTE/ROGER WHITE, RAY HALLEE | SILENT NIGHT | GOOD KING WENCESLAS | 1949 | $1.50 | $3.00 |
| 1 | 502 | THE TEDDY BEAR CAROLEERS, MARIE GERARD, BARBARA TOUCHETTE | O COME, ALL YE FAITHFUL | THE FIRST NOEL | | $1.50 | $3.00 |
| 1 | 503 | ? | IT CAME UPON A MIDNIGHT CLEAR | JOY TO THE WORLD | | $1.50 | $3.00 |
| 1 | 504 | ROGER WHITE, BOBOLINK CHRISTMAS SINGERS | TWAS THE NIGHT BEFORE CHRISTMAS | HARK THE HERALD ANGELS SING/O LITTLE TOWN OF BETHLEHEM | | $1.50 | $3.00 |
| 1 | 505 | THE LINCOLN SINGERS/ROY HALLEE | THERE WAS A CROOKED MAN | OLD WOMAN WHO LIVED IN A SHOE | | $1.50 | $3.00 |
| 1 | 506 | GERRY TOUCHETTE/THE LINCOLN SINGERS | TO MARKET, TO MARKET | THE GINGERBREAD MAN | | $2.00 | $4.00 |
| 1 | 507 | ROGER WHITE & THE LINCOLN SINGERS/THE LINCOLN PLAYERS | RUM-DE-DIDDLE, THE RUNAWAY FIDDLE | OATS, PEAS, BEANS AND BARLEY | | $2.00 | $4.00 |
| 1 | 508 | GERRY TOUCHETTS/ROY HALLEE, JOANNE MORELAND | DING DONG BELL | GOOSEY GOOSEY GANDER | | $2.00 | $4.00 |
| 1 | 509 | ROGER WHITE & THE LINCOLN SINGERS/JOANNE MORELAND, GERRY TOUCHETTE | THE THREE BILLYGOATS | GEORGIE PORGIE | | $2.00 | $4.00 |
| 1 | 510 | GERRY TOUCHETTS/ROY HALLEE, JOANNE MORELAND | A FROG HE WOULD A WOOING GO | BILLY BOY | | $2.00 | $4.00 |
| 1 | 517 | ? | THE EMPEROR'S NEW CLOTHES | LITTLE BOY BLUE/WHERE HAS MY LITTLE DOG GONE? | 1950 | $2.00 | $4.00 |
| 1 | 518 | ROY HALLEE, THE LINCOLN SINGERS | THE MIKADO (PT. 1) | THE MIKADO (PT. 2) | | $2.00 | $4.00 |
| 1 | 519 | ROGER WHITE, GERRY BEITZEL, THE LINCOLN SINGERS | H.M.S. PINAFORE (PT. 1) | H.M.S. PINAFORE (PT. 2) | | $2.00 | $4.00 |
| 1 | 520 | ROGER WHITE, LOREN BECKER/? | THE FIRE ENGINE PARADE | HEY DIDDLE DIDDLE/A TRIP TO NEW YORK | | $2.00 | $4.00 |
| 1 | 521 | MARION ROSETTE, SALLY SWEETLAND/MARION ROSETTE | MOTHER GOOSE PARTY | PUSSY CAT, PUSSY CAT/A HUNTING WE WILL GO | | $2.00 | $4.00 |
| 1 | 522 | ROY HALLEE/ROGER WHITE & THE LINCOLN PLAYERS | THE OLD CHISHOLM TRAIL | SHE'LL BE COMIN' ROUND THE MOUNTAIN | | $2.00 | $4.00 |
| 1 | 523 | ROGER WHITE & THE LINCOLN PLAYERS/ROY HALLEE & THE LINCOLN PLAYERS | COWBOY'S OLD HORSE | CASEY JONES | | $2.00 | $4.00 |
| 1 | 524 | WHITE, HALLEE, BEITZEL, MORELAND, ENOCH LIGHT ORCH./NOT LISTED | THE TRAVELING MUSICIANS | SING A SONG OF SIXPENCE/THE MUFFIN MAN | | $2.00 | $4.00 |
| 1 | 525 | ROGER WHITE, SALLY SWEETLAND/ROY HALLEE | PINOCCHIO | HOP O' MY THUMB | | $2.00 | $4.00 |
| 1 | 526 | ROY HALLEE, GERRY BEITZE/ROY HALLEE | RUMPLESTILTSKIN | PAT-A-CAKE/OVER IN THE MEADOW | | $2.00 | $4.00 |
| 1 | 527 | SALLY SWEETLAND, ROY HALLEE/SALLY SWEETLAND | THE CITY MOUSE AND THE COUNTRY MOUSE | RIDE A COCK HORSE/FIDDLE-DE-DEE | | $2.00 | $4.00 |
| 1 | 528 | GERRY BEITZEL, JOANNE MORELAND, LOREN BECKER/MARION ROSETTE | SNOW WHITE AND THE SEVEN DWARFS | THE LION AND THE MOUSE/FRERE JACQUES (BROTHER JOHN) | | $2.00 | $4.00 |
| 1 | 529 | SALLY SWEETLAND/JOANNE MORELAND, GERRY BEITZEL, ROGER WHITE | WYNKEN, BLYNKEN AND NOD | RAPUNZEL | | $2.00 | $4.00 |
| 1 | 530 | ? | SANTA CLAUS IS FLYING THRU THE SKY | DECK THE HALLS/GOD REST YE MERRY GENTLEMEN | | $2.00 | $4.00 |
| 1 | 539 | ROGER WHITE, ROY HALLEE/GERRY BEITZEL & THE LINCOLN PLAYERS | THE FISHERMAN AND THE FLOUNDER | THREE BLIND MICE | 1949 | $2.00 | $4.00 |
| 1 | 540 | GERRY BEITZEL/GERRY TOUCHETTE, JOANNE MORELAND | NIGHT SONG FOR LITTLE ONE | THE ALPHABET SONG | | $2.00 | $4.00 |
| 1 | 541 | MARIE GERARD, THE LINCOLN PLAYERS/GERRY BEITZEL, THE LINCOLN PLAYERS | CHICKEN LICKEN | KATIE THE KANGAROO | | $4.00 | $8.00 |
| 1 | 542 | ROY HALLEE, ROGER WHITE/ROGER WHITE | THE ELVES AND THE SHOEMAKER | THE FROG AND THE OX | | $2.00 | $4.00 |
| 1 | 543 | GERRY BEITZEL, JOANNE MORELAND/GERRY TOUCHETTE, ROY HALLEE | CHARLIE HAD A CHOO CHOO | OLD MOTHER HUBBARD | | $2.00 | $4.00 |
| 1 | 544 | GERRY BEITZEL, MARIE GERARD/ROY HALLEE, GERRY BEITZEL | A MONKEY WHO WANTED TO FLY | HUMPTY DUMPTY | | $2.00 | $4.00 |
| 6 | ALB #L-27 (505-10) | THE LINCOLN SINGERS, ETC. | SONGS & STORIES FOR CHILDREN: SEE SINGLE TITLES 505 - 510 | SONGS & STORIES FOR CHILDREN: SEE SINGLE TITLES 505 - 510 | | $10.00 | $20.00 |

## LINDSTROM 6" SINGLES

| # REC | DISC # | ARTIST | A TITLE | B TITLE | YEAR | G/VG | EX/NMT |
|---|---|---|---|---|---|---|---|
| 1 | 101 | NOT LISTED | OLD KING COLE | LITTLE BO PEEP | 193? | $4.00 | $8.00 |
| 1 | 102 | NOT LISTED | MARY HAD A LITTLE LAMB | LITTLE BOY BLUE | | $4.00 | $8.00 |
| 1 | 110 | NOT LISTED | LONDON BRIDGE IS FALLING DOWN | THREE LITTLE PIGS | | $4.00 | $8.00 |
| 1 | 113 | NOT LISTED | THE HOUSE THAT JACK BUILT | THREE BLIND MICE | | $4.00 | $8.00 |
| 1 | 130 | NOT LISTED | THERE WAS A CROOKED MAN | BAA BAA BLACK SHEEP | | $4.00 | $8.00 |

## LINDSTROM 7" SINGLES

| # REC | DISC # | ARTIST | A TITLE | B TITLE | YEAR | G/VG | EX/NMT |
|---|---|---|---|---|---|---|---|
| 1 | 701 | NOT LISTED | LAZY MARY WILL YOU GET UP | HAPPY BIRTHDAY TO YOU | 193? | $4.00 | $8.00 |
| 1 | 702 | NOT LISTED | LONDON BRIDGE IS FALLING DOWN | I HAD A LITTLE DOGGY | | $4.00 | $8.00 |
| 1 | 703 | NOT LISTED | THE FARMER IN THE DELL | GOOD MORNING MERRY SUNSHINE | | $4.00 | $8.00 |
| 1 | 704 | NOT LISTED | JACK AND JILL | OH DEAR WHAT CAN THE MATTER BE | | $4.00 | $8.00 |
| 1 | 705 | NOT LISTED | LITTLE BO PEEP | TWINKLE TWINKLE LITTLE STAR | | $4.00 | $8.00 |
| 1 | 706 | NOT LISTED | OLD KING COLE | LITTLE BOY BLUE | | $4.00 | $8.00 |
| 1 | 711 | NOT LISTED | DOLL DANCE | THE WEDDING OF THE PAINTED DOLL | | $4.00 | $8.00 |
| 1 | 712 | NOT LISTED | WALTZ-CLOG | TAP DANCE | | $4.00 | $8.00 |
| 1 | 713 | NOT LISTED | POLKA | MINUET | | $4.00 | $8.00 |
| 1 | 714 | NOT LISTED | PARADE OF THE WOODEN SOLDIERS | TOM THUMB'S DREAM | | $4.00 | $8.00 |
| 1 | 715 | NOT LISTED | LITTLE DROPS OF WATER | THE BIRD BAND | | $4.00 | $8.00 |
| 1 | 716 | NOT LISTED | JINGLE BELLS | TEN LITTLE DARKIES | | $4.00 | $8.00 |
| 1 | 717 | NOT LISTED | WINTER | DOLLS | | $4.00 | $8.00 |
| 1 | 718 | NOT LISTED | COLUMBIA, THE GEM OF THE OCEAN | STAR SPANGLED BANNER | | $4.00 | $8.00 |

## LIONEL MAIN CHILDREN'S SERIES 6" SINGLES SOUND EFFECTS RECORDS 5", 6", 10" SINGLES, REGULAR AND PICTURE DISCS

| SET # | # REC | DISC # | MAIN TITLE | ARTIST | YEAR | G/VG | EX/NMT |
|---|---|---|---|---|---|---|---|
| 49700-100 | 1 | 100 | LONDON BRIDGE, ETC./DID YOU EVER SEE A LASSIE, ETC. | JUDY WILLIAMS, JACK RUSSELL, HONEY DREAMERS | 195? | $5.00 | $10.00 |
| 49700-101 | 1 | 101 | ROUND THE MULBERRY BUSH/HERE WE GO LOOBY LOO | JUDY WILLIAMS, JACK RUSSELL, HONEY DREAMERS | | $5.00 | $10.00 |
| 49700-102 | 1 | 102 | TWINKLE TWINKLE LITTLE STAR/BRAHMS' LULLABY | ? | | $5.00 | $10.00 |
| 49700-103 | 1 | 103 | OLD KING COLE, ETC./POP GOES THE WEASEL, ETC. | ? | | $5.00 | $10.00 |
| 49710-104 | 1 | 104 | POLLY WOLLY DOODLE, BLUE TAIL FLY/THE ARKANSAS TRAVELER | ? | | $5.00 | $10.00 |
| 49710-105 | 1 | 105 | BUFFALO GALS, DOWN IN THE VALLEY/WHOOPEE TI YI YO, SKIP TO MY LOU | ? | | $5.00 | $10.00 |
| 49710-106 | 1 | 106 | OLD FOLKS AT HOME, OH SUSANNA/CLEMENTINE, ON TOP OF OLD SMOKEY | ? | | $5.00 | $10.00 |
| 49710-107 | 1 | 107 | PONY BOY, RED RIVER VALLEY/HOME ON THE RANGE | ? | | $5.00 | $10.00 |
| 49720-108 | 1 | 108 | JINGLE BELLS, JOLLY OLD ST. NICHOLAS/NOEL, COME ALL YE FAITHFUL | HUGH PERETTE, CHORUS DIR./JUNE WINTERS | | $5.00 | $10.00 |
| 49720-109 | 1 | 109 | SILENT NIGHT/WE WISH YOU A MERRY CHRISTMAS, DECK THE HALLS | JUNE WINTERS | | $5.00 | $10.00 |
| 49720-110 | 1 | 110 | OH HOLY NIGHT/GOD REST YE MERRY GENTLEMEN, RING CHRISTMAS BELLS | JUNE WINTERS | | $5.00 | $10.00 |
| 49720-111 | 1 | 111 | TWAS THE NIGHT BEFORE CHRISTMAS | ? | | $5.00 | $10.00 |
| 49730-112 | 1 | 112 | THE LITTLE RED HEN | AL JAVELON | | $5.00 | $10.00 |
| 49730-113 | 1 | 113 | THE THREE GOATS | AL JAVELON | | $5.00 | $10.00 |
| 49730-114 | 1 | 114 | THE FOX & THE GRAPES/THE CITY MOUSE & THE COUNTRY MOUSE | ? | | $5.00 | $10.00 |
| 49730-115 | 1 | 115 | THE LION & THE MOUSE/THE FROG & THE OX | ? | | $5.00 | $10.00 |
| 49750-117 | 1 | 117 | DANCE TUNES FOR LITTLE FOLKS: H AND D STOMP/ ARKANSAS REEL | ? | | $5.00 | $10.00 |
| 49740-118 | 1 | 118 | PATRIOTIC SONGS AND MARCHES #1: EL CAPITAN/THE THUNDER MARCH | ? | | $5.00 | $10.00 |
| 49740-119 | 1 | 119 | PATRIOTIC SONGS AND MARCHES #2: CAISSON SONG/SEM-PER FIDELIS | NOT LISTED | | $5.00 | $10.00 |
| 49740-120 | 1 | 120 | PATRIOTIC SONGS AND MARCHES #3: LIBERTY BELL MARCH/THE STARS AND STRIPES | ? | | $5.00 | $10.00 |

LISTEN-LOOK PICTURE BOOK
LITTLE RED RIDING HOOD
$10.00

LITTLE CHIP RECORDS
A TRIP TO THE ZOO
$1.00

LITTLE FOLK FAVORITES
ALADDIN'S LAMP
$25.00

## LIONEL MAIN CHILDREN'S SERIES 6" SINGLES SOUND EFFECTS RECORDS 5", 6", 10" SINGLES, REGULAR AND PICTURE DISC

| SET # | # REC | DISC # | MAIN TITLE | ARTIST | YEAR | G/VG | EX/NMT |
|---|---|---|---|---|---|---|---|
| 49740-121 | 1 | 121 | PATRIOTIC SONGS AND MARCHES #4: COLUMBIA THE GEM OF THE OCEAN/EYES OF TEXAS | ? | | $5.00 | $10.00 |
| 49750-122 | 1 | 122 | DANCE TUNES FOR LITTLE FOLKS #1: THE CLARINET POLKA/THE HELENA POLKA | ? | | $5.00 | $10.00 |
| 49750-123 | 1 | 123 | DANCE TUNES FOR LITTLE FOLKS #2: MERRY WIDOW WALTZ/BLUE DANUBE WALTZ | ? | | $5.00 | $10.00 |
| 49750-124 | 1 | 124 | DANCE TUNES FOR LITTLE FOLKS #3: EL CHOCLO-TANGO/A MEDIZ LUZ-RHUMBA | ? | | $5.00 | $10.00 |
| 49700-140 | 1 | 140 | BABES IN TOYLAND | ? | | $5.00 | $10.00 |
| NO # (6") | 1 | NO # | WHISTLES AND BELLS AND PUFFING LIONEL TRAINS | AUTHENTIC TRAIN SOUNDS | | $12.00 | $25.00 |
| NO # (6") | 1 | 3/14 | LIONEL TRAINS: WHISTLE SIGNALS/IN ACTION | AUTHENTIC WHISTLE SIGNALS/BILL STERN | 1947 | $30.00 | $60.00 |
| NO # (6") | 1 | NO # | LIONEL TRAIN SOUND EFFECTS (FLEXI PIC-DISC) | AUTHENTIC TRAIN SOUNDS | 51 + 54 | $25.00 | $50.00 |
| NO # (10") | 1 | NO # | LIONEL TRAIN SOUND EFFECTS (PROMOTIONAL RECORD) | AUTHENTIC TRAIN SOUNDS | 1947 | $12.00 | $25.00 |
| NO # (5") | 1 | NO # | I'M A LIONEL (TOOT TOOT) ENGINEER | AUTHENTIC TRAIN SOUNDS | 1955 | $25.00 | $50.00 |

## LIONEL-SPEAR 6" SINGLES

| # REC | DISC # | MAIN TITLE | ARTIST | A TITLE | B TITLE | YEAR | G/VG | EX/NMT |
|---|---|---|---|---|---|---|---|---|
| 1 | 49700-1 | BABES IN TOYLAND | ? | | | | $3.00 | $6.00 |
| 1 | 49700-1 | LONDON BRIDGE, ETC./DID YOU EVER SEE A LASSIE, ETC. | JUDY WILLIAMS, JACK RUSSELL, HONEY DREAMERS | LONDON BRIDGE, BAA BAA BLACK SHEEP, HUMPTY DUMPTY | DID YOU EVER SEE A LASSIE, LITTLE BOY BLUE, MARY HAD A LITTLE LAMB | 1962 | $3.00 | $6.00 |
| 1 | 49700-2 | ROUND THE MULBERRY BUSH/HERE WE GO LOOBY LOO | JUDY WILLIAMS, JACK RUSSELL, HONEY DREAMERS | ROUND THE MULBERRY BUSH | HERE WE GO LOOBY LOO | | $3.00 | $6.00 |
| 1 | 49700-3 | TWINKLE TWINKLE LITTLE STAR/BRAHMS' LULLABY | ? | TWINKLE TWINKLE LITTLE STAR | BRAHMS' LULLABY | | $3.00 | $6.00 |
| 1 | 49700-4 | OLD KING COLE, ETC./POP GOES THE WEASEL, ETC. | ? | OLD KING COLE, PUSSY CAT PUSSY CAT, SING A SONG OF SIX PENCE | POP GOES THE WEASEL, ETC. | | $3.00 | $6.00 |
| 1 | 49710-1 | POLLY WOLLY DOODLE, BLUE TAIL FLY/THE ARKANSAS TRAVELER | ? | POLLY WOLLY DOODLE, BLUE TAIL FLY | THE ARKANSAS TRAVELER | | $3.00 | $6.00 |
| 1 | 49710-2 | BUFFALO GALS, DOWN IN THE VALLEY/WHOOPEE TI YI YO, SKIP TO MY LOU | ? | BUFFALO GALS, DOWN IN THE VALLEY | WHOOPEE TI YI YO, SKIP TO MY LOU | | $3.00 | $6.00 |
| 1 | 49710-3 | OLD FOLKS AT HOME, OH SUSANNA/CLEMENTINE, ON TOP OF OLD SMOKEY | ? | OLD FOLKS AT HOME, OH SUSANNA | CLEMENTINE, ON TOP OF OLD SMOKEY | | $3.00 | $6.00 |

LITTLE FOLK FAVORITES
MY HORSE TOPPER
$25.00

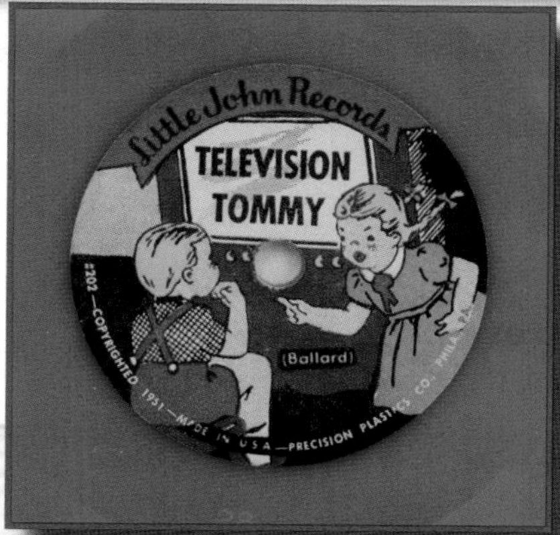


LITTLE JOHN RECORDS
TELEVISION TOMMY
$10.00

LITTLE PAL RECORDS
LITTLE BOY BLUE
$8.00

## LIONEL-SPEAR 6" SINGLES

| # REC | DISC # | MAIN TITLE | ARTIST | A TITLE | B TITLE | G/VG | EX/NMT |
|---|---|---|---|---|---|---|---|
| 1 | 49710-4 | PONY BOY, RED RIVER VALLEY/HOME ON THE RANGE | ? | PONY BOY, RED RIVER VALLEY | HOME ON THE RANGE | $3.00 | $6.00 |
| 1 | 49720-1 | JINGLE BELLS, JOLLY OLD ST. NICHOLAS/NOEL, COME ALL YE FAITHFUL | HUGH PERETTE, CHORUS DIR./ JUNE WINTERS | JINGLE BELLS, JOLLY OLD ST. NICHOLAS | NOEL, COME ALL YE FAITHFUL | $3.00 | $6.00 |
| 1 | 49720-2 | SILENT NIGHT/WE WISH YOU A MERRY CHRISTMAS, DECK THE HALLS | JUNE WINTERS | SILENT NIGHT | WE WISH YOU A MERRY CHRISTMAS, DECK THE HALLS | $3.00 | $6.00 |
| 1 | 49720-3 | OH HOLY NIGHT/GOD REST YE MERRY GENTLEMEN, RING CHRISTMAS BELLS | JUNE WINTERS | OH HOLY NIGHT | GOD REST YE MERRY GENTLEMEN, RING CHRISTMAS BELLS | $3.00 | $6.00 |
| 1 | 49720-4 | TWAS THE NIGHT BEFORE CHRISTMAS | ? | TWAS THE NIGHT BEFORE CHRISTMAS (PT. 1) | TWAS THE NIGHT BEFORE CHRISTMAS (PT. 2) | $3.00 | $6.00 |
| 1 | 49730-1 | THE LITTLE RED HEN | AL JAVELON | THE LITTLE RED HEN (PT. 1) | THE LITTLE RED HEN (PT. 2) | $3.00 | $6.00 |
| 1 | 49730-2 | THE THREE GOATS | AL JAVELON | THE THREE GOATS (PT. 1) | THE THREE GOATS (PT. 2) | $3.00 | $6.00 |
| 1 | 49730-3 | THE FOX & THE GRAPES/THE CITY MOUSE & THE COUNTRY MOUSE | ? | THE FOX AND THE GRAPES | THE CITY MOUSE AND THE COUNTRY MOUSE | $3.00 | $6.00 |
| 1 | 49730-4 | THE LION & THE MOUSE/THE FROG & THE OX | ? | THE LION & THE MOUSE | THE FROG AND THE OX | $3.00 | $6.00 |
| 1 | 49740-1 | PATRIOTIC SONGS AND MARCHES #1: EL CAPITAN/THE THUNDER MARCH | ? | EL CAPITAN | THE THUNDER MARCH | $3.00 | $6.00 |
| 1 | 49740-2 | PATRIOTIC SONGS AND MARCHES #2: CAISSON SONG/SEMPER FIDELIS | NOT LISTED | CAISSON SONG | SEMPER FIDELIS | $3.00 | $6.00 |
| 1 | 49740-3 | PATRIOTIC SONGS AND MARCHES #3: LIBERTY BELL MARCH/THE STARS AND STRIPES | ? | LIBERTY BELL MARCH | THE STARS AND STRIPES | $3.00 | $6.00 |
| 1 | 49740-4 | PATRIOTIC SONGS AND MARCHES #4: COLUMBIA THE GEM OF THE OCEAN/EYES OF TEXAS | ? | COLUMBIA THE GEM OF THE OCEAN | EYES OF TEXAS | $3.00 | $6.00 |
| 1 | 49750-1 | DANCE TUNES FOR LITTLE FOLKS: H AND D STOMP/ARKANSAS REEL | ? | H AND D STOMP | ARKANSAS REEL | $3.00 | $6.00 |
| 1 | 49750-2 | DANCE TUNES FOR LITTLE FOLKS #1: THE CLARINET POLKA/THE HELENA POLKA | ? | THE CLARINET POLKA | THE HELENA POLKA | $3.00 | $6.00 |
| 1 | 49750-3 | DANCE TUNES FOR LITTLE FOLKS #2: MERRY WIDOW WALTZ/BLUE DANUBE WALTZ | ? | MERRY WIDOW WALTZ | BLUE DANUBE WALTZ | $3.00 | $6.00 |
| 1 | 49750-4 | DANCE TUNES FOR LITTLE FOLKS #3: EL CHOCLO-TANGO/A MEDIZ LUZ-RHUMBA | ? | EL CHOCLO-TANGO | A MEDIZ LUZ-RHUMBA | $3.00 | $6.00 |

## LISTEN-LOOK PICTURE BOOK (MUSIC YOU ENJOY) 7" SINGLES IN BOOK

| # REC | DISC # | MAIN TITLE | ARTIST | YEAR | G/VG | EX/NMT |
|---|---|---|---|---|---|---|
| 1 | LL-1 | LITTLE RED RIDING HOOD | NOT LISTED | 1941 | $5.00 | $10.00 |
| 1 | LL-2 | ALICE IN WONDERLAND | NOT LISTED | | $5.00 | $10.00 |
| 1 | LL-3 | THE THREE LITTLE PIGS | NOT LISTED | | $5.00 | $10.00 |
| 1 | LL-4 | LITTLE BLACK SAMBO | NOT LISTED | | $15.00 | $30.00 |
| 1 | LL-5 | MYRTLE THE TURTLE | NOT LISTED | | $5.00 | $10.00 |
| 1 | LL-6 | CINDERELLA | NOT LISTED | | $5.00 | $10.00 |

## LITTLE CHIP 7" SINGLES

| # REC | DISC # | MAIN TITLE | ARTIST | YEAR | ALSO ISSUED ON REMINGTON | G/VG | EX/NMT |
|---|---|---|---|---|---|---|---|
| 1 | 1 | CINDERELLA | UNCLE MAC | 196? | J-51 | $1.00 | $2.00 |
| 1 | 2 | THE CUCKOO CLOCK/THE MOUSE'S BIRTHDAY PARTY | SCOTTY MACGREGOR | | 108 | $1.00 | $2.00 |
| 1 | 3 | PETE PETERSEN'S HOUSE/THE SNOW BELLS | SCOTTY MACGREGOR | | 1009 | $1.00 | $2.00 |
| 1 | 4 | OH SUSANNA, DE CAMPTOWN RACES, THE BLUE TAIL FLY | SCOTTY MACGREGOR | | 55 | $1.00 | $2.00 |
| 1 | 5 | SLEEPING BEAUTY | SCOTTY MACGREGOR | | 52 | $1.00 | $2.00 |
| 1 | 6 | ALADDIN AND THE WONDERFUL LAMP | SCOTTY MACGREGOR | | 100 | $1.00 | $2.00 |
| 1 | 7 | TIME TO GET UP/IT'S SLEEPY TIME | SCOTTY MACGREGOR | | 1004 | $1.00 | $2.00 |
| 1 | 8 | HAPPY BIRTHDAY | SCOTTY MACGREGOR | | 112 | $1.00 | $2.00 |
| 1 | 9 | THE GINGERBREAD BOY | SCOTTY MACGREGOR | | 104 | $1.00 | $2.00 |
| 1 | 10 | BON-BON STREET/THE STORY OF THE NARCISSUS | SCOTTY MACGREGOR | | 109 | $1.00 | $2.00 |
| 1 | 11 | WHY THE GIRAFFE LAUGHED | SCOTTY MACGREGOR | | 105 | $1.00 | $2.00 |
| 1 | 12 | SLEEPY TIME | ? | | NONE | $1.00 | $2.00 |
| 1 | 13 | THE BOUNCING BALL/THE LONGEST TRAIN | SCOTTY MACGREGOR | | 103 | $1.00 | $2.00 |
| 1 | 14 | LITTLE RED RIDING HOOD | SCOTTY MACGREGOR, CYNTHIA STONE | | 53 | $1.00 | $2.00 |
| 1 | 15 | THE THREE LITTLE PIGS | SCOTTY MACGREGOR | | 102 | $1.00 | $2.00 |
| 1 | 16 | JOHNNY ON HIS BICYCLE/TOMMY AND HIS WAGON | SCOTTY MACGREGOR | | 1007 | $1.00 | $2.00 |
| 1 | 17 | CLICKITY-CLACKITY TRAIN/MONKEY SHINES | SCOTTY MACGREGOR | | 1005 | $1.00 | $2.00 |
| 1 | 18 | THE STORY OF THE TEN LITTLE INDIANS | SCOTTY MACGREGOR | | 58 | $1.00 | $2.00 |
| 1 | 19 | PETER RABBIT | UNCLE MAC | | 57 | $1.00 | $2.00 |
| 1 | 20 | THE ANIMAL PARADE/THE LITTLE BROWN DUCK | SCOTTY MACGREGOR | | 107 | $1.00 | $2.00 |
| 1 | 21 | THE CIRCUS ELEPHANT | SCOTTY MACGREGOR | | 101 | $1.00 | $2.00 |
| 1 | 22 | THE OLD GRAY MARE, THE MAN ON THE FLYING TRAPEZE/ THE BIRD ORCHESTRA | SCOTTY MACGREGOR | | 1013 | $1.00 | $2.00 |
| 1 | 23 | THE LITTLE MATCH GIRL | UNCLE MAC & THE KIDDIE PLAYHOUSE | | 106 | $1.00 | $2.00 |
| 1 | 24 | THE UGLY DUCKLING | ? | | 1010 | $1.00 | $2.00 |
| 1 | 25 | HOUSE TOWN FIRE ENGINE | ? | | NONE | $1.00 | $2.00 |
| 1 | 26 | TEN LITTLE INDIANS/OLD MACDONALD HAD A FARM, ETC. | ? | | 54 | $1.00 | $2.00 |
| 1 | 27 | THE SNOW QUEEN | ? | | 61 | $1.00 | $2.00 |
| 1 | 28 | EDNA AND THE TOOTHBRUSH | SCOTTY MACGREGOR, CYNTHIA STONE | | K-202 | $4.00 | $8.00 |
| 1 | 29 | LITTLE TINY | ? | | 1020 | $1.00 | $2.00 |
| 1 | 30 | THE HAPPY DANCING CLOWN | ? | | 115 | $1.00 | $2.00 |
| 1 | 31 | EDNA AND THE MAGIC CEREAL | SCOTTY MACGREGOR, CYNTHIA STONE | | K-203 | $4.00 | $8.00 |
| 1 | 32 | IT'S SANTA CLAUS/JINGLE BELLS | SCOTTY MACGREGOR | | 1001 | $1.00 | $2.00 |
| 1 | 33 | THE RED SHOES | THE FAIRY TALE PLAYERS | | 62 | $1.00 | $2.00 |
| 1 | 34 | THE PRINCESS AND THE MAGIC BIRD | ? | | 1014 | $1.00 | $2.00 |
| 1 | 35 | EDNA AND THE THUNDERMAN | SCOTTY MACGREGOR, CYNTHIA STONE | | K-204 | $4.00 | $8.00 |
| 1 | 36 | THE ENCHANTED CASTLE | UNCLE MAC & THE KIDDIE PLAYHOUSE | | 63 | $1.00 | $2.00 |
| 1 | 37 | THE WILD SWANS | ? | | 116 | $1.00 | $2.00 |
| 1 | 38 | THE EMPEROR'S NEW CLOTHES | ? | | 1015 | $1.00 | $2.00 |
| 1 | 39 | EDNA AND THE ANIMAL MIX-UP | SCOTTY MACGREGOR, CYNTHIA STONE | | K-206 | $4.00 | $8.00 |
| 1 | 40 | THE GOLDEN SNUFF BOX | UNCLE MAC & THE KIDDIE PLAYHOUSE | | 64 | $1.00 | $2.00 |
| 1 | 41 | THE STEADFAST TIN SOLDIER | THE FAIRYTALE PLAYERS | | 117 | $1.00 | $2.00 |
| 1 | 42 | A TRIP TO THE ZOO | UNCLE MAC & THE KIDDIE PLAYHOUSE | | 1016 | $1.00 | $2.00 |
| 1 | 43 | THE PRINCESS AND THE PEA | THE FAIRY TALE PLAYERS | | 65 | $1.00 | $2.00 |
| 1 | 44 | EDNA IN BUNNYTOWN | SCOTTY MACGREGOR, CYNTHIA STONE | | K-205 | $4.00 | $8.00 |

## LITTLE CHIP 7" SINGLES

| # REC | DISC # | MAIN TITLE | ARTIST | ALSO ISSUED ON REMINGTON | G/VG | EX/NMT |
|---|---|---|---|---|---|---|
| 1 | 45 | THE ROBOT MAN | ? | 118 | $5.00 | $10.00 |
| 1 | 46 | THE PRINCESS' DOLL | ? | 1017 | $1.00 | $2.00 |
| 1 | 47 | THE CLOCK THAT WOULDN'T TALK | ? | 66 | $1.00 | $2.00 |
| 1 | 48 | THE TINDER BOX | THE FAIRYTALE PLAYERS | 119 | $1.00 | $2.00 |
| 1 | 49 | THE FUNNIEST STORY EVER TOLD | UNCLE MAC & THE KIDDIE PLAYHOUSE | 1018 | $1.00 | $2.00 |
| 1 | 50 | HOW THE BIRDS LEARNED TO SING | UNCLE MAC & THE KIDDIE PLAYHOUSE | 67 | $1.00 | $2.00 |
| 1 | 51 | THE AIRPLANE THAT WOULDN'T FLY | UNCLE MAC & THE KIDDIE PLAYHOUSE | 120 | $3.00 | $6.00 |
| 1 | 52 | THE TOY RACING CAR | UNCLE MAC & THE KIDDIE PLAYHOUSE | 1019 | $3.00 | $6.00 |

## LITTLE FOLKS FAVORITES 10" SINGLES

| SET # | # REC | DISC # | MAIN TITLE | ARTIST | A TITLE | B TITLE | YEAR | G/VG | EX/NMT |
|---|---|---|---|---|---|---|---|---|---|
| LF-100 | 1 | PB1/2 | PUSS IN BOOTS | BILL ROBERTS AND BETTY JAYNE | PUSS IN BOOTS, PT. 1 | PUSS IN BOOTS, PT. 2 | 194? | $2.50 | $5.00 |
| LF-101 | 1 | FD1/2 | THE FAIRIES AND THE DANDELIONS | BILL ROBERTS AND BETTY JAYNE | THE FAIRIES AND THE DANDELIONS, PT. 1 | THE FAIRIES AND THE DANDELIONS, PT. 2 | | $2.50 | $5.00 |
| LF-102 | 1 | AL1/2 | ALADDIN'S LAMP | BEBE DANIELS | ALADDIN'S LAMP | ALADDIN'S LAMP | | $12.00 | $25.00 |
| LF-103 | 1 | ? | THE DOLL WHO RAN AWAY | BEBE DANIELS | THE DOLL WHO RAN AWAY | THE DOLL WHO RAN AWAY | | $12.00 | $25.00 |
| LF-104 | 1 | SS1/2 | SINBAD THE SAILOR | GENE RAYMOND | SINBAD THE SAILOR, PT. 1 | SINBAD THE SAILOR, PT. 2 | | $3.00 | $6.00 |
| LF-105 | 1 | TS1/2 | TOMMY THE TOY SOLDIER | GENE RAYMOND | TOMMY THE TOY SOLDIER, PT. 1 | TOMMY THE TOY SOLDIER, PT. 2 | | $3.00 | $6.00 |
| LF-106 | 1 | HT1/2 | MY HORSE TOPPER | BILL BOYD (HOPALONG CASSIDY) | MY HORSE TOPPER, PT. 1 | MY HORSE TOPPER, PT. 1 | | $12.00 | $25.00 |
| LF-107 | 1 | BB1/2 | BILLY AND THE BANDIT | BILL BOYD (HOPALONG CASSIDY) | BILLY AND THE BANDIT, PT. 1 | BILLY AND THE BANDIT, PT. 2 | | $12.00 | $25.00 |
| LF-FM-108 | 1 | ? | NURSERY RHYMES: HEY DIDDLE DIDDLE DUMPLING + 5 OTHERS | NORMAN KRAEFT | HEY DIDDLE DIDDLE DUMPLING + 5 OTHERS | JACK & JILL + 5 OTHERS | | $2.50 | $5.00 |
| LF-FM-109 | 1 | LF35L/36L | NURSERY RHYMES: POP GOES THE WEASEL + 4 OTHERS | NORMAN KRAEFT | POP GOES THE WEASEL + 4 OTHERS | THERE WAS A CROOKED MAN + 5 OTHERS | | $2.50 | $5.00 |
| LF-FM-110 | 1 | LF5000/1 | CINDERELLA | NORM PIERCE | CINDERELLA, PT. 1 | CINDERELLA, PT. 2 | | $2.50 | $5.00 |
| LF-FM-111 | 1 | LF50002/3 | RUMPELSTILTSKIN | NORM PIERCE | RUMPELSTILTSKIN, PT. 1 | RUMPELSTILTSKIN, PT. 2 | | $2.50 | $5.00 |
| LF-FM-112 | 1 | LF5004/5 | GOLDILOCKS AND THE THREE BEARS | NORM PIERCE | GOLDILOCKS AND THE THREE BEARS, PT. 1 | GOLDILOCKS AND THE THREE BEARS, PT. 2 | | $2.50 | $5.00 |
| LF-FM-113 | 1 | LF5006/7 | LITTLE RED RIDING HOOD | NORM PIERCE | LITTLE RED RIDING HOOD, PT. 1 | LITTLE RED RIDING HOOD, PT. 2 | | $2.50 | $5.00 |
| LF-FM-114 | 1 | LF5008/9 | THREE LITTLE PIGS | NORM PIERCE | THREE LITTLE PIGS | THREE LITTLE PIGS | | $2.50 | $5.00 |
| LF-FM-117 | 1 | LF5014/15 | RIME GAME: DING DONG BELL + 3 OTHERS | ? | DING DONG BELL + 5 OTHERS | 12 DIFFERENT NURSERY RHYMES | | $10.00 | $20.00 |

## LITTLE FOLKS FAVORITES 10" SINGLES

| SET # | # REC | DISC # | MAIN TITLE | ARTIST | YEAR | G/VG | EX/NMT |
|---|---|---|---|---|---|---|---|
| (NO. 1) | 2 | PB1/FD2 - PB2/FD1 | PUSS IN BOOTS/THE FAIRIES & THE DANDELIONS | BILL ROBERTS AND BETTY JAYNES | 194? | $3.00 | $6.00 |
| (NO. 2) | 2 | AL1/DRA2 - AL2/DRA1 | ALADDIN'S LAMP/THE DOLL THAT RAN AWAY | BEBE DANIELS | | $25.00 | $50.00 |
| (NO. 3) | 2 | SS1/TS2 - SS2/TS1 | SINBAD THE SAILOR/TOMMY THE TOY SOLDIER | GENE RAYMOND | | $3.00 | $6.00 |
| (NO. 4) | 2 | AF1/3 - 2/4 | ANIMAL CRACKER FAIR | MA PERKINS | | $3.00 | $6.00 |
| (NO. 5) | 2 | BB1/HT2 - BB2/HT1 | BILLY & THE BANDIT/MY HORSE TOPPER | WILLIAM BOYD (AS HOPALONG CASSIDY) | | $25.00 | $50.00 |
| (NO. 6) | 2 | RC1/2 - 2/4 | ROBINSON CRUSOE | JOHN LODER | | $3.00 | $6.00 |
| (NO. 7) | 2 | GG1/3 - 2/4 | THE GALLANT GRENADIERS | JOHN LODER | | $3.00 | $6.00 |

## LITTLE JOHN 5" SINGLES

| # REC | DISC # | ARTIST | A TITLE | B TITLE | YEAR | G/VG | EX/NMT |
|---|---|---|---|---|---|---|---|
| 1 | 101 | NOT LISTED | HAPPY BIRTHDAY CAKE | THE DOLL'S TEA PARTY | 1950 | $1.00 | $2.00 |
| 1 | 102 | NOT LISTED | FUNNY CIRCUS CLOWN | THE GINGER BREAD MAN | | $1.00 | $2.00 |
| 1 | 103 | NOT LISTED | RIDIN' THE FIRE ENGINE | BOY WITH THE MATCHES | | $2.00 | $4.00 |
| 1 | 104 | NOT LISTED | THERE GO THE INJUNS | HERE COME THE COWBOYS | | $2.00 | $4.00 |
| 1 | 105 | NOT LISTED | THE ICICLE MAN | BOW WOW RIVER | | $1.00 | $2.00 |
| 1 | 106 | NOT LISTED | LITTLE LOST PUPPY | BIG TOY BAND PARADE | | $1.00 | $2.00 |
| 1 | 107 | NOT LISTED | PAPER DOLL COULDN'T CRY | LITTLE POLLY POLITE | | $1.00 | $2.00 |
| 1 | 108 | NOT LISTED | POPPIN' POPCORN | POOR LITTLE LOLLIPOP BEAR | | $1.00 | $2.00 |
| 1 | 109 | NOT LISTED | Z-I-P WENT THE ROCKET SHIP | ON THE MERRY GO ROUND | | $5.00 | $10.00 |
| 1 | 110 | NOT LISTED | JIMINY CRICKET BOO | SLEDDIN' ON A SNOWY HILL | | $1.00 | $2.00 |
| 1 | 201 | NOT LISTED | SPACE-GUN JIMMY | LITTLE 2-GUN JOE | 1951 | $5.00 | $10.00 |
| 1 | 202 | NOT LISTED | SMOKEY THE OLD COW POKEY | TELEVISION TOMMY | | $5.00 | $10.00 |
| 1 | 203 | NOT LISTED | ZOOMIN' IN THE MOONSHIP | MAGIC CANDY MAN | | $5.00 | $10.00 |
| 1 | 204 | NOT LISTED | JOLLY POLLY PARROT | BILLY WITH ONE ROLLER SKATE | | $1.00 | $2.00 |
| 1 | 205 | NOT LISTED | HAPPY LITTLE BLUEBIRD | PERCY, THE CATFACE DOG | | $1.00 | $2.00 |
| 1 | 206 | NOT LISTED | CRYBABY DOLL | TORTONI THE PINK-EARED PONY | | $1.00 | $2.00 |
| 1 | 207 | NOT LISTED | LITTLE BO PEEP | POLLY WOLLY DOODLE | | $1.00 | $2.00 |
| 1 | 208 | NOT LISTED | FARMER IN THE DELL | BILLY BOY | | $1.00 | $2.00 |
| 1 | 209 | NOT LISTED | MARY HAD A LITTLE LAMB | JACK AND JILL | | $1.00 | $2.00 |
| 1 | 210 | NOT LISTED | TEN LITTLE INDIANS | A TISKET, A TASKET | | $1.00 | $2.00 |
| 1 | X-1 | NOT LISTED | CHRISTMAS BELLS | O LITTLE TOWN OF BETHLEHEM | 1952 | $1.00 | $2.00 |
| 1 | X-2 | NOT LISTED | LET'S TRIM THE CHRISTMAS TREE | AWAY IN A MANGER | | $1.00 | $2.00 |
| 1 | X-3 | NOT LISTED | SANTA'S LITTLEST REINDEER | THE FIRST NOEL | | $1.00 | $2.00 |
| 1 | X-4 | NOT LISTED | MERRY CHRISTMAS SONG | IT CAME UPON A MIDNIGHT CLEAR | | $1.00 | $2.00 |
| 1 | X-5 | NOT LISTED | HANG UP THE STOCKINGS | SILENT NIGHT | | $1.00 | $2.00 |
| 1 | X-6 | NOT LISTED | HURRY UP SANTA CLAUS | O COME ALL YE FAITHFUL | | $1.00 | $2.00 |
| 1 | X-7 | NOT LISTED | WE WISH YOU A MERRY CHRISTMAS | WHILE SHEPHERDS WATCHED THEIR FLOCKS | | $1.00 | $2.00 |
| 1 | X-8 | NOT LISTED | HARK! THE HERALD ANGELS SING | JOLLY OLD ST. NICHOLAS | | $1.00 | $2.00 |
| 1 | X-9 | NOT LISTED | JOY TO THE WORLD | I HEARD THE BELLS ON CHRISTMAS DAY | | $1.00 | $2.00 |
| 1 | X-10 | NOT LISTED | O CHRISTMAS TREE | JINGLE BELLS | | $1.00 | $2.00 |

## LITTLE MASTER MUSIC YOU ENJOY 7" ALBUMS

| SET # | # REC | DISC # | MAIN TITLE | ARTIST | YEAR | G/VG | EX/NMT |
|---|---|---|---|---|---|---|---|
| 1-A | 4 | LM 1 – 4 | STRAUSS: BLUE DANUBE WALTZ, ETC. | DR. SIGMUND SPAETH, DIRECTOR | 1941 | $3.00 | $6.00 |
| 2-A | 4 | LM 5 – 8 | TCHAIKOVSKY: CHINESE DANCE, TREPAK, ETC. | DR. SIGMUND SPAETH, DIRECTOR | | $3.00 | $6.00 |
| 3-A | 4 | LM 9 – 12 | MOZART: DON JUAN MINUET, ETC. | DR. SIGMUND SPAETH, DIRECTOR | | $3.00 | $6.00 |
| 4-A | 4 | LM 14 – 7 | SIBELIUS: FINLANDIA, ETC. | DR. SIGMUND SPAETH, DIRECTOR | | $3.00 | $6.00 |
| 5-A | 4 | LM 18 – 21 | WAGNER: PRELUDE, ACT 3, LOHENGRIN, ETC. | DR. SIGMUND SPAETH, DIRECTOR | | $3.00 | $6.00 |
| 6-A | 4 | LM 22 – 5 | TCHAIKOVSKY: DANCE OF THE TOY PIPES, ETC. | DR. SIGMUND SPAETH, DIRECTOR | | $3.00 | $6.00 |

## LITTLE PAL 7" SINGLES AND ALBUMS

| # REC | DISC # | ARTIST | A TITLE | B TITLE | YEAR | ALSO ISSUED ON | G/VG | EX/NMT |
|---|---|---|---|---|---|---|---|---|
| 1 | 1001 | IRVING KAUFMAN/ ERNEST HARE | JACK AND JILL | OLD KING COLE | 1938 | LITTLE TOTS 100, PLAYTIME 201 | $4.00 | $8.00 |
| 1 | 1002 | VERNON DALHART/ IRVING KAUFMAN | LITTLE BO-PEEP | MARY HAD A LITTLE LAMB | | LITTLE TOTS 101, PLAYTIME 202 | $4.00 | $8.00 |
| 1 | 1003 | JANE BARTLETT/IR-VING KAUFMAN | ROCK-A-BYE BABY | SING A SONG OF SIXPENCE | | LITTLE TOTS 102, PLAYTIME 203 | $4.00 | $8.00 |
| 1 | 1004 | ARTHUR FIELDS/ ARTHUR HALL | I HAD A LITTLE DOGGY | MOTHER TABBYSKINS | | LITTLE TOTS 121, PLAYTIME 221 | $4.00 | $8.00 |
| 1 | 1005 | ARTHUR HALL | GO ROUND THE MUL-BERRY BUSH | OATS, PEAS AND BEANS | | LITTLE TOTS 106, PLAYTIME 207 | $4.00 | $8.00 |
| 1 | 1006 | ARTHUR HALL | LONDON BRIDGE IS FALLING DOWN | THE FARMER IN THE DELL | | LITTLE TOTS 107, PLAYTIME 208 | $4.00 | $8.00 |
| 1 | 1007 | ARTHUR HALL | LAZY MARY WILL YOU GET UP | TEN LITTLE INDIANS | | LITTLE TOTS 108, PLAYTIME 209 | $4.00 | $8.00 |

## LITTLE WONDER 5" SINGLES AND GENERIC ALBUMS

| # REC | DISC # | ARTIST | A TITLE | B TITLE | YEAR | G/VG | EX/NMT |
|---|---|---|---|---|---|---|---|
| 1 | 793 | HENRY BURR? | LONDON BRIDGE | N/A | | $3.00 | $6.00 |
| 1 | 794 | HENRY BURR? | THREE BLIND MICE | N/A | | $3.00 | $6.00 |
| 1 | 799 | HENRY BURR | GOOSEY GANDER, RING AROUND A ROSY | N/A | | $3.00 | $6.00 |
| 1 | 812 | HENRY BURR? | TWINKLE TWINKLE LITTLE STAR | N/A | | $3.00 | $6.00 |
| 1 | 813 | HENRY BURR | LITTLE BOY BLUE | N/A | | $3.00 | $6.00 |
| 1 | 814 | HENRY BURR? | ROCK-A-BYE BABY | N/A | | $3.00 | $6.00 |
| 1 | 820 | HENRY BURR | JUST A BABY'S PRAYER AT TWILIGHT | N/A | | $3.00 | $6.00 |
| 1 | 846 | ? | TEN LITTLE INDIANS | N/A | | $3.00 | $6.00 |
| 1 | 855 | HENRY BURR? | HEY DIDDLE DIDDLE | N/A | | $3.00 | $6.00 |
| 1 | 856 | HENRY BURR | HOME SWEET HOME | N/A | | $3.00 | $6.00 |
| 1 | 874 | HENRY BURR | I SAW THREE SHIPS | N/A | | $3.00 | $6.00 |
| 1 | 875 | HENRY BURR? | SING A SONG OF SIXPENCE | N/A | | $3.00 | $6.00 |
| 1 | 876 | HENRY BURR | THREE BLIND MICE | N/A | | $3.00 | $6.00 |
| 1 | 878 | HENRY BURR? | DANCE A BABY DIDDY | N/A | | $3.00 | $6.00 |
| 1 | 912 | DON RICHARDSON? | ARKANSAS TRAVELER, SWANEE RIVER | N/A | | $3.00 | $6.00 |
| 1 | 942 | SHANNON FOUR? | HUMPTY DUMPTY | N/A | | $3.00 | $6.00 |
| 1 | 943 | SHANNON FOUR? | LITTLE JACK HORNER, ALPHABET SONG | N/A | | $3.00 | $6.00 |
| 1 | 945 | SHANNON FOUR? | MOTHER, MAY I GO INTO SWIM? | N/A | | $3.00 | $6.00 |
| 1 | 946 | LEWIS JAMES? | CALENDAR SONG | N/A | | $3.00 | $6.00 |
| 1 | 947 | LEWIS JAMES? | TEN LITTLE NIGGERS | N/A | | $12.00 | $25.00 |
| 1 | 965 | ? | MEDLEY OF KIDDIES' SONGS (PT. 1) | N/A | | $3.00 | $6.00 |
| 1 | 966 | ? | MEDLEY OF KIDDIES' SONGS (PT. 2) | N/A | | $3.00 | $6.00 |
| 1 | 971 | ? | O LITTLE TOWN OF BETHLEHEM | N/A | 1919 | $3.00 | $6.00 |
| 1 | 972 | PRINCE'S ORCHESTRA | TOY SYMPHONY | N/A | | $3.00 | $6.00 |
| 1 | 975 | ? | CHRISTMAS MORNING WITH THE KIDDIES | N/A | | $5.00 | $10.00 |
| 1 | 1229 | CAMPBELL AND BURR | LULLABY TIME | N/A | 1920 | $4.00 | $8.00 |
| 1 | 1527 | ? | SILENT NIGHT | N/A | 1921 | $6.00 | $12.00 |
| 1 | 1550 | IRVING KAUFMAN | TEN LITTLE FINGERS AND TEN LITTLE TOES | N/A | | $6.00 | $12.00 |
| 1 | 1573 | ? | PLANTATION LULLABY | N/A | | $6.00 | $12.00 |

## LONDON 10" 2 RECORD GATEFOLD SETS

| SET # | # REC | DISC # | MAIN TITLE | ARTIST | YEAR | G/VG | EX/NMT |
|---|---|---|---|---|---|---|---|
| JS-1 | 2 | 20001 – 3 | CINDERELLA | MARGARET LOCKWOOD | 1950 | $2.00 | $4.00 |
| JS-2 | 2 | 20005 – 6 | MUFFIN THE MULE AND HIS FRIENDS, NO. 1 | ANNETTE MILLS | | $3.00 | $6.00 |
| JS-3 | 2 | 20003 – 4 | ELSIE AND ELMER OUT WEST | JAN MINER, PAUL ARNOLD | | $12.00 | $25.00 |
| JS-4 | 2 | 20007 – 8 | MUFFIN THE MULE AND HIS FRIENDS, NO. 2 | ANNETTE MILLS | | $3.00 | $6.00 |
| JS-5 | 2 | 20010 – 11 | THUMBELINA | ? | | $2.00 | $4.00 |
| JS-6 | 2 | 20016 – 17 | ELSIE'S CHRISTMAS PACKAGE | PAUL ARNOLD, JAN MINER QUARTET, EDDIE DAVIS' ORCH. | | $12.00 | $25.00 |
| JS-7 | 2 | 20018 – 19 | BUNTY THE BEAR AND HIS FRIENDS | UNCLE JOHN RUST | | $5.00 | $10.00 |

## LONDON 10" SINGLES

| # REC | DISC # | ARTIST | A TITLE | B TITLE | YEAR | G/VG | EX/NMT |
|---|---|---|---|---|---|---|---|
| 1 | 20009 | MERRIE PAULET, MICHAEL BALFOUR, THE KEYNOTES | WELCOME TO CHRISTMAS (PT. 1) | WELCOME TO CHRISTMAS (PT. 2) | 1950 | $1.00 | $2.00 |
| 1 | 20012 | THE KEYNOTES, MALCOLM LOCKYER QUARTET | TEDDY BEARS' PICNIC | THE DICKY BIRD HOP | | $2.00 | $4.00 |
| 1 | 20013 | CURT MASSEY, TONY VALE ORCH. | GABBY THE GOBBLER | DOWN AT UNCLE BILL'S | | $3.00 | $6.00 |
| 1 | 20014 | JAN MINER, PAUL ARNOLD | ELSIE'S FAVORITE NURSERY RHYMES (PT. 1) | ELSIE'S FAVORITE NURSERY RHYMES (PT. 2) | | $8.00 | $15.00 |
| 1 | 20015 | JAN MINER, PAUL ARNOLD | MORE OF ELSIE'S FAVORITE NURSERY RHYMES (PT. 1) | MORE OF ELSIE'S FAVORITE NURS-ERY RHYMES (PT. 2) | | $8.00 | $15.00 |
| 1 | 20021 | AL MORGAN | LITTLE RED CABOOSE | ROSIE THE ELEPHANT | | $2.00 | $4.00 |
| 1 | 1482 | FRANK WEIR | THE LITTLE SHOEMAKER | THE NEVER-NEVER LAND | | $2.00 | $4.00 |
| 1 | L-1851 | CYRIL STAPLETON ORCH. | CHILDREN'S MARCHING SONG | INN OF THE SIXTH HAPPINESS | | $2.00 | $4.00 |

## LYRIC 10" DOUBLES AND SINGLES

| # REC | DISC # | MAIN TITLE | ARTIST | YEAR | ALSO IS-SUED ON | G/VG | EX/NMT |
|---|---|---|---|---|---|---|---|
| 1 | KK-1 | KIDDY BANDWAGON | EILEEN O'CONNELL | 194? | KAROUSEL | $3.00 | $6.00 |
| 1 | KK-2 | KIDDY KARNIVAL | ? | | KAROUSEL | $3.00 | $6.00 |
| 1 | KK-3 | TINY TOWN THEATRE | EILEEN O'CONNELL | | KAROUSEL | $3.00 | $6.00 |
| 1 | KK-4 | TINY WIND-UP TIME | FLOYD WORTHINGTON | | KAROUSEL | $5.00 | $10.00 |
| 1 | 406 | CRADLE SONG (BRAHMS)/CRADLE SONG (WALLACE) | ? | | | $2.00 | $4.00 |
| 1 | 409 | PINOCCHIO | DICK DEFREITAS, EVELYN WRAY, ETC. | | | $2.00 | $4.00 |
| 1 | 411 | RUMPLESTILTSKIN | DICK DEFREITAS, EVELYN WRAY, ETC. | | | $2.00 | $4.00 |
| 1 | 412 | JACK AND THE BEANSTALK | DICK DEFREITAS, EVELYN WRAY, ETC. | | | $2.00 | $4.00 |
| 1 | 413 | SLEEPING BEAUTY | DICK DEFREITAS, EVELYN WRAY, ETC. | | | $2.00 | $4.00 |
| 1 | ? | CINDERELLA | DICK DEFREITAS, EVELYN WRAY, ETC. | | | $2.00 | $4.00 |
| 1 | ? | LITTLE RED RIDING HOOD | DICK DEFREITAS, EVELYN WRAY, ETC. | | | $2.00 | $4.00 |
| 1 | ? | SLUMBER SONG/VENETIAN SONG | ? | | | $2.00 | $4.00 |
| 1 | ? | CRADLE SONG (BRAHMS)/THE LITTLE SANDMAN (BRAHMS) | ? | | | $2.00 | $4.00 |
| 2 | 501 | PAGLIACCI | FLOYD WORTHINGTON, JOHN BARAGREY, ETC. | | | $5.00 | $10.00 |
| 2 | 600 | OLYMPIA THE MECHANICAL DOLL | EILEEN O'CONNELL | | | $5.00 | $10.00 |
| 2 | 601 | THE PRINCESS AND THE PAUPER | DICK DEFREITAS, EILEEN O'CONNELL, FLOYD WORTHINGTON | | | $5.00 | $10.00 |
| 2 | ? | CARMEN | ? | | | $5.00 | $10.00 |

# M

## MACGREGOR MISCELLANEOUS 10" SINGLES

| # REC | DISC # | ARTIST | A TITLE | B TITLE | YEAR | G/VG | EX/NMT |
|---|---|---|---|---|---|---|---|
| 1 | FT-001 | NOT LISTED | CINDERELLA | CINDERELLA | 194? | $3.00 | $6.00 |
| 1 | FT-002 | NOT LISTED | SNOW WHITE & THE SEVEN DWARFS | SNOW WHITE & THE SEVEN DWARFS | | $3.00 | $6.00 |
| 1 | 400 | JACK RIVER BOYS | SCHOTTISCHE | HEEL & TOE POLKA | | $1.00 | $2.00 |
| 1 | 699 | FRANK MESSINA & THE MAVERICKS | HOKEY-POKEY | BUNNY HOP | | $5.00 | $10.00 |

## MACGREGOR SQUARE DANCE SERIES 10" SINGLES

| SET # | # REC | DISC # | MAIN TITLE | ARTIST | YEAR | G/VG | EX/NMT |
|---|---|---|---|---|---|---|---|
| ALBUM # 1 | 5 (12") | ? | DANCE MASTER: LITTLE LIZZA JANE, ETC. | GARY CASHMAN, WYNN GRANGER | 195? | $5.00 | $10.00 |
| ALBUM # 2 | ? | ? | ? | ? | | $4.00 | $8.00 |
| ALBUM # 3 | ? | ? | ? | ? | | $4.00 | $8.00 |
| ALBUM # 4 | 4 | ? | SQUARE DANCES: THE PINE TREE, ETC. | FENTON "JONESY" JONES | | $4.00 | $8.00 |
| ALBUM # 5 | ? | ? | ? | ? | | $4.00 | $8.00 |
| ALBUM # 6 | ? | ? | ? | ? | | $4.00 | $8.00 |
| ALBUM # 7 | 4 | ? | SQUARE DANCES: DARLING NELLIE GRAY, ETC. | FENTON "JONESY" JONES | | $4.00 | $8.00 |
| ALBUM # 8 | 4 | ? | SQUARE DANCES: I WANT A GIRL, ETC. | FENTON "JONESY" JONES | | $4.00 | $8.00 |
| ALBUM # 9 | ? | ? | ? | ? | | $4.00 | $8.00 |
| ALBUM # 10 | 4 (12") | ? | WALTZES FOR SQUARE DANCERS | FENTON "JONESY" JONES | | $4.00 | $8.00 |
| ALBUM # 11 | 4 | ? | SQUARE DANCES: TEXAS TORNADO, ETC. | FENTON "JONESY" JONES | | $4.00 | $8.00 |

MAGIC PHONOGRAPH AND RECORD
HANSEL AND GRETEL
$40.00

MAGIC TALKING BOOKS
THE SPEEDY LITTLE TAXI
$10.00

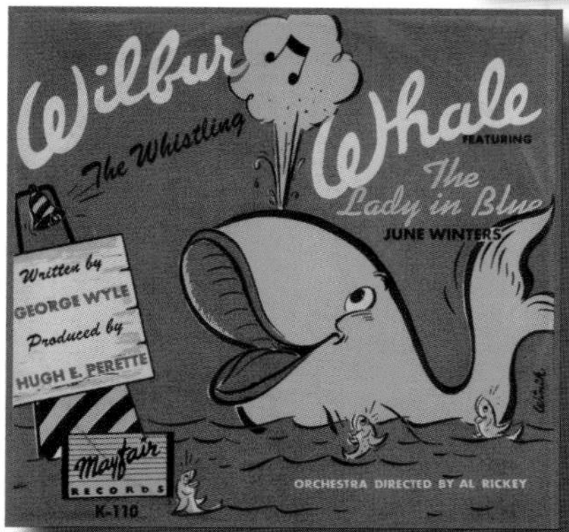


MAYFAIR RECORDS
WILBUR THE WHISTLING WHALE
$4.00

## MAGIC PHONOGRAPH AND RECORD, THE

| # REC | DISC # | MAIN TITLE | ARTIST | YEAR | G/VG | EX/NMT |
|---|---|---|---|---|---|---|
| 1 | NO # | THE NIGHT BEFORE CHRISTMAS | NOT LISTED | 1955 | $20.00 | $40.00 |
| 1 | NO # | CHILDREN'S PRAYERS | NOT LISTED | | $20.00 | $40.00 |
| 1 | NO # | LEARNING THE ALPHABET | NOT LISTED | | $20.00 | $40.00 |
| 1 | NO # | HANSEL AND GRETEL | NOT LISTED | | $20.00 | $40.00 |
| 1 | NO # | NURSERY RHYMES | NOT LISTED | | $20.00 | $40.00 |
| 1 | NO # | ALADDIN AND HIS LAMP | NOT LISTED | | $20.00 | $40.00 |
| 1 | NO # | CINDERELLA | NOT LISTED | | $20.00 | $40.00 |
| 1 | NO # | TEN LITTLE INDIANS | NOT LISTED | | $20.00 | $40.00 |
| 1 | NO # | TEACHING HOW TO COUNT | NOT LISTED | | $20.00 | $40.00 |

## MAGIC TALKING BOOKS 6" SINGLES INTEGRATED INTO BOOK COVER

| # REC | DISC # | MAIN TITLE | ARTIST | YEAR | G/VG | EX/NMT |
|---|---|---|---|---|---|---|
| 1 | T-1 | THE SINGING MOTHER GOOSE BOOK: THREE FAVORITE MOTHER GOOSE SONGS | FRANK MILANO, JIMMY CARROLL, MUSICAL DIR. | 1955 | $5.00 | $10.00 |
| 1 | T-2 | THE SINGING HAPPY BIRTHDAY BOOK: HAPPY BIRTHDAY TO YOU | JIMMY CARROLL, MUSICAL DIR. | | $5.00 | $10.00 |
| 1 | T-3 | THE SPEEDY LITTLE TAXI: THE BUSY-BUSY TRAFFIC SONG | JAMES MACKLIN, JIMMY CARROLL, MUSICAL DIR. | | $5.00 | $10.00 |
| 1 | T-4 | NOAH'S ARK: ALL AROUND THE ARK | JAMES MACKLIN, JIMMY CARROLL, MUSICAL DIR. | | $5.00 | $10.00 |
| 1 | T-5 | THE MAGIC ABC BOOK: LET US LEARN OUR ABC'S | JAMES MACKLIN, JIMMY CARROLL, MUSICAL DIR. | | $5.00 | $10.00 |
| 1 | T-6 | THE MUSICAL TOY PARADE: VICTOR HERBERT'S MARCH OF THE TOYS | JIMMY CARROLL, MUSICAL DIR. | | $5.00 | $10.00 |
| 1 | T-7 | THE NOISY BABY ANIMALS: OLD MACDONALD HAD A FARM | JAMES MACKLIN, JIMMY CARROLL, MUSICAL DIR. | | $5.00 | $10.00 |
| 1 | T-8 | THE LITTLE CIRCUS TRAIN THAT LED THE PARADE: SONG OF THE CIRCUS | JAMES MACKLIN, JIMMY CARROLL, MUSICAL DIR. | | $5.00 | $10.00 |
| 1 | T-9 | THE SINGING HANSEL AND GRETEL BOOK: BROTHER WILL YOU DANCE WITH ME? | SHERRY MADISON, JIMMY CARROLL, MUSICAL DIR. | | $5.00 | $10.00 |
| 1 | T-10 | THE TALE OF PETER RABBIT: I'M A HAPPY HOPPY BUNNY | FRANK MILANO, JIMMY CARROLL, MUSICAL DIR. | | $5.00 | $10.00 |
| 1 | T-11 | BLACK BEAUTY: THE BALLAD OF BLACK BEAUTY | OZNI BROWN, JIMMY CARROLL, MUSICAL DIR. | | $10.00 | $20.00 |
| 1 | T-12 | DAVID AND GOLIATH: THE SONG OF DAVID | JIMMY CARROLL, MUSICAL DIR. | | $10.00 | $20.00 |
| 1 | T-13 | THE LITTLE BUS THAT LIKED HOME BEST: THE CHUGGITY BUS SONG | JIMMY CARROLL, MUSICAL DIR. | | $10.00 | $20.00 |
| 1 | T-14 | THE SINGING BABY BOOK: BRAHMS' CRADLE SONG | ? | | $10.00 | $20.00 |
| 1 | T-15 | THE LITTLE PUPPY WHO LEARNED TO BEHAVE: THE BAD LITTLE GOOD LITTLE PUPPY | ? | | $10.00 | $20.00 |
| 1 | T-16 | THE STORY OF HEIDI: HEIDI'S SONG | ? | | $10.00 | $20.00 |
| 1 | T-17 | MUSICAL NIGHT BEFORE CHRISTMAS: NIGHT BEFORE CHRISTMAS SONG | JIMMY CARROLL, MUSICAL DIR. | | $10.00 | $20.00 |
| 1 | T-18 | SINGING BOOK OF CHRISTMAS CAROLS: THREE FAVORITE CAROLS | ? | | $10.00 | $20.00 |
| 1 | T-19 | DAVY CROCKETT AND THE INDIANS: STRAIGHT SHOOTIN' DAVY | JIMMY CARROLL, MUSICAL DIR. | | $15.00 | $30.00 |
| 1 | T-20 | DAVY CROCKETT AND THE FLATBOAT: FLATBOAT 'ROUND THE BEND | ? | | $15.00 | $30.00 |

## MAGIC-TONE 10" SINGLES

| SET # | # REC | DISC # | ARTIST | A TITLE | B TITLE | G/VG | EX/NMT |
|---|---|---|---|---|---|---|---|
| M-1 | 1 | M-3005 | MERRILL E. JOELS | THE TIN SOLDIER | THE NIGHTINGALE | $3.00 | $6.00 |
| M-2 | 1 | M-3006 | MERRILL E. JOELS | THE NUTCRACKER SUITE | PETER AND THE WOLF | $1.50 | $3.00 |
| M-3 | 1 | M-3007 | FLOYD WORTHINGTON | THE NIGHT BEFORE CHRISTMAS | CHRISTMAS CAROLS | $1.50 | $3.00 |
| M-4 | 1 | M-3008 | FLOYD WORTHINGTON | OL' FAITHFUL | COW-BOY SONGS | $1.50 | $3.00 |
| M-5 | 1 | ? | ? | LITTLE SALLY SAMBA | THE LITTLE RHUMBA BAND | $1.50 | $3.00 |
| M-6 | 1 | ? | ? | LET'S GO TO THE CIRCUS | ANIMAL SONGS | $1.50 | $3.00 |
| M-7 | 1 | M-3017 | FLOYD WORTHINGTON | PONY EXPRESS | BUFFALO BILL'S WILD WEST SHOW | $1.50 | $3.00 |
| M-8 | 1 | ? | ? | THE TOY TRAIN (THAT RAN AWAY) | SONGS ABOUT TRAINS | $1.50 | $3.00 |
| M-9 | 1 | M-3019 | JEAN ELLSPERMAN | CHILDREN'S PRAYERS | CHILDREN'S LULLABIES | $1.50 | $3.00 |
| M-10 | 1 | M-3010 | THE G&S TROUBADOURS | THE MIKADO, PT. 1 | THE MIKADO, PT. 2 | $1.50 | $3.00 |
| M-11 | 1 | M-3011 | THE G&S TROUBADOURS | H.M.S. PINAFORE, PT. 1 | H.M.S. PINAFORE, PT. 2 | $1.50 | $3.00 |
| M-15 | 1 | M-3015 | ANTHONY RIVERS | THE STORY & MUSIC OF FRANZ SCHUBERT, PT. 1 | THE STORY & MUSIC OF FRANZ SCHUBERT, PT. 2 | $1.50 | $3.00 |
| M-16 | 1 | ? | ? | THE LITTLE TOWN OF BETHLEHEM | THE CHRISTMAS TREE | $1.50 | $3.00 |
| M-17 | 1 | M-3020 | FLOYD WORTHINGTON | JOHNNY GOES TO THE CITY | DOWN ON THE FARM | $1.50 | $3.00 |
| M-18 | 1 | ? | ? | SAILING SAILING | SAILOR SONGS | $1.50 | $3.00 |
| M-19 | 1 | M-3013 | JEAN ELLSPERMAN | A CHILD'S GARDEN OF VERSES, PT. 1 | A CHILD'S GARDEN OF VERSES, PT. 2 | $1.50 | $3.00 |
| M-20 | 1 | M-3022 | TOMMY SHEARIN | THE TOY PLANE (THAT LEARNED TO FLY) | SONGS ABOUT PLANES | $3.00 | $6.00 |
| M-21 | 1 | M-3029 | TOMMY SHEARIN | CHOPIN FOR CHILDREN, PT. 1 | CHOPIN FOR CHILDREN, PT. 2 | $1.50 | $3.00 |
| M-24 | 1 | M-3024 | LAWRENCE CHELSI | CHILDREN'S SONGS OF FRANCE, PT. 1 | CHILDREN'S SONGS OF FRANCE, PT. 2 | $1.50 | $3.00 |
| M-26 | 1 | M-3026 | LAWRENCE CHELSI | CHILDREN'S SONGS OF ITALY, PT. 1 | CHILDREN'S SONGS OF ITALY, PT. 2 | $1.50 | $3.00 |
| M-100 | 1 | M-3106 | THE MAGIC-TONE ORCHESTRA | WALTZES: BLUE DANUBE, VIENNA WOODS | THE EMPEROR WALTZ, VIENNA LIFE | $1.50 | $3.00 |
| M-101 | 1 | M-3105 | THE MAGIC-TONE VILLAGERS | SQUARE DANCES: POP GOES THE WEASEL, THE IRISH WASHER-WOMAN | MISS MCLEOD'S REEL, SPEED THE PLOW | $1.50 | $3.00 |

## MAJESTIC 10" ALBUMS AND SINGLES

| SET # | # REC | DISC # | MAIN TITLE | ARTIST | YEAR | ALSO ISSUED ON | G/VG | EX/NMT |
|---|---|---|---|---|---|---|---|---|
| M 8 | 4 | 1079 – 82 | SONGS FOR LITTLE FOLKS | BOB HANNON | 1946 | MERCURY MMP-50 | $15.00 | $30.00 |
| M 9 | 3 | 5005 – 7 | TALES OF ANCIENT HEROES | LEW AYRES | | MERCURY MMP-57 - 49 | $10.00 | $20.00 |
| M 19 | 3 | 1141 – 3 | KIDDIE KLASSICS | BOB HANNON | | MERCURY MMP-58 | $15.00 | $30.00 |
| N/A | 1 | 11029 | THE LITTLE BOY'S LETTER TO SANTA/EASY TO PLEASE | JIMMY SELPH | | | $1.00 | $2.00 |

## MANOR 10" DOUBLES AND SINGLES

| SET # | # REC | DISC # | MAIN TITLE | ARTIST | YEAR | G/VG | EX/NMT |
|---|---|---|---|---|---|---|---|
| 102 | 2 | 8006 – 7 | HANSEL & GRETEL | LEW LEHR | 194? | $5.00 | $10.00 |
| K-1 | 1 | ? | CINDERELLA | LEW LEHR | | $5.00 | $10.00 |
| K-2 | 1 | 8027 | AT THE OLD TOY SHOP/THE TALE OF WILLIAM TELL | LEW LEHR | | $5.00 | $10.00 |
| K-3 | 1 | ? | THE BARNYARD BALL/THE SLY LITTLE FOX | LEW LEHR | | $5.00 | $10.00 |
| K-4 | 1 | ? | "SARAH" COME BACK TO THE RANGE/BORSHT BELT BLUES | LEW LEHR | | $5.00 | $10.00 |

## MATTEL MICKEY MOUSE CLUB, THE NEWSREEL 6" SINGLES

| SET # | # REC | DISC # | MAIN TITLE | ARTIST | YEAR | G/VG | EX/NMT |
|---|---|---|---|---|---|---|---|
| SERIES A (VER 1) | 1 | A-1/2 | TOUCHDOWN MICKEY/DANCE OF THE LEOPARD BOYS* | JIMMIE DODD | 1956 | $8.00 | $15.00 |
| SERIES A (VER.2) | 1 | A-1/2 | TOUCHDOWN MICKEY/NO SAIL* | JIMMIE DODD | | $8.00 | $15.00 |
| SERIES B | 1 | B-1/2 | MICKEY THE MAIL PILOT/PECULIAR PENGUINS* | JIMMIE DODD | | $8.00 | $15.00 |
| SERIES C | 1 | C-1/2 | TWO GUN MICKEY/DON DONALD* | JIMMIE DODD | | $8.00 | $15.00 |
| SERIES D | 1 | D-1/2 | ELMER ELEPHANT/THE GORILLA MYSTERY* | JIMMIE DODD | | $8.00 | $15.00 |
| SERIES E | 1 | E-1/2 | THE TORTOISE AND THE HARE/THE BRAVE LITTLE TAILOR* | JIMMIE DODD | | $8.00 | $15.00 |
| SERIES F | 1 | F-1/2 | THE THREE LITTLE PIGS/YE OLDEN DAYS* | JIMMIE DODD | | $8.00 | $15.00 |
| SERIES J | 1 | J-1/2 | AT THE WATERHOUSE (FROM "AFRICAN LION")/THE BUFFALO BATTLE (FROM "VANISHING PRAIRIE")* | JIMMIE DODD | | $10.00 | $20.00 |
| SERIES K | 1 | K-1/2 | WATER BIRDS/BEAR COUNTRY* | JIMMIE DODD | | $10.00 | $20.00 |
| SERIES R | 1 | R-1/2 | FROGVILLE, USA/ON SILENT WINGS* | JIMMIE DODD | | $8.00 | $15.00 |
| SERIES S | 1 | S-1/2 | THE HIPPO WHO GOOFED/TEEN-AGE TOREADORS* | JIMMIE DODD | | $8.00 | $15.00 |

*SUBTRACT $5.00 IF FILM STRIPS ARE MISSING.

## MATTEL PICTURE DISC 7" "MUSICAL MARS"

| SET # | # REC | DISC # | MAIN TITLE | ARTIST | YEAR | G/VG | EX/NMT |
|---|---|---|---|---|---|---|---|
| NO # | 5 | | THE LEGEND OF DAVY CROCKETT | NOT LISTED | 1955 | $150.00 | $300.00 |
| | | 1 | DAVY CROCKETT — HUNTER | NOT LISTED | | | |
| | | 2 | DAVY CROCKETT — INDIAN FIGHTER | NOT LISTED | | | |
| | | 3 | DAVY CROCKETT — FRONTIERSMAN | NOT LISTED | | | |
| | | 4 | DAVY CROCKETT — GOES TO CONGRESS | NOT LISTED | | | |
| | | 5 | DAVY CROCKETT — ALAMO DEFENDER | NOT LISTED | | | |
| NO # | 5 | | YOUR TRIP TO DISNEYLAND | NOT LISTED | | $25.00 | $50.00 |
| | | 6 | INTRODUCTION TO DISNEYLAND | NOT LISTED | | | |
| | | 7 | TOMORROWLAND | NOT LISTED | | | |
| | | 8 | FANTASYLAND | NOT LISTED | | | |
| | | 9 | FRONTIERLAND | NOT LISTED | | | |
| | | 10 | ADVENTURELAND | NOT LISTED | | | |
| NO # | 5 | | YOUR OWN MICKEY MOUSE CLUB | NOT LISTED | | $35.00 | $70.00 |
| | | 11 | MICKEY MOUSE CLUB MARCH, SONG | NOT LISTED | | | |
| | | 12 | CARTOON TIME | NOT LISTED | | | |
| | | 13 | JOE MCDONALD MUSICAL ON THE FARM | NOT LISTED | | | |
| | | 14 | MICKEY MOUSE CLUB CIRCUS DAY | NOT LISTED | | | |
| | | 15 | TOOT-TOOT TALEN ROUNDUP | NOT LISTED | | | |
| N/A | N/A | N/A | LOOSE RECORDS (DISNEYLAND, MICKEY MOUSE CLUB) | N/A | | $5.00 | $10.00 |
| N/A | N/A | N/A | LOOSE RECORDS (DAVY CROCKETT) | N/A | | $12.00 | $25.00 |

## MAYFAIR 10" SINGLES

| # REC | DISC # | MAIN TITLE | ARTIST | A TITLE | B TITLE | YEAR | G/VG | EX/NMT |
|---|---|---|---|---|---|---|---|---|
| 1 | K-100 | LITTLE RED HEN/THE THREE GOATS | DAVID KURLAN | LITTLE RED HEN | THE THREE GOATS | 195? | $1.50 | $3.00 |
| 1 | K-101 | GOLDILOCKS & THE 3 BEARS/ THE ELEPHANT & THE JACK-RABBIT | DAVID KURLAN | GOLDILOCKS & THE 3 BEARS | THE ELEPHANT & THE JACKRAB-BIT | | $1.50 | $3.00 |
| 1 | K-102 | THE LITTLE FIR TREE* | DAVID KURLAN | THE LITTLE FIR TREE, PT. 1 | THE LITTLE FIR TREE, PT. 2 | | $1.50 | $3.00 |
| 1 | K-103 | LET'S GO TO THE ZOO | DAVID KURLAN | LET'S GO TO THE ZOO (PT. 1) | LET'S GO TO THE ZOO (PT. 2) | | $1.50 | $3.00 |
| 1 | K-104 | SING, DANCE, PLAY WITH THE LADY IN BLUE | JUNE WINTERS, THE LADY IN BLUE | TWINKLE TWINKLE + 3 OTHERS | TEN LITTLE INDIANS + 4 OTHERS | | $1.50 | $3.00 |
| 1 | K-105 | MOTHER GOOSE PARADE | JUNE WINTERS, THE LADY IN BLUE | MOTHER GOOSE PARADE, SIDE 1 | MOTHER GOOSE PARADE, SIDE 2 | | $1.50 | $3.00 |
| 1 | K-106 | PARADE OF THE WOODEN SOL-DIERS/OLD MCDONALD HAD A FARM | JUNE WINTERS, THE LADY IN BLUE | PARADE OF THE WOODEN SOLDIERS | OLD MCDONALD HAD A FARM | | $1.50 | $3.00 |
| 1 | K-107 | HANSEL & GRETEL'S DANCE/ ALL THROUGH THE NIGHT | JUNE WINTERS, THE LADY IN BLUE | HANSEL & GRETEL'S DANCE | ALL THROUGH THE NIGHT | | $1.50 | $3.00 |
| 1 | K-108 | CHRISTOPHER COLUMBUS/ GEORGE WASHINGTON | JUNE WINTERS, THE LADY IN BLUE | CHRISTOPHER COLUMBUS | GEORGE WASHINGTON | | $1.50 | $3.00 |
| 1 | K-109 | ABE LINCOLN/BETSY ROSS | JUNE WINTERS, THE LADY IN BLUE | ABE LINCOLN | BETSY ROSS | | $1.50 | $3.00 |
| 1 | K-110 | WILBUR THE WHISTLING WHALE | JUNE WINTERS, THE LADY IN BLUE | WILBUR THE WHISTLING WHALE, SIDE 1 | WILBUR THE WHISTLING WHALE, SIDE 2 | | $4.00 | $8.00 |
| 1 | K-111 | MUSIC BOX | JUNE WINTERS, THE LADY IN BLUE | MUSIC BOX, SIDE 1: LISTEN TO THE MUSIC BOX + 4 OTHERS | MUSIC BOX, SIDE 2: OLD KING COLE + 4 OTHERS | | $1.50 | $3.00 |
| 1 | K-112 | MAGIC CARPET (DISC 1): ST. PATRICK'S DAY IN THE MORN-ING, ETC. | JUNE WINTERS, THE LADY IN BLUE | MAGIC CARPET, SIDE 1: ST. PATRICK'S DAY IN THE MORN-ING + 2 OTHERS | MAGIC CARPET, SIDE 2: LITTLE MARIONETTES + 2 OTHERS | | $1.50 | $3.00 |
| 1 | K-113 | MAGIC CARPET (DISC 2): BOY & GIRL POLKA, ETC.** | JUNE WINTERS, THE LADY IN BLUE | MAGIC CARPET, SIDE 3: BOY & GIRL POLKA + 2 OTHERS | MAGIC CARPET, SIDE 4: BUB-LITCHKI + 2 OTHERS | | $1.50 | $3.00 |
| 1 | K-114 | KIDDIE BARN DANCE | JUNE WINTERS, THE LADY IN BLUE | KIDDIE BARN DANCE: LITTLE BROWN JUG + 2 OTHERS | KIDDIE BARN DANCE: SKIP TURN-A-LOO + 2 OTHERS | | $1.50 | $3.00 |
| 1 | K-115 | LITTLE WILLIE | JUNE WINTERS, THE LADY IN BLUE | LITTLE WILLIE, SIDE 1 | LITTLE WILLIE, SIDE 2 | | $1.50 | $3.00 |

*REC-O-CARD **IN GATEFOLD COMBINATION

## MAYFAIR 10" SINGLES

| # REC | DISC # | MAIN TITLE | ARTIST | A TITLE | B TITLE | G/VG | EX/NMT |
|---|---|---|---|---|---|---|---|
| 1 | K-116 | KIDDIE KONGA | JUNE WINTERS, THE LADY IN BLUE | KIDDIE KONGA, SIDE 1 | KIDDIE KONGA, SIDE 2 | $1.50 | $3.00 |
| 1 | K-117 | HAPPY BIRTHDAY | JUNE WINTERS, THE LADY IN BLUE | HAPPY BIRTHDAY, SIDE 1 | HAPPY BIRTHDAY, SIDE 2 | $1.50 | $3.00 |
| 1 | K-118 | LITTLE BAG-PIPE | JUNE WINTERS, THE LADY IN BLUE | LITTLE BAG-PIPE, SIDE 1 | LITTLE BAG-PIPE, SIDE 2 | $1.50 | $3.00 |
| 1 | K-119 | AESOP'S FABLES | JUNE WINTERS, THE LADY IN BLUE | THE CITY MOUSE & THE COUNTRY MOUSE, THE LION & THE MOUSE | THE FROG & THE OX, THE FOX & THE GRAPES | $1.50 | $3.00 |
| 1 | K-120 | KIDDIE LAND BALL ROOM | JUNE WINTERS, THE LADY IN BLUE | KIDDIE LAND BALL ROOM, SIDE 1 | KIDDIE LAND BALL ROOM, SIDE 2 | $1.50 | $3.00 |
| 1 | K-121 | PONY BOY | UNCLE STU WAYNE | PONY BOY, SIDE 1 | PONY BOY, SIDE 2 | $1.50 | $3.00 |
| 1 | K-122 | TWO FRONT TEETH | JUNE WINTERS, THE LADY IN BLUE | TWO FRONT TEETH, SIDE 1 | TWO FRONT TEETH, SIDE 2 | $1.50 | $3.00 |
| 1 | K-123 | SQUIRT, THE LITTLE FIRE ENGINE | STUART WAYNE (UNCLE STU) | SQUIRT, THE LITTLE FIRE ENGINE, SIDE 1 | SQUIRT, THE LITTLE FIRE ENGINE, SIDE 2 | $2.00 | $4.00 |
| 1 | K-124 | CONEY ISLAND | JUNE WINTERS, THE LADY IN BLUE | CONEY ISLAND, SIDE 1 | CONEY ISLAND, SIDE 2 | $4.00 | $8.00 |
| 1 | K-125 | BARNACLE BILL | STUART WAYNE (UNCLE STU) | BARNACLE BILL, SIDE 1 | BARNACLE BILL, SIDE 2 | $1.50 | $3.00 |
| 1 | K-126 | MARCH OF THE TOYS/ WHAT'S MY FAVORITE TOY? | JUNE WINTERS, THE LADY IN BLUE | MARCH OF THE TOYS | WHAT'S MY FAVORITE TOY? | $1.50 | $3.00 |
| 1 | K-127 | THE WEDDING OF THE PAINTED DOLL/THE LAND OF HATCHY-MILATCHY | JUNE WINTERS, THE LADY IN BLUE | THE WEDDING OF THE PAINTED DOLL | THE LAND OF HATCHY-MILATCHY | $2.00 | $4.00 |
| 1 | K-128 | ALICE IN WONDERLAND* | JUNE WINTERS, THE LADY IN BLUE | ALICE IN WONDERLAND, I'M LATE | ALL IN A GOLDEN AFTERNOON, THE UNBIRTHDAY SONG | $8.00 | $15.00 |
| 1 | K-129 | ME & MY TEDDY BEAR/PEPI THE PUPPET | JUNE WINTERS, THE LADY IN BLUE | ME AND MY TEDDY BEAR | PEPI THE PUPPET | $1.50 | $3.00 |

*DISNEY

## MAYFAIR 10" ALBUMS

| SET # | # RECS | DISC # | MAIN TITLE | ARTIST | YEAR | G/VG | EX/NMT |
|---|---|---|---|---|---|---|---|
| M1 | 2 | K-100 - 101 | ONCE UPON A TIME: LITTLE RED HEN/GOLDILOCKS | DAVID KURLAN | 195? | $3.00 | $6.00 |
| M4 | 2 | K-104 - 105 | NURSERY RHYMES: THE LADY IN BLUE/MOTHER GOOSE PARADE | THE LADY IN BLUE | | $3.00 | $6.00 |
| M5 | 2 | K-106 - 107 | KIDDIE HIT PARADE: PARADE OF THE WOODEN SOLDIERS/ALL THROUGH THE NIGHT | THE LADY IN BLUE | | $3.00 | $6.00 |
| M6 | 2 | K 108 - 109 | YOUNG AMERICA FOR YOUNG AMERICANS: CHRISTOPHER COLUMBUS/ ABE LINCOLN, BETSY ROSS | THE LADY IN BLUE | | $3.00 | $6.00 |
| M7 | 2 | K 112 - 113 | MAGIC CARPET: MAGIC CARPET/MEXICAN CLAP HAND SONG | THE LADY IN BLUE | | $3.00 | $6.00 |

## MELODEE 10" ALBUMS

| SET # | # REC | DISC # | MAIN TITLE | ARTIST | YEAR | G/VG | EX/NMT |
|---|---|---|---|---|---|---|---|
| MA-10 | 2 | M-101/4 - 2/3 | PINOCCHIO | RICHARD JAMES | 194? | $2.50 | $5.00 |
| MA-12 | 2 | M-121/4 - 2/3 | SNOW WHITE AND THE SEVEN DWARFS | RICHARD JAMES | | $2.50 | $5.00 |
| MA-14 | 2 | M-141/4 - 2/3 | IRVING CAESAR'S SONGS OF SAFETY | JOEY NASH | | $5.00 | $10.00 |
| MA-16 | 2 | M-161/4 - 2/3 | SLEEPING BEAUTY | RICHARD JAMES | | $2.50 | $5.00 |
| MA-18 | 2 | M-181/4 - 2/3 | CINDERELLA | RICHARD JAMES | | $2.50 | $5.00 |
| MA-20 | 2 | M-201/4 - 2/3 | FAVORITE NURSERY SONGS AND GAMES | BARBARA ASHLEY | | $2.50 | $5.00 |
| MA-22 | 2 | M-221/4 - 2/3 | ALICE IN WONDERLAND | GRACE COPPIN | | $2.50 | $5.00 |
| MA-26 | 2 | M-261/4 - 2/3 | FREEDOM SONGS | JOEY NASH | | $2.50 | $5.00 |
| MA-28 | 2 | M-281/4 - 2/3 | SONGS CHILDREN LOVE | JOEY NASH; WALTER DAMROSCH, EDITOR | | $2.50 | $5.00 |

## MELODEE 10" SINGLES

| SET # | # REC | DISC # | MAIN TITLE | ARTIST | YEAR | G/VG | EX/NMT |
|---|---|---|---|---|---|---|---|
| M-100 | 1 | ? | FAVORITE NURSERY SONGS (PT. 1) | BARBARA ASHLEY | 194? | $1.50 | $3.00 |
| M-101 | 1 | ? | FAVORITE NURSERY SONGS (PT. 2) | BARBARA ASHLEY | | $1.50 | $3.00 |
| M-102 | 1 | M-141/M-144 | IRVING CAESAR'S SING A SONG OF SAFETY (PT. 1) | JOEY NASH | | $2.00 | $4.00 |
| M-103 | 1 | M-142/M-143 | IRVING CAESAR'S SING A SONG OF SAFETY (PT. 2) | JOEY NASH | | $2.00 | $4.00 |
| M-104 | 1 | M-4 | SINBAD THE SAILOR | RICHARD JAMES | | $1.50 | $3.00 |
| M-105 | 1 | M-5 | ALADDIN'S LAMP | RICHARD JAMES | | $1.50 | $3.00 |

## MELODEE 10" SINGLES

| SET # | # REC | DISC # | MAIN TITLE | ARTIST | G/VG | EX/NMT |
|---|---|---|---|---|---|---|
| M-106 | 1 | ? | CANDYLAND | JOEY NASH; WALTER DAMROSCH, EDITOR | $5.00 | $10.00 |
| M-107 | 1 | ? | PINOCCHIO | RICHARD JAMES | $1.50 | $3.00 |
| M-108 | 1 | ? | SNOW WHITE | RICHARD JAMES | $1.50 | $3.00 |
| M-109 | 1 | M-161/M-162 | SLEEPING BEAUTY | RICHARD JAMES | $1.50 | $3.00 |
| M-110 | 1 | M-181/M-182 | CINDERELLA | RICHARD JAMES | $1.50 | $3.00 |
| NO # | 1 | M-221/M-222 | ALICE IN WONDERLAND | GRACE COPPIN | $1.50 | $3.00 |

## MELODEE 10" 2-ALBUMS

| SET # | DISC # | MAIN TITLE | ARTIST | G/VG | EX/NMT |
|---|---|---|---|---|---|
| MA-10 | M-101/4 - 2/3 | PINOCCHIO | RICHARD JAMES | $3.00 | $6.00 |
| MA-12 | M-121/4 - 2/3 | SNOW WHITE AND THE SEVEN DWARFS | RICHARD JAMES | $3.00 | $6.00 |
| MA-14 | M-141/4 - 2/3 | IRVING CAESAR'S SONGS OF SAFETY | JOEY NASH | $5.00 | $10.00 |
| MA-16 | M-161/4 - 2/3 | SLEEPING BEAUTY | RICHARD JAMES | $3.00 | $6.00 |
| MA-18 | M-181/4 - 2/3 | CINDERELLA | RICHARD JAMES | $3.00 | $6.00 |
| MA-20 | M-201/4 - 2/3 | FAVORITE NURSERY SONGS AND GAMES | BARBARA ASHLEY | $3.00 | $6.00 |
| MA-22 | M-221/4 - 2/3 | ALICE IN WONDERLAND | GRACE COPPIN | $3.00 | $6.00 |
| MA-26 | M-261/4 - 2/3 | FREEDOM SONGS | JOEY NASH | $3.00 | $6.00 |
| MA-28 | M-281/4 - 2/3 | SONGS CHILDREN LOVE | JOEY NASH, WALTER DAMROSCH, EDITOR | $4.00 | $8.00 |

## MENORAH 7" SINGLES AND ALBUMS

| SET # | # REC | DISC # | MAIN TITLE | ARTIST | YEAR | G/VG | EX/NMT |
|---|---|---|---|---|---|---|---|
| NO # | 1 | B-34 | WHY IS THIS NIGHT DIFFERENT? | ? | 1949 | $3.00 | $5.00 |
| NO # | 1 | S 1/2 | GOOD MORNING/THE LITTLE MUSICIAN | EVE LIPPMAN, GLADYS GEWIRTZ | | $2.00 | $4.00 |
| NO # | 1 | S 3/4 | A TRIP TO ISRAEL/LET'S DANCE | EVE LIPPMAN, GLADYS GEWIRTZ | | $2.00 | $4.00 |
| NO # | 1 | S 5/6 | ANIMAL FRIENDS/POOR LITTLE APPLE | EVE LIPPMAN, GLADYS GEWIRTZ | | $2.00 | $4.00 |
| NO # | 1 | S 7/8 | CHALUTZIM/TOY TRAIN | EVE LIPPMAN, GLADYS GEWIRTZ | | $2.00 | $4.00 |
| MP-1 | 4 | P 1/2 - 7/8 | HAPPY CHANUKAH! (PICTURE-DISC BOXED SET) | EVE LIPPMAN, GLADYS GEWIRTZ | | $175.00 | $350.00 |
| - | - | P 1/2 - 7/8 | BRACHOT/MAOZ TSUR | EVE LIPPMAN, GLADYS GEWIRTZ | | $35.00 | $75.00 |
| - | - | P 3/4 | THE CHANUKAH STORY | EVE LIPPMAN, GLADYS GEWIRTZ | | $35.00 | $75.00 |
| - | - | P 5/6 | CANDLE DANCE/WHEN CHANUKAH COMES | EVE LIPPMAN, GLADYS GEWIRTZ | | $35.00 | $75.00 |
| - | - | P 7/8 | LET'S MAKE LATKES/DREYDL DANCE | EVE LIPPMAN, GLADYS GEWIRTZ | | $35.00 | $75.00 |
| S-50 | 2 | SIDE 1/2 - 3/4 | MENORAH'S LITTLE SEDER | GLADYS GEWIRTZ, MOSHE LEIFMAN | 1951 | $3.00 | $6.00 |

## MENORAH 10" SINGLES AND ALBUMS

| SET # | # REC | MAIN TITLE | ARTIST | YEAR | G/VG | EX/NMT |
|---|---|---|---|---|---|---|
| E-101 | 1 | BAR MITZVAH BROCHOS (STUDY RECORD) | SOLOMON SCHWARTZ | 1948 | $2.00 | $4.00 |
| G-1 | 2 | MOTHER GOOSE SONGS FOR JEWISH CHILDREN | GLADYS GEWIRTZ | 1950 | $3.00 | $6.00 |
| H-1 | 2 | CHANUKAH IN SONG | GLADYS GEWIRTZ | | $3.00 | $6.00 |
| H-2 | 2 | PURIM'S HERE | ? | | $3.00 | $6.00 |
| H-3 | 2 | PESACH | ? | | $3.00 | $6.00 |
| H-4 | 1 | SHAVUOT TIME | ? | | $2.00 | $4.00 |
| H-5 | 1 | THE HIGH HOLY DAYS | GLADYS GEWIRTZ | 1949 | $2.00 | $4.00 |
| H-6 | 2 | SUCCOT AND SIMCHAT TORAH | GLADYS GEWIRTZ | | $3.00 | $6.00 |

## MERCURY CHILDCRAFT SERIES 10" SINGLES

| # REC | DISC # | MAIN TITLE | ARTIST | A TITLE | B TITLE | YEAR | ALSO ISSUED ON | G/VG | EX/NMT |
|---|---|---|---|---|---|---|---|---|---|
| 1 | 1 | OLD MOTHER GOOSE: KING OF FRANCE..., ETC. | NOT LISTED | KING OF FRANCE WITH 40,000 MEN, ETC. | LITTLE ROBIN REDBREAST/ COCK-A-DOODLE DOO, ETC. | 1953 | MMP-68 | $2.00 | $4.00 |
| 1 | 2 | MOTHER GOOSE PARADE: HEY DIDDLE DIDDLE, ETC. | NOT LISTED | HEY DIDDLE DIDDLE/ HUMPTY DUMPTY | OH DEAR WHAT CAN THE MATTER BE/JACK SPRAT/HICKORY DICKORY DOCK | | MMP-69 | $2.00 | $4.00 |
| 1 | 3 | NURSERY FAVORITES: SEE-SAW, MARGERY DAW, ETC. | NOT LISTED | SEE SAW MARGERY DAW, ETC. | THIS LITTLE PIG WENT TO MARKET, ETC. | | MMP-70 | $2.00 | $4.00 |
| 1 | 4 | NURSERY RHYMES: DIDDLE DIDDLE DUMPLING, ETC. | NOT LISTED | DIDDLE DIDDLE DUMPING/TWINKLE TWINKLE LITTLE STAR | HOT CROSS BUNS/PAT-A-CAKE/ THREE BLIND MICE | | | $2.00 | $4.00 |

MAYFAIR RECORDS
WEDDING OF THE PAINTED DOLL
$4.00

MELODEE RECORDS
IRVING CEASAR'S SING A SONG OF SAFETY (PT. 1)
$4.00

MERCURY RECORDS
TUNES FOR WEE FOLKS: THE TELEPHONE SONG
$8.00

## MENORAH 10" SINGLES AND ALBUMS

| # REC | DISC # | MAIN TITLE | ARTIST | A TITLE | B TITLE | G/VG | EX/NMT |
|---|---|---|---|---|---|---|---|
| 1 | 5 | SONGS FOR PLAYING: ONE TWO BUCKLE MY SHOE, ETC. | KITTY KALLEN | ONE TWO BUCKLE MY SHOE/ RING-AROUND-A-ROSY | DING DONG BELL/LITTLE JACK HORNER/JACK AND JILL | $2.00 | $4.00 |
| 1 | 6 | MERRY MELODIES: BOW WOW SAYS THE DOG, ETC. | KITTY KALLEN | BOW WOW SAYS THE DOG/ PETER PETER | WEE WILLIE WINKIE/LITTLE MISS MUFFET/BYE BABY BUNTING, ETC. | $2.00 | $4.00 |
| 1 | 7 | TUNES FOR TOYS: CLOCK SONG, ETC. | HUGH PERETTI | CLOCK SONG/STEEPLE BELL/ROCKING HORSE | RAINDROPS/TEAKETTLE/HOW DO YOU DO/SLEEPYHEAD | $2.00 | $4.00 |
| 1 | 8 | TUNES FOR WEE FOLKS: THE TELEPHONE SONG/YOUR PAL TEDDY | HUGH PERETTI | THE TELEPHONE SONG | YOUR PAL TEDDY | $4.00 | $8.00 |
| 1 | 9 | FOLK SONGS OF OUR LAND: OH SUSANNAH, ETC. | JACK RUSSELL | OH SUSANNAH/GIT ALONG LITTLE DOGIES | THE ARKANSAS TRAVELER/CASEY JONES | $2.00 | $4.00 |
| 1 | 10 | FOLK SONGS OF OTHER LANDS: THE LITTLE MARIONETTES, ETC. | JACK RUSSELL | THE LITTLE MARIONETTES/ TROT, MY | A FUNNY LITTLE MAN CALLED AIKEN DRUM/FUNICULI, FUNICULA | $2.00 | $4.00 |
| 1 | 11 | HANSEL AND GRETEL | RICHARD HAYES, JUNE WINTERS | PART 1 | PART 2 | $2.00 | $4.00 |
| 1 | 12 | THE SHOEMAKER AND THE ELVES | JUNE WINTERS | PART 1 | PART 2 | $2.00 | $4.00 |
| 1 | CMG-13 | PETER AND THE WOLF | BORIS KARLOFF | PART 1 | PART 2 | $8.00 | $15.00 |
| 1 | CMG-14 | BILLY GOATS GRUFF | BORIS KARLOFF | PART 1 | PART 2 | $8.00 | $15.00 |
| 1 | CMG-15 | GREAT MUSIC FOR YOUNG FOLKS: THE MERRY FARMER (SCHUMANN), ETC. | NOT LISTED | THE MERRY FARMER, ETC. | VALSE/A MUSIC BOX, ETC. | $2.00 | $4.00 |
| 1 | CMG-16 | SONGS FOR SLEEPYHEADS: NOW TO SLEEP, ETC. | NOT LISTED | NOW TO SLEEP/REST BABY REST, ETC. | OF OUR LAND/HUSH LITTLE BABY/ MOZART LULLABY | $2.00 | $4.00 |
| 1 | CMG-17 | SOLDIER SONGS OF OUR LAND: ANCHORS AWEIGHT (NAVY), ETC. | NOT LISTED | ANCHORS AWEIGH/THE CAISSONS GO ROLLING ALONG | FROM THE HALLS OF MONTEZUMA/ THE U.S. AIR FORCE, ETC. | $2.00 | $4.00 |
| 1 | CMG-18 | SONGS OF OUR PATRIOTS: AMERICA THE BEAUTIFUL, ETC. | NOT LISTED | AMERICA THE BEAUTIFUL, ETC. | COLUMBIA THE GEM OF THE OCEAN, ETC. | $2.00 | $4.00 |
| 1 | CM-19 | HILLBILLY AND PLAY PARTY SONGS: RIG A JIG JIG | NOT LISTED | BIG ROCK CANDY MOUNTAIN, ETC. | POP GOES THE WEASEL/SHOO FLY (DON'T BOTHER ME), ETC. | $2.00 | $4.00 |
| 1 | CM-20 | CAMPFIRE SONGS: HOME ON THE RANGE, ETC. | NOT LISTED | BLOW THE MAN DOWN/ HOME ON THE RANGE, ETC. | RED RIVER VALLEY/CHARLIE IS MY DARLING, ETC. | $2.00 | $4.00 |
| 1 | CM-21 | FATHER GANDER: OLD FATHER GANDER, ETC. | BEN ARONIN | OLD FATHER GANDER/WHY | TO WASHINGTON, TO WASHINGTON/ THE SINGER FROM SINGAPORE | $2.00 | $4.00 |
| 1 | CM-22 | NEW MOTHER GOOSE: WHAT SHALL I BE, ETC. | BEN ARONIN | WHAT SHALL I BE/RAGGEDY RIG | TINY TOM TIDDLE/SLEEPYTIME HOLLOW | $2.00 | $4.00 |
| 1 | CM-23 | FUN FAIR: WHEN THE CIRCUS COMES TO TOWN | NOT LISTED | WHEN THE CIRCUS COMES TO TOWN/THE JOLLY FARMER, ETC. | AT THE ZOO/LET'S GO TO THE COUNTRY FAIR | $2.00 | $4.00 |
| 1 | CM-24 | THE HARE AND THE TORTOISE, ETC./ MY LITTLE TOY BOAT, ETC. | NOT LISTED | THE HARE AND THE TORTOISE/MY TINY TWO-WHEEL SCOOTER | MY LITTLE TOY BOAT/MY LITTLE CHOO-CHOO TRAIN | $2.00 | $4.00 |
| 1 | CM-25 | SONGS FOR CHRISTMAS: COME ALL YE FAITHFUL, ETC. | NOT LISTED | COME ALL YE FAITHFUL/O LITTLE TOWN OF BETHLEHEM | HARK THE HERALD ANGELS SING/SILENT NIGHT | $2.00 | $4.00 |

## MERCURY CHILDCRAFT SERIES 10" SINGLES

| # REC | DISC # | MAIN TITLE | ARTIST | A TITLE | B TITLE | G/VG | EX/NMT |
|---|---|---|---|---|---|---|---|
| 1 | CM-26 | RUDOLPH THE RED-NOSED REINDEER, FROSTY THE SNOWMAN/THE NIGHT BEFORE CHRISTMAS | NOT LISTED | RUDOLPH THE RED-NOSED REINDEER/FROSTY THE SNOWMAN | THE NIGHT BEFORE CHRISTMAS | $2.00 | $4.00 |
| 1 | CM-27 | COWBOY SONGS: OH THAT STRAWBERRY ROAN, ETC. | CURTIS BIEVER & HIS ORCH. | OH THAT STRAWBERRY ROAN/COOL WATER | TUMBLING TUMBLEWEEDS/THE LAST ROUND-UP | $2.00 | $4.00 |
| 1 | CM-28 | CAPTAIN SNORTER'S BURIED TREASURE | CURTIS BIEVER & HIS ORCH. | PART 1 | PART 2 | $5.00 | $10.00 |
| 1 | CM-29 | CHOO CHOO TO THE FARM | CURTIS BIEVER & HIS ORCH. | PART 1 | PART 2 | $2.00 | $4.00 |
| 1 | CM-30 | SLEEPING BEAUTY | CURTIS BIEVER & HIS ORCH. | PART 1 | PART 2 | $2.00 | $4.00 |
| 1 | CM-31 | HAPPY BIRTHDAY PARTY | JUNE WINTERS, HUGO PERETTI & ORCH. | HAPPY BIRTHDAY PARTY | PART 2 | $2.00 | $4.00 |
| 1 | CM-32 | SIDEWALK SONGS | ARNOLD AMARU, HUGO PERETTI & ORCH. | PART 1 | PART 2 | $2.00 | $4.00 |
| 1 | CM-33 | PINOCCHIO | NORMAN PRESCOTT, HUGO PERETTI & ORCH. | PART 1 | PART 2 | $2.00 | $4.00 |
| 1 | CM-34 | THE UGLY DUCKLING | NORMAN PRESCOTT, SALLY SWEETLAND, CURTIS BIEVER & ORCH. | PART 1 | PART 2 | $2.00 | $4.00 |
| 1 | CM-35 | ROCKET TO THE MOON | HUGO PERETTI & ORCH. | PART 1 | PART 2 | $15.00 | $30.00 |
| 1 | CM-36 | JACK AND THE BEANSTALK | HUGO PERETTI & ORCH. | PART 1 | PART 2 | $2.00 | $4.00 |
| 1 | CM-37 | WALT DISNEY'S "ALICE IN WONDERLAND": IN A WORLD OF MY OWN, ETC. | RICHARD HAYES, ROBERTA QUINLAN, HUGH PERETTI & ORCH. | PART 1 | PART 2 | $20.00 | $40.00 |
| 1 | CM-38 | THE BARBER OF SEVILLE | KEN NORDINE: BILL WALKER & ORCH. | PART 1 | PART 2 | $3.00 | $6.00 |
| 1 | CM-39 | THE HAPPY PRINCE | PAUL TOMAINE, HUGO PERETTI & ORCH. | PART 1 | PART 2 | $2.00 | $4.00 |
| 1 | CM-40 | PETER PONSIL LOST HIS TONSIL | GWEN DAVIES, HUGO PERETTI & ORCH. | PART 1 | PART 2 | $5.00 | $10.00 |
| 1 | CM-41 | AMAHL AND THE NIGHT VISITORS | HUGO PERETTI | PART 1 | PART 2 | $3.00 | $6.00 |
| 1 | CM-42 | SNOW WHITE AND THE SEVEN DWARFS | HUGO PERETTI & ORCH. | PART 1 | PART 2 | $3.00 | $6.00 |
| 1 | CM-43 | THE STAR SPANGLED BANNER/AMERICA | HUGO PERETTI & ORCH. | THE STAR SPANGLED BANNER | AMERICA | $3.00 | $6.00 |
| 1 | MC-44 | BEST LOVED MARCHES FOR CHILDREN: STARS & STRIPES FOREVER, ETC. | HUGO PERETTI & ORCH. | AMERICAN PATROL, ETC. | THE GIRL I LEFT BEHIND, ETC. | $2.00 | $4.00 |
| 1 | MC-45 | DAVID AND GOLIATH/THE STORY OF NOAH'S ARK | BOB EMERICK, HUGO PERETTI & ORCH. | DAVID AND GOLIATH | NOAH'S ARK | $2.00 | $4.00 |
| 1 | MC-46 | THE SORCERER'S APPRENTICE | HUGO PERETTI & ORCH. | PART 1 | PART 2 | $2.00 | $4.00 |
| 1 | MC-47 | THE BUNNY HOP/THE HOKEY POKEY | HUGO PERETTI ORCH. & CHORUS | THE BUNNY HOP | THE HOKEY POKEY | $4.00 | $8.00 |
| 1 | MC-48 | SQUARE DANCES FOR CHILDREN | JOE MAYBROWN & HIS MOUNTAINEERS | THE HINKEY DINKEY SQUARE DANCE | THE IRISH WASHERWOMAN, ETC. | $2.00 | $4.00 |
| 1 | MC-49 | AIDA | ? | PART 1 | PART 2 | $2.00 | $4.00 |
| 1 | CM-50 | FIRST TRIP TO THE DENTIST | GWEN DAVIES, HUGO PERETTI & ORCH. | PART 1 | PART 2 | $3.00 | $6.00 |
| 1 | MC-51 | THE WHISTLER AND HIS DOG/CHOO CHOO TRAIN RIDE | HUGO PERETTI & ORCH. | WHISTLER AND HIS DOG | CHOO CHOO TRAIN RIDE | $2.00 | $4.00 |
| 1 | CM-52 | THE CHRISTMAS TREE | CLAUDE RAINS, HUGO PERETTI & ORCH. | PART 1 | PART 2 | $5.00 | $10.00 |
| 1 | CM-53 | A CHRISTMAS CAROL | CLAUDE RAINS, HUGO PERETTI & ORCH. | PART 1 | PART 2 | $5.00 | $10.00 |
| 1 | CM-54 | CHRISTMAS CAROLS | ? | PART 1 | PART 2 | $2.00 | $4.00 |
| 1 | MC-55 | 20,000 LEAGUES UNDER THE SEA | GILBERT MACK, HUGO PERETTI & ORCH. | PART 1 | PART 2 | $3.00 | $6.00 |
| 1 | MC-56 | PETER PONSIL GOES TO SCHOOL | GWEN DAVIES, HUGO PERETTI & ORCH. | PART 1 | PART 2 | $5.00 | $10.00 |
| 1 | MC-57 | REAL TRAIN SOUNDS | BOB EMERICKS, TRAIN CONDUCTOR | PART 1 | PART 2 | $4.00 | $8.00 |
| 1 | MC-58 | NUTCRACKER SUITE | ROBERT EMERICK, MINNEAPOLIS SYMPHONY ORCH.; ANTAL DORATI, COND. | PART 1 | PART 2 | $2.00 | $4.00 |

## MERCURY CHILDCRAFT SERIES 10" SINGLES

| # REC | DISC # | MAIN TITLE | ARTIST | A TITLE | B TITLE | G/VG | EX/NMT |
|---|---|---|---|---|---|---|---|
| 1 | MC-59 | CONCERT IN THE PARK: THE BAND PLAYED ON, ETC. | HUGO PERETTI'S BAND & CHORUS | PART 1 | PART 2 | $2.00 | $4.00 |
| 1 | MC-60 | THE GINGERBREAD BOY | GILBERT MACK, GWEN DAVIES, HUGO PERETTI & ORCH. | PART 1 | PART 2 | $2.00 | $4.00 |
| 1 | MC-61 | SHOWBOAT | GILBERT MACK, HUGO PERETTI & ORCH. | PART 1 | PART 2 | $2.00 | $4.00 |
| 1 | MC-62 | THE WEDDING OF THE PAINTED DOLL | HUGO PERETTI ORCH. & CHORUS | THE WEDDING OF THE PAINTED DOLL | THE OWL AND THE PUSSY CAT | $4.00 | $8.00 |
| 1 | MC-63 | THE LORD'S PRAYER/THE 23RD PSALM | MONTY WOOLEY, HUGO PERETTI & ORCH. | THE LORD'S PRAYER | THE 23RD PSALM | $2.00 | $4.00 |
| 1 | MC-64 | A CHILD'S GARDEN OF VERSES | MONTY WOOLEY, HUGO PERETTI & ORCH. | PART 1 | PART 2 | $2.00 | $4.00 |

## MERCURY PLAYCRAFT SERIES 10" SINGLES

| # REC | DISC # | MAIN TITLE | ARTIST | A TITLE | B TITLE | YEAR | G/VG | EX/NMT |
|---|---|---|---|---|---|---|---|---|
| 1 | MP-1 | DOGGIE IN THE WINDOW/I WANNA BE A COWBOY'S SWEETHEART | PATTI PAGE | DOGGIE IN THE WINDOW | I WANNA BE A COWBOY'S SWEETHEART | 1951 | $12.00 | $25.00 |
| 1 | MP-2 | WALT DISNEY'S "THE MAGIC FLYING CARPET" | MICKEY MOUSE, MINNIE MOUSE, DONALD DUCK, AND PLUTO | PART 1 | PART 2 | 1952 | $20.00 | $40.00 |
| 1 | MP-3 | WALT DISNEY'S "ALADDIN AND HIS WONDERFUL LAMP" | MICKEY MOUSE, MINNIE MOUSE, DONALD DUCK, AND PLUTO | PART 1 | PART 2 | | $20.00 | $40.00 |
| 1 | MP-4 | THE ADVENTURES OF CHIQUITA THE CHIHUAHUA | GILBERT MACK, XAVIER CUGAT | PART 1 | PART 2 | | $8.00 | $15.00 |
| 1 | MP-5 | DADDY'S LITTLE BOY/DADDY'S LITTLE GIRL | EDDY HOWARD | DADDY'S LITTLE BOY | DADDY'S LITTLE GIRL | | $3.00 | $6.00 |
| 1 | MP-6 | ARFIE, THE DOGGIE IN THE WINDOW | PATTI PAGE, GILBERT MACK, ARNOLD AMARU | PART 1 | PART 2 | 1953 | $5.00 | $10.00 |
| 1 | MP-7 | SUPER CIRCUS MENAGERIE | TV CAST: CLAUDE KIRCHNER, MARY HARTLINE, THE SUPER CIRCUS BAND, ET AL. | PART 1 | PART 2 | | $15.00 | $30.00 |
| 1 | MP-8 | SUPER CIRCUS CLOWN ALLEY | TV CAST: CLAUDE KIRCHNER, MARY HARTLINE, THE SUPER CIRCUS BAND, ET AL. | PART 1 | PART 2 | | $15.00 | $30.00 |
| 1 | MP-9 | THE SUPER CIRCUS BAND | TV CAST: CLAUDE KIRCHNER, MARY HARTLINE, THE SUPER CIRCUS BAND, ET AL. | PART 1 | PART 2 | | $15.00 | $30.00 |
| 1 | MP-10 | SUPER CIRCUS SIDE SHOW | TV CAST: CLAUDE KIRCHNER, MARY HARTLINE, THE SUPER CIRCUS BAND, ET AL. | PART 1 | PART 2 | | $15.00 | $30.00 |
| 1 | MP-11 | ARFIE CATCHES AN ECHO/ARFIE GOES TO SCHOOL | PATTI PAGE, HUGO PERETTI ORCH. | ARFIE GOES TO SCHOOL | ARFIE CATCHES AN ECHO | 1954 | $5.00 | $10.00 |
| 1 | MP-12 | I WANNA' GO SKATING WITH WILLIE/PRETTY SNOWFLAKES | PATTI PAGE | PRETTY SNOWFLAKES | I WANNA' GO SKATING WITH WILLIE | | $5.00 | $10.00 |
| 1 | MP-13 | KIDDIE KONGA | THE LADY IN BLUE (JUNE WINTERS) | PART 1 | PART 2 | | $3.00 | $6.00 |
| 1 | MP-14 | VICTOR HERBERT'S "MARCH OF THE TOYS"/MY FAVORITE TOY | THE LADY IN BLUE (JUNE WINTERS) | MARCH OF THE TOYS | THAT'S MY FAVORITE TOY | | $3.00 | $6.00 |
| 1 | MP-15 | ARFIE GOES TO SCHOOL | PATTI PAGE, HUGO PERETTI ORCH. | PART 1 | PART 2 | | $5.00 | $10.00 |
| 1 | MP-16 | PETER RABBIT/EASTER MORNIN' | RUSTY DRAPER | PETER RABBIT | EASTER MORNIN' | | $4.00 | $8.00 |
| 1 | MP-17 | AT THE FAIR | PAUL WINCHELL AND JERRY MAHONEY | PART 1 | PART 2 | | $15.00 | $30.00 |
| 1 | MP-18 | DID YOU EVER FALL IN LOVE WITH A TEDDY BEAR/MR. FUZZY BEAR | THE LADY IN BLUE (JUNE WINTERS), HUGO PERETTI ORCH. | MR. FUZZY BEAR | TEDDY BEAR'S SONG | | $3.00 | $6.00 |
| 1 | MP-19 | THE HAPPY CLOCK/THE PARADE OF THE WOODEN SOLDIERS | THE LADY IN BLUE (JUNE WINTERS), HUGO PERETTI ORCH. | PARADE OF THE WOODEN SOLDIERS | THE HAPPY CLOCK | | $3.00 | $6.00 |

## MERCURY PLAYCRAFT SERIES 10" SINGLES

| # REC | DISC # | MAIN TITLE | ARTIST | A TITLE | B TITLE | YEAR | G/VG | EX/NMT |
|---|---|---|---|---|---|---|---|---|
| 1 | MP-20 | SUPER CIRCUS PARADE | TV CAST: CLAUDE KIRCHNER, MARY HARTLINE, THE SUPER CIRCUS BAND, ET AL. | PART 1 | PART 2 | | $15.00 | $30.00 |
| 1 | MP-21 | SUPER CIRCUS TRAIN | TV CAST: CLAUDE KIRCHNER, MARY HARTLINE, THE SUPER CIRCUS BAND, ET AL. | PART 1 | PART 2 | | $15.00 | $30.00 |
| 1 | MP-22 | HAPPY BIRTHDAY/BIMBO | EDDY HOWARD & ORCH. | BIMBO | HAPPY BIRTHDAY | | $3.00 | $6.00 |
| 1 | MP-23 | THE MAMA DOLL SONG/I'M ALLAGAZIRL THE MAGIC GIRL | PATTI PAGE, JACK RAEL ORCH. | THE MAMA DOLL SONG | I'M ALLAGAZIRL THE MAGIC GIRL | | $5.00 | $10.00 |
| 1 | MP-24 | THE LITTLE SHOEMAKER/PUPALINA | THE GAYLORDS, GEORGE ANNIS ORCH. | THE LITTLE SHOEMAKER | PUPALINA | | $3.00 | $6.00 |
| 1 | MP-25 | TWINKLE TOES/DANCE MR. SNOWMAN DANCE | THE CREW-CUTS, DAVID CARROLL ORCH. | TWINKLE TOES | DANCE MR. SNOWMAN DANCE | | $8.00 | $15.00 |
| 1 | MP-26 | SING ALONG WITH RUSTY/? | RUSTY DRAPER, HUGO PERETTI ORCH. | SING ALONG WITH RUSTY | ? | | $4.00 | $8.00 |
| 1 | MP-27 | THE BALLAD OF DAVY CROCKETT/LAZY MULE | RUSTY DRAPER, DAVID CARROLL ORCH. | THE BALLAD OF DAVY CROCKETT | LAZY MULE | 1955 | $6.00 | $12.00 |
| 1 | MP-28 | NOBODY LIKES A CRYBABY/THE FROGGIE LOVE SONG | PATTI PAGE, JACK RAEL ORCH. | NOBODY LIKES A CRY BABY | THE FROGGIE LOVE SONG | | $5.00 | $10.00 |
| 1 | MP-29 | EATIN' GOOBER PEAS/? | RUSTY DRAPER | EATIN' GOOBER PEAS | ? | | $4.00 | $8.00 |
| 1 | MP-30 | LITTLE WILLIE, THE LEADER OF THE BAND | JUNE WINTERS, THE LADY IN BLUE, HUGO PERETTI ORCH. | PART 1 | PART 2 | | $3.00 | $6.00 |
| 1 | MP-31 | LEARNIN' MY LATIN/REPEAT AFTER ME | PATTI PAGE | LEARNIN' MY LATIN | REPEAT AFTER ME | | $4.00 | $8.00 |
| 1 | MP-32 | TOOTLES THE TUG/ON THE GOOD SHIP LOLLIPOP | JUNE WINTERS | TOOTLES THE TUG | ON THE GOOD SHIP LOLLIPOP | | $3.00 | $6.00 |
| 1 | MP-33 | THE LITTLE WHITE DUCK/HATCHY MILATCHY | THE LADY IN BLUE (JUNE WINTERS), HUGO PERETTI ORCH. | THE LITTLE WHITE DUCK | HATCHY MILATCHY | | $3.00 | $6.00 |
| 1 | MP-34 | THE THREE LITTLE KITTENS/I'M A LITTLE TEAPOT | HUGO PERETTI ORCH. & CHORUS/TOBY DEANE, HUGO PERETTI ORCH. | I'M A LITTLE TEAPOT | THE THREE LITTLE KITTENS | 1956 | $4.00 | $8.00 |
| 1 | MP-35 | LOVE AND MARRIAGE/STANDING ON THE CORNER | ? | LOVE AND MARRIAGE | STANDING ON THE CORNER | 1957 | $2.00 | $4.00 |

## MERCURY MINIATURE PLAYHOUSE 10" SERIES SINGLES AND ALBUMS

| SET # | # REC | DISC # | MAIN TITLE | ARTIST | YEAR | G/VG | EX/NMT | REMARKS |
|---|---|---|---|---|---|---|---|---|
| MMP-AA1 | 3 | 7000 – 2 | HERMAN ERMINE IN RABBIT TOWN | JOHN GARFIELD | 1946 | $12.00 | $25.00 | |
| MMP-A2 | 2 | 7003 – 4 | WILLIE AND HANNIBAL IN MOUSELAND | JACK CARSON | | $12.00 | $25.00 | |
| MMP-3 | 2 | 7005 – 6 | CAPTAIN BILL MEETS FEARY O'LEARY | DON DOOLITTLE | | $12.00 | $25.00 | |
| MMP-4 | 2 | 7007 – 8 | NURSERY RHYME TIME | DICK "TWO TON" BAKER | | $4.00 | $8.00 | |
| MMP-5 | 2 | 7010 – 11 | CHRISTMAS PARTY: THE NIGHT BEFORE CHRISTMAS, ETC. | DICK "TWO TON" BAKER | | $4.00 | $8.00 | |
| MMP-6 | 2 | 7012 – 3 | ALPHABET FUN FROM A TO Z | IREENE WICKER, THE SINGING LADY | | $4.00 | $8.00 | |
| MMP-7 | 2 | 7014 – 5 | THIS IS CHRISTMAS | IREENE WICKER, THE SINGING LADY | | $4.00 | $8.00 | ALSO ISSUED AS THE LEGEND OF THE CHRISTMAS ROSE |
| MMP-8 | 2 | 7016 – 7 | GOLDILOCKS AND THE THREE BEARS | IREENE WICKER, THE SINGING LADY | | $4.00 | $8.00 | |
| MMP-9 | 2 | 7018 – 9 | SING A SILLY SONG: I LIKE YOU, YOU'RE SILLY, ET AL. | DICK "TWO TON" BAKER | | $4.00 | $8.00 | |
| MMP-10 | 2 | 7020 – 1 | DICK TRACY IN THE CASE OF THE MIDNIGHT MARAUDER | JIM AMECHE (AS DICK TRACY) | | $45.00 | $90.00 | |
| MMP-11 | 1 | 7022 (12") | BOOMER THE BASS DRUM | DICK "TWO TON" BAKER | | $8.00 | $15.00 | |
| MMP-12 | 2 | 7023 – 4 | NEW MOTHER GOOSE RHYMES | BEN ARONIN | | $8.00 | $15.00 | WITH BOOK |
| MMP-13 | 2 | 7025 – 6 | THE LITTLE LOST STAR (FEATURING JUMP JUMP) | MARY MCCONNELL | | $4.00 | $8.00 | |
| MMP-14 | 1 | 7027 | THE PRINCESS AND THE PEA | ROBERT BAILEY | | $4.00 | $8.00 | |
| MMP-15 | 3 | 7028 – 30 | KING THRUSHBEARD | ROBERT BAILEY | | $4.00 | $8.00 | |

## MERCURY MINIATURE PLAYHOUSE 10" SERIES SINGLES AND ALBUMS

| SET # | # REC | DISC # | MAIN TITLE | ARTIST | YEAR | G/VG | EX/NMT |
|---|---|---|---|---|---|---|---|
| MMP-16 | 3 | 7031 - 3 | THE FISHERMAN AND THE FLOUNDER/THE ELVES AND THE SHOEMAKER | ROBERT BAKER | | $4.00 | $8.00 |
| MMP-17 | 2 | 7034 - 5 | JUMP JUMP AND SLEEPY SLIM THE TIRED LION | MARY MCCONNELL | | $3.00 | $6.00 |
| MMP-18 | 2 | 7036 - 7 | JUMP JUMP AND THE UGLY DUCKLING | MARY MCCONNELL | | $3.00 | $6.00 |
| MMP-19 | 1 | 7038 | SPARKLE PLENTY'S BIRTHDAY PARTY | BEN ARONIN | | $25.00 | $50.00 |
| MMP-20 | 2 | 7039 - 40 | KEN MURRAY'S "BILL AND COO" | ELIZABETH WALTERS, LIONEL NEWMAN ORCHESTRA | 1948 | $15.00 | $30.00 |
| MMP-21 | 2 | 7041 - 2 | JOY CITY | SHERMAN MARKS | | $3.00 | $6.00 |
| MMP-22 | 2 | 7043 - 4 | MAKING HABITS FUN | BEN ARONIN | | $3.00 | $6.00 |
| MMP-23 | 2 | 7045 - 6 | MOTHER GOOSE AND FATHER GANDER RHYMES | BEN ARONIN | | $3.00 | $6.00 |
| MMP-24 | 1 | 7047 | I WUV A WABBIT/I'M A LITTLE TEAPOT | DICK "TWO TON" BAKER | | $3.00 | $6.00 |
| MMP-25 | 1 | 7048 | LONELY LITTLE PETUNIA/EVERYBODY HAS A LAUGHING PLACE | DICK "TWO TON" BAKER | 1947 | $5.00 | $10.00 |
| MMP-27 | 1 | 7050 | LITTLE JACK HORNER | BEN ARONIN | | $2.00 | $4.00 |
| MMP-28 | 1 | 7051 | LITTLE MISS MUFFET | BEN ARONIN | | $2.00 | $4.00 |
| MMP-29 | 1 | 7052 | LITTLE BOY BLUE | BEN ARONIN | | $2.00 | $4.00 |
| MMP-30 | 1 | 7053 | LITTLE BO PEEP | BEN ARONIN | | $2.00 | $4.00 |
| MMP-31 | 1 | 7054 | EDWARD LEAR'S "NONSENSE ALPHABET" | GILBERT MACK | | $8.00 | $15.00 |
| MMP-32 | 1 | 7049 | EDWARD LEAR'S "ANOTHER NONSENSE ALPHABET" | GILBERT MACK | | $8.00 | $15.00 |
| MMP-33 | 1 | 7050 | MOTHER GOOSE PICTURERIMES: LITTLE MISS MUFFET/LONDON BRIDGE | BEN ARONIN | | $2.00 | $4.00 |
| MMP-34 | 1 | 7051 | MOTHER GOOSE PICTURERIMES: RING AROUND THE ROSIE/LITTLE JACK HORNER | BEN ARONIN | | $2.00 | $4.00 |
| MMP-35 | 1 | 7052 | MOTHER GOOSE PICTURERIMES: LITTLE BO PEEP/LUCY LOCKET | BEN ARONIN | | $2.00 | $4.00 |
| MMP-36 | 1 | 7053 | MOTHER GOOSE PICTURERIMES: LITTLE BOY BLUE/'ROUND THE MULBERRY BUSH | BEN ARONIN | | $2.00 | $4.00 |
| MMP-39 | 1 | 7059 | CHOO CHOO TRAIN RIDE/THE WHISTLER AND HIS DOG | MERCURY NOVELTY ORCHESTRA | | $2.00 | $4.00 |
| MMP-43 | 1 | 1079 | WHEN GRANDMA DANCED THE MINUET, JOLLY FARMER/SPRING, BELLS IN THE STEEPLE | BOB HANNON | | $4.00 | $8.00 |
| MMP-44 | 1 | 1080 | MY LITTLE TOY BOAT/THE WIND AND THE BREEZE | BOB HANNON | | $4.00 | $8.00 |
| MMP-45 | 1 | 1081 | MY TINY SCOOTER, IN THE GOOD OLD WINTER TIME/DOWN WHERE THE RAINBOW ENDS, DANCE AND BE MERRY | BOB HANNON | | $4.00 | $8.00 |
| MMP-46 | 1 | 1082 | AT THE ZOO/WHEN THE CIRCUS COMES TO TOWN | BOB HANNON | | $4.00 | $8.00 |
| MMP-47 | 1 | ? | TALES OF THE GREAT BIBLE HEROES: NOAH | LEW AYRES | | $3.00 | $6.00 |
| MMP-48 | 1 | ? | TALES OF THE GREAT BIBLE HEROES: DAVID & THE KING/DAVID AND GOLIATH | LEW AYRES | | $3.00 | $6.00 |
| MMP-49 | 1 | ? | TALES OF THE GREAT BIBLE HEROES: SHADRACH, MESHACH AND ABEDNEGO/DANIEL | LEW AYRES | | $3.00 | $6.00 |
| MMP-50 | 4 | 1079 - 82 | SONGS FOR LITTLE FOLKS: ALBUM CONTAINING MMP 43 - 46 | BOB HANNON | | $15.00 | $30.00 |
| MMP-52 | 1 | 2522 | MY LITTLE PUP/MYRTLE THE TURTLE | DICK "TWO TON" BAKER | 1949 | $3.00 | $6.00 |
| MMP-53 | 1 | 2772/2921 | ELLY THE ELEGANT ELEPHANT/LOOEY THE LOCOMOTIVE | DICK "TWO TON" BAKER | | $3.00 | $6.00 |
| MMP-54 | 2 | 2924 - 5 | OUR BODY IS A LITTLE HOUSE (PT. 1/2) | DICK "TWO TON" BAKER | | $3.00 | $6.00 |
| MMP-55 | 1 | MMP-55 | COME TO MY PARTY, ETC. | BOB HANNON | | $4.00 | $8.00 |
| MMP-56 | 1 | MMP-56 | I HAVE A PUP AND KITTY, ETC. | BOB HANNON | | $4.00 | $8.00 |
| MMP-57 | 1 | MMP-57 | THE WALRUS AND THE CARPENTER, ETC. | BOB HANNON | | $4.00 | $8.00 |
| MMP-58 | 3 | MMP 55-57 | KIDDIE KLASSICS: ALBUM CONTAINING MMP 55 - 57 | BOB HANNON | | $15.00 | $30.00 |
| MMP-59 | 1 | 2986-7 | GUS THE GOPHER AND HIS PAL TWO TON BAKER | DICK "TWO TON" BAKER | | $4.00 | $8.00 |
| MMP-60 | 1 | 2988-9 | GUS THE GOPHER AND HIS PAL TWO TON BAKER SAVES CHRISTMAS | DICK "TWO TON" BAKER | | $4.00 | $8.00 |
| MMP-61 | 1 | ? | TEN LITTLE INDIANS, ETC. | MERCURY NOVELTY ORCHESTRA | | $1.00 | $2.00 |
| MMP-62 | 1 | ? | ARE YOU SLEEPING, ETC. | MERCURY NOVELTY ORCHESTRA | | $1.00 | $2.00 |
| MMP-63 | 1 | 3210-1 | ONE LITTLE CANDLE ON A TWO LAYER CAKE/THE BOY WITH THE RIP IN HIS PANTS | DICK "TWO TON" BAKER | | $1.00 | $2.00 |
| MMP-64 | 1 | ? | NURSERY SONGS | MERCURY NOVELTY ORCHESTRA | | $1.00 | $2.00 |

## MERCURY MINIATURE PLAYHOUSE 10" SERIES SINGLES AND ALBUMS

| SET # | # REC | DISC # | MAIN TITLE | ARTIST | YEAR | G/VG | EX/NMT |
|---|---|---|---|---|---|---|---|
| MMP-65 | 1 | ? | BUFFALO BILLY/ANNIE OAKLEY | ROBERTA QUINLAN | | $1.00 | $2.00 |
| MMP-66 | 1 | ? | CRADLE SONGS | MERCURY NOVELTY ORCHESTRA | | $1.00 | $2.00 |
| MMP-67 | 1 | 2962-2016 | RUDOLPH THE RED NOSED REINDEER/BLUETAIL FLY | EDDY HOWARD | | $1.00 | $2.00 |
| MMP-68 | 1 | ? | OLD MOTHER GOOSE | NOT LISTED | | $1.00 | $2.00 |
| MMP-69 | 1 | ? | MOTHER GOOSE PARADE | NOT LISTED | | $1.00 | $2.00 |
| MMP-70 | 1 | ? | NURSERY FAVORITES | NOT LISTED | | $1.00 | $2.00 |
| MMP-71 | 1 | ? | MOTHER GOOSE SONGS FOR SINGING | NOT LISTED | | $1.00 | $2.00 |
| MMP-74 | 1 | 1911/09-3664 | SILENT NIGHT, O COME ALL YE FAITHFUL/PUNKY PUNKIN | DING DONG BELL SINGERS/ROBERTA QUIN-LAN | 1950 | $1.00 | $2.00 |
| MMP-76 | 1 | 3762-3 | FROSTY THE SNOWMAN/TUBBY THE TUBA SONG | DICK "TWO TON" BAKER, JERRY MURAD'S HARMONICATS | | $3.00 | $6.00 |
| MMP-77 | 2 | 3208 – 9 | PETER COTTONTAIL/CINDERELLA WORK SONG | DICK "TWO TON" BAKER | | $3.00 | $6.00 |
| MMP-78 | 1 | 3900 – 1 | JEST 'FORE CHRISTMAS/THE NIGHT BEFORE CHRISTMAS | FRAN WEIGEL | | $1.00 | $2.00 |
| MMP-81 | 1 | ? | DADDY'S LITTLE BOY/DADDY'S LITTLE GIRL | ? | | $1.00 | $2.00 |
| MMP-82 | 1 | ? | SYNCOPATED CLOCK/GAY CANARY | AL TRACE | 1951 | $2.00 | $4.00 |

## MERCURY MINIATURE PLAYHOUSE 7" SERIES SINGLES AND GENERIC BOXES

| # REC | DISC # | MAIN TITLE | ARTIST | A TITLE | B TITLE | YEAR | G/VG | EX/NMT |
|---|---|---|---|---|---|---|---|---|
| 1 | 100-7 | MOTHER GOOSE IN SONG AND STORY: LAZY MARY, ETC. | GILBERT MACK, THE MOTHER GOOSE SINGERS | LAZY MARY, POLLY PUT THE KET-TLE ON, COCK A DOODLE DOO | GEORGIE PORGIE, MARY HAD A LITTLE LAMB | 1948 | $1.00 | $2.00 |
| 1 | 101-7 | MOTHER GOOSE IN SONG AND STORY: SING A SONG OF SIXPENCE, ETC. | GILBERT MACK, THE MOTHER GOOSE SINGERS | SING A SONG OF SIXPENCE, DING DONG BELL, THE MUFFIN MAN | PETER PIPER, LITTLE BO PEEP | | $1.00 | $2.00 |
| 1 | 102-7 | MOTHER GOOSE IN SONG AND STORY: THE BEAR WENT OVER THE MOUN-TAIN, ETC. | GILBERT MACK, THE MOTHER GOOSE SINGERS | THE BEAR WENT OVER THE MOUNTAIN, CROOKED MAN | BOBBY SHAFTOE, A FROG HE WOULD A WOOING GO | | $1.00 | $2.00 |
| 1 | 103-7 | MOTHER GOOSE IN SONG AND STORY: HOT CROSS BUNS, ETC. | GILBERT MACK, THE MOTHER GOOSE SINGERS | HOT CROSS BUNS, PAT A CAKE | THREE BLIND MICE, OLD MACDONALD HAD A FARM | | $1.00 | $2.00 |
| 1 | 104-7 | SINGING GAMES: A TIS-KET, A TASKET/RING AROUND THE ROSIE, LOOBY-LOO | GILBERT MACK, THE MOTHER GOOSE SINGERS | A TISKET A TASKET | RING AROUND THE ROSIE, LOOBY LOO | | $1.00 | $2.00 |
| 1 | 105-7 | SINGING GAMES: LON-DON BRIDGE/MUL-BERRY BUSH | GILBERT MACK, THE MOTHER GOOSE SINGERS | LONDON BRIDGE | MULBERRY BUSH | | $1.00 | $2.00 |
| 1 | 106-7 | SINGING GAMES: TEN LITTLE INDIANS, ETC. | GILBERT MACK, THE MOTHER GOOSE SINGERS | TEN LITTLE INDIANS | DID YOU EVER SEE A LASSIE, THIS IS THE WAY THE GENTLE-MEN RIDE | | $1.00 | $2.00 |
| 1 | 107-7 | SINGING GAMES: FARMER IN THE DELL/ ROUND AND ROUND THE VILLAGE | GILBERT MACK, THE MOTHER GOOSE SINGERS | FARMER IN THE DELL | ROUND AND ROUND THE VIL-LAGE | | $1.00 | $2.00 |
| 1 | 108-7 | LULLABIES: SLEEP BABY SLEEP, ETC. | ANNE VINCENT, SUZANNE BLOCH | SLEEP BABY SLEEP, BRAHMS LULLABY | THE SANDMAN COMES, WIN-KUM WINKUM | | $1.00 | $2.00 |
| 1 | 109-7 | LULLABIES: THE CHILD AND THE STAR | ANNE VINCENT, SUZANNE BLOCH | THE CHILD AND THE STAR | ROCKABYE BABY, ALL THROUGH THE NIGHT | | $1.00 | $2.00 |
| 1 | 110-7 | LULLABIES: GO TO SLEEP MY LITTLE BABY/ GO TELL AUNT RODIE | JEAN RITCHIE | GO TO SLEEP MY LITTLE BABY | GO TELL AUNT RODIE | | $2.00 | $4.00 |
| 1 | 111-7 | LULLABIES: HUSH LITTLE BABY/LITTLE SHOES | JEAN RITCHIE | HUSH LITTLE BABY | LITTLE SHOES | | $2.00 | $4.00 |
| 1 | 112-7 | ROUNDS & ROUNDELAYS: ROW, ROW, ROW YOUR BOAT/SKIN & BONES | ? | SWEETLY SINGS THE DONKEY | HOP AROUND, SKIP AROUND | | $2.00 | $4.00 |
| 1 | 113-7 | ROUNDS & ROUNDELAYS: OH, HOW LOVELY IS THE EVENING/THIS OLD MAN | JEAN RITCHIE, DING DONG BELL SINGERS | ROW ROW ROW YOUR BOAT | SKIN AND BONES | | $2.00 | $4.00 |
| 1 | 114-7 | ROUNDS & ROUNDELAYS: ARE YOU SLEEPING?/ THERE WAS A TAILOR HAD A MOUSE | JEAN RITCHIE, DING DONG BELL SINGERS | OH HOW LOVELY IS THE EVENING | THIS OLD MAN | | $2.00 | $4.00 |

MERCURY RECORDS
CAPTAIN SNORTER'S BURIED TREASURE
$10.00

MERCURY RECORDS
PETER PONSIL LOST HIS TONSIL
$10.00

MERCURY RECORDS
SQUARE DANCES FOR CHILDREN
$4.00

## MERCURY MINIATURE PLAYHOUSE 7" SERIES SINGLES AND GENERIC BOXES

| # REC | DISC # | MAIN TITLE | ARTIST | A TITLE | B TITLE | G/VG | EX/NMT |
|---|---|---|---|---|---|---|---|
| 1 | 115-7 | ROUNDS & ROUNDELAYS: SWEETLY SINGS THE DONKEY/ HOP AROUND, SKIP AROUND | JEAN RITCHIE, DING DONG BELL SINGERS | ARE YOU SLEEPING | THERE WAS A TAILOR HAD A MOUSE | $2.00 | $4.00 |
| 1 | 116-7 | CHILDREN'S CHRISTMAS CAROLS: HARK! THE HERALD ANGELS SING/LITTLE BIDDY BABY | ? | HARK! THE HERALD ANGELS SING | LITTLE BIDDY BABY | $2.00 | $4.00 |
| 1 | 117-7 | CHILDREN'S CHRISTMAS CAROLS: COME ALL YE FAITHFUL/THERE WAS A LITTLE PIG WENT OUT TO DIG | ? | COME ALL YE FAITHFUL | THERE WAS A LITTLE PIG WENT OUT TO DIG | $2.00 | $4.00 |
| 1 | 118-7 | CHILDREN'S CHRISTMAS CAROLS: OH LITTLE TOWN OF BETHLE-HEM/AWAY IN THE MANGER | ? | OH LITTLE TOWN OF BETHLEHEM | AWAY IN THE MANGER | $2.00 | $4.00 |
| 1 | 119-7 | CHILDREN'S CHRISTMAS CAROLS: SILENT NIGHT/WASSAIL SONG | JEAN RITCHIE, DING DONG BELL SINGERS | SILENT NIGHT | WASSAIL SONG | $2.00 | $4.00 |

## MERCURY MISCELLANEOUS 10" SINGLES AND ALBUMS

| # REC | DISC # | ARTIST | A TITLE | B TITLE | G/VG | EX/NMT |
|---|---|---|---|---|---|---|
| 1 | 3019 | ? | FROM DISNEY'S "MAKE MINE MUSIC": WITHOUT YOU | ? | $3.00 | $6.00 |
| 1 | 3047 | DICK "TWO TON" BAKER | ZIP A DEE DOO DAH | RICKETY RICKSHAW MAN | $3.00 | $6.00 |
| 1 | 5329 | DICK "TWO TON" BAKER | I'M JUST A LITTLE PANSY | ? | $2.00 | $4.00 |
| 1 | 5392 | DICK "TWO TON" BAKER | MY LITTLE PUP | ? | $2.00 | $4.00 |
| 1 | 5397 | DICK "TWO TON" BAKER | PETER COTTONTAIL | FROM DISNEY'S "CINDERELLA": THE WORK SONG | $3.00 | $6.00 |
| 1 | 5399 | DICK "TWO TON" BAKER | CINDERELLA | PETER COTTONTAIL | $3.00 | $6.00 |
| 1 | 5615 | ROBERTA QUINLAN | ALICE IN WONDERLAND | GOTTA FIND SOMEBODY TO LOVE | $3.00 | $6.00 |
| 1 | 5627 (A-89 ALBUM?) | RICHARD HAYES, ROBERTA QUINLAN | ALICE IN WONDERLAND: THEME SONG | IN THE WORLD OF MY DREAMS | $3.00 | $6.00 |
| 1 | 5639 (A-89 ALBUM?) | RICHARD HAYES, ROBERTA QUINLAN | ALICE IN WONDERLAND: I'M LATE, THE CAUCUS RACE | UNBIRTHDAY SONG | $3.00 | $6.00 |
| 1 | 5722 | EDDY HOWARD ORCH. | UNCLE MISTLETOE | WHEN CHRISTMAS ROLLS AROUND | $2.00 | $4.00 |
| 1 | 5760 | RUSS CARLYLE ORCH. | SANTA LOOKS JUST LIKE MY DADDY | ONLY YOU | $2.00 | $4.00 |
| 1 | 5475 | EDDY HOWARD ORCH. | DADDY'S LITTLE BOY | THEY PUT THE LIGHTS OUT | $2.00 | $4.00 |
| 1 | 5883 | DICK "TWO TON" BAKER | I'M A LONELY LITTLE PETUNIA | THE COCOANUT SONG | $3.00 | $6.00 |
| 1 | 70070 | PATTI PAGE | THE DOGGIE IN THE WINDOW | A WOMAN IS STRANGE | $4.00 | $8.00 |
| 1 | 70124 | BABY PAMELA RICH | EASTER BUNNY SONG | GOODY GOODY GUMDROPS | $2.00 | $4.00 |
| 1 | 70207 | BABY PAMELA RICH | I WANNA GO TO SCHOOL | GOD BLESS US ALL | $2.00 | $4.00 |
| 1 | 70229 | PAUL WINCHELL AND JERRY MA-HONEY, HUGO PERETTI ORCH. | THE FRIENDLY POLKA | A WOMAN IS STRANGE | $5.00 | $10.00 |
| 1 | 70555 | RUSTY DRAPER | THE BALLAD OF DAVY CROCKETT | I'VE BEEN THINKING | $4.00 | $8.00 |
| 3 | A-89 (ALBUM) | ? | ALICE IN WONDERLAND | ALICE IN WONDERLAND | $8.00 | $15.00 |

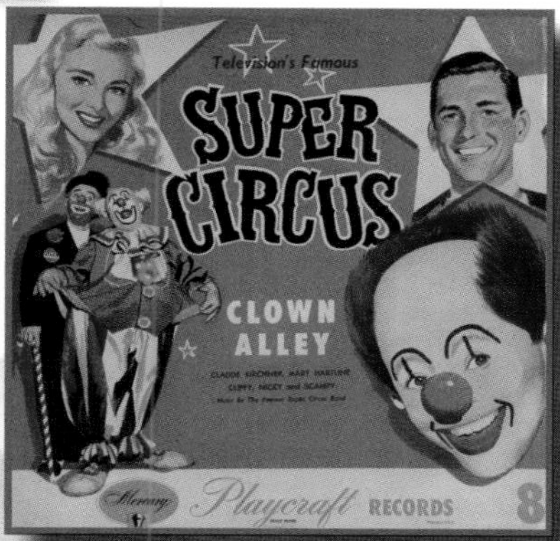

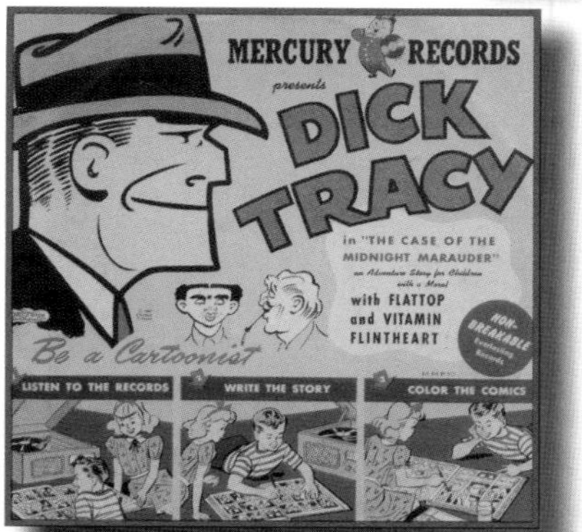


MERCURY RECORDS
SUPER CIRCUS CLOWN ALLEY
$30.00

MERCURY RECORDS
NOBODY LIKES A CRYBABY
$10.00

MERCURY RECORDS
DICK TRACY IN
$90.00

## MERRY-GO-ROUND BOOKS (MUSETTE) 7" SINGLES WITH BOOKS

| # REC | DISC # | MAIN TITLE | ARTIST | YEAR | G/VG | EX/NMT |
|---|---|---|---|---|---|---|
| 1 | FR 1/2 | ALL BY MYSELF (FRANCE): THERE WAS A LITTLE MAN, ETC. | WILMA ROBBINS, CHESTER LUDGIN, TED PODNOS, ORCH. | 1954 | $4.00 | $8.00 |
| 1 | IT 1/2 | LITTLE BETTINA MAKE BELIEVE (ITALY): THE FAIR OF MAST' ANDREA, ETC. | WILMA ROBBINS, CHESTER LUDGIN, TED PODNOS, ORCH. | | $4.00 | $8.00 |
| 1 | NOR 1/2 | LITTLE OLD LADY OF CLIFFSIDE (NORWAY): LITTLE FISHES, ETC. | WILMA ROBBINS, CHESTER LUDGIN, TED PODNOS, ORCH. | | $4.00 | $8.00 |
| 1 | IR 1/2 | THE DAY THE CLOUDS BUMPED NOSES (IRELAND): SHEPHERD BOY, ETC. | WILMA ROBBINS, CHESTER LUDGIN, TED PODNOS, ORCH. | | $4.00 | $8.00 |

## MERRY-GO-SOUND 10" DOUBLES AND ONE SINGLE

| SET # | # REC | DISC # | MAIN TITLE | ARTIST | YEAR | G/VG | EX/NMT |
|---|---|---|---|---|---|---|---|
| TP-1 | 2 | 101/102 | RUMPLESTILTSKIN | MERRY-GO-SOUND PLAYERS, TED COTT, DIR. | 1947 | $3.00 | $6.00 |
| TP-2 | 2 | 103/104 | SEVEN AT A BLOW | MERRY-GO-SOUND PLAYERS, TED COTT, DIR. | | $3.00 | $6.00 |
| TP-3 | 2 | 105/106 | MOTHER GOOSE PARTY | DICK BROWN, MERRY-GO-SOUND PLAYERS, TED COTT, DIR. | | $3.00 | $6.00 |
| NO # | 1 | 107 | OLD MACDONALD HAD A FARM | PAUL CONRAD, MERRY-GO-SOUND PLAYERS, TED COTT, DIR. | | $2.00 | $4.00 |
| TP-5 | 2 | 109/110 | TOM THUMB | BARRY THOMSON, MERRY-GO-SOUND PLAYERS, TED COTT, DIR. | | $3.00 | $6.00 |
| TP-6 | 2 | 111/112 | AESOP'S FABLES | DICK BROWN, BARRY THOMSON, MERRY-GO-SOUND PLAYERS, TED COTT, DIR. | | $3.00 | $6.00 |
| TP-7 | 2 | 113/114 | CHILDREN'S OPRY HOUSE | BARRY THOMSON, MERRY-GO-SOUND PLAYERS, TED COTT, DIR. | | $3.00 | $6.00 |
| TP-8 | 2 | 115/116 | WHO'S WHO AT THE ZOO | BOB ROSS, LEONARD SHERER, BARRY THOMSON, MERRY-GO-SOUND ORCH.; TED COTT, DIR. | | $3.00 | $6.00 |

## MGM L-SERIES 10" DOUBLES AND ONE SINGLE

| SET # | # REC | DISC # | MAIN TITLE | ARTIST | YEAR | G/VG | EX/NMT |
|---|---|---|---|---|---|---|---|
| L-1 | 2 | 10066 – 7 (50001 – 2) | IRVING THE UNEMPLOYED HORSE | ALLAN MELVIN | 1947 | $10.00 | $20.00 |
| L-2 | 2 | 10064 – 5 | MOTHER GOOSE PARADE | BETTY MARTIN | | $2.00 | $4.00 |
| L-3 | 2 | 50003 – 4 (10195 – 6) | TUGBOAT DANNY | RAY DARBY, MORRIS SURDIN | 1948 | $4.00 | $8.00 |
| L-4 | 2 | 50005 – 6 | HORTON HATCHES THE EGG | MARVIN MILLER, DR. SEUSS | | $10.00 | $20.00 |
| L-5 | 2 | 50007 – 8 | THE PRIDE OF KENTUCKY | ALLAN MELVIN | | $4.00 | $8.00 |
| L-6 | 2 | 50012 – 3 | SONGS OF HEALTH | IRVING CAESAR | | $4.00 | $8.00 |
| L-7 | 2 | 50014 – 5 | FLICK, THE LITTLE FIRE ENGINE | ROBERT DANN | 1949 | $8.00 | $15.00 |
| L-8 | 2 | 50016 – 7 | THE BARCLEY'S OF BROADWAY | FRED ASTAIRE AND GINGER ROGERS | | $25.00 | $50.00 |
| L-9 | 2 | 50018 – 9 | THE WIZARD OF OZ | LEE FORESTER & CHORUS, JOEL HERRON ORCH. | | $10.00 | $20.00 |
| L-10 | 2 | 50028 – 9 | THE MIRACLE OF THE MUSIC SHOP | ROBERT DANN | | $3.00 | $6.00 |
| L-11 | 2 | 50022 – 3 | THE LITTLE GINGER BREAD MAN | BETTY MARTIN | | $2.00 | $4.00 |
| L-12 | 2 | 50026 – 7 | A KIDDIE KARNIVAL | KORN KOBBLERS | | $4.00 | $8.00 |
| L-14 | 2 | 60007 – 8 | PAT AND THE PIXIES | JERRY BARTELL | 1950 | $4.00 | $8.00 |
| L-15 | 1 | 60004 – 5 | JINGLE BELLS, ETC./RUDOLPH THE RED-NOSED REINDEER, ETC. | KORN KOBBLERS | | $2.00 | $4.00 |
| L-16 | 2 | 60015 – 16 | DRIPPY (THE RUNAWAY RAINDROP) | KEENAN WYNN | 1951 | $8.00 | $15.00 |
| L-17 | 2 | 60021 – 2 | TOM AND JERRY IN "JOHANN MOUSE" | BRET MORRISON | | $15.00 | $30.00 |

## MGM S-SERIES 10" SINGLES

| SET # | # REC | DISC # | MAIN TITLE | ARTIST | A TITLE | B TITLE | YEAR | G/VG | EX/NMT |
|---|---|---|---|---|---|---|---|---|---|
| S-1 | 1 | 50021 | TEDDY BEARS' PICNIC/THE MOSQUITO PARADE | PHILIP GREEN | TEDDY BEARS' PICNIC | THE MOSQUITO PARADE | 1949 | $2.00 | $4.00 |
| S-2 | 1 | ? | THE MULBERRY BUSH/DID YOU EVER SEE A LASSIE, LOOBY LOU | DONALD DAME | THE MULBERRY BUSH | DID YOU EVER SEE A LASSIE, LOOBY LOU | | $2.00 | $4.00 |
| S-3 | 1 | ? | THE THREE LITTLE PIGS | BETTY MARTIN | PART 1 | PART 2 | | $2.00 | $4.00 |
| S-4 | 1 | 50024 | THERE WERE THREE INDIANS | DWIGHT WEIST, ISH-TI-OPI | PART 1 | PART 2 | | $2.00 | $4.00 |
| S-6 | 1 | 50027 | LOOBY LOU/THE MULBERRY BUSH, DID YOU EVER SEE A LASSIE | DONALD DAME | LOOBY LOU | THE MULBERRY BUSH, DID YOU EVER SEE A LASSIE | | $2.00 | $4.00 |
| S-7 | 1 | 50032 | PARADE OF THE WOODEN SOLDIERS/THE TOYMAKERS' DREAM | THE SONG SPINNERS | PARADE OF THE WOODEN SOLDIERS | THE TOYMAKERS' DREAM | | $2.00 | $4.00 |
| S-8 | 1 | 50033 | FANTISSIMO (THE LITTLE HORSE WITH BELLS IN HIS HEART) | BETTY GARRETT | PART 1 | PART 2 | 1950 | $10.00 | $20.00 |
| S-9 | 1 | 60001 | PETER COTTONTAIL/THE LITTLE WHITE HORSE & THE MARE | DERRY FALLIGANT | PETER COTTONTAIL | THE LITTLE WHITE DUCK | | $2.00 | $4.00 |
| S-10 | 1 | 60009 | NURSERY SONGS: LONDON BRIDGE IS FALLING DOWN, ETC. | BETTY MARTIN | PART 1 | PART 2 | | $2.00 | $4.00 |
| S-12 | 1 | 60011 | I'M A LITTLE TEAPOT/HUMPTY DUMPTY'S HOLIDAY | JUDY VALENTINE | I'M A LITTLE TEA POT | HUMPTY DUMPTY'S HOLIDAY | | $2.00 | $4.00 |
| S-13 | 1 | ? | PUNKY PUNKIN' | | PUNKY PUNKIN' | GUFFY THE GOOFY GOBBLER | | $2.00 | $4.00 |
| S-14 | 1 | ? | CINDERELLA | | PART 1 | PART 2 | | $2.00 | $4.00 |
| S-15 | 1 | 60013 | GUESS WHO I AM/GUESS WHAT I AM | THE MELODEONS | GUESS WHO I AM | GUESS WHAT I AM | | $2.00 | $4.00 |
| S-16 | 1 | 60010 | SONNY THE BUNNY/PETER COTTONTAIL | SALLY SWEETLAND, TOMMY TUCKER ORCH./DERRY FALLIGANT, THE THREE COTTONTOPS | PETER COTTONTAIL | SONNY THE BUNNY | 1951 | $2.00 | $4.00 |
| S-17 | 1 | NONE | FROSTY THE SNOWMAN/CHRISTMAS COMES BUT ONCE A YEAR | JIMMY DURANTE | FROSTY THE SNOWMAN | CHRISTMAS COMES BUT ONCE A YEAR | | $8.00 | $15.00 |
| S-18 | 1 | NONE | TOM AND JERRY MEET SANTA CLAUS | BRET MORRISON | PART 1 | PART 2 | | $12.00 | $25.00 |
| S-19 | 1 | NONE | TOM AND JERRY AND THE FIRE ENGINE | BRET MORRISON | PART 1 | PART 2 | | $12.00 | $25.00 |
| S-20 | 1 | NONE | TOM AND JERRY AND THE ROCKET SHIP TO THE MOON | BRET MORRISON | PART 1 | PART 2 | 1952 | $15.00 | $30.00 |
| S-21 | 1 | NONE | TOM AND JERRY IN THE WILD WEST | BRET MORRISON | PART 1 | PART 2 | | $12.00 | $25.00 |
| S-22 | 1 | NONE | TOM AND JERRY ON THE FARM | BRET MORRISON | PART 1 | PART 2 | | $12.00 | $25.00 |
| S-23 | 1 | NONE | TOM AND JERRY FIND ALADDIN'S LAMP | BRET MORRISON | PART 1 | PART 2 | | $12.00 | $25.00 |
| S-24 | 1 | NONE | TOM AND JERRY AND CHARLIE & THE CHOO CHOO TRAIN | BRET MORRISON | PART 1 | PART 2 | | $12.00 | $25.00 |
| S-25 | 1 | NONE | TOM AND JERRY AND OLD MACDONALD'S BARNYARD BAND | BRET MORRISON | PART 1 | PART 2 | | $12.00 | $25.00 |
| S-26 | 1 | NONE | TOM AND JERRY MEET ROBIN HOOD | BRET MORRISON | PART 1 | PART 2 | | $12.00 | $25.00 |
| S-27 | 1 | NONE | TOM AND JERRY AND THE TEXAS RANGERS | BRET MORRISON | PART 1 | PART 2 | | $12.00 | $25.00 |
| S-28 | 1 | NONE | TOM AND JERRY AND THE TUG BOAT | BRET MORRISON | PART 1 | PART 2 | | $12.00 | $25.00 |
| S-30 | 1 | NONE | THE KING'S NEW CLOTHES | FRANK LOESSER | PART 1 | PART 2 | | $5.00 | $10.00 |
| S-31 | 1 | NONE | THE UGLY DUCKLING/THE INCH WORM | FRANK LOESSER | THE UGLY DUCKLING | THE INCH WORM | | $5.00 | $10.00 |
| S-32 | 1 | NONE | TOM AND JERRY IN NURSERY RHYMELAND | BRET MORRISON | PART 1 | PART 2 | | $12.00 | $25.00 |
| S-34 | 1 | 30759 | HI-LILI, HI-LO/LILI AND THE PUPPETS | LESLIE CARON, MEL FERRER | HI-LILI, HI-LO | LILI AND THE PUPPETS | | $15.00 | $30.00 |
| S-35 | 1 | NONE | CASEY AT THE BAT | LIONEL BARRYMORE | PART 1 | PART 2 | | $15.00 | $30.00 |
| S-37 | 1 | NONE | SANTA AND THE DOODLE-LI-BOOP/THE STORY OF SANTA CLAUS | SAM ULANO/SANTA CLAUS | SANTA AND THE DOODLE-LI-BOOP | THE STORY OF SANTA CLAUS | | $5.00 | $10.00 |
| | 1 | 12243 | FORBIDDEN PLANET/THEME FROM THE SWAN | DAVID ROSE & HIS ORCH. | FORBIDDEN PLANET | THEME FROM THE SWAN | | $25.00 | $50.00 |

## MGM ALBUMS 10"

| SET # | # RECS | DISC # | MAIN TITLE | ARTIST | YEAR | G/VG | EX/NMT | REMARKS |
|---|---|---|---|---|---|---|---|---|
| 4 | 4 | 30021 – 4 | THE UNFINISHED DANCE | WALTER PIDGEON | 1947 | $5.00 | $10.00 | |
| 10A | 3 | 30045 – 7 | HALLOWEEN | LIONEL BARRYMORE | | $8.00 | $15.00 | |
| 12A | 4 | 30054 – 7 | THE BEAR THAT WASN'T | KEENAN WYNN | | $50.00 | $10.00 | |
| 13 | 4 | 10077 – 80 | A KIDDIE KORNCERT | THE KORN KOBBLERS | | $10.00 | $20.00 | |
| 14 | 4 | 30064 – 7 | SONGS OF FRIENDSHIP | IRVING CAESAR | | $10.00 | $20.00 | |
| 15 | 4 | 30069 – 72 | CHRISTMAS HYMNS AND CAROLS | CANTERBURY CHOIR, MAKLIN MARROW, COND | | $3.00 | $6.00 | |
| 16A | 4 | 30074 – 7 | A CHRISTMAS CAROL | LIONEL BARRYMORE, RICHARD HALE | | $8.00 | $15.00 | |
| 18 | 4 | 30085 – 8 | THE KING'S MEN: RED RIVER VALLEY, ETC. | THE KING'S MEN | | $2.00 | $4.00 | |
| 34A | 3 | 30155 – 7 | JOHNNY APPLESEED | KATE SMITH | | $10.00 | $20.00 | |
| 44A | 2 | 30213 – 4 | CHRISTMAS CAROLS | CANTERBURY CHOIR, MAKLIN MARROW, COND | | $2.00 | $4.00 | |
| 46A | 3 | 30215 – 7 | RIP VAN WINKLE | LIONEL BARRYMORE | 1949 | $8.00 | $15.00 | |
| 51A | 2 | 60002 – 3 | TOM AND JERRY AT THE CIRCUS | FRANCIS DESALES | 1950 | $20.00 | $40.00 | WITH BOOK SEWN IN |
| 110 | 3 | 30661 - 3 | ALI BABA AND THE FORTY THIEVES | LIONEL BARRYMORE | | $8.00 | $15.00 | |

## MGM 10" SINGLES

| # REC | DISC # | ARTIST | A TITLE | B TITLE | YEAR | G/VG | EX/NMT |
|---|---|---|---|---|---|---|---|
| 1 | 10139 | BOB WILLS & HIS TEXAS PLAY BOYS | CLOSED FOR REPAIRS | LITTLE COWBOY LULLABY | 1947 | $5.00 | $10.00 |
| 1 | 10178 | THE KING'S MEN | PECOS BILL | LITTLE TOOT | | $5.00 | $10.00 |
| 1 | 10512 | BOB WILLS & HIS TEXAS PLAYBOYS | WHEN IT'S CHRISTMAS ON THE RANGE | SANTA'S ON HIS WAY | – | $5.00 | $10.00 |
| 1 | 10523 | BLUE BARRON & HIS MUSIC | CHRISTMAS TIME | SANTA CLAUS IS COMIN' TO TOWN | – | $1.00 | $2.00 |
| 1 | 10557 | BOB HOUSTON | LEPRECHAUN LULLABY | JUST A KISS APART | 1949 | $1.00 | $2.00 |
| 1 | 10607 | BILLY ECKSTINE | YOU GO TO MY HEAD | OVER THE RAINBOW (FROM THE WIZARD OF OZ | - | $2.00 | $4.00 |
| 1 | 10657 | JUDY VALENTINE | I'D LIKE TO WRAP YOU UP | CINDERELLA WORK SONG | - | $2.00 | $4.00 |
| 1 | 10675 | DERRY FALLIGANT | PETER COTTONTAIL | LITTLE WHITE HORSE AND THE MARE | 1950 | $1.00 | $2.00 |
| 1 | 10959 | THE MELODEONS | THE LOLLIPOP TREE | THE UNBIRTHDAY SONG | | $1.00 | $2.00 |
| 1 | 11016 | LEROY HOLMES & HIS ORCHESTRA | LITTLE LEAGUE | TAKE ME OUT TO THE BALL GAME | | $3.00 | $6.00 |
| 1 | 11097 | TOMMY EDWARDS | CHRISTMAS IS FOR CHILDREN | KRIS KRINGLE | 1951 | $1.00 | $2.00 |
| 1 | 11098 | TEX BENEKE & HIS ORCHESTRA | THE SANTA CLAUS PARADE | A ROOTIN' TOOTIN' SANTA | | $1.00 | $2.00 |
| 1 | 11099 | MILTON DELUGG | SHAKE HANDS WITH SANTA CLAUS | THIRTY TWO FEET AND EIGHT LITTLE TAILS | | $1.00 | $2.00 |
| 1 | 11375 | BLUE BARRON | SANTA CLAUS LULLABY | THE LITTLE MATCH GIRL | | $1.00 | $2.00 |
| 1 | 11381 | BETTY CLARK | I SAW MOMMY KISSING SANTA CLAUS | YOU CAN FLY! YOU CAN FLY! | | $1.00 | $2.00 |
| 1 | 11411 | BUDDY DE FRANCO ORCH. | SUMMERTIME | OVER THE RAINBOW | | $1.00 | $2.00 |
| 1 | 11437 | LESLIE "UGGAMS" CRAYNE | EASTER BUNNY DAY | PERCY, THE PALE FACED POLAR BEAR | 1953 | $5.00 | $10.00 |
| 1 | 11476 | LESLIE "UGGAMS" CRAYNE | MY CANDY APPLE (PT. 1) | MY CANDY APPLE (PT. 2) | | $5.00 | $10.00 |
| 1 | 11624 | TOMMY EDWARDS | IT'S CHRISTMAS ONCE AGAIN | EVERYDAY IS CHRISTMAS | | $2.00 | $4.00 |
| 1 | 11625 | LITTLE RITA FAYE | I FELL OUT OF A CHRISTMAS TREE | THE MIRACLE OF CHRISTMAS | | $4.00 | $8.00 |
| 1 | 11626 | LESLIE "UGGAMS" CRAYNE | MISSUS SANTA CLAUS (PT. 1) | MISSUS SANTA CLAUS (PT. 2) | | $4.00 | $8.00 |
| 1 | 11755 | LESLIE "UGGAMS" CRAYNE | EV'RY LITTLE PIGGY'S GOT A CURLY TAIL | PALSY WALSY LAND | | $4.00 | $8.00 |
| 1 | 11757 | LITTLE RITA FAYE | DON'T YOU PLAY WITH BILLY | MOMMIE'S LITTLE HELPER | | $3.00 | $6.00 |
| 1 | 11867 | RITA FAYE | I WANT SANTA CLAUS FOR CHRISTMAS | THERE REALLY IS A SANTA CLAUS | | $3.00 | $6.00 |
| 1 | 11868 | LESLIE UGGAMS & FRED NORMAN | THE FAT FAT MAN. (WITH THE WHITE WHITE BEARD) | UNCLE SANTA. (SANTA BABY) | | $4.00 | $8.00 |
| 1 | 11870 | FRANK PETTY TRIO | JINGLE BELLS-MAMBO | RUDOLPH THE RED-NOSED REINDEER - MAMBO | | $1.00 | $2.00 |
| 1 | 11941 | JAMES BROWN & THE TRAIL WINDERS | THE BALLAD OF DAVY CROCKETT | HE'S A ROCKIN' HORSE COWBOY | 1955 | $5.00 | $10.00 |
| 1 | 11944 | RAY HANEY RIOGRANDE PLAYBOYS | LITTLE ONE, LEAN ONE, LONG ONE | WALKING AROUND OUTSIDE | | $1.00 | $2.00 |
| 1 | 11960 | JONI JAMES | WHEN YOU WISH UPON A STAR | IS THIS THE END OF THE LINE? | | $2.00 | $4.00 |
| 1 | 11963 | MARION SISTERS W JOE LIPMAN | HE'S A TRAMP | THE SIAMESE CAT SONG | | $2.00 | $4.00 |
| 1 | 11967 | KAY ARMEN | BELLA NOTTE | LA LA LU | | $4.00 | $8.00 |
| 1 | 11968 | FRANK PETTY TRIO | 10 LITTLE FINGERS, 10 LITTLE TOES | UNDER DOUBLE EAGLE MARCH | | $1.00 | $2.00 |

## MGM S-SERIES 10" SINGLE

| # REC | DISC # | ARTIST | A TITLE | B TITLE | YEAR | G/VG | EX/NMT |
|---|---|---|---|---|---|---|---|
| 1 | 12092 | ART MOONEY ORCH. | NUTTIN' FOR CHRISTMAS | SANTA LOOKS JUST LIKE DADDY | | $2.00 | $4.00 |
| 1 | 12243 | DAVID ROSE & ORCH. | FORBIDDEN PLANET | THEME FROM "THE SWAN" | 1956 | $25.00 | $50.00 |
| 1 | 12350 | JAMES BROWN & THE TRAIL WINDERS | FORWARD HO! | GHOST TOWN | | $5.00 | $10.00 |
| 1 | 12367 | BARRY GORDON | ZOOMAH, THE SANTA CLAUS FROM MARS | I LIKE CHRISTMAS | 1956 | $12.00 | $25.00 |
| 1 | 13316 | JOHNNY TILLOTSON | ANGEL (FROM DISNEY'S "THOSE CAL-LOWAYS") | I DON'T WANT TO LOVE YOU (LIKE I DO) | 1965 | $5.00 | $10.00 |
| 1 | 30176 | JIMMY DURANTE, BETTY GARRETT | THE PUSSY CAT SONG (NYOW! NYOT NYOW!) | ANY STATE IN THE FORTY EIGHT IS GREAT | 1948 | $5.00 | $10.00 |
| 1 | 30257 | JIMMY DURANTE | FROSTY THE SNOWMAN | CHRISTMAS COMES BUT ONCE A YEAR | 1950 | $5.00 | $10.00 |
| 1 | 30258 | LIONEL BARRYMORE | A VISIT FROM ST. NICHOLAS | NO ROOM AT THE INN | | $3.00 | $6.00 |
| 1 | 50009 | FRANKLIN MACCORMACK | I LIKE CHRISTMAS | MY NEW YEAR'S WISH FOR YOU | | $1.00 | $2.00 |

## MONTGOMERY WARD 10" SINGLES

| # REC | DISC # | MAIN TITLE | ARTIST | YEAR | G/VG | EX/NMT |
|---|---|---|---|---|---|---|
| 1 | M-4902 | FARMER IN THE DELL, ETC. | COMPILED BY RAY GOLD | 193? | $4.00 | $8.00 |
| 1 | M-7063 | SONGS FROM SHIRLEY TEMPLE SHOWS | ? | | $8.00 | $15.00 |
| 1 | M-7201 | POPEYE CARTOON SONGS | ORIGINAL CARTOON VOICES | | $15.00 | $30.00 |
| 1 | M-7211 | THE ORPHAN'S BENEFIT/MICKEY'S GRAND OPERA | ORIGINAL CARTOON VOICES | | $15.00 | $30.00 |
| 1 | M-7212 | MICKEY'S MOVING DAY/THE GRASSHOPPER AND THE ANTS | ORIGINAL CARTOON VOICES | | $15.00 | $30.00 |
| 1 | M-7549 | THE STORY BOOK BALL/DANCE OF THE TINKER TOYS | JIMMY RAY/KIDDIE KLOWNS ORCH. | | $3.00 | $6.00 |

## MOPPET 10" SINGLES

| SET # | # REC | DISC # | ARTIST | A TITLE | B TITLE | YEAR | G/VG | EX/NMT |
|---|---|---|---|---|---|---|---|---|
| 7001 | 1 | KS 1/2 | ? | ? | ? | 1954 | $4.00 | $8.00 |
| 7002 | 1 | KS 3/4 | ? | ? | ? | | $4.00 | $8.00 |
| 7003 | 1 | KS 5/6 | DICK "TWO TON" BAKER | CLINK-CLANK (IN MY PIGGY BANK) | THE FROGGY SONG | | $4.00 | $8.00 |
| 7004 | 1 | KS 7/8 | DICK "TWO TON" BAKER | I'M A LITTLE WEENIE | RUB-A-DUB DUB | | $4.00 | $8.00 |
| 7005 | 1 | KS 9/10 | ? | ? | ? | | $4.00 | $8.00 |
| 7006 | 1 | KS 11/12 | ? | ? | ? | | $4.00 | $8.00 |
| 7007 | 1 | KS 13/14 | SHERIFF SCOTTY | YOU'LL NEVER LOSE A FRIEND | ROCKIN' HORSE RODEO | | $10.00 | $20.00 |
| 7008 | 1 | KS 15/16 | SHERIFF SCOTTY | THE WONDERFUL LAND OF NU (PT. 1) | THE WONDERFUL LAND OF NU (PT. 2) | | $10.00 | $20.00 |

## MOUSKETEER T-V 7" SINGLES

| # REC | DISC # | MAIN TITLE | ARTIST | YEAR | G/VG | EX/NMT |
|---|---|---|---|---|---|---|
| 1 | 300-1/2 | DUMBO | NOT LISTED | CA. 1956 | $2.00 | $4.00 |
| 1 | 300-3/4 | PETER PAN | NOT LISTED | | $2.00 | $4.00 |
| 1 | 300-5/6 | PINOCCHIO | NOT LISTED | | $2.00 | $4.00 |
| 1 | 300-7/8 | SNOW WHITE | NOT LISTED | | $2.00 | $4.00 |
| 1 | 300-9/10 | BAMBI | NOT LISTED | | $2.00 | $4.00 |

## MUSETTE MUSICAL RADIO SCRIPT 10" SINGLES WITH BOOK

| # REC | DISC # | MAIN TITLE | ARTIST | YEAR | ALSO ISSUED ON | G/VG | EX/NMT |
|---|---|---|---|---|---|---|---|
| 1 | 343 | GINGERBREAD BOY | MILTON CROSS | 1940 | CARAVAN C-5 | $10.00 | $20.00 |
| 1 | 344 | CINDERELLA | MILTON CROSS | | CARAVAN C-2 | $10.00 | $20.00 |
| 1 | 345 | LITTLE RED RIDING HOOD | MILTON CROSS | | CARAVAN C-3 | $10.00 | $20.00 |
| 1 | 346 | SLEEPING BEAUTY | MILTON CROSS | | CARAVAN C-9 | $10.00 | $20.00 |
| 1 | 76510/1 | MOLLY PITCHER | MILTON CROSS | | | $10.00 | $20.00 |
| 1 | 76512/3 | LITTLE BLACK SAMBO | MILTON CROSS | | CARAVAN C-7 | $40.00 | $80.00 |
| 1 | Z 1/2 | CHRISTMAS EVE IN A TOY SHOP | MILTON CROSS | 1943 | CARAVAN C-8 | $10.00 | $20.00 |
| 1 | Z 3/4 | YOUNG BENJAMIN FRANKLIN | MILTON CROSS | | | $10.00 | $20.00 |
| 1 | Z 5/6 | YOUNG GEORGE WASHINGTON | MILTON CROSS | | | $10.00 | $20.00 |
| 1 | Z 7/8 | PUSS IN BOOTS | MILTON CROSS | | CARAVAN C-1 | $10.00 | $20.00 |

## MUSETTE JACK AND JILL SERIES 7" SINGLES WITH BOOK

| # REC | DISC # | ARTIST | A TITLE | B TITLE | YEAR | G/VG | EX/NMT |
|---|---|---|---|---|---|---|---|
| 1 | JJ-1 | TED DONALDSON, JACK & JILL SINGERS | JACK AND JILL, BAA BAA BLACK SHEEP | LONDON BRIDGE, LITTLE JACK HORNER | 1942 | $5.00 | $10.00 |
| 1 | JJ-2 | TED DONALDSON, JACK & JILL SINGERS | OLD KING COLE, PUSSY CAT | HUMPTY DUMPTY, MARY HAD A LITTLE LAMB | | $5.00 | $10.00 |
| 1 | JJ-3 | TED DONALDSON, JACK & JILL SINGERS | TWINKLE TWINKLE LITTLE STAR, ALPHABET SONG | HI DIDDLE DIDDLE, YANKEE DOODLE | | $5.00 | $10.00 |
| 1 | JJ-4 | TED DONALDSON, JACK & JILL SINGERS | POP GOES THE WEASEL, HICKORY DICKORY DOCK | ROUND THE MULBERRY BUSH | | $5.00 | $10.00 |
| 1 | JJ-5 | TED DONALDSON, JACK & JILL SINGERS | FARMER IN THE DELL, SING A SONG OF SIXPENCE | JINGLE BELLS | | $5.00 | $10.00 |
| 1 | JJ-6 | TED DONALDSON, JACK & JILL SINGERS | THREE BLIND MICE, ROW ROW ROW | TOM TOM THE PIPER'S SON, BYE BABY BUNTING | | $5.00 | $10.00 |

## MUSETTE ZOO-ZOO SONGS 5" SQUARE PICTURE DISCS IN PANELS

| # REC | DISC # | MAIN TITLE | ARTIST | YEAR | G/VG | EX/NMT |
|---|---|---|---|---|---|---|
| 1 | 1 | THE CHRISTMAS BUG/THE ELEPHANT AND THE TURTLE | SCOTTY MACGREGOR | 1947 | $25.00 | $50.00 |
| 1 | 2 | THE HAPPY LITTLE BUMBLE BEE/THE LITTLE BEAR WHO HAD NO HAIR | SCOTTY MACGREGOR | | $25.00 | $50.00 |
| 1 | 3 | THE DING-DONG SCHOOL/THE FOX AND HIS FRIENDS | SCOTTY MACGREGOR | | $25.00 | $50.00 |
| 1 | 4 | HOP, SKIP AND JUMP/THE PUPPY TALE | SCOTTY MACGREGOR | | $25.00 | $50.00 |
| 1 | 5 | THE LITTLE FISHY/THE SLOW, SLOW TURTLE | SCOTTY MACGREGOR | | $25.00 | $50.00 |

## MUSETTE SUPERMAN 7" PICTURE DISCS IN BOOK

| SET # | # REC | DISC # | MAIN TITLE | ARTIST | YEAR | G/VG | EX/NMT | REMARKS |
|---|---|---|---|---|---|---|---|---|
| NO. 1 | 2 | 1-2 | THE FLYING TRAIN | ORIGINAL RADIO CAST | 1947 | $50.00 | $100.00 | PRICE SHOWN IS FOR BOOK & RECORDS |
| NO. 2 | 2 | 1-2 | THE MAGIC RING | ORIGINAL RADIO CAST | | $50.00 | $100.00 | PRICE SHOWN IS FOR BOOK & RECORDS |
| N/A | N/A | N/A | VALUE OF LOOSE RECORDS FROM EITHER SET | | | $10.00 | $20.00 | |

## MUSETTE MISCELLANEOUS 10" SINGLES AND DOUBLES

| SET # | # REC | DISC # | MAIN TITLE | ARTIST | YEAR | G/VG | EX/NMT |
|---|---|---|---|---|---|---|---|
| M-001 | 1 | DA 1/2 | A CHILD'S DAY (RECORD # 1) | JANE MAYER, TED PODNOS ORCH. | 1953 | $3.00 | $6.00 |
| M-001 | 1 | DA 3/4 | A CHILD'S DAY (RECORD # 2) | JANE MAYER, TED PODNOS ORCH. | | | |
| NO # | 2 | NO. 1/2 | SING A SONG OF FRIENDSHIP (MUSETTE RECORDBOOK) | IRVING CAESAR | 194? | $20.00 | $40.00 |

## MUSICAL SOUND BOOKS EDWARD MACDOWELL SERIES 10" SINGLES

| # REC | DISC # | MAIN TITLE | ARTIST | YEAR | G/VG | EX/NMT |
|---|---|---|---|---|---|---|
| 1 | MSB 1 | OF A TAYLOR AND A BEAR | LILLIAN BALDWIN; SONDRA BIANCA, PIANIST | 1954 | $1.00 | $2.00 |
| 1 | MSB 2 | OF BR'ER RABBIT | LILLIAN BALDWIN; SONDRA BIANCA, PIANIST | | $1.00 | $2.00 |
| 1 | MSB 3 | TO A WATER LILY | LILLIAN BALDWIN; SONDRA BIANCA, PIANIST | | $1.00 | $2.00 |
| 1 | MSB 4 | FROM AN INDIAN LODGE | LILLIAN BALDWIN; SONDRA BIANCA, PIANIST | | $1.00 | $2.00 |
| 1 | MSB 5 | TO A WILD ROSE | LILLIAN BALDWIN; SONDRA BIANCA, PIANIST | | $1.00 | $2.00 |
| 1 | MSB 6 | WITCHES DANCE: TO A HUMMINGBIRD/WILL O' THE WISP | LILLIAN BALDWIN; SONDRA BIANCA, PIANIST | | $1.00 | $2.00 |
| 1 | MSB 7 | THE WITCH/THE CLOWN | LILLIAN BALDWIN; SONDRA BIANCA, PIANIST | | $1.00 | $2.00 |
| 1 | MSB 8 | AD 1620 | LILLIAN BALDWIN; SONDRA BIANCA, PIANIST | | $1.00 | $2.00 |

## MUSICAL SOUND BOOKS TINY MASTERPIECES (1954) 10" SINGLES

| # REC | DISC # | ARTIST | A TITLE | B TITLE | YEAR | G/VG | EX/NMT |
|---|---|---|---|---|---|---|---|
| 1 | MSB 21 | LILLIAN BALDWIN; SONDRA BIANCA, PIANIST | HICKORY DICKORY DOCK | THE NORTH WIND DOTH BLOW | 1954 | $1.00 | $2.00 |
| 1 | MSB 22 | LILLIAN BALDWIN; SONDRA BIANCA, PIANIST | AT WORK (A CHILD'S DAY) | DANCE OF THE SWALLOWS/PUSSY IS ILL | | $1.00 | $2.00 |
| 1 | MSB 23 | LILLIAN BALDWIN; SONDRA BIANCA, PIANIST | MY DEAR MUMMIE | SUNBEAM PLAY | | $1.00 | $2.00 |
| 1 | MSB 24 | LILLIAN BALDWIN; SONDRA BIANCA, PIANIST | THE FIRST SWALLOW | MAZURKA OF THE MICE/THE FOX | | $1.00 | $2.00 |
| 1 | MSB 25 | LILLIAN BALDWIN; SONDRA BIANCA, PIANIST | ROUNDELAY/LONDONDERRY AIR | WALTZ IN A FLAT | | $1.00 | $2.00 |
| 1 | MSB 26 | LILLIAN BALDWIN; SONDRA BIANCA, PIANIST | LITTLE WINDMILLS IN THE BREEZE | SISTER MONICA | | $1.00 | $2.00 |
| 1 | MSB 27 | LILLIAN BALDWIN; SONDRA BIANCA, PIANIST | MINUET IN G | MARCH IN D | | $1.00 | $2.00 |

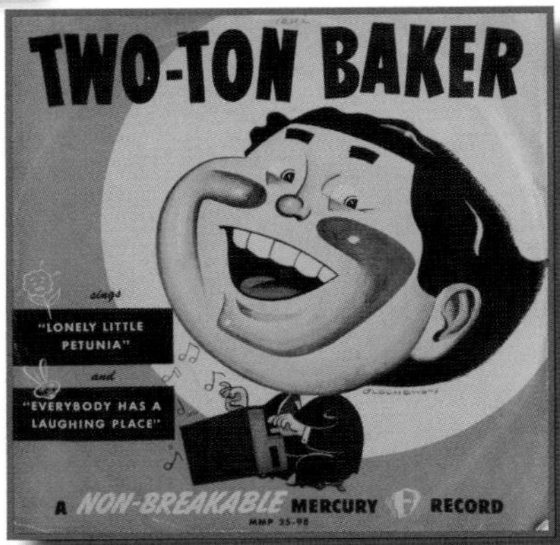


MERCURY RECORDS
LONELY LITTLE PETUNIA
$10.00

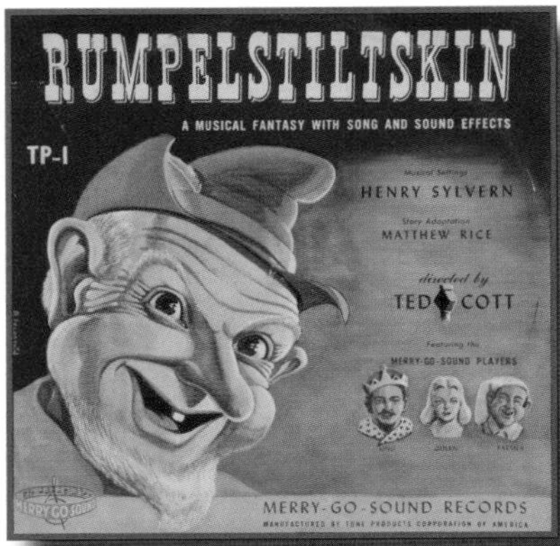


MERRY-GO-SOUND RECORDS
RUMPLESTILTSKIN
$6.00

MGM RECORDS
IRVING THE UNEMPLOYED HORSE
$20.00

## MUSICAL SOUND BOOKS TINY MASTERPIECES (1954) 10" SINGLES

| # REC | DISC # | MAIN TITLE | ARTIST | YEAR | G/VG | EX/NMT |
|---|---|---|---|---|---|---|
| 1 | MSB-78001 | HANDEL: WATER MUSIC — SELECTIONS | PHILHARMONIA ORCHESTRA OF HAMBURG; HANS-JURGEN WALTHER, COND. | 1954 | $1.00 | $2.00 |
| 1 | MSB-78002 | HANDEL: FIREWORKS MUSIC — SELECTIONS | PHILHARMONIA ORCHESTRA OF HAMBURG; HANS-JURGEN WALTHER, COND. | | $1.00 | $2.00 |
| 1 | MSB-78003 | MOZART: THE LITTLE NOTHINGS, ETC. | PHILHARMONIA ORCHESTRA OF HAMBURG; HANS-JURGEN WALTHER, COND. | | $1.00 | $2.00 |
| 1 | MSB-78004 | MOZART: EINE KLEINE NACHTMUSIK, ETC. | PHILHARMONIA ORCHESTRA OF HAMBURG; HANS-JURGEN WALTHER, COND. | | $1.00 | $2.00 |
| 1 | MSB-78005 | GHYS: AMARYLLIS/SCHUBERT: MARCHE MILITAIRE | PHILHARMONIA ORCHESTRA OF HAMBURG; HANS-JURGEN WALTHER, COND. | | $1.00 | $2.00 |
| 1 | MSB-78006 | SCHUMANN: SCENES FROM CHILDHOOD | SONDRA BIANCA, PIANIST | | $1.00 | $2.00 |
| 1 | MSB-78007 | SCHUMANN: SCENES FROM CHILDHOOD | SONDRA BIANCA, PIANIST | | $1.00 | $2.00 |
| 1 | MSB-78008 | BIZET: CHILDREN'S GAMES | SONDRA BIANCA, FELICE TAKAJIAN | | $1.00 | $2.00 |
| 1 | MSB-78009 | BIZET: CHILDREN'S GAMES | SONDRA BIANCA, FELICE TAKAJIAN | | $1.00 | $2.00 |
| 1 | MSB-78010 | SAINT-SAENS: CARNIVAL OF THE ANIMALS | SONDRA BIANCA, GERHARDT ARNOLDI, PHIL. ORCH. OF HAMBURG | | $1.00 | $2.00 |
| 1 | MSB-78011 | SAINT-SAENS: CARNIVAL OF THE ANIMALS | SONDRA BIANCA, GERHARDT ARNOLDI, PHIL. ORCH. OF HAMBURG | | $1.00 | $2.00 |
| 1 | MSB-78012 | SAINT-SAENS: CARNIVAL OF THE ANIMALS | SONDRA BIANCA, GERHARDT ARNOLDI, PHIL. ORCH. OF HAMBURG | | $1.00 | $2.00 |
| 1 | MSB-78013 | RAVEL: THE MOTHER GOOSE SUITE | SONDRA BIANCA, PIANIST | | $1.00 | $2.00 |
| 1 | MSB-78014 | RAVEL: THE MOTHER GOOSE SUITE | SONDRA BIANCA, PIANIST | | $1.00 | $2.00 |
| 1 | MSB-78015 | PIERNE: ENTRANCE OF THE LITTLE FAUNS/MARCH OF THE LITTLE LEAD SOLDIERS | PHILHARMONIA ORCHESTRA OF HAMBURG; HANS-JURGEN WALTHER, COND. | | $1.00 | $2.00 |
| 1 | MSB-78016 | POLDINI: THE DANCING DOLL/LLADOV: DANCE OF THE MOS-QUITO, THE MUSIC BOX | SONDRA BIANCA, PIANIST | | $1.00 | $2.00 |
| 1 | MSB-78017 | LLADOV: THE ENCHANTED LAKE | PHILHARMONIA ORCHESTRA OF HAMBURG; HANS-JURGEN WALTHER, COND. | | $1.00 | $2.00 |
| 1 | MSB-78018 | MACDOWELL: FROM UNCLE REMUS, OF BR'ER RABBIT/A DE-SERTED FARM | SONDRA BIANCA, PIANIST | | $1.00 | $2.00 |

## MUSICAL SOUND BOOKS RED SECTION 10" SINGLES

| # REC | DISC # | MAIN TITLE | ARTIST | YEAR | G/VG | EX/NMT |
|---|---|---|---|---|---|---|
| 1 | MSB-78019 | BOCCHERINI: MINUET/TCHAIKOVSKY: STRING QUAR-TET NO. | THE BARTELS ENSEMBLE OF HAMBURG | 1953 | $1.00 | $2.00 |
| 1 | MSB-78020 | THE NELL GWYN SUITE,T ETC. | PHILHARMONIA ORCHESTRA OF HAMBURG; HANS-JURGEN WALTHER, COND. | | $1.00 | $2.00 |
| 1 | MSB-78021 | STRAUSS: BLUE DANUBE WALTZ/GOUNOD: FUNERAL MARCH OF A MARIONETTE | PHILHARMONIA ORCHESTRA OF HAMBURG; HANS-JURGEN WALTHER, COND. | | $1.00 | $2.00 |
| 1 | MSB-78022 | QUILTER: A CHILDREN'S OVERTURE | PHILHARMONIA ORCHESTRA OF HAMBURG; HANS-JURGEN WALTHER, COND. | | $1.00 | $2.00 |
| 1 | MSB-78023 | OH VERMELAND!/LONDONDERRY AIR | PHILHARMONIA ORCHESTRA OF HAMBURG; HANS-JURGEN WALTHER, COND. | | $1.00 | $2.00 |

## MUSICAL SOUND BOOKS RED SECTION 10" SINGLES

| # REC | DISC # | MAIN TITLE | ARTIST | YEAR | G/VG | EX/NMT |
|---|---|---|---|---|---|---|
| 1 | MSB-78024 | DOTT: JUBA DANCE, ETC./SKILTON: WAR DANCE, DUBENSKY: GOSSIPS | PHILHARMONIA ORCHESTRA OF HAMBURG; HANS-JURGEN WALTHER, COND. | | $1.00 | $2.00 |
| 1 | MSB-78025 | MENDELSSOHN: A MIDSUMMER NIGHT'S DREAM | PHILHARMONIA ORCHESTRA OF HAMBURG; HANS-JURGEN WALTHER, COND. | | $1.00 | $2.00 |
| 1 | MSB-78026 | MENDELSSOHN: A MIDSUMMER NIGHT'S DREAM | PHILHARMONIA ORCHESTRA OF HAMBURG; HANS-JURGEN WALTHER, COND. | | $1.00 | $2.00 |
| 1 | MSB-78027 | MENDELSSOHN: A MIDSUMMER NIGHT'S DREAM | PHILHARMONIA ORCHESTRA OF HAMBURG; HANS-JURGEN WALTHER, COND. | | $1.00 | $2.00 |
| 1 | MSB-78028 | MENDELSSOHN: A MIDSUMMER NIGHT'S DREAM | PHILHARMONIA ORCHESTRA OF HAMBURG; HANS-JURGEN WALTHER, COND. | | $1.00 | $2.00 |
| 1 | MSB-78029 | GRIEG: PEER GYNT MUSIC | PHILHARMONIA ORCHESTRA OF HAMBURG; HANS-JURGEN WALTHER, COND. | | $1.00 | $2.00 |
| 1 | MSB-78030 | GRIEG: PEER GYNT MUSIC | PHILHARMONIA ORCHESTRA OF HAMBURG; HANS-JURGEN WALTHER, COND. | | $1.00 | $2.00 |
| 1 | MSB-78031 | GRIEG: PEER GYNT MUSIC | PHILHARMONIA ORCHESTRA OF HAMBURG; HANS-JURGEN WALTHER, COND. | | $1.00 | $2.00 |
| 1 | MSB-78032 | GRIEG: MARCH OF THE DWARFS/MARCH OF ALLEGIANCE | PHILHARMONIA ORCHESTRA OF HAMBURG; HANS-JURGEN WALTHER, COND. | | $1.00 | $2.00 |
| 1 | MSB-78033 | TCHAIKOVSKY: THE NUTCRACKER SUITE | PHILHARMONIA ORCHESTRA OF HAMBURG; HANS-JURGEN WALTHER, COND. | | $1.00 | $2.00 |
| 1 | MSB-78034 | TCHAIKOVSKY: THE NUTCRACKER SUITE | PHILHARMONIA ORCHESTRA OF HAMBURG; HANS-JURGEN WALTHER, COND. | | $1.00 | $2.00 |
| 1 | MSB-78035 | TCHAIKOVSKY: THE NUTCRACKER SUITE | PHILHARMONIA ORCHESTRA OF HAMBURG; HANS-JURGEN WALTHER, COND. | | $1.00 | $2.00 |
| 1 | MSB-78036 | DEBUSSY: THE CHILDREN'S CORNER SUITE | SONDRA BIANCA, PIANIST | | $1.00 | $2.00 |
| 1 | MSB-78037 | DEBUSSY: THE CHILDREN'S CORNER SUITE | SONDRA BIANCA, PIANIST | | $1.00 | $2.00 |
| 1 | MSB-78038 | COATES: THE THREE BEARS | SONDRA BIANCA, PIANIST | | $1.00 | $2.00 |

## MUSICAL SOUND BOOKS BLUE SECTION 10" SINGLES

| # REC | DISC # | MAIN TITLE | ARTIST | YEAR | G/VG | EX/NMT |
|---|---|---|---|---|---|---|
| 1 | MSB-78039 | SCARLATTI: THE CAT'S FUGUE, PASTORALE/BACH: MINUET, MARCH | HANNELORE UNRUH, HARPSICHORDIST | 1954 | $1.00 | $2.00 |
| 1 | MSB-78040 | BACH: SUITE NO. 3 IN D MAJ: AIR/GAVOTTES I & II | PHILHARMONIA ORCHESTRA OF HAMBURG; HANS-JURGEN WALTHER, COND. | | $1.00 | $2.00 |
| 1 | MSB-78041 | BACH: SUITE NO. 3 IN D MAJOR: BOURREE, GIGUE/CHRISTMAS ORATORIO: 2 CHORALES | BALDWIN-WALLACE BACH FEST. CHORUS | | $1.00 | $2.00 |
| 1 | MSB-78042 | HAYDN: THE SURPRISE SYMPHONY (ANDANTE)/THE EMPEROR'S HYMN | THE BARTELS ENSEMBLE | | $1.00 | $2.00 |
| 1 | MSB-78043 | HAYDN: THE TOY SYMPHONY | PHILHARMONIA ORCHESTRA OF HAMBURG; HANS-JURGEN WALTHER, COND. | | $1.00 | $2.00 |
| 1 | MSB-78044 | CHOPIN: POLONAISE IN A MAJOR OP 40/PRELUDE IN D FLAT NO. 15 | ? | | $1.00 | $2.00 |
| 1 | MSB-78045 | TOCH: PINOCCHIO — A MERRY OVERTURE | PHILHARMONIA ORCHESTRA OF HAMBURG; HANS-JURGEN WALTHER, COND. | | $1.00 | $2.00 |
| 1 | MSB-78046 | GLUCK: DANCE OF THE FURIES/DANCE OF THE HAPPY SPIRITS | PHILHARMONIA ORCHESTRA OF HAMBURG; HANS-JURGEN WALTHER, COND. | | $1.00 | $2.00 |
| 1 | MSB-78047 | ROSSINI: OVERTURE TO WILLIAM TELL | PHILHARMONIA ORCHESTRA OF HAMBURG; HANS-JURGEN WALTHER, COND. | | $1.00 | $2.00 |
| 1 | MSB-78048 | ROSSINI: OVERTURE TO WILLIAM TELL/VERDI: TRIUMPHAL MARCH FROM AIDA | PHILHARMONIA ORCHESTRA OF HAMBURG; HANS-JURGEN WALTHER, COND. | | $1.00 | $2.00 |
| 1 | MSB-78049 | WAGNER: THE VALKYRIES | PHILHARMONIA ORCHESTRA OF HAMBURG; HANS-JURGEN WALTHER, COND. | | $1.00 | $2.00 |
| 1 | MSB-78050 | RIMSKY-KORSAKOV: SONG OF INDIA, FLIGHT OF THE BUMBLEBEE/DANCE OF THE CLOWNS | PHILHARMONIA ORCHESTRA OF HAMBURG; HANS-JURGEN WALTHER, COND. | | $1.00 | $2.00 |
| 1 | MSB-78051 | HUMPERDINCK: HANSEL AND GRETEL | PHILHARMONIA ORCHESTRA OF HAMBURG; HANS-JURGEN WALTHER, COND. | | $1.00 | $2.00 |

## MUSICAL SOUND BOOKS MUSIC TO REMEMBER 10" SINGLES

| # REC | DISC # | MAIN TITLE | ARTIST | YEAR | G/VG | EX/NMT |
|---|---|---|---|---|---|---|
| 1 | 78101 | CORELLI: SUITE FOR STRINGS* | HAMBURG CHAMBER ORCHESTRA; HANS-JURGEN WALTHER, CONDUCTOR | 1954 | $1.00 | $2.00 |
| 1 | 78102 | PROKOFIEV: CLASSICAL SYMPHONY* | PHILHARMONIA ORCHESTRA OF HAMBURG; HANS-JURGEN WALTHER, COND. | | $1.00 | $2.00 |
| 1 | 78103 | BOLZONI: MINUETTO* | HAMBURG CHAMBER ORCHESTRA; HANS-JURGEN WALTHER, CONDUCTOR | | $1.00 | $2.00 |
| 1 | 78104 | STRAUSS: VOICES OF SPRING/SHOSTAKOVICH: THE GOLDEN AGE (POLKA)* | PHILHARMONIA ORCHESTRA OF HAMBURG; HANS-JURGEN WALTHER, COND. | | $1.00 | $2.00 |

*CLASSIC DANCE TYPES: THE BEGINNING OF INSTRUMENTAL MUSIC

## MUSICAL SOUND BOOKS MUSIC TO REMEMBER 10" SINGLES

| # REC | DISC # | MAIN TITLE | ARTIST | G/VG | EX/NMT |
|---|---|---|---|---|---|
| 1 | 78105 | BRAHMS: LIEBESLIEDER WALTZES* | SONDRA BIANCA AND GERHARD ARNOLDI, PIANISTS | $1.00 | $2.00 |
| 1 | 78106 | BRAHMS: LIEBESLIEDER WALTZES* | SONDRA BIANCA AND GERHARD ARNOLDI, PIANISTS | $1.00 | $2.00 |
| 1 | 78107 | CHOPIN: WALTZ IN C-SHARP MINOR/FANTASIE IMROMPTU* | SONDRA BIANCA, PIANIST | $1.00 | $2.00 |
| 1 | 78108 | TCHAIKOVSKY:SLEEPING BEAUTY WALTZ/SIBELIUS: VALSE TRIESTE* | PHILHARMONIA ORCHESTRA OF HAMBURG; HANS-JURGEN WALTHER, COND. | $1.00 | $2.00 |
| 1 | 78109 | SMETANA: THE BARTERED BRIDE** | PHILHARMONIA ORCHESTRA OF HAMBURG; HANS-JURGEN WALTHER, COND. | $1.00 | $2.00 |
| 1 | 78110 | BRAHMS: HUNGARIAN DANCES 5 & 6** | PHILHARMONIA ORCHESTRA OF HAMBURG; HANS-JURGEN WALTHER, COND. | $1.00 | $2.00 |
| 1 | 78111 | DVORAK: SLAVONIC DANCES 1, 3** | PHILHARMONIA ORCHESTRA OF HAMBURG; HANS-JURGEN WALTHER, COND. | $1.00 | $2.00 |
| 1 | 78112 | DVORAK: SLAVONIC DANCE 10/MUSSORGSKY: GOPAK** | PHILHARMONIA ORCHESTRA OF HAMBURG; HANS-JURGEN WALTHER, COND. | $1.00 | $2.00 |
| 1 | 78113 | GRAINGER: SHEPHERD'S HEY/COUNTRY GARDENS, MOLLY ON THE SHORE (DANCES)** | PHILHARMONIA ORCHESTRA OF HAMBURG; HANS-JURGEN WALTHER, COND. | $1.00 | $2.00 |
| 1 | 78114 | LECUONA: MALAGUENA/CAILLET: POP GOES THE WEASEL (VARIATIONS)** | PHILHARMONIA ORCHESTRA OF HAMBURG; HANS-JURGEN WALTHER, COND. | $1.00 | $2.00 |
| 1 | 78115 | MEXICANA (THREE MEXICAN SONGS)** | PHILHARMONIA ORCHESTRA OF HAMBURG; HANS-JURGEN WALTHER, COND. | $1.00 | $2.00 |
| 1 | 78116 | MENDELSSOHN: WAR MARCH OF THE PRIESTS/ GOUNOD: CORTEGE FROM THE QUEEN OF SHEBA*** | PHILHARMONIA ORCHESTRA OF HAMBURG; HANS-JURGEN WALTHER, COND. | $1.00 | $2.00 |
| 1 | 78117 | WAGNER: FESTIVAL MARCH FROM TANNHAUSER*** | PHILHARMONIA ORCHESTRA OF HAMBURG; HANS-JURGEN WALTHER, COND. | $1.00 | $2.00 |
| 1 | 78118 | TCHAIKOVSKY: SYMPHONY PATETIQUE (MARCH-SCHERZO)*** | PHILHARMONIA ORCHESTRA OF HAMBURG; HANS-JURGEN WALTHER, COND. | $1.00 | $2.00 |
| 1 | 78119 | GOUNOD: FUNERAL MARCH OF A MARIONETTE/ HALVORSEN: TRIUMPHAL ENTRANCE OF THE BOYARDS*** | PHILHARMONIA ORCHESTRA OF HAMBURG; HANS-JURGEN WALTHER, COND. | $1.00 | $2.00 |
| 1 | 78120 | ELGAR: POMP CIRCUMSTANCE NO. 1/SOUSA: THE STARS & STRIPES FOREVER*** | PHILHARMONIA ORCHESTRA OF HAMBURG; HANS-JURGEN WALTHER, COND. | $1.00 | $2.00 |
| 1 | 78121 | WEBER: INVITATION TO THE DANCE**** | PHILHARMONIA ORCHESTRA OF HAMBURG; HANS-JURGEN WALTHER, COND. | $1.00 | $2.00 |
| 1 | 78122 | CHABRIER: RHAPSODY ESPANA**** | PHILHARMONIA ORCHESTRA OF HAMBURG; HANS-JURGEN WALTHER, COND. | $1.00 | $2.00 |
| 1 | 78123 | GRIEG: HEAR WOUNDS, THE LAST SPRING**** | PHILHARMONIA ORCHESTRA OF HAMBURG; HANS-JURGEN WALTHER, COND. | $1.00 | $2.00 |
| 1 | 78124 | SAINT-SAENS: THE DANCE OF DEATH**** | PHILHARMONIA ORCHESTRA OF HAMBURG; HANS-JURGEN WALTHER, COND. | $1.00 | $2.00 |
| 1 | 78125 | SAINT-SAENS: PHAETON**** | PHILHARMONIA ORCHESTRA OF HAMBURG; HANS-JURGEN WALTHER, COND. | $1.00 | $2.00 |
| 1 | 78126 | SAINT-SAENS: OMPHALE'S SPINNING WHEEL**** | PHILHARMONIA ORCHESTRA OF HAMBURG; HANS-JURGEN WALTHER, COND. | $1.00 | $2.00 |
| 1 | 78127 | RESPIGHI: THE PINES OF ROME: ...OF THE VILLA BORGHESE/...NEAR A CATACOMB**** | PHILHARMONIA ORCHESTRA OF HAMBURG; HANS-JURGEN WALTHER, COND. | $1.00 | $2.00 |
| 1 | 78128 | RESPIGHI: THE PINES OF ROME: ...OF THE JANICULUM/...OF THE APPIAN WAY**** | PHILHARMONIA ORCHESTRA OF HAMBURG; HANS-JURGEN WALTHER, COND. | $1.00 | $2.00 |
| 1 | 78129 | SIEGMEISTER: MORNING IN THE HILLS/CAMP MEETING**** | PHILHARMONIA ORCHESTRA OF HAMBURG; HANS-JURGEN WALTHER, COND. | $1.00 | $2.00 |
| 1 | 78130 | SIEGMEISTER: LAZY AFTERNOON/SATURDAY NIGHT**** | PHILHARMONIA ORCHESTRA OF HAMBURG; HANS-JURGEN WALTHER, COND. | $1.00 | $2.00 |
| 1 | 78131 | WEBER: OBERON: OVERTURE***** | PHILHARMONIA ORCHESTRA OF HAMBURG; HANS-JURGEN WALTHER, COND. | $1.00 | $2.00 |
| 1 | 78132 | NICOLAI: THE MERRY WIVES OF WINDSOR***** | PHILHARMONIA ORCHESTRA OF HAMBURG; HANS-JURGEN WALTHER, COND. | $1.00 | $2.00 |
| 1 | 78133 | WAGNER: LOHENGRIN: PRELUED, ACT III/WEDDING MUSIC***** | PHILHARMONIA ORCHESTRA OF HAMBURG; HANS-JURGEN WALTHER, COND. | $1.00 | $2.00 |
| 1 | 78134 | WAGNER: SIEGFRIED: FOREST MURMURS***** | PHILHARMONIA ORCHESTRA OF HAMBURG; HANS-JURGEN WALTHER, COND. | $1.00 | $2.00 |
| 1 | 78135 | WAGNER: MASTERSINGERS OF NUREMBERG: DANCE OF THE APPRENTICES, ET AL. ***** | PHILHARMONIA ORCHESTRA OF HAMBURG; HANS-JURGEN WALTHER, COND. | $1.00 | $2.00 |
| 1 | 78136 | BIZET: SUITE FROM CARMEN: SOLDIERS CHANGING THE GUARD/GYPSY DANCE***** | PHILHARMONIA ORCHESTRA OF HAMBURG; HANS-JURGEN WALTHER, COND. | $1.00 | $2.00 |
| 1 | 78137 | BIZET: SUITE FROM CARMEN: INTERMEZZO/ MARCH OF THE SMUGGLERS***** | PHILHARMONIA ORCHESTRA OF HAMBURG; HANS-JURGEN WALTHER, COND. | $1.00 | $2.00 |
| 1 | 78138 | GILBERT: IOLANTHE: OVERTURE***** | PHILHARMONIA ORCHESTRA OF HAMBURG; HANS-JURGEN WALTHER, COND. | $1.00 | $2.00 |
| 1 | 78139 | WOLF-FERRARI: THE JEWELS OF THE MADONNA: INTERMEZZI ACTS I & II***** | PHILHARMONIA ORCHESTRA OF HAMBURG; HANS-JURGEN WALTHER, COND. | $1.00 | $2.00 |
| 1 | 78140 | ? | PHILHARMONIA ORCHESTRA OF HAMBURG; HANS-JURGEN WALTHER, COND. | $1.00 | $2.00 |
| 1 | 78141 | ? | PHILHARMONIA ORCHESTRA OF HAMBURG; HANS-JURGEN WALTHER, COND. | $1.00 | $2.00 |
| 1 | 78142 | ? | PHILHARMONIA ORCHESTRA OF HAMBURG; HANS-JURGEN WALTHER, COND. | $1.00 | $2.00 |
| 1 | 78143 | ? | PHILHARMONIA ORCHESTRA OF HAMBURG; HANS-JURGEN WALTHER, COND. | $1.00 | $2.00 |
| 1 | 78144 | BEETHOVEN: RAGE OVER A LOST PENNY: RONDO, CAPRICCIOSO | PHILHARMONIA ORCHESTRA OF HAMBURG; HANS-JURGEN WALTHER, COND. | $1.00 | $2.00 |

*CLASSIC DANCE TYPES: THE BEGINNING OF INSTRUMENTAL MUSIC **TONE POEMS: MUSIC WITH POETIC IDEAS ***THE MARCH: A RHYTHMIC FORM OF MANY MOODS ****NATIONAL DANCES: THE TOUCH OF LOCAL COLOR *****THE STAGE: MUSIC FROM THE THEATER

## PETER PAN MAIN SERIES INCLUDING L, P, AND X SERIES 7" SINGLES

| # REC | DISC # | ARTIST | A TITLE | B TITLE | YEAR | ALSO ISSUED ON | G/VG | EX/NMT |
|---|---|---|---|---|---|---|---|---|
| 1 | 385 | FRANKIE STARR, PPO, VK/? | THE LITTLE ENGINE THAT COULD | ? | | | $1.00 | $2.00 |
| 1 | 387 | MICHAEL REED, PPO, VK/ JACK ARTHUR, VK | TUBBY THE TUBA | BLUE TAIL FLY, SKIP TO MY LOU, CLEMENTINE, MEXICAN HAT DANCE | | | $2.00 | $4.00 |
| 1 | 388 | ?/JA, PPO, VK | SWINGIN' ON A STAR | STARS AND STRIPES FOREVER | | | $1.00 | $2.00 |
| 1 | 389 | THE BRIGADIERS, PPO, VK/JA, VK | THE JONES BOY | GET ALONG LITTLE DOGIE, POLLY WOLLY DOODLE | | 372-B | $1.00 | $2.00 |
| 1 | 390 | MICHAEL REED, PPO, VK/ JA, VK | EASTER PARADE | TEDDY BEARS ON PARADE (AKA THE TEDDY BEARS POLKA) | | | $1.00 | $2.00 |
| 1 | 392 | PPO, VK/DANNY STEVENS, THE FOUR SERGEANTS, PPO, VK | THE SYNCOPATED CLOCK | THE LITTLE TIN SOLDIER (AND THE LITTLE TOY DRUM) | | 357-A | $1.00 | $2.00 |
| 1 | 393 | PPO, VK/THE FAIRYLAND PLAYERS | DOWN BY THE STATION | THE ALPHABET SONG | | | $1.00 | $2.00 |
| 1 | 395 | LEE ADAMS, PPO, VK/ PPO, PM | LET'S ALL SING LIKE THE BIRDIES SING | GOOD MORNING MERRY SUNSHINE, RIG A JIG JIG | | | $1.00 | $2.00 |
| 1 | 396 | TIPPY BROWN, PPO, VK/ JA, VK | CHOO'N GUM | CLEMENTINE, MEXICAN HAT DANCE | | | $1.00 | $2.00 |
| 1 | 397 | DALE LORING, PPO, VK/ JA, VK | OPEN UP YOUR HEART (AND LET THE SUNSHINE IN) | JESUS LOVES ME, CHILDREN OF THE HEAVENLY KING | 1955 | | $1.00 | $2.00 |
| 1 | 398 A/ 2297 B | DALE LORING, PPO, VK/ PPO, PM | COUNT YOUR BLESSINGS | ALL AROUND MULBERRY BUSH: DID YOU EVER SEE A LASSIE, BABY BUNTING | | | $1.00 | $2.00 |
| 1 | 398 A/ 398 B | DALE LORING, PPO, VK/BW | COUNT YOUR BLESSINGS | HOME ON THE RANGE, CHISHOLM TRAIL | | | $1.00 | $2.00 |
| 1 | 399 | LEE ADAMS, THE CRICKETS, PPO, VK/BW | TWEEDLEE DEE | BIG ROCK CANDY MOUNTAIN, CAMPTOWN RACES, OH SUSANNA | | | $1.00 | $2.00 |
| 1 | 400 | ?/PPO | THIS OLD HOUSE | OLD MACDONALD HAD A FARM | | | $1.00 | $2.00 |
| 1 | 402 | PPO, VK/BW | ORGAN GRINDER'S SWING | HOME ON THE RANGE, THE OLD CHISHOLM TRAIL | | | $1.00 | $2.00 |
| 1 | 403 | BOB TOWERS, PPO, VK/ JA: VK | THE BALLAD OF DAVY CROCKETT | RED RIVER VALLEY, ARKANSAS TRAVELER | | | $3.00 | $6.00 |
| 1 | 404 | BETTY WELLS, JIMMY WES, PPO, SYL STEWART, DIR.(SS)/JA, VK | LITTLE SIR ECHO | PONY BOY, BUFFALO GALS | | | $1.00 | $2.00 |
| 1 | 405 | MICHAEL REED, PPO, VK/ JA, VK | WAY BACK HOME | FOLK SONGS: BLUE TAIL FLY, SKIP TO MY LOU | | | $1.00 | $2.00 |
| 1 | 406 | JOHNNY SWIFT, PPO, VK/ PPO, PM | POPCORN MAN | BILLY BOY | | | $1.00 | $2.00 |
| 1 | 408 | LEE ADAMS, PPO, VK/ PPO, VK | GRANDFATHER'S CLOCK | THE STARS AND STRIPES FOREVER | | | $1.00 | $2.00 |
| 1 | 409 | LEE ADAMS, THE CRICKETS, PPO, VK/JA, PPO, VK | WHERE WILL THE DIMPLE BE? | MARCHING SONGS: STARS AND STRIPES FOREVER, YANKEE DOODLE | | | $1.00 | $2.00 |
| 1 | 410 | ?/JA, PPO, VK | DANCE WITH ME HENRY | MARCHING SONGS | | | $1.00 | $2.00 |
| 1 | 411 | FRANKIE STAR, THE CRICKETS, PPO, VK/JA, VK | THE BERRY TREE | TEDDY BEARS ON PARADE (AKA THE TEDDY BEARS POLKA) | | | $1.00 | $2.00 |
| 1 | 412 | PPO, VK/JOHNNY CORVO, PPO, THE SATISFIERS, VK | HEY, MR. BANJO | PONY ON THE MERRY-GO-ROUND | | | $1.00 | $2.00 |
| 1 | 413 | PPO, VK/JA, PPO, VK | THE YELLOW ROSE OF TEXAS | MARCHING SONGS: STARS AND STRIPES FOREVER, YANKEE DOODLE | | | $1.00 | $2.00 |
| 1 | 414 | FRANKIE STAR, THE CRICKETS, PPO, VK/JA, VK | TINA MARIE | RED RIVER VALLEY, ARKANSAS TRAVELER | | | $1.00 | $2.00 |
| 1 | 415 | FRANKIE STAR, PPO, VK/ JA, PPO, VK | A BOY IN BUCKSKIN (AND A GAL IN CALICO) | STARS AND STRIPES FOREVER | 1956 | | $1.00 | $2.00 |
| 1 | 416 | THE CRICKETS, PPO, SS/ LINDA BARRIE, PPO, VK | FUNNY LITTLE BUNNIES | SILLY EASTER BONNET | | | $1.00 | $2.00 |
| 1 | 417 | PPO, VK | TAP DANCE RECORD, PT I: EAST SIDE, WEST SIDE, THE BAND PLAYED ON | TAP DANCE RECORD — PT. II: A BICYCLE BUILT FOR TWO; EAST SIDE, WEST SIDE | | | $4.00 | $8.00 |
| 1 | 418 | PPO, VK/PPO, PM | MEXICAN CLAP HANDS — CHIAPENACAS | FRERE JACQUES | | | $1.00 | $2.00 |
| 1 | 420 | THE HIGHLAND LADS, PPO, SS/PPO, VK | MY BONNIE LASSIE | RIFLE REGIMENT | | | $1.00 | $2.00 |
| 1 | 421 | FRANKIE STARR, PPO, SS/ PETER PAN CAROLEERS, VK | THERE'S NO PLACE LIKE HOME FOR THE HOLIDAYS | AWAY IN A MANGER | | | $1.00 | $2.00 |

## PETER PAN MAIN SERIES INCLUDING L, P, AND X SERIES 7" SINGLES

| # REC | DISC # | ARTIST | A TITLE | B TITLE | YEAR | ALSO ISSUED ON | G/VG | EX/NMT |
|---|---|---|---|---|---|---|---|---|
| 1 | 422 | PPO, SS/HANK WILSON, SUE BAXTER, VK | YOUNG ABE LINCOLN | OH SUSANNAH | | | $1.00 | $2.00 |
| 1 | 423 | PPO, VK | BONNIE BLUE GAL | THE HIGH SCHOOL CADETS | | | $1.00 | $2.00 |
| 1 | 424 | PPO, VK | DOGFACE SOLDIER | MARCH FAVORITES | | | $1.00 | $2.00 |
| 1 | 425 | MICHAEL REED, PPO, SS/JA, VK | I BELIEVE | SAVIOR, TEACH ME DAY BY DAY | | | $1.00 | $2.00 |
| 1 | 426 | BILLY LOWE, PPO/THE CREWMAN, PPO | 16 TONS | I'VE BEEN WORKING ON THE RAILROAD | | | $3.00 | $6.00 |
| 1 | 427 | BUDDY EDWARDS, PPO: VK/LEE ADAMS, PPO, VK | LOVE AND MARRIAGE | SOMEDAY MY PRINCE WILL COME (WD'S SNOW WHITE) | | | $1.00 | $2.00 |
| 1 | 428 | JIMMY GILBERT, PPO, VK/LAURA LESLIE, PPO, VK | DUNGAREE DOLL | I'VE GOT NO STRINGS (WD'S PINOCCHIO) | | | $2.00 | $4.00 |
| 1 | 429 | LINDA & BILL MARINE, VK/LAURA LESLIE, PPO, VK | LITTLE CHILD | WHEN YOU WISH UPON A STAR (WD'S PINOCCHIO) | | | $2.00 | $4.00 |
| 1 | 430 | MICHAEL REED, THE RANGERS, PPO, SS/FRANKIE STARR, JOHNNIE CORVO | ANGELS IN THE SKY | WHISTLE WHILE YOU WORK (WD'S SNOW WHITE) | | | $2.00 | $4.00 |
| 1 | 431 | WILLIAM MARINE/CONNIE DESMOND | THE LORD'S PRAYER | NOW I LAY ME DOWN TO SLEEP | | | $1.00 | $2.00 |
| 1 | 432 | GABBY DIXON, PPO, VK/DALE LORING, PPO | JUKE BOX BABY | THE WORLD OWES ME A LIVING (WD'S THE GRASSHOPPER AND THE ANTS) | | | $2.00 | $4.00 |
| 1 | 433 | BOBBY REYNOLDS, PPO, VK | HOT DIGGITY | WHO'S AFRAID OF THE BIG BAD WOLF (WD'S THE THREE LITTLE PIGS) | | | $2.00 | $4.00 |
| 1 | 434 | MICHAEL REED, PPO, SS/LEE ADAMS, PPO, VK | TUTTI-FRUTTI | THE DWARFS' YODEL SONG (THE SILLY SONG), (WD'S SNOW WHITE) | | | $2.00 | $4.00 |
| 1 | 435 | LINDA BROWN, PPO, SS/JIMMY BLAINE, PPO, VK | BOLL WEEVIL | GIVE A LITTLE WHISTLE (WD'S PINOCCHIO) | | | $2.00 | $4.00 |
| 1 | 436 | DANNY LANE, PPO, SS/JOHNNIE CORVO, PPO, THE SATISFIERS, VK | ROCK ISLAND LINE | PONY ON THE MERRY-GO-ROUND | | | $1.00 | $2.00 |
| 1 | 437 | THE PLAYMATES, PPO, VK/FRANKIE STAR, PPO, VK | WHEN THE RED ROBIN COMES BOB BOB BOBBIN' ALONG | WHISTLE WHILE YOU WORK (WD'S SNOW WHITE) | | | $2.00 | $4.00 |
| 1 | 438 | THE PLAYMATES, PPO, SS/FRANKIE STAR, PPO, VK | WD'S ZIP-A-DEE-DOO-DAH | GIVE A LITTLE WHISTLE (WD'S PINOCCHIO) | | | $2.00 | $4.00 |
| 1 | 439 | THE RANGERS, PPO, VK/LEE ADAMS, PPO | YOU ARE MY SUNSHINE | HEIGH-HO (DWARFS MARCHING SONG), (WD'S SNOW WHITE) | | | $2.00 | $4.00 |
| 1 | 440 | NAOMI FORD, PPO, VK/LAURA LESLIE, PPO, VK | WHAT EVER WILL BE WILL BE | BLUDDLE-UDDLE-UN-DUM (WD'S SNOW WHITE) | | | $2.00 | $4.00 |
| 1 | 441 | PETER PAN SHOWBOAT CAST/LAURA LESLIE, JIMMY POLACK, PPO, VK | WAITING FOR THE ROBERT E. LEE | PAPER OF PINS | | | $1.00 | $2.00 |
| 1 | 442 | JOE DAVIS, PPO, MARTY KASEN, DIR./JIMMY BLAINE, PPO | HAPPINESS STREET | HI DIDDLE DEE DEE (WD'S PINOCCHIO) | | 370 | $2.00 | $4.00 |
| 1 | 443 | JOE DAVIS, PPO, VK/LAURA LESLIE, PPO | IN THE MIDDLE OF THE HOUSE | WHEN I SEE AN ELEPHANT FLY (WD'S DUMBO) | | | $2.00 | $4.00 |
| 1 | 444 | PAULA LESTER, PPO, VK/BOBBY DIXON, JOHNNY SWIFT, PPO, VK | TONIGHT YOU BELONG TO ME | APPLE ON A STICK | | | $1.00 | $2.00 |
| 1 | 445 | LEE BARTON, PPO/BW | CINDY, OH CINDY | THE BIG ROCK CANDY MOUNTAIN | | | $1.00 | $2.00 |
| 1 | 446 | JERRY JACK, PPO/THE RANGERS, PPO, VK | GREEN DOOR | YOU ARE MY SUNSHINE | | 439 | $1.00 | $2.00 |
| 1 | 447 | SUGAR BEAT, PPO/JA, VK | BLUEBERRY HILL | TEDDY BEARS ON PARADE (AKA THE TEDDY BEARS POLKA) | | 342 | $1.00 | $2.00 |
| 1 | 448 A/437 A | PHIL GRAY, PPO/THE PLAYMATES, PPO | ROCK-A-BYE YOUR BABY WITH A DIXIE MELODY | WHEN THE RED ROBIN COMES BOB BOB BOBBIN' ALONG | | | $1.00 | $2.00 |
| 1 | 449 | ?/PPO, PM | GONNA GET ALONG WITHOUT YOU NOW | BILLY BOY | | 408-B, 212-A | $1.00 | $2.00 |
| 1 | 450 A/437 B | SLIPPER KANE, PPO/FRANKIE STAR, PPO, VK | THE AUCTIONEER | WHISTLE WHILE YOU WORK (WD'S SNOW WHITE) | | | $2.00 | $4.00 |
| 1 | 451 A/398 B | LES STARKER, PPO/BW | WRINGLE WRANGLE | ARKANSAS TRAVELER, RED RIVER VALLEY | | | $1.00 | $2.00 |

## PETER PAN MAIN SERIES INCLUDING L, P, AND X SERIES 7" SINGLES

| # REC | DISC # | ARTIST | A TITLE | B TITLE | YEAR | ALSO ISSUED ON | G/VG | EX/NMT |
|---|---|---|---|---|---|---|---|---|
| 1 | 452 A/ 405 B | THE PROMINEERS, PPO/ JA, VK | THE BANANA BOAT SONG | FOLK SONGS: BLUE TAIL FLY, SKIP TO MY LOU | | | $1.00 | $2.00 |
| 1 | 453 | THE COWBOY RANGERS, JA | HOME ON THE RANGE/CHISHOLM TRAIL | RED RIVER VALLEY, ARKANSAS TRAVELER | | | $1.00 | $2.00 |
| 1 | 454 | JERRY MARKS, PPO/CONNIE DESMOND | THE BIBLE TELLS ME SO | NOW I LAY ME DOWN TO SLEEP | | | $1.00 | $2.00 |
| 1 | 455 | JERRY MARKS, PPO/JOHNNIE CORVO, PPO, THE SATISFIERS, VK | THE HOKEY POKEY | PONY ON THE MERRY-GO-ROUND | | | $1.00 | $2.00 |
| 1 | 456 A/ 2298 A | TERRY GLEASON, PPO/ DANNY STEVENS, THE FOUR SERGEANTS, PPO, VK | MARIANNE | THE LITTLE TIN SOLDIER (AND THE LITTLE TOY DRUM) | | | $1.00 | $2.00 |
| 1 | 457 | ? | STASHU PANDOWSKI | BOY FRIEND POLKA | | | $1.00 | $2.00 |
| 1 | 458 A/ 345 B | BOB MITCHELL, PPO/JACK RUSSELL, PPO, VK | ROUND AND ROUND | YOU'RE A GRAND OLD FLAG | | | $1.00 | $2.00 |
| 1 | 459 A/ 382 B | HARRY LOGAN, PPO/ BOBBY DIXON, LINDA BARRIE, THE HAPPY THREE, PPO, VK | MAMA LOOK A BOO-BOO | LITTLE GOLDIE GOLDFISH | | 382-B, 354-A, 459 | $2.00 | $4.00 |
| 1 | 460 | A. STARR, PPO/PPO, PM | FREIGHT TRAIN | POP GOES THE WEASEL, I HAD A LITTLE NUT TREE | 1957 | | $1.00 | $2.00 |
| 1 | 461 | MICHAEL REED, PPO/PPO, PM | THE GIRL WITH THE GOLDEN BRAIDS | ALL AROUND THE MULBERRY BUSH | | | $1.00 | $2.00 |
| 1 | 462 | PPO, H. LAPIDUS, DIR/JA, THE SONG SPINNERS, DON COPE, DIR. | BRAHMS' LULLABY | SLEEP, BABY, SLEEP; DIDDLE DIDDLE DUMPLING, MY SON JOHN | | | $1.00 | $2.00 |
| 1 | 463 | DEBBY BROOKS, PPO/PPO | TAMMY | CLEMENTINE | | | $1.00 | $2.00 |
| 1 | 464 | ?/PPO | HONEYCOMB | OH DEM GOLDEN SLIPPERS | | | $1.00 | $2.00 |
| 1 | 465 | JA, PAUL TAUBMAN & ORCH. | GOLDILOCKS | GOLDILOCKS | | | $1.00 | $2.00 |
| 1 | 466 | JA, DON COPE, DIR. | GOLDILOCKS | LITTLE RED RIDING HOOD | | | $1.00 | $2.00 |
| 1 | 468 | JA, THE SATISFIERS, PPO, VK | HANSEL AND GRETEL (SIDE 1) | HANSEL AND GRETEL (SIDE 2) | | | $1.00 | $2.00 |
| 1 | 468 A/ L-14 B | JA, THE SATISFIERS, PPO, VK/JA, TOBY DEANE, PPO, VK | HANSEL AND GRETEL | CINDERELLA | | | $1.00 | $2.00 |
| 1 | 469 | PPO/JA, VK | SWEETIE BEAR | COUNTING SONG, PONY BOY | | 625 B | $1.00 | $2.00 |
| 1 | 470 | PPO, H. LAPIDUS, DIR. | SWEETIE PIE | SWEETIE PIE | | | $4.00 | $8.00 |
| 1 | 471 | MICHAEL REED, PPO, H. LAPIDUS, DIR | TAKE ME OUT TO THE BALLGAME | ROUND AND ROUND | | | $3.00 | $6.00 |
| 1 | 472 | JA, PPO, H. LAPIDUS, DIR. | RED RIVER VALLEY | JESSE JAMES | | | $1.00 | $2.00 |
| 1 | 473 | LEE BARTON, PPO, H. LAPIDUS, DIR. | CINDY OH CINDY, SQUARING UP TIME | JACK WAS A SAILOR, SQUID JIGGING GROUND | | | $1.00 | $2.00 |
| 1 | 474 | PPO | POPEYE* | POPEYE | | | $4.00 | $8.00 |
| 1 | 475 | DANNY STEVENS, THE FOUR SERGEANTS, PPO, VK/JA, PPO, VK | THE LITTLE TIN SOLDIER (AND THE LITTLE TOY DRUM) | MARCHING SONGS: STARS AND STRIPES FOREVER, YANKEE DOODLE | | | $8.00 | $15.00 |
| 1 | 476 | JA, PPO, VK/BW | BUFFALO BILLY | THE BIG ROCK CANDY MOUNTAIN | | | $1.00 | $2.00 |
| 1 | 477 | THE FAIRYLAND PLAYERS, JUSTINE STONE, DIR./ PPO, PM | MARY HAD A LITTLE LAMB, TWINKLE, TWINKLE LITTLE STAR, SING A SONG OF SIXPENCE | ALL AROUND THE MULBERRY BUSH, DID YOU EVER SEE A LASSIE? BYE BABY BUNTING | | | $1.00 | $2.00 |
| 1 | 478 | PPO | WYATT EARP | WYATT EARP | | | $4.00 | $8.00 |
| 1 | 479 | PPO | BUFFALO BILL | BUFFALO BILL | | | $4.00 | $8.00 |
| 1 | 480 | PPO | WILD BILL HICKOK | WILD BILL HICKOK | | | $4.00 | $8.00 |
| 1 | 481 | JA, THE SONG SPINNERS, DON COPE, DIR. | HUMPTY DUMPTY, A TISKET A TASKET, JACK AND JILL | SLEEP, BABY, SLEEP; DIDDLE DIDDLE DUMPLING, MY SON JOHN | | | $1.00 | $2.00 |
| 1 | 482 | JA, THE SONG SPINNERS, DON COPE, DIR. | POLLY PUT THE KETTLE ON, OATS, PEAS AND BEANS, PEAS PORRIDGE HOT | LITTLE MISS MUFFET, LITTLE JACK HORNER, JACK SPRAT ATE NO FAT | | | $1.00 | $2.00 |
| 1 | 483 | JA, THE SONG SPINNERS, DON COPE, DIR. | THE THREE LITTLE KITTENS, PUSSY CAT PUSSY CAT, I LOVE A LITTLE PUSSY | OLD MOTHER HUBBARD, WHERE! OH WHERE! HAS MY LITTLE DOG GONE, HARK! HARK! THE DOGS DO BARK | | | $1.00 | $2.00 |

*POPEYE (LAUNCHES HIS NEW SONG HIT)

## PETER PAN MAIN SERIES INCLUDING L, P, AND X SERIES 7" SINGLES

| # REC | DISC # | ARTIST | A TITLE | B TITLE | YEAR | ALSO ISSUED ON | G/VG | EX/NMT |
|---|---|---|---|---|---|---|---|---|
| 1 | 484 | PPO/THE FAIRYLAND PLAYERS | DOWN BY THE STATION | BAD BRAHMA BULL | | | $1.00 | $2.00 |
| 1 | 485 | PPO | I'VE BEEN WORKING ON THE RAILROAD, TRAIN SOUND EFFECTS | WHERE YOU WORKA JOHN? SHE'LL BE COMING ROUND THE MOUNTAIN | | | $4.00 | $8.00 |
| 1 | 486 | PPO/BILL LEEDS, PPO | BEAUTIFUL DREAMER | CAMPTOWN RACES | | | $1.00 | $2.00 |
| 1 | 487 | PPO, VK | IN THE GOOD OLD SUMMERTIME, I WANT A GAL | STROLLING THROUGH PARK ONE DAY, OLD MACDONALD HAD A FARM | 1959 | | $1.00 | $2.00 |
| 1 | 488 | CAWANDA'S GROUP | SHA SHA GALOR, YARBOU, BANJA JE EN GAY | ASAWANDA AYILONGO, ELUNDE, YOW COW LE | | | $4.00 | $8.00 |
| 1 | 489 | LEE ADAMS, PPO, VK/PAT DEANE, PPO, VK | ON TOP OF OLD SMOKY | CUDDLE UP A LITTLE CLOSER | | | $1.00 | $2.00 |
| 1 | 490 | DAVID ROSS, THE MULLEN SISTERS, PPO, VK | SLEEPING BEAUTY | SLEEPING BEAUTY | | | $1.00 | $2.00 |
| 1 | 491 | PPO | POKY THE PIG'S POLKA PARTY: POKY PIG POLKA | POKY THE PIG'S POLKA PARTY: BONGO POLKA | | | $1.00 | $2.00 |
| 1 | 492 | KEN ROBERTS, PPO; DON COPE, DIR. | FELIX AND HIS FRIENDS | FELIX AND HIS FRIENDS | | | $8.00 | $15.00 |
| 1 | 493 | KEN ROBERTS, PPO; DON COPE, DIR. | POPEYE'S FAVORITE SEA SONGS: SAILING, SAILING, NANCY LEE | POPEYE'S FAVORITE SEA SONGS: BLOW THE MAN DOWN, A LIFE ON THE OCEAN WAVE | | | $7.00 | $14.00 |
| 1 | 494 | THE FAIRYLAND PLAYERS; JUSTIN STONE, DIR. | THREE BLIND MICE, THERE WAS A CROOKED MAN, LITTLE BO PEEP | THE ALPHABET SONG | | 112/113 | $1.00 | $2.00 |
| 1 | 495 | VICKI DALE, PPO, VK/ BOBBY DIXON, JOHNNY SWIFT, PPO, VK | BUNNY HOP | APPLE ON A STICK | | 355-A, 383 | $1.00 | $2.00 |
| 1 | 496 | DAVID RICHARDS, PPO, VK/JA, VK | WD'S LITTLE TOOT | PANCHO THE CIRCUS DONKEY | | | $2.00 | $4.00 |
| 1 | 497 | JOHN BRADFORD, BOBBY HOOKEY, PPO, VK/PPO | LITTLE BRAVE SAMBO | PINOCCHIO | | | $8.00 | $15.00 |
| 1 | 498 (V.1) | JA, PPO | THREE LITTLE PIGS | THREE LITTLE PIGS | | | $1.00 | $2.00 |
| 1 | 498 (V.2) | JA, PPO/JA, PAUL TAUBMAN & ORCH. | THREE LITTLE PIGS | GOLDILOCKS | | | $1.00 | $2.00 |
| 1 | 499 | PPO | OLD KING COLE, HEY DIDDLE DIDDLE, LITTLE TOMMY TUCKER | LITTLE BOY BLUE, ROCK-A-BYE BABY | | | $1.00 | $2.00 |
| 1 | 500 | MOOK LEANI & GROUP, VK | ALOHA | HAWAIIAN WAR CHANT | | | $3.00 | $6.00 |
| 1 | 501 | JANE & PEGGY, PPO, VK/ PPO, VK | THE DOGGIE IN THE WINDOW | RINGS ON HER FINGERS | | | $2.00 | $4.00 |
| 1 | 502 | JERRY MARKS, PPO/JOHNNIE CORVO, PPO | THE HOKEY POKEY | PONY ON THE MERRY-GO-ROUND | | | $2.00 | $4.00 |
| 1 | 503 | THE RANGERS, PPO, VK/ PPO | YOU ARE MY SUNSHINE | DOWN IN THE VALLEY | | | $1.00 | $2.00 |
| 1 | 504 | PPO | LITTLE RED RIDING HOOD | LITTLE RED RIDING HOOD | | | $1.00 | $2.00 |
| 1 | 505 | VICTOR JORY, TOBY DEANE, PPO; VK, DIRECTOR | PETER PAN | PETER PAN | | | $4.00 | $8.00 |
| 1 | 506 | JERRY MARKS, PPO, PPO | THE BIBLE TELLS ME SO | OH DEM GOLDEN SLIPPERS | | | $1.00 | $2.00 |
| 1 | 507 | AL GOODMAN, PPO, VK | I'VE BEEN WORKING ON THE RAILROAD, SHORTNIN' BREAD | THE OLD GRAY MARE, DAISY BELL | | | $1.00 | $2.00 |
| 1 | 508 | PPO, VK/BETTY BONNIE, PPO, VK | JACK AND THE BEANSTALK | THE GINGERBREAD MAN | | | $1.00 | $2.00 |
| 1 | 509 | PPO, VK | GOODNIGHT LADIES, ON THE BANKS OF THE WABASH | LITTLE ANNIE ROONEY, THERE IS A TAVERN IN THE TOWN | | | $1.00 | $2.00 |
| 1 | 510 | BOBBY NICHOLAS, ANNIE WET, PPO, VK/PPO | IN A LITTLE RED SCHOOLHOUSE | SCHOOL DAYS | | | $1.00 | $2.00 |
| 1 | 511 | JA, MARILYN REESE, THE HONEYDREAMERS, VK | TINA THE BALLERINA | TINA THE BALLERINA | | | $8.00 | $15.00 |
| 1 | 512 | BETTY HARRIS, PPO, VK/ JACK RUSSELL, PPO, VK | I'M A LITTLE TEAPOT | I'M A YANKEE DOODLE DANDY | | | $1.00 | $2.00 |
| 1 | 513 | BETTY HARRIS, PPO, VK | ON THE GOOD SHIP LOLLIPOP | CHOCOLATE TRAIN | | | $1.00 | $2.00 |
| 1 | 514 | PPO, PM | OLD MACDONALD HAD A FARM | LOOBY LOO | | | $1.00 | $2.00 |

## PETER PAN MAIN SERIES INCLUDING L, P, AND X SERIES 7" SINGLES

| # REC | DISC # | ARTIST | A TITLE | B TITLE | YEAR | ALSO ISSUED ON | G/VG | EX/NMT |
|---|---|---|---|---|---|---|---|---|
| 1 | 515 | PPO, VK | THE STAR-SPANGLED BANNER | AMERICA THE BEAUTIFUL | | | $1.00 | $2.00 |
| 1 | 516 | JA, PPO, VK/BW | PETER RABBIT | PETER RABBIT | | | $1.00 | $2.00 |
| 1 | 517 | JP, THE SONG SPINNERS; DON COPE, DIR. | HUMPTY DUMPTY, A TISKET A TASKET, JACK AND JILL | OLD MOTHER HUBBARD, WHERE! OH WHERE! HAS MY LITTLE DOG GONE, HARK! HARK! THE DOGS DO BARK | | | $1.00 | $2.00 |
| 1 | 518 | BOB RYAN TRIO | CIELITO LINDO | CHIPANECAS | | | $1.00 | $2.00 |
| 1 | 519 | BOB CLAYTON TRIO | IN MY MERRY OLDSMOBILE | WAIT TILL THE SUN SHINES, NELLIE | | 568 | $5.00 | $10.00 |
| 1 | 520 | BOB MITCHELL, PPO/MICHAEL REED, PPO; H. LAPIDUS, DIR. | ON A BICYCLE BUILT FOR TWO | TAKE ME OUT TO THE BALLGAME | | | $3.00 | $6.00 |
| 1 | 521 | PPO | WASHINGTON POST MARCH, THE THUNDERER | YANKEE DOODLE, THE STARS & STRIPES FOREVER | | | $1.00 | $2.00 |
| 1 | 522 | PPO, PM/PPO | BILLY BOY | POP GOES THE WEASEL, I HAD A LITTLE NUT TREE | | | $1.00 | $2.00 |
| 1 | 523 | DELL SHARBET, THE HONEYDREAMERS | THE UGLY DUCKLING | THE UGLY DUCKLING | | | $1.00 | $2.00 |
| 1 | 524 | MITCHELL REED, THE RANGERS, PPO, SS/PPO | ANGELS IN THE SKY | NOW THE DAY IS DONE | | | $1.00 | $2.00 |
| 1 | 525 | PPO | RED WING | RED RIVER VALLEY | | | $1.00 | $2.00 |
| 1 | 526 | THE PETER PAN PIXIES | COUNTING SONG | GLOW WORM | | | $1.00 | $2.00 |
| 1 | 527 | DELL SHARBET, THE HONEYDREAMERS | THUMBELINA | THUMBELINA | | | $1.00 | $2.00 |
| 1 | 528 | PPO | MIGHTY MOUSE IN TOYLAND (PT. 1) | MIGHTY MOUSE IN TOYLAND (PT. 2) | | | $10.00 | $20.00 |
| 1 | 529 | PPO | LITTLE WHITE DUCK | SHE WORE A YELLOW RIBBON | | | $1.00 | $2.00 |
| 1 | 530 | DICK EDWARDS, PPO/PPO | PETER COTTONTAIL | HARRIGAN | | | $1.00 | $2.00 |
| 1 | 531 (P19 A/531 B | PPO | CHILDREN'S MARCHING SONG (NICK NACK PADDY WHACK) | IN THE EVENING BY THE MOONLIGHT | | | $1.00 | $2.00 |
| 1 | 532 | PPO | DO-RE-MI | OH SUSANNA | | | $1.00 | $2.00 |
| 1 | 533 | THE CADET MARCHING BAND & CHORUS | MARINES' HYMN | ANCHORS AWEIGH | 1960 | | $1.00 | $2.00 |
| 1 | 534 | THE GRASSHOPPERS | ROW, ROW, ROW YOUR BOAT | THE BIG ROCK CANDY MOUNTAIN | | | $1.00 | $2.00 |
| 1 | 535 | MARTY MARTIN & HIS SIX-SHOOTERS | PONY BOY | BLUE TAIL FLY | | | $1.00 | $2.00 |
| 1 | 536 | KEN ROBERTS, PPO; DON COPE, DIR. | FELIX AND HIS FRIENDS | FELIX AND HIS FRIENDS | | | $8.00 | $15.00 |
| 1 | 537 A/ 340 B | THE MERRY MICE (EKE, ZEKE & SQUEEK)/JACK RUSSELL, PPO, VK | WHEN THE SAINTS GO MARCHING IN | I'M A YANKEE DOODLE DANDY | | | $1.00 | $2.00 |
| 1 | 537 A/ 537 B | THE MERRY MICE (EKE, ZEKE & SQUEEK)/PPO, VK | WHEN THE SAINTS GO MARCHING IN | RED RIVER VALLEY | | | $1.00 | $2.00 |
| 1 | 538 | FRED BURTON, THE WILSON AVE. SINGERS | IN THE SHADE OF THE OLD APPLE TREE | WAIT TILL THE SUN SHINES, NELLIE | | | $1.00 | $2.00 |
| 1 | 539 | PPO | HERE COMES THE BRIDE | WHEN WE WERE M-A-DOUBLE-R-I-E-D | | | $1.00 | $2.00 |
| 1 | 540 | PPO | THREE LITTLE KITTENS | OLD MOTHER HUBBARD, WHERE! OH WHERE! HAS MY LITTLE DOG GONE | | | $1.00 | $2.00 |
| 1 | 541 | PPO | TREASURE ISLAND | TREASURE ISLAND | | | $1.00 | $2.00 |
| 1 | 542 | PPO | JESUS LOVES ME | CHILDREN OF THE HEAVENLY KING | | | $1.00 | $2.00 |
| 1 | 543 | PPO/JA, PPO | STAND UP FOR JESUS | SAVIOR TEACH ME DAY BY DAY | | | $1.00 | $2.00 |
| 1 | 544 | BETTY HARRIS, PPO/JA, PPO | ME AND MY TEDDY BEAR | TEDDY BEARS ON PARADE (AKA THE TEDDY BEARS POLKA) | | | $1.00 | $2.00 |
| 1 | 545 | PPO | POPEYE | POPEYE | | | $8.00 | $15.00 |
| 1 | 546 | THE FAIRYLAND PLAYERS | THREE BLIND MICE, THERE WAS A CROOKED MAN, LITTLE BO PEEP | THE FARMER IN THE DELL | | | $1.00 | $2.00 |
| 1 | 547 | JA, PPO | SNOW WHITE | SNOW WHITE | | | $2.00 | $4.00 |

## PETER PAN MAIN SERIES INCLUDING L, P, AND X SERIES 7" SINGLES

| # REC | DISC # | ARTIST | A TITLE | B TITLE | YEAR | ALSO ISSUED ON | G/VG | EX/NMT |
|---|---|---|---|---|---|---|---|---|
| 1 | 548 | JOHNNY JONES, PPO/PPO | SMOKEY THE BEAR | GET ALONG LITTLE DOGIE, POLLY WOLLY DOODLE | | | $5.00 | $10.00 |
| 1 | 549 | PPO | ALPHABET SONG | CHOCOLATE TRAIN | | | $1.00 | $2.00 |
| 1 | 550 | RAY HALLEE, PPO, VK/PPO | LITTLE RED CABOOSE | SWEET BETSY FROM PIKE | | | $1.00 | $2.00 |
| 1 | 551 | PPO | LONDON BRIDGE | THE MUFFIN MAN, SWEET & LOW | | | $1.00 | $2.00 |
| 1 | 553 | PPO, VK | PARADE OF THE WOODEN SOLDIERS | WE'RE OFF TO SEE THE PARADE | | | $1.00 | $2.00 |
| 1 | 554 | JA, TOBY DEANE, PPO | CINDERELLA | CINDERELLA | | | $2.00 | $4.00 |
| 1 | 556 | MICHAEL REED, PPO/BOBBY DIXON, JOHNNY SWIFT, PPO, VK | TUBBY THE TUBA | LITTLE GOLDIE GOLDFISH | | | $3.00 | $6.00 |
| 1 | 557 | PPO, VK | JACK AND THE BEANSTALK | JACK AND THE BEANSTALK | | | $1.00 | $2.00 |
| 1 | 558 | SHORTY MCMILLEN, PPO, PPO | CHEYENNE | BLUE TAIL FLY, SKIP TO MY LOU | | | $5.00 | $10.00 |
| 1 | 560 | JA, PPO | THE VALIANT LITTLE TAILOR | THE VALIANT LITTLE TAILOR | | | $1.00 | $2.00 |
| 1 | 561 | PPO/THE HIGHLAND LADS, PPO, SS | THE LITTLE DUTCH GIRL AND THE LITTLE DUTCH BOY | MY BONNIE LIES OVER THE OCEAN | | | $1.00 | $2.00 |
| 1 | 562 | PPO | DEM DRY BONES | CAMPTOWN RACES | | | $1.00 | $2.00 |
| 1 | 563 | PPO | MACNAMARA'S BAND | MARY'S A GRAND OLD NAME | | | $1.00 | $2.00 |
| 1 | 564 | PPO | ROUND THE VILLAGE | GOOD MORNING MARY SUNSHINE, RIG-A-JIG-JIG | | | $1.00 | $2.00 |
| 1 | 565 | PPO | ALICE IN WONDERLAND | ALICE IN WONDERLAND | | | $3.00 | $6.00 |
| 1 | 566 | PPO | HERE WE GO LOOBY LOO | ALL AROUND THE MULBERRY BUSH | | | $1.00 | $2.00 |
| 1 | 567 | PPO | FUNDAY SCHOOL SONGS: IN A LITTLE RED SCHOOLHOUSE, SCHOOL DAYS | THE ALPHABET SONG | | | $1.00 | $2.00 |
| 1 | 568 | PPO | SING ALONG TRAVELIN' SONGS: IN MY MERRY OLDSMOBILE, ON A BICYCLE BUILT FOR TWO | I'VE BEEN WORKING ON THE RAILROAD | | 519 | $5.00 | $10.00 |
| 1 | 569 | PPO | BONNIE SONGS FOR LADS & LASSIES, DID YOU EVER SEE A LASSIE, MY BONNIE LIES OVER THE OCEAN | MY BONNIE LASSIE | 1962 | | $1.00 | $2.00 |
| 1 | 570 | PPO | ME AND MY SHADOW | LITTLE SIR ECHO | | | $1.00 | $2.00 |
| 1 | 571 | PPO | FOLK SONGS USA: BLUE TAIL FLY, SKIP TO MY LOU | FOLK SONGS USA: TURKEY IN THE STRAW, SHE'LL BE COMIN' ROUND THE MOUNTAIN | | | $1.00 | $2.00 |
| 1 | 572 | PPO | BIG BRASS BAND: 76 TROMBONES | BIG BRASS BAND: I LOVE A PARADE | | | $1.00 | $2.00 |
| 1 | 573 | PPO | PARADE OF THE WOODEN SOLDIERS (FROM "BABES IN TOYLAND") | LITTLE TIN SOLDIER & LITTLE TIN DRUM (FROM "BABES IN TOYLAND") | | | $1.00 | $2.00 |
| 1 | 574 | SINGING GRASSHOPPERS | DIXIE | SWANEE RIVER | | | $1.00 | $2.00 |
| 1 | 575 | PPO | LARIAT SAM'S STORY: PEOPLE CATCHER | LARIAT SAM'S STORY: PEOPLE CATCHER | | | $4.00 | $8.00 |
| 1 | 576 | DAYTON ALLEN, ORIGINAL TV SOUND TRACK VOICES | DEPUTY DAWG: BIG CHIEF NO TREATY | DEPUTY DAWG: BIG CHIEF NO TREATY | | | $8.00 | $15.00 |
| 1 | 577 | HARRY WELCH, PPO | POPEYE: SKINDIVER | POPEYE: SKINDIVER | | | $8.00 | $15.00 |
| 1 | 578 | HARRY WELCH, PPO | POPEYE: JEEP JEEP | POPEYE: JEEP JEEP | | | $8.00 | $15.00 |
| 1 | 579 | HARRY WELCH, PPO | POPEYE: FLEAS A CROWD | POPEYE: FLEAS A CROWD | | | $8.00 | $15.00 |
| 1 | 580 | HARRY WELCH, PPO | POPEYE: WHERE THERE'S A WILL | POPEYE: WHERE THERE'S A WILL | | | $8.00 | $15.00 |
| 1 | 581 | TOM MORRISON | MIGHTY MOUSE AND THE GIANT CAT | MIGHTY MOUSE AND THE GIANT CAT | | | $10.00 | $20.00 |
| 1 | 582 | JIMMY NELSON | JOKE ALONG WITH JIMMY NELSON AND HIS FRIENDS | JOKE ALONG WITH JIMMY NELSON AND HIS FRIENDS | | | $8.00 | $15.00 |

## PETER PAN MAIN SERIES INCLUDING L, P, AND X SERIES 7" SINGLES

| # REC | DISC # | ARTIST | A TITLE | B TITLE | YEAR | ALSO ISSUED ON | G/VG | EX/NMT |
|---|---|---|---|---|---|---|---|---|
| 1 | 583 | ORIGINAL VOICES OF TV SHOW, PPO | THE MAGIC LAND OF ALLA-KA-ZAM: ALLA-KA-ZAM THEME | THE MAGIC LAND OF ALLA-KA-ZAM: PRESTO-MAGIC | | | $8.00 | $15.00 |
| 1 | 584 | ARNOLD STANG, PPO | THE ELEPHANT WHO FORGOT | PERCY THE POLITE SEAL | | | $4.00 | $8.00 |
| 1 | 585 | PPO | SPACE SONGS: TRIP IN A ROCKET SHIP | SPACE SONGS: ON THE MOON | | | $10.00 | $20.00 |
| 1 | 586 | PPO | HAPPY TRAIN | CHOCOLATE TRAIN | | | $1.00 | $2.00 |
| 1 | 587 | PPO | HA HA THE CLOWN | CIRCUS BAND | | | $1.00 | $2.00 |
| 1 | 588 | JA, PPO, VK | TEDDY BEAR DANCE | TEDDY BEARS ON PARADE (AKA THE TEDDY BEARS POLKA) | | | $1.00 | $2.00 |
| 1 | 589 | CAPTAIN KANGAROO, PPO | THE TREASURE HOUSE KEYS | KNOCK KNOCK | | | $5.00 | $10.00 |
| 1 | 590 | CAPTAIN KANGAROO: MR. GREEN JEANS, PPO | WHEN A BUNNY WANTS A CARROT | THE TREASURE HOUSE BAND ON PARADE | | | $5.00 | $10.00 |
| 1 | 591 | CAPTAIN KANGAROO, PPO | GRANDFATHER'S CLOCK | MUSICAL MOOSE | | | $5.00 | $10.00 |
| 1 | 592 | ARNOLD STANG, PPO | CLOCK THAT WENT TOCK TICK | CLOCK THAT WENT TOCK TICK | | | $8.00 | $15.00 |
| 1 | 593 | PPO | SING A SONG OF PRESIDENTS: GEORGE WASHINGTON | SING A SONG OF PRESIDENTS: JOHN F. KENNEDY | | | $10.00 | $20.00 |
| 1 | 594 | ? | NEW LITTLE BABY | ? | | | $1.00 | $2.00 |
| 1 | 595 | PPO | SING A SONG OF ARITHMETIC: ADDITION | SING A SONG OF ARITHMETIC: SUBTRACTION | | | $1.00 | $2.00 |
| 1 | 596 | DAYTON ALLEN, ORIGINAL TV SOUND TRACK VOICES | DEPUTY DAWG: 2" INCH WORM | DEPUTY DAWG: 2" INCH WORM | | | $8.00 | $15.00 |
| 1 | 597 | PPO | SINGING VOICES OF MEXICO: VOCABULARY | SINGING VOICES OF MEXICO: TOM TAMBOR | | | $1.00 | $2.00 |
| 1 | 598 | PPO | COUNTING SONG (JOHN BROWN HAD A LITTLE INDIAN) | HICKORY DICKORY DOCK, MISTRESS MARY, QUITE CONTRARY | 1964 | | $1.00 | $2.00 |
| 1 | 599 | ? | DANCE OF THE SUGAR PLUM FAIRY | WALTZ OF THE FLOWERS | | | $1.00 | $2.00 |
| 1 | 600 | FREDDY HALL, PPO | THE MAN ON THE FLYING TRAPEZE | AFTER THE BALL | | | $1.00 | $2.00 |
| 1 | 601 | ? | SCARLET RIBBONS | GOODNIGHT, IRENE | | | $1.00 | $2.00 |
| 1 | 602 | PPO | CASPER, THE FRIENDLY GHOST: THEME SONG | IN THE EVENING BY THE MOONLIGHT | | | $8.00 | $15.00 |
| 1 | 603 | THE THREE STOOGES | THE STORY OF THE MAGIC LAMP | THE STORY OF THE MAGIC LAMP | | | $8.00 | $15.00 |
| 1 | 604 | LARRY HARMON, HENRY CALVIN (ORIGINAL ANIMATED VOICES) | LAUREL & HARDY: CHILLER, DILLER THRILLER | LAUREL & HARDY: CHILLER, DILLER THRILLER | | | $8.00 | $15.00 |
| 1 | 605 | ? | SUPERCAR: FLIGHT OF FANCY | ? | | | $8.00 | $15.00 |
| 1 | 606 | PPO | WHAT'S THE GOOD WORD: ANTONYM ISLAND | WHAT'S THE GOOD WORD: SING A SONG OF SYNONYMS | | | $1.00 | $2.00 |
| 1 | 607 | PPO | IT'S ABOUT TIME: MINUTE HAND AND HOUR HAND DUET | IT'S ABOUT TIME: MINUTE HAND MARCH | | | $1.00 | $2.00 |
| 1 | 608 | PIXIES PEE-WEE, POKEY & POO, PPO | PEPINO, THE ITALIAN MOUSE | SAILING, SAILING | | | $1.00 | $2.00 |
| 1 | 609 | PPO | THE SHOEMAKER AND THE ELVES | THE SHOEMAKER AND THE ELVES | | | $1.00 | $2.00 |
| 1 | 610 | PPO | DAYS OF THE WEEK | MONTHS OF THE YEAR | | | $1.00 | $2.00 |
| 1 | 611 | ? | SONGS ABOUT WORDS | SONGS ABOUT WORDS | | | $1.00 | $2.00 |
| 1 | 612 | PPO | THE STORY OF A MIRACLE | THE STORY OF A MIRACLE | | | $1.00 | $2.00 |
| 1 | 613 | THE THREE STOOGES | THE PRINCESS AND THE PEA | THE PRINCESS AND THE PEA | | | $8.00 | $15.00 |
| 1 | 614 | PPO | I AM A TRAIN | I AM A TRUCK | | | $2.00 | $4.00 |
| 1 | 615 | ARNOLD STANG, PPO | THE HAPPY HIPPO | ? | | | $8.00 | $15.00 |
| 1 | 616 | ? | SONGS ABOUT GOOD HABITS | ? | | | $1.00 | $2.00 |
| 1 | 617 | LEN STOKES & THE SONG SPINNERS, PAUL TAUBMAN & ORCH. | THE BIG RED FIRE ENGINE | THE BIG RED FIRE ENGINE | | | $1.00 | $2.00 |

PETER PAN RECORDS
I'M A LITTLE TEAPOT
$2.00

PETER PAN RECORDS
MIGHTY MOUSE IN TOYLAND
$20.00

PETER PAN RECORDS
LITTLE GOLDIE GOLDFISH
$8.00

## PETER PAN MAIN SERIES INCLUDING L, P, AND X SERIES 7" SINGLES

| # REC | DISC # | ARTIST | A TITLE | B TITLE | YEAR | ALSO ISSUED ON | G/VG | EX/NMT |
|---|---|---|---|---|---|---|---|---|
| 1 | 618 | ? | SONGS ABOUT INVENTORS | ? | | | $1.00 | $2.00 |
| 1 | 619 | CAPTAIN KANGAROO, PPO | THE TALE OF THE TOOTLE-BIRD | THE TALE OF THE TOOTLEBIRD | | | $5.00 | $10.00 |
| 1 | 620 | PPO | THE WIZARD OF OZ | THE WIZARD OF OZ | | | $2.00 | $4.00 |
| 1 | 621 | PPO | RUMPELSTILTSKIN | RUMPELSTILTSKIN | | | $1.00 | $2.00 |
| 1 | 622 | PPO | KING MIDAS | KING MIDAS | | | $1.00 | $2.00 |
| 1 | 623 | PPO | THE ADVENTURES OF SIMPLE SIMON | THE ADVENTURES OF SIMPLE SIMON | | | $1.00 | $2.00 |
| 1 | 624 | PPO | THE FURTHER ADVENTURES OF WYNKEN, BLYNKEN AND NOD | THE FURTHER ADVENTURES OF WYNKEN, BLYNKEN AND NOD | | | $1.00 | $2.00 |
| 1 | 625 | PPO | PUFF THE MAGIC DRAGON | SWEETIE BEAR | | | $4.00 | $8.00 |
| 1 | 626 | PPO | A SPOONFUL OF SUGAR | WE SAIL THE OCEAN BLUE, OVER THE SUMMER SEA | | | $2.00 | $4.00 |
| 1 | 627 | PPO | SUPER-CALI-FRAGIL-ISTIC-EXPI-ALI-DOCIOUS | THE GREEN GRASS GREW ALL AROUND | | | $3.00 | $6.00 |
| 1 | 628 | PPO | CHUGGA CHUGGA CHOO | THE LITTLE TRAIN THAT CAUGHT COLD | | | $1.00 | $2.00 |
| 1 | 629 | PPO | AESOP'S FABLES: THE MILK-MAID AND HER PAIL | AESOP'S FABLES: THE MILKMAID AND HER PAIL | | | $1.00 | $2.00 |
| 1 | 630 | PPO | PEOPLE (FROM THE BROAD-WAY SHOW "FUNNY GIRL") | WHEN I FIRST CAME TO THIS LAND | | | $3.00 | $6.00 |
| 1 | 631 | ? | HELLO DOLLY | ? | | | $3.00 | $6.00 |
| 1 | 632 | PPO | SONGS ABOUT GOOD HEALTH: YOUR MOUTH IS A HOUSE, BE NEAT | SONGS ABOUT GOOD HEALTH: THE BATHROOM, WHEN YOU'VE HAD A BATH | | | $1.00 | $2.00 |
| 1 | 633 | PPO | SONGS ABOUT GOOD MAN-NERS: SPECIAL EXPRESSION SONG | SONGS ABOUT GOOD MANNERS: KIND-NESS & CONSIDERATION, WHEN YOUR LITTLE FRIENDS COME TO VISIT YOU | | | $1.00 | $2.00 |
| 1 | 634 | PPO | SONGS ABOUT YOUR FAMILY | SONGS ABOUT YOUR FAMILY | | | $1.00 | $2.00 |
| 1 | 635 | PPO | SONGS ABOUT COMMUNITY HELPERS | SONGS ABOUT COMMUNITY HELPERS | | | $1.00 | $2.00 |
| 1 | 636 | PPO | TRAIN SCHOOL | MAIL TRAIN | | | $1.00 | $2.00 |
| 1 | 637 | PPO | THAT'S WHAT WE LEARN IN SCHOOL | THE GREEN GRASS GREW ALL AROUND | | | $1.00 | $2.00 |
| 1 | 638 | PPO | THE STORY OF PUSS IN BOOTS | THE STORY OF PUSS IN BOOTS | | | $1.00 | $2.00 |
| 1 | 639 | PPO | RAPUNZEL | RAPUNZEL | | | $1.00 | $2.00 |
| 1 | 640 | PPO | PANDORA | PANDORA | | | $1.00 | $2.00 |

## PETER PAN MAIN SERIES INCLUDING L, P, AND X SERIES 7" SINGLES

| # REC | DISC # | ARTIST | A TITLE | B TITLE | YEAR | ALSO ISSUED ON | G/VG | EX/NMT |
|---|---|---|---|---|---|---|---|---|
| 1 | X-6 (V.1) | BOBBY NICHOLAS, PPO, VK/THE CAROLEERS, VK | SANTA CLAUS IS COMIN TO TOWN | SILENT NIGHT | | | $1.00 | $2.00 |
| 1 | X-6 A/ NN-6 B | THE CAROLEERS, VK | SANTA CLAUS IS COMING TO TOWN | JOLLY OLD SAINT NICK | | | $1.00 | $2.00 |
| 1 | X-6 A/ NX-6 B | BOBBY NICHOLAS, PPO, VK/THE CAROLEERS, VK | SANTA CLAUS IS COMING TO TOWN | AWAY IN A MANGER | | | $1.00 | $2.00 |
| 1 | X-7 | SUZY WILLIAMS, PPO, VK/ BOBBY BURNS, PPO, VK | I SAW MOMMY KISSING SANTA CLAUS | CHRISTMAS CHOPSTICKS ('TWAS THE NIGHT BEFORE CHRISTMAS) | | | $1.00 | $2.00 |
| 1 | X-8 | JACK RUSSELL, THE HONEYDREAMERS, VK | WHITE CHRISTMAS | ADESTE FIDELES | | | $1.00 | $2.00 |
| 1 | X-9 | DAVID ROSS, THE MULLEN SISTERS, PPO, VK | THE NATIVITY | THE NATIVITY | | | $1.00 | $2.00 |
| 1 | X-10 | LAURA LESLIE, PPO, VK/ THE CAROLEERS, VK | SLEIGH RIDE | O LITTLE TOWN OF BETHLEHEM | | | $1.00 | $2.00 |
| 1 | X-11 | MICHAEL REED, PPO, VK/ THE CAROLEERS, VK | WINTER WONDERLAND | IT CAME UPON A MIDNIGHT CLEAR, AWAY IN THE MANGER | | | $1.00 | $2.00 |
| 1 | X-12 | JESSE CRAWFORD | O COME ALL YE FAITHFUL, IT CAME UPON A MIDNIGHT CLEAR | O LITTLE TOWN OF BETHLEHEM, HARK! THE HERALD ANGELS SING | | | $1.00 | $2.00 |
| 1 | X-14 | SUE RICHARDS, BOB ASHLEY, PPO, SS | SNOW FLAKES | WE THREE KINGS/I SAW THREE SHIPS | | | $1.00 | $2.00 |
| 1 | X-15 | FRANKIE STARR, PPO, SS/ PPO, VK | HOME FOR THE HOLIDAYS | AWAY IN A MANGER | | | $1.00 | $2.00 |
| 1 | X-16 | GABBY DIXON & THE CRICKETS, PPO, VK/GABE DRAKE, PPO, VK | WHEN SANTA CLAUS GETS YOUR LETTER | SING A KRIS KRINGLE JINGLE | | | $1.00 | $2.00 |
| 1 | X-17 | LAURA LESLIE, PPO, SS/ THE CAROLEERS | THE NIGHT BEFORE CHRISTMAS SONG | OH CHRISTMAS TREE (O TANNENBAUM) | | | $1.00 | $2.00 |
| 1 | X-18 | FRANKIE STARR, PPO, SS/ THE STARBRIGHTS | THIRTY-TWO FEET AND EIGHT LITTLE TAILS | UP ON A HOUSETOP | | | $2.00 | $4.00 |
| 1 | X-19 | BOBBY STEWART, PPO, VK | I'M GETTIN' NUTTIN' FOR CHRISTMAS | JOLLY OLD ST. NICHOLAS | | | $2.00 | $4.00 |
| 1 | X-20 | PPO, VK | RUDOLPH THE RED-NOSED REINDEER | I HEARD THE BELLS ON CHRISTMAS DAY | | | $2.00 | $4.00 |
| 1 | X-23 | DICK EDWARDS, PPO, VK/ THE CAROLEERS, VK | FROSTY THE SNOWMAN | GOD REST YE MERRY GENTLEMEN, JOY TO THE WORLD/DECK THE HALLS | | | $1.00 | $2.00 |
| 1 | X-24 | THE CAROLEERS, VK | JINGLE BELLS, SILENT NIGHT | GO TELL IT ON THE MOUNTAIN, GOOD KING WENCESLAS | | | $1.00 | $2.00 |
| 1 | X-25 | JOHNNY KAY, THE CAROLEERS, VK | HARK THE HERALD ANGELS SING, O LITTLE TOWN OF BETHLEHEM | DECK THE HALLS WITH BOUGHS OF HOLLY/JOY TO THE WORLD | | | $1.00 | $2.00 |
| 1 | X-26 (V.1) | THE CAROLEERS, PPO | THE NIGHT BEFORE CHRISTMAS, OH COME ALL YE FAITHFUL | THE FIRST NOEL, IT CAME UPON A MIDNIGHT CLEAR | | | $1.00 | $2.00 |
| 1 | X-26 (V.2) | JOHNNY KAY, THE CAROLEERS, VK | THE FIRST NOEL, RING OUT WILD BELLS | IT CAME UPON A MIDNIGHT CLEAR, ADESTE FIDELES | | | $1.00 | $2.00 |
| 1 | X-27 | SANTA'S ELVES | THE CHIPMUNK SONG | THE LITTLE TIN SOLDIER AND THE LITTLE TOY DRUM | | | $2.00 | $4.00 |
| 1 | X-28 | SUZY WILLIAMS, PPO, VK/ THE CAROLEERS | I SAW MOMMY KISSING SANTA CLAUS | RING OUT WILD BELLS | | | $2.00 | $4.00 |
| 1 | X-29 | PPO | THE LITTLE DRUMMER BOY | 32 FEET AND 8 LITTLE TAILS | | | $1.00 | $2.00 |
| 1 | X-30 | MADELAINE, PPO | DOMINIQUE | SAINTE NUIT | | | $2.00 | $4.00 |
| 1 | X-31 | BOBBY STEWART, PPO | I'M GETTING NUTTIN' FOR CHRISTMAS | SING A KRIS KRINGLE JINGLE | | | $2.00 | $4.00 |
| 1 | X-32 | THE CAROLEERS | HARK THE HERALD ANGELS SING, O COME ALL YE FAITHFUL | DECK THE HALLS WITH BOUGHS OF HOLLY, JOY TO THE WORLD | | | $1.00 | $2.00 |
| 1 | X-34 | PPO | SILENT NIGHT | WE THREE KINGS, I SAW THREE SHIPS | | | $1.00 | $2.00 |
| 1 | X-35 | PPO | THE TWELVE DAYS OF CHRISTMAS | SLEIGH RIDE, JINGLE BELLS | | | $1.00 | $2.00 |
| 1 | X-37 | PPO | DECK THE HALLS WITH BOUGHS OF HOLLY/HARK THE HERALD ANGELS SING | O LITTLE TOWN OF BETHLEHEM/SING A KRIS KRINGLE JINGLE | | | $1.00 | $2.00 |

## PETER PAN 10" SERIES SINGLES

| # REC | DISC # | ARTIST | A TITLE | B TITLE | YEAR | G/VG | EX/NMT |
|---|---|---|---|---|---|---|---|
| 1 | 342 | JANE & PEGGY, PETER PAN PLAYERS (PPO); VICKY KASEN (VK), DIR./ JACK ARTHUR (JA), PPO, VK | THE DOGGIE IN THE WINDOW | TEDDY BEARS ON PARADE | 1949 | $3.00 | $6.00 |
| 1 | 501 | JA, VK | PANCHO THE CIRCUS DONKEY | PANCHO THE CIRCUS DONKEY | | $2.00 | $4.00 |
| 1 | 502 | PPO, VK | HAPPY BIRTHDAY TO YOU | HAPPY BIRTHDAY TO YOU | | $1.00 | $2.00 |
| 1 | 503 | JA, PPO, VK | TEDDY BEARS PICNIC | TEDDY BEARS ON POLKA ( AKA THE TEDDY BEARS PARADE) | | $2.00 | $4.00 |
| 1 | 507 | PPO, VK/? | BUFFALO BILLY | I FOUND MY MOMMA | | $1.00 | $2.00 |
| 1 | 510 | DAVID ROSS, THE MULLEN SISTERS, PPO, VK | SLEEPING BEAUTY | SLEEPING BEAUTY | | $2.00 | $4.00 |
| 1 | 511 | DAVID ROSS, THE MULLEN SISTERS, PPO, VK | THE NATIVITY | THE NATIVITY | | $1.00 | $2.00 |
| 1 | 513 | MICHAEL REED, PPO, VK/JOHN CORVO, THE SATISFIERS, EARL SHELDON ORCH. | BIMBO | OZZIE THE OSTRICH | | $2.00 | $4.00 |
| 1 | 514 | JA, PPO, THE SATISFIERS, VK | HANSEL AND GRETEL | HANSEL AND GRETEL | | $1.00 | $2.00 |
| 1 | 516 | MICHAEL REED, PPO, VK/VICTOR JORY, PPO, VK | OVER THE RAINBOW | FROM "THE NUTCRACKER SUITE": MARCH MINIATURE, DANCE OF THE SUGAR PLUM FAIRY | | $2.00 | $4.00 |
| 1 | 519 | TOBY DEANE, PPO, VK/PPO, PM | I'M GONNA GET WELL TODAY | COUNTING SONG, HICKORY DICKORY, MARY CONTRARY | | $1.00 | $2.00 |
| 1 | 520 | LAURA LESLIE, PPO, VK/WENDY WILLIAMS, BOBBY DIXON, PPO, VK | SOME DAY MY PRINCE WILL COME (WD'S SNOW WHITE) | IN THE LAND OF LEMONADE AND LOLLIPOPS | | $2.00 | $4.00 |
| 1 | 521 | LEE ADAMS, PPO, VK/BOBBY DIXON, LINDA BARRIE, THE HAPPY THREE, PPO, VK | WHO'S AFRAID OF THE BIG BAD WOLF (WD'S THE THREE LITTLE PIGS) | LITTLE GOLDIE GOLDFISH | | $3.00 | $6.00 |
| 1 | 522 | LAURA LESLIE, PPO, VK/BETTY BONNIE, PPO, VK | WHEN YOU WISH UPON A STAR (WD'S PINOCCHIO) | THE GINGERBREAD MAN | | $2.00 | $4.00 |
| 1 | 523 | FRANKIE STARR, PPO, VK/JA, PPO, VK | WHISTLE WHILE YOU WORK (WD'S SNOW WHITE) | SNOW WHITE | | $2.00 | $4.00 |
| 1 | 524 | JIMMY BLAINE, PPO, VK/JOHN BRADFORD, BOBBY HOOKEY, PPO, VK | GIVE A LITTLE WHISTLE (WD'S PINOCCHIO) | PINOCCHIO | | $2.00 | $4.00 |
| 1 | 525 | LEE ADAMS, PPO, VK/PPO, VK | HEIGH-HO (DWARFS MARCHING SONG), (WD'S SNOW WHITE) | THE HIGH SCHOOL CADETS/OUR DIRECTOR | | $2.00 | $4.00 |
| 1 | 526 | LAURA LESLIE, PPO, VK/WENDY WILLIAMS, PPO, VK | WHEN I SEE AN ELEPHANT FLY (WD'S DUMBO) | SQUEE GEE (THE HAPPY LITTLE CLOWN) | | $3.00 | $6.00 |
| 1 | 527 | JIMMY BLAINE, PPO, VK/DANNY STEVENS, THE FOUR SERGEANTS, PPO, VK | HI DIDDLE DEE DEE (WALT DISNEY'S (WD'S) PINOCCHIO) | THE LITTLE TIN SOLDIER (AND THE LITTLE TOY DRUM) | | $2.00 | $4.00 |
| 1 | 528 | DALE LORING, PPO/BOBBY DIXON, JOHNNY SWIFT, PPO, VK | THE WORLD OWES ME A LIVING (WD'S THE GRASSHOPPER AND THE ANTS) | APPLE ON A STICK | | $2.00 | $4.00 |
| 1 | 529 | LEE ADAMS, PPO, VK/LAURA LESLIE, PPO, VK | THE DWARFS' YODEL SONG (THE SILLY SONG) (WD'S SNOW WHITE) | LITTLE POLLY PARAKEET | | $2.00 | $4.00 |
| 1 | 530 | LAURA LESLIE, PPO, VK/VICTOR JORY, PPO, VK | I'VE GOT NO STRINGS (WD'S PINOCCHIO) | FROM "THE NUTCRACKER SUITE": DANCE OF THE SHEPHERDS, WALTZ OF THE FLOWERS | | $3.00 | $6.00 |
| 1 | 531 | LAURA LESLIE, PPO, VK/JOHN CORVO, THE SATISFIERS, PPO, VK | BLUDDLE-UDDLE-UN-DUM (WD'S SNOW WHITE) | PONY ON THE MERRY-GO-ROUND | | $2.00 | $4.00 |
| 1 | 533 | BOBBY NICHOLAS, PPO, VK/THE CAROLEERS, VK | SANTA CLAUS IS COMING TO TOWN | JINGLE BELLS, ADESTE FIDELES | | $1.00 | $2.00 |
| 1 | 1024 | BETTY JANE, VK/THE CAROLEERS | I SAW MOMMY KISSING SANTA CLAUS | JINGLE BELLS, ADESTE FIDELES | | $1.00 | $2.00 |
| 1 | 2115 | JA, THE SONG SPINNERS; DON COPE, DIR. | OLD KING COLE, ETC. | HUMPTY DUMPTY, ETC. | | $1.00 | $2.00 |
| 1 | 2117 | JA, THE SONG SPINNERS; DON COPE, DIR. | LITTLE MISS MUFFET, ETC. | THE THREE LITTLE KITTENS, ETC. | | $1.00 | $2.00 |
| 1 | 2119 | JA; DON COPE, DIR. | GOLDILOCKS | LITTLE RED RIDING HOOD | | $1.00 | $2.00 |
| 1 | 2120 | PPO | OH DEAR! WHAT CAN THE MATTER BE, BILLY BOY | HICKORY DICKORY DOCK, ETC. | | $1.00 | $2.00 |
| 1 | 2226 | BILLY WILLIAMS (BW) & HIS COWBOY RANGERS; DON COPE, DIR. | SHE'LL BE COMIN' ROUND THE MOUNTAIN, ETC. | OLD MACDONALD HAD A FARM | | $1.00 | $2.00 |
| 1 | 2227 | BW | HOME ON THE RANGE, THE OLD CHISHOLM TRAIL | CAMPTOWN RACES, OH! SUSANNA | | $1.00 | $2.00 |

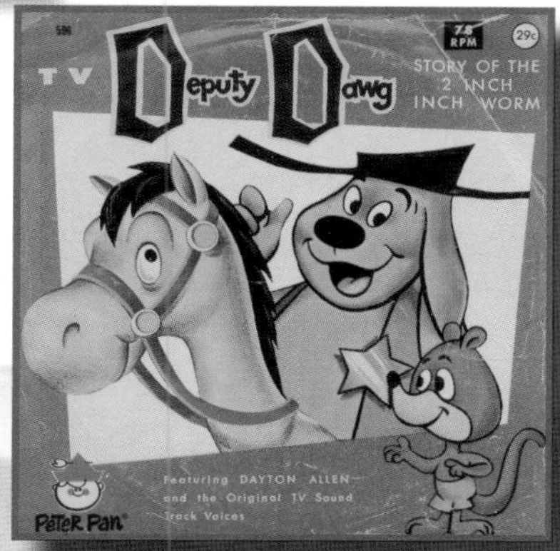


PETER PAN RECORDS
DEPUTY DAWG 2" INCH WORM
$15.00

PETER PAN RECORDS
DRAG THE MAGIC PUFFIN
$10.00

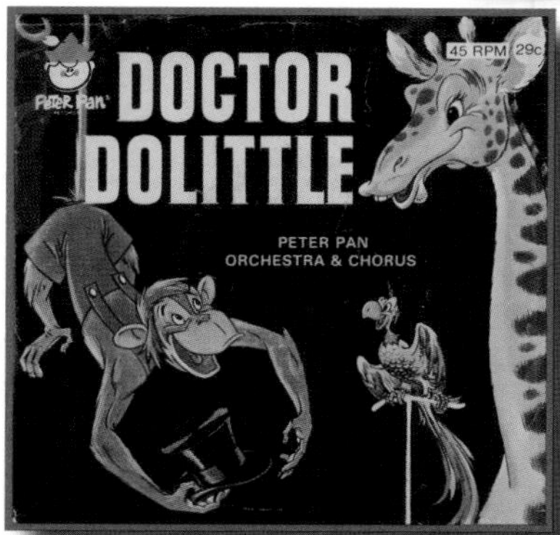


PETER PAN RECORDS
DOCTOR DOLITTLE
$15.00

## PETER PAN 10" SERIES SINGLES

| # REC | DISC # | ARTIST | A TITLE | B TITLE | YEAR | G/VG | EX/NMT |
|---|---|---|---|---|---|---|---|
| 1 | 2228 | JA, PAUL TAUBMAN & ORCH., DON COPE, DIR. | THREE LITTLE PIGS | THREE LITTLE PIGS | | $1.00 | $2.00 |
| 1 | 2229 | JA, PAUL TAUBMAN & ORCH., DON COPE, DIR. | PETER RABBIT | PETER RABBIT | | $1.00 | $2.00 |
| 1 | 2231 | THE CAROLEERS | SILENT NIGHT, O LITTLE TOWN OF BETHLEHEM | JINGLE BELLS, ADESTE FIDELES | 1949 | $1.00 | $2.00 |
| 1 | 2233 | THE CAROLEERS | THE NIGHT BEFORE CHRISTMAS | IT CAME UPON A MIDNIGHT CLEAR, ETC. | | $1.00 | $2.00 |
| 1 | 2235 | LEN STOKES & THE SONG SPINNERS, PAUL TAUBMAN & ORCH. | THE BIG RED FIRE ENGINE | THE BIG RED FIRE ENGINE | | $1.00 | $2.00 |
| 1 | 2237 | LEN STOKES & THE SONG SPINNERS, PAUL TAUBMAN & ORCH. | CIRCUS (THE BIGGEST SHOW IN TOWN) | CIRCUS (THE BIGGEST SHOW IN TOWN) | | $1.00 | $2.00 |
| 1 | 2238 | JOHN BRADFORD, BOBBY HOOKEY, PPO, VK | PINOCCHIO | PINOCCHIO | | $1.00 | $2.00 |
| 1 | 2239 | JOHN BRADFORD, BOBBY HOOKEY, PPO, VK | LITTLE BRAVE SAMBO | LITTLE BRAVE SAMBO | | $8.00 | $15.00 |
| 1 | 2240 | PPO; JUSTIN STONE, DIR. | ALPHABET SONG, ETC. | MARY HAD A LITTLE LAMB, ETC. | | $1.00 | $2.00 |
| 1 | 2241 | JA, TOBY DEANE, PPO, VK | CINDERELLA | CINDERELLA | | $1.00 | $2.00 |
| 1 | 2242 | JA, PPO, VK | PUFF & TOOT | PUFF & TOOT | | $2.00 | $4.00 |
| 1 | 2243 | JA, PPO, VK | SNOW WHITE | SNOW WHITE | | $1.00 | $2.00 |
| 1 | 2244 | JA, BOBBY HOOKEY; HUGO PA-RETTI, DIR. | TREASURE ISLAND | TREASURE ISLAND | | $1.00 | $2.00 |
| 1 | 2245 | JA, PPO, VK | WE'RE OFF TO SEE THE PARADE, ETC. | THE CAISSONS GO ROLLING ALONG, ETC. | | $1.00 | $2.00 |
| 1 | 2246 | JA, VK | GET ALONG LITTLE DOGGIE, ETC. | BLUE TAIL FLY, ETC. | | $1.00 | $2.00 |
| 1 | 2247 | JA, JANICE PAGE, PPO, VK | ALICE IN WONDERLAND | ALICE IN WONDERLAND | | $1.00 | $2.00 |
| 1 | 2248 | JA, VK | JESUS LOVES ME, ETC. | SAVIOR, TEACH ME DAY BY DAY | | $1.00 | $2.00 |
| 1 | 2249 | JA, VK | STAND UP FOR JESUS, ETC. | JESUS CALLS US, ETC. | | $1.00 | $2.00 |
| 1 | 2250 | DICK EDWARDS, PPO, VK | PEEK-A-BOO | PEEK-A-BOO | | $1.00 | $2.00 |
| 1 | 2251 | DICK EDWARDS, TOBY DEANE, PPO, VK | HENNY PENNY | THE LITTLE RED HEN | | $1.00 | $2.00 |
| 1 | 2252 | DICK EDWARDS, PPO, VK/THE CAROLEERS | RUDOLPH THE RED-NOSED REIN-DEER | DECK THE HALLS, ETC. | | $1.00 | $2.00 |
| 1 | 2253 | JOE DEANE, SOMER ALBERG, PPO, VK | DINKY | DINKY | | $10.00 | $20.00 |
| 1 | 2254 | SOMER ALBERG, PPO, VK | MIGHTY MOUSE IN TOYLAND | MIGHTY MOUSE IN TOYLAND | | $10.00 | $20.00 |
| 1 | 2255 | PPO, VK/JA, PPO, VK | THE LITTLE WHITE DUCK | PONY BOY, ETC. | | $1.00 | $2.00 |
| 1 | 2256 | DICK EDWARDS, PPO, VK/THE CAROLEERS | FROSTY THE SNOWMAN | SILENT NIGHT | | $1.00 | $2.00 |

## PETER PAN 10" SERIES SINGLES

| # REC | DISC # | ARTIST | A TITLE | B TITLE | YEAR | G/VG | EX/NMT |
|---|---|---|---|---|---|---|---|
| 1 | 2256 | DICK EDWARDS, PPO, VK/JA, BOBBY HOOKEY, PPO, VK | FROSTY THE SNOWMAN | THE LITTLE RED WAGON | | $5.00 | $10.00 |
| 1 | 2257 | DICK EDWARDS, PPO, VK/JA, VK | PETER COTTONTAIL | BLUE TAIL FLY, ETC. | | $1.00 | $2.00 |
| 1 | 2258 | JA, BOBBY HOOKEY, PPO, VK | THE LITTLE RED WAGON | THE LITTLE RED WAGON | | $5.00 | $10.00 |
| 1 | 2259 | JA, VK | BUFFALO BILLY | GET ALONG LITTLE DOGGIE, ETC. | | $1.00 | $2.00 |
| 1 | 2260 | LOREN BECKER, PPO, VK/SOMER ALBERG, PPO, VK | PARADE OF THE WOODEN SOLDIERS | TOYLAND | | $1.00 | $2.00 |
| 1 | 2261 | JA, MARILYN REESE, THE HONEYDREAMERS, VK | TINA THE BALLERINA | TINA THE BALLERINA | | $8.00 | $15.00 |
| 1 | 2262 | JA, MARILYN REESE, THE HONEYDREAMERS, VK | MAKE BELIEVE | MAKE BELIEVE | | $1.00 | $2.00 |
| 1 | 2263 | JIM GOODE, JA, VK | TRAIN SOUND EFFECTS | TRAIN SOUND EFFECTS | | $4.00 | $8.00 |
| 1 | 2264 | JACK RUSSELL, THE HONEYDREAMERS, VK/THE CAROLEERS | WHITE CHRISTMAS | JINGLE BELLS | | $1.00 | $2.00 |
| 1 | 2265 | BETTY HARRIS, VK/DICK EDWARDS, TOBY DEANE, PPO, VK | ME AND MY TEDDY BEAR | THE LITTLE RED HEN | | $1.00 | $2.00 |
| 1 | 2266 | JA, PAUL TAUBMAN & ORCH./JA, VK | GOLDILOCKS AND THE THREE BEARS | PANCHO THE CIRCUS DONKEY | | $2.00 | $4.00 |
| 1 | 2267 | JA, PPO/JA, BOBBY HOOKEY, PPO, VK | LITTLE RED RIDING HOOD | THE LITTLE RED WAGON | | $5.00 | $10.00 |
| 1 | 2268 | JOYA LOMBARDI, BRUCE MARSHALL, RAY HEATHERTON, VK | THE BOBBSEY TWINS | THE BOBBSEY TWINS | | $5.00 | $10.00 |
| 1 | 2269 | VICTOR JORY, TOBY DEANE; VK, DIRECTOR | PETER PAN | PETER PAN | | $3.00 | $6.00 |
| 1 | 2270 | VICTOR JORY, VK | PETER AND THE WOLF | PETER AND THE WOLF | | $3.00 | $6.00 |
| 1 | 2271 | RAY HALLEE, PPO, VK/JACK ARTHUR, VK | THE LITTLE RED CABOOSE | GET ALONG LITTLE DOGGIE, ETC. | | $1.00 | $2.00 |
| 1 | 2272 | DICK EDWARDS, PPO, VK/JA, VK | SMOKEY THE BEAR | BLUE TAIL FLY, ETC. | | $1.00 | $2.00 |
| 1 | 2273 | BOBBY NICHOLAS, PPO, VK/THE CAROLEERS, VK | SANTA IS COMING TO TOWN | JINGLE BELLS, ADESTE FIDELES | | $1.00 | $2.00 |
| 1 | 2274 | SOMER ALBERG, PPO, VK/JOE DEANE, SOMER ALBERG, PPO, VK | MIGHTY MOUSE IN TOYLAND | DINKY | | $10.00 | $20.00 |
| 1 | 2275 | SUZY WILLIAMS, PPO, VK/THE CAROLEERS | I SAW MOMMY KISSING SANTA CLAUS | SILENT NIGHT | | $1.00 | $2.00 |
| 1 | 2276 | JANE & PEGGY, PPO, VK/JA, PPO, VK | THE DOGGIE IN THE WINDOW | TEDDY BEARS ON PARADE | | $3.00 | $6.00 |
| 1 | 2277 | JOHNNY SWIFT, TOM BURNS, PPO, VK/JA, VK | TELL ME A STORY | FOLK SONGS: BLUE TAIL FLY, ETC. | | $1.00 | $2.00 |
| 1 | 2278 | TOBY DEANE, PPO, VK | JINGLE DINGLE | JINGLE DINGLE | | $5.00 | $10.00 |
| 1 | 2279 | BETTY HARRIS, PPO, VK/THE FAIRYLAND PLAYERS, JUSTIN STONE, DIR. | I'M A LITTLE TEA POT | SLEEPYTOWN TRAIN | | $1.00 | $2.00 |
| 1 | 2280 | BETTY HARRIS, PPO, VK/BW | ON THE GOOD SHIP LOLLIPOP | SHE'LL BE COMIN' ROUND THE MOUNTAIN, ETC. | | $1.00 | $2.00 |
| 1 | 2281 | JACK RUSSELL, PPO, VK/JACK HORN, PPO, VK | I'M A YANKEE DOODLE DANDY, YOU'RE A GRAND OLD FLAG | HERE COMES THE BAND: AMERICA'S FAVORITE MARCHING SONGS | | $1.00 | $2.00 |
| 1 | 2282 | DAVID RICHARDS, PPO, VK/THE FAIRYLAND PLAYERS; JUSTIN STONE, DIR. | LITTLE TOOT | SLEEPYTOWN TRAIN | | $1.00 | $2.00 |
| 1 | 2283 | DAVID RICHARDS, PPO, VK/PPO, VK | THE MUSIC GOES 'ROUND AND ROUND | JACK AND THE BEANSTALK | | $1.00 | $2.00 |
| 1 | 2284 | BOBBY NICHOLAS, ANNIE WET, PPO, VK/PPO; PEGGY MARSHALL, DIR. | IN A LITTLE RED SCHOOLHOUSE | BILLY BOY, ETC. | | $1.00 | $2.00 |
| 1 | 2286 | PPO, VK | THE HIGH SCHOOL CADETS | OUR DIRECTOR | | $1.00 | $2.00 |
| 1 | 2288 | PETER PAN SQUARE DANCE PLAYERS & CALLER | SQUARE DANCES FOR JUNIORS WITH CALLS: TAKE A PEEK | SQUARE DANCES FOR JUNIORS WITH CALLS: CLIMBING UP THE GOLDEN STAIRS | | $1.00 | $2.00 |
| 1 | 2290 | VICKI DALE, PPO, VK/BOBBY BURNS, PPO, VK | I WANT A HIPPOPOTAMUS FOR CHRISTMAS | CHRISTMAS CHOPSTICKS ('TWAS THE NIGHT BEFORE CHRISTMAS) | | $1.00 | $2.00 |
| 1 | 2291 | VICKI DALE, PPO, VK/SOMER ALBERG, PPO, VK | ARE MY EARS ON STRAIGHT | TOYLAND | | $1.00 | $2.00 |
| 1 | 2292 | BOBBY DIXON, PPO, VK/JA, VK | GOD BLESS US ALL | TEDDY BEARS ON PARADE (AKA TEDDY BEARS POLKA) | | $1.00 | $2.00 |
| 1 | 2293 | BETTY BONNIE, PPO, VK | THE GINGERBREAD MAN | WHEN YOU WISH UPON A STAR | | $2.00 | $4.00 |

## PETER PAN 10" SERIES SINGLES

| # REC | DISC # | ARTIST | A TITLE | B TITLE | YEAR | G/VG | EX/NMT |
|---|---|---|---|---|---|---|---|
| 1 | 2294 | PPO, VK | OLD MACDONALD HAD A FARM | OH SUSANNA | | $1.00 | $2.00 |
| 1 | 2295 | BOBBY DIXON, LINDA BARRIE, THE HAPPY THREE, PPO, VK/PPO | LITTLE GOLDIE GOLDFISH | OH DEAR! WHAT CAN THE MATTER BE | | $3.00 | $6.00 |
| 1 | 2296 | VICTOR JORY | PRESTO — THE MAGIC RECORD: THE FABULOUS ADVENTURES OF TOMMY & HIS FRIENDS | | | $4.00 | $8.00 |
| 1 | 2297 | BOBBY DIXON, JOHNNY SWIFT, PPO, VK/PPO, PEGGY MARSHALL, DIR. | APPLE ON A STICK | ALL AROUND THE MULBERRY BUSH, ETC. | | $1.00 | $2.00 |
| 1 | 2298 | DANNY STEVENS, THE FOUR SERGEANTS, PPO, VK/? | THE LITTLE TIN SOLDIER (AND THE LITTLE TOY DRUM) | ? | | $1.00 | $2.00 |
| 1 | 2299 | WENDY WILLIAMS, BOBBY DIXON, PPO, VK/? | IN THE LAND OF LOLLIPOPS AND LEMONADE | ? | | $1.00 | $2.00 |
| 1 | L-10 | JOHN BRADFORD, BOBBY HOOKEY, PPO, VK | PINOCCHIO | PINOCCHIO | | $1.00 | $2.00 |
| 1 | X-4 B/ X-7 B | MORT LAWRENCE, VK/BOBBY BURNS, PPO, VK | THE NIGHT BEFORE CHRISTMAS | CHRISTMAS CHOPSTICKS ('TWAS THE NIGHT BEFORE CHRISTMAS) | | $1.00 | $2.00 |

## PETER PAN 7", PAPER COVER AND SPIRAL BOUND ALBUMS

| SET # | # REC | DISC # | MAIN TITLE | ARTIST | G/VG | EX/NMT |
|---|---|---|---|---|---|---|
| NO. 1 (PAPER COVER) | 4 | ? | ? | ? | $3.00 | $6.00 |
| NO. 2 (PAPER COVER) | 4 | ? | ? | ? | $3.00 | $6.00 |
| NO. 3 (PAPER COVER) | 4 | 218, 220, 222, 226 | A CHRISTMAS ALBUM | THE CAROLEERS | $3.00 | $6.00 |
| NO. 1 (SPIRAL BOUND) | 4 | ? | CHRISTMAS RECORD ALBUM | ? | $3.00 | $6.00 |
| NO. 2 (SPIRAL BOUND) | 4 | ? | SANTA'S MUSIC SHOP | ? | $3.00 | $6.00 |
| NO. 3 (SPIRAL BOUND) | 4 | ? | STORYTIME: FAVORITE MUSICAL STORIES | ? | $3.00 | $6.00 |
| NO. 4 (SPIRAL BOUND) | 4 | ? | MOTHER GOOSE | ? | $3.00 | $6.00 |
| NO # (8" X 12" CARDBOARD FOLDER) | 4 | X1, X4, X10B/X15B, X11B/X16B | CHRISTMAS ALBUM | THE CAROLEERS, ETC. | $3.00 | $6.00 |

## PHOEBE JAMES CREATIVE RHYTHMS FOR CHILDREN 10" SINGLES

| # REC | DISC # | MAIN TITLE | ARTIST | YEAR | G/VG | EX/MT |
|---|---|---|---|---|---|---|
| 1 | AED 1 | ANIMAL RHYTHMS | PHOEBE JAMES | 196? | $1.00 | $2.00 |
| 1 | AED 2 | FREE RHYTHMS | PHOEBE JAMES | | $1.00 | $2.00 |
| 1 | AED 3 | ANIMAL RHYTHMS WITH SOUND EFFECTS | PHOEBE JAMES | | $1.00 | $2.00 |
| 1 | AED 4 | GARDEN VARIETIES | PHOEBE JAMES | | $1.00 | $2.00 |
| 1 | AED 5 | FUNDAMENTAL RHYTHMS | PHOEBE JAMES | | $1.00 | $2.00 |
| 1 | AED 6 | TRAINS | PHOEBE JAMES | | $1.00 | $2.00 |
| 1 | AED 7 | BOAT RHYTHMS | PHOEBE JAMES | | $1.00 | $2.00 |
| 1 | AED 8 | BRANDING CATTLE — LA COSTILLA | PHOEBE JAMES | | $1.00 | $2.00 |
| 1 | AED 9 | THE GINGERBREAD BOY AND THE BILLY GOATS GRUFF | PHOEBE JAMES | | $1.00 | $2.00 |
| 1 | AED 10 | AN INDIAN DANCE AND DRUM BEATS | PHOEBE JAMES | | $1.00 | $2.00 |
| 1 | AED 11 | FIRE! FIRE! — A MARCH | PHOEBE JAMES | | $1.00 | $2.00 |
| 1 | AED 12 | FAVORITE ACTION SONGS | PHOEBE JAMES | | $1.00 | $2.00 |
| 1 | AED 13 | FARM ANIMALS | PHOEBE JAMES | | $1.00 | $2.00 |
| 1 | AED 14 | CHRISTMAS RHYTHMS | PHOEBE JAMES | | $1.00 | $2.00 |
| 1 | AED 15 | HALLOWE'EN RHYTHMS | PHOEBE JAMES | | $3.00 | $6.00 |
| 1 | AED 16 | THE STORY OF SUGAR: PLANTING, ETC. | PHOEBE JAMES | | $1.00 | $2.00 |
| 1 | AED 17 | THE STORY OF SUGAR: HARVESTING BY HAND, ETC. | PHOEBE JAMES | | $1.00 | $2.00 |
| 1 | AED 18 | THE STORY OF PINEAPPLE (3RD TO 8TH) | PHOEBE JAMES | | $1.00 | $2.00 |
| 1 | AED 19 | THE STORY OF LUMBER (3RD TO 8TH) | PHOEBE JAMES | | $1.00 | $2.00 |
| 1 | AED 20 | RHYTHM ORCHESTRA | PHOEBE JAMES | | $1.00 | $2.00 |
| 1 | AED 21 | NURSERY SCHOOL RHYTHMS | PHOEBE JAMES | | $1.00 | $2.00 |
| 1 | AED 22 | SEA LIFE RHYTHMS | PHOEBE JAMES | | $1.00 | $2.00 |

## PHONODISC SHAPED PICTURE DISCS, 5" PLAYING SURFACE

| REC # | DISC # | MAIN TITLE | ARTIST | YEAR | G/VG | EX/NMT | REMARKS |
|---|---|---|---|---|---|---|---|
| 1 | 5A-40 (PD) | A MESSAGE FROM SANTA/A RECORD FROM SANTA | NOT LISTED | 194? | $8.00 | $15.00 | |
| 1 | A4/A5 (PD) | A RECORD FROM THE EASTER BUNNY | SCOTTY MACGREGOR | | $8.00 | $15.00 | WITH MAILER |
| 1 | ? | BIRTHDAY GREETINGS (PANDA) | ? | | $8.00 | $15.00 | |

## PHONODISC STORYTIME SERIES 7" SINGLES

| # REC | DISC # | ARTIST | A TITLE | B TITLE | YEAR | G/VG | EX/NMT |
|---|---|---|---|---|---|---|---|
| 1 | 7-1 | SCOTT MACGREGOR | THE FOX AND HIS FRIENDS, PRETTY LITTLE ZEBRA | THE SLOW SLOW TURTLE, NURSERY MEDLEY | 1948 | $2.00 | $4.00 |
| 1 | 7-2 | ? | THE ANIMALS WENT TOT THE PARK, WILLIE THE SPIDER | LET'S GO OUT TOGETHER | | $2.00 | $4.00 |
| 1 | 7-3 | ? | PUSSY CAT, PUSSY CAT, ETC. | BAA BAA BLACK SHEEP, ETC. | | $2.00 | $4.00 |
| 1 | 7-4 | ? | LUCK LOCKET, ETC. | JACK AND JILL, ETC. | | $2.00 | $4.00 |
| 1 | 7-5 | MAX RICH | THE PUSSY CAT AND THE FIDDLE | UP WITH THE DAWN | | $2.00 | $4.00 |
| 1 | 7-6 | ED LEWIS AND WALLY RUSSELL | OH SUSANNA, OLD CHISHOLM TRAIL | BIG ROCK CANDY MOUNTAIN, ETC. | | $2.00 | $4.00 |
| 1 | 7-7 | ? | ? | ? | | $2.00 | $4.00 |
| 1 | 7-8 | ED LEWIS AND WALLY RUSSELL | OLD MACDONALD HAD A FARM | WOOLIE BOOGIE BEE | | $2.00 | $4.00 |
| 1 | 7-57 | UNCLE NACE/SCOTTY MACGREGOR | HAPPY BIRTHDAY | HAPPY BIRTHDAY ANIMALS | | $2.00 | $4.00 |

## PICTO TOONS 6" SINGLE-SIDE, BOXED WITH TOYS

| # REC | DISC # | MAIN TITLE | ARTIST | YEAR | G/VG | EX/NMT | REMARKS |
|---|---|---|---|---|---|---|---|
| 1 | 502-A | LITTLE BOY BLUE | NOT LISTED | 1958 | $25.00 | $50.00 | BOXED RECORD, PICTURE PUZZLES, STAND-UP FIGURES, MFG. SELCHOW & RIGHTER |
| 1 | 502-B | HEY DIDDLE DIDDLE | NOT LISTED | | $25.00 | $50.00 | |
| 1 | 502-C | SING A SONG OF SIXPENCE | NOT LISTED | | $25.00 | $50.00 | |
| 1 | 502-D | MONDAY'S CHILD | NOT LISTED | | $25.00 | $50.00 | |
| 1 | 502-E | ROCK A BYE BABY | NOT LISTED | | $25.00 | $50.00 | |
| 1 | 502-F | BAA, BAA BLACK SHEEP | NOT LISTED | | $25.00 | $50.00 | |

## PICTORIAL 6" PICTURE DISCS IN FOLDER

| # REC | DISC # | ARTIST | A TITLE | B TITLE | YEAR | G/VG | EX/NMT |
|---|---|---|---|---|---|---|---|
| 1 | 10,001* | NOT LISTED | THREE LITTLE KITTENS | JACK AND JILL | 1928 | $35.00 | $75.00 |
| 1 | 10,002* | NOT LISTED | LITTLE BO PEEP | OLD KING COLE | | $35.00 | $75.00 |
| 1 | 10,003* | NOT LISTED | MARY HAD A LITTLE LAMB | TOM TOM THE PIPER'S SON | | $35.00 | $75.00 |
| 1 | 10,004** | NOT LISTED | OLD MOTHER GOOSE | DING DONG BELL | | $35.00 | $75.00 |
| 1 | 10,005** | NOT LISTED | SING A SONG OF SIXPENCE | LITTLE BOY BLUE | | $35.00 | $75.00 |
| 1 | 10,006** | NOT LISTED | OLD MOTHER HUBBARD | HEY DIDDLE DIDDLE | | $35.00 | $75.00 |

*MOTHER GOOSE (PART ONE) **MOTHER GOOSE (PART TWO). NOTE: ADD $75.00 FOR FOLDER.

## PICTURTONE MAIN SERIES 7" PICTURE DISCS, BOXED SETS

| SET # | # REC | DISC # | MAIN TITLE | ARTIST | A TITLE | B TITLE | YEAR | G/VG | EX/NMT |
|---|---|---|---|---|---|---|---|---|---|
| VOL. 1 | 3 | | TREASURE TALES* | DAVID KURLAN | | | CA 1948 | $15.00 | $30.00 |
| | | 10166/10266 | | DAVID KURLAN | A STORY WITHOUT AN END | BELLING THE CAT | | $3.00 | $6.00 |
| | | 10366/10466 | | DAVID KURLAN | THE CAMEL AND THE MONKEY | THE PRINCESS AND THE PEA | | $3.00 | $6.00 |
| | | 10566/10666 | | DAVID KURLAN | THE FISHERMAN AND THE GENIE | THE POT OF JAM | | $3.00 | $6.00 |
| VOL. 2 | 3 | | TREASURE TALES | DAVID KURLAN | | | | $15.00 | $30.00 |
| | | 10766/10866 | | DAVID KURLAN | THE BEGGAR AND THE WOMAN WHO PECKED | THE CAT AND THE FOX | | $3.00 | $6.00 |
| | | 10966/11066 | | DAVID KURLAN | WHEN THE KING SNEEZES | THE BOY WHO CRIED WOLF! | | $3.00 | $6.00 |
| | | 11166/11266 | | DAVID KURLAN | SWEET SOUP | THE TOWN MOUSE AND THE COUNTRY MOUSE | | $3.00 | $6.00 |
| VOL. 3 | 3 | | MUSICAL TALES | THE MERRY SINGERS | | | | $15.00 | $30.00 |
| | | M301/302 | | THE MERRY SINGERS | OLD MACDONALD HAD A FARM | POLLY PUT THE KETTLE ON | | $3.00 | $6.00 |
| | | M303/304 | | THE MERRY SINGERS | THREE BLIND MICE | WE'LL ALL GO A-SINGING | | $3.00 | $6.00 |
| | | M305/306 | | THE MERRY SINGERS | YANKEE DOODLE | DOING THE HOKEY-POKEY | | $3.00 | $6.00 |
| VOL. 4 | 3 | | MUSICAL TALES | THE MERRY SINGERS | | | | $15.00 | $30.00 |
| | | M307/308 | | THE MERRY SINGERS | SKIP TO MY LOU | THREE LITTLE KITTENS | | $3.00 | $6.00 |
| | | M309/310 | | THE MERRY SINGERS | POP! GOES THE WEASEL | OH DEAR! WHAT CAN THE MATTER BE? | | $3.00 | $6.00 |

*PRICE SHOWN ON VOL. # LINE INCLUDES RECORDS AND BOX.

## PICTURTONE MAIN SERIES 7" PICTURE DISCS, BOXED SETS

| SET # | # REC | DISC # | MAIN TITLE | ARTIST | A TITLE | B TITLE | G/VG | EX/NMT |
|---|---|---|---|---|---|---|---|---|
| | | M311/312 | | THE MERRY SINGERS | A FROG WENT A-WALKING | TEN LITTLE INDIANS | $3.00 | $6.00 |
| VOL. 5 | 3 | | FOLK SONGS | THE MERRY SINGERS | | | $15.00 | $30.00 |
| | | S571/572 | | THE MERRY SINGERS | THE BLUE-TAIL FLY | FUNICULI, FUNICULA | $3.00 | $6.00 |
| | | S573/574 | | THE MERRY SINGERS | THE ERIE CANAL | FRERE JACQUES | $3.00 | $6.00 |
| | | S575/576 | | THE MERRY SINGERS | DO YOU KEN JOHN PEEL | OH SUSANNAH! | $3.00 | $6.00 |
| VOL. 6 | 3 | | FOLK DANCES | THE MERRY SINGERS | | | $15.00 | $30.00 |
| | | D451/452 | | THE MERRY SINGERS | TURKEY IN THE STRAW | CAROUSEL (A SWEDISH FOLK DANCE) | $3.00 | $6.00 |
| | | D453/454 | | THE MERRY SINGERS | TAKE A LITTLE PEEK | THE KERRY DANCE | $3.00 | $6.00 |
| | | D455/456 | | THE MERRY SINGERS | SHOO FLY DON'T BOTHER ME | THE MEXICAN HAT DANCE | $3.00 | $6.00 |
| VOL. 7 | 3 | | FOLK SONGS | THE MERRY SINGERS | | | $15.00 | $30.00 |
| | | S577/578 | | THE MERRY SINGERS | CLEMENTINE | SWEET BETSY FROM PIKE | $3.00 | $6.00 |
| | | S579/580 | | THE MERRY SINGERS | PAPER OF PINS | I'VE BEEN WORKIN' ON THE RAILROAD | $3.00 | $6.00 |
| | | S581/582 | | THE MERRY SINGERS | CASEY JONES | THE GIRL I LEFT BE-HIND ME | $3.00 | $6.00 |
| VOL. 8 | 3 | | FOLK DANCES | THE MERRY SINGERS | | | $15.00 | $30.00 |
| | | D457/458 | | THE MERRY SINGERS | ARKANSAS TRAVELER | LA JESUCITA | $3.00 | $6.00 |
| | | D459/460 | | THE MERRY SINGERS | BUFFALO GALS | WALTZING MATILDA | $3.00 | $6.00 |
| | | D461/462 | | THE MERRY SINGERS | MISS JENNY JONES | THE CAMPBELLS ARE COMIN' | $3.00 | $6.00 |
| VOL. 9 | 3 | | PLAY-PARTY SONGS | THE MERRY SINGERS, CECE BLAKE | | | $15.00 | $30.00 |
| | | P 11/12 | | THE MERRY SINGERS, CECE BLAKE | FARMER IN THE DELL | IN AND OUT THE WIN-DOW | $3.00 | $6.00 |
| | | P 13/14 | | THE MERRY SINGERS, CECE BLAKE | RING AROUND A ROSY | PLANTING CORN | $3.00 | $6.00 |
| | | P 15/16 | | THE MERRY SINGERS | ON THE BRIDGE AT AVIGNON | ALL AROUND THE MUL-BERRY BUSH | $3.00 | $6.00 |
| VOL. 10 | 3 | | HOLIDAY SONGS | THE MERRY SINGERS | | | $15.00 | $30.00 |
| | | H 91/92 | | THE MERRY SINGERS | RING DONG-DING DONG | CHRISTMAS COMES BUT ONCE A YEAR | $3.00 | $6.00 |
| | | H 93/94 | | THE MERRY SINGERS | JOLLY OLD ST. NICHOLAS | DECK THE HALLS WITH BOUGHS OF HOLLY | $3.00 | $6.00 |
| | | H 95/96 | | THE MERRY SINGERS | THE FIRST NOEL | JINGLE BELLS | $3.00 | $6.00 |
| VOL. 11 | 3 | | GILBERT AND SULLIVAN FOR YOUNG FOLK: THE MIKADO | THE MERRY SINGERS | | | $25.00 | $50.00 |
| | | GSS 1/2 | | THE MERRY SINGERS | HERE'S A HOW-DE-DO | A WANDERING MINSTREL | $6.00 | $12.00 |
| | | GSS 3/4 | | THE MERRY SINGERS | LORD HIGH EXECUTIONER | THREE LITTLE MAIDS | $6.00 | $12.00 |
| | | GSS 5/6 | | THE MERRY SINGERS | THE FLOWER THAT BLOOM IN THE SPRING | TIT-WILLOW | $6.00 | $12.00 |
| VOL. 12 | 3 | | GILBERT AND SUL-LIVAN FOR YOUNG FOLK: THE H.M.S. PINAFORE | THE MERRY SINGERS | | | $25.00 | $50.00 |
| | | GSS 7/8 | | THE MERRY SINGERS | CAREFULLY ON TIPTOE STEALING | I AM THE CAPTAIN OF THE PINAFORE | $6.00 | $12.00 |
| | | GSS 9/10 | | THE MERRY SINGERS | WE SAIL THE OCEAN BLUE | I'M CALLED LITTLE BUTTERCUP | $6.00 | $12.00 |
| | | GSS 11/12 | | THE MERRY SINGERS | WHEN I WAS A LAD | I AM THE MONARCH OF THE SEA | $6.00 | $12.00 |
| VOL. 16 | 3 | | GILBERT AND SULLIVAN FOR YOUNG FOLK: THE PIRATES OF PENZANCE | THE MERRY SINGERS | | | $25.00 | $50.00 |
| | | GSS 13/14 | | THE MERRY SINGERS | WHEN FREDERIC WAS A LAD | THE FOEMAN BARES HIS STEEL | $6.00 | $12.00 |
| | | GSS 15/16 | | THE MERRY SINGERS | THE PIRATE'S SONG | A POLICEMAN'S LOT IS NOT A HAPPY ONE | $6.00 | $12.00 |

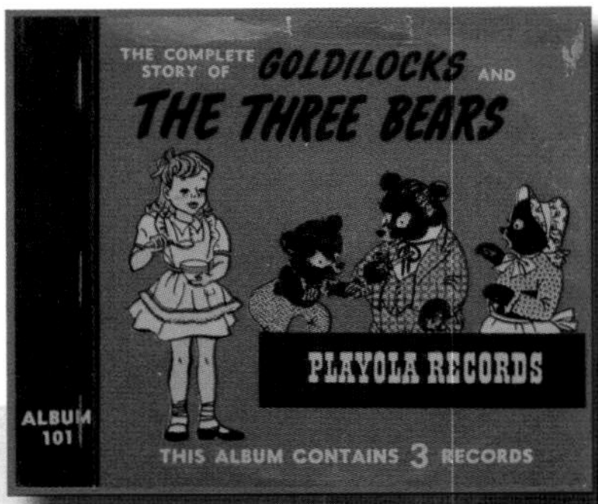


PICTURTONE RECORDS
SKIP TO MY LOU
$6.00

PIX RECORDS
DEEDLE DEEDLE DUMPLING
$80.00

PLAYOLA RECORDS
GOLDILOCKS AND THE THREE BEARS
$2.00

## PICTURTONE MAIN SERIES 7" PICTURE DISCS, BOXED SETS

| SET # | # REC | DISC # | MAIN TITLE | ARTIST | A TITLE | B TITLE | G/VG | EX/NMT |
|---|---|---|---|---|---|---|---|---|
| | | GSS 17/18 | | THE MERRY SINGERS | MODEL OF A MODERN MAJOR-GENERAL | WITH CATLIKE TREAD | $6.00 | $12.00 |
| VOL. 17 | 3 | | GILBERT AND SULLIVAN FOR YOUNG FOLK: TRIAL BY JURY/IOLANTHE | THE MERRY SINGERS | | | $25.00 | $50.00 |
| | | GSS 19/20 | | THE MERRY SINGERS | TINK-A-TANK, TINK-A-TANK | THE JUDGE'S SONG | $6.00 | $12.00 |
| | | GSS 21/22 | | THE MERRY SINGERS | ALL THE YOUNG LADIES I KNOW | FAINT HEART NEVER WON FAIR LADY | $6.00 | $12.00 |
| | | GSS 23/24 | | THE MERRY SINGERS | WHEN YOU'RE LYING AWAKE | IF WE'RE WEAK ENOUGH TO TARRY | $6.00 | $12.00 |
| VOL. ? | 3 | | IRVING CAESAR'S SONGS | THE MERRY SINGERS | | | $35.00 | $70.00 |
| | | ICS 1/2 | | THE MERRY SINGERS | AN AUTOMOBILE HAS TWO BIG EYES | HOT AND COLD WATER | $8.00 | $15.00 |
| | | ICS 3/4 | | THE MERRY SINGERS | WHEN YOU RIDE A BICYCLE | LEANING OUT OF WINDOWS, NEVER BE AFRAID OF ANYTHING | $8.00 | $15.00 |
| | | ICS 5/6 | | THE MERRY SINGERS | ? | ? | $8.00 | $15.00 |
| | | | IRVING CAESAR'S SONGS | THE MERRY SINGERS | | | $35.00 | $70.00 |
| VOL. ? | 3 | ICS 7/8 | | THE MERRY SINGERS | YOU'RE WATCHING A PARADE | STICKS AND STONES | $8.00 | $15.00 |
| | | ICS 9/10 | | THE MERRY SINGERS | REMEMBER YOUR NAME AND ADDRESS | WHEN YOU SWIM | $8.00 | $15.00 |
| | | ICS 11/12 | | THE MERRY SINGERS | STAY AWAY FROM THE RAILROAD TRACKS | WHEN JOHNNY CLIMBS FENCES | $8.00 | $15.00 |
| VOL. ? | 3 | | MARCHING SONGS | THE MERRY SINGERS | | | $15.00 | $30.00 |
| | | MAR1/2 | | THE MERRY SINGERS | THE GRENADIERS | LA MARSEILLAISE | $3.00 | $6.00 |
| | | MAR3/4 | | THE MERRY SINGERS | WHEN JOHNNY COMES MARCHING HOME | BATTLE HYMN OF THE REPUBLIC | $3.00 | $6.00 |
| | | MAR5/6 | | THE MERRY SINGERS | COLUMBIA, THE GEM OF THE OCEAN | WILLIE TAKE YOUR LITTLE DRUM | $3.00 | $6.00 |
| VOL. ? | 3 | | SPRING SONGS | THE MERRY SINGERS | | | $35.00 | $70.00 |
| | | SPR 1/2 | | THE MERRY SINGERS | SPRING IS HERE | EASTER CAROL | $8.00 | $15.00 |
| | | SPR 3/4 | | THE MERRY SINGERS | SPRING SONG | EASTER BELLS RING GLADLY | $8.00 | $15.00 |
| | | SPR 5/6 | | THE MERRY SINGERS | BUNNY OH BUNNY | SONG OF PETER RABBIT | $8.00 | $15.00 |
| NO # | 1 | NO # | | NOT LISTED | ALPHABET RECORD (WITH PICTURTONE RECORD-BOOK) | | $12.00 | $25.00 |
| NO # | 1 | NO # | | NOT LISTED | ALPHABET RECORD (WITHOUT BOOK) | | $3.00 | $6.00 |

## PICTURTONE GREETINGSONG SERIES 7" SINGLE SIDE PICTURE DISCS WITH MAILER

| DISC # | ARTIST | A TITLE | B TITLE | YEAR | G/VG | EX/NMT |
|---|---|---|---|---|---|---|
| G-201 S/S | NOT LISTED | AS ANNIVERSARY BELLS RING ON | N/A | CA 1948 | $5.00 | $10.00 |
| G-202 S/S | NOT LISTED | CONGRATULATIONS ON THIS DAY | N/A | | $5.00 | $10.00 |
| G-203 S/S | NOT LISTED | FOR YOU WHO SAY "I DO" | N/A | | $5.00 | $10.00 |
| G-204 S/S | NOT LISTED | (CHEER UP) HURRY UP AND GET WELL SOON | N/A | | $5.00 | $10.00 |
| G-205 S/S | NOT LISTED | HELLO BOUNCIN' BABY | N/A | | $5.00 | $10.00 |
| G-206 S/S | NOT LISTED | BIRTHDAY GREETINGS | N/A | | $5.00 | $10.00 |
| G-207 S/S | NOT LISTED | TO THE SWEETEST GIRL IN THE WORLD | N/A | | $5.00 | $10.00 |
| G-208 S/S | NOT LISTED | TO THE SWEETEST GUY IN THE WORLD | N/A | | $5.00 | $10.00 |
| G-209 S/S | NOT LISTED | MOTHER DEAR | N/A | | $5.00 | $10.00 |
| G-210 S/S | NOT LISTED | MY DEAR DAD | N/A | | $5.00 | $10.00 |
| G-211 S/S | NOT LISTED | MY FAVORITE RELATION IS YOU | N/A | | $5.00 | $10.00 |
| G-212 S/S | NOT LISTED | WHAT I'D GIVE TO BE HOME TODAY | N/A | | $5.00 | $10.00 |
| G-214 S/S | NOT LISTED | HAPPY BIRTHDAY, HOORAY! | N/A | | $5.00 | $10.00 |
| G-215 S/S | NOT LISTED | GOOD LUCK ON YOUR BIRTHDAY | N/A | | $5.00 | $10.00 |
| G-216 S/S | NOT LISTED | A BIRTHDAY SONG OF LOVE, SWEETHEART | N/A | | $5.00 | $10.00 |

## PIED PIPER (MUSIC YOU ENJOY) 7" SERIES SINGLES AND BOXED SETS

| # REC | DISC # | ARTIST | A TITLE | B TITLE | YEAR | ALSO ISSUED ON | G/VG | EX/NMT |
|---|---|---|---|---|---|---|---|---|
| 1 | PP-1 | NOT LISTED | CARRY ME BACK TO OLD VIRGINNY | OH SUSANNA | 194? | | $1.00 | $2.00 |
| 1 | PP-2 | NOT LISTED | SKATERS WALTZ | BLUE DANUBE | | | $1.00 | $2.00 |
| 1 | PP-3 | NOT LISTED | WALTZ OF THE FLOWERS | SCHUBERT WALTZ | | | $1.00 | $2.00 |
| 1 | PP-4 | NOT LISTED | MARCH OF A MARIONETTE | MARCH OF THE 3 KINGS | | | $1.00 | $2.00 |
| 1 | PP-5 | NOT LISTED | MARCHE LORRAINE | HAIL COLUMBIA | | | $1.00 | $2.00 |
| 1 | PP-6 | NOT LISTED | MARCH MILITAIRE | TRAMP THE BOYS ARE MARCHING | | | $1.00 | $2.00 |
| 1 | PP-7 | NOT LISTED | MARCH OF THE DWARFS | MARCH SLAV | | | $1.00 | $2.00 |
| 1 | PP-8 | NOT LISTED | TURKEY IN THE STRAW | THE ARKANSAS TRAVELER | | | $1.00 | $2.00 |
| 1 | PP-9 | NOT LISTED | COMIN' THRU THE RYE | OLD FOLKS AT HOME | | | $1.00 | $2.00 |
| 1 | PP-10 | NOT LISTED | POLKA | WHEN THEY PLAYED THE POLKA | | | $1.00 | $2.00 |
| 1 | PP-11 | NOT LISTED | THE IRISH WASHERWOMAN | LA CUCUARACHA | | | $1.00 | $2.00 |
| 1 | PP-12 | NOT LISTED | CAMPTOWN RACES | MINUET | | | $1.00 | $2.00 |
| 1 | PP-14 | NOT LISTED | FARMER IN THE DELL | A TISKET, A TASKET; PUSSY CAT | | KIDDIE RECORDS | $1.00 | $2.00 |
| 1 | PP-15 | NOT LISTED | LONDON BRIDGE IS FALLING DOWN | HI DIDDLE DIDDLE, JACK HORNER | | KIDDIE RECORDS | $1.00 | $2.00 |
| 1 | PP-16 | NOT LISTED | TWINKLE TWINKLE LITTLE STAR | SING A SONG OF SIXPENCE | | KIDDIE RECORDS | $1.00 | $2.00 |
| 1 | PP-17 | NOT LISTED | LITTLE BO PEEP | MARY HAD A LITTLE LAMB | | KIDDIE RECORDS | $1.00 | $2.00 |
| 1 | PP-18 | NOT LISTED | JACK AND JILL | ALL AROUND THE MULBERRY BUSH | | KIDDIE RECORDS | $1.00 | $2.00 |
| 1 | PP-19 | THE ED. LEWIS TRIO | HOME ON THE RANGE | WAITING FOR THE WAGON | | KIDDIE RECORDS | $1.00 | $2.00 |
| 1 | PP-20 | NOT LISTED | GIT ALONG LITTLE DOGGIE | LONE PRAIRIE | | KIDDIE RECORDS | $1.00 | $2.00 |
| 1 | PP-21 | NOT LISTED | COMIN' ROUND THE MOUNTAIN | GOODBYE OLD PAINT | | KIDDIE RECORDS | $1.00 | $2.00 |
| 1 | PT | NOT LISTED | THE RED RIVER VALLEY | THE CHISHOLM TRAIL | | KIDDIE RECORDS | $1.00 | $2.00 |
| 1 | PP-23 | THE ED. LEWIS TRIO | HUMPTY DUMPTY | LITTLE MISS MUFFET | | KIDDIE RECORDS | $1.00 | $2.00 |
| 1 | PP-24 | THE ED. LEWIS TRIO | THREE LITTLE KITTENS | BAA BAA BLACK SHEEP | | KIDDIE RECORDS | $1.00 | $2.00 |
| 1 | PP-25 | THE ED. LEWIS TRIO | ROCK-A-BYE BABY | POLLY WOLLY DOODLE | | KIDDIE RECORDS | $1.00 | $2.00 |
| 1 | PP-26 | THE ED. LEWIS TRIO | JINGLE BELLS | THREE BLIND MICE | | KIDDIE RECORDS | $1.00 | $2.00 |
| 1 | PP-27 | THE ED. LEWIS TRIO | SIMPLE SIMON | WHERE HAS MY LITTLE DOG GONE | | KIDDIE RECORDS | $1.00 | $2.00 |
| 1 | PP-28 | THE ED. LEWIS TRIO | LITTLE BOY BLUE | THE OLD WOMAN IN THE SHOE | | KIDDIE RECORDS | $1.00 | $2.00 |
| 1 | PP-29 | THE ED. LEWIS TRIO | YANKEE DOODLE | TEN LITTLE INDIANS | | KIDDIE RECORDS | $1.00 | $2.00 |

## PIED PIPER (MUSIC YOU ENJOY) 7" SERIES SINGLES AND BOXED SETS

| # REC | DISC # | MAIN TITLE | ARTIST | YEAR | G/VG | EX/NMT |
|---|---|---|---|---|---|---|
| 1 | PP-50 | FARMER IN THE DELL, ETC. | NOT LISTED | 195? | $1.00 | $2.00 |
| 1 | PP-51 | TWINKLE TWINKLE LITTLE STAR, ETC. | NOT LISTED | | $1.00 | $2.00 |
| 1 | PP-52 | ROCK-A-BYE BABY, ETC. | NOT LISTED | | $1.00 | $2.00 |
| 1 | PP-53 | LITTLE BO PEEP, ETC. | NOT LISTED | | $1.00 | $2.00 |
| 1 | PP-54 | MARY HAD A LITTLE LAMB, ETC. | NOT LISTED | | $1.00 | $2.00 |
| 1 | PP-55 | LITTLE BOY BLUE, ETC. | NOT LISTED | | $1.00 | $2.00 |
| 1 | PP-56 | GOODBYE OLD PAINT, ETC. | NOT LISTED | | $1.00 | $2.00 |
| 1 | PP-57 | COMIN' ROUND THE MOUNTAIN, ETC. | NOT LISTED | | $1.00 | $2.00 |

## PIX 10" PICTURE DISCS, SINGLE SIDE, BOXED SETS

| # REC | DISC # | MAIN TITLE | ARTIST | YEAR | G/VG | EX/NMT |
|---|---|---|---|---|---|---|
| 1 | 101 S/S | MARY HAD A LITTLE LAMB | WILLIAM ADAMS, ROBERT NOLAND | 1941 | $40.00 | $80.00 |
| 1 | 102 S/S | HUMPTY DUMPTY | WILLIAM ADAMS, ROBERT NOLAND | | $40.00 | $80.00 |
| 1 | 103 S/S | LITTLE MISS MUFFET | WILLIAM ADAMS, ROBERT NOLAND | | $40.00 | $80.00 |
| 1 | 104 S/S | LITTLE JACK HORNER | WILLIAM ADAMS, ROBERT NOLAND | | $40.00 | $80.00 |
| 1 | 105 S/S | HEY DIDDLE DIDDLE | WILLIAM ADAMS, ROBERT NOLAND | | $40.00 | $80.00 |
| 1 | 106 S/S | THE OLD WOMAN IN THE SHOE | WILLIAM ADAMS, ROBERT NOLAND | | $40.00 | $80.00 |
| 1 | 107 S/S | HICKORY DICKORY DOCK | WILLIAM ADAMS, ROBERT NOLAND | | $40.00 | $80.00 |
| 1 | 108 S/S | JACK AND JILL | WILLIAM ADAMS, ROBERT NOLAND | | $40.00 | $80.00 |
| 1 | 109 S/S | DEEDLE DEEDLE DUMPLING | WILLIAM ADAMS, ROBERT NOLAND | | $40.00 | $80.00 |

## PIXIE 10" SINGLES

| # REC | DISC # | MAIN TITLE | ARTIST | YEAR | G/VG | EX/NMT |
|---|---|---|---|---|---|---|
| 1 | P-1 | REAL COWBOY SONGS | LEONARD STOKES | 194? | $1.50 | $3.00 |
| 1 | P-2 | REAL SAILOR SONGS | LEONARD STOKES | | $1.50 | $3.00 |
| 1 | P-3 | DOWN BY THE STATION | WARREN GARNDER | | $1.50 | $3.00 |
| 1 | P-4 | MARCHES FOR CHILDREN | JACK SLOANE | | $1.50 | $3.00 |
| 1 | P-5 | SONGS FOR TODDLERS | ? | | $1.50 | $3.00 |
| 1 | P-6 | LET'S GO TO THE ZOO | ? | | $1.50 | $3.00 |
| 1 | P-7 | STEPHEN FOSTER FOR CHILDREN | GLEN CROSS | | $1.50 | $3.00 |
| 1 | P-8 | SING ME A LULLABY | GLEN CROSS | | $1.50 | $3.00 |
| 1 | P-9 | NIGHT BEFORE CHRISTMAS/JINGLE BELLS | GILBERT MACK | | $1.50 | $3.00 |
| 1 | P-10 | POLLY WOLLY DOODLE | JACK SLOANE | | $1.50 | $3.00 |

## PLASCO MAIN SERIES 7" SINGLES IN BOX WITH TOY FURNITURE

| # REC | DISC # | ARTIST | A TITLE | B TITLE | YEAR | G/VG | EX/NMT |
|---|---|---|---|---|---|---|---|
| 1 | 1/2 | CECILE ROY | DRUMMER BOY | MANNERS | 1949 | $1.00 | $2.00 |
| 1 | 3/4 | CECILE ROY | I WANT A DOLL HOUSE | PLAYING TOGETHER | | $1.00 | $2.00 |
| 1 | 5/6 | CECILE ROY | SLEEPY TIME | GETTING UP | | $1.00 | $2.00 |
| 1 | 7/8 | CECILE ROY | SETTING THE TABLE | ALICE IN WONDERLAND | | $1.00 | $2.00 |
| 1 | 9/10 | CECILE ROY | THE THISTLE | BUDDY'S GARDEN | | $1.00 | $2.00 |
| 1 | 11/12 | CECILE ROY | THE LITTLE ROSE | BUDDY'S BUTTERFLY | | $1.00 | $2.00 |
| 1 | 13/14 | CECILE ROY | CHRISTMAS EVE | PLASCO TOYS | | $1.00 | $2.00 |
| 1 | 15/16 | CECILE ROY | BO BO BO SKE DEETON | COUNTY FAIR | | $1.00 | $2.00 |
| N/A | N/A | N/A | BOXED SET W/TOY FURNITURE | PLASCO TOYS | | $50.00 | $100.00 |

## PLASCO CPC SERIES 7" SINGLES IN BOX WITH TOY FURNITURE

| # REC | DISC # | ARTIST | A TITLE | B TITLE | G/VG | EX/NMT |
|---|---|---|---|---|---|---|
| 1 | C.P.C. 1/5 | CECILE ROY | A COWBOY'S LIFE IS FUN | THE OLD BARN DANCE | $1.00 | $2.00 |
| 1 | C.P.C. 2/6 | CECILE ROY | CHUCK WAGON SONG | CALLING A SQUARE DANCE | $1.00 | $2.00 |
| 1 | C.P.C. 17/18 | CECILE ROY | EVERYBODY'S WORKING FOR ME | TODAY IS MY BIRTHDAY | $1.00 | $2.00 |

## RECORD GUILD OF AMERICA PICTURE DISCS 7" SINGLES AND BOXED SETS

| # REC | DISC # | ARTIST | A TITLE | B TITLE | YEAR | G/VG | EX/NMT |
|---|---|---|---|---|---|---|---|
| 1 | 1001-P | ST. PATRICK'S CATHEDRAL BOY CHORISTERS* | IT CAME UPON A MIDNIGHT CLEAR | JOY TO THE WORLD | 1948 | $3.00 | $6.00 |
| 1 | 1002-P | ST. PATRICK'S CATHEDRAL BOY CHORISTERS* | O LITTLE TOWN OF BETHLEHEM | FIRST NOEL | | $3.00 | $6.00 |
| 1 | 1003-P | REX CHORUS & BAND* | JINGLE BELLS | AULD LANG SYNE | | $3.00 | $6.00 |
| 1 | 1004-P | DARREN MCGAVIN, REX CHORUS* | THE NIGHT BEFORE CHRISTMAS (PT. 1) | THE NIGHT BEFORE CHRISTMAS (PT. 2) | | $3.00 | $6.00 |
| 1 | 2001-P | ANDY GAINEY, MUSIC HALL CHORUS & ORCH.* | BLUE TAIL FLY | CARRY ME BACK TO OLD VIR-GINNY | | $8.00 | $15.00 |
| 1 | 2002-P | RUE KNAPP, TEX JAMES BAND* | RED RIVER VALLEY | COCKLES AND MUSSELS | | $3.00 | $6.00 |
| 1 | 2003-P | ANDY GAINEY, MUSIC HALL CHORUS & ORCH.* | WORKIN' ON THE RAILROAD | ERIE CANAL | | $3.00 | $6.00 |
| 1 | 2004-P | ANDY GAINEY, PHIL & DOTTIE PROUD, MUSIC HALL CHORUS & ORCH.* | CAMPTOWN RACES | LITTLE BROWN JUG | | $3.00 | $6.00 |
| 1 | 3001-P | RANDOLPH SINGERS, TOM BROWN BAND* | THE FARMER IN THE DELL | THE MUFFIN MAN | | $3.00 | $6.00 |
| 1 | 3002-P | RANDOLPH SINGERS, TOM BROWN BAND* | ALL AROUND THE MULBERRY BUSH | A TISKET A TASKET | | $3.00 | $6.00 |
| 1 | 3003-P | DOTTIE & PHIL PROUD, MUSIC HALL CHORUS & ORCH.* | HAPPY BIRTHDAY | FOR HE'S A JOLLY GOOD FELLOW | | $3.00 | $6.00 |
| 1 | 3004-P | ANDY GAINEY, DOTTIE PROUD, MUSIC HALL CHORUS & ORCH.* | MEXICAN HAT DANCE | SKIP TO MY LOU | | $3.00 | $6.00 |
| 1 | 4001-P | DOTTIE & PHIL PROUD, MUSIC HALL ORCH.* | OLD MACDONALD | WHERE HAS MY LITTLE DOG GONE | | $3.00 | $6.00 |
| 1 | 4002-P | RANDOLPH SINGERS, TOM BROWN BAND* | TEN LITTLE INDIANS | HEY DIDDLE DIDDLE, MISS MUFFET | | $3.00 | $6.00 |
| 1 | 4003-P | ? | A HUNTING WE WILL GO | RIDE A COCK HORSE | | $3.00 | $6.00 |
| 1 | 4004-P | JENEFER BUNKER, MUSIC HALL ORCH.* | ALPHABET SONG | COUNTING SONG | | $3.00 | $6.00 |
| 1 | 5001-P | JENEFER BUNKER, MUSIC HALL ORCH.* | TWINKLE TWINKLE LITTLE STAR | PRETTY POLLY | | $3.00 | $6.00 |
| 1 | 5002-P | DOTTIE PROUD, MUSIC HALL & ORCH.* | ROCK-A-BYE BABY | PETER PETER PUMPKIN EATER | | $3.00 | $6.00 |
| 1 | 5003-P | JENEFER BUNKER, MUSIC HALL ORCH.* | MARY HAD A LITTLE LAMB | THREE LITTLE KITTENS | | $3.00 | $6.00 |
| 1 | 5004-P | DOTTIE PROUD, MUSIC HALL CHORUS & ORCH.* | JACK AND JILL | LITTLE BO PEEP, MARY MARY | | $3.00 | $6.00 |
| 1 | 6001-P | RUE KNAPP, BILL HARTT, TEX JAMES BAND* | NIGHT HERDING SONG | HOME ON THE RANGE | | $3.00 | $6.00 |
| 1 | 6002-P | BILL HARTT, DOUG MARTIN, ANDY GAINEY, TEX JAMES CHORUS & BAND* | GIT ALONG LITTLE DOGIE | WHISTLING RODEO POLKA | | $3.00 | $6.00 |
| 1 | 6003-P | ANDY GAINEY, RUE KNAPP, DOUG MARTIN, TEX JAMES BAND* | OLD CHISHOLM TRAIL | THE LONE PRAIRIE | | $3.00 | $6.00 |
| 1 | 6004-P | ANDY GAINEY, DOTTIE PROUD, TEX JAMES BAND* | OLD DAN TUCKER | BUFFALO GALS | | $3.00 | $6.00 |
| 1 | T-1010 | NOT LISTED. SEE LABEL NOTES FOR DETAILS ON ARTISTS.** | JACK AND THE BEANSTALK | THE EMPEROR'S NEW CLOTHES | | $3.00 | $6.00 |
| 1 | T-1011 | NOT LISTED. SEE LABEL NOTES FOR DETAILS ON ARTISTS.** | TOM THUMB | ALADDIN AND THE WONDERFUL LAMP | | $3.00 | $6.00 |
| 1 | T-1012 | NOT LISTED. SEE LABEL NOTES FOR DETAILS ON ARTISTS.** | SNOW DROP AND THE DWARFS (AKA SNOW WHITE) | RUM-PEL-STILT-SKIN | | $3.00 | $6.00 |
| 1 | T-1013 | NOT LISTED. SEE LABEL NOTES FOR DETAILS ON ARTISTS.** | CINDERELLA | THE UGLY DUCKLING | | $3.00 | $6.00 |
| 1 | S-2010 | NOT LISTED. SEE LABEL NOTES FOR DETAILS ON ARTISTS.** | HEY DIDDLE DIDDLE DUMPLING, COCK A DOODLE DOO | GOOSEY GOOSEY GANDER, HICKET PICKET MY BLACK HEN | | $3.00 | $6.00 |
| 1 | S-2011 | NOT LISTED. SEE LABEL NOTES FOR DETAILS ON ARTISTS.** | PEASE PORRIDGE HOT, COB-BLER COBBLER | SLEEP BABY SLEEP, BYE BABY BUNTING | | $3.00 | $6.00 |
| 1 | S-2012 | NOT LISTED. SEE LABEL NOTES FOR DETAILS ON ARTISTS.** | LITTLE BO PEEP, MARY MARY QUITE CONTRARY | SEE SAW MARGERY DAW, THIS LITTLE PIG | | $3.00 | $6.00 |
| 1 | S-2013 | NOT LISTED. SEE LABEL NOTES FOR DETAILS ON ARTISTS.** | LITTLE BOY BLUE, SING A SONG OF SIXPENCE | HUMPTY DUMPTY, SIMPLE SIMON | | $3.00 | $6.00 |
| 1 | S-2014 | NOT LISTED. SEE LABEL NOTES FOR DETAILS ON ARTISTS.** | THERE WAS A LITTLE GIRL, HICKORY DICKORY DOCK | OLD KING COLE, THERE WAS A CROOKED MAN | | $3.00 | $6.00 |
| 1 | S-2015 | NOT LISTED. SEE LABEL NOTES FOR DETAILS ON ARTISTS.** | A DILLAR A DOLLAR, TO MAR-KET TO MARKET | HOT CROSS BUNS, BAA BAA BLACK SHEEP | | $3.00 | $6.00 |
| 1 | S-2016 | NOT LISTED. SEE LABEL NOTES FOR DETAILS ON ARTISTS.** | HEY DIDDLE DIDDLE, LITTLE MISS MUFFET | PUSSY CAT PUSSY CAT, TOM TOM THE PIPER'S SON | | $3.00 | $6.00 |
| 1 | S-2017 | NOT LISTED. SEE LABEL NOTES FOR DETAILS ON ARTISTS.** | OLD MOTHER HUBBARD, WHERE O WHERE HAS MY LITTLE DOG GONE | LITTLE TOMMY TUCKER, JACK BE NIMBLE | | $3.00 | $6.00 |
| 1 | S-2018 | NOT LISTED. SEE LABEL NOTES FOR DETAILS ON ARTISTS.** | JACK SPRATT, DING DONG BELL | THERE WAS AN OLD WOMAN, LITTLE JACK HORNER | | $3.00 | $6.00 |

*VINYLITE **CARDBOARD

RECORD GUILD OF AMERICA
GIT ALONG LITTLE DOGIE
$6.00

RECORD GUILD OF AMERICA FLASH GORDON: CITY OF SEA CAVES
$50.00

RECORD GUILD OF AMERICA
HARK THE HERALD ANGELS SING
$3.00

## RECORD GUILD OF AMERICA PICTURE DISCS 7" SINGLES AND BOXED SETS

| # REC | DISC # | ARTIST | A TITLE | B TITLE | G/VG | EX/NMT |
|---|---|---|---|---|---|---|
| 1 | S-2019 | NOT LISTED. SEE LABEL NOTES FOR DETAILS ON ARTISTS.* | BILLY BOY | THREE LITTLE KITTENS | $3.00 | $6.00 |
| 1 | S-2020 | NOT LISTED. SEE LABEL NOTES FOR DETAILS ON ARTISTS.* | PAT A CAKE | LUCY LOCKET | $3.00 | $6.00 |
| 1 | S-2021 | NOT LISTED. SEE LABEL NOTES FOR DETAILS ON ARTISTS.* | POLLY PUT THE KETTLE ON | TEN LITTLE INDIANS | $3.00 | $6.00 |
| 1 | S-2022 | NOT LISTED. SEE LABEL NOTES FOR DETAILS ON ARTISTS.* | GEORGIE PORGIE | RIDE A COCK HORSE | $3.00 | $6.00 |
| 1 | S-2023 | NOT LISTED. SEE LABEL NOTES FOR DETAILS ON ARTISTS.* | FIDDLE DEE DEE | JACK AND JILL | $3.00 | $6.00 |
| 1 | S-2024 | NOT LISTED. SEE LABEL NOTES FOR DETAILS ON ARTISTS.* | PRETTY POLLY | THREE BLIND MICE | $3.00 | $6.00 |
| 1 | S-2025 | NOT LISTED. SEE LABEL NOTES FOR DETAILS ON ARTISTS.* | RUB-A-DUB-DUB | PETER PIPER | $3.00 | $6.00 |
| 1 | S-2026 | NOT LISTED. SEE LABEL NOTES FOR DETAILS ON ARTISTS.* | EARLY TO BED EARLY TO RISE | ROCKABYE BABY | $3.00 | $6.00 |
| 1 | S-2027 | NOT LISTED. SEE LABEL NOTES FOR DETAILS ON ARTISTS.* | MARY HAD A LITTLE LAMB | PETER PETER PUMPKIN EATER | $3.00 | $6.00 |
| 1 | S-2028 | NOT LISTED. SEE LABEL NOTES FOR DETAILS ON ARTISTS.* | TWINKLE TWINKLE LITTLE STAR | RAIN RAIN GO AWAY | $3.00 | $6.00 |
| 1 | S-3010 | NOT LISTED. SEE LABEL NOTES FOR DETAILS ON ARTISTS.* | SILENT NIGHT | NOEL NOEL | $3.00 | $6.00 |
| 1 | S-3011 | NOT LISTED. SEE LABEL NOTES FOR DETAILS ON ARTISTS.* | COME ALL YE FAITHFUL | IT CAME UPON A MIDNIGHT CLEAR | $3.00 | $6.00 |
| 1 | S-3012 | NOT LISTED. SEE LABEL NOTES FOR DETAILS ON ARTISTS.* | JINGLE BELLS | AULD LANG SYNE | $3.00 | $6.00 |
| 1 | G-4010 | NOT LISTED. SEE LABEL NOTES FOR DETAILS ON ARTISTS.* | A TISKET A TASKET | DID YOU EVER SEE A LASSIE | $3.00 | $6.00 |
| 1 | G-4011 | NOT LISTED. SEE LABEL NOTES FOR DETAILS ON ARTISTS.* | THE FARMER IN THE DELL | ALL AROUND THE MULBERRY BUSH | $3.00 | $6.00 |
| 1 | G-4012 | NOT LISTED. SEE LABEL NOTES FOR DETAILS ON ARTISTS.* | A HUNTING WE WILL GO | LONDON BRIDGE IS FALLING DOWN | $3.00 | $6.00 |
| 1 | G-4013 | NOT LISTED. SEE LABEL NOTES FOR DETAILS ON ARTISTS.* | LAZY MARY WILL YOU GET UP | OPEN THE GATES AS HIGH AS THE SKY | $3.00 | $6.00 |
| 1 | G-4014 | NOT LISTED. SEE LABEL NOTES FOR DETAILS ON ARTISTS.* | ROUND THE VILLAGE | LOOBY LOO | $3.00 | $6.00 |
| 1 | G-4015 | NOT LISTED. SEE LABEL NOTES FOR DETAILS ON ARTISTS.* | OH YES WE'VE SEEN THE MUFFIN MAN | NOBODY KNOWS WHAT MAKES OATS, PEAS, BEANS AND BARLEY GROW | $3.00 | $6.00 |
| 1 | M-5010 | NOT LISTED. SEE LABEL NOTES FOR DETAILS ON ARTISTS.* | ARKANSAS TRAVELER | CLEMENTINE | $3.00 | $6.00 |
| 1 | M-5011 | NOT LISTED. SEE LABEL NOTES FOR DETAILS ON ARTISTS.* | BLUE TAIL FLY | CAMPBELLS ARE COMING | $3.00 | $6.00 |
| 1 | M-5012 | NOT LISTED. SEE LABEL NOTES FOR DETAILS ON ARTISTS.* | POP GOES THE WEASEL | TURKEY IN THE STRAW | $3.00 | $6.00 |
| 1 | M-5013 | NOT LISTED. SEE LABEL NOTES FOR DETAILS ON ARTISTS.* | LITTLE BROWN JUG | MEXICAN HAT DANCE | $3.00 | $6.00 |
| 1 | M-5014 | NOT LISTED. SEE LABEL NOTES FOR DETAILS ON ARTISTS.* | OH DEAR WHAT CAN THE MATTER BE | OLD MACDONALD HAD A FARM | $3.00 | $6.00 |
| 1 | M-5015 | NOT LISTED. SEE LABEL NOTES FOR DETAILS ON ARTISTS.* | OH SUSANNA | SKIP TO MY LOU | $3.00 | $6.00 |
| 1 | M-5016 | NOT LISTED. SEE LABEL NOTES FOR DETAILS ON ARTISTS.* | COCKLES AND MUSSELS | ALOUETTE | $3.00 | $6.00 |
| 1 | M-5017 | NOT LISTED. SEE LABEL NOTES FOR DETAILS ON ARTISTS.* | DOWN IN THE VALLEY | ERIE CANAL | $3.00 | $6.00 |
| 1 | M-5018 | NOT LISTED. SEE LABEL NOTES FOR DETAILS ON ARTISTS.* | HOME SWEET HOME | DIXIE | $3.00 | $6.00 |
| 1 | M-5019 | NOT LISTED. SEE LABEL NOTES FOR DETAILS ON ARTISTS.* | CAMPTOWN RACES | CARRY ME BACK TO OLD VIRGINNY | $3.00 | $6.00 |
| 1 | M-5020 | NOT LISTED. SEE LABEL NOTES FOR DETAILS ON ARTISTS.* | RED RIVER VALLEY | WORKING ON THE RAILROAD | $3.00 | $6.00 |
| 1 | E-6010 | NOT LISTED. SEE LABEL NOTES FOR DETAILS ON ARTISTS.* | ALPHABET SONG | COUNTING SONG | $3.00 | $6.00 |

*CARDBOARD

## RECORD GUILD OF AMERICA PICTURE DISCS 7" SINGLES AND BOXED SETS

| # REC | DISC # | ARTIST | A TITLE | B TITLE | G/VG | EX/NMT |
|---|---|---|---|---|---|---|
| 1 | E-6011 | NOT LISTED. SEE LABEL NOTES FOR DETAILS ON ARTISTS.* | HAPPY BIRTHDAY | FOR HE'S A JOLLY GOOD FELLOW | $3.00 | $6.00 |
| 1 | C-7010 | NOT LISTED. SEE LABEL NOTES FOR DETAILS ON ARTISTS.* | NIGHT BEFORE CHRISTMAS (PT. 1) | NIGHT BEFORE CHRISTMAS (PT. 2) | $3.00 | $6.00 |
| 1 | C-7011 | NOT LISTED. SEE LABEL NOTES FOR DETAILS ON ARTISTS.* | O COME, ALL YE FAITHFUL | DECK THE HALLS | $3.00 | $6.00 |
| 1 | C-7012 | NOT LISTED. SEE LABEL NOTES FOR DETAILS ON ARTISTS.* | SILENT NIGHT | HARK THE HERALD ANGELS SING | $3.00 | $6.00 |
| 1 | C-7013 | NOT LISTED. SEE LABEL NOTES FOR DETAILS ON ARTISTS.* | THE FIRST NOEL | WASSAIL SONG | $3.00 | $6.00 |
| 1 | C-7014 | NOT LISTED. SEE LABEL NOTES FOR DETAILS ON ARTISTS.* | AULD LANG SYNE | JOY TO THE WORLD | $3.00 | $6.00 |
| 1 | C-7015 | NOT LISTED. SEE LABEL NOTES FOR DETAILS ON ARTISTS.* | JINGLE BELLS | WE THREE KINGS | $3.00 | $6.00 |
| 1 | F-301 | NOT LISTED. SEE LABEL NOTES FOR DETAILS ON ARTISTS.** | FLASH GORDON: CITY OF SEA CAVES (PT. 1) | FLASH GORDON: CITY OF SEA CAVES (PT. 2) | $25.00 | $50.00 |
| 1 | F-401 | NOT LISTED. SEE LABEL NOTES FOR DETAILS ON ARTISTS.** | RED RYDER: HERMIT'S GOLD (PT. 1) | RED RYDER: HERMIT'S GOLD (PT. 2) | $20.00 | $40.00 |
| 1 | F-501 | NOT LISTED. SEE LABEL NOTES FOR DETAILS ON ARTISTS.** | TERRY AND THE PIRATES: THE MILLION DOLLAR RUBY (PT. 1) | TERRY AND THE PIRATES: THE MILLION DOLLAR RUBY (PT. 2) | $20.00 | $40.00 |
| 1 | F-601 | NOT LISTED. SEE LABEL NOTES FOR DETAILS ON ARTISTS.** | POPEYE: PIRATE TREASURE (PT. 1) | POPEYE: PIRATE TREASURE (PT. 2) | $25.00 | $50.00 |
| 1 | N-101 | NOT LISTED. SEE LABEL NOTES FOR DETAILS ON ARTISTS.*** | SANTA'S SURPRISE (PT. 1) | SANTA'S SURPRISE (PT. 2) | $8.00 | $15.00 |
| 1 | N-102 | NOT LISTED. SEE LABEL NOTES FOR DETAILS ON ARTISTS.**** | SLEEPY BUNNY AND THE RAIN-BOW (PT. 1) | SLEEPY BUNNY AND THE RAIN-BOW (PT. 2) | $8.00 | $15.00 |

*CARDBOARD **CARTOON SERIES ***DIE-CUT **** VINYLITE

## RECORD GUILD OF AMERICA PICTURE PLAY 7" SINGLES SERIES

| # REC | DISC # | ARTIST | A TITLE | B TITLE | G/VG | EX/NMT |
|---|---|---|---|---|---|---|
| 1 | C-1 | NOT LISTED. SEE LABEL NOTES FOR DETAILS ON ARTISTS. | YELLOW ROSE OF TEXAS | COWBOY ROUND-UP | $10.00 | $20.00 |
| 1 | C-2 | NOT LISTED. SEE LABEL NOTES FOR DETAILS ON ARTISTS. | LET'S ALL SING LIKE THE BIRD-IES SING | A TISKET, A TASKET | $10.00 | $20.00 |
| 1 | C-3 | NOT LISTED. SEE LABEL NOTES FOR DETAILS ON ARTISTS. | PONY BOY | MAN ON THE FLYING TRAPEZE | $10.00 | $20.00 |
| 1 | C-4 | NOT LISTED. SEE LABEL NOTES FOR DETAILS ON ARTISTS. | HEY MR. BANJO | TEDDY BEAR | $10.00 | $20.00 |
| 1 | C-5 | NOT LISTED. SEE LABEL NOTES FOR DETAILS ON ARTISTS. | PEG O' MY HEART | SKATING TIME | $10.00 | $20.00 |
| 1 | C-6 | NOT LISTED. SEE LABEL NOTES FOR DETAILS ON ARTISTS. | OVER THE RAINBOW | TOY TOWN | $10.00 | $20.00 |
| 1 | C-7 | NOT LISTED. SEE LABEL NOTES FOR DETAILS ON ARTISTS. | MOTHER GOOSE | PLAY TIME | $10.00 | $20.00 |
| 1 | C-8 | NOT LISTED. SEE LABEL NOTES FOR DETAILS ON ARTISTS. | THE BIBLE TELLS ME SO | ONCE UPON A TIME | $10.00 | $20.00 |
| 1 | C-9 | NOT LISTED. SEE LABEL NOTES FOR DETAILS ON ARTISTS. | OLD MACDONALD | ZOO PARADE | $10.00 | $20.00 |
| 1 | C-10 | NOT LISTED. SEE LABEL NOTES FOR DETAILS ON ARTISTS. | MARCHES FOR TOTS | TRAIN TIME | $10.00 | $20.00 |
| 1 | C-11 | NOT LISTED. SEE LABEL NOTES FOR DETAILS ON ARTISTS. | DOGGIE IN THE WINDOW | PLAY GAME ACTIVITY | $10.00 | $20.00 |
| 1 | C-12 | NOT LISTED. SEE LABEL NOTES FOR DETAILS ON ARTISTS. | HAPPY BIRTHDAY | PARTY TIME | $10.00 | $20.00 |
| 1 | PP-1 | NOT LISTED. SEE LABEL NOTES FOR DETAILS ON ARTISTS.* | TEDDY BEARS PICNIC | RING, RING THE BANJO | $50.00 | $100.00 |
| 1 | PP-2 | NOT LISTED. SEE LABEL NOTES FOR DETAILS ON ARTISTS.* | RAILROAD IN THE MIDDLE OF THE HOUSE | MARY HAD A LITTLE LAMB | $50.00 | $100.00 |
| 1 | PP-3 | NOT LISTED. SEE LABEL NOTES FOR DETAILS ON ARTISTS.* | JACK AND THE BEANSTALK | SNOW WHITE | $50.00 | $100.00 |
| 1 | PP-4 | NOT LISTED. SEE LABEL NOTES FOR DETAILS ON ARTISTS.* | RED WING | SHORTNIN' BREAD | $50.00 | $100.00 |
| 1 | PP-5 | NOT LISTED. SEE LABEL NOTES FOR DETAILS ON ARTISTS.* | HEIGH-HO, HEIGH-HO | DING DONG BELL | $50.00 | $100.00 |
| 1 | PP-6 | NOT LISTED. SEE LABEL NOTES FOR DETAILS ON ARTISTS.* | ABC COUNTING SONG | JACK AND JILL | $50.00 | $100.00 |
| 1 | PP-7 | NOT LISTED. SEE LABEL NOTES FOR DETAILS ON ARTISTS.* | LISTEN TO THE MOCKING BIRD | LITTLE BO PEEP | $50.00 | $100.00 |
| 1 | PP-8 | NOT LISTED. SEE LABEL NOTES FOR DETAILS ON ARTISTS.* | LITTLE WHITE DUCK | THREE LITTLE KITTENS | $50.00 | $100.00 |
| 1 | PP-9 | NOT LISTED. SEE LABEL NOTES FOR DETAILS ON ARTISTS.* | PARADE OF SOLDIERS | HAND ME DOWN MY WALKING CANE | $50.00 | $100.00 |
| 1 | PP-11 | NOT LISTED. SEE LABEL NOTES FOR DETAILS ON ARTISTS.* | SQUARE DANCE JAMBOREE | SHE WORE A YELLOW RIBBON | $50.00 | $100.00 |
| 1 | PP-12 | NOT LISTED. SEE LABEL NOTES FOR DETAILS ON ARTISTS.* | THREE BLIND MICE | HAPPY BIRTHDAY | $50.00 | $100.00 |

*ANIMATION RECORD

## RECORD GUILD OF AMERICA 7" SINGLES SERIES

| SET # | # REC | DISC # | MAIN TITLE | ARTIST | A TITLE | B TITLE | YEAR | G/VG | EX/NMT |
|---|---|---|---|---|---|---|---|---|---|
| 1 | 4 | ? | MOTHER GOOSE SONGS* | NOT LISTED. SEE LABEL NOTES FOR DETAILS ON ARTISTS. | ** | ** | 1948 | $10.00 | $20.00 |
| 2 | 4 | ? | TINY TUNES | NOT LISTED. SEE LABEL NOTES FOR DETAILS ON ARTISTS. | ** | ** | | $10.00 | $20.00 |
| 3 | 4 | ? | HAPPY TIME SONGS | NOT LISTED. SEE LABEL NOTES FOR DETAILS ON ARTISTS. | ** | ** | | $10.00 | $20.00 |
| 4 | 4 | S-2022/3/4, G-4010 | PLAYTIME SONGS | NOT LISTED. SEE LABEL NOTES FOR DETAILS ON ARTISTS. | ** | ** | | $10.00 | $20.00 |

*PRICES ARE FOR BOXES WITH RECORDS COMPLETE. **SEE INDIVIDUAL RECORD LISTINGS WITH RECORDS COMPLETE.

## RECORD GUILD OF AMERICA TRADE-A-RECORD BOXED SETS 7" PICTURE DISCS

| SET # | # REC | DISC # | MAIN TITLE | ARTIST | A TITLE | B TITLE | G/VG | EX/NMT |
|---|---|---|---|---|---|---|---|---|
| 5 | 4 | ? | GAME SONGS | NOT LISTED. SEE LABEL NOTES FOR DETAILS ON ARTISTS. | * | * | $10.00 | $20.00 |
| 6 | 4 | ? | FAIRY TALES | NOT LISTED. SEE LABEL NOTES FOR DETAILS ON ARTISTS. | * | * | $10.00 | $20.00 |
| 7 | 4 | ? | NURSERY SONGS | NOT LISTED. SEE LABEL NOTES FOR DETAILS ON ARTISTS. | * | * | $10.00 | $20.00 |
| 8 | 4 | ? | FOLK SONGS | NOT LISTED. SEE LABEL NOTES FOR DETAILS ON ARTISTS. | * | * | $10.00 | $20.00 |
| 9 | 4 | ? | FAVORITE SONGS | NOT LISTED. SEE LABEL NOTES FOR DETAILS ON ARTISTS. | * | * | $10.00 | $20.00 |
| 10 | 4 | 7011, 12, 14, 15 | CHRISTMAS SONGS | NOT LISTED. SEE LABEL NOTES FOR DETAILS ON ARTISTS. | * | * | $10.00 | $20.00 |
| 11 | 4 | ? | AMERICAN SONGS | NOT LISTED. SEE LABEL NOTES FOR DETAILS ON ARTISTS. | * | * | $10.00 | $20.00 |
| 12 | 4 | F-301 TO F-601 | CARTOON COMICS | NOT LISTED. SEE LABEL NOTES FOR DETAILS ON ARTISTS. | * | * | $120.00 | $240.00 |
| 13 | 4 | 5001 TO 4 P | NURSERY FAVORITES | NOT LISTED. SEE LABEL NOTES FOR DETAILS ON ARTISTS. | * | * | $10.00 | $20.00 |
| 14 | 4 | 4001 TO 4 P | SMALL FRY FAVORITES | NOT LISTED. SEE LABEL NOTES FOR DETAILS ON ARTISTS. | * | * | $10.00 | $20.00 |
| 15 | 4 | 3001 TO 4 P | PARTY GAMES | NOT LISTED. SEE LABEL NOTES FOR DETAILS ON ARTISTS. | * | * | $10.00 | $20.00 |
| 16 | 4 | 2001 TO 4 P | FOLK TUNES | NOT LISTED. SEE LABEL NOTES FOR DETAILS ON ARTISTS. | * | * | $15.00 | $30.00 |
| 17 | 4 | 6001 TO 4 P | COWBOY FAVORITES | NOT LISTED. SEE LABEL NOTES FOR DETAILS ON ARTISTS. | * | * | $10.00 | $20.00 |
| 18 | 4 | 1001 TO 4 P | CHRISTMAS FAVORITES | NOT LISTED. SEE LABEL NOTES FOR DETAILS ON ARTISTS. | * | * | $10.00 | $20.00 |
| NO # | N/A | VARIES | GENERIC BOX | NOT LISTED. SEE LABEL NOTES FOR DETAILS ON ARTISTS. | * | * | $5.00 | $10.00 |

*SEE INDIVIDUAL RECORD LISTINGS FOR TITLES.

## RECORD GUILD OF AMERICA NON-PICTURE DISCS 7" SINGLES

| # REC | DISC # | ARTIST | A TITLE | B TITLE | YEAR | G/VG | EX/NMT |
|---|---|---|---|---|---|---|---|
| 1 | V-101 | NOT LISTED | SILENT NIGHT | WE THREE KINGS | 1948 | $1.50 | $3.00 |
| 1 | V-102 | NOT LISTED | HARK THE HERALD ANGELS SING | WASSAIL SONG | | $1.50 | $3.00 |
| 1 | V-103 | NOT LISTED | COME ALL YE FAITHFUL | DECK THE HALLS WITH HOLLY | | $1.50 | $3.00 |
| 1 | V-104 | NOT LISTED | SANTA'S SURPRISE (PT. 1) | SANTA'S SURPRISE (PT. 2) | | $1.50 | $3.00 |
| 1 | V-105 | NOT LISTED | JOY TO THE WORLD | IT CAME UPON A MIDNIGHT CLEAR | | $1.50 | $3.00 |
| 1 | V-106 | NOT LISTED | THE FIRST NOEL | LITTLE TOWN OF BETHLEHEM | | $1.50 | $3.00 |
| 1 | V-201 | NOT LISTED | DOWN IN THE VALLEY | CLEMENTINE | | $1.50 | $3.00 |
| 1 | V-202 | NOT LISTED | DIXIE | HOME SWEET HOME | | $1.50 | $3.00 |
| 1 | V-203 | NOT LISTED | ARKANSAS TRAVELER | TURKEY IN THE STRAW | | $1.50 | $3.00 |
| 1 | V-204 | NOT LISTED | O SUSANNA | POP GOES THE WEASEL | | $1.50 | $3.00 |
| 1 | V-205 | NOT LISTED | BLUE TAIL FLY | CARRY ME BACK TO OLD VIRGINNY | | $4.00 | $8.00 |
| 1 | V-301 | NOT LISTED | LOOBY LOU | DID YOU EVER SEE A LASSIE | | $1.50 | $3.00 |
| 1 | V-302 | NOT LISTED | ROUND THE VILLAGE | OPEN THE GATES | | $1.50 | $3.00 |
| 1 | V-303 | NOT LISTED | LONDON BRIDGE | LUCY LOCKET | | $1.50 | $3.00 |
| 1 | V-304 | NOT LISTED | ALOUETTE | PAT A CAKE | | $1.50 | $3.00 |
| 1 | V-306 | NOT LISTED | ALL AROUND THE MULBERRY BUSH | A TISKET A TASKET | | $1.50 | $3.00 |
| 1 | V-401 | NOT LISTED | BILLY BOY | LAZY MARY | | $1.50 | $3.00 |
| 1 | V-402 | NOT LISTED | OATS, PEAS, BEANS | EARLY TO BED | | $1.50 | $3.00 |
| 1 | V-403 | NOT LISTED | RAIN RAIN GO AWAY | OLD WOMAN IN A SHOE, JACK HORNER | | $1.50 | $3.00 |
| 1 | V-404 | NOT LISTED | RUB-A-DUB DUB | PETER PIPER | | $1.50 | $3.00 |
| 1 | V-501 | NOT LISTED | FIDDLE DEE DEE | PEASE PORRIDGE, COBBLER, COBBLER | | $1.50 | $3.00 |
| 1 | V-502 | NOT LISTED | POLLY PUT THE KETTLE ON | GEORGIE PORGIE | | $1.50 | $3.00 |
| 1 | V-503 | NOT LISTED | OH DEAR WHAT CAN THE MATTER BE | HICKORY DICKORY DOCK, THERE WAS A LITTLE GIRL | | $1.50 | $3.00 |
| 1 | V-504 | NOT LISTED | THREE BLIND MICE | DING DONG BELL, JACK SPRATT | | $1.50 | $3.00 |
| 1 | V-506 | NOT LISTED | PETER PETER PUMPKIN EATER | ROCKABYE BABY | | $1.50 | $3.00 |
| 1 | V-507 | NOT LISTED | THREE LITTLE KITTENS | MARY HAD A LITTLE LAMB | | $1.50 | $3.00 |

RECORD GUILD OF AMERICA
THE DOGGIE IN THE WINDOW
$4.00

RECORD GUILD OF AMERICA
ROOTIN' TOOTIN' COWBOY
$3.00

RECORD GUILD OF AMERICA
I SAW MOMMY KISSING SANTA CLAUS
$3.00

## RECORD GUILD OF AMERICA NON-PICTURE DISCS 7" SINGLES

| # REC | DISC # | ARTIST | A TITLE | B TITLE | G/VG | EX/NMT |
|---|---|---|---|---|---|---|
| 1 | V-508 | NOT LISTED | THE CAMPBELL'S ARE COMING | JACK AND JILL | $1.50 | $3.00 |
| 1 | V-601 | ARIZONA CLIFF MARTIN/NOT LISTED | RUDOLPH THE RED-NOSED REINDEER | SILENT NIGHT | $1.50 | $3.00 |
| 1 | V-602 | ARIZONA CLIFF MARTIN/NOT LISTED | FROSTY THE SNOWMAN | COME ALL YE FAITHFUL | $1.50 | $3.00 |
| 1 | V-603 | NOT LISTED | ALICE IN WONDERLAND (PT. 1) | ALICE IN WONDERLAND (PT. 2) | $1.50 | $3.00 |
| 1 | V-604 | NOT LISTED | MARCHES FOR CHILDREN (PT. 1) | MARCHES FOR CHILDREN (PT. 2) | $1.50 | $3.00 |
| 1 | V-700 | GUILD PLAYERS & ORCH. | MR. BUNNY AND THE RAINBOW (PT. 1) | MR. BUNNY AND THE RAINBOW (PT. 2) | $1.50 | $3.00 |
| 1 | V-701 | GUILD PLAYERS & ORCH. | THE EMPEROR'S NEW CLOTHES | JACK AND THE BEANSTALK | $1.50 | $3.00 |
| 1 | V-702 | GUILD PLAYERS & ORCH. | ALADDIN AND THE WONDERFUL LAMP | TOM THUMB | $1.50 | $3.00 |
| 1 | V-703 | GUILD PLAYERS & ORCH. | RUMPELSTILTSKIN | SNOW WHITE (AKA SNOW DROP) | $1.50 | $3.00 |
| 1 | V-704 | GUILD PLAYERS & ORCH. | UGLY DUCKLING | CINDERELLA | $1.50 | $3.00 |
| 1 | V-705 | GUILD PLAYERS & ORCH. | PETER RABBIT (PT. 1) | PETER RABBIT (PT. 2) | $1.50 | $3.00 |
| 1 | V-706 | WARREN GARDNER, GUILD ORCH. | DOWN BY THE STATION (PT. 1) | DOWN BY THE STATION (PT. 2) | $1.50 | $3.00 |
| 1 | V-707 | BERN HOFFMAN, GUILD ORCH. | PETER AND THE WOLF (PT. 1) | PETER AND THE WOLF (PT. 2) | $1.50 | $3.00 |
| 1 | V-708 | LEONARD STOKES, GUILD ORCH. | GOING TO SEA (PT. 1) | GOING TO SEA (PT. 2) | $1.50 | $3.00 |
| 1 | V-709 | WARREN GARDNER, GUILD ORCH. | FOLLOW THE LEADER (PT. 1) | FOLLOW THE LEADER (PT. 2) | $1.50 | $3.00 |
| 1 | V-710 | ARIZONA CLIFF MARTIN/GUILD ORCH. | PETER COTTONTAIL | THE CAMPBELL'S ARE COMING | $1.50 | $3.00 |
| 1 | V-711 | PAT ELLI/JIMMIE BLAINE | I SAW MOMMY KISSING SANTA CLAUS | GOING TO BOSTON | $1.50 | $3.00 |
| 1 | V-712 | PAT ELLI, GUILD ORCH./JIMMY BLAINE | TELL ME A STORY | BIG ROCK CANDY MOUNTAIN | $1.50 | $3.00 |
| 1 | V-713 | ARLENE JAMES/ART GENTRY, GUILD ORCH. | THAT DOGGIE IN THE WINDOW | PLAY ALONG SONGS/SWING, SWING | $2.00 | $4.00 |
| 1 | V-714 | JEFF CLARK, RICHARD RHODES & ORCH. | PETER PAN (PT. 1) | PETER PAN (PT. 2) | $1.50 | $3.00 |
| 1 | V-715 | GUILD PLAYERS & ORCH. | CHRISTMAS PARTY (PT. 1) | CHRISTMAS PARTY (PT. 2) | $1.50 | $3.00 |
| 1 | V-716 | GILBERT MACK, GUILD ORCH. | TRIP TO THE ZOO (PT. 1) | TRIP TO THE ZOO (PT. 2) | $1.50 | $3.00 |
| 1 | V-717 | DICK KOLLMAR, CISNEY PLAYERS | THREE LITTLE PIGS (PT. 1) | THREE LITTLE PIGS (PT. 2) | $1.50 | $3.00 |
| 1 | V-718 | DICK KOLLMAR, CISNEY PLAYERS | GOLDILOCKS (PT. 1) | GOLDILOCKS (PT. 2) | $1.50 | $3.00 |
| 1 | V-719 | DICK KOLLMAR, CISNEY PLAYERS | LITTLE RED RIDING HOOD (PT. 1) | LITTLE RED RIDING HOOD (PT. 2) | $1.50 | $3.00 |
| 1 | V-720 | GUY MARTIN, TINY TOWN TRIO | POPO THE PUP (PT. 1) | POPO THE PUP (PT. 2) | $1.50 | $3.00 |
| 1 | V-721 | ? | LITTLE RED ENGINE (PT. 1) | LITTLE RED ENGINE (PT. 2) | $1.50 | $3.00 |
| 1 | V-722 | GUY MARTIN, TINY TOWN TRIO, GUILD ORCH. | BIG LITTLE DRUM (PT. 1) | BIG LITTLE DRUM (PT. 2) | $1.50 | $3.00 |
| 1 | V-723 | TINY TOWN TRIO, RAY BLACK ORCH. | ORGAN GRINDER MAN (PT. 1) | ORGAN GRINDER MAN (PT. 2) | $1.50 | $3.00 |
| 1 | V-724 | NORMAN STANLEY, GUILD ORCH. | TOOT TOOT TOODLES (PT. 1) | TOOT TOOT TOODLES (PT. 2) | $1.50 | $3.00 |
| 1 | V-725 | GWEN DAVIES, GUILD ORCH. | ME TOO (PT. 1) | ME TOO (PT. 2) | $1.50 | $3.00 |

## RECORD GUILD OF AMERICA NON-PICTURE DISCS 7" SINGLES

| # REC | DISC # | ARTIST | A TITLE | B TITLE | G/VG | EX/NMT |
|---|---|---|---|---|---|---|
| 1 | V-726 | BOB EMERICK, GUILD QUINTET & ORCH. | FIRE IN THE TOY SHOP (PT. 1) | FIRE IN THE TOY SHOP (PT. 2) | $1.50 | $3.00 |
| 1 | V-727 | BOB EMERICK, GUILD QUINTET & ORCH. | PARADE OF THE SOLDIERS (PT. 1) | PARADE OF THE SOLDIERS (PT. 2) | $1.50 | $3.00 |
| 1 | V-728 | MERRILL JOELS, GLEN OSIER, ORCH. | HANSEL AND GRETEL (PT. 1) | HANSEL AND GRETEL (PT. 2) | $1.50 | $3.00 |
| 1 | V-729 | GUILD VOCALISTS AND ORCH. | MAGIC TRAIN (PT. 1) | MAGIC TRAIN (PT. 2) | $1.50 | $3.00 |
| 1 | V-730 | GUILD SINGERS & ORCH. | THREE LITTLE FISHES (PT. 1) | THREE LITTLE FISHES (PT. 2) | $1.50 | $3.00 |
| 1 | V-731 | RAY HEATHERTON, GUILD ORCH. | HOCUS POCUS (PT. 1) | HOCUS POCUS (PT. 2) | $1.50 | $3.00 |
| 1 | V-732 | GUILD SINGERS & ORCH. | HAPPY GO LUCKY (PT. 1) | HAPPY GO LUCKY (PT. 2) | $1.50 | $3.00 |
| 1 | V-733 | RANCH HANDS, GUILD ORCH. | COWBOYS AND INDIANS (PT. 1) | COWBOYS AND INDIANS (PT. 2) | $1.50 | $3.00 |
| 1 | V-734 | RAY HEATHERTON, GUILD ORCH. | TEDDY BEARS HOP (PT. 1) | TEDDY BEARS HOP (PT. 2) | $1.50 | $3.00 |
| 1 | V-735 | GUILD PARTY MAKERS, GUILD ORCH. | HAPPY BIRTHDAY (PT. 1) | HAPPY BIRTHDAY (PT. 2) | $1.50 | $3.00 |
| 1 | V-1010 | NOT LISTED | JACK AND THE BEANSTALK | THE EMPEROR'S NEW CLOTHES | $1.00 | $2.00 |
| 1 | V-1011 | NOT LISTED | TOM THUMB | ALADDIN AND THE WONDERFUL LAMP | $1.00 | $2.00 |
| 1 | V-1012 | NOT LISTED | SNOW DROP AND THE DWARFS | RUM-PEL-STILT-SKIN | $1.00 | $2.00 |
| 1 | V-1013 | NOT LISTED | CINDERELLA | THE UGLY DUCKLING | $1.00 | $2.00 |
| 1 | V-2014 | NOT LISTED | THERE WAS A LITTLE GIRL, HICKORY DICKORY DOCK | OLD KING COLE, THERE WAS A CROOKED MAN | $1.00 | $2.00 |
| 1 | V-2015 | NOT LISTED | A DILLAR A DOLLAR, TO MARKET TO MARKET | HOT CROSS BUMS, BAA BAA BLACK SHEEP | $1.00 | $2.00 |
| 1 | V-2016 | NOT LISTED | HEY DIDDLE DIDDLE, LITTLE MISS MUFFET | PUSSY CAT, PUSSY CAT, TOM TOM THE PIPER'S SON | $1.00 | $2.00 |
| 1 | V-2017 | NOT LISTED | OLD MOTHER HUBBARD, WHERE O WHERE HAS MY LITTLE DOG GONE | LITTLE TOMMY TUCKER, JACK THE NIMBLE | $1.00 | $2.00 |
| 1 | V-2018 | NOT LISTED | JACK SPRATT, DING DONG BELL | THERE WAS AN OLD WOMAN, LITTLE JACK HORNER | $1.00 | $2.00 |
| 1 | V-2019 | NOT LISTED | BILLY BOY | THREE LITTLE KITTENS | $1.00 | $2.00 |
| 1 | V-2020 | NOT LISTED | PAT A CAKE | LUCY LOCKET | $1.00 | $2.00 |
| 1 | V-2021 | NOT LISTED | POLLY PUT THE KETTLE ON | TEN LITTLE INDIANS | $1.00 | $2.00 |
| 1 | V-2022 | NOT LISTED | GEORGIE PORGIE | RIDE A COCK HORSE | $1.00 | $2.00 |
| 1 | V-2023 | NOT LISTED | FIDDLE DEE DEE | JACK AND JILL | $1.00 | $2.00 |
| 1 | V-2024 | NOT LISTED | PRETTY POLLY | THREE BLIND MICE | $1.00 | $2.00 |
| 1 | V-2025 | NOT LISTED | RUB A DUB DUB | PETER PIPER | $1.00 | $2.00 |
| 1 | V-2026 | NOT LISTED | EARLY TO BED EARLY TO RISE | ROCKABYE BABY | $1.00 | $2.00 |
| 1 | V-2027 | NOT LISTED | MARY HAD A LITTLE LAMB | PETER PETER PUMPKIN EATER | $1.00 | $2.00 |
| 1 | V-2028 | NOT LISTED | TWINKLE TWINKLE LITTLE STAR | RAIN RAIN GO AWAY | $1.00 | $2.00 |
| 1 | V-3010 | NOT LISTED | SILENT NIGHT | NOEL NOEL | $1.00 | $2.00 |
| 1 | V-3011 | NOT LISTED | COME ALL YE FAITHFUL | IT CAME UPON A MIDNIGHT CLEAR | $1.00 | $2.00 |
| 1 | V-3012 | NOT LISTED | JINGLE BELLS | AULD LANG SYNE | $1.00 | $2.00 |
| 1 | V-4010 | NOT LISTED | A TISKET A TASKET | DID YOU EVER SEE A LASSIE | $1.00 | $2.00 |
| 1 | V-4011 | NOT LISTED | THE FARMER IN THE DELL | ALL AROUND THE MULBERRY BUSH | $1.00 | $2.00 |
| 1 | V-4012 | NOT LISTED | A HUNTING WE WILL GO | LONDON BRIDGE IS FALLING DOWN | $1.00 | $2.00 |
| 1 | V-4013 | NOT LISTED | LAZY MARY WILL YOU GET UP! | OPEN THE GATES AS HIGH AS THE SKY | $1.00 | $2.00 |
| 1 | V-4014 | NOT LISTED | ROUND THE VILLAGE | LOOBY LOO | $1.00 | $2.00 |
| 1 | V-5010 | NOT LISTED | ARKANSAS TRAVELER | CLEMENTINE | $1.00 | $2.00 |
| 1 | V-5011 | NOT LISTED | BLUE TAIL FLY | CAMPBELL'S ARE COMING | $1.00 | $2.00 |
| 1 | V-5012 | NOT LISTED | POP GOES THE WEASEL | TURKEY IN THE STRAW | $1.00 | $2.00 |
| 1 | V-5013 | NOT LISTED | LITTLE BROWN JUG | MEXICAN HAT DANCE | $1.00 | $2.00 |
| 1 | V-5017 | NOT LISTED | DOWN IN THE VALLEY | ERIE CANAL | $1.00 | $2.00 |
| 1 | V-5018 | NOT LISTED | HOME SWEET HOME | DIXIE | $1.00 | $2.00 |
| 1 | V-5019 | NOT LISTED | CAMPTOWN RACES | CARRY ME BACK TO OLD VIRGINNY | $1.00 | $2.00 |
| 1 | V-5020 | NOT LISTED | RED RIVER VALLEY | WORKING ON THE RAILROAD | $1.00 | $2.00 |
| 1 | V-6010 | NOT LISTED | ALPHABET SONG | COUNTING SONG | $1.00 | $2.00 |
| 1 | V-6011 | NOT LISTED | HAPPY BIRTHDAY | FOR HE'S A JOLLY GOOD FELLOW | $1.00 | $2.00 |
| 1 | V-7010 | NOT LISTED | THE NIGHT BEFORE CHRISTMAS (PT. 1) | THE NIGHT BEFORE CHRISTMAS (PT. 2) | $1.00 | $2.00 |
| 1 | V-7011 | NOT LISTED | O COME ALL YE FAITHFUL | DECK THE HALLS | $1.00 | $2.00 |
| 1 | V-7012 | NOT LISTED | SILENT NIGHT | HARK THE HERALD ANGELS SING | $1.00 | $2.00 |
| 1 | V-7013 | NOT LISTED | THE FIRST NOEL | WASSAIL SONG | $1.00 | $2.00 |
| 1 | V-7014 | NOT LISTED | AULD LANG SYNE | JOY TO THE WORLD | $1.00 | $2.00 |
| 1 | V-7015 | NOT LISTED | JINGLE BELLS | WE THREE KINGS | $1.00 | $2.00 |
| 1 | V-7016 | NOT LISTED | IT CAME UPON A MIDNIGHT CLEAR | OH LITTLE TOWN OF BETHLEHEM | $1.00 | $2.00 |

## RECORD GUILD OF AMERICA TRADE-A-RECORD BOXED SETS 7" NON-PICTURE DISCS

| SET # | # REC | DISC # | MAIN TITLE | ARTIST | A TITLE | B TITLE | YEAR | G/VG | EX/NMT |
|---|---|---|---|---|---|---|---|---|---|
| 1 | 4 | 2010 - 13 | MOTHER GOOSE SONGS | NOT LISTED. SEE LABEL NOTES FOR DETAILS ON ARTISTS. | ? | ? | 1948 | $10.00 | $20.00 |
| 2 | 4 | ? | TINY TUNES | NOT LISTED. SEE LABEL NOTES FOR DETAILS ON ARTISTS. | ? | ? | | $10.00 | $20.00 |
| 3 | 4 | ? | HAPPY TIME SONGS | NOT LISTED. SEE LABEL NOTES FOR DETAILS ON ARTISTS. | ? | ? | | $10.00 | $20.00 |
| 4 | 4 | ? | PLAYTIME SONGS | NOT LISTED. SEE LABEL NOTES FOR DETAILS ON ARTISTS. | ? | ? | | $10.00 | $20.00 |
| 5 | 4 | ? | GAME SONGS | NOT LISTED. SEE LABEL NOTES FOR DETAILS ON ARTISTS. | ? | ? | | $10.00 | $20.00 |
| 6 | 4 | ? | FAIRY TALES | NOT LISTED. SEE LABEL NOTES FOR DETAILS ON ARTISTS. | ? | ? | | $10.00 | $20.00 |
| 7 | 4 | ? | NURSERY SONGS | NOT LISTED. SEE LABEL NOTES FOR DETAILS ON ARTISTS. | ? | ? | | $10.00 | $20.00 |
| 8 | 4 | ? | FOLK SONGS | NOT LISTED. SEE LABEL NOTES FOR DETAILS ON ARTISTS. | ? | ? | | $10.00 | $20.00 |
| 9 | 4 | 4014, 5014 - 16 | FAVORITE SONGS | NOT LISTED. SEE LABEL NOTES FOR DETAILS ON ARTISTS. | ? | ? | | $10.00 | $20.00 |
| 10 | 4 | ? | CHRISTMAS SONGS | NOT LISTED. SEE LABEL NOTES FOR DETAILS ON ARTISTS. | ? | ? | | $10.00 | $20.00 |
| 11 | 4 | ? | AMERICAN SONGS | NOT LISTED. SEE LABEL NOTES FOR DETAILS ON ARTISTS. | ? | ? | | $10.00 | $20.00 |
| 12 | 4 | ? | CHRISTMAS CAROLS | NOT LISTED. SEE LABEL NOTES FOR DETAILS ON ARTISTS. | ? | ? | | $10.00 | $20.00 |

## RECORD GUILD OF AMERICA 10" SINGLES SERIES

| # REC | DISC # | MAIN TITLE | ARTIST | A TITLE | B TITLE | YEAR | G/VG | EX/NMT |
|---|---|---|---|---|---|---|---|---|
| 1 | R-117/118 | MOTHER GOOSE: LITTLE BO PEEP, ETC./HEY DIDDLE DIDDLE, ETC. | DOTTIE PROUD, MUSIC HALL CHORUS & ORCH. (MHO)/INEZ MANIER, JANE DAVIES, DOTTIE PROUD, MHO | MOTHER GOOSE (SIDE 1) | (SIDE 2) | 1953 | $1.50 | $3.00 |
| 1 | R-119/120 | LULLABYE NURSERY SONGS: ROCKABYE BABY, ETC./EARLY TO BED, ETC. | DOTTIE PROUD, JANE DAVIS, MHO/PHIL PROUD, ANDY GAINEY, JENEFER BUNKER, MHO | LULLABYE NURSERY SONGS (SIDE 1) | (SIDE 2) | | $1.50 | $3.00 |
| 1 | R-121/122 | TINY TUNES: THERE WAS A LITTLE GIRL, ETC./ HUMPTY DUMPTY, ETC. | JANE DAVIS, BOB DAVIS, PHIL PROUD, DOROTHY PROUD, MHO | TINY TUNES (SIDE 1) | (SIDE 2) | | $1.50 | $3.00 |
| 1 | R-123/124 | PLAY-GAMES ACTIVITY SONGS: A TISKET, A TASKET, ETC./THE FARMER IN THE DELL, ETC. | RANDOLPH SINGERS, TOM BROWN BAND | PLAY-GAMES ACTIVITY SONGS (SIDE 1) | (SIDE 2) | | $1.50 | $3.00 |
| 1 | R-125/126 | HAPPY BIRTHDAY, FOR HE'S A JOLLY GOOD FELLOW/ALPHABET SONG, COUNTING SONG | DOTTIE & PHIL PROUD, MHO/ JENEFER BUNKER, DOTTIE PROUD, MHO | ABC BIRTHDAY PARTY (SIDE 1) | (SIDE 2) | | $1.50 | $3.00 |
| 1 | R-127/128 | SMALL FRY FAVORITES: OH SUSANNA, ALOUETTE/ARKANSAS TRAVELER, WORKIN' ON THE RAILROAD | ANDY GAINEY, MHO/ANDY GAINEY, DARREN MCGAVIN, MHO | SMALL FRY FAVORITES (SIDE 1) | (SIDE 2) | | $1.50 | $3.00 |
| 1 | R-129/130 | FAMILY SING SONG: ?/OLD MACDONALD, CLEMENTINE | ?/DOTTIE & PHIL PROUD, MHO | FAMILY SING SONG (SIDE 1) | (SIDE 2) | | $1.50 | $3.00 |
| 1 | R-131/132 | DANCE JAMBOREE: SKIP TO MY LOU, CAMPBELLS ARE COMING/TURKEY IN THE STRAW, MEXICAN HAT DANCE | ANDY GAINEY, JENEFER BUNKER, PHIL PROUD, MHO/ANDY GAINEY, DOTTIE PROUD, MHO | DANCE JAMBOREE (SIDE 1) | (SIDE 2) | | $1.50 | $3.00 |
| 1 | R-133/134 | COWBOY SONGS: CHISHOLM TRAIL, GET ALONG LITTLE DOGGIE/ RED RIVER VALLEY, LONE PRAIRIE | ANDY GAINEY, DOUG MARTIN, TEX JAMES BAND/RUE KNAPP, DOC MCCROCK, TEX JAMES BAND | COWBOY SONGS (SIDE 1) | (SIDE 2) | | $1.50 | $3.00 |
| 1 | R-135/136 | WESTERN SONGS: WHISTLING RODEO POLKA, HOME ON THE RANGE/ BUFFALO GALS, OLD DAN TUCKER | DOC MCCROCK, BILL HART, RUE KNAPP, TEX JAMES BAND/ DOUG MARTIN, ANDY GAINEY, DOTTIE PROUD, TEX JAMES BAND | WHISTLING RODEO POLKA/ HOME ON THE RANGE (SIDE 1) | BUFFALO GALS/OLD DAN TUCKER | | $1.50 | $3.00 |

## RECORD GUILD OF AMERICA 10" SINGLES SERIES

| # REC | DISC # | MAIN TITLE | ARTIST | A TITLE | B TITLE | G/VG | EX/NMT |
|---|---|---|---|---|---|---|---|
| 1 | R-137/138 | CHRISTMAS SONG FAVORITES: JINGLE BELLS, DECK THE HALLS/FIRST NOEL, JOY TO THE WORLD | RUTH COTTINGHAM, PHIL PROUD, REX CHORUS & BAND/LITA DARWIN, REX CHORUS & BAND | CHRISTMAS SONG FAVORITES (SIDE 1) | (SIDE 2) | $1.50 | $3.00 |
| 1 | R-139/140 | SILENT NIGHT, COME ALL YE FAITHFUL/LITTLE TOWN OF BETHLEHEM, IT CAME UPON A MIDNIGHT CLEAR | ST. PATRICK'S BOYS CHOIR | SILENT NIGHT, ETC. | LITTLE TOWN OF BETHLEHEM, ETC. | $1.50 | $3.00 |
| 1 | R-141 | RUDOLPH THE RED-NOSED REINDEER/SANTA'S SURPRISE | ARIZONA CLIFF MARTIN, MHO/MUSIC HALL DRAMA GROUP & ORCH. | RUDOLPH THE RED-NOSED REINDEER | OLD MACDONALD/CLEMENTINE | $1.50 | $3.00 |
| 1 | R-166 | FROSTY THE SNOWMAN/NIGHT BEFORE CHRISTMAS | ARIZONA CLIFF MARTIN, MHO/MUSIC HALL DRAMA GROUP & ORCH. | FROSTY THE SNOWMAN | THE NIGHT BEFORE CHRISTMAS | $1.50 | $3.00 |
| 1 | R-168 | ALICE IN WONDERLAND | GUILD DRAMA GROUP | ALICE IN WONDERLAND (PT. 1) | ALICE IN WONDERLAND (PT. 2) | $1.50 | $3.00 |
| 1 | R-170 | MARCHES FOR CHILDREN: MARCHE MILITAIRE, ETC./MARINE HYMN, ETC. | GUILD BAND | MARCHES FOR CHILDREN (PT. 1) | MARCHES FOR CHILDREN (PT. 2) | $1.50 | $3.00 |
| 1 | R-202 | ROOTIN' TOOTIN' COWBOY | LEONARD STOKES, GUILD ORCH. (GO)/GLEN CROSS, GO | ROOTIN' TOOTIN' COWBOY | ROOTIN' TOOTIN' COWBOY | $1.50 | $3.00 |
| 1 | R-204 | SAILING TO SEA: SEA SONGS FOR CHILDREN | LEONARD STOKES, GUILD ORCH. (GO) | SAILING TO SEA | SEA SONGS | $1.50 | $3.00 |
| 1 | R-206 | DOWN BY THE STATION/FARE THEE WELL | WARREN GARDNER, GO/JACK SLOANE, GO | DOWN BY THE STATION | FAIR THEE WELL | $1.50 | $3.00 |
| 1 | R-208 | PLAYLAND PARTY: FOLLOW THE LEADER/SOUNDS OF THIS & THAT | WARREN GARDNER, GO | FOLLOW THE LEADER | SOUNDS OF THIS AND THAT | $1.50 | $3.00 |
| 1 | R-210 | SLEEPY SANDMAN: GOOD NIGHT LULLABYES/HUSH LITTLE BABY | GLENN CROSS, GO | GOOD NIGHT LULLABYES | HUSH LITTLE BABY | $1.50 | $3.00 |
| 1 | R-212 | THE LITTLE RED HEN | DORA RICHMAN, GO | THE LITTLE RED HEN (PT. 1) | THE LITTLE RED HEN (PT. 2) | $1.50 | $3.00 |
| 1 | R-214 | PETER RABBIT | DORA RICHMAN, GO | PETER RABBIT (PT. 1) | PETER RABBIT (PT. 2) | $1.50 | $3.00 |
| 1 | R-216 | THE LION AND THE DONKEY | DORA RICHMAN, GO | THE LION AND THE DONKEY (PT. 1) | THE LION AND THE DONKEY (PT. 2) | $1.50 | $3.00 |
| 1 | R-218 | JACK AND THE BEANSTALK, THE EMPEROR'S NEW CLOTHES/TOM THUMB, ALADDIN & THE WONDERFUL LAMP | GUILD PLAYERS: JAMES MONKS, CLIFF CARPENTER, MARTIN WOLFSON, HESTER SONDERGAARD | JACK AND THE BEANSTALK/THE EMPEROR'S NEW CLOTHES | TOM THUMB/ALADDIN | $1.50 | $3.00 |
| 1 | R-220 | SNOW WHITE, RUMPELSTILTSKIN/CINDERELLA, UGLY DUCKLING | GUILD PLAYERS: JAMES MONKS, CLIFF CARPENTER, MARTIN WOLFSON, HESTER SONDERGAARD | SNOW WHITE/RUMPELSTILTSKIN | CINDERELLA/UGLY DUCKLING | $1.50 | $3.00 |
| 1 | R-222 | COME TO THE ZOO | GILBERT MACK, GO | COME TO THE ZOO | COME TO THE ZOO | $1.50 | $3.00 |
| 1 | R-224 | PETER AND THE WOLF/MARCHES FOR CHILDREN | BERN HOFFMAN, GO/JACK SLOANE, GO | PETER AND THE WOLF | MARCHES FOR CHILDREN | $1.50 | $3.00 |
| 1 | 5-300 | MR. BUNNY AND THE RAINBOW/CAMPTOWN RACES, THE GLENDY BURK | GUILD PLAYERS, GO/GLENN CROSS, GO | MR. BUNNY AND THE RAINBOW | CAMPTOWN RACES/THE GLENDY BURKE | $1.50 | $3.00 |
| 1 | 5-302 | THREE LITTLE PIGS | DICK KOLLMAR, CISNEY PLAYERS | THREE LITTLE PIGS (PT. 1) | THREE LITTLE PIGS (PT. 2) | $1.50 | $3.00 |
| 1 | 5-304 | CINDERELLA | DICK KOLLMAR, CISNEY PLAYERS | CINDERELLA (PT. 1) | CINDERELLA (PT. 2) | $1.50 | $3.00 |
| 1 | 5-306 | LITTLE RED RIDING HOOD | DICK KOLLMAR, CISNEY PLAYERS | LITTLE RED RIDING HOOD (PT. 1) | LITTLE RED RIDING HOOD (PT. 2) | $1.50 | $3.00 |
| 1 | 5-308 | GOLDILOCKS AND THE THREE BEARS | DICK KOLLMAR, CISNEY PLAYERS | GOLDILOCKS AND THE THREE BEARS (PT. 1) | GOLDILOCKS AND THE THREE BEARS (PT. 2) | $1.50 | $3.00 |
| 1 | 5-310 | NEARER MY GOD TO THEE, JESUS GOOD ABOVE ALL OTHER/ROCK OF AGES, ABIDE WITH ME | RANDOLPH SINGERS, DAVID RANDOLPH, DIR. | NEARER MY GOD TO THEE | 3 OTHER HYMNS | $1.50 | $3.00 |
| 1 | 5-312 | JESUS GENTLEST SAVIOR, CROWN HIM WITH MANY CROWNS/BRIGHTLY GLEAMS OUR BANNER, O SANCTISSIMA | PAULIST CHORISTERS, BRIAN SULLIVAN | JESUS GENTLEST SAVIOR | BRIGHTLY GLEAMS OUR BANNER | $1.50 | $3.00 |

## ROBIN HOOD 7" BOXED SETS

| SET # | # REC | DISC # | MAIN TITLE | ARTIST | A TITLE | B TITLE | G/VG | EX/NMT |
|---|---|---|---|---|---|---|---|---|
| | | 713 | | NOT LISTED | 3. THE ELEPHANT TRUNK | 4. LEE STACY, WORLD FAMOUS MIDGET, 5. THE MIDGET AND GIANT SING I'VE BEEN WORKING ON THE RAILROAD | | |
| | | 714 | | NOT LISTED | 6. THE TALKING FLEA, 7. CIRCUS FIREWORKS | 8. THE BIG ARENA AND BILLY THE WONDER BOY | | |
| | | 715 | | NOT LISTED | 9. BOBO, THE CLOWN | 10. THE ACROBATS, 11. THE GRAND FINALE | | |
| 44 | 4 | | 16 SONGS AND STORIES FOR A RAINY DAY | | | | $3.00 | $6.00 |
| | | 716 | | THE ROBIN HOOD PLAYERS | RAIN RAIN GO AWAY, GREEN GRASS GREW ALL AROUND | TEN LITTLE INDIANS | | |
| | | 717 | | THE ROBIN HOOD PLAYERS | POP GOES THE WEASEL | THREE BLIND MICE, ETC. | | |
| | | 718 | | THE ROBIN HOOD PLAYERS | LITTLE BO PEEP, FARMER IN THE DELL | ROW ROW ROW YOUR BOAT, THE GINGERBREAD MAN | | |
| | | 719 | | THE ROBIN HOOD PLAYERS | LONDON BRIDGE, ETC. | BAA BAA BLACK SHEEP, ETC. | | |
| 45 | 4 | | ? | | | | $3.00 | $6.00 |
| | | 720 | | ? | ? | ? | | |
| | | 721 | | ? | ? | ? | | |
| | | 722 | | ? | ? | ? | | |
| | | 723 | | ? | ? | ? | | |
| 46 | 4 | | ? | | | | $3.00 | $6.00 |
| | | 724 | | ? | THE OLD RUGGED CROSS | THE LORD'S PRAYER | | |
| | | 725 | | ? | ? | ? | | |
| | | 726 | | ? | ? | ? | | |
| | | 727 | | ? | ROCK OF AGES | 23RD PSALM, AMEN | | |
| N/A | | SINGLE RECORDS | N/A | N/A | N/A | N/A | $.50 | $1.00 |

## ROCKING HORSE (PETER PAN) 7" SERIES SINGLES AND BOXED SETS

| # REC | DISC # | ARTIST | A TITLE | B TITLE | YEAR | ALSO ISSUED ON | G/VG | EX/NMT |
|---|---|---|---|---|---|---|---|---|
| 1 | PL-A 100/101 | THE FAIRYLAND PLAYERS; JUSTIN STONE, DIR. | WYNKEN, BLYNKEN & NOD (PT. 1) | WYNKEN, BLYNKEN & NOD (PT. 2) | 1947 | PETER PAN | $1.00 | $2.00 |
| 1 | PL-A 102/103 | THE FAIRYLAND PLAYERS; JUSTIN STONE, DIR. | LULLABY & GOOD NIGHT | NURSERY RHYMES: MARY HAD A LITTLE LAMB, ETC. | | PETER PAN | $1.00 | $2.00 |
| 1 | PL-A 104/105 | THE FAIRYLAND PLAYERS; JUSTIN STONE, DIR. | SLEEPY TOWN TRAIN (PT. 1) | SLEEPY TOWN TRAIN (PT. 2) | | PETER PAN | $1.00 | $2.00 |
| 1 | PL-A 106/107 | THE FAIRYLAND PLAYERS; JUSTIN STONE, DIR. | THE OLD ELM TREE (PT. 1) | THE OLD ELM TREE (PT. 2) | | PETER PAN | $1.00 | $2.00 |
| 1 | PL-A 108/109 | THE FAIRYLAND PLAYERS; JUSTIN STONE, DIR. | DOWN ON THE FARM (PT 1) | DOWN ON THE FARM (PT 2) | | PETER PAN | $1.00 | $2.00 |
| 1 | PL-A 112/113 | THE FAIRYLAND PLAYERS; JUSTIN STONE, DIR. | MOTHER GOOSE SONGS: THREE BLIND MICE, ETC. | ALPHABET SONG | | PETER PAN | $1.00 | $2.00 |
| 1 | PL-A 115 | JACK ARTHUR, THE SONG SPINNERS; DON COPE, DIR. | MUSICAL NURSERY RHYMES: OLD KING COLE, ETC. | MUSICAL NURSERY RHYMES: LITTLE BOY BLUE, ETC. | | PETER PAN | $1.00 | $2.00 |
| 1 | PL-A 116 | JACK ARTHUR, THE SONG SPINNERS; DON COPE, DIR. | SONGS ON BEING CAREFUL: HUMPTY-DUMPTY, ETC. | SLEEP, BABY, SLEEP, DIDDLE DIDDLE DUMPLING MY SON JOHN | | PETER PAN | $1.00 | $2.00 |
| 1 | PL-A 117 | JACK ARTHUR, THE SONG SPINNERS; DON COPE, DIR. | NURSERY RHYMES ON EATING: LITTLE MISS MUFFET, ETC. | NURSERY RHYMES ON EATING: POLLY PUT THE KETTLE ON | | PETER PAN | $1.00 | $2.00 |
| 1 | PL-A 118 | JACK ARTHUR, THE SONG SPINNERS; DON COPE, DIR. | ANIMAL SONGS: THE THREE LITTLE KITTENS | ANIMAL SONGS: OLD MOTHER HUBBARD | | PETER PAN | $1.00 | $2.00 |
| 1 | PL-A 119 | JACK ARTHUR; DON COPE, DIR. | GOLDILOCKS (PT. 1) | GOLDILOCKS (PT. 2) | | PETER PAN | $1.00 | $2.00 |
| 1 | PL-A 120 | JACK ARTHUR; DON COPE, DIR. | LITTLE RED RIDING HOOD (PT. 1) | LITTLE RED RIDING HOOD (PT. 2) | | PETER PAN | $1.00 | $2.00 |
| 1 | PL-A 126 | MORT LAWRENCE; VICKY KASEN, DIR. | THE NIGHT BEFORE CHRISTMAS (PT. 1)* | THE NIGHT BEFORE CHRISTMAS (PT. 2) | | PETER PAN | $1.00 | $2.00 |

*I HAVE SLV WITH #126; RECORD IS 222/223.

REMINGTON JUNIOR RECORDS
THE AIRPLANE THAT WOULD NOT FLY
$10.00

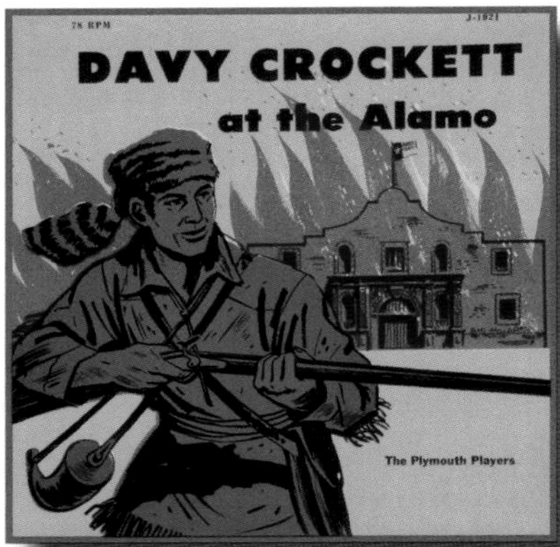


REMINGTON JUNIOR RECORDS
DAVY CROCKETT AT THE
ALAMO $15.00

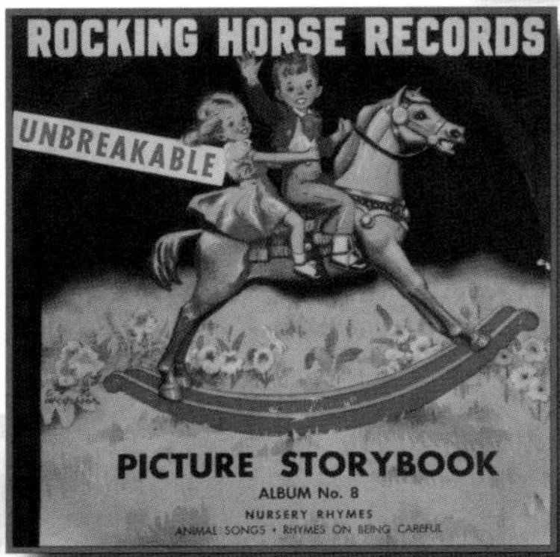


ROCKING HORSE RECORDS
NURSERY RHYMES
$10.00

## ROCKING HORSE (PETER PAN) 7" SERIES SINGLES AND BOXED SETS

| # REC | DISC # | ARTIST | A TITLE | B TITLE | YEAR | ALSO ISSUED ON | G/VG | EX/NMT |
|---|---|---|---|---|---|---|---|---|
| 1 | PL-A 218/219 | THE FAIRYLAND PLAYERS; VICKY KASEN, DIR. | SILENT NIGHT | ADESTE FIDELES (OH COME ALL YE FAITHFUL) | | PETER PAN | $1.00 | $2.00 |
| 1 | PL A 220/221 | THE FAIRYLAND PLAYERS; VICKY KASEN, DIR. | JINGLE BELLS | O LITTLE TOWN OF BETHLEHEM | | PETER PAN | $1.00 | $2.00 |
| 1 | PL-A 222/223 | THE FAIRYLAND PLAYERS; VICKY KASEN, DIR. | THE NIGHT BEFORE CHRISTMAS (PT. 1) | THE NIGHT BEFORE CHRISTMAS (PT. 2) | | PETER PAN | $1.00 | $2.00 |
| 1 | PL A 224/225 | THE FAIRYLAND PLAYERS; VICKY KASEN, DIR. | HAPPY BIRTHDAY | FOR HE'S A JOLLY GOOD FELLOW | | PETER PAN | $1.00 | $2.00 |

## ROCKING HORSE (PETER PAN) PICTURE STORYBOOK SERIES 7" ALBUMS

| SET # | # REC | DISC # | MAIN TITLE | ARTIST | YEAR | G/VG | EX/NMT |
|---|---|---|---|---|---|---|---|
| ALBUM #5 | 3 | 100, 119, 120 | LITTLE RED RIDING HOOD, ETC. | THE FAIRYLAND PLAYERS JACK ARTHUR; DON COPE, DIR. | 1947 | $5.00 | $10.00 |
| ALBUM #6 | 3 | 104/5, 106/7, 108/9 | MUSICAL STORIES: DOWN ON THE FARM, ETC. | THE FAIRYLAND PLAYERS; JUSTIN STONE, DIR. | | $5.00 | $10.00 |
| ALBUM #7 | 3 | 102/3, 112/3, 117 | MOTHER GOOSE SONGS ON RHYMES & EATING | THE FAIRYLAND PLAYERS/JACK ARTHUR, THE SONG SPINNERS | | $5.00 | $10.00 |
| ALBUM #8 | 3 | 115, 116, 118 | NURSERY RHYMES | JACK ARTHUR, THE SONG SPINNERS; DON COPE, DIR. | | $5.00 | $10.00 |
| ALBUM #9 | 3 | 218/9, 220/1, 222/3 | CHRISTMAS CAROLS & SONGS | THE FAIRYLAND PLAYERS; VICKY KASEN, DIR. | | $5.00 | $10.00 |
| BOXED SET | 3 | ANY COMBO | N/A | N/A | | $6.00 | $12.00 |

## ROYALE 10" DOUBLES

| SET # | # REC | MAIN TITLE | ARTIST | YEAR | G/VG | EX/NMT |
|---|---|---|---|---|---|---|
| PL-1 | 2 | NURSERY RHYMES | UNCLE DON CARNEY | 195? | $3.00 | $6.00 |
| PL-2 | 2 | 13 MUSICAL STORIES | UNCLE DON CARNEY | | $3.00 | $6.00 |
| UD-1 | 2 | CIRCUS DAY WITH UNCLE DON | UNCLE DON CARNEY | | $5.00 | $10.00 |
| UD-2 | 2 | UNCLE DON ON THE FARM | UNCLE DON CARNEY | | $5.00 | $10.00 |
| UD 3 | 2 | AN AIRPLANE TRIP WITH UNCLE DON | UNCLE DON CARNEY | | $5.00 | $10.00 |
| UD-4 | 2 | UNCLE DON TELL ME A STORY | UNCLE DON CARNEY | | $4.00 | $8.00 |

## RUSSELL 10" SINGLES

| # REC | DISC # | ARTIST | A TITLE | B TITLE | YEAR | G/VG | EX/NMT |
|---|---|---|---|---|---|---|---|
| 1 | 1 | NOT LISTED | BICYCLE BUILT FOR TWO, LITTLE ANNIE ROONEY | PEGGY O'NEIL | 195? | $1.00 | $2.00 |
| 1 | 2 | NOT LISTED | EXACTLY LIKE YOU, GOOD MORNING | HAP HAP HAPPY DAY | | $1.00 | $2.00 |
| 1 | 3 | NOT LISTED | ANCHORS AWEIGH, PARADE OF THE WOODEN SOLDIERS | STARS AND STRIPES FOREVER | | $1.00 | $2.00 |
| 1 | 4 | NOT LISTED | SHINE ON HARVEST MOON | JEALOUS | | $1.00 | $2.00 |
| 1 | 5 | NOT LISTED | BLUE SKIES, LIZA, WHO | I KNOW THAT YOU KNOW | | $1.00 | $2.00 |
| 1 | 6 | NOT LISTED | COQUETTE, THE DARKTOWN STRUTTER'S BALL | HONEYSUCKLE ROSE, ROSETTA | | $1.00 | $2.00 |
| 1 | 7 | NOT LISTED | TEA FOR TWO | ? | | $1.00 | $2.00 |

## RUSSELL 10" SINGLES

| # REC | DISC # | ARTIST | A TITLE | B TITLE | G/VG | EX/NMT |
|---|---|---|---|---|---|---|
| 1 | 8 | NOT LISTED | FOR ME AND MY GAL | ? | $1.00 | $2.00 |
| 1 | 9 | NOT LISTED | CHARMAINE, FALLING IN LOVE WITH LOVE | I'LL SEE YOU AGAIN, MERRY WIDOW WALTZ | $1.00 | $2.00 |
| 1 | 10 | NOT LISTED | TURKEY IN THE STRAW | YANKEE DOODLE | $1.00 | $2.00 |
| 1 | 11 | NOT LISTED | NOLA | ? | $1.00 | $2.00 |
| 1 | 12 | NOT LISTED | CHICKEN REEL | ? | $1.00 | $2.00 |
| 1 | 13 | NOT LISTED | LADY BE GOOD | ? | $1.00 | $2.00 |
| 1 | 14 | NOT LISTED | BASIN STREET BALL | ? | $1.00 | $2.00 |
| 1 | 15 | NOT LISTED | DOLL DANCE | WEDDING OF THE PAINTED DOLL | $1.00 | $2.00 |
| 1 | 16 | NOT LISTED | I CAN'T GIVE YOU ANYTHING BUT LOVE, IT DON'T MEAN A THING | MOUNTAIN GREENERY, PUTTIN' ON THE RITZ | $1.00 | $2.00 |
| 1 | 17 | NOT LISTED | LET ME CALL YOU SWEETHEART | WHEN IRISH EYES ARE SMILING | $1.00 | $2.00 |
| 1 | 18 | NOT LISTED | LOUISE | YOU MADE ME LOVE YOU | $1.00 | $2.00 |
| 1 | 19 | NOT LISTED | AMERICAN PATROL | ? | $1.00 | $2.00 |
| 1 | 20 | NOT LISTED | ME AND MY SHADOW | SLEEPY TIME GAL | $1.00 | $2.00 |
| 1 | 21 | NOT LISTED | TWELFTH (12TH) STREET RAG | BYE BYE BLUES | $1.00 | $2.00 |
| 1 | 22 | NOT LISTED | AMOR | ? | $1.00 | $2.00 |
| 1 | 23 | NOT LISTED | GLOW-WORM | SLEEPING BEAUTY WALTZ | $1.00 | $2.00 |
| 1 | 24 | NOT LISTED | VALSE BLUETTE, CHOPIN PRELUDE | WALTZ OF THE FLOWERS (TCHAIKOVSKY) | $1.00 | $2.00 |
| 1 | 25 | NOT LISTED | MAZURKA (CHOPIN) | QUI VIVE GALOP | $1.00 | $2.00 |
| 1 | 26 | NOT LISTED | GRAND VAISE BRILLENTE, NOCTURNE (CHOPIN) | MINUET WALTZ, VALSE (CHOPIN) | $1.00 | $2.00 |
| 1 | 27 | NOT LISTED | A PRETTY GIRL IS LIKE A MELODY | ? | $1.00 | $2.00 |
| 1 | 28 | NOT LISTED | IT HAD TO BE YOU | ? | $1.00 | $2.00 |
| 1 | 29 | NOT LISTED | ARTIST'S LIFE | MAZURKA (STRAUSS), FAUST BALLET | $1.00 | $2.00 |
| 1 | 30 | NOT LISTED | ALEGRIAS | PASO DOBLE, GERROTIN | $1.00 | $2.00 |
| 1 | 31 | NOT LISTED | LES CYGNETS, LE SPECTRE DE LA ROSE | VALSE IN E MINOR (CHOPIN), WALTZ (LEVITSKY) | $1.00 | $2.00 |
| 1 | 32 | NOT LISTED | COPPELLA WALTZ | NAILA | $1.00 | $2.00 |
| 1 | 33 | NOT LISTED | THE WATER BUG | WATER LILIES | $1.00 | $2.00 |
| 1 | 34 | NOT LISTED | JARABE TAPATIO (MEXICAN HAT DANCE) | ? | $1.00 | $2.00 |
| 1 | 35 | NOT LISTED | SPANISH GYPSY DANCE | VALS ARAGONES, TWO GUITARS | $1.00 | $2.00 |
| 1 | 36 | NOT LISTED | BALLET BOOGIE | PAVANNE (GOULD) | $1.00 | $2.00 |
| 1 | 37 | NOT LISTED | IRISH WASHERWOMAN | KERRY DANCE, SAILOR'S HORNPIPE | $1.00 | $2.00 |
| 1 | 38 | NOT LISTED | WHISTLE WHILE YOU WORK | ? | $1.00 | $2.00 |
| 1 | 39 | NOT LISTED | NO CAN DO | YOU ARE MY LUCKY STAR | $1.00 | $2.00 |
| 1 | 40 | NOT LISTED | HUMORESQUE (TCHAIKOVSKY) | VIENNA LIFE | $1.00 | $2.00 |
| 1 | 41 | NOT LISTED | DANCE OF THE HOURS | SLEEPING BEAUTY WALTZ | $1.00 | $2.00 |
| 1 | 42 | NOT LISTED | THE BALLET DANCER | ROMANCE (RUBINSTEIN) | $1.00 | $2.00 |
| 1 | 43 | NOT LISTED | FAUST WALTZ, SCHON ROSMARIN (KREISLER) | RUSTIC DANCE | $1.00 | $2.00 |
| 1 | 44 | NOT LISTED | LE SECRET | VALSE IMPROMPTU (UPCRAFT) | $1.00 | $2.00 |
| 1 | 45 | NOT LISTED | JALOUSIE (JEALOUSY) | ? | $1.00 | $2.00 |
| 1 | 46 | NOT LISTED | SWAMP FIRE | ? | $1.00 | $2.00 |
| 1 | 47 | NOT LISTED | THE BELLS OF ST. MARY'S | IN THE CHAPEL IN THE MOONLIGHT | $1.00 | $2.00 |
| 1 | 48 | NOT LISTED | OH, MARIE | THREE O'CLOCK IN THE MORNING | $1.00 | $2.00 |
| 1 | 49 | NOT LISTED | DANCE CAPRICE | A MINIATURE MUSIC BOX | $1.00 | $2.00 |
| 1 | 50 | NOT LISTED | DANCE OF THE SCARECROWS | ECHO WALTZ | $1.00 | $2.00 |
| 1 | 51 | NOT LISTED | OLD MACDONALD HAD A FARM | POLLY WOLLY DOODLE | $1.00 | $2.00 |
| 1 | 52 | NOT LISTED | ARKANSAS TRAVELER | ? | $1.00 | $2.00 |
| 1 | 53 | NOT LISTED | ORCHIDS IN THE MOONLIGHT | ? | $1.00 | $2.00 |
| 1 | 54 | NOT LISTED | CARIOCA | ? | $1.00 | $2.00 |
| 1 | 55 | NOT LISTED | BONGOMANIA | CHRISTOPHER COLUMBUS | $1.00 | $2.00 |
| 1 | 56 | NOT LISTED | ESPANA CANI | ? | $1.00 | $2.00 |
| 1 | 57 | NOT LISTED | LITTLE BROWN GAL | MY LITTLE GRASS SHACK | $1.00 | $2.00 |
| 1 | 58 | NOT LISTED | BEYOND THE REEF | MALIHINI MALE | $1.00 | $2.00 |
| 1 | 59 | NOT LISTED | SCALAWAG | ? | $1.00 | $2.00 |
| 1 | 60 | NOT LISTED | CO-ED ON A HOLIDAY | ? | $1.00 | $2.00 |

## RUSSELL 10" SINGLES

| # REC | DISC # | ARTIST | A TITLE | B TITLE | G/VG | EX/NMT |
|---|---|---|---|---|---|---|
| 1 | 61 | NOT LISTED | THE GHOST DANCE | THAT SHUFFLIN' RAG | $1.00 | $2.00 |
| 1 | 62 | NOT LISTED | RHYTHM IN MY NURSERY RHYMES | ? | $1.00 | $2.00 |
| 1 | 63 | NOT LISTED | IN OUR LITTLE WOODEN SHOES | ? | $1.00 | $2.00 |
| 1 | 64 | NOT LISTED | THE DONKEY SERENADE | ? | $1.00 | $2.00 |
| 1 | 65 | NOT LISTED | ON THE GOOD SHIP LOLLIPOP | ? | $1.00 | $2.00 |
| 1 | 66 | NOT LISTED | DIXIE | ? | $1.00 | $2.00 |
| 1 | 67 | NOT LISTED | THE SIDEWALKS OF NEW YORK | ? | $1.00 | $2.00 |
| 1 | 68 | NOT LISTED | NARCISSUS | ? | $1.00 | $2.00 |
| 1 | 69 | NOT LISTED | CHIAPANECAS (CLAP HANDS) | ? | $1.00 | $2.00 |
| 1 | 70 | NOT LISTED | DANCING TAMBOURINE | ? | $1.00 | $2.00 |
| 1 | 71 | NOT LISTED | ANIMAL CRACKERS IN MY SOUP | ? | $1.00 | $2.00 |
| 1 | 72 | NOT LISTED | HOOP-DEE-DOO | ME AND MY TEDDY BEAR | $1.00 | $2.00 |
| 1 | 73 | NOT LISTED | ROMANY LIFE | TREPAK (TCHAIKOVSKY) | $1.00 | $2.00 |
| 1 | 74 | NOT LISTED | I'M AN OLD COWHAND | WYOMING | $1.00 | $2.00 |
| 1 | 75 | NOT LISTED | DAGGER DANCE | PALE MOON | $1.00 | $2.00 |
| 1 | 76 | NOT LISTED | ORIENTAL DANCE | ? | $1.00 | $2.00 |
| 1 | 77 | NOT LISTED | LITTLE LOTUS FLOWER | ? | $1.00 | $2.00 |
| 1 | 78 | NOT LISTED | TENEMAHA | ? | $1.00 | $2.00 |
| 1 | 79 | NOT LISTED | GALOP (FROM "ORPHEUS") | ? | $1.00 | $2.00 |
| 1 | 80 | NOT LISTED | JOY OF SPRING | ? | $1.00 | $2.00 |
| 1 | 81 | NOT LISTED | INSPIRATION WALTZ | ? | $1.00 | $2.00 |
| 1 | 82 | NOT LISTED | MARY HAD A LITTLE LAMB | ? | $1.00 | $2.00 |
| 1 | 83 | NOT LISTED | LIMEHOUSE BLUES | ? | $1.00 | $2.00 |
| 1 | 84 | NOT LISTED | NORWEGIAN DANCE | ? | $1.00 | $2.00 |
| 1 | 85 | NOT LISTED | BALLIN' THE JACK | ? | $1.00 | $2.00 |
| 1 | 86 | NOT LISTED | PENGUINS ON PARADE | ? | $1.00 | $2.00 |
| 1 | 87 | NOT LISTED | THE A B C SONG | ? | $1.00 | $2.00 |
| 1 | 88 | NOT LISTED | PUNCH AND JUDY DANCE | ? | $1.00 | $2.00 |
| 1 | 89 | NOT LISTED | HINDUSTAN | ? | $1.00 | $2.00 |
| 1 | 90 | NOT LISTED | CARAVAN | ? | $1.00 | $2.00 |
| 1 | 91 | NOT LISTED | PETITE BALLET | ? | $1.00 | $2.00 |
| 1 | 92 | NOT LISTED | CARMELITE | ? | $1.00 | $2.00 |
| 1 | 93 | NOT LISTED | BLUE PRELUDE | ? | $1.00 | $2.00 |
| 1 | 94 | NOT LISTED | AVALON | ? | $1.00 | $2.00 |
| 1 | 95 | NOT LISTED | THE LAND OF MAKE BELIEVE | ? | $1.00 | $2.00 |
| 1 | 96 | NOT LISTED | MICKEY MOUSE'S BIRTHDAY PARTY | ? | $5.00 | $10.00 |
| 1 | 97 | NOT LISTED | WOODLAND NYMPHS | ? | $1.00 | $2.00 |
| 1 | 98 | NOT LISTED | THE SHEIK OF ARABY | ? | $1.00 | $2.00 |
| 1 | 99 | NOT LISTED | ACH DU LIEBER AUGUSTINE | ? | $1.00 | $2.00 |
| 1 | 100 | NOT LISTED | JUS' VAMPIN' | ? | $1.00 | $2.00 |
| 1 | 101 | NOT LISTED | SYNCOPATED CLOCK | ? | $1.00 | $2.00 |
| 1 | 102 | NOT LISTED | BATTEMENT FRAPPE | PETITE BATTEMENT, PLIE ET RELEVE | $1.00 | $2.00 |
| 1 | 103 | NOT LISTED | GRANDE BATTEMENT | ROND DE JAMBE | $1.00 | $2.00 |
| 1 | 104 | NOT LISTED | BATTEMENT TENDU, RELEVE | PASSE, COU DE PIED | $1.00 | $2.00 |
| 1 | 105 | NOT LISTED | BOURRE CHANGE, PAS DE BASQUE, PORT DE BRAS | JETE, CHANGEMENT | $1.00 | $2.00 |
| 1 | 106 | NOT LISTED | TRICK OR TREAT | ? | $1.00 | $2.00 |
| 1 | 107 | NOT LISTED | COPY-CAT SHADOW | ? | $1.00 | $2.00 |
| 1 | 108 | NOT LISTED | SANTA HAS HIS EYE ON YOU | ? | $1.00 | $2.00 |
| 1 | 109 | NOT LISTED | EV'RY SHOW MUST HAVE A FINALE | YOU GOTTA BE A FOOTBALL HERO | $1.00 | $2.00 |
| 1 | 110 | NOT LISTED | I HAVE A PAIR OF ROLLER SKATES | ? | $1.00 | $2.00 |
| 1 | 111 | NOT LISTED | ONLY IN MY DREAMS | ? | $1.00 | $2.00 |
| 1 | 112 | NOT LISTED | THE BAND PLAYED ON | SWEET ROSIE O'GRADY | $1.00 | $2.00 |
| 1 | 113 | NOT LISTED | BY THE LIGHT OF THE SILVERY MOON | POOR BUTTERFLY | $1.00 | $2.00 |

ROBIN HOOD RECORDS
A DAY OF FUN AT THE CIRCUS
$6.00

ROCKING HORSE RECORDS
WYNKEN, BLYNKEN & NOD
$2.00

RUSSELL RECORDS
HOW D'YE DO MY PARTNER
$2.00

## RUSSELL 10" SINGLES

| # REC | DISC # | ARTIST | A TITLE | B TITLE | G/VG | EX/NMT |
|---|---|---|---|---|---|---|
| 1 | 114 | NOT LISTED | MY BLUE HEAVEN | YOU'RE THE CREAM IN MY COFFEE | $1.00 | $2.00 |
| 1 | 115 | NOT LISTED | LITTLE BROWN JUG | ? | $1.00 | $2.00 |
| 1 | 116 | NOT LISTED | FIVE FOOT TWO, EYES OF BLUE | ? | $1.00 | $2.00 |
| 1 | 117 | NOT LISTED | MINUET IN G (PADEREWSKI) | MINUET IN G (BEETHOVEN) | $1.00 | $2.00 |
| 1 | 118 | NOT LISTED | GAVOTTE (FROM "MIGNON") | PIZZICATI (DELLBES) | $1.00 | $2.00 |
| 1 | 119 | NOT LISTED | YES SIR, THAT'S MY BABY | ? | $1.00 | $2.00 |
| 1 | 120 | NOT LISTED | JARABE TAPATIO (MEXICAN HAT DANCE) | ? | $1.00 | $2.00 |
| 1 | 121 | NOT LISTED | TALES OF THE VIENNA WOODS | ? | $1.00 | $2.00 |
| 1 | 122 | NOT LISTED | BLUE DANUBE | ? | $1.00 | $2.00 |
| 1 | 123 | NOT LISTED | YANKEE ROSE | ? | $1.00 | $2.00 |
| 1 | 124 | NOT LISTED | SWANEE RIVER | ? | $1.00 | $2.00 |
| 1 | 125 | NOT LISTED | MARCHE MILLTAIRE | ? | $1.00 | $2.00 |
| 1 | 126 | NOT LISTED | HUNGARIAN DANCE NO. 5 | ? | $1.00 | $2.00 |
| 1 | 127 | NOT LISTED | HAPPY FEET | ? | $1.00 | $2.00 |
| 1 | 128 | NOT LISTED | PRETTY BABY | ? | $1.00 | $2.00 |
| 1 | 129 | NOT LISTED | PIZZICATO POLKA (STRAUSS) | SPINNING SONG | $1.00 | $2.00 |
| 1 | 130 | NOT LISTED | COUNTRY GARDENS | SPANISH DANCE NO. 1 | $1.00 | $2.00 |
| 1 | 131 | NOT LISTED | BABY FACE | ? | $1.00 | $2.00 |
| 1 | 132 | NOT LISTED | ROSE ROOM | WHISPERING | $1.00 | $2.00 |
| 1 | 133 | NOT LISTED | DANCING DOLL (POUPEE VALSANTE) | THE MAMA DOLL SONG, POUPEE VALSANTE (DANCING DOLL) | $1.00 | $2.00 |
| 1 | 134 | NOT LISTED | DANCE OF THE SUGAR PLUM FAIRY | THE GOLDEN WEDDING | $1.00 | $2.00 |
| 1 | 135 | NOT LISTED | ON THE SUNNY SIDE OF THE STREET | SHINE | $1.00 | $2.00 |
| 1 | 136 | NOT LISTED | DARK EYES | MELODY IN F | $1.00 | $2.00 |
| 1 | 137 | NOT LISTED | STEPPIN' OUT WITH MY BABY | ? | $1.00 | $2.00 |
| 1 | 138 | NOT LISTED | BAMBALINA | ? | $1.00 | $2.00 |
| 1 | 139 | NOT LISTED | I'M A LITTLE TEAPOT | ? | $1.00 | $2.00 |
| 1 | 140 | NOT LISTED | THE MOON IS BLUE | ? | $1.00 | $2.00 |
| 1 | 141 | NOT LISTED | JOSEPHINE | ONCE IN LOVE WITH AMY | $1.00 | $2.00 |
| 1 | 142 | NOT LISTED | VAMP TILL READY | ? | $1.00 | $2.00 |
| 1 | 143 | NOT LISTED | MARGIE | DANCER'S BOOGIE | $1.00 | $2.00 |
| 1 | 144 | NOT LISTED | CASEY JONES | ? | $1.00 | $2.00 |
| 1 | 145 | NOT LISTED | STARDUST | TENDERLY | $1.00 | $2.00 |
| 1 | 146 | NOT LISTED | A FINE ROMANCE | I GOT RHYTHM, THERE'S NO BUSINESS LIKE SHOW BUSINESS | $1.00 | $2.00 |
| 1 | 147 | NOT LISTED | CLAIR DE LUNE | ELEGIE | $1.00 | $2.00 |
| 1 | 148 | NOT LISTED | FINE AND DANDY | SUNDAY, THIS CAN'T BE LOVE | $1.00 | $2.00 |

## RUSSELL 10" SINGLES

| # REC | DISC # | ARTIST | A TITLE | B TITLE | G/VG | EX/NMT |
|---|---|---|---|---|---|---|
| 1 | 149 | NOT LISTED | AMARYLLIS | SALUT D'AMOUR | $1.00 | $2.00 |
| 1 | 150 | NOT LISTED | ANYTHING GOES, WHO CARES? | HALLELUJAH, THOU SWELL | $1.00 | $2.00 |
| 1 | 151 | NOT LISTED | BALLET MUSIC FROM "ROSAMUNDE" | SCARF DANCE | $1.00 | $2.00 |
| 1 | 152 | NOT LISTED | THE BALLAD OF DAVY CROCKETT | SHORTNIN' BREAD | $5.00 | $10.00 |
| 1 | 153 | NOT LISTED | BUTTONS AND BOWS | A GAL IN CALICO | $1.00 | $2.00 |
| 1 | 154 | NOT LISTED | JINGLE JANGLE JINGLE | RAGTIME COWBOY JOE | $1.00 | $2.00 |
| 1 | 155 | NOT LISTED | THE CAISSONS GO ROLLING ALONG | STRIKE UP THE BAND | $1.00 | $2.00 |
| 1 | 156 | NOT LISTED | DON'T GIVE UP THE SHIP | THE MARINES' HYMN, YOU'RE A GRAND OLD FLAG | $1.00 | $2.00 |
| 1 | 157 | NOT LISTED | GIVE ME THAT OLD SOFT SHOE, A STRAW HAT AND A CANE | SOFT SHOE SONG | $1.00 | $2.00 |
| 1 | 158 | NOT LISTED | CECILIA | MARY'S A GRAND OLD NAME | $1.00 | $2.00 |
| 1 | 159 | NOT LISTED | GIVE A LITTLE WHISTLE | SWINGING ON A STAR | $2.00 | $4.00 |
| 1 | 160 | NOT LISTED | MR. GHOST GOES TO TOWN, TAIN'T NO SIN | SATAN TAKES A HOLIDAY | $1.00 | $2.00 |
| 1 | 161 | NOT LISTED | CHEROKEE, TOTEM TOM TOM | PASS THAT PEACE PIPE | $1.00 | $2.00 |
| 1 | 162 | NOT LISTED | SCHOOL DAYS | TAKE ME OUT TO THE BALL GAME | $1.00 | $2.00 |
| 1 | 163 | NOT LISTED | ALABAMA JUBILEE, LOUISIANA HAYRIDE | ALABAMY BOUND, SWEET GEORGIA BROWN | $1.00 | $2.00 |
| 1 | 164 | NOT LISTED | NAGASAKI | ? | $2.00 | $4.00 |
| 1 | 165 | NOT LISTED | BY HECK | DOIN' WHAT COMES NATURALLY | $1.00 | $2.00 |
| 1 | 166 | NOT LISTED | COUNTRY STYLE, SIOUX CITY SUE | GOOFUS | $1.00 | $2.00 |
| 1 | 167 | NOT LISTED | ALEXANDER'S RAGTIME BAND | THE DARKTOWN STRUTTER'S BALL | $1.00 | $2.00 |
| 1 | 168 | NOT LISTED | JA-DA | ZIP-A-DEE DOO-DAH | $2.00 | $4.00 |
| 1 | 700 | NOT LISTED | MARY HAD A LITTLE LAMB, ETC. | WEE WILLIE WINKIE, ETC. | $1.00 | $2.00 |
| 1 | 702 | NOT LISTED | LOBBY LOO, ETC. | HERE WE GO ROUND THE MULBERRY BUSH, ETC. | $1.00 | $2.00 |
| 1 | 703 | NOT LISTED | ROUND AND ROUND THE VILLAGE, ETC. | THREE LITTLE KITTENS, ETC. | $1.00 | $2.00 |
| 1 | 704 | NOT LISTED | POP GOES THE WEASEL, ETC. | ROCKABYE BABY, ETC. | $1.00 | $2.00 |
| 1 | 705 | NOT LISTED | WOODLAND NYMPHS | LITTLE POLLY FLINDERS, ETC. | $1.00 | $2.00 |
| 1 | 725 | NOT LISTED | HOW D'YE DO, MY PARTNER, ETC. | CHIMES OF DUNKIRK, ETC. | $1.00 | $2.00 |
| 1 | 726 | NOT LISTED | DANISH DANCE OF GREETING , ETC. | I SEE YOU, ETC. | $1.00 | $2.00 |
| 1 | 727 | NOT LISTED | JOLLY IS THE MILLER, CAROUSEL | THE MUFFIN MAN | $1.00 | $2.00 |

# S

## SACRED SUNDAY SCHOOL SERIES 7" SINGLES AND ALBUMS

| # REC | DISC # | ARTIST | A TITLE | B TITLE | YEAR | G/VG | EX/NMT |
|---|---|---|---|---|---|---|---|
| 1 | 701 | TINY EVELYN/RADIO KIDS BIBLE CLUB | DO LITTLE CHILDREN LOVE THE LORD | THE B-I-B-L-E, ETC. | 1952 | $.50 | $1.00 |
| 1 | 702 | SUSIE & RADIO KIDS BIBLE CLUB/ RADIO KIDS BIBLE CLUB | WONDERFUL WORDS OF LIFE (SAFE AM I) | ALL THROUGH THE NIGHT | | $.50 | $1.00 |
| 1 | 703 | RADIO KIDS BIBLE CLUB | SUNSHINE, SUNSHINE, ETC. | ALL FOR JESUS | | $.50 | $1.00 |
| 1 | 704 | RADIO KIDS BIBLE CLUB | A LITTLE CHILD OF SEVEN, ETC. | DO LORD, DO REMEMBER ME/ RADIO KIDS BIBLE CLUB | | $.50 | $1.00 |
| 1 | 705 | RADIO KIDS BIBLE CLUB | OPEN THE DOOR FOR THE CHILDREN | JEWELS | | $.50 | $1.00 |
| 1 | 706 | RADIO KIDS BIBLE CLUB | JESUS LOVES THE LITTLE CHILDREN/HE LOVES ME | TELL ME THE STORY OF JESUS | | $.50 | $1.00 |
| 1 | 707 | RADIO KIDS BIBLE CLUB | JESUS LOVES ME/THIS I KNOW | WE'LL BE DWELLING TOGETHER, ETC. | | $.50 | $1.00 |
| 1 | 708 | UNCLE EARLE (UE) | FOR GOD SO LOVED THE WORLD | I'M SO HAPPY/I HAVE THE JOY, JOY | | $.50 | $1.00 |
| 1 | 709 | UE | JESUS WANTS ME FOR A SUNBEAM/CLIMB UP SUNSHINE MOUNTAIN | WONDERFUL JESUS IS TO ME, ETC. | | $.50 | $1.00 |
| 1 | 710 | UE | ARE WE DOWNHEARTED? ETC. | SINCE JESUS CAME INTO MY HEART/HOW DID MOSES PART THE RED SEA | | $.50 | $1.00 |
| 1 | 711 | UE | THE GOSPEL STORY FOR CHILDREN (JESUS LOVES ME) | THE GOSPEL STORY FOR CHILDREN (JESUS LOVES ME) | | $.50 | $1.00 |
| 1 | 801 | UE/UE SUNDAY SCHOOL SINGERS | OUR WONDERFUL WORLD | SUNLIGHT IN MY SOUL TODAY | 1953 | $.50 | $1.00 |
| 1 | 802 | UE, BILL AND KATHY/UE'S SUNDAY SCHOOL SINGERS | GARDEN OF EDEN | THE GOSPEL EXPRESS | | $.50 | $1.00 |
| 1 | 803 | UE, BILL AND KATHY/UE'S SUNDAY SCHOOL SINGERS | SATAN ENTERS THE GARDEN | JUST WHISTLE A HAPPY SONG | | $.50 | $1.00 |
| 1 | 804 | UE & BILL, UE'S SUNDAY SCHOOL SING-ERS | CAIN AND ABEL | AMAZING GRACE | | $.50 | $1.00 |

## SACRED SUNDAY SCHOOL SERIES 7" SINGLES AND ALBUMS

| # REC | DISC # | ARTIST | A TITLE | B TITLE | YEAR | G/VG | EX/NMT |
|---|---|---|---|---|---|---|---|
| 1 | 805 | BILL AND KATHY/UE'S SUNDAY SCHOOL SINGERS | NOAH'S BIG BOAT | NOAH WAS SAFE IN THE ARK | | $.50 | $1.00 |
| 1 | 851 | ? | BABY JESUS IN THE TEMPLE | ? | | $.50 | $1.00 |
| 1 | 852 | ? | THE BOY WHO WAS LEFT BEHIND | OH, FOR A THOUSAND TONGUES | | $.50 | $1.00 |
| 1 | 853 | BILL AND KATHY/UE'S SUNDAY SCHOOL SINGERS | JOHN THE BAPTIST | BRING THEM IN | | $.50 | $1.00 |
| 1 | 854 | ? | JESUS IS BAPTIZED | TELL ME THE STORY OF JESUS | | $.50 | $1.00 |
| 1 | 855 | UE, BILL AND KATHY/UE'S SUNDAY SCHOOL SINGERS | JESUS IS TEMPTED BY SATAN | WHISPER A PRAYER | | $.50 | $1.00 |
| 1 | 858 | ? | THE CHRISTMAS SHEPHERDS | IT CAME UPON A MIDNIGHT CLEAR/HARK! THE HERALD ANGELS SING | | $.50 | $1.00 |
| N/A | | N/A | ALBUM HOLDERS WITH 10 RECORDS | | | $5.00 | $10.00 |

## SACRED BIBLE STORYMAN SERIES 10" ALBUMS AND SINGLES

| SET # | # REC | DISC # | MAIN TITLE | ARTIST | YEAR | G/VG | EX/NMT |
|---|---|---|---|---|---|---|---|
| BS-1 | 3 | 39-41 | NOAH AND THE ARK + LOT'S WIFE | ED COLMANS | 1952 | $6.00 | $12.00 |
| BS-2 | 1 | 42 | SAMSON AND THE LION | ED COLMANS | | $2.00 | $4.00 |

## SCOTT-FORESMAN 10" ALBUMS

| SET # | # REC | DISC # | MAIN TITLE | ARTIST | YEAR | G/VG | EX/NMT |
|---|---|---|---|---|---|---|---|
| NO # | 3 | | SOUNDS AROUND US | MAY HILL ARBUTHNOT | 1951 | $18.00 | $35.00 |
| | | E1CB - 1552/3 | AROUND THE HOUSE | MAY HILL ARBUTHNOT | | | |
| | | EOCB - 5322/3 | AROUND THE FARM | MAY HILL ARBUTHNOT | | | |
| | | E1CB - 1554/5 | AROUND THE TOWN | MAY HILL ARBUTHNOT | | | |
| NO # | 3 | | POETRY TIME | WAYNE GRIFFIN | | $5.00 | $10.00 |
| | | EOCB - 4562/60 | JIGS & JINGLES | WAYNE GRIFFIN | | | |
| | | EOCB - 4548/9 | TALKING TIME | WAYNE GRIFFIN | | | |
| | | EOCB - 4561/3 | IN THE COUNTRY/WHAT SHALL WE DO TODAY | WAYNE GRIFFIN | | | |

## SIGNATURE 10" DOUBLE ALBUMS AND GATEFOLDS

| SET # | # REC | DISC # | MAIN TITLE | ARTIST | YEAR | G/VG | EX/NMT | REMARKS |
|---|---|---|---|---|---|---|---|---|
| C-1 | 2 | 12001 - 2 | THE STORY OF CELESTE | VICTOR JORY | 1946 | $6.00 | $12.00 | ALBUM |
| C-2 | 2 | 12003 - 4 | DAVID AND GOLIATH | VICTOR JORY | | $6.00 | $12.00 | ALBUM |
| C-3 | 2 | 12005 - 6 | PAUL BUNYAN | VICTOR JORY | | $5.00 | $10.00 | ALBUM |
| CF-1 | 2 | 12007 - 8 | LITTLE STORIES FOR LITTLE PEOPLE | MONICA LEWIS | | $3.00 | $6.00 | GATEFOLD COVER |
| CF-2 | 2 | 12009 - 10 | WILD BILL (RIDES AGAIN) | VICTOR JORY | 1948 | $4.00 | $8.00 | GATEFOLD COVER |

## SILVER BURDETT 10" SINGLES

| SET # | # REC | DISC # | MAIN TITLE | ARTIST | YEAR | ALSO ISSUED ON | G/VG | EX/NMT | REMARKS |
|---|---|---|---|---|---|---|---|---|---|
| 8241 | 1 | 54058-9 | MUSIC THROUGH THE DAY — ALBUM 1, BOOK 1 | NOT LISTED | 1960 | COLUMBIA | $1.00 | $2.00 | GRADE 1 |
| 8242 | 1 | 54060-1 | MUSIC THROUGH THE DAY — ALBUM 2, BOOK 1 | NOT LISTED | | | $1.00 | $2.00 | |
| 8243 | 1 | 54062-3 | MUSIC THROUGH THE DAY — ALBUM 3, BOOK 1 | NOT LISTED | | | $1.00 | $2.00 | |
| 8244 | 1 | 54064-5 | MUSIC THROUGH THE DAY — ALBUM 4, BOOK 1 | NOT LISTED | | | $1.00 | $2.00 | |
| 8245 | 1 | 54066-7 | MUSIC THROUGH THE DAY — ALBUM 5, BOOK 1 | NOT LISTED | | | $1.00 | $2.00 | |
| 8246 | 1 | 54068-9 | MUSIC THROUGH THE DAY — ALBUM 6, BOOK 1 | NOT LISTED | | | $1.00 | $2.00 | |
| 8247 | 1 | 54070-1 | MUSIC THROUGH THE DAY — ALBUM 7, BOOK 1 | NOT LISTED | | | $1.00 | $2.00 | |
| 8248 | 1 | 54072-3 | MUSIC THROUGH THE DAY — ALBUM 8, BOOK 1 | NOT LISTED | | | $1.00 | $2.00 | |
| 8249 | 1 | 54074-5 | MUSIC THROUGH THE DAY — ALBUM 9, BOOK 1 | NOT LISTED | | | $1.00 | $2.00 | |
| 8250 | 1 | 54076-7 | MUSIC THROUGH THE DAY — ALBUM 10, BOOK 1 | NOT LISTED | | | $1.00 | $2.00 | |

## SILVER BURDETT 10" SINGLES

| SET # | # REC | DISC # | MAIN TITLE | ARTIST | G/VG | EX/NMT | REMARKS |
|---|---|---|---|---|---|---|---|
| NO # | 1 | FR974-5 | MUSIC THROUGH THE DAY — ALBUM 11, BOOK 1 | NOT LISTED | $1.00 | $2.00 | |
| NO # | 1 | FR976-7 | MUSIC THROUGH THE DAY — ALBUM 12, BOOK 1 | NOT LISTED | $1.00 | $2.00 | |
| NO # | 1 | FR978-9 | MUSIC THROUGH THE DAY — ALBUM 13, BOOK 1 | NOT LISTED | $1.00 | $2.00 | |
| NO # | 1 | FR980-1 | MUSIC THROUGH THE DAY — ALBUM 14, BOOK 1 | NOT LISTED | $1.00 | $2.00 | |
| NO # | 1 | FR982-3 | MUSIC THROUGH THE DAY — ALBUM 15, BOOK 1 | NOT LISTED | $1.00 | $2.00 | |
| 8251 | 1 | 54251-2 | MUSIC IN OUR TOWN — ALBUM 1, BOOK 2 | NOT LISTED | $1.00 | $2.00 | GRADE 2 |
| 8252 | 1 | 54253-4 | MUSIC IN OUR TOWN — ALBUM 2, BOOK 2 | NOT LISTED | $1.00 | $2.00 | |
| 8253 | 1 | 54255-6 | MUSIC IN OUR TOWN — ALBUM 3, BOOK 2 | NOT LISTED | $1.00 | $2.00 | |
| 8254 | 1 | 54257-8 | MUSIC IN OUR TOWN — ALBUM 4, BOOK 2 | NOT LISTED | $1.00 | $2.00 | |
| 8255 | 1 | 54259-60 | MUSIC IN OUR TOWN — ALBUM 5, BOOK 2 | NOT LISTED | $1.00 | $2.00 | |
| 8256 | 1 | 54261-2 | MUSIC IN OUR TOWN — ALBUM 6, BOOK 2 | NOT LISTED | $1.00 | $2.00 | |
| 8257 | 1 | 54263-4 | MUSIC IN OUR TOWN — ALBUM 7, BOOK 2 | NOT LISTED | $1.00 | $2.00 | |
| 8258 | 1 | 54265-6 | MUSIC IN OUR TOWN — ALBUM 8, BOOK 2 | NOT LISTED | $1.00 | $2.00 | |
| 8259 | 1 | 54267-8 | MUSIC IN OUR TOWN — ALBUM 9, BOOK 2 | NOT LISTED | $1.00 | $2.00 | |
| 8260 | 1 | 54269-70 | MUSIC IN OUR TOWN — ALBUM 10, BOOK 2 | NOT LISTED | $1.00 | $2.00 | |
| NO # | 1 | FR984-5 | MUSIC IN OUR TOWN — ALBUM 11, BOOK 2 | NOT LISTED | $1.00 | $2.00 | |
| NO # | 1 | FR986-7 | MUSIC IN OUR TOWN — ALBUM 12, BOOK 2 | NOT LISTED | $1.00 | $2.00 | |
| NO # | 1 | FR988-9 | MUSIC IN OUR TOWN — ALBUM 13, BOOK 2 | NOT LISTED | $1.00 | $2.00 | |
| NO # | 1 | FR990-1 | MUSIC IN OUR TOWN — ALBUM 14, BOOK 2 | NOT LISTED | $1.00 | $2.00 | |
| NO # | 1 | FR992-3 | MUSIC IN OUR TOWN — ALBUM 15, BOOK 2 | NOT LISTED | $1.00 | $2.00 | |
| 8261 | 1 | 56421-2 | MUSIC NOW AND LONG AGO — ALBUM 1, BOOK 3 | NOT LISTED | $1.00 | $2.00 | GRADE 3 |
| 8262 | 1 | 56423-4 | MUSIC NOW AND LONG AGO — ALBUM 2, BOOK 3 | NOT LISTED | $1.00 | $2.00 | |
| 8263 | 1 | 56425-6 | MUSIC NOW AND LONG AGO — ALBUM 3, BOOK 3 | NOT LISTED | $1.00 | $2.00 | |
| 8264 | 1 | 56427-8 | MUSIC NOW AND LONG AGO — ALBUM 4, BOOK 3 | NOT LISTED | $1.00 | $2.00 | |
| 8265 | 1 | 56429-30 | MUSIC NOW AND LONG AGO — ALBUM 5, BOOK 3 | NOT LISTED | $1.00 | $2.00 | |
| 8266 | 1 | 56431-2 | MUSIC NOW AND LONG AGO — ALBUM 6, BOOK 3 | NOT LISTED | $1.00 | $2.00 | |
| 8267 | 1 | 56433-4 | MUSIC NOW AND LONG AGO — ALBUM 7, BOOK 3 | NOT LISTED | $1.00 | $2.00 | |
| 8268 | 1 | 56435-6 | MUSIC NOW AND LONG AGO — ALBUM 8, BOOK 3 | NOT LISTED | $1.00 | $2.00 | |
| 8269 | 1 | 56437-8 | MUSIC NOW AND LONG AGO — ALBUM 9, BOOK 3 | NOT LISTED | $1.00 | $2.00 | |
| 8270 | 1 | 56439-40 | MUSIC NOW AND LONG AGO — ALBUM 10, BOOK 3 | NOT LISTED | $1.00 | $2.00 | |
| NO # | 1 | FR994-5 | MUSIC NOW AND LONG AGO — ALBUM 11, BOOK 3 | NOT LISTED | $1.00 | $2.00 | |
| NO # | 1 | FR996-7 | MUSIC NOW AND LONG AGO — ALBUM 12, BOOK 3 | NOT LISTED | $1.00 | $2.00 | |
| NO # | 1 | FR998-9 | MUSIC NOW AND LONG AGO — ALBUM 13, BOOK 3 | NOT LISTED | $1.00 | $2.00 | |
| NO # | 1 | FR1000-1 | MUSIC NOW AND LONG AGO — ALBUM 14, BOOK 3 | NOT LISTED | $1.00 | $2.00 | |
| NO # | 1 | FR1002-3 | MUSIC NOW AND LONG AGO — ALBUM 15, BOOK 3 | NOT LISTED | $1.00 | $2.00 | |
| 8271 | 1 | 54094-5 | MUSIC NEAR AND FAR — ALBUM 1, BOOK 4 | NOT LISTED | $1.00 | $2.00 | |
| 8272 | 1 | 54096-7 | MUSIC NEAR AND FAR — ALBUM 2, BOOK 4 | NOT LISTED | $1.00 | $2.00 | |
| 8273 | 1 | 54098-9 | MUSIC NEAR AND FAR — ALBUM 3, BOOK 4 | NOT LISTED | $1.00 | $2.00 | |
| 8274 | 1 | 54100-1 | MUSIC NEAR AND FAR — ALBUM 4, BOOK 4 | NOT LISTED | $1.00 | $2.00 | |
| 8275 | 1 | 54102-3 | MUSIC NEAR AND FAR — ALBUM 5, BOOK 4 | NOT LISTED | $1.00 | $2.00 | |
| 8276 | 1 | 54104-5 | MUSIC NEAR AND FAR — ALBUM 6, BOOK 4 | NOT LISTED | $1.00 | $2.00 | |
| 8277 | 1 | 54106-7 | MUSIC NEAR AND FAR — ALBUM 7, BOOK 4 | NOT LISTED | $1.00 | $2.00 | |
| 8278 | 1 | 54108-9 | MUSIC NEAR AND FAR — ALBUM 8, BOOK 4 | NOT LISTED | $1.00 | $2.00 | |
| 8279 | 1 | 54110-1 | MUSIC NEAR AND FAR — ALBUM 9, BOOK 4 | NOT LISTED | $1.00 | $2.00 | |
| 8280 | 1 | 54112-3 | MUSIC NEAR AND FAR — ALBUM 10, BOOK 4 | NOT LISTED | $1.00 | $2.00 | |
| NO # | 1 | FR1006-7 | MUSIC NEAR AND FAR — ALBUM 11, BOOK 4 | NOT LISTED | $1.00 | $2.00 | |
| NO # | 1 | FR1008-9 | MUSIC NEAR AND FAR — ALBUM 12, BOOK 4 | NOT LISTED | $1.00 | $2.00 | |
| NO # | 1 | FR1010-11 | MUSIC NEAR AND FAR — ALBUM 13, BOOK 4 | NOT LISTED | $1.00 | $2.00 | |
| NO # | 1 | FR1-12-13 | MUSIC NEAR AND FAR — ALBUM 14, BOOK 4 | NOT LISTED | $1.00 | $2.00 | |
| NO # | 1 | FR1014015 | MUSIC NEAR AND FAR — ALBUM 15, BOOK 4 | NOT LISTED | $1.00 | $2.00 | |
| 8281 | 1 | 56877-8 | MUSIC IN OUR COUNTRY — ALBUM 1, BOOK 5 | NOT LISTED | $1.00 | $2.00 | GRADE 5 |
| 8282 | 1 | 56879-80 | MUSIC IN OUR COUNTRY — ALBUM 2, BOOK 5 | NOT LISTED | $1.00 | $2.00 | |
| 8283 | 1 | 56881-2 | MUSIC IN OUR COUNTRY — ALBUM 3, BOOK 6 | NOT LISTED | $1.00 | $2.00 | |
| 8284 | 1 | 56883-4 | MUSIC IN OUR COUNTRY — ALBUM 4, BOOK 6 | NOT LISTED | $1.00 | $2.00 | |

## SILVER BURDETT 10" SINGLES

| SET # | # REC | DISC # | MAIN TITLE | ARTIST | G/VG | EX/NMT | REMARKS |
|---|---|---|---|---|---|---|---|
| 8285 | $1.00 | 56885-6 | MUSIC IN OUR COUNTRY — ALBUM 5, BOOK 5 | NOT LISTED | $1.00 | $2.00 | |
| 8286 | 1 | 56887-8 | MUSIC IN OUR COUNTRY — ALBUM 6, BOOK 5 | NOT LISTED | $1.00 | $2.00 | |
| 8287 | 1 | 56889-90 | MUSIC IN OUR COUNTRY — ALBUM 7, BOOK 5 | NOT LISTED | $1.00 | $2.00 | |
| 8288 | 1 | 56891-2 | MUSIC IN OUR COUNTRY — ALBUM 8, BOOK 5 | NOT LISTED | $1.00 | $2.00 | |
| 8289 | 1 | 56893-4 | MUSIC IN OUR COUNTRY — ALBUM 9, BOOK 5 | NOT LISTED | $1.00 | $2.00 | |
| 8290 | 1 | 56895-6 | MUSIC IN OUR COUNTRY — ALBUM 10, BOOK 5 | NOT LISTED | $1.00 | $2.00 | |
| NO # | 1 | FR1016-17 | MUSIC IN OUR COUNTRY — ALBUM 11, BOOK 5 | NOT LISTED | $1.00 | $2.00 | |
| NO # | 1 | FR1018-19 | MUSIC IN OUR COUNTRY — ALBUM 12, BOOK 5 | NOT LISTED | $1.00 | $2.00 | |
| NO # | 1 | FR1020-1 | MUSIC IN OUR COUNTRY — ALBUM 13, BOOK 5 | NOT LISTED | $1.00 | $2.00 | |
| NO # | 1 | FR1022-3 | MUSIC IN OUR COUNTRY — ALBUM 14, BOOK 5 | NOT LISTED | $1.00 | $2.00 | |
| NO # | 1 | FR1024-5 | MUSIC IN OUR COUNTRY — ALBUM 15, BOOK 5 | NOT LISTED | $1.00 | $2.00 | |
| 8291 | 1 | 55960-1 | MUSIC AROUND THE WORLD — ALBUM 1, BOOK 6 | NOT LISTED | $1.00 | $2.00 | GRADE 6 |
| 8292 | 1 | 55962-3 | MUSIC AROUND THE WORLD — ALBUM 2, BOOK 6 | NOT LISTED | $1.00 | $2.00 | |
| 8293 | 1 | 55964-5 | MUSIC AROUND THE WORLD — ALBUM 3, BOOK 6 | NOT LISTED | $1.00 | $2.00 | |
| 8294 | 1 | 55966-7 | MUSIC AROUND THE WORLD — ALBUM 4, BOOK 6 | NOT LISTED | $1.00 | $2.00 | |
| 8295 | 1 | 55968-9 | MUSIC AROUND THE WORLD — ALBUM 5, BOOK 6 | NOT LISTED | $1.00 | $2.00 | |
| 8296 | 1 | 55970-1 | MUSIC AROUND THE WORLD — ALBUM 6, BOOK 6 | NOT LISTED | $1.00 | $2.00 | |
| 8297 | 1 | 55972-3 | MUSIC AROUND THE WORLD — ALBUM 7, BOOK 6 | NOT LISTED | $1.00 | $2.00 | |
| 8298 | 1 | 55974-5 | MUSIC AROUND THE WORLD — ALBUM 8, BOOK 6 | NOT LISTED | $1.00 | $2.00 | |
| 8299 | 1 | 55976-7 | MUSIC AROUND THE WORLD — ALBUM 9, BOOK 6 | NOT LISTED | $1.00 | $2.00 | |
| 8300 | 1 | 55978-9 | MUSIC AROUND THE WORLD — ALBUM 10, BOOK 6 | NOT LISTED | $1.00 | $2.00 | |
| NO # | 1 | FR1026-7 | MUSIC AROUND THE WORLD — ALBUM 11, BOOK 6 | NOT LISTED | $1.00 | $2.00 | |
| NO # | 1 | FR1028-9 | MUSIC AROUND THE WORLD — ALBUM 12, BOOK 6 | NOT LISTED | $1.00 | $2.00 | |
| NO # | 1 | FR1030-1 | MUSIC AROUND THE WORLD — ALBUM 13, BOOK 6 | NOT LISTED | $1.00 | $2.00 | |
| NO # | 1 | FR1032-3 | MUSIC AROUND THE WORLD — ALBUM 14, BOOK 6 | NOT LISTED | $1.00 | $2.00 | |
| NO # | 1 | FR1034-5 | MUSIC AROUND THE WORLD — ALBUM 15, BOOK 6 | NOT LISTED | $1.00 | $2.00 | |

## SILVER BURDETT NEW MUSIC HORIZONS 10" SINGLES

| SET # | # REC | MAIN TITLE | ARTIST | YEAR | ALSO ISSUED ON | G/VG | EX/NMT |
|---|---|---|---|---|---|---|---|
| NO # | 4 | SONGS FROM MUSIC FOR EARLY CHILDHOOD | NOT LISTED | 1950 – 1951 | COLUMBIA MJV-141 | $4.00 | $8.00 |
| 1-B | 2 | LET'S STEP ALONG, ETC. | NOT LISTED | | COLUMBIA MJV-132 | $2.00 | $4.00 |
| 2 | 2 | OUR ANIMAL FRIENDS, ETC. | NOT LISTED | | COLUMBIA MJV-77 | $2.00 | $4.00 |
| 2-B | 2 | SONGS FOR HOLIDAYS, ETC. | NOT LISTED | | COLUMBIA MJV-133 | $2.00 | $4.00 |
| 3 | 2 | PLAYING OUTDOORS, ETC. | NOT LISTED | | COLUMBIA MJV-78 | $2.00 | $4.00 |
| 3-B | 2 | OUR COUNTRY, ETC. | NOT LISTED | | COLUMBIA MJV-134 | $2.00 | $4.00 |
| 4 | 2 | SAILING THE SEAS, ETC. | NOT LISTED | | COLUMBIA MJV-79 | $2.00 | $4.00 |
| 4-B | 2 | FOLK SONGS, ETC. | NOT LISTED | | COLUMBIA MJV-135 | $2.00 | $4.00 |
| 5 | 2 | DANCING SONGS FROM EUROPE, ETC. | NOT LISTED | | COLUMBIA MJV-80 | $2.00 | $4.00 |
| 5-B | 2 | MORE FUN WITH HARMONY, ETC. | NOT LISTED | | COLUMBIA MJV-136 | $2.00 | $4.00 |
| 6 | 2 | GREAT MASTERS, ETC. | NOT LISTED | | COLUMBIA MJV-81 | $2.00 | $4.00 |
| 6-B | 2 | AMERICAN SONGS, ETC. | NOT LISTED | | COLUMBIA MJV-137 | $2.00 | $4.00 |
| NO # | 4 | SONGS FROM WORLD MUSIC HORIZONS | NOT LISTED | | COLUMBIA MJV-118 | $4.00 | $8.00 |
| NO # | 4 | SONGS FROM AMERICAN MUSIC HORIZONS | NOT LISTED | | COLUMBIA MJV-119 | $4.00 | $8.00 |

## SILVERTONE RECORD CLUB 12" SINGLES AND ALBUMS

| # REC | DISC # | MAIN TITLE | ARTIST | YEAR | G/VG | EX/NMT |
|---|---|---|---|---|---|---|
| 1 | 8A | BUNKEY THE MONKEY (WHO WANTED TO SEE THE WORLD) | CLAYTON COLLYER | 1950 | $25.00 | $50.00 |
| 1 | 43A | BUNKEY THE MONKEY IN YELLOWSTONE PARK | CLAYTON COLLYER | | $15.00 | $30.00 |
| 3 | 1000 (NBR 90A-1A-2A) | HANSEL AND GRETEL | CHICAGO THEATER OF THE AIR | | $12.00 | $25.00 |

SACRED-SUNDAY SCHOOL
SAMSON AND THE LION
$4.00

SACRED-SUNDAY SCHOOL
ARE WE DOWNHEARTED
$1.00

SIGNATURE RECORDS
WILD BILL RIDES AGAIN
$8.00

## SIMMEL-MESERVEY 12" SINGLES

| # REC | DISC # | MAIN TITLE | ARTIST | YEAR | G/VG | EX/NMT |
|---|---|---|---|---|---|---|
| 1 | 12387/8 | TUNEFUL TALES (SERIES 1): THE THREE LITTLE PIGS | MARTHA BLAIR FOX | 194? | $5.00 | $10.00 |
| 1 | 12394/5 | TUNEFUL TALES (SERIES 1): THE LITTLE ENGINE THAT COULD | MARTHA BLAIR FOX | | $5.00 | $10.00 |
| 1 | 12397/8 | TUNEFUL TALES (SERIES 1): JOHNNY CAKE | MARTHA BLAIR FOX | | $5.00 | $10.00 |
| 1 | 12404/5 | TUNEFUL TALES (SERIES 1): THE SHOEMAKER & THE ELVES | MARTHA BLAIR FOX | | $5.00 | $10.00 |
| 1 | 12408/9 | TUNEFUL TALES (SERIES 1): THE LAUGHING JACK O'LANTERN | MARTHA BLAIR FOX | | $5.00 | $10.00 |
| 1 | 12434/5 | TUNEFUL TALES (SERIES 1): WHITE EASTER RABBIT | MARTHA BLAIR FOX | | $5.00 | $10.00 |
| 1 | 12464/5 | TUNEFUL TALES (SERIES 1): THE NUTCRACKER & KING MOUSE | MARTHA BLAIR FOX | | $5.00 | $10.00 |

## SIMMEL-MESERVEY 12" SINGLES

| SET # | # REC | DISC # | MAIN TITLE | ARTIST | YEAR | G/VG | EX/NMT |
|---|---|---|---|---|---|---|---|
| M-100 (10") | 3 | M109/10 - 113/14 | HAPPY HABITS: THE DISGRACEFUL PIG, ETC. | ARTHUR Q. BRYAN | 194? | $12.00 | $25.00 |
| ? | 2 | ? | CLASSICAL DANCE RHYTHMS | EDDISON VON OTTENFELD | | $2.00 | $4.00 |
| NO # (12") | 7 | 12377, 94, 7, 404, 8, 34, 64 (12") | TUNEFUL TALES SERIES 1: THREE LITTLE PIGS + 6 OTHER STORIES | MARTHA BLAIR FOX | 1946 | $10.00 | $20.00 |

## SIMON SAYS RECORD GUILD OF AMERICA 7" SINGLES

| # REC | DISC # | MAIN TITLE | ARTIST | A TITLE | B TITLE | YEAR | G/VG | EX/NMT |
|---|---|---|---|---|---|---|---|---|
| 1 | A-1 | ALOUETTE/ LITTLE BOY BLUE, SING A SONG OF SIXPENCE | NOT LISTED — SEE LABEL NOTES FOR MORE DETAIL. | ALOUETTE | LITTLE BOY BLUE, SING A SONG OF SIXPENCE | 195? | $1.00 | $2.00 |
| 1 | A-2 | SEE SAW MARGERY DAW/? | NOT LISTED — SEE LABEL NOTES FOR MORE DETAIL. | SEE SAW MARGERY DAW | ? | | $1.00 | $2.00 |
| 1 | A-3 | GOOSEY GOOSEY GANDER, MY BLACK HEN/? | NOT LISTED — SEE LABEL NOTES FOR MORE DETAIL. | GOOSEY GOOSEY GANDER, MY BLACK HEN | ? | | $1.00 | $2.00 |
| 1 | A-4 | LITTLE TOMMY TUCKER, JACK BE NIMBLE | NOT LISTED — SEE LABEL NOTES FOR MORE DETAIL. | LITTLE TOMMY TUCKER | JACK BE NIMBLE | | $1.00 | $2.00 |
| 1 | A-5 | THREE LITTLE KIT-TENS/? | NOT LISTED — SEE LABEL NOTES FOR MORE DETAIL. | THREE LITTLE KITTENS | ? | | $1.00 | $2.00 |
| 1 | A-6 | SIMPLE SIMON/? | NOT LISTED — SEE LABEL NOTES FOR MORE DETAIL. | SIMPLE SIMON | ? | | $1.00 | $2.00 |
| 1 | A-7 | THREE BLIND MICE/? | NOT LISTED — SEE LABEL NOTES FOR MORE DETAIL. | THREE BLIND MICE | ? | | $1.00 | $2.00 |
| 1 | A-8 | DIXIE | NOT LISTED — SEE LABEL NOTES FOR MORE DETAIL. | DIXIE | CARRY ME BACK TO OLD VIRGINNY | | $1.00 | $2.00 |
| 1 | A-9 | BAA BAA BLACK SHEEP/? | NOT LISTED — SEE LABEL NOTES FOR MORE DETAIL. | BAA BAA BLACK SHEEP | ? | | $1.00 | $2.00 |
| 1 | A-10 | THE UGLY DUCK-LING/TOM THUMB | NOT LISTED — SEE LABEL NOTES FOR MORE DETAIL. | THE UGLY DUCKLING | TOM THUMB | | $1.00 | $2.00 |

## SIMON SAYS RECORD GUILD OF AMERICA 7" SINGLES

| # REC | DISC # | MAIN TITLE | ARTIST | A TITLE | B TITLE | G/VG | EX/NMT |
|---|---|---|---|---|---|---|---|
| 1 | A-11 | I'VE BEEN WORKING ON THE RAILROAD/ERIE CANAL | NOT LISTED — SEE LABEL NOTES FOR MORE DETAIL. | WORKING ON THE RAILROAD | ERIE CANAL | $1.00 | $2.00 |
| 1 | A-12 | MY SON JOHN, COCK A DOODLE DOO/ THE EMPEROR'S NEW CLOTHES | NOT LISTED — SEE LABEL NOTES FOR MORE DETAIL. | MY SON JOHN | THE EMPEROR'S NEW CLOTHES | $1.00 | $2.00 |
| 1 | A-13 | LITTLE BO PEEP/SLEEP BABY SLEEP, BYE BABY BUNTING | NOT LISTED — SEE LABEL NOTES FOR MORE DETAIL. | LITTLE BO PEEP | SLEEP BABY SLEEP, BYE BABY BUNTING | $1.00 | $2.00 |
| 1 | A-14 | JACK AND THE BEANSTALK/ RUMPLESTILTSKIN | NOT LISTED — SEE LABEL NOTES FOR MORE DETAIL. | JACK AND THE BEANSTALK | RUMPLESTILTSKIN | $1.00 | $2.00 |
| 1 | A-15 | A DILLER A DOLLAR, TO MARKET TO MARKET/ SNOWDROP | NOT LISTED — SEE LABEL NOTES FOR MORE DETAIL. | TO MARKET TO MARKET | SNOWDROP | $1.00 | $2.00 |
| 1 | A-16 | THERE WAS A LITTLE GIRL, HICKORY DICKORY DOCK/ ROUNDUP TIME | NOT LISTED — SEE LABEL NOTES FOR MORE DETAIL. | HICKORY DICKORY DOCK | ROUNDUP TIME | $1.00 | $2.00 |
| 1 | A-17 | HEY DIDDLE DIDDLE, LITTLE MISS MUFFET/MOLLY MALONE | NOT LISTED — SEE LABEL NOTES FOR MORE DETAIL. | HEY DIDDLE DIDDLE | MOLLY MALONE | $1.00 | $2.00 |
| 1 | A-18 | OH WHERE OH WHERE HAS MY LITTLE DOG GONE?/? | NOT LISTED — SEE LABEL NOTES FOR MORE DETAIL. | OH WHERE OH WHERE HAS MY LITTLE DOG GONE? | ? | $1.00 | $2.00 |
| 1 | A-19 | PEAS PORRIDGE HOT/? | NOT LISTED — SEE LABEL NOTES FOR MORE DETAIL. | PEAS PORRIDGE HOT | ? | $1.00 | $2.00 |
| 1 | A-20 | PUSSYCAT PUSSYCAT/? | NOT LISTED — SEE LABEL NOTES FOR MORE DETAIL. | PUSSYCAT PUSSYCAT | ? | $1.00 | $2.00 |
| 1 | A-21 | ALPHABET SONG/? | NOT LISTED — SEE LABEL NOTES FOR MORE DETAIL. | ALPHABET SONG | ? | $1.00 | $2.00 |
| 1 | A-22 | THE FARMER IN THE DELL/? | NOT LISTED — SEE LABEL NOTES FOR MORE DETAIL. | THE FARMER IN THE DELL | ? | $1.00 | $2.00 |
| 1 | A-23 | LONDON BRIDGE/? | NOT LISTED — SEE LABEL NOTES FOR MORE DETAIL. | LONDON BRIDGE | ? | $1.00 | $2.00 |
| 1 | A-24 | HAPPY BIRTHDAY/POP GOES THE WEASEL | NOT LISTED — SEE LABEL NOTES FOR MORE DETAIL. | HAPPY BIRTHDAY | POP GOES THE WEASEL | $1.00 | $2.00 |
| 1 | A-27 | SILENT NIGHT/JOY TO THE WORLD | NOT LISTED — SEE LABEL NOTES FOR MORE DETAIL. | SILENT NIGHT | JOY TO THE WORLD | $1.00 | $2.00 |
| 1 | A-28 | JINGLE BELLS/DECK THE HALLS WITH BOUGHS OF HOLLY | NOT LISTED — SEE LABEL NOTES FOR MORE DETAIL. | JINGLE BELLS | DECK THE HALLS | $1.00 | $2.00 |
| 1 | A-29 | OH COME ALL YE FAITHFUL/WE ARE NOT BEGGARS | NOT LISTED — SEE LABEL NOTES FOR MORE DETAIL. | OH COME ALL YE FAITHFUL | WE ARE NOT BEGGARS | $1.00 | $2.00 |
| 1 | A-32 | THE NIGHT BEFORE CHRISTMAS/? | NOT LISTED — SEE LABEL NOTES FOR MORE DETAIL. | THE NIGHT BEFORE CHRISTMAS | ? | $1.00 | $2.00 |

## SINGSPIRATION HAPPY-TIME 7" DOUBLES

| SET # | # REC | DISC # | ARTIST | A TITLE | B TITLE | YEAR | G/VG | EX/NMT |
|---|---|---|---|---|---|---|---|---|
| 1H | 2 | | | | | 1949 | $1.00 | $2.00 |
| | | H-2500 | WENDELL P. LOVELESS | NOAH'S ARK | THE BIBLE ZOO | | | |
| | | H-2501 | HELEN MCALERNEY BARTH AND AL SMITH | THE NUMBERING SONG | HAPPY ALL THE TIME | | | |
| 2H | 2 | | | | | | $1.00 | $2.00 |
| | | H-2502 | WENDELL P. LOVELESS | SAMUEL | JONAH AND THE WHALE | | | |
| | | H-2503 | HELEN MCALERNEY BARTH AND AL SMITH | THE WISE MAN AND THE FOOLISH MAN | JESUS IS THE SHEPHERD | | | |
| 3H | 2 | | | | | | $1.00 | $2.00 |
| | | H-2504 | WENDELL P. LOVELESS | JOSHUA AND THE WALLS OF JERICHO | JESUS HEALS THE BLIND MAN | | | |
| | | H-2505 | HELEN MCALERNEY BARTH AND AL SMITH | HAPPY DAY EXPRESS | WHOSOEVER WILL TO THE LORD MAY COME | | | |
| 4H | 2 | | | | | | $1.00 | $2.00 |
| | | H-2506 | WENDELL P. LOVELESS | JESUS STOPS A STORM | THE HEART HOUSE | | | |
| | | H-2507 | HELEN MCALERNEY BARTH AND AL SMITH | JEWELS | SHADRACH, MESHACH AND ABEDNEGO | | | |
| 5H | 2 | | | | | | $1.00 | $2.00 |
| | | H-2508 | WENDELL P. LOVELESS | ELIJAH THE PROPHET | MARY AND THE PIG | 1950 | | |
| | | H-2509 | HELEN MCALERNEY BARTH AND AL SMITH | JESUS WANTS ME FOR A SUNBEAM | | | | |

## SINGSPIRATION HAPPY-TIME 7" DOUBLES

| SET # | # REC | DISC # | ARTIST | A TITLE | B TITLE | YEAR | G/VG | EX/NMT |
|---|---|---|---|---|---|---|---|---|
| ? | 1 | H-2514 | ? | NOAH WAS SAFE | BOYS & GIRLS FOR JESUS | | ¢.50 | $1.00 |
| 6H | 2 | | | | | | $1.00 | $2.00 |
| | | H-2515 | WENDELL P. LOVELESS/ UNCLE BEN | DAVID AND GOLIATH | BE ON TIME | | | |
| | | H-2516 | HELEN MCALERNEY BARTH AND AL SMITH | ALPHABET SONG | JESUS LOVES ME | | | |
| 7H | 2 | | | | | | $1.00 | $2.00 |
| | | H-2517 | UNCLE BEN/WENDELL P. LOVELESS | THE FOX WHO LOST HIS TAIL | AN ESCAPE FROM JAIL | | | |
| | | H-2518 | HELEN MCALERNEY BARTH AND AL SMITH | THE DAY OF THE WEEK SONG | JESUS THE WONDERFUL FRIEND | | | |
| 8H | 2 | | | | | | $1.00 | $2.00 |
| | | H-2519 | UNCLE BEN/WENDELL P. LOVELESS | THE STORY OF A POSTAGE STAMP | THE SHIPWRECK | | | |
| | | H-2520 | HELEN MCALERNEY BARTH AND AL SMITH | THE BIRDS UPON THE TREE TOPS | OH, BE CAREFUL | | | |
| 9H | 2 | | | | | | $1.00 | $2.00 |
| | | H-2521 | UNCLE BEN/WENDELL P. LOVELESS | THE FIRST TRAIN WHISTLE | DANIEL AND THE LIONS | | | |
| | | H-2522 | HELEN MCALERNEY BARTH AND AL SMITH | WHY WORRY WHEN YOU CAN PRAY | PRAYER SONG | | | |
| 10H | 2 | | | | | | $1.00 | $2.00 |
| | | H-2523 | ? | ? | ? | | | |
| | | H-2524 | ? | ? | ? | | | |
| 11H | 2 | | | | | | $1.00 | $2.00 |
| | | H-2525 | ? | ? | ? | | | |
| | | H-2526 | ? | ? | ? | | | |
| 12H | 2 | | | | | 1951 | $1.00 | $2.00 |
| | | H-2527 | WENDELL P. LOVELESS | THREE CHILDREN IN A FURNACE | WHO OWNS YOUR FACE | | | |
| | | H-2528 | HELEN MCALERNEY BARTH AND AL SMITH | GIVE ME OIL IN MY LAMP | MY HEART WAS BLACK WITH SIN | | | |

## SINGSPIRATION SONGTIME 7" DOUBLES

| SET # | # REC | DISC # | ARTIST | A TITLE | B TITLE | YEAR | G/VG | EX/NMT |
|---|---|---|---|---|---|---|---|---|
| ST-1 | 2 | | | | | 195? | $1.00 | $2.00 |
| | | S-2601 | UNCLE DON DEVOS | THE LORD IS COUNTING ON YOU | OPEN UP YOUR HEART | | | |
| | | S-2602 | UNCLE DON DEVOS | SAMUEL | THE NOBLEMAN'S SON | | | |
| ST-10 | 2 | | | | | | $1.00 | $2.00 |
| | | S-2610 | BACK TO THE BIBLE YOUTH CHOIR | IT IS NO SECRET | ONWARD, CHRISTIAN SOLDIERS | | | |
| | | S-2611 | BACK TO THE BIBLE YOUTH CHOIR | HARVEST CALL | THE B-I-B-L-E, ALPHABET CHORUS, I'M H-A-P-P-Y | | | |
| ST-11 | 2 | | | | | | $1.00 | $2.00 |
| | | ? | ? | TEN LITTLE CHILDREN, ETC. | I'M IN THE LORD'S ARMY, ETC. | | | |
| | | ? | ? | TOO SMALL | JESUS LOVES EVEN ME | | | |
| ST-12 | 2 | | | | | | $1.00 | $2.00 |
| | | ? | ? | JESUS SON OF GOD | MY ALL TO THEE, JEWELS | | | |
| | | ? | ? | POOR LITTLE BLACK SHEEP | WHY DO I SING ABOUT JESUS | | | |

## SINGSPIRATION SUNNY SONGS SERIES 7" SINGLES

| # REC | DISC # | ARTIST | A TITLE | B TITLE | YEAR | G/VG | EX/NMT |
|---|---|---|---|---|---|---|---|
| 1 | SS 1 | BACK TO THE BIBLE HOUR — KIDS CHOIR | FATHER WE THANK YOU | ALL THROUGH THE WEEK AND SUNDAY GO TO MEETIN' | 195? | $.50 | $1.00 |
| 1 | SS 2 | BACK TO THE BIBLE HOUR — KIDS CHOIR | IS THERE ANYBODY HERE WHO LOVES MY JESUS | DON'T YOU GET WEARY, ETC. | | $.50 | $1.00 |
| 1 | SS 3 | BACK TO THE BIBLE HOUR — KIDS CHOIR | JOSHUA FIT THE BATTLE OF JERICHO | ASSURANCE MARCH | | $.50 | $1.00 |

## TEDDY BEAR 8" SINGLES

| # REC | DISC # | ARTIST | A TITLE | B TITLE | YEAR | G/VG | EX/NMT |
|---|---|---|---|---|---|---|---|
| 1 | 201 | THE TEDDY BEAR (TB) SINGERS & ORCHESTRA/ROY HALEE & THE TB ORCHESTRA | OLD MACDONALD HAD A FARM | HICKORY, DICKORY, DOCK | 1949 | $1.50 | $3.00 |
| 1 | 202 | JERRY BEITZEL & ROY HALEE/THE TB SINGERS | LITTLE BOY BLUE | ROW ROW ROW | | $1.50 | $3.00 |
| 1 | 203 | THE TB SINGERS & ORCHESTRA/ROBERT NOLAND & THE TB SINGERS | JINGLE BELLS | THE BEAR WENT OVER THE MOUNTAIN | | $1.50 | $3.00 |
| 1 | 204 | BOB MOODY & THE TB ORCHESTRA/ BOB MOODY & THE TB SINGERS | RED RIVER VALLEY | CLEMENTINE | | $1.50 | $3.00 |
| 1 | 205 | BOB MOODY & THE TB SINGERS | HOME ON THE RANGE | I'VE BEEN WORKING ON THE RAILROAD | | $1.50 | $3.00 |
| 1 | 206 | BOB MOODY & THE TB ORCHESTRA/ BOB MOODY & THE TB SINGERS | LONE PRAIRIE | WHOOPEE TI YI YO | | $1.50 | $3.00 |
| 1 | 207 | THE TB SINGERS & ORCHESTRA/ROY HALEE & THE TB ORCHESTRA | THE FARMER IN THE DELL | TOM, TOM THE PIPER'S SON | | $1.50 | $3.00 |
| 1 | 208 | JERRY BEITZEL, JOHANNE MORELAND & THE TB ORCHESTRA/JERRY BEITZEL & THE TB ORCHESTRA | LAZY MARY | ROCK-A-BYE BABY | | $1.50 | $3.00 |
| 1 | 209 | THE TB SINGERS & ORCHESTRA/JERRY BEITZEL & THE TB SINGERS | LITTLE BO-PEEP | TWINKLE, TWINKLE | | $1.50 | $3.00 |
| 1 | 210 | THE TB SINGERS & ORCHESTRA/JERRY BEITZEL & THE TB ORCHESTRA | MARY HAD A LITTLE LAMB | GOLDILOCKS AND THE THREE BEARS | | $1.50 | $3.00 |
| 1 | 211 | ROY HALEE, JERRY BEITZEL & THE TB ORCHESTRA/ROY HALEE & THE TB ORCHESTRA | POP GOES THE WEASEL | THE PIED PIPER | | $1.50 | $3.00 |
| 1 | 212 | THE TB SINGERS & ORCHESTRA/JERRY BEITZEL, ROY HALEE & THE TB ORCHESTRA | LONDON BRIDGE | LITTLE RED RIDING HOOD | | $1.50 | $3.00 |
| 1 | 251 | THE TB PLAYERS | OLD KING COLE | LITTLE RED HEN | | $1.50 | $3.00 |
| 1 | 252 | THE TB PLAYERS | OUR BIRTHDAY PARTY | FUNNY BUNNY | | $1.50 | $3.00 |
| 1 | 253 | THE TB PLAYERS | THREE LITTLE PIGS | KATIE THE KANGAROO | | $3.00 | $6.00 |
| 1 | 254 | JERRY BEITZEL/ROGER WHITE & ROY HALEE | WHAT CAN THE MATTER BE | HOBBLEDY HORSE | | $1.50 | $3.00 |
| 1 | 255 | THE TB PLAYERS/JERRY BEITZEL & GERRY TOUCHETTE | LOOBY LOO | THE WEEZ WUMP | | $2.00 | $4.00 |
| 1 | 256 | JERRY TOUCHETTE/ROY HALEE | SLEEPYTIME FOR DOLLY | PADDY THE BAKERY BOY | | $1.50 | $3.00 |
| 1 | 257 | ? | TEN LITTLE INDIANS | BRAVE LITTLE SAMBO | | $5.00 | $10.00 |
| 1 | 258 | THE TB PLAYERS/JERRY BEITZEL & THE TB PLAYERS | THREE LITTLE KITTENS | CINDERELLA | | $1.50 | $3.00 |
| 1 | 259 | ROGER WHITE & JERRY BEITZEL | H.M.S. PINAFORE (PT. 1) | H.M.S. PINAFORE (PT. 2) | | $1.50 | $3.00 |
| 1 | 260 | JERRY BEITZEL/ROY HALEE & THE TB SINGERS | JACK AND THE BEANSTALK | OH SUZANNA | | $1.50 | $3.00 |
| 1 | 261 | ROY HALEE & THE TB SINGERS | THE MIKADO (PT. 1) | THE MIKADO (PT. 2) | | $1.50 | $3.00 |
| 1 | 265 | ROBERT NOLAN, THE TB SINGERS & ORCH./ROGER WHITE | JINGLE BELLS | TWAS THE NIGHT BEFORE CHRISTMAS | | $1.50 | $3.00 |
| 1 | 266 | MARIE GERARD & BARBARA TOUCHETTE/ROGER WHITE & ROY HALEE | SILENT NIGHT | GOOD KING WENCESLAS | | $1.50 | $3.00 |
| 1 | 267 | MARIE GERARD & BARBARA TOUCHETTE/THE TB CAROLEERS | O COME, ALL YE FAITHFUL | THE FIRST NOEL | | $1.50 | $3.00 |
| 1 | 268 | THE TB CAROLEERS | IT CAME UPON A MIDNIGHT CLEAR | JOY TO THE WORLD | | $1.50 | $3.00 |

## TOPS FOR TOTS FIRST ISSUE 7" SINGLES

| # REC | DISC # | ARTIST | A TITLE | B TITLE | YEAR | G/VG | EX/NMT |
|---|---|---|---|---|---|---|---|
| 1 | V-1 | TOBY DEANE, THE TOPS ORCH. | NELLIE NEAT | MARY HAD A LITTLE LAMB | 1952 | $1.00 | $2.00 |
| 1 | V-11 | TOPS ORCH. | SKIP TO MY LOU | DID YOU EVER SEE A LASSIE? | | $1.00 | $2.00 |
| 1 | V-14 | BOB KENNEDY, TOPS ORCH. | TEN LITTLE INDIANS | OH DEAR WHAT CAN THE MATTER BE? | | $1.00 | $2.00 |
| 1 | V-15 | ? | LAZY MARY | GOOD MORNING MARY SUNSHINE | | $1.00 | $2.00 |
| 1 | V-17 | ? | BRAHMS' LULLABY | ROCKABYE BABY | | $1.00 | $2.00 |
| 1 | V-18 | ? | CAMPTOWN RACES | AMERICA THE BEAUTIFUL | | $1.00 | $2.00 |
| 1 | V-19 | TOPS ORCH. | ARKANSAS TRAVELER | FIDDLE DEE DEE | | $1.00 | $2.00 |
| 1 | V-20 | TOBY DEANE/KAY ARMEN | THE FARMER IN THE DELL | THE COUNTING SONG | | $1.00 | $2.00 |
| 1 | V-23 | THE TOPPERS CAST & ORCH. | POP GOES THE WEASEL | HIPPITY HOP BUNNY | | $1.00 | $2.00 |

## TOPS FOR TOTS FIRST ISSUE 7" SINGLES

| # REC | DISC # | ARTIST | A TITLE | B TITLE | G/VG | EX/NMT |
|---|---|---|---|---|---|---|
| 1 | V-24 | ? | YANKEE DOODLE | LAUGH LAUGH PHONOGRAPH | $3.00 | $6.00 |
| 1 | V-25 | THE TOPS CAST & ORCH. | THREE BLIND MICE | WOULD YOU RATHER BE AN ELEPHANT | $1.00 | $2.00 |
| 1 | V-26 | ? | I TISKET, I TASKET | DINKY THE DOGGIE | $1.00 | $2.00 |
| 1 | V-27 | GWEN ALDEN/PAT LANE | BAA, BAA, BLACK SHEEP | BE YOUR MOTHER'S LITTLE HELPER | $1.00 | $2.00 |
| 1 | V-28 | GINNY GIBSON, VOCO ORCH. | JACK AND THE BEANSTALK | ONE TWO BUCKLE MY SHOE | $1.00 | $2.00 |
| 1 | V-29 | BOB KENNEDY/BERNIE KNEE, GINNY GIBSON | HANSEL AND GRETEL | ROW ROW ROW YOUR BOAT | $1.00 | $2.00 |
| 1 | V-30 | BERNIE KNEE | LITTLE RED RIDING HOOD | LOOBY LOO | $1.00 | $2.00 |
| 1 | V-31 | FRAN PARKER/STAN BAKER, BARRY KEANE, THE TOPPER ORCH. | GOLDILOCKS AND THE THREE BEARS (PT. 1) | GOLDILOCKS AND THE THREE BEARS (PT. 2) | $1.00 | $2.00 |
| 1 | V-32 | TOBY DEAN, BOB MALLIT | THE THREE LITTLE PIGS (PT. 1) | THE THREE LITTLE PIGS (PT. 2) | $1.00 | $2.00 |
| 1 | V-33 | BOB KENNEDY, GINNY GIBSON | CINDERELLA (PT. 1) | CINDERELLA (PT. 2) | $1.00 | $2.00 |
| 1 | V-34 | TODD MANNERS, GINNY GIBSON | ALICE IN WONDERLAND (PT. 1) | ALICE IN WONDERLAND (PT. 2) | $1.00 | $2.00 |
| 1 | V-35 | BUD ROMAN, LAURIE WAYNE, RAY BAXTER ORCH./ BOB KENNEDY, TOPS ORCH. | TELL ME A STORY | OH SUZANNA | $1.00 | $2.00 |
| 1 | V-36 | PAT FARWELL | A TRIP IN A ROCKET SHIP (PT. 1) | A TRIP IN A ROCKET SHIP (PT.2) | $5.00 | $10.00 |
| 1 | V-37 | BETSY GAY | WEE WILLIE THE WHALE | WEE WILLIE THE WHALE | $3.00 | $6.00 |
| 1 | V-38 | BETSY GAY | THE ZEBRA WHO LOST HER STRIPES | THE SLY OLD FOX | $2.00 | $4.00 |
| 1 | V-39 | PAT FARWELL | BENNY THE HUNGRY GOAT (PT. 1) | BENNY THE HUNGRY GOAT (PT. 2) | $1.00 | $2.00 |
| 1 | V-40 | GENE GULLIKSEN | THE HAPPY CLOCKS | THE BARNYARD BALL | $1.00 | $2.00 |
| 1 | V-41 | MIMI MARTEL, THE HAL LOMAN ORCH./BOB KENNEDY, TOPS ORCH. | DOGGIE IN THE WINDOW | A FROG WENT WALKING | $2.00 | $4.00 |
| 1 | V-100 | BEN ZEPPA, LEW RAYMOND ORCH. | HERE COMES PETER COTTONTAIL | EASTER PARADE | $1.00 | $2.00 |
| 1 | VX-101 | THE MARINERS/BOB KENNEDY, VOCO ORCH. | JINGLE BELLS | I WISH I WAS SANTA CLAUS | $1.00 | $2.00 |
| 1 | V-517 | (MARIE MENDOZA), THE TOPS CHORUS & ORCH./ STEVEN NELSON, THE TOPPERS ORCH. | HAPPY BIRTHDAY | JOLLY GOOD FELLOW | $1.00 | $2.00 |
| 1 | V-533 | ? | HOME ON THE RANGE | WHAT WOULD YOU RATHER BE | $1.00 | $2.00 |
| 1 | V-534 | SMOKEY JAMES, THE TOPS RANCHERS CHORUS & ORCH. | THE LONE PRAIRIE | SOURWOOD MOUNTAIN | $1.00 | $2.00 |
| 1 | V-535 | THE VOCO RANGERS | RED RIVER VALLEY | SCARECROW IN THE CORNFIELD | $1.00 | $2.00 |
| 1 | V-536 | ? | THE BIG ROCK CANDY MOUNTAIN | THE OL' CHISHOLM TRAIL | $1.00 | $2.00 |
| 1 | V-537 | THE TOPS RANGERS/ANN WHITE, THE TOPPERS ORCH. | SHE'LL BE COMIN' ROUND THE MOUNTAIN | SPUNKY THE MONKEY | $1.00 | $2.00 |
| 1 | V-538 | ? | GET ALONG LITTLE DOGGIE | BUSTER THE BRONCO BUSTER | $1.00 | $2.00 |
| 1 | VX-624 | ? | JOY TO THE WORLD | HARK THE HERALD ANGELS SING | $1.00 | $2.00 |
| 1 | VX-625 | ? | GOD REST YE MERRY GENTLEMEN | DECK THE HALLS | $1.00 | $2.00 |
| 1 | VX-628 | THE TOPS CHORALEERS, THE TOPPERS ORCH. | SILENT NIGHT | O COME ALL YE FAITHFUL | $1.00 | $2.00 |
| 1 | VX-629 | ? | LITTLE TOWN OF BETHLEHEM | SANTA CLAUS COMES CALLING | $1.00 | $2.00 |
| 1 | VX-630 | TOPS ORCH. | SANTA'S TOY SHOP | THE FIRST NOEL | $1.00 | $2.00 |
| 1 | VX-631 | ? | THE NIGHT BEFORE CHRISTMAS (PT. 1) | THE NIGHT BEFORE CHRISTMAS (PT. 2) | $1.00 | $2.00 |
| 1 | VX-632 | ? | I SAW MOMMY KISSING SANTA CLAUS | I WISH I WERE SANTA CLAUS | $1.00 | $2.00 |

*SLV IS TOPS, LBL IS VOCO.

## TOPS FOR TOTS SECOND ISSUE 7" SINGLES

| # REC | DISC # | ARTIST | A TITLE | B TITLE | YEAR | G/VG | EX/NMT |
|---|---|---|---|---|---|---|---|
| 1 | V-10 | PAT FARWELL, THE TOPS CAST & ORCH. | THE CROCODILE WHO CRIED (SIDE 1) | THE CROCODILE WHO CRIED (SIDE 2) | 195? | $1.00 | $2.00 |
| 1 | V-11 | PAT FARWELL, GENE GULLIKSEN | MAGIC FLYING SONG (SIDE 1) | MAGIC FLYING SONG (SIDE 2) | | $1.00 | $2.00 |
| 1 | V-12 | THE TOPS CAST & ORCH. | BRAVE LITTLE COWBOY | BRAVE LITTLE COWBOY | | $1.00 | $2.00 |
| 1 | V-13 | BERNIE KNEE/THE TOPS CAST & ORCH. | AROUND THE WORLD IN A BUBBLE | PATRIOTIC SONGS | | $1.00 | $2.00 |
| 1 | V-14 | BOB KENNEDY, TOPS ORCH. | TEN LITTLE INDIANS | OH DEAR, WHAT CAN THE MATTER BE? | | $1.00 | $2.00 |

## TOPS FOR TOTS SECOND ISSUE 7" SINGLES

| # REC | DISC # | ARTIST | A TITLE | B TITLE | G/VG | EX/NMT |
|---|---|---|---|---|---|---|
| 1 | V-16 | TOPS ORCH., TOBY DEANE | SIMPLE SIMON | OLD MACDONALD HAD A FARM | $1.00 | $2.00 |
| 1 | V-17 | THE TOPS CAST & ORCH. | FIRE ENGINE PARADE | TRAVELING MUSICIANS | $1.00 | $2.00 |
| 1 | V-19 | THE TOPS CAST & ORCH. | PINOCCHIO | HOP O' MY THUMB | $1.00 | $2.00 |
| 1 | V-20 | THE TOPS CAST & ORCH. | OLD WOMAN WHO LIVED IN A SHOE | DING DONG BELL | $1.00 | $2.00 |
| 1 | V-21 | THE TOPS CAST & ORCH. | BRAVE LITTLE SAMBO | THREE BILLY GOATS | $5.00 | $10.00 |
| 1 | V-22 | THE TOPS CAST & ORCH. | I'VE BEEN WORKING ON THE RAILROAD | PADDY THE BAKERY BOY | $1.00 | $2.00 |
| 1 | V-23 | THE TOPS CAST & ORCH. | ALPHABET SONG | TO MARKET TO MARKET | $1.00 | $2.00 |
| 1 | V-24 | THE TOPS CAST & ORCH. | MOTHER GOOSE PARTY | THREE LITTLE KITTENS | $1.00 | $2.00 |
| 1 | V-25 | THE TOPS CAST & ORCH. | THREE BLIND MICE | THE ELVES AND THE SHOEMAKER | $1.00 | $2.00 |
| 1 | V-26 | THE TOPS CAST & ORCH. | PIED PIPER | THERE WAS A CROOKED MAN | $1.00 | $2.00 |
| 1 | V-27 | GWEN ALDEN/PAT LANE | BAA BAA BLACK SHEEP | OLD MOTHER HUBBARD | $1.00 | $2.00 |
| 1 | V-28 | JEAN LONG/STAN BAKER, EDDIE HOWARD, THE TOPPER ORCH. | JACK AND THE BEANSTALK | THE FISHERMAN AND THE FLOUNDER | $1.00 | $2.00 |
| 1 | V-29 | THE TOPS CAST & ORCH. | THE GINGERBREAD MAN | THE BEAR WENT OVER THE MOUNTAIN | $1.00 | $2.00 |
| 1 | V-30 | BERNIE KNEE | LITTLE RED RIDING HOOD | THE ALPHABET SONG | $1.00 | $2.00 |
| 1 | V-31 | FRAN PARKER/STAN BAKER, BARRY KEANE, THE TOPPER ORCH. | GOLDILOCKS AND THE THREE BEARS | THE FROG AND THE OX | $1.00 | $2.00 |
| 1 | V-32 | TOBY DEAN, BOB MALLIT/? | THE THREE LITTLE PIGS | FIDDLE-DE-DEE | $1.00 | $2.00 |
| 1 | V-33 | BOB KENNEDY, GINNY GIBSON | CINDERELLA (PT. 1) | CINDERELLA (PT. 2) | $1.00 | $2.00 |
| 1 | V-34 | NOT LISTED | AT THE BAR X RANCH | COWBOY SONGS | $1.00 | $2.00 |
| 1 | V-35 | BUD ROMAN, LAURIE WAYNE, RAY BAXTER ORCH./BOB KENNEDY, TOPS ORCH. | TELL ME A STORY | O SUZANNA | $1.00 | $2.00 |
| 1 | V-36 | PAT FARWELL | A TRIP IN A ROCKETSHIP (PT. 1) | A TRIP IN A ROCKETSHIP (PT. 2) | $5.00 | $10.00 |
| 1 | V-37 | BETSY GAY | WEE WILLIE THE WHALE (PT. 1) | WEE WILLIE THE WHALE (PT. 2) | $3.00 | $6.00 |
| 1 | V-38 | BETSY GAY | THE ZEBRA WHO LOST HER STRIPES (PT. 1) | THE ZEBRA WHO LOST HER STRIPES (PT. 2) | $2.00 | $4.00 |
| 1 | V-39 | PAT FARWELL | BENNY THE HUNGRY GOAT (PT. 1) | BENNY THE HUNGRY GOAT (PT. 2) | $1.00 | $2.00 |
| 1 | V-40 | GENE GULLIKSEN | THE HAPPY CLOCKS (PT. 1) | THE HAPPY CLOCKS (PT. 2) | $1.00 | $2.00 |
| 1 | V-41 | MIMI MARTEL, HAL LOMEN ORCH./BOB KENNEDY, TOPS ORCH. | THE DOGGIE IN THE WINDOW | A FROG WENT WALKING | $2.00 | $4.00 |
| 1 | V-42 | THE TOPPERS ORCH. | FARMER IN THE DELL | A MONKEY WHO WANTED TO FLY | $1.00 | $2.00 |
| 1 | V-43 | THE TOPS PLAYERS & ORCH. | THE CIRCUS TRAIN (PT. 1) | THE CIRCUS TRAIN (PT. 2) | $1.00 | $2.00 |
| 1 | V-44 | ? | THREE WISE MONKEYS | ? | $1.00 | $2.00 |
| 1 | V-45 | THE TOPS CAST & ORCH. | LITTLE BOY BLUE | THE LION AND THE MOUSE | $1.00 | $2.00 |
| 1 | V-46 | JOAN HARRIS/THE TOPS PLAYERS & ORCH. | TRAFFIC LIGHT | HEY DIDDLE DIDDLE | $1.00 | $2.00 |
| 1 | V-47 | THE TOPPERS CAST & ORCH./FRAN PARKER, TOPPERS CAST & ORCH. | HUMPTY DUMPTY | FRERES JACQUES (BROTHER JOHN) | $1.00 | $2.00 |
| 1 | V-48 | FRAN PARKER & THE TOPPERS ORCH./THE TOPS PLAYERS & ORCH. | RIDE A COCK HORSE | LONDON BRIDGE | $1.00 | $2.00 |
| 1 | V-49 | JOAN HARRIS/THE TOPS CHORUS & ORCH. | MAMA'S LITTLE HELPER | CHARLIE HAD A CHOO CHOO | $1.00 | $2.00 |
| 1 | V-50 | SETH THOMPSON, THE TOPPERS ORCH./DICK ROGERS, THE TOPPERS ORCH. | MONKEY DOODLE DOO | HICKORY DICKORY DOCK | $1.00 | $2.00 |
| 1 | V-51 | JOAN HARRIS, THE TOPPERS ORCH./THE TOPS PLAYERS & ORCH. | GOLDIE THE GOLDFISH | OLD KING COLE | $1.00 | $2.00 |
| 1 | V-52 | EDDIE HOWARD, THE TOPPERS ORCH./THE TOPS PLAYERS & ORCH. | JACK AND JILL | PAT A CAKE | $1.00 | $2.00 |
| 1 | V-53 | THE TOPPERS CAST & ORCH. | POP GOES THE WEASEL | A TRIP TO NEW YORK | $2.00 | $4.00 |
| 1 | V-54 | FRAN PARKER, JUDY KELLY, THE TOPPERS CAST & ORCH./FRAN PARKER, THE TOPPERS ORCH. | SING A SONG OF SIXPENCE | NIGHT SONG FOR LITTLE ONE | $1.00 | $2.00 |
| 1 | V-55 | THE TOPS ORCH. | THE MUFFIN MAN | CHICKEN LICKEN | $1.00 | $2.00 |
| 1 | V-56 | EDMOND KARLSRUD/TOBY DEANE | DAN THE FIREMAN | NURSERY SONGS | $2.00 | $4.00 |
| 1 | V-57 | HELEN CARROLL & THE SWAN TONES/THE TOPS CHORALEERS | THE ENCHANTED FOREST | LULLABY TIME | $2.00 | $4.00 |
| 1 | V-58 | TOBY DEANE/HELEN CARROLL & THE SWAN TONES | THE FAIRYLAND EXPRESS | MOTHER GOOSE SONGS | $2.00 | $4.00 |
| 1 | V-59 | THE TOPS CAST & ORCH. | COUNTING SONG | LAZY MARY | $1.00 | $2.00 |
| 1 | V-517 | (MARIE MENDOZA), THE TOPS CHORUS & ORCH./STEVEN NELSON, THE TOPPERS ORCH. | HAPPY BIRTHDAY | WHERE HAS MY LITTLE DOG GONE? | $1.00 | $2.00 |

TALKING BOOK RECORDS
THE FARMER IN THE DELLL
$30.00

TEDDY BEAR RECORDS
KATIE THE KANGEROO
$6.00

TOTS N' TEENS RECORDS
TWAS A NIGHT BEFORE CHRISTMAS
$2.00

## TOPS FOR TOTS SECOND ISSUE 7" SINGLES

| # REC | DISC # | ARTIST | A TITLE | B TITLE | G/VG | EX/NMT |
|---|---|---|---|---|---|---|
| 1 | V-534 | SMOKEY JAMES, THE TOPS RANCHERS CHORUS & ORCH. | THE LONE PRAIRIE | WHOOPEE TI YI YO | $1.00 | $2.00 |
| 1 | V-535 | ? | THE BALLAD OF DAVEY CROCKETT | CLEMENTINE | $4.00 | $8.00 |
| 1 | V-536 | ? | THE BIG ROCK CANDY MOUNTAIN | THE OLD CHISHOLM TRAIL | $1.00 | $2.00 |
| 1 | V-537 | THE TOPS RANGERS/ANN WHITE, THE TOPPERS ORCH. | SHE'LL BE COMIN' ROUND THE MOUNTAIN | A-HUNTING WE WILL GO | $1.00 | $2.00 |
| 1 | VX-601 | THE MARINERS/JACK WILLIAMS, THE TOPPERS ORCH. | JINGLE BELLS | TWAS THE NIGHT BEFORE CHRISTMAS | $1.00 | $2.00 |
| 1 | VX-602 | THE TOPS CHORALEERS, THE TOPPERS ORCH. | SILENT NIGHT | O COME ALL YE FAITHFUL | $1.00 | $2.00 |
| 1 | VX-603 | ? | I SAW MOMMY KISSING SANTA CLAUS | SANTA'S TOY SHOP | $1.00 | $2.00 |
| 1 | VX-604 | BUD ROMAN, THE FRANKIE MARTIN ORCH./ TED WHITE, THE TOPPERS CHORUS & ORCH. | RUDOLPH THE RED-NOSED REINDEER | SANTA IS FLYING THROUGH THE SKY | $1.00 | $2.00 |

## TOPS FOR TOTS 7" ALBUMS

| SET # | # REC | DISC # | MAIN TITLE | ARTIST | A TITLE | B TITLE | G/VG | EX/NMT |
|---|---|---|---|---|---|---|---|---|
| ALBUM # 4G | 4 | V-14, 16 + 515, 523 (VOCO #S) | KIDDIE FAVORITES | VARIOUS | SEE INDIVIDUAL VOCO RECORD NUMBERS FOR TITLES. | SEE INDIVIDUAL VOCO RECORD NUMBERS FOR TITLES. | $6.00 | $12.00 |
| ALBUM # 4N | 4 | V-20, 23 + 518, 539 (VOCO #S) | MOTHER GOOSE FAVORITES | VARIOUS | SEE INDIVIDUAL VOCO RECORD NUMBERS FOR TITLES. | SEE INDIVIDUAL VOCO RECORD NUMBERS FOR TITLES. | $6.00 | $12.00 |
| ALBUM # 4W | 4 | 533, 4, 6, 8 (VOCO #S) | WESTERN FAVORITES | VARIOUS | SEE INDIVIDUAL VOCO RECORD NUMBERS FOR TITLES. | SEE INDIVIDUAL VOCO RECORD NUMBERS FOR TITLES. | $6.00 | $12.00 |
| ALBUM # 4X | 4 | VX-101, 528, 530, 531 (VOCO #S) | CHRISTMAS FAVORITES | VARIOUS | SEE INDIVIDUAL VOCO RECORD NUMBERS FOR TITLES. | SEE INDIVIDUAL VOCO RECORD NUMBERS FOR TITLES. | $6.00 | $12.00 |

## TOPS FOR TOTS 10" SINGLES

| # REC | DISC # | ARTIST | A TITLE | B TITLE | YEAR | ALSO ISSUED ON | G/VG | EX/NMT |
|---|---|---|---|---|---|---|---|---|
| 1 | TC-11 | TOBY DEANE/HELEN CARROL & THE SWAN TONES | MOTHER GOOSE SONGS | THE FAIRYLAND EXPRESS | 1950 | VOCO | $1.00 | $2.00 |
| 1 | TC-12 | HELEN CARROL & THE SWAN TONES/THE TOPS CHORALEERS | THE ENCHANTED FOREST | LULLABY TIME | | VOCO | $2.00 | $4.00 |
| 1 | TC-13 | EDMOND KARLSRUD/TOBY DEANE | DAN THE FIREMAN | NURSERY SONGS | | VOCO | $1.00 | $2.00 |
| 1 | TC-14 | BERNIE KNEE & THE TOPS RANGERS | AT THE BAR-X RANCH | COWBOY SONGS | | VOCO | $1.00 | $2.00 |
| 1 | TC-15 | BERNIE KNEE/THE TOPS CHORALEERS | AROUND THE WORLD IN A BUBBLE | LITTLE PATRIOT SONGS | | VOCO | $1.00 | $2.00 |
| 1 | TC-16 | NOT LISTED | THE SOUND EFFECTS MAN | LITTLE SONGS FOR LITTLE ONES | | VOCO | $1.00 | $2.00 |
| 1 | TC-17 | TOBY DEANE, BOB MALLIT & TOPS ORCHESTRA | THREE LITTLE PIGS | SONGS OF THE FARM | | VOCO | $1.00 | $2.00 |
| 1 | TC-18 | BOB KENNEDY & TOBY DEANE/BOB KENNEDY | GOLDILOCKS AND THE THREE BEARS | A FROG WENT WALKING, POLLY WOLLY DOODLE | | VOCO | $1.00 | $2.00 |
| 1 | TC-19 | BUD ROMAN & LAURIE WAYNE (AGE 7)/PAT FARWELL | TELL ME A STORY | SMARTY CAT AND THE FIDDLE | | | $1.00 | $2.00 |

## TOPS FOR TOTS 10" SINGLES

| # REC | DISC # | ARTIST | A TITLE | B TITLE | ALSO ISSUED ON | G/VG | EX/NMT |
|---|---|---|---|---|---|---|---|
| 1 | TC-20 | PAT FARWELL/BETSY GAY | A TRIP IN A ROCKET SHIP | THE CUCKOO POLKA | | $4.00 | $8.00 |
| 1 | TC-21 | BETSY GAY | WEE WILLIE THE WHALE | POOLA DOES THE HULA | | $3.00 | $6.00 |
| 1 | TC-22 | BETSY GAY/AL TRACE & THE SILLY SYMPHONETTES | THE ZEBRA WHO LOST HER STRIPES | THE SLY OLD FOX | | $2.00 | $4.00 |
| 1 | TC-23 | PAT FARWELL/AL TRACE & THE SILLY SYMPHONETTES | BENNY THE HUNGRY GOAT | THE OLD TOY SHOP | | $1.00 | $2.00 |
| 1 | TC-24 | GENE GULLICKSEN/AL TRACE & THE SILLY SYMPHONETTES | THE HAPPY CLOCKS | THE BARNYARD BALL | | $1.00 | $2.00 |
| 1 | TC-25 | PAT FARWELL | THE ORCHESTRA WHO WOULDN'T (SIDE 1) | THE ORCHESTRA WHO WOULDN'T (SIDE 2) | | $1.00 | $2.00 |
| 1 | TC-26 | PAT FARWELL, GENE GULLIKSEN | THE MAGIC FLYING SONG (SIDE 1) | THE MAGIC FLYING SONG (SIDE 2) | | $1.00 | $2.00 |
| 1 | TC-27 | MIMI MARTEL/AL TRACE & THE SILLY SYMPHONETTES | THE DOGGIE IN THE WINDOW | THE GOAT SONG | | $2.00 | $4.00 |
| 1 | TC-28 | PAT FARWELL | THE CROCODILE WHO CRIED (SIDE 1) | THE CROCODILE WHO CRIED (SIDE 2) | | $1.00 | $2.00 |
| 1 | TC-29 | BETSY GAY, PAT FARWELL | MAKE BELIEVE COWBOY | BRAVE LITTLE COWBOY | | $1.00 | $2.00 |
| 1 | TX-102 | TOBY DEANE & THE HUMMING BIRDS/THE TOPS CHORALEERS | ALICE IN CHRISTMAS WONDERLAND | CHRISTMAS CAROLS (SILENT NIGHT/O COME ALL YE FAITHFUL) | VOCO | $1.00 | $2.00 |
| 1 | TX-103 | BOB KENNEDY & THE HUMMING BIRDS/THE TOPS PLAYERS | JINGLE BELLS | SANTA'S TOY SHOP | VOCO | $1.00 | $2.00 |
| 1 | TX-104 | JUDY HARRIET WITH THE TOPPERS/BOB KENNEDY, TOPS CHORALEERS | I SAW MOMMY KISSING SANTA CLAUS | I WISH I WERE SANTA CLAUS/DECK THE HALLS | VOCO | $1.00 | $2.00 |
| 1 | 309 | BUD ROMAN & THE TOPPERS/THE MUSIC HALL DRAMA GROUP | FROSTY THE SNOWMAN | THE NIGHT BEFORE CHRISTMAS | | $1.00 | $2.00 |
| 1 | 1003 | BUD ROMAN/THE CHORALEERS | RUDOLPH THE RED NOSED REINDEER | SANTA CLAUS COMES CALLING | | $1.00 | $2.00 |
| 1 | 1020 | AUTHENTIC TRAIN SOUNDS | RAILROAD SOUNDS (AUTHENTIC TRAIN SOUND EFFECTS) SIDE 1 | RAILROAD SOUNDS (AUTHENTIC TRAIN SOUND EFFECTS) SIDE 2 | | $4.00 | $8.00 |

## TOPS FOR TOTS TOP SINGLES SERIES 10"

| # REC | DISC # | MAIN TITLE | ARTIST | YEAR | ALSO ISSUED ON | G/VG | EX/NMT |
|---|---|---|---|---|---|---|---|
| 1 | 309 | FROSTY THE SNOW MAN/THE NIGHT BEFORE CHRISTMAS | BUD ROMAN & THE TOPPERS/THE MUSIC HALL DRAMA GROUP | 195? | TOPS FOR TOTS | $1.00 | $2.00 |
| 1 | 1003 | RUDOLPH THE RED-NOSED REINDEER/CHRISTMAS FAVORITES | BUD ROMAN/THE CHORALEERS | | TOPS FOR TOTS | $1.00 | $2.00 |
| 1 | 1004 | WHITE CHRISTMAS/SILENT NIGHT | CLIFF HOLLAND | | | $1.00 | $2.00 |
| 1 | 1020 | RAILROAD SOUNDS | AUTHENTIC TRAIN SOUND EFFECTS | | TOPS FOR TOTS | $3.00 | $6.00 |
| 1 | 1037 | CIRCUS TRAIN/BENNY THE HUNGRY GOAT, POOLA DOES THE HULA | JOHNNY HOLIDAY/PAT FARWELL, BETSY GAY | | | $1.00 | $2.00 |
| 3 | 18-X-1 (RX 1010-2) | 18 CHRISTMAS FAVORITES | TOPS ORCHESTRA & CHORISTERS | | | $3.00 | $6.00 |
| 1 | TX-104 | I SAW MOMMY KISSING SANTA CLAUS/I WISH THAT I WERE SANTA CLAUS, DECK THE HALLS | JUDY HARRIET WITH THE TOPPERS/BOB KENNEDY | | TOPS FOR TOTS | $1.00 | $2.00 |
| 1 | R-254 | THE BALLAD OF DAVY CROCKETT/IT MAY SOUND SILLY | THE RHYTMAIRES | | | $5.00 | $10.00 |

## TOTS 'N TEENS (REGAL) 7" BOXED SETS

| SET # | # REC | DISC # | MAIN TITLE | ARTIST | A TITLE | B TITLE | YEAR | G/VG | EX/NMT |
|---|---|---|---|---|---|---|---|---|---|
| R-30 | 4 | | SONG STORIES | | | | 194? | $6.00 | $12.00 |
| | | 115 | | IREENE WICKER | GOLDILOCKS AND THE THREE BEARS (PT. 1) | GOLDILOCKS AND THE THREE BEARS (PT. 2) | | | |
| | | 116 | | IREENE WICKER | JACK AND THE BEANSTALK | THE MAGIC HEN | | | |
| | | 117 | | IREENE WICKER | LITTLE RED RIDING HOOD | A DILLAR A DOLLAR | | | |
| | | 118 | | IREENE WICKER | HI DIDDLE DIDDLE | CINDERELLA | | | |
| R-31 | 4 | | TUNES FOR TOTS N' TEENS (AKA MELODY ROUNDUP) | | | | | $6.00 | $12.00 |
| | | 109 | | MURRAY PHILLIPS | PONY BOY | I'VE BEEN WORKING ON THE RAILROAD | | | |
| | | 110 | | MURRAY PHILLIPS | DOWN IN THE VALLEY | SKIP TO MY LOU | | | |

## TOTS 'N TEENS (REGAL) 7" BOXED SETS

| SET # | # REC | DISC # | MAIN TITLE | ARTIST | A TITLE | B TITLE | G/VG | EX/NMT |
|---|---|---|---|---|---|---|---|---|
| | | 111 | | MURRAY PHILLIPS | THE GAY MUSICIAN | CLAP, CLAP, BOW, PAW PAW PATCH | | |
| | | 112 | | MURRAY PHILLIPS | LITTLE BOY BLUE, OLD KING COLE | TWINKLE TWINKLE LITTLE STAR, SIMPLE SIMON | | |
| R-32 | 4 | | CHRISTMAS SONG STORIES | | | | $6.00 | $12.00 |
| | | 119 | | IREENE WICKER | A NIGHT BEFORE CHRISTMAS (PT. 1) | A NIGHT BEFORE CHRISTMAS (PT. 2) | | |
| | | 121 | | IREENE WICKER | DICKENS' CHRISTMAS CAROL (PT. 1) | DICKENS' CHRISTMAS CAROL (PT. 2) | | |
| | | 122 | | IREENE WICKER | SILENT NIGHT | JINGLE BELLS | | |
| | | 123 | | IREENE WICKER | O COME, ALL YE FAITHFUL | DECK THE HALLS, I SAW THREE SAILS | | |
| R-33 | 4 | | NURSERY RHYMES, VOL. 1 | | | | $6.00 | $12.00 |
| | | 124 | | IREENE WICKER | MISTRESS MARY, ETC. | THREE BLIND MICE, ETC. | | |
| | | 125 | | IREENE WICKER | OLD KING COLE, ETC. | THE OWL AND THE PUSSY CAT, ETC. | | |
| | | 126 | | IREENE WICKER | JACK AND JILL, ETC. | LITTLE COCK SPARROW, ETC. | | |
| | | 127 | | IREENE WICKER | PETER PETER PUMPKIN EATER, ETC. | WHERE HAS MY LITTLE DOG GONE, ETC. | | |
| R-34 | 4 | | LULLABIES | | | | $6.00 | $12.00 |
| | | 128 | | IREENE WICKER | LULLABY (BRAHMS) MOZART | SLEEP OH MY DARLING SLEEP | | |
| | | 129 | | IREENE WICKER | SWEET AND LOW | ALL THROUGH THE NIGHT | | |
| | | 130 | | IREENE WICKER | ROCKABYE BABY, SLEEP MY LITTLE ONE | MIGHTY LAK A ROSE | | |
| | | 131 | | IREENE WICKER | CURLY HEAD BABY | KENTUCKY BABE | | |
| R-35 | 4 | | NURSERY RHYMES, VOL. 2 | | | | $6.00 | $12.00 |
| | | 132 | | IREENE WICKER | MARY HAD A LITTLE LAMB, ETC. | PUSSY CAT, ETC. | | |
| | | 133 | | IREENE WICKER | COO COO COO COO, ETC. | LITTLE BOY BLUE, ETC. | | |
| | | 134 | | IREENE WICKER | HUMPTY DUMPTY, ETC. | HICKORY DICKORY DOCK, ETC. | | |
| | | 135 | | IREENE WICKER | I HAD A LITTLE HEN, ETC. | ABCD, THIRTY DAYS HATH SEPTEMBER, ETC. | | |
| R-36 | 4 | | AMERICANA | | | | $6.00 | $12.00 |
| | | 136 | | BOYD HEATH | BLUE TAIL FLY | OLD FOLKS AT HOME | | |
| | | 137 | | BOYD HEATH | LITTLE BROWN JUG | A FROGGY WOULD A WOOING GO | | |
| | | 138 | | BOYD HEATH | OH SUSANNA | TURKEY IN THE STRAW | | |
| | | 139 | | BOYD HEATH | COMIN' ROUND THE MOUNTAIN | POLLY WOLLY DOODLE | | |
| R-37 | 4 | | RANGER ROUND UP | | | | $6.00 | $12.00 |
| | | 140 | | BOYD HEATH | SWEET BETSY FROM PIKE | RED RIVER VALLEY | | |
| | | 141 | | BOYD HEATH | THE GAL I LEFT BEHIND ME | HOME ON THE RANGE | | |
| | | 142 | | BOYD HEATH | I WAS BORN 10,000 YEARS AGO | BIG ROCK CANDY MOUNTAIN | | |
| | | 143 | | BOYD HEATH | OLD CHISHOLM TRAIL | WHOOPEE TI YI YO | | |
| R-38 | 4 | | SEA SONGS? | BOYD HEATH | | | $6.00 | $12.00 |
| | | 144 | | BOYD HEATH | BLOW THE MAN DOWN | MY BONNIE LIES OVER THE OCEAN | | |
| | | 145 | | BOYD HEATH | THE SEASICK SAILOR | SAILING, SAILING | | |
| | | 146 | | BOYD HEATH | RIO GRANDE | A CAPITAL SHIP | | |
| | | 147 | | BOYD HEATH | ? | ? | | |
| N/A | | N/A | | N/A | LOOSE SINGLE RECORDS | LOOSE SINGLE RECORDS | $1.00 | $2.00 |

## TOYTIME RECORD AND PICTURE BOOK 7" BOXED SETS

| # REC | DISC # | MAIN TITLE | ARTIST | YEAR | G/VG | EX/NMT |
|---|---|---|---|---|---|---|
| 1 | TT-100 | BEAUTY AND THE BEAST | HILDA LA CENTRA | 1941? | $10.00 | $20.00 |
| 1 | TT-105 | JACK AND THE BEANSTALK | HILDA LA CENTRA | | $10.00 | $20.00 |
| 1 | TT-110 | WILLIAM TELL | HILDA LA CENTRA | | $10.00 | $20.00 |
| 1 | TT-115 | THE GOLDEN GOOSE | HILDA LA CENTRA | | $10.00 | $20.00 |
| 1 | TT-120 | ALI BABA | HILDA LA CENTRA | | $10.00 | $20.00 |
| 1 | TT-125 | SLEEPING BEAUTY | HILDA LA CENTRA | | $10.00 | $20.00 |

TOPS FOR TOTS RECORDS
DAN THE FIREMAN
$2.00

TOPS FOR TOTS RECORDS
THE ENCHANTED FOREST
$4.00

TOPS FOR TOTS RECORDS
A TRIP IN A ROCKETSHIP
$10.00

## TOY TOON 6" PICTURE DISCS

| # REC | DISC # | ARTIST | A TITLE | B TITLE | YEAR | G/VG | EX/NMT |
|---|---|---|---|---|---|---|---|
| 1 | P11/11A | NOT LISTED | HAPPY BIRTHDAY | FOR HE'S A JOLLY GOOD FELLOW | 195? | $5.00 | $10.00 |
| 1 | P12/12A | NOT LISTED | CINDERELLA | SNOW WHITE AND THE 7 DWARFS | | $5.00 | $10.00 |
| 1 | P13/13A | NOT LISTED | GOLDILOCKS AND THE THREE BEARS | THREE LITTLE PIGS | | $5.00 | $10.00 |
| 1 | P14/14A | NOT LISTED | SONGS FROM MOTHER GOOSE (PT. 1) | SONGS FROM MOTHER GOOSE (PT. 2) | | $5.00 | $10.00 |
| 1 | P15/15A | NOT LISTED | JACK AND THE BEANSTALK | HANSEL AND GRETEL | | $5.00 | $10.00 |
| 1 | P16/16A | NOT LISTED | LITTLE RED RIDING HOOD | ALICE IN WONDERLAND | | $5.00 | $10.00 |
| 1 | P17/17A | NOT LISTED | ROBIN HOOD | I'VE BEEN WORKING ON THE RAILROAD | | $5.00 | $10.00 |
| 1 | P18/18A | NOT LISTED | PINOCCHIO | SNOOPY SNIFFER | | $5.00 | $10.00 |
| 1 | P19/19A | NOT LISTED | SONG OF CAPTAIN HOOK | PETER PAN | | $5.00 | $10.00 |
| 1 | P20/20A | NOT LISTED | TEN LITTLE INDIANS | SKIP TO MY LOU | | $5.00 | $10.00 |
| 1 | P21/21A | NOT LISTED | ALPHABET SONG | COUNTING SONG | | $5.00 | $10.00 |
| 1 | P22/22A | NOT LISTED | GOOD MORNING MARY SUNSHINE | LAZY MARY | | $5.00 | $10.00 |

## TRANSOGRAM 4" SINGLES

| # REC | DISC # | ARTIST | A TITLE | B TITLE | YEAR | G/VG | EX/NMT |
|---|---|---|---|---|---|---|---|
| 1 | TRS-2606/7 | ? | ONE TWO, BUCKLE MY SHOE, THE ABC SONG | OLD KING COLE, JACK SPRAT, TOM TOM, THE PIPER'S SON | 195? | $1.00 | $2.00 |
| 1 | TRS-2608/9 | ? | THE FARMER IN THE DELL, POP GOES THE WEASEL | THIS LITTLE PIGGY WENT TO MARKET, BAA BAA BLACK SHEEP | | $1.00 | $2.00 |
| 1 | TRS-2610/11 | ? | SIMPLE SIMON, THERE WAS AN OLD WOMAN WHO LIVED IN A SHOE | COCK-A-DOODLE-DOO; PUSSY CAT, PUSSY CAT | | $1.00 | $2.00 |
| 1 | TRS-2612/13 | ? | LITTLE BOY BLUE, LITTLE JACK HORNER, HUMPTY DUMPTY | TWINKLE TWINKLE LITTLE STAR | | $1.00 | $2.00 |
| 1 | TRS-2614/15 | ? | THE CAT AND THE MOUSE, THERE WAS A CROOKED MAN | SONG OF SIXPENCE, LITTLE TOMMY TUCKER | | $1.00 | $2.00 |
| 1 | TRS-2616/17 | ? | MARY HAD A LITTLE LAMB, JACK BE NIMBLE | THREE LITTLE KITTENS | | $1.00 | $2.00 |
| 1 | TRS-2618/19 | ? | THREE BLIND MICE, HICKORY DICKORY DOCK, HEY DIDDLE DIDDLE | JACK AND JILL, LONDON BRIDGE | | $1.00 | $2.00 |
| 1 | TRS-2620/21 | ? | POLLY PUT THE KETTLE ON, PEASE PORRIDGE HOT | TEN LITTLE INDIANS, THE MULBERRY BUSH | | $1.00 | $2.00 |
| 1 | TRS-2622/23 | ? | SHORTNIN' BREAD, A TISKET A TASKET | LET'S ALL JOIN HANDS, LET'S DANCE LOOBY LOO (LOOPY LOO) | | $1.00 | $2.00 |
| 1 | TRS-2624/25 | ? | OLD MACDONALD HAD A FARM | THE HAND CLAPPING SONG, THIS OLD MAN | | $1.00 | $2.00 |
| 1 | TRS-2626/27 | ? | DECK THE HALL, WE WISH YOU A MERRY CHRISTMAS | O CHRISTMAS TREE, O CHRISTMAS TREE | | $1.00 | $2.00 |
| 1 | TRS.2628/29 | ? | SILENT NIGHT | JINGLE BELLS | | $1.00 | $2.00 |
| 1 | TRS.2630/31 | ? | HARK! THE HERALS ANGELS SING | O, COME ALL YE FAITHFUL | | $1.00 | $2.00 |
| 1 | TRS-2632/33 | ? | OH DEAR WHAT CAN THE MATTER BE | ALOUETTE, FRERE JACQUES | | $1.00 | $2.00 |

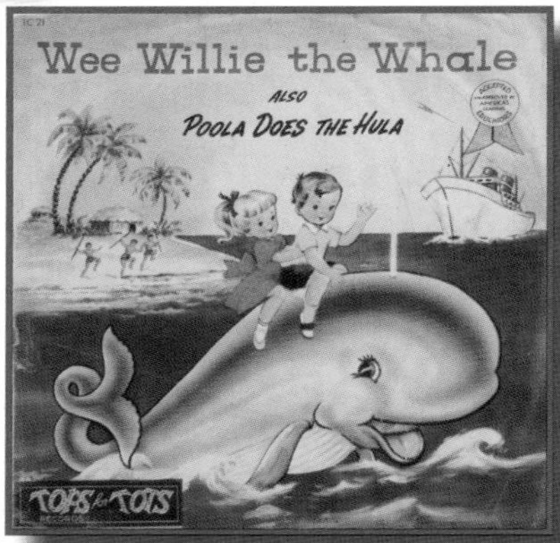


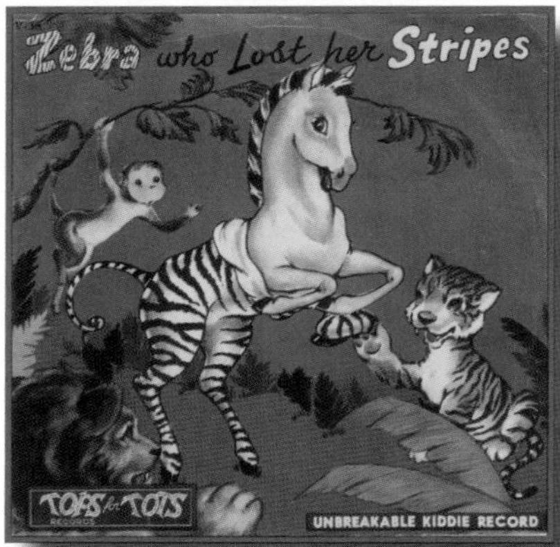

TOPS FOR TOTS RECORDS
WEE WILLIE THE WHALE
$6.00

TOPS FOR TOTS RECORDS
THE ZEBRA WHO LOST HER STRIPES
$4.00

TOYTIME RECORD AND PICTURE BOOKS
BEAUTY AND THE BEAST
$20.00

## TREASURE 7" SINGLES

| # REC | DISC # | ARTIST | A TITLE | B TITLE | YEAR | ALSO ISSUED ON | G/VG | EX/NMT |
|---|---|---|---|---|---|---|---|---|
| 1 | 1601 | ? | KATIE THE KANGAROO | OATS PEAS BEANS AND BARLEY | 1951 | WONDERLAND JUNIOR | $4.00 | $8.00 |
| 1 | 1602 | ? | TEN LITTLE INDIANS | LITTLE BO PEEP | | WONDERLAND JUNIOR | $1.50 | $3.00 |
| 1 | 1603 | ? | THREE LITTLE KITTENS | PUSSY CAT, PUSSY CAT/A HUNTING WE WILL GO | | WONDERLAND JUNIOR | $1.50 | $3.00 |
| 1 | 1604 | ? | THE MIKADO, PART 2 | THE MIKADO, PART 2 | | WONDERLAND JUNIOR | $1.50 | $3.00 |
| 1 | 1605 | ? | HMS PINAFORE, PART 1 | HMS PINAFORE, PART 2 | | WONDERLAND JUNIOR | $1.50 | $3.00 |
| 1 | 1606 | ? | THE PIRATES OF PENZANCE, PART 1 | THE PIRATES OF PENZANCE, PART 2 | | WONDERLAND JUNIOR | $1.50 | $3.00 |
| 1 | 1607 | ? | THERE WAS A CROOKED MAN | TO MARKET, TO MARKET | | WONDERLAND JUNIOR | $1.50 | $3.00 |
| 1 | 1608 | ? | BILLY BOY | PAT-A-CAKE/OVER IN THE MEADOW | | WONDERLAND JUNIOR | $1.50 | $3.00 |
| 1 | 1609 | THE TREASURE TROUPE | A FROG HE WOULD A-WOOING GO | DID YOU EVER SEE A LASSIE? | | WONDERLAND JUNIOR | $1.50 | $3.00 |
| 1 | 1610 | BOB MOODY & THE TREASURE TROUPE | CLEMENTINE | HOME ON THE RANGE | | WONDERLAND JUNIOR | $1.50 | $3.00 |
| 1 | 1611 | BOB MOODY & THE TREASURE TROUPE/BOB MOODY | I'VE BEEN WORKING ON THE RAILROAD | RED RIVER VALLEY | | WONDERLAND JUNIOR | $1.50 | $3.00 |
| 1 | 1612 | ? | ROCK CANDY MOUNTAIN | CASEY JONES | | WONDERLAND JUNIOR | $1.50 | $3.00 |
| 1 | 1613 | ROGER WHITE & THE TREASURE TROUPE/ROY HALLEE | COWBOY'S OLD HORSE | LONE PRAIRIE | | WONDERLAND JUNIOR | $1.50 | $3.00 |
| 1 | 1614 | ? | SHE'LL BE COMIN' ROUND THE MOUNTAIN | THE OLD CHISHOLM TRAIL | | WONDERLAND JUNIOR | $1.50 | $3.00 |
| 1 | 1615 | ? | OLD KING COLE | WHAT CAN THE MATTER BE? | | WONDERLAND JUNIOR | $1.50 | $3.00 |
| 1 | 1616 | ? | LAZY MARY | HEY DIDDLE DIDDLE/WHERE HAS MY LITTLE DOG GONE? | | WONDERLAND JUNIOR | $1.50 | $3.00 |
| 1 | 1617 | ? | FIDDLE-DE-DEE | LITTLE BOY BLUE/MARY HAD A LITTLE LAMB | | WONDERLAND JUNIOR | $1.50 | $3.00 |
| 1 | 1618 | GERRY GERARD, JOHANNE MORELAND, TREASURE ORCH./ROY HALLEE, GERRY BEITZEL, TREASURE ORCH. | THE ALPHABET SONG | HICKORY DICKORY DOCK/SING A SONG OF SIXPENCE | | WONDERLAND JUNIOR | $1.50 | $3.00 |
| 1 | 1619 | THE TREASURE TROUPE | HAPPY BIRTHDAY | LONDON BRIDGE | | WONDERLAND JUNIOR | $1.50 | $3.00 |
| 1 | 1620 | ROGER WHITE, GERRY TOUCHETTE/THE WONDERLAND PLAYERS | HUMPTY DUMPTY | THREE BLIND MICE | | WONDERLAND JUNIOR | $1.50 | $3.00 |
| 1 | 1621 | ? | POP GOES THE WEASEL | FARMER IN THE DELL | | WONDERLAND JUNIOR | $1.50 | $3.00 |
| 1 | 1622 | ? | THREE LITTLE PIGS | HOBBLEDY HORSE | | WONDERLAND JUNIOR | $1.50 | $3.00 |

TOY TOON RECORDS
SONG OF CAPTAIN HOOK
$10.00

TREASURE RECORDS
RUM-DE-DIDDLE THE RUNAWAY FIDDLE
$3.00

TUNES FOR TOTS RECORDS
CHOO-CHOO-TRAIN
$2.00

## TREASURE 7" SINGLES

| # REC | DISC # | ARTIST | A TITLE | B TITLE | YEAR | ALSO ISSUED ON | G/VG | EX/NMT |
|---|---|---|---|---|---|---|---|---|
| 1 | 1623 | ? | FUNNY BUNNY | CHICKEN LICKEN | | WONDERLAND JUNIOR | $1.50 | $3.00 |
| 1 | 1624 | ? | SLEEPYTIME FOR DOLLY | DING DONG BELL | | WONDERLAND JUNIOR | $1.50 | $3.00 |
| 1 | 1625 | ? | BRAVE LITTLE SAMBO | THE WEEZ WUMP | | WONDERLAND JUNIOR | $5.00 | $10.00 |
| 1 | 1626 | ? | RAPUNZEL, PART 1 | RAPUNZEL, PART 2 | | WONDERLAND JUNIOR | $1.50 | $3.00 |
| 1 | 1627 | ? | JACK AND THE BEANSTALK | THE EMPEROR'S NEW CLOTHES | | WONDERLAND JUNIOR | $1.50 | $3.00 |
| 1 | 1628 | SALLY SWEETLAND, THE TREASURE ORCH./JOANNE MORELAND, GERRY GERARD, TREASURE ORCH. | OLD WOMAN WHO LIVED IN A SHOE | GEORGIE PORGIE | | WONDERLAND JUNIOR | $1.50 | $3.00 |
| 1 | 1629 | ? | THE GINGERBREAD MAN | THE CITY MOUSE AND THE COUNTRY MOUSE | | WONDERLAND JUNIOR | $1.50 | $3.00 |
| 1 | 1630 | ? | CINDERELLA | WYNKEN, BLYNKEN AND NOD | | WONDERLAND JUNIOR | $1.50 | $3.00 |
| 1 | 1631 | ? | THREE BILLYGOATS GRUFF | THE LION AND THE MOUSE | | WONDERLAND JUNIOR | $1.50 | $3.00 |
| 1 | 1632 | ? | GOLDILOCKS AND THE THREE BEARS | THE RUNAWAY CHOO-CHOO TRAIN | | WONDERLAND JUNIOR | $1.50 | $3.00 |
| 1 | 1633 | ? | LITTLE RED RIDING HOOD | A MONKEY WHO WANTED TO FLY | | WONDERLAND JUNIOR | $1.50 | $3.00 |
| 1 | 1634 | ? | THE PIED PIPER | PADDY THE BAKERY BOY | | WONDERLAND JUNIOR | $1.50 | $3.00 |
| 1 | 1635 | ? | THE LITTLE RED HEN | NIGHT SONG FOR LITTLE ONE | | WONDERLAND JUNIOR | $1.50 | $3.00 |
| 1 | 1636 | ? | MOTHER GOOSE PARTY | THE FROG AND THE OX | | WONDERLAND JUNIOR | $1.50 | $3.00 |
| 1 | 1637 | ? | OLD MACDONALD HAD A FARM | GOOSEY GOOSEY GANDER | | WONDERLAND JUNIOR | $1.50 | $3.00 |
| 1 | 1638 | ? | OLD MOTHER HUBBARD | THE SHOEMAKER AND THE ELVES | | WONDERLAND JUNIOR | $1.50 | $3.00 |
| 1 | 1639 | THE TREASURE TROUPE | THE TRAVELING MUSICIANS | PINOCCHIO | | WONDERLAND JUNIOR | $1.50 | $3.00 |
| 1 | 1640 | | SNOW WHITE AND THE SEVEN DWARFS, PART 1 | SNOW WHITE AND THE SEVEN DWARFS, PART 2 | | WONDERLAND JUNIOR | $1.50 | $3.00 |
| 1 | 1641 | THE TREASURE TROUPE/ROGER WHITE, ROY HALLEE, TREASURE ORCH. | RUM-DE-DIDDLE THE RUNAWAY FIDDLE | THE FISHERMAN AND THE FOUNDER | | WONDERLAND JUNIOR | $1.50 | $3.00 |
| 1 | 1642 | ? | ALICE IN WONDERLAND, PART 1 | ALICE IN WONDERLAND, PART 2 | | WONDERLAND JUNIOR | $1.50 | $3.00 |
| 1 | 1643 | ? | RUDOLPH THE RED-NOSED REINDEER | SANTA CLAUS IS FLYING THROUGH THE SKY | | WONDERLAND JUNIOR | $1.50 | $3.00 |
| 1 | 1644 | ? | FROSTY THE SNOW MAN | TWAS THE NIGHT BEFORE CHRISTMAS | | WONDERLAND JUNIOR | $1.50 | $3.00 |

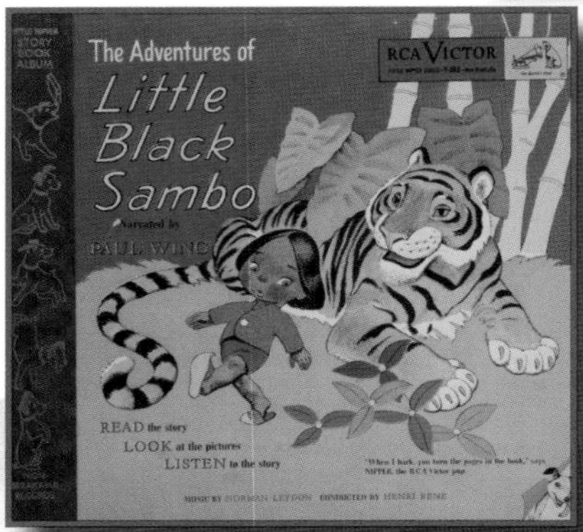


VARSITY RECORDS 12 NURSERY SONGS $4.00

VICTOR RECORDS ADVENTURES IN MUSIC— MELODY $40.00

VICTOR RECORDS THE ADVENTURES OF LITTLE BLACK SAMBO $100.00

## TREASURE 7" SINGLES

| # REC | DISC # | ARTIST | A TITLE | B TITLE | ALSO ISSUED ON | G/VG | EX/NMT |
|---|---|---|---|---|---|---|---|
| 1 | 1645 | ? | JINGLE BELLS | HARK THE HERALD ANGELS SING/O LITTLE TOWN OF BETHLEHEM | WONDERLAND JUNIOR | $1.50 | $3.00 |
| 1 | 1646 | ? | SILENT NIGHT | GOOD KING WENCESLAS | WONDERLAND JUNIOR | $1.50 | $3.00 |
| 1 | 1647 | ? | O COME ALL YE FAITHFUL | DECK THE HALLS/GOD REST YE MERRY GENTLEMEN | WONDERLAND JUNIOR | $1.50 | $3.00 |
| 1 | 1648 | ? | IT CAME UPON A MIDNIGHT CLEAR | JOY TO THE WORLD | WONDERLAND JUNIOR | $1.50 | $3.00 |

## TUNES FOR TOTS 7" SINGLES

| # REC | DISC # | ARTIST | A TITLE | B TITLE | YEAR | G/VG | EX/NMT |
|---|---|---|---|---|---|---|---|
| 1 | 4001 | CAROLE CHRISTY/EILEEN SCOTT | MAMA DOLL SONG | I SAW MOMMY KISSING SANTA CLAUS | 195? | $1.00 | $2.00 |
| 1 | 4003 | BILL RUFF | THE BALLAD OF DAVY CROCKETT (PT. 1) | THE BALLAD OF DAVY CROCKET (PT. 2) | | $3.00 | $6.00 |
| 1 | 4004 | THE NUNN SISTERS | OPEN UP YOUR HEART (PT. 1) | OPEN UP YOUR HEART (PT. 2) | | $1.00 | $2.00 |
| 1 | 4006 | EILEEN SCOTT/DICK WARREN | CHOO-CHOO TRAIN | DAFFODILLY DUCK | | $1.00 | $2.00 |
| 1 | 4007 | WOODIE WOODELL/DOLL NUNN | ELFIE THE ELF | I SAW MOMMY KISSING SANTA CLAUS | | $1.00 | $2.00 |
| 1 | 4010 | DICK WARREN, DOLLY NUNN | THE CAT AND THE FIDDLE, A TISKET, A TASKET | MISTRESS MARY, QUITE CONTRARY, SEE SAW MARJORY DAW | | $1.00 | $2.00 |
| 1 | 4011 | EILEEN SCOTT | ROCK-A-BYE BABY, SLEEP BABY SLEEP | BYE BABY BUNTING, TWINKLE TWINKLE LITTLE STAR | | $1.00 | $2.00 |
| 1 | 4013 | JACK DANIELS/TERRY BUTER | RUDOLPH THE RED-NOSED REINDEER | C-H-R-I-S-T-M-A-S | | $1.00 | $2.00 |

# V

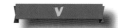

## VARSITY PLAYLAND SERIES 10" SINGLES AND ONE 3-RECORD SET

| # REC | DISC # | MAIN TITLE | ARTIST | YEAR | G/VG | EX/NMT |
|---|---|---|---|---|---|---|
| 1 | CH-1 | 7 NURSERY SONGS | UNCLE DON CARNEY | 195? | $2.00 | $4.00 |
| 1 | CH-2 | 12 NURSERY SONGS | UNCLE DON CARNEY | | $2.00 | $4.00 |
| 1 | CH-3 | 9 NURSERY SONGS | UNCLE DON CARNEY | | $2.00 | $4.00 |
| 1 | CH-4 | 15 NURSERY SONGS | UNCLE DON CARNEY | | $2.00 | $4.00 |
| 1 | CH-5 | 13 MUSICAL STORIES | UNCLE DON CARNEY | | $2.00 | $4.00 |
| 1 | CH-6 | 9 MUSICAL STORIES | UNCLE DON CARNEY | | $2.00 | $4.00 |
| 1 | CH-7 | 9 MUSICAL STORIES | UNCLE DON CARNEY | | $2.00 | $4.00 |
| 1 | CH-8 | 9 MUSICAL STORIES | UNCLE DON CARNEY | | $2.00 | $4.00 |
| 1 | CH-9 | 7 MUSICAL GAMES | UNCLE DON CARNEY | | $2.00 | $4.00 |
| 3 | CH-10, 11, 12 (E-58) | UNCLE DON AT THE ZOO | UNCLE DON CARNEY | | $6.00 | $12.00 |
| 3 | 8156-8 | PINOCCHIO | BUDDY CLARK | | $35.00 | $70.00 |

## VICTOR RCA VICTOR "M" ALBUMS 10" AND 12"

| SET # | # REC | DISC # | MAIN TITLE | ARTIST | YEAR | G/VG | EX/NMT |
|---|---|---|---|---|---|---|---|
| DM- 905 (12") | 3 | 11-8206 - 8 | KIPLING'S JUNGLE BOOK | SABU | | $8.00 | $15.00 |
| DM-1020 (12") | 3 | 11-8915 - 7 | NUTCRACKER SUITE | EUGENE ORMANDY, COND. | | $3.00 | $6.00 |
| M-1030 | 3 | 10-1182 - 4 | KIPLING SONGS | NORMAN CORDON | | $5.00 | $10.00 |
| M-1062 (12") | 4 | 11-9225 - 8 | RCA VICTOR'S CHILDREN'S TREASURY OF MUSIC (VOL. 1) | VARIOUS CONDUCTORS | | $3.00 | $6.00 |
| M-1063 (12") | 4 | 11-9229 - 32 | RCA VICTOR'S CHILDREN'S TREASURY OF MUSIC (VOL. 2) | VARIOUS CONDUCTORS | | $3.00 | $6.00 |
| M-1064 (12") | 4 | 11-9223 - 6 | RCA VICTOR'S CHILDREN'S TREASURY OF MUSIC (VOL. 3) | VARIOUS CONDUCTORS | | $3.00 | $6.00 |
| MO-1077 (12") | 4 | 11-9313 - 6 | CHRISTMAS HYMNS AND CAROLS | ROBERT SHAW & THE VICTOR CHORALE | | $3.00 | $6.00 |
| DM-1327 | 3 | 10-1488 - 10 | CHILDREN'S CORNER SUITE | LEOPOLD STOKOWSKI, COND. | | $3.00 | $6.00 |

## VICTOR RCA VICTOR "P" ALBUMS 10"

| SET # | # REC | DISC # | MAIN TITLE | ARTIST | YEAR | G/VG | EX/NMT |
|---|---|---|---|---|---|---|---|
| P-18 (DIE-CUT COVER) | 3 | 26477 - 9 | PINOCCHIO | ORIGINAL DISNEY FILM CAST | 1940 | $50.00 | $100.00 |
| P-18 (REGULAR COVER) | 3 | 26477 - 9 | PINOCCHIO | ORIGINAL DISNEY FILM CAST | | $25.00 | $50.00 |
| P-20 | 2 | 26516 - 7 | BALLAD FOR AMERICANS | PAUL ROBESON | | $15.00 | $30.00 |
| P-35 | 3 | 26698 - 700 | ROBIN HOOD | JUNIOR PROGRAMS COMPANY | 1941 | $5.00 | $10.00 |
| P-38 | 4 | 26701 - 4 | HANSEL AND GRETEL | JUNIOR PROGRAMS OPERA COMPANY | | $5.00 | $10.00 |
| P-84 | 4 | 27550 - 3 | ROUND THE CAMPFIRE | TEXAS JIM ROBERTSON | | $5.00 | $10.00 |
| P-90 | 4 | 27558 - 1 | ADVENTURES OF MARCO POLO | JUNIOR PROGRAMS COMPANY | | $5.00 | $10.00 |
| P-101 | 3 | 27660 - 2 | DUMBO* | ORIGINAL DISNEY FILM CAST | | $25.00 | $50.00 |
| P-112 | ? | 27761 - ? | PETER AND THE WOLF (INSTRUMENTAL) | LEW WHITE, ORGAN | | $5.00 | $10.00 |
| P-117 | 5 | 27812 - 6 | SONGS OF THE SERVICE | VICTOR MILITARY BAND | | $8.00 | $15.00 |
| P-120 | 4 | 27833 - 6 | H.M.S. PINAFORE | THE VICTOR LIGHT OPERA ORCHESTRA & CHORUS | 1942 | $5.00 | $10.00 |
| P-143 | 3 | 20-1739 - 41 | THE NUTCRACKER SUITE | SPIKE JONES | 1945 | $10.00 | $20.00 |
| P-168 | 4 | 20-2076 - 9 | COWBOY CLASSICS | SONS OF THE PIONEERS | 1946 | $8.00 | $15.00 |
| P-197 | 3 | 20-3859 - 61 | FAVORITE CHRISTMAS SONGS | DENNIS DAY, MITCHELL BOYCHOIR | 1950 | $3.00 | $6.00 |

*TWO COVER VARIATIONS, ILLUSTRATED AND PLAIN.

## VICTOR RCA VICTOR MISCELLANEOUS ALBUMS 10" AND 12"

| SET # | # REC | DISC # | MAIN TITLE | ARTIST | YEAR | G/VG | EX/NMT |
|---|---|---|---|---|---|---|---|
| AC-23 (12") | 5 | 36151 - 5 | GEMS FROM GILBERT AND SULLIVAN OPERETTAS | LIGHT OPERA COMPANY | | $3.00 | $6.00 |
| DG-29 (12") | 4 | 36414 - 7 | A CHRISTMAS CAROL (INTERNATIONAL SERIES) | ERNEST CHAPPELL | | $3.00 | $6.00 |
| K-12 (12"?) | ? | ? | DUMBO | ? | | $25.00 | $50.00 |
| K-13 (12") | 6 | 46-0015 - 20 | ALICE IN WONDERLAND | EVA LE GALLIENNE | | $25.00 | $50.00 |
| S-24 (10") | 3 | V-603 - 5 | FRENCH NURSERY RHYMES AND SONGS | VARIOUS FRENCH CHILDREN'S CHOIRS | 1939 | $3.00 | $6.00 |

## VICTOR RCA VICTOR "VBY" AND "VY" SERIES 7" DOUBLES

| SET # | # REC | DISC # | MAIN TITLE | ARTIST | YEAR | G/VG | EX/NMT |
|---|---|---|---|---|---|---|---|
| VBY-1 | 2 | E2VK-7553/4 - 5/6 | CINDERELLA | IAN MARTIN | 1952 | $2.00 | $4.00 |
| VBY-2 | 2 | E2VK-7557/8 - 59/60 | SNOW WHITE AND THE SEVEN DWARFS | NELSON OLMSTED | | $2.00 | $4.00 |
| VBY-3 | 2 | E2VK-7561/2 - 3/4 | SLEEPING BEAUTY | IAN MARTIN | | $2.00 | $4.00 |
| VBY-4 | 2 | E2VK-7565/6 - 7/8 | THE STORY OF PAUL BUNYAN | RALPH CAMARGO | | $2.00 | $4.00 |
| VBY-5 | 2 | E2VK-7569/70 - 1/2 | BUFFALO BILL AND THE PONY EXPRESS | RALPH CAMARGO | | $2.00 | $4.00 |
| VBY-6 | 2 | E2VK-7573/4 5/6 | MOTHER GOOSE PLAY SONGS | GLEN RIGGS | | $2.00 | $4.00 |
| VBY-7 | 2 | E2VK-7577/8 - 9/80 | MOTHER GOOSE BIRTHDAY PARTY | GLEN RIGGS | | $2.00 | $4.00 |
| VBY-8 | 2 | E2VK-75-81/2 - 3/4 | THE NUTCRACKER SUITE | NORMAN LEYDEN | | $2.00 | $4.00 |
| VBY-9 | 2 | E2VK-7746/7 - 8/9 | MIGHTY MOUSE'S FIRST ADVENTURE | TODD RUSSELL | | $15.00 | $30.00 |
| VBY-10 | 2 | E2VK-? | MIGHTY MOUSE SAVES DINKY | TODD RUSSELL | | $15.00 | $30.00 |
| VBY-11 | 2 | E2VK-7585/6 - 7/8 | LITTLE JOHNNY EVERYTHING | SANDY FUSSELL | | $10.00 | $20.00 |
| VBY-12 | 2 | E2VK-7589/90 - 91/2 | FUN ON A RAINY DAY WITH LITTLE JOHNNY EVERYTHING | SANDY FUSSELL | | $10.00 | $20.00 |
| VY-2000 | 2 | E2VK-6175/6 - 7/8 | DONALD DUCK IN "TRICK OR TREAT"* | ORIGINAL DISNEY VOICES | | $15.00 | $30.00 |

*GATEFOLD

## VICTOR RCA VICTOR "VBY" AND "VY" SERIES 7" DOUBLES

| SET # | # REC | DISC # | MAIN TITLE | ARTIST | G/VG | EX/NMT |
|---|---|---|---|---|---|---|
| VY-2001 | 2 | E2VK-6183/4 - 5/6 | MICKEY MOUSE'S CANDY MINE | ORIGINAL DISNEY VOICES | $15.00 | $30.00 |
| VY-2002 | 2 | E2VK-6179/80 - 81/2 | MICKEY MOUSE & PLUTO IN "THE WHAT-ZIS AND WHO-ZIS" | ORIGINAL DISNEY VOICES | $15.00 | $30.00 |
| VY-2003 | 2 | E2VK-6187/8 - 89/90 | KUKLA FRAN & OLLIE AND THE WISHING WELL | FRAN ALLISON | $15.00 | $30.00 |
| VY-2004 | 2 | E2VK-6191/2 - 93/4 | KUKLA FRAN & OLLIE AT THE FAIR | FRAN ALLISON | $15.00 | $30.00 |
| VY-2005 | 2 | E2VK-6319/20 - 1/2 | ROBIN HOOD | JOHN RUST | $8.00 | $15.00 |
| VY-2006 | 2 | E2VK-6315/6 - 7/8 | ALADDIN | ED HERLIHY | $8.00 | $15.00 |
| VY-2007 | 2 | E2VK-6311/2 - 3/4 | HANSEL & GRETEL | JANE PICKENS | $8.00 | $15.00 |
| VY-2008 | 2 | E2VK-6195/6 - 7/8 | CAPTAIN VIDEO AND HIS VIDEO RANGERS | ORIGINAL CAST OF TV SHOW | $25.00 | $50.00 |
| VY-2009 | 2 | E2VK-6199/200 - 1/2 | CAPTAIN VIDEO AND THE CAPTIVES OF SATURN | ORIGINAL CAST OF TV SHOW | $25.00 | $50.00 |
| VY-2010 | 2 | E2VK-6303/4 - 5/6 | LITTLE NIPPER FIRE CHIEF | FRANK MILANO | $8.00 | $15.00 |
| VY-2011 | 2 | E2VK-6307/8 - 9/10 | LITTLE NIPPER AND THE RAILROAD TRAIN | FRANK MILANO | $8.00 | $15.00 |
| VY-4000 | 4 | E2VK-6568/9 - 74/5 | ADVENTURES IN MUSIC — MELODY | ORIGINAL DISNEY FILM CAST | $20.00 | $40.00 |
| VY-4001 | 4 | E2VK-6560/1 - 66/7 | PETER PAN | BOBBY DRISCOLL, KATHRYN BEAUMONT | $20.00 | $40.00 |
| VY-4003 | ? | ? | A TOOT & A WHISTLE & A PLUNK & A BOOM | ? | $15.00 | $30.00 |

## VICTOR RCA VICTOR "Y" SERIES 10" SINGLES AND ALBUMS

| SET # | # REC | DISC # | MAIN TITLE | ARTIST | YEAR | ALSO ISSUED ON | G/VG | EX/NMT | REMARKS |
|---|---|---|---|---|---|---|---|---|---|
| Y-1 | 1 | 39-3000 | 3 LITTLE PIGS/ORPHAN'S BENEFIT | WALT DISNEY CAST | 1944 | Y1, Y32 | $10.00 | $20.00 | |
| Y-2 | 1 | 39-3001 | UNCLE MAC'S NURSERY RHYMES | UNCLE MAC | | Y15 | $5.00 | $10.00 | SINGLE |
| Y-3 | 1 | 39-3002 | ROCK-A-BYE PARADE/DUCKLINGS ON PARADE | VAUGHN DE LEATH | | Y16 | $10.00 | $20.00 | SINGLE |
| Y-4 | 3 | 39-3003 - 5 | MOTHER GOOSE NURSERY RHYMES | MARILYN MILLER, BOBBY HASTINGS | | | $5.00 | $10.00 | ENVELOPE |
| Y-5 | 3 | 39-3006 - 8 | LET'S PLAY AIRPLANE/LET'S PLAY TRAIN | HELEN MYERS | | Y12, Y23 | $5.00 | $10.00 | |
| Y-6 | 3 | 41-0000 - 2 | SNOW WHITE AND THE SEVEN DWARFS | ORIGINAL DISNEY CAST | | Y17, Y33 | $25.00 | $50.00 | |
| Y-7 | 1 | 39-3033 | THE SHEEP AND THE PIG WHO SET UP HOUSEKEEPING | GUDRUN THORNE-THOMSEN | 1945 | Y18 | $5.00 | $10.00 | |
| Y-8 | 1 | 39-3034 | THE THREE BILLY GOATS GRUFF/ANSWER THREE QUESTIONS, IF YOU CAN | GUDRUN THORNE-THOMSEN | | Y19 | $5.00 | $10.00 | |
| Y-9 | 1 | 41-0003 | THE NIGHT BEFORE CHRISTMAS/JINGLE BELLS FANTASY | MILTON CROSS | | Y20 | $5.00 | $10.00 | |
| Y-10 | 1 | 39-3038 | WHAT IS GOD LIKE?/THE SONG OF GROWING THINGS | KAROLYN HARRIS | 1946 | Y21 | $5.00 | $10.00 | |
| Y-11 | 2 | 41-0014 - 5 | HELLO I'M ADELINE | ROLAND WINTERS, ELLEN MERRILL | | Y22 | $15.00 | $30.00 | |
| Y-12 | 2 | 41-0016 - 7 | LET'S PLAY AIRPLANE/LET'S PLAY TRAIN | HELEN MYERS | | BC-52Y5, Y23 | $5.00 | $10.00 | |
| Y-13 | 2 | 41-0018 - 9 | IN WHICH A HOUSE IS BUILT AT POOH CORNER FOR EEYORE | ROBERT SHAW | | Y24 | $15.00 | $30.00 | |
| Y-14 | 1 | 45-5094 | 3 LITTLE PIGS/ORPHAN'S BENEFIT | WALT DISNEY CAST | 1947 | Y1, Y32 | $10.00 | $20.00 | |
| Y-15 | 1 | 45-5095 | UNCLE MAC'S NURSERY RHYMES | UNCLE MAC | | Y2 | $5.00 | $10.00 | |
| Y-16 | 1 | 45-5096 | ROCK-A-BYE PARADE/DUCKLINGS ON PARADE | VAUGHN DE LEATH | | Y3 | $10.00 | $20.00 | |
| Y-17 | 3 | 45-5097 - 9 | SNOW WHITE AND THE SEVEN DWARFS | ORIGINAL DISNEY CAST | | Y6, Y33 | $25.00 | $50.00 | |
| Y-18 | 1 | 45-5104 | THE SHEEP AND THE PIG WHO SET UP HOUSEKEEPING | GUDRUN THORNE-THOMSEN | | Y7 | $5.00 | $10.00 | |
| Y-19 | 1 | 45-5105 | THE THREE BILLY GOATS GRUFF/ANSWER THREE QUESTIONS, IF YOU CAN | GUDRUN THORNE-THOMSEN | | Y8 | $5.00 | $10.00 | |
| Y-20 | 1 | 45-5106 | THE NIGHT BEFORE CHRISTMAS/JINGLE BELLS FANTASY | MILTON CROSS | | Y9 | $5.00 | $10.00 | |
| Y-21 | 1 | 45-5107 | WHAT IS GOD LIKE?/THE SONG OF GROWING THINGS | KAROLYN HARRIS | | Y10 | $5.00 | $10.00 | |
| Y-22 | 2 | 45-5112 - 3 | HELLO I'M ADELINE | ROLAND WINTERS, ELLEN MERRILL | | Y11 | $15.00 | $30.00 | |
| Y-23 | 2 | 45-5114 - 5 | LET'S PLAY AIRPLANE/LET'S PLAY TRAIN | HELEN MYERS | | Y5, Y12 | $5.00 | $10.00 | ALBUM |
| Y-24 | 2 | 45-5116 - 7 | IN WHICH A HOUSE IS BUILT AT POOH CORNER FOR EEYORE | ROBERT SHAW | | Y13 | $15.00 | $30.00 | ALBUM |
| Y-25 | 3 | 45-5151 - 3 | SONGS FOR LITTLE PEOPLE | LEWIS JAMES | 1948 | | $5.00 | $10.00 | |
| Y-26 | 2 | 45-5188 - 9 | CHRISTOPHER ROBIN SONGS | ALEC TEMPLETON | 1948 | | $25.00 | $50.00 | |

## VICTOR RCA VICTOR "Y" SERIES 10" SINGLES AND ALBUMS

| SET # | # REC | DISC # | MAIN TITLE | ARTIST | YEAR | ALSO ISSUED ON | G/VG | EX/NMT |
|---|---|---|---|---|---|---|---|---|
| Y-27 | 2 | 45-5192 - 3 | SONGS OF RAGGEDY ANN AND ANDY | JACK ARTHUR | | Y35 | $20.00 | $40.00 |
| Y-30 | 2 | 45-5204 - 5 | ADVENTURES IN MOTHER GOOSE LAND | JACK ARTHUR | 1949 | Y34 | $5.00 | $10.00 |
| Y-31 | 2 | 45-5809 - 10 (12") | HOLIDAYS IN SONG | JACK ARTHUR | | | $3.00 | $6.00 |
| Y-32 | 1 | 45-5094 | THE THREE LITTLE PIGS | WALT DISNEY CAST | | Y1, Y14 | $10.00 | $20.00 |
| Y-33 | 2 | 45-5256 - 7 | SNOW WHITE AND THE SEVEN DWARFS* | WALT DISNEY CAST | | Y6, Y17 | $25.00 | $50.00 |
| Y-34 | 2 | 45-5204 - 5 | ADVENTURES IN MOTHER GOOSE LAND* | JACK ARTHUR | | Y30 | $5.00 | $10.00 |
| Y-35 | 2 | 45-5192 - 3 | SONGS OF RAGGEDY ANN AND ANDY | JACK ARTHUR | | Y27 | $20.00 | $40.00 |
| Y-301 | 3 | 39-3009 - 11 | LITTLE BLACK SAMBO/LITTLE BLACK SAMBO AND THE MONKEY PEOPLE | PAUL WING | 1944 | BC6 | $50.00 | $10.00 |
| Y-302 | 3 | 39-3012 - 4 | WINNIE THE POOH GOES VISITING | CRAIG MCDONNELL | | BC7 | $25.00 | $50.00 |
| Y-303 | 3 | 39-3015 - 7 | LITTLE BLACK SAMBO'S JUNGLE BAND | PAUL WING | | BC17, Y316, Y334, Y392 | $40.00 | $80.00 |
| Y-304 | 3 | 39-3018 - 20 | 500 HATS OF BARTHOLOMEW CUBBINS | PAUL WING | | BC26, Y317, Y-339 | $25.00 | $50.00 |
| Y-305 | 1 | 39-3021 | LONDON BRIDGE/THE FARMER IN THE DELL | MADGE TUCKER | | Y-335 | $4.00 | $8.00 |
| Y-306 | 1 | 39-3022 | RUMPLESTILTSKIN | HELEN MYERS | | | $4.00 | $8.00 |
| Y-307 | 3 | 39-3023 - 5 | THE LITTLE ENGINE THAT COULD | PAUL WING | | BC36, Y307, Y341, Y384 | $10.00 | $20.00 |
| Y-308 | 3 | 39-3026 - 8 | ONE STRING FIDDLE | PAUL WING | | BC-41, Y-319, Y-341 | $5.00 | $10.00 |
| Y-309 | 1 | 39-3029 | SONGS OF THE ZOO | JOHN AND LUCY ALLISON | | Y-337 | $5.00 | $10.00 |
| Y-310 | 3 | 39-3030 - 2 | BERTRAM AND THE BABY DINOSAUR | PAUL WING | | BC41 | $15.00 | $30.00 |
| Y-311 | 3 | 39-3035 - 7 | THE CHRISTMAS ADVENTURE OF BILLY AND BETTY | ERNEST CHAPPELL, BETTY PHILSON | | BC-46 | $5.00 | $10.00 |
| Y-312 | 2 | 41-0008 - 9 | LITTLE BLACK SAMBO | PAUL WING | | BC-6, Y-333, Y-383 | $50.00 | $10.00 |
| Y-313 | 1 | 42-0000 | HOME ON THE RANGE/TAKE ME BACK TO MY BOOTS AND SADDLE | JOHN CHARLES THOMAS | | | $4.00 | $8.00 |
| Y-314 | 1 | 39-3039 | WHEN THE HUSBAND KEPT HOUSE | GUDRUM THORNE-THOMSEN | | Y338 | $4.00 | $8.00 |
| Y-315 | 1 | 1441 | THE STARS AND STRIPES FOREVER/EL CAPITAN MARCH | LEOPOLD STOKOWSKI | | | $5.00 | $10.00 |
| Y-316 | 2 | 41-0004 - 5 | LITTLE BLACK SAMBO'S JUNGLE BAND | PAUL WING | | Y-303 | $40.00 | $80.00 |
| Y-317 | 2 | 41-0010 - 1 | 500 HATS OF BARTHOLOMEW CUBBINS | PAUL WING | | BC26, Y304, Y-339 | $25.00 | $50.00 |
| Y-318 | 2 | 41-0012 - 3 | THE LITTLE ENGINE THAT COULD | PAUL WING | | BC36, Y307, Y341, Y384 | $10.00 | $20.00 |
| Y-319 | 2 | 41-0006 - 7 | ONE STRING FIDDLE | PAUL WING | | BC-41, Y-308, Y-340 | $5.00 | $10.00 |
| Y-320 | 2 | 41-0020 - 1 | THE UNSUCCESSFUL ELF | PAUL WING | 1946 | Y-342 | $5.00 | $10.00 |
| Y-321 | 2 | 41-0022 - 3 | THE PANCAKE/THE FARMERS BRIDE | GUDRUM THORNE-THOMSEN | | Y-343 | $5.00 | $10.00 |
| Y-322 | 2 | 45-0003 - 4 | PEE-WEE THE PICCOLO** | PAUL WING | | Y-344 | $15.00 | $30.00 |
| Y-323 | 2 | 45-0005 - 6 | PETER AND THE WOLF | STERLING HOLLOWAY | | Y-345, Y-386 | $12.00 | $25.00 |
| Y-324 | 2 | 41-0024 - 5 | 'ERBERT'S 'APPY BIRTHDAY | ROLAND WINTERS | | Y-346 | $10.00 | $20.00 |
| Y-325 | 2 | 41-0036 - 7 | RAPUNZEL | DAME MAY WHITTY | | Y-347 | $5.00 | $10.00 |
| Y-326 | 2 | 41-0028 - 9 | LITTLE BLACK SAMBO AND THE TWINS | PAUL WING | | Y-348 | $40.00 | $80.00 |
| Y-327 | 2 | 45-5083 - 4 | CINDERELLA** | JEANETTE MCDONALD | 1947 | | $8.00 | $15.00 |
| Y-328 | 2 | 45-5085 - 6 | UNCLE REMUS** | NORMAN CORDON | | | $10.00 | $20.00 |
| Y-329 | 2 | 45-5087 - 8 | PETER CHURCHMOUSE** | PAUL WING | | | $10.00 | $20.00 |
| Y-330 | 3 | 45-5089 - 1 | THE TWELVE DANCING PRINCESSES** | MICHAEL MARTIN & LEE ROGOW | | | $15.00 | $30.00 |
| Y-331 | 2 | 45-5800 - 1 (12") | PAN, THE PIPER***** | PAUL WING | | | $15.00 | $30.00 |
| Y-332 | 2 | 45-5092 - 3 | THE PRETTIEST SONG IN THE WHOLE WORLD** | DAME MAY WHITTY | | | $6.00 | $12.00 |
| Y-333 | 2 | 45-5100 - 1 | LITTLE BLACK SAMBO** | PAUL WING | | BC-6, Y-312, Y-383 | $50.00 | $100.00 |
| Y-334 | 2 | 45-5102 - 3 | LITTLE BLACK SAMBO'S JUNGLE BAND | PAUL WING | | BC-17, Y-309, Y-316, Y-392 | $40.00 | $80.00 |
| Y-335 | 1 | 45-5108 | LONDON BRIDGE/THE FARMER IN THE DELL | MADGE TUCKER | | Y-305 | $4.00 | $8.00 |
| Y-337 | 1 | 45-5110 | SONGS OF THE ZOO | JOHN AND LUCY ALLISON | | Y-309 | $4.00 | $8.00 |
| Y-338 | 1 | 45-5111 | WHEN THE HUSBAND KEPT HOUSE | GUDRUM THORNE-THOMSEN | | Y-314 | $4.00 | $8.00 |
| Y-339 | 2 | 45-5118 - 9 | 500 HATS OF BARTHOLOMEW CUBBINS | PAUL WING | | BC-26, Y-304, Y-317 | $25.00 | $50.00 |

*STORY BOOK ALBUM **ALBUM ***GATEFOLD

## VICTOR RCA VICTOR "Y" SERIES 10" SINGLES AND ALBUMS

| SET # | # REC | DISC # | MAIN TITLE | ARTIST | YEAR | ALSO ISSUED ON | G/VG | EX/NMT |
|---|---|---|---|---|---|---|---|---|
| Y-340 | 2 | 45-5120 - 1 | ONE STRING FIDDLE** | PAUL WING | | BC-41, Y-308, Y-319 | $5.00 | $10.00 |
| Y-341 | 2 | 45-5122 - 3 | THE LITTLE ENGINE THAT COULD** | PAUL WING | | BC-36, Y-307, Y-318, Y-384 | $10.00 | $20.00 |
| Y-342 | 2 | 45-5124 - 5 | THE UNSUCCESSFUL ELF***** | PAUL WING | | Y-320 | $5.00 | $10.00 |
| Y-343 | 2 | 45-5126 - 7 | THE PANCAKE/THE FARMER'S BRIDE | GUDRUM THORNE-THOMSEN | | Y-321 | $5.00 | $10.00 |
| Y-344 | 2 | 45-5128 - 9 | PEE-WEE THE PICCOLO | PAUL WING | | Y-322 | $15.00 | $30.00 |
| Y-345 | 2 | 45-5130 - 1 | PETER AND THE WOLF | STERLING HOLLOWAY | | Y-323, Y-386 | $12.00 | $25.00 |
| Y-346 | 2 | 45-5132 - 3 | 'ERBERT'S 'APPY BIRTHDAY** | ROLAND WINTERS | | Y-324 | $10.00 | $20.00 |
| Y-347 | 2 | 45-5134 - 5 | RAPUNZEL** | DAME MAY WHITTY | | Y-325 | $5.00 | $10.00 |
| Y-348 | 2 | 45-5136 - 7 | LITTLE BLACK SAMBO AND THE TWINS** | PAUL WING | | Y-326 | $40.00 | $80.00 |
| Y-349 | 3 | 45-5138 - 9 | PINOCCHIO** | CLIFF EDWARDS | | P-18, Y-385 | $25.00 | $50.00 |
| Y-350 | 3 | 45-5141 - 3 | DUMBO** | SHIRLEY TEMPLE | | P-101 | $25.00 | $50.00 |
| Y-351 | 2 | 45-5804 - 5 (12") | HOW TO PLAY BASEBALL** | JOE E. BROWN | | | $75.00 | $150.00 |
| Y-352 | 2 | 45-5154 - 5 | 'ERBERT AND THE PIRATE** | ROLAND WINTERS | | | $10.00 | $20.00 |
| Y-353 | 2 | 45-5156 - 7 | RUDOLPH THE RED-NOSED REINDEER | PAUL WING | | | $4.00 | $8.00 |
| Y-354 | 2 | 45-5158 - 9 | RUMPLESTILTSKIN** | ROLAND WINTERS | | Y-306 | $4.00 | $8.00 |
| Y-355 | 2 | 45-5160 - 1 | LITTLE GNAWMAN***** | GEORGE ROCKWELL | | | $5.00 | $10.00 |
| Y-356 | 2 | 45-5162 - 3 | THE DOLL IN THE GRASS/THE LAD AND THE NORTH WIND** | GUDRUM THORNE-THOMSEN | | | $4.00 | $8.00 |
| Y-357 | 2 | 45-5168 - 8 | WHY THE CHIMES RANG | TED MALONE, NARRATOR | | | $10.00 | $20.00 |
| Y-358 | 2 | 45-5174 - 5 | JOHNNY STRANGER | RAY MIDDLETON, NARRATOR | | | $10.00 | $20.00 |
| Y-359 | 2 | 45-5164 - 5 | MUSICAL NONSENSE | SPIKE JONES AND HIS CITY SLICKERS | | | $10.00 | $20.00 |
| Y-360 | 2 | 45-5166 - 7 | THE PIED PIPER OF HAMELIN | ALEC TEMPLETON | | | $5.00 | $10.00 |
| Y-361 | 2 | 45-5170 - 1 | MOLLY WHUPPIE | JOHN CRONAN | 1948 | | $8.00 | $15.00 |
| Y-362 | 2 | 45-5172 - 3 | LITTLE FREDDIE AND HIS FIDDLE | GUDRUM THORNE-THOMSEN | | | $5.00 | $10.00 |
| Y-363 | 2 | 45-5176 - 7 | THE HAPPY HARMONICA | JOHN SEBASTIAN | | | $5.00 | $10.00 |
| Y-364 | 2 | 45-5178 - 9 | ALADDIN AND HIS WONDERFUL LAMP | TURHAN BEY | | | $5.00 | $10.00 |
| Y-365 | 2 | 45-5180 - 1 | THE FURTHER ADVENTURES OF TUBBY THE TUBA | RAY MIDDLETON | | | $10.00 | $20.00 |
| Y-366 | 2 | 45-5182 - 3 | BILLY-ON-A-BIKE | VAUGHN MONROE | | | $8.00 | $15.00 |
| Y-367 | 2 | 45-5184 - 5 | ST. CATHERINE AND THE MIRACULOUS MEDAL | TED MALONE | | | $4.00 | $8.00 |
| Y-368 | 3 | 45-5213 - 5 | JOHNNY APPLESEED | DENNIS DAY | | Y-390 | $25.00 | $50.00 |
| Y-369 | 2 | 45-5186 - 7 | MELODY TIME | ROY ROGERS, SONS OF THE PIONEERS | | | $25.00 | $50.00 |
| Y-370 | 2 | 45-5190 - 1 | HAPPY THE HUMBUG HAS A BIRTHDAY | DAVID WAYNE | | | $10.00 | $20.00 |
| Y-373 | 2 | 45-5198 - 9 | SYLVESTER THE SEAL | EDDIE MAYEHOFF | | | $8.00 | $15.00 |
| Y-374 | 2 | 45-5202 - 3 | THE WEDDING OF THE PRINCESS | PAUL WING | | | $5.00 | $10.00 |
| Y-375 | 3 | 45-5216 - 8 | PECOS BILL | ROY ROGERS, SONS OF THE PIONEERS | | Y-389 | $25.00 | $50.00 |
| Y-376 | 2 | 45-5222 - 3 | THE BOY WHO SANG FOR THE KING | DENNIS DAY | | | $5.00 | $10.00 |
| Y-377 | 2 | 45-5224 - 5 | HOW THE CIRCUS LEARNED TO SMILE | SPIKE JONES AND HIS CITY SLICKERS | | Y-387 | $12.00 | $25.00 |
| Y-382 | 3 | 45-5246 - 8 | DUMBO** | SHIRLEY TEMPLE | 1949 | | $25.00 | $50.00 |
| Y-383 | 2 | 45-5249 - 50 | LITTLE BLACK SAMBO (STORY BOOK ALBUM)* | PAUL WING | | BC-6, Y-312, Y-333 | $50.00 | $100.00 |
| Y-384 | 2 | 45-5251 - 2 | THE LITTLE ENGINE THAT COULD* | PAUL WING | | BC-36, Y-307, Y-318, Y-341 | $10.00 | $20.00 |
| Y-385 | 2 | 45-5253 - 4 | PINOCCHIO* | CLIFF EDWARDS | | | $25.00 | $50.00 |
| Y-386 | 2 | 45-5130 - 1 | PETER AND THE WOLF* | STERLING HOLLOWAY | | Y-323, Y-345 | $12.00 | $25.00 |
| Y-387 | 2 | 45-5224 - 5 | HOW THE CIRCUS LEARNED TO SMILE* | SPIKE JONES AND HIS CITY SLICKERS | | Y-377 | $12.00 | $25.00 |
| Y-388 | 2 | 45-5208 - 9 | LORE OF THE WEST | ROY ROGERS, GABBY HAYES | | Y-394 | $25.00 | $50.00 |
| Y-389 | 3 | 45-5216 - 8 | PECOS BILL | ROY ROGERS, SONS OF THE PIONEERS | | Y-375 | $25.00 | $50.00 |

*STORY BOOK ALBUM **ALBUM ***GATEFOLD

## VICTOR RCA VICTOR "Y" SERIES 10" SINGLES AND ALBUMS

| SET # | # REC | DISC # | MAIN TITLE | ARTIST | YEAR | ALSO ISSUED ON | G/VG | EX/NMT | REMARKS |
|---|---|---|---|---|---|---|---|---|---|
| Y-390 | 3 | 45-5213 – 5 | JOHNNY APPLESEED** | DENNIS DAY | | Y-368 | $25.00 | $50.00 | ALBUM |
| Y-391 | 3 | 45-5219 – 21 | BAMBI* | SHIRLEY TEMPLE | | | $25.00 | $50.00 | STORY BOOK ALBUM |
| Y-392 | 2 | 45-5270 – 1 | LITTLE BLACK SAMBO'S JUNGLE BAND | PAUL WING | | BC17, Y303, Y316, Y334 | $4.00 | $8.00 | STORY BOOK ALBUM |
| Y-394 | 2 | 45-5208 – 9 | LORE OF THE WEST | ROY ROGERS AND GABBY HAYES | | Y-388 | $25.00 | $50.00 | ALBUM (GATE-FOLD) |
| Y-395 | 3 | 45-5219 – 21 | BAMBI | SHIRLEY TEMPLE | | | $25.00 | $50.00 | ALBUM (WHITE SPINE) |
| Y-397 | 2 | 45-5258 – 9 | HOWDY DOODY AND THE AIR-O-DOODLE | BOB SMITH AND HOWDY DOODY | | | $20.00 | $40.00 | |
| Y-398 | 1 | 45-5255 | A STAR ON THE CHRISTMAS TREE | BILLY THE BROWNIE | | | $4.00 | $8.00 | |
| Y-399 | 2 | 45-5260 – 1 | WALT DISNEY'S CINDERELLA | ILENE WOODS | 1950 | | $25.00 | $50.00 | ALBUM |
| Y-400 | 1 | 45-5262 | THE BRAVE ENGINEER (THE STORY OF CASEY JONES) | JERRY COLONNA | | | $10.00 | $20.00 | DISNEY |
| Y-401 | 1 | 45-5263 | FUN ON OLD MACDONALD'S FARM | CLIFF EDWARDS | | | $4.00 | $8.00 | NIPPER JUNIOR |
| Y-402 | 1 | 45-5264 | FUN WITH MOTHER GOOSE | CLIFF EDWARDS | | | $4.00 | $8.00 | NIPPER JUNIOR |
| Y-403 | 1 | 45-5265 | FUN ALL DAY LONG | CLIFF EDWARDS | | | $4.00 | $8.00 | NIPPER JUNIOR |
| Y-404 | 1 | 45-5266 | A-B-C FUN/1-2-3 FUN | CLIFF EDWARDS | | | $4.00 | $8.00 | NIPPER JUNIOR |
| Y-405 | 1 | 45-5267 | COWBOY FUN***** | TEXAS JIM ROBERTSON | | | $4.00 | $8.00 | NIPPER JUNIOR |
| Y-406 | 1 | 45-5268 | PETER COTTONTAIL/STARS ARE THE WINDOWS OF HEAVEN | FRAN ALLISON | | | $4.00 | $8.00 | NIPPER JUNIOR |
| Y-407 | 1 | 45-5269 | THE MAN ON THE FLYING TRAPEZE/ BLOWING BUBBLE GUM | SPIKE JONES AND HIS CITY SLICKERS | | | $12.00 | $25.00 | NIPPER JUNIOR |
| Y-408 | 1 | 45-5272 | SUNDAY SCHOOL SONGS | JACK BERCH | | | $4.00 | $8.00 | NIPPER JUNIOR |
| Y-409 | 1 | 45-5273 | LITTLE RED RIDING HOOD/THE GINGERBREAD BOY | GLEN RIGGS | | | $4.00 | $8.00 | NIPPER JUNIOR |
| Y-410 | 1 | 45-5274 | GOLDILOCKS AND THE THREE BEARS/CHICKEN LICKEN | GLEN RIGGS | | | $4.00 | $8.00 | NIPPER JUNIOR |
| Y-411 | 1 | 45-5275 | THE TEDDY BEARS' PICNIC/ME AND MY TEDDY BEAR | JACK BERCH | | | $4.00 | $8.00 | NIPPER JUNIOR |
| Y-412 | 1 | 45-5276 | THE TORTOISE AND THE HARE/THE LITTLE RED HEN | GLEN RIGGS | | | $4.00 | $8.00 | NIPPER JUNIOR |
| Y-413 | 2 | 45-5277 – 8 | ROY ROGER'S RODEO | ROY ROGERS | | | $15.00 | $30.00 | STORY BOOK ALBUM |
| Y-414 | 2 | 45-5279 – 80 | HOWDY DOODY'S LAUGHING CIRCUS | BOB SMITH AND HOWDY DOODY | | | $20.00 | $40.00 | |
| Y-415 | 2 | 45-5281 – 2 | UNCLE WIGGILY | PAUL WING | | | $20.00 | $40.00 | STORY BOOK ALBUM |
| Y-416 | 2 | 45-5283 – 4 | WALT DISNEY'S TREASURE ISLAND | BOBBY DRISCOLL | | | $8.00 | $15.00 | |
| Y-417 | 1 | 45-5285 | MY TWO FRONT TEETH/RUDOLPH THE RED-NOSED REINDEER | SPIKE JONES AND HIS CITY SLICKERS | | | $12.00 | $25.00 | NIPPER JUNIOR |
| Y-418 | 1 | 45-5286 | FROSTY THE SNOWMAN/GABBY THE GOBBLER | ROY ROGERS | | | $15.00 | $30.00 | |
| Y-419 | 1 | 45-5287 | THE CHRISTMAS TREE ANGEL/ CHRISTMAS IN MY HEART | FRAN ALLISON | | | $4.00 | $8.00 | NIPPER JUNIOR |
| Y-420 | 1 | 45-5288 | 1001 WESTERN NIGHTS (NO. 1) | GEORGE "GABBY" HAYES | | | $12.00 | $25.00 | |
| Y-421 | 1 | 45-5289 | PARADE OF THE WOODEN SOL-DIERS/THE TOYMAKERS DREAM | MINDY CARSON | | | $4.00 | $8.00 | NIPPER JUNIOR |
| Y-422 | 1 | 45-5290 | THE FIRST CHRISTMAS | PERRY COMO | | | $4.00 | $8.00 | NIPPER JUNIOR |
| Y-423 | 2 | 45-52-91 – 2 | HAPPY MOTHER GOOSE | FRAN ALLISON AND BURR TILLSTROM | | | $15.00 | $30.00 | |

*STORY BOOK ALBUM **ALBUM ***GATEFOLD

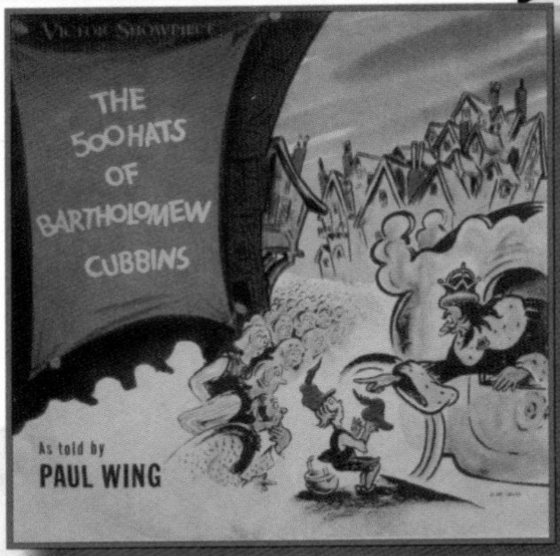


VICTOR RECORDS
CAPTAIN VIDEO AND THE CAPTIVES OF SATURN
$50.00

VICTOR RECORDS
DANCE OF THE BOGEY MEN
$600.00

VICTOR RECORDS
THE 500 HATS OF BARTHOLMEW CUBBINS
$50.00

## VICTOR RCA VICTOR "Y" SERIES 10" SINGLES AND ALBUMS

| SET # | # REC | DISC # | MAIN TITLE | ARTIST | YEAR | G/VG | EX/NMT | REMARKS |
|---|---|---|---|---|---|---|---|---|
| Y-424 | 1 | 45-5302 | 1001 WESTERN NIGHTS (NO. 2) | GEORGE "GABBY" HAYES | | $12.00 | $25.00 | |
| Y-425 | 2 | 45-5312 – 3 | SONGS BY KUKLA, FRAN AND OLLIE | FRAN ALLISON AND BURR TILLSTROM | | $25.00 | $50.00 | |
| Y-426 | 1 | 45-5298 | JACK AND THE BEANSTALK/THE SHOE-MAKER AND THE ELVES | PAUL WING | 1951 | $4.00 | $8.00 | |
| Y-427 | 1 | 45-5299 | THE BRAVE TIN SOLDIER/SEVEN AT ONE BLOW | PAUL WING | | $4.00 | $8.00 | |
| Y-428 | 1 | 45-5300 | TOM THUMB/PUSS AND BOOTS | PAUL WING | | $4.00 | $8.00 | |
| Y-429 | 1 | 45-5301 | PETER RABBIT/RUMPLESTILTSKIN | PAUL WING | | $4.00 | $8.00 | |
| Y-430 | 1 | 45-5303 | BIRTHDAY FUN/UNBIRTHDAY SONG | DENNIS DAY | | $4.00 | $8.00 | |
| Y-431 | 1 | 45-5304 | FAVORITE HYMNS FOR CHILDREN | DENNIS DAY | | $4.00 | $8.00 | |
| Y-432 | 1 | 45-5314 | MR. TELEVISION | MILTON BERLE AND DON-ALD DUCK W/MICKEY MOUSE | | $35.00 | $75.00 | |
| Y-433 | 1 | 45-5315 | MR. ANIMATED CARTOON | MILTON BERLE AND DON-ALD DUCK W/MICKEY MOUSE | | $35.00 | $75.00 | |
| Y-434 | 1 | 45-5293 | ALICE AND THE WHITE RABBIT | ED WYNN AND KATHRYN BEAUMONT | | $15.00 | $30.00 | |
| Y-435 | 1 | 45-5294 | ALICE AND THE MAD TEA PARTY | ED WYNN AND KATHRYN BEAUMONT | | $15.00 | $30.00 | |
| Y-436 | 1 | 45-5295 | ALICE AND THE TRIAL | ED WYNN AND KATHRYN BEAUMONT | | $15.00 | $30.00 | |
| Y-437 | 2 | 45-5296 – 7 | ALICE IN WONDERLAND | ED WYNN AND KATTHRYN BEAUMONT | | $25.00 | $50.00 | GIANT STORY BOOK ALBUM |
| Y-438 | 2 | 45-5316 – 7 | WINNIE THE POOH NO. 1: HEFFALUMP, TIG-GER | JAMES STEWART | | $25.00 | $50.00 | STORY BOOK ALBUM |
| Y-439 | 2 | 45-5318 – 9 | WINNIE THE POOH NO. 2: EEYORE, KANGA | JAMES STEWART | | $25.00 | $50.00 | STORY BOOK ALBUM |
| Y-440 | 2 | 45-5306-7 | A CHRISTMAS CAROL | CHARLES LAUGHTON | | $5.00 | $10.00 | STORY BOOK ALBUM |
| Y-441 | 2 | 45-5308 – 9 | RUDOLPH'S SECOND CHRISTMAS | PAUL WING | | $4.00 | $8.00 | |
| Y-442 | 2 | 45-5310 – 1 | HOWDY DOODY'S CHRISTMAS PARTY | BOB SMITH AND HOWDY DOODY | | $25.00 | $50.00 | |
| Y-443 | 1 | 45-5327 | THE MASKED MARAUDER | ROY ROGERS | 1952 | $15.00 | $30.00 | |
| Y-444 | 1 | 45-5328 | THE TELEVISION AMBUSH | ROY ROGERS | | $15.00 | $30.00 | NIPPER JUNIOR |
| Y-445 | 1 | 45-5325 | HOWDY DOODY'S DO'S AND DON'TS | BOB SMITH AND HOWDY DOODY | | $20.00 | $40.00 | NIPPER JUNIOR |
| Y-446 | 1 | 45-5326 | IT'S HOWDY DOODY TIME | BOB SMITH AND HOWDY DOODY | | $30.00 | $60.00 | NIPPER JUNIOR |
| Y-447 | 1 | 45-5329 | SNOW WHITE AND SNEEZY | DENNIS DAY | | $15.00 | $30.00 | |
| Y-448 | 1 | 45-5330 | SNOW WHITE AND DOPEY | DENNIS DAY | | $15.00 | $30.00 | |
| Y-449 | 1 | 45-5331 | AT SPACE ACADEMY | TOM CORBETT — SPACE CADET CAST | | $40.00 | $80.00 | |

## VICTOR RCA VICTOR "Y" SERIES 10" SINGLES AND ALBUMS

| SET # | # REC | DISC # | MAIN TITLE | ARTIST | YEAR | G/VG | EX/NMT |
|---|---|---|---|---|---|---|---|
| Y-450 | 1 | 45-5332 | RESCUE IN SPACE | TOM CORBETT — SPACE CADET CAST | | $40.00 | $80.00 |
| Y-453 | 1 | 45-5333 | LITTLE NIPPER RIDDLES/LITTLE NIPPER MARCH | PAUL WING | | $5.00 | $10.00 |
| Y-454 | 1 | 45-5334 | DICK WHITTINGTON AND HIS CAT/RAPUNZEL | PAUL WING | | $4.00 | $8.00 |
| Y-455 | 1 | 45-5335 | THREE BILLY GOATS GRUFF/THE UGLY DUCKLING | PAUL WING | | $4.00 | $8.00 |
| Y-456 | 1 | 45-5337 | HYMNS OF CATHOLIC DEVOTION (VOL. 1) | ST. PATRICK'S CATHOLIC CHOIRESTERS | | $4.00 | $8.00 |
| Y-457 | 1 | 45-5338 | HYMNS OF CATHOLIC DEVOTION (VOL. 2) | ST. PATRICK'S CATHOLIC CHOIRESTERS | | $4.00 | $8.00 |
| Y-458 | 1 | E2VB-5913/4 | WHEN I GET BACK FROM MY VACATION/ICE CREAM | PAUL WINCHELL AND JERRY MAHONEY | | $20.00 | $40.00 |
| Y-459 | 1 | E2VB-6822/3 | SMOKEY THE BEAR/HORACE THE HORSE | EDDY ARNOLD | | $10.00 | $20.00 |
| Y-460 | 1 | E2VB-5283/0675 | THIRTY-TWO FEET — EIGHT LITTLE TAILS/SUZY SNOWFLAKE | DALE EVANS | | $12.00 | $25.00 |
| Y-461 | 1 | E2VB-6984/5 | SOCKO THE SMALLEST SNOWBALL/BARNYARD CHRISTMAS | SPIKE JONES AND HIS CITY SLICKERS | | $12.00 | $25.00 |
| Y-462 | 1 | E2VB-5280/2 | TEXAS FOR ME/CHICKERY CHICK | DALE EVANS | | $12.00 | $25.00 |
| Y-463 | 1 | E2VB-7756/7 | NEVER SMILE AT A CROCODILE/YOU CAN FLY! YOU CAN FLY! YOU CAN FLY! | HUGO WINTERHALTER | 1953 | $10.00 | $20.00 |
| Y-464 | 1 | E2VB-7764/6 | THUMBELINA/THE UGLY DUCKLING | JUDY VALENTINE | | $4.00 | $8.00 |
| Y-465 | 1 | ? | PETER COTTONTAIL/MOTHER GOOSE MEDLEY | SPIKE JONES AND HIS CITY SLICKERS | | $12.00 | $25.00 |
| Y-466 | 1 | E3VB-0217/8 | MOTHER GOOSE MEDLEY/GOING TO BED AT NIGHT | MISS FRANCIS | | $8.00 | $15.00 |
| Y-467 | 1 | E3VB-0223/4 | DING DONG SCHOOL SONG/FUN WITH INSTRUMENTS | MISS FRANCIS | | $8.00 | $15.00 |
| Y-468 | 1 | E3VB-0219/20 | RIDING ALONG/BELLS | MISS FRANCIS | | $8.00 | $15.00 |
| Y-469 | 1 | E3VB-0221/22 | LARRY THE LIGHTNING BUG | MISS FRANCIS | 1954 | $8.00 | $15.00 |
| Y-470 | 1 | E3VB-1683/4 | STORMY THE THOROUGHBRED | RALPH CAMARGO | | $8.00 | $15.00 |
| Y-471 | 1 | E3VB-1681/2 | BEN AND ME | MERRILL JOELS | | $8.00 | $15.00 |
| Y-472 | 1 | E3VB-0117/2002 | CAPTAIN OF THE SPACE SHIP/A TOOT, A WHISTLE, A PLUNK AND A BOOM | SPIKE JONES AND HIS CITY SLICKERS | | $25.00 | $50.00 |
| Y-475 | 1 | E3VB-0273/8 | PETER WENT TO SLEEP/WHAT IS AN OPPOSITE | MISS FRANCIS | | $8.00 | $15.00 |
| Y-476 | 1 | E3VB-0272/6 | THE FROG THAT JUMPED THE WRONG WAY | MISS FRANCIS | | $8.00 | $15.00 |
| Y-477 | 1 | E3VB-0274/7 | WALKING DOWN THE STREET/INSTRUMENTS YOU CAN PLAY | MISS FRANCIS | | $8.00 | $15.00 |
| Y-478 | 1 | E3VB-0275/9 | THE MUSIC MAKES YOU | MISS FRANCIS | | $8.00 | $15.00 |
| Y-483 | 1 | E4TB-4607/8 | CINDERELLA | ILENE WOODS | | $10.00 | $20.00 |
| Y-484 | 1 | E4TB-4904/5 | SNOW WHITE AND THE SEVEN DWARFS | DENNIS DAY AND ILENE WOODS | | $10.00 | $20.00 |
| Y-485 | 1 | E4TB-4915/6 | ALICE IN WONDERLAND | ED WYNN AND KATHRYN BEAUMONT | | $10.00 | $20.00 |
| Y-486 | 1 | E4TB-4913/4 | PETER PAN | BOBBY DRISCOLL AND KATHRYN BEAU-MONT | | $10.00 | $20.00 |
| Y-487 | 1 | E3VB-1601/1353 | TWELVE DAYS OF CHRISTMAS | PERRY COMO | | $4.00 | $8.00 |
| Y-488 | 1 | E3VB-1338/9 | PERRY COMO FOR CHRISTMAS | PERRY COMO | | $4.00 | $8.00 |
| Y-489 | 1 | ? | THE LITTLE SHOEMAKER/VERA'S VERANDA | ? | | $4.00 | $8.00 |
| Y-490 | 1 | E4VB-5511/5448 | A PRESENT FOR SANTA CLAUS/SITTIN' ON SANTA CLAUS' LAP | EDDY ARNOLD & JO ANN (DAUGHTER) | | $15.00 | $30.00 |
| Y-491 | 1 | E4VB-5401/2 | I GOT A COLD FOR CHRISTMAS/THERE'LL ALWAYS BE A CHRISTMAS | THE AMES BROTHERS | | $4.00 | $8.00 |
| Y-492 | 1 | E4TB-1025/6 | THE HORSE IN STRIPED PAJAMAS/WHY, DADDY? | EDDY ARNOLD & JO ANN (DAUGHTER) | | $15.00 | $30.00 |
| Y-601 | 1 | 4321 | HUNGARIAN DANCES: 5 & 6 | BOSTON "POPS" ORCHESTRA; ARTHUR FIEDLER, COND. | | $2.00 | $4.00 |
| Y-602 (12") | 1 | 11932 | NATOMA: DAGGER DANCE | BOSTON "POPS" ORCHESTRA; ARTHUR FIEDLER, COND. | | $2.00 | $4.00 |
| Y-603 (12") | 1 | 12527 | COPPÉLIA BALLET SUITE: DANCE OF THE AUTOMA-TONS, WALTZ AND CZARDAS (DELIBES) | BOSTON "POPS" ORCHESTRA; ARTHUR FIEDLER, COND. | | $2.00 | $4.00 |
| Y-604 (12") | 1 | 15425 | BLUE DANUBE WALTZ (J. STRAUSS) | PHILADELPHIA ORCHESTRA; LEOPOLD STOKOWSKI, COND. | 1944 | $2.00 | $4.00 |
| Y-605 (12") | 1 | 41-5000 | SYMPHONY NO. 5, IN C MINOR (BEETHOVEN) | VICTOR SYMPHONY ORCH., CHARLES O'CONNELL, COND. | | $2.00 | $4.00 |
| Y-606 | 1 | 42-0001 | WILLIAM TELL OVERTURE (ROSSINI) | BOSTON "POPS" ORCHESTRA; ARTHUR FIEDLER, COND. | | $2.00 | $4.00 |
| Y-607 (12") | 1 | 42-5000 | PEER GYNT SUITE NO. 1, OP. 46 | CINCINNATI SYMPH ORCH., EUGENE GO-OSSENS, COND. | | $2.00 | $4.00 |
| Y-608 | 2 | 45-5802 - 3 | THE COMEDY OF ERRORS (FUN WITH MISTER SHAKESPEARE) | CHARLES COBURN, HAROLD STOKES & ORCH. | 1947 | $2.00 | $4.00 |
| Y-609 | 3 | 45-5144 - 6 | ROBIN HOOD | JUNIOR PROGRAMS COMPANY | | $5.00 | $10.00 |

## VICTOR RCA VICTOR "Y" SERIES 10" SINGLES AND ALBUMS

| SET # | # REC | DISC # | MAIN TITLE | ARTIST | YEAR | ALSO ISSUED ON | G/VG | EX/NMT | REMARKS |
|---|---|---|---|---|---|---|---|---|---|
| Y-610 | 4 | 45-5147 – 50 | HANSEL AND GRETEL | JUNIOR PROGRAMS OPERA COMPANY | | P-38 | $5.00 | $10.00 | |
| Y-611 (12") | 2 | 45-5806 – 7 | PRINCE VALIANT AND THE OUTLAWS | DOUGLAS FAIRBANKS, JR, PAUL CROSET & CAST | 1948 | | $25.00 | $50.00 | |
| Y-2015 | 2 | E3VB-0171/4 – 0172/3 | THE LITTLEST STORK | JOAN CRAWFORD, ANDRÉ PREVIN ORCH. | | | $25.00 | $50.00 | ALBUM |
| Y-2016 | 4 | E3VB-1268/9 – 1274/5 | LUDWIG BEMELMANS' "MADELINE" + ROSEBUD, THE LONESOME PINE, SUNSHINE | NELSON OLMSTEAD | | | $25.00 | $50.00 | ALBUM |
| Y-2017 | 2 | E3VB-1939/42 – 1940/1 | HOWDY DOODY AND SANTA CLAUS | HOWDY DOODY, BUFFALO BILL, TV SHOW CAST | | | $50.00 | $100.00 | |
| Y-2018 | 2 | E3VB-1966/9 – 1967/8 | HOWDY DOODY AND MOTHER GOOSE | HOWDY DOODY, BUFFALO BILL, TV SHOW CAST | | | $50.00 | $100.00 | |
| Y-2019 | 2 | E4TB-3851/5 – 3852/3 | HOWDY DOODY AND YOU | HOWDY DOODY, BUFFALO BILL, TV SHOW CAST | | | $50.00 | $100.00 | |
| Y-2020 | 2 | E4TB-4101/4 – 4102/3 | HOWDY DOODY'S MAGIC JUKE BOX | HOWDY DOODY, BUFFALO BILL, TV SHOW CAST | | | $50.00 | $100.00 | |
| Y-2021 | 2 | E4TB-4190/3 – 4191/2 | HOWDY DOODY'S CRYSTAL BALL | HOWDY DOODY, BUFFALO BILL, TV SHOW CAST | | | $50.00 | $100.00 | |
| Y-2022 | 2 | E4TB-3965/8 – 3966/7 | HOWDY DOODY AND THE MUSICAL FOREST | HOWDY DOODY, BUFFALO BILL, TV SHOW CAST | | | $50.00 | $100.00 | |
| Y-2023 | 2 | F2RB-3403/6 – 3404/5 | PAN THE PIPER | PAUL WING | 1955 | | $10.00 | $20.00 | STORY BOOK ALBUM |
| Y-4001 | 2 | E2VB-6560/6 – 6562/4 | PETER PAN | KATHRYN BEAUMONT, BOBBY DRISCOLL | | | $15.00 | $30.00 | STORY BOOK ALBUM |
| Y-4002 | 1 | EV3B-1915/6 | THE BIRD CALL GAME | BERT HARWELL | | | $4.00 | $8.00 | |
| Y-4003 | ? | ? | A TOOT & A WHISTLE & A PLUNK & A BOOM | ? | | | $15.00 | $30.00 | |
| Y-4004 | 2 | E4TB-4701/4 – 4702/3 | 20,000 LEAGUES UNDER THE SEA | WILLIAM REDFIELD, BERNARD LENROW, ET AL. | 1954 | | $15.00 | $30.00 | STORY BOOK ALBUM |

## VICTOR RCA VICTOR EDUCATIONAL SERIES 10" ALBUMS

| SET # | # REC | DISC # | MAIN TITLE | ARTIST | YEAR | G/VG | EX/NMT |
|---|---|---|---|---|---|---|---|
| E-71 | 4 | 5000 – 3 | RECORD LIBRARY FOR ELEMENTARY SCHOOLS: RHYTHMIC ACTIVITIES (V. 1, PRIMARY GRADES) | RCA VICTOR ORCH., ARDON CORNWELL, ET AL. CONDUCTORS | 1947 | $3.00 | $6.00 |
| E-72 | 4 | 5004 – 7 | RECORD LIBRARY FOR ELEMENTARY SCHOOLS: RHYTHMIC ACTIVITIES (V. 2, PRIMARY GRADES) | RCA VICTOR ORCH., ARDON CORNWELL, ET AL. CONDUCTORS | | $3.00 | $6.00 |
| E-73 | 4 | 5008 – 11 | RECORD LIBRARY FOR ELEMENTARY SCHOOLS: RHYTHMIC ACTIVITIES (V. 3, PRIMARY GRADES) | RCA VICTOR ORCH., ARDON CORNWELL, ET AL. CONDUCTORS | | $3.00 | $6.00 |
| E-74 | 4 | 5012 – 15 | RECORD LIBRARY FOR ELEMENTARY SCHOOLS: RHYTHMIC ACTIVITIES (V. 4, UPPER GRADES) | RCA VICTOR ORCH., ARDON CORNWELL, ET AL. CONDUCTORS | | $3.00 | $6.00 |
| E-75 | 4 | 5016 – 19 | RECORD LIBRARY FOR ELEMENTARY SCHOOLS: RHYTHMIC ACTIVITIES (V. 5, UPPER GRADES) | RCA VICTOR ORCH., ARDON CORNWELL, ET AL. CONDUCTORS | | $3.00 | $6.00 |
| E-76 | 4 | 5020 – 23 | RECORD LIBRARY FOR ELEMENTARY SCHOOLS: RHYTHMIC ACTIVITIES (V. 6, UPPER GRADES) | RCA VICTOR ORCH., ARDON CORNWELL, ET AL. CONDUCTORS | | $3.00 | $6.00 |
| E-77 | 4 | 5024 – 27 | RECORD LIBRARY FOR ELEMENTARY SCHOOLS: LISTENING ACTIVITIES (V. 1, PRIMARY GRADES) | RCA VICTOR ORCH., ARDON CORNWELL, ET AL. CONDUCTORS | | $3.00 | $6.00 |
| E-78 | 4 | 5028 – 31 | RECORD LIBRARY FOR ELEMENTARY SCHOOLS: LISTENING ACTIVITIES (V. 2, PRIMARY GRADES) | RCA VICTOR ORCH., ARDON CORNWELL, ET AL. CONDUCTORS | | $3.00 | $6.00 |
| E-79 | 4 | 5032 – 35 | RECORD LIBRARY FOR ELEMENTARY SCHOOLS: LISTENING ACTIVITIES (V. 3, PRIMARY GRADES) | RCA VICTOR ORCH., ARDON CORNWELL, ET AL. CONDUCTORS | | $3.00 | $6.00 |
| E-80 | 4 | 5036 – 39 | RECORD LIBRARY FOR ELEMENTARY SCHOOLS: LISTENING ACTIVITIES (V. 4, UPPER GRADES) | RCA VICTOR ORCH., ARDON CORNWELL, ET AL. CONDUCTORS | | $3.00 | $6.00 |
| E-81 | 4 | 5040 – 43 | RECORD LIBRARY FOR ELEMENTARY SCHOOLS: LISTENING ACTIVITIES (V. 5, UPPER GRADES) | RCA VICTOR ORCH., ARDON CORNWELL, ET AL. CONDUCTORS | | $3.00 | $6.00 |
| E-82 | 4 | 5044 – 47 | RECORD LIBRARY FOR ELEMENTARY SCHOOLS: LISTENING ACTIVITIES (V. 6, UPPER GRADES) | RCA VICTOR ORCH., ARDON CORNWELL, ET AL. CONDUCTORS | | $3.00 | $6.00 |
| E-83 | 4 | 5048 – 51 | RECORD LIBRARY FOR ELEMENTARY SCHOOLS: SINGING ACTIVITIES (V. 1, PRIMARY GRADES) | RCA VICTOR ORCH., ARDON CORNWELL, ET AL. CONDUCTORS | | $3.00 | $6.00 |
| E-84 | 4 | 5052 – 55 | RECORD LIBRARY FOR ELEMENTARY SCHOOLS: SINGING ACTIVITIES (V. 4, UPPER GRADES) | RCA VICTOR ORCH., ARDON CORNWELL, ET AL. CONDUCTORS | | $3.00 | $6.00 |
| E-85 | 4 | 5056 – 59 | RECORD LIBRARY FOR ELEMENTARY SCHOOLS: SINGING ACTIVITIES (V. 5, UPPER GRADES) | RCA VICTOR ORCH., ARDON CORNWELL, ET AL. CONDUCTORS | | $3.00 | $6.00 |
| E-86 | 4 | 5060 – 63 | RECORD LIBRARY FOR ELEMENTARY SCHOOLS: SINGING ACTIVITIES (V. 6, UPPER GRADES) | RCA VICTOR ORCH., ARDON CORNWELL, ET AL. CONDUCTORS | | $3.00 | $6.00 |

## VICTOR RCA VICTOR EDUCATIONAL SERIES 10" ALBUMS

| SET # | # REC | DISC # | MAIN TITLE | ARTIST | YEAR | G/VG | EX/NMT |
|---|---|---|---|---|---|---|---|
| E-87 | 4 | 5064 - 67 | RECORD LIBRARY FOR ELEMENTARY SCHOOLS: SINGING GAMES FOR PRIMARY GRADES | RCA VICTOR ORCH.; ARDON CORNWELL, ET AL., CONDUCTORS | | $3.00 | $6.00 |
| E-88 | 4 | 5068 - 71 | RECORD LIBRARY FOR ELEMENTARY SCHOOLS: MUSIC AT CHRISTMAS TIME FOR ELEMENTARY GRADES | JEAN PRIVETTE, ET AL., RCA VICTOR ORCH.; ARDON CORNWELL, COND. | | $3.00 | $6.00 |
| E-89 | 4 | 5072 - 75 | RECORD LIBRARY FOR ELEMENTARY SCHOOLS: MUSIC OF AMERICAN INDIANS | HOPI INDIAN CHANTERS (#5072), RCA VICTOR ORCH.; ARDON CORNWELL, ET AL., CONDUCTORS | | $10.00 | $20.00 |
| E-90 | 4 | 5076 - 79 | RECORD LIBRARY FOR ELEMENTARY SCHOOLS: MUSIC FOR RHYTHM BANDS FOR PRIMARY GRADES | RCA VICTOR ORCH.; ARDON CORNWELL, ET AL., CONDUCTORS | | $3.00 | $6.00 |
| E-91 | 3 | 5080 - 82 | RECORD LIBRARY FOR ELEMENTARY SCHOOLS: PATRIOTIC SONGS | RCA MIXED CHORUS; DON CRAIG, DIR. | | $3.00 | $6.00 |
| NO # | 1 | ? | DEMONSTRATION RECORD FOR TEACHERS | RCA VICTOR ORCH.; ARDON CORNWELL, ET AL., CONDUCTORS | | $5.00 | $10.00 |
| E-94 | 4 | 6000 - 3 | A SINGING SCHOOL: OUR FIRST MUSIC — BOOK 1 (1ST GRADE) | ROBERT SHAW CHORALE MEMBERS | 1949 | $10.00 | $20.00 |
| E-95 | 6 | 6004 - 9 | A SINGING SCHOOL: OUR SONGS — BOOK 2 (2ND GRADE) | ROBERT SHAW CHORALE MEMBERS | | $10.00 | $20.00 |
| E-96 | 5 | 6010 - 14 | A SINGING SCHOOL: MERRY MUSIC — BOOK 3 (3RD GRADE) | ROBERT SHAW CHORALE MEMBERS | | $10.00 | $20.00 |
| E-97 | 5 | 6015 - 19 | A SINGING SCHOOL: WE SING — BOOK 4 (4TH GRADE) | ROBERT SHAW CHORALE MEMBERS | | $10.00 | $20.00 |
| E-98 | 5 | 6020 - 25 | A SINGING SCHOOL: OUR LAND OF SONG — BOOK 5 (5TH GRADE) | ROBERT SHAW CHORALE MEMBERS | | $10.00 | $20.00 |
| E-99 | 5 | 6025 - 29 | A SINGING SCHOOL: MUSIC EVERYWHERE - BOOK 6 (6TH GRADE) | ROBERT SHAW CHORALE MEMBERS | | $10.00 | $20.00 |
| E-100 | 6 | 6054 - 9 | A SINGING SCHOOL: SING OUT! — BOOK 7 (7TH GRADE) | ROBERT SHAW CHORALE MEMBERS | | $10.00 | $20.00 |
| E-101 | 6 | 6060 - 5 | A SINGING SCHOOL: LET MUSIC RING! — BOOK 8 (8TH GRADE) | ROBERT SHAW CHORALE MEMBERS | | $10.00 | $20.00 |
| E-102 | 5 | 6040 - 4 | A SINGING SCHOOL: HAPPY SINGING (1ST TO 4TH GRADE) | ROBERT SHAW CHORALE MEMBERS | | $10.00 | $20.00 |
| E-103 | 5 | 6045 - 9 | A SINGING SCHOOL: MUSIC IN THE AIR (1ST TO 8TH GRADE) | ROBERT SHAW CHORALE MEMBERS | | $10.00 | $20.00 |
| E-104 | 4 | 6050 - 53 | INSTRUMENTS OF THE ORCHESTRA | NOT LISTED | | $5.00 | $10.00 |
| NO # | 1 | EO-EB-6152 | DEMONSTRATION RECORD FROM A SINGING SCHOOL | ROBERT SHAW CHORALE MEMBERS | | $10.00 | $20.00 |

## VICTOR RCA VICTOR FOLK DANCE SERIES 10" SINGLES

| # REC | DISC # | MAIN TITLE | ARTIST | YEAR | G/VG | EX/NMT |
|---|---|---|---|---|---|---|
| 1 | 45-6169 | ACE OF DIAMONDS/BLEKING | RCA VICTOR FOLK DANCE ORCHESTRA | 1952 | $1.00 | $2.00 |
| 1 | 45-6170 | GUSTAF'S SKOAL/LOTT'IST TOD | RCA VICTOR FOLK DANCE ORCHESTRA | | $1.00 | $2.00 |
| 1 | 45-6171 | KLAPPDANS/SHOEMAKER'S DANCE | RCA VICTOR FOLK DANCE ORCHESTRA | | $1.00 | $2.00 |
| 1 | 45-6172 | SEVEN JUMPS/BINGO | RCA VICTOR FOLK DANCE ORCHESTRA | | $1.00 | $2.00 |
| 1 | 45-6173 | NORWEGIAN MOUNTAIN MARCH/TRA-LA-LA JA SAA | RCA VICTOR FOLK DANCE ORCHESTRA | | $1.00 | $2.00 |
| 1 | 45-6174 | SELLENGER'S ROUND/GATHERING PEASCODS | RCA VICTOR FOLK DANCE ORCHESTRA | | $1.00 | $2.00 |
| 1 | 56-6175 | GREEN SLEEVES/RIBBON DANCE | RCA VICTOR FOLK DANCE ORCHESTRA | | $1.00 | $2.00 |
| 1 | 45-6176 | CRESTED HEN/CHIMES OF DUNKIRK | RCA VICTOR FOLK DANCE ORCHESTRA | | $1.00 | $2.00 |
| 1 | 45-6177 | COME LET US BE JOYFUL, BUMMEL SCHOTTISCHE/ OH SUSANNA | RCA VICTOR FOLK DANCE ORCHESTRA | | $1.00 | $2.00 |
| 1 | 45-6178 | THE IRISH WASHERWOMAN/ | RCA VICTOR FOLK DANCE ORCHESTRA | | $1.00 | $2.00 |
| 1 | 45-6179 | CARROUSEL, KINDERPOLKA/HIGHLAND FLING, HIGHLAND SCHOTTISCHE | RCA VICTOR FOLK DANCE ORCHESTRA | | $1.00 | $2.00 |
| 1 | 45-6180 | VIRGINIA REEL/POP GOES THE WEASEL | RCA VICTOR FOLK DANCE ORCHESTRA | | $1.00 | $2.00 |
| 1 | 45-6181 | MINUET MAYPOLE DANCE | RCA VICTOR FOLK DANCE ORCHESTRA | | $1.00 | $2.00 |
| 1 | 45-6182 | TURN AROUND ME, HANSEL AND GRETEL/THE WHEAT, CSHEBOGAR | RCA VICTOR FOLK DANCE ORCHESTRA | | $1.00 | $2.00 |
| 1 | 45-6183 | TANTOLI/DANCE OF GREETING | RCA VICTOR FOLK DANCE ORCHESTRA | | $1.00 | $2.00 |
| 1 | 45-6184 | BLACKBERRY QUADRILLE/SOLDIER'S JOY | WOODHULL'S OLD TYME MASTERS | | $1.00 | $2.00 |

## VICTOR RCA VICTOR LET'S SQUARE DANCE SERIES 10" SINGLES

| SET # | # REC | DISC # | MAIN TITLE | ARTIST | YEAR | G/VG | EX/NMT | REMARKS |
|---|---|---|---|---|---|---|---|---|
| E-3000 | 4 | 6199 - 202 | LET'S SQUARE DANCE - ALBUM NO. 1 (GRADES 3, 4) | RICHARD KRAUS, CALLER, RCA VICTOR SQUARE DANCE ORCH. | 1956 | $2.00 | $4.00 | FOR AGES 8 - 10 |
| E-3001 | 4 | 6203 - 6 | LET'S SQUARE DANCE - ALBUM NO. 2 (GRADES 5, 6) | RICHARD KRAUS, CALLER, RCA VICTOR SQUARE DANCE ORCH. | | $2.00 | $4.00 | FOR AGES 10 - 12 |
| E-3002 | 4 | 6207 - 10 | LET'S SQUARE DANCE - ALBUM NO. 3 (GRADES 7, 8) | RICHARD KRAUS, CALLER, RCA VICTOR SQUARE DANCE ORCH. | | $2.00 | $4.00 | FOR AGES 12 - 14 |
| E-3003 | 4 | 6211 - 14 | LET'S SQUARE DANCE - ALBUM NO. 4 (GRADES 9, 10) | RICHARD KRAUS, CALLER, RCA VICTOR SQUARE DANCE ORCH. | | $2.00 | $4.00 | FOR AGES 14 - 16 |
| E-3004 | 5 | 6215 - 19 | LET'S SQUARE DANCE - ALBUM NO. 5 (GRADES 11, 12) | RICHARD KRAUS, CALLER, RCA VICTOR SQUARE DANCE ORCH. | | $2.00 | $4.00 | FOR AGES 16 - 18 |

## VICTOR RCA VICTOR BLUEBIRD MISCELLANEOUS 10" SINGLES

| # REC | DISC # | ARTIST | A TITLE | B TITLE | YEAR | G/VG | EX/NMT |
|---|---|---|---|---|---|---|---|
| 1 | B-5102 | JAMES HARKINS | MEDLEY OF CHILDREN'S SONGS | MEDLEY OF CHILDREN'S SONGS | 1932 | $1.00 | $2.00 |
| 1 | B-5178 | BILL SCOTTI ORCH. | WHO'S AFRAID OF THE BIG BAD WOLF | ? | 1933 | $5.00 | $10.00 |
| 1 | B-5270 | JAMES HARKINS | MEDLEY OF CHILDREN'S SONGS: POP GOES THE WEASEL, ETC. | MEDLEY OF CHILDREN'S SONGS | | $1.00 | $2.00 |
| 1 | B-6158 | CLIFFORD JOHNS | FARMER IN THE DELL, TO MARKET, TOM TOM | RING AROUND THE ROSEY MEDLEY, LONDON BRIDGE | 1935 | $1.00 | $2.00 |
| 1 | B-6159 | CLIFFORD JOHNS | LITTLE TOMMY TUCKER | ROBIN SING FOR ME, TEN LITTLE INDIANS | | $1.00 | $2.00 |
| 1 | B-6723 | FLOYD BUCKLEY SONGS FOR CHILDREN | I'M POPEYE THE SAILOR MAN (PT. 1) | I'M POPEYE THE SAILOR MAN (PT. 2) | 1936 | $10.00 | $20.00 |
| 1 | B-6724 | FLOYD BUCKLEY SONGS FOR CHILDREN | I'M POPEYE THE SAILOR MAN (PT. 3) | I'M POPEYE THE SAILOR MAN (PT. 4) | | $10.00 | $20.00 |
| 1 | B-7343 | SHEP FIELDS & HIS RIPPLING RHYTHM ORCH. | WHISTLE WHILE YOU WORK | ? | 1938 | $5.00 | $10.00 |
| 1 | B-7773 | THE KIDDIE KLOWNS ORCHESTRA | THE STORY BOOK BALL | DANCE OF THE TINKER TOYS | | $1.00 | $2.00 |
| 1 | B-10570 | GLENN MILLER | WHEN YOU WISH UPON A STAR | GAUCHO SERENADE | 1941 | $4.00 | $8.00 |
| 1 | B-11556 | TEDDY POWELL ORCH. | LOVE IS A SONG (FROM BAMBI) | TAPESTRY IN BLUE | | $3.00 | $6.00 |
| 1 | B-11586 | SPIKE JONES AND HIS CITY SLICKERS | DER FUHERER'S FACE | I WANNA GO BACK TO WEST VIRGINIA | 1942 | $10.00 | $20.00 |

## VICTOR RCA VICTOR VICTOR MISCELLANEOUS SINGLE SIDE 7", 8" AND 10" SINGLES

| # REC | DISC # | MAIN TITLE | ARTIST | YEAR | G/VG | EX/NMT |
|---|---|---|---|---|---|---|
| 1 | A-60 | MOTHER GOOSE RHYMES | WILLIAM HOOLEY | 1900 | $4.00 | $8.00 |
| 1 | A-853 | SONGS FOR LITTLE FOLKS: THE FAIRY BOAT | GILBERT GERARD | 1901 | $4.00 | $8.00 |
| 1 | A-854 | SONGS FOR LITTLE FOLKS: THE WEDDING OF THE FROG & THE MOUSE | GILBERT GERARD | 1901 | $4.00 | $8.00 |
| 1 | A-855 | SONGS FOR LITTLE FOLKS: WILLIKENS & HIS DINAH | GILBERT GERARD | 1901 | $4.00 | $8.00 |
| 1 | A-856 | THE FABLE OF THE GOAT AND THE OX | GILBERT GERARD | 1901 | $4.00 | $8.00 |
| 1 | A-858 | A TRIP TO THE CIRCUS | GILBERT GERARD | 1901 | $4.00 | $8.00 |
| 1 | A-859 | MOTHER GOOSE & OTHER RHYMES | GILBERT GERARD | 1901 | $4.00 | $8.00 |
| 1 | M-3462 (10") | MOTHER GOOSE AND OTHER RHYMES | GILBERT GERARD | 1901 | $4.00 | $8.00 |
| 1 | A-1641 | THREE LITTLE OWLS, NAUGHTY LITTLE MICE | CAL STEWART | 1902 | $4.00 | $8.00 |
| 1 | M-859 (10") | MOTHER GOOSE & OTHER RHYMES | SPENCER AND GIRARD | 1902 | $4.00 | $8.00 |
| 1 | 2626 (7" + 10") | MOTHER GOOSE | BOB ROBERTS | 1904 | $4.00 | $8.00 |
| 1 | 2642 (10") | MOTHER GOOSE: STORIES ADAM TOLD TO EVE | HAYDN QUARTET | 1904 | $4.00 | $8.00 |
| 1 | 2738 | POP GOES THE WEASEL MEDLEY | CHARLES D'ALMAINE | 1904 | $4.00 | $8.00 |
| 1 | 2877 | DANCING IN THE BARN | VICTOR DANCE ORCH. | 1904 | $4.00 | $8.00 |
| 1 | 4554 (8") | CHILDREN'S SERIES, NO. 2: PUNCH & JUDY | LEN SPENCER | 1906 | $4.00 | $8.00 |
| 1 | 4759 (8") | CHILDREN'S SERIES, NO. 1: OLD MOTHER HUBBARD, ETC. | ALFRED HOLT | 1906 | $4.00 | $8.00 |
| 1 | 4809 (8") | CHILDREN'S SERIES, NO. 3: WYNKEN, BLYNKEN & NOD | EDGAR DAVENPORT | 1906 | $4.00 | $8.00 |
| 1 | 5202 (8") | TEDDY BEARS' PICNIC: NAUGHTY TEDDY BEARS | VICTOR ORCHESTRA | 1907 | $5.00 | $10.00 |
| 1 | 5067 | THREE LITTLE OWLS, NAUGHTY LITTLE MICE | CAL STEWART | 1907 | $4.00 | $8.00 |
| 1 | 5191 | CHILDREN'S SERIES # 4: THE TEDDY BEARS' LULLABY | HARRY MACDONOUGH | 1907 | $4.00 | $8.00 |
| 1 | 5594 (10") | TEDDY BEARS' PICNIC | ARTHUR PRYOR'S BAND | 1908 | $5.00 | $10.00 |

VICTOR RECORDS
LET'S SQUARE DANCE
$4.00

VICTOR RECORDS
LITTLE BLACK SAMBO AND THE TWINS
$80.00

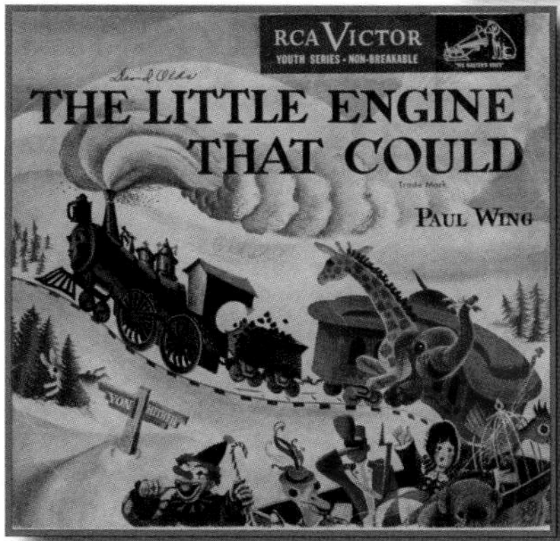


VICTOR RECORDS
THE LITTLE ENGINE THAT COULD
$20.00

## VICTOR RCA VICTOR VICTOR MISCELLANEOUS DOUBLE-SIDE 10" SINGLES

| # REC | DISC # | ARTIST | A TITLE | B TITLE | YEAR | G/VG | EX/NMT |
|---|---|---|---|---|---|---|---|
| | 21696 | SALLY HAMLIN | JACK & THE BEANSTALK, PT. 1 | JACK & THE BEANSTALK, PT. 2 | | $1.00 | $2.00 |
| | 21697 | SALLY HAMLIN | CINDERELLA, PT. 1 | CINDERELLA, PT. 2 | | $1.00 | $2.00 |
| | 21698 | SALLY HAMLIN | THE LITTLE KITTEN THAT WOULD NOT WASH ITS FACE, PT. 1 | THE LITTLE KITTEN THAT WOULD NOT WASH ITS FACE, PT. 2 | | $1.00 | $2.00 |
| | 21699 | SALLY HAMLIN | THE LITTLE DOG THAT WOULD NOT WAG ITS TAIL, PT. 1 | THE LITTLE DOG THAT WOULD NOT WAG ITS TAIL, PT. 2 | | $1.00 | $2.00 |
| | 21823 | SALLY HAMLIN | ABOU BEN ADHEM, ETC. | YEAR'S AT THE SPRING, ETC. | | $1.00 | $2.00 |
| | 21824 | SALLY HAMLIN | THE DEAR LITTLE HEN | THE LITTLE ENGINE THAT COULD | | $1.00 | $2.00 |
| | 21825 | SALLY HAMLIN | LITTLE ORPHANT ANNIE | SEEIN' THINGS AT NIGHT | | $1.00 | $2.00 |
| | 21826 | SALLY HAMLIN | JABBBERWOCKY | THE WALRUS & THE CARPENTER | | $1.00 | $2.00 |
| 1 | 22098 | NEW LIGHT SYMPHONY ORCH. | CHILDREN'S OVERTURE (PT. 1) | CHILDREN'S OVERTURE (PT. 2) | 1929 | $1.00 | $2.00 |
| 1 | 22099 | NEW LIGHT SYMPHONY ORCH. | CHILDREN'S OVERTURE (PT. 3) | CHILDREN'S OVERTURE (PT. 4) | | $1.00 | $2.00 |
| 1 | 22133 | LEWIS JAMES | SONGS FOR LITTLE PEOPLE (PT. 1) | SONGS FOR LITTLE PEOPLE (PT. 2) | | $5.00 | $10.00 |
| 1 | 22134 | LEWIS JAMES | SONGS FOR LITTLE PEOPLE (PT. 3) | SONGS FOR LITTLE PEOPLE (PT. 4) | | $5.00 | $10.00 |
| 1 | 22135 | LEWIS JAMES | SONGS FOR LITTLE PEOPLE (PT. 5) | SONGS FOR LITTLE PEOPLE (PT. 6) | | $5.00 | $10.00 |
| 1 | 22175 | VICTOR ORCHESTRA | HANSEL & GRETEL: BAREFOOT GOSLINGS, ETC. | HANSEL & GRETEL: SAND-MAN'S SONG, ETC. | | $1.00 | $2.00 |
| 1 | 22176 | VICTOR ORCHESTRA | HANSEL & GRETEL: CHILDREN'S PRAYER | HANSEL & GRETEL: WITCHES RIDE, ETC. | | $1.00 | $2.00 |
| 1 | 22620 | ANNA HOWARD | SONGS FOR CHILDREN: PLAYING BALL, ETC. | SONGS FOR CHILDREN: ON THE WAY TO SCHOOL, ETC. | 1930 | $1.00 | $2.00 |
| 1 | 22764 | VICTOR ORCHESTRA | MARCHES FOR CHILDREN: MARCH FROM "AIDA" | MARCHES FOR CHILDREN: SOLDIERS' CHORUS ("IL TRO-VATORE") | 1931 | $1.00 | $2.00 |
| 1 | 22765 | VICTOR ORCHESTRA | SKIPS FOR CHILDREN: LA PIFFERARI (THE RABBIT) | PHRASING: THEME FROM SO-NATA IN A (MOZART) | | $1.00 | $2.00 |
| 1 | 22766 | VICTOR ORCHESTRA | RHYTHM BAND: POLLY PUT THE KETTLE ON: ETC. | MARCHES FOR CHILDREN: COME LASSIES AND LADS, ETC. | | $1.00 | $2.00 |
| 1 | 22993 | ANNA HOWARD | SONGS FOR CHILDREN: OVER THE HEATHER, ETC. | SONGS FOR CHILDREN: BRAHMS' LULLABY, ETC. | | $1.00 | $2.00 |
| 1 | 24410 | FLORENCE CASE, CHARLES YONTZ | WHO'S AFRAID OF THE BIG BAD WOLF | MICKEY MOUSE AND MINNIE'S IN TOWN | 1933 | $5.00 | $10.00 |
| 1 | 24530 | ALEXANDER SCHMIDT | CHILDREN'S SONGS: GIRLS AND BOYS, ETC. | OVER THE HILLS & FAR AWAY, ETC. | | $1.00 | $2.00 |
| 1 | 24616 | RAYMOND PAIGE & ORCH. | THE WISE LITTLE HEN | THE GRASSHOPPER & THE ANTS | 1934 | $5.00 | $10.00 |
| 1 | 25419 | WAYNE KING & HIS ORCH. | MICKEY MOUSE'S BIRTHDAY PARTY | NURSERY RHYMES: LONDON BRIDGE, ETC. | | $5.00 | $10.00 |

## VICTOR RCA VICTOR VICTOR MISCELLANEOUS DOUBLE-SIDE 10" SINGLES

| # REC | DISC # | ARTIST | A TITLE | B TITLE | YEAR | G/VG | EX/NMT |
|---|---|---|---|---|---|---|---|
| 1 | 26455 | SAMMY KAYE ORCH. | WHEN YOU WISH UPON A STAR | TURN ON THE OLD MUSIC BOX | 1936 | $3.00 | $6.00 |
| 1 | 26466 | HAL KEMP & HIS ORCH. | GIVE A LITTLE WHISTLE | I'VE GOT NO STRINGS | 1939 | $5.00 | $10.00 |
| 1 | 26477 | CLIFF EDWARDS | WHEN YOU WISH UPON A STAR | GIVE A LITTLE WHISTLE | | $5.00 | $10.00 |
| 1 | 26504 | KENNY BAKER | WHEN YOU WISH UPON A STAR | ? | | $3.00 | $6.00 |
| 1 | 27499 | SAMMY KAYE ORCH. | THE RELUCTANT DRAGON | ? | 1941 | $5.00 | $10.00 |
| 1 | 45053 | VICTOR HERBERT'S ORCHESTRA | NUTCRACKER SUITE: DANSE ARABE | NUTCRACKER SUITE: DANSE CHINOISE, DANSE DES MIRLITONS | | $1.00 | $2.00 |
| 1 | 45082 | KITTY CHEATHAM | NURSERY RHYMES — NO 1: LITTLE BOY BLUE, ETC. | NURSERY RHYMES NO. 2: BAA BAA BLACK SHEEP, ETC. | 1916 | $1.00 | $2.00 |
| 1 | 45085 | CHARLES KELLOGG, BIRD IMITATIONS | NARCISSUS | SERENADE | | $1.00 | $2.00 |
| 1 | 45092 | REINALD WERRENRATH | I ATTEMPT FROM LOVE'S SICKNESS TO FLY | MY MOTHER BIDS ME BIND MY HAIR | | $1.00 | $2.00 |
| 1 | 45109 | REINALD WERRENRATH | FUZZY WUZZY | THE GYPSY TRAIL | | $1.00 | $2.00 |
| 1 | 45135 | REINALD WERRENRATH | AMERICA, STAR SPANGLED BANNER | SILENT NIGHT, HOLY NIGHT | | $1.00 | $2.00 |
| 1 | 45190 | JAMES WHITCOMB RILEY | LITTLE ORPHANT ANNIE | THE RAGGEDY MAN | | $5.00 | $10.00 |
| 1 | 45321 | LUCY ISABELLE MARSH | PEER GYNT SUITE: SOLVEJG'S CRADLE SONG | THE FIRST PRIMROSE | | $1.00 | $2.00 |
| 1 | 45387 | ROYAL DADMUN | A ROUNDUP LULLABY | ROUNDED UP IN GLORY | | $1.00 | $2.00 |
| 1 | 55054 | VICTOR HERBERT'S ORCHESTRA | BABES IN TOYLAND: MARCH OF THE TOYS | NAUGHTY MARIETTA | | $1.00 | $2.00 |
| 1 | 55092 | CHARLES KELLOGG, BIRD IMITATIONS | SOUNDS OF THE FOREST, PT. 1 | SOUNDS OF THE FOREST, PT. 2 | | $1.00 | $2.00 |
| 1 | 55095 | JAMES WHITCOMB RILEY | LOCKERBY BOOK: OUT TO OLD AUNT MARY'S | RHYMES OF CHILDHOOD: HAPPY LITTLE CRIPPLE | 1918 | $1.00 | $2.00 |
| 1 | 55096 | COMM. ROBERT PEARY | DISCOVERY OF THE NORTH POLE | A DASH FOR THE SOUTH POLE | | $10.00 | $20.00 |
| 1 | 55104 | VICTOR HERBERT'S ORCHESTRA | BABES IN TOYLAND: MILITARY BALL | BADINAGE | | $1.00 | $2.00 |
| 1 | 55108 | LUCY ISABELLE MARSH | PEER GYNT SUITE: SOLVEIG'S CRADLE SONG | THE SWALLOWS | 1919 | $1.00 | $2.00 |
| 1 | 55136 | ERNEST T. SETON | THREE SIOUX SCOUTS, PT. 1 | THREE SIOUX SCOUTS, PT. 2 | 1921 | $1.00 | $2.00 |
| 1 | 72166 | EVA GAUTHIER | PONT D'AVIGNON, ETC. | AS TU VU LA CASQUETTE, ETC. | | $1.00 | $2.00 |
| 1 | 73366 | INTERNATIONAL NOVELTY ORCH. | PARADE OF THE WOODEN SOLDIERS | TWINKLING STAR | | $1.00 | $2.00 |
| 1 | 82092 | SINFONIA TONTA | EL RATON VOLADOR (THE FLYING MOUSE) | ? | | $2.00 | $4.00 |

## VICTOR RCA VICTOR VICTOR MISCELLANEOUS DOUBLE-SIDE 12" SINGLES

| # REC | DISC # | ARTIST | A TITLE | B TITLE | YEAR | G/VG | EX/NMT |
|---|---|---|---|---|---|---|---|
| 1 | 35028 | ARTHUR PRYOR'S BAND | MY MARYLAND FANTASIE | DEATH OF CUSTER | 1908 | $1.00 | $2.00 |
| 1 | 35157 | ARTHUR PRYOR'S BAND | STABAT MATER-CUJUS ANIMAM | FUNERAL MARCH (CHOPIN) | 1910 | $1.00 | $2.00 |
| 1 | 35188 | ARTHUR PRYOR'S BAND | KNEE-DEEP IN JUNE | KENTUCKY BABE | 1911 | $1.00 | $2.00 |
| 1 | 35204 | VICTOR MILITARY BAND | OUR DIRECTOR'S MARCH | ROYAL TRUMPETER'S MARCH | | $1.00 | $2.00 |
| 1 | 35225 | ELIZABETH WHEELER | MOTHER GOOSE NO. 2: BEAN PORRIDGE HOT, ETC. | VOWEL SONGS | 1912 | $1.00 | $2.00 |
| 1 | 35243 | VICTOR CONCERT ORCH. | SURPRISE SYMPHONY (NO. 94 IN G): "ALLEGRO" (HAYDN) | SURPRISE SYMPHONY (NO. 94 IN G): "ANDANTE" (HAYDN) | | $1.00 | $2.00 |
| 1 | 35244 | VICTOR CONCERT ORCH. | SURPRISE SYMPHONY (NO. 94 IN G): "ADAGIO" (HAYDN) | SURPRISE SYMPHONY (NO. 94 IN G): "MINUETTO" (HAYDN) | | $1.00 | $2.00 |
| 1 | 35262 | GEORGENE FAULKNER | GOLDILOCKS & THE THREE BEARS | CHICKEN LITTLE | 1913 | $2.00 | $4.00 |
| 1 | 35265 | VESSELLA & HIS ITALIAN BAND | AIDA (VERDI): GRAND MARCH | RONDO CAPRICCIOSO (MENDELSSOHN) | | $1.00 | $2.00 |
| 1 | 35276 | VESSELLA & HIS ITALIAN BAND | MORNING, NOON AND NIGHT IN VIENNA (VON SUPPE) | ALESSANDRO STRADELLA OVERTURE (FLOTOW) | | $1.00 | $2.00 |
| 1 | 35290 | WILLIAM DE WOLF | CASEY AT THE BAT | MAN WHO FANNED CASEY | | $8.00 | $15.00 |
| 1 | 35291 | HARRY HUMPHREY | DECLARATION OF INDEPENDENCE | DECLARATION OF INDEPENDENCE | | $3.00 | $6.00 |
| 1 | 35293 | GEORGENE FAULKNER | PANCAKE STORY | THE FOX AS HERDSMAN | | $2.00 | $4.00 |
| 1 | 35311 | VICTOR CONCERT ORCH. | MILITARY SYMPHONY (NO. 100 IN G MAJOR): ALLEGRO | MILITARY SYMPHONY (NO. 100 IN G): ALLEGRETTO | | $1.00 | $2.00 |
| 1 | 35324 | VICTOR ORCHESTRA | HUNT IN THE BLACK FOREST | IN A CLOCK STORE | | $1.00 | $2.00 |
| 1 | 35350 | CORA MEL PATTEN | DOLL'S WOOING, THE SUGAR PLUM TREE | JEST 'FORE CHRISTMAS, THE SUGAR-PLUM TREE | | $1.00 | $2.00 |

VICTOR RECORDS
LITTLE JOHNNY EVERYTHING
$20.00

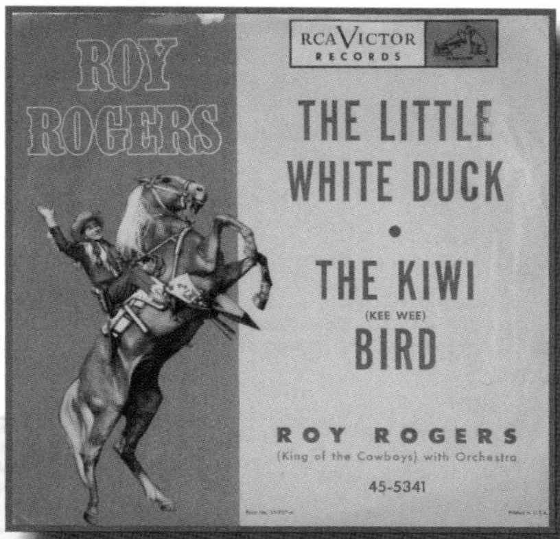


VICTOR RECORDS
LITTLE WHITE DUCK
$6.00

VICTOR RECORDS
LUDWIG BEMELMAN'S MADELINE
$2.00

## VICTOR RCA VICTOR VICTOR MISCELLANEOUS DOUBLE-SIDE 12" SINGLES

| # REC | DISC # | ARTIST | A TITLE | B TITLE | YEAR | G/VG | EX/NMT |
|---|---|---|---|---|---|---|---|
| 1 | 35351 | HARRY HUMPHREY | MEDLEY: SEA SONGS | MEDLEY: WAR SONGS | | $1.00 | $2.00 |
| 1 | 35377 | HARRY HUMPHREY | LINCOLN'S GETTYSBURG ADDRESS | GIVE ME LIBERTY OR GIVE ME DEATH! | | $8.00 | $15.00 |
| 1 | 35378 | ELSIE BAKER | THE BEAR STORY THAT ALEX YIST MADE UP | THE BEAR STORY THAT ALEX YIST MADE UP | | $2.00 | $4.00 |
| 1 | 35398 | ELSIE BAKER | HOME, SWEET HOME | OLD FOLKS AT HOME | | $1.00 | $2.00 |
| 1 | 35412 | VICTOR ORATORIO CHORUS | IT CAME UPON THE MIDNIGHT CLEAR | WHILE SHEPHERDS WATCHED THEIR FLOCKS AT NIGHT | | $1.00 | $2.00 |
| 1 | 35413 | VICTOR LIGHT OPERA CO. | GEMS FROM ROBIN HOOD (PT. 1) | GEMS FROM ROBIN HOOD (PT. 2) | | $2.00 | $4.00 |
| 1 | 35418 | GEORGENE FAULKNER | THE GINGERBREAD BOY | THE NIGHT BEFORE CHRISTMAS | | $2.00 | $4.00 |
| 1 | 35443 | OLIVE KLINE | TROVATORE (VERDI): HOME TO OUR MOUNTAINS | TROVATORE: MISERERE | 1915 | $1.00 | $2.00 |
| 1 | 35447 | PAULINE POTTER | CINDERELLA | LITTLE RED RIDING HOOD | | $2.00 | $4.00 |
| 1 | 35448 | JULIUS SCHENDEL | PAPILLON, RUSTLE OF SPRING | WALKURE: MAGIC FIRE SCENE | | $2.00 | $4.00 |
| 1 | 35467 | SOUSA'S BAND | THE DYING POET | THE LAST HOPE | | $1.00 | $2.00 |
| 1 | 35470 | VICTOR CONCERT ORCH. | PEER GYNT: MORNING | PEER GYNT: DEATH OF ASE | | $1.00 | $2.00 |
| 1 | 35482 | VICTOR CONCERT ORCH. | SYMPHONY IN G MINOR (MOZART): ALLEGRO MOLTO (1ST MVT.) | SYMPHONY IN G MINOR: ANDANTE (2ND MVT.) | | $1.00 | $2.00 |
| 1 | 35489 | VICTOR CONCERT ORCH. | SYMPHONY IN G MINOR (MOZART): MENUETTO (3RD MVT.) | SYMPHONY IN G MINOR: ALLEGRO (4TH MVT.) | | $1.00 | $2.00 |
| 1 | 35513 | VICTOR MIXED CHORUS | MEDLEYS: SONGS OF IRELAND | MEDLEYS: SONGS OF SCOTLAND | 1916 | $1.00 | $2.00 |
| 1 | 35525 | PATRICK CONWAY'S BAND | STEPHEN FOSTER GEMS | MEMORIES OF THE WAR (1861 – 1863) | | $1.00 | $2.00 |
| 1 | 35530 | PATRICK CONWAY'S BAND | HENRY VIII: MORRIS DANCE, HENRY VII: SHEPHERD'S DANCE | NELL GWYNN: COUNTRY DANCE | | $1.00 | $2.00 |
| 1 | 35532 | VICTOR MILITARY BAND | CUPID AND THE BUTTERFLY | DOROTHY THREE-STEP | | $1.00 | $2.00 |
| 1 | 35543 | VICTOR CONCERT ORCH. | MORNING, NOON AND NIGHT IN VIENNA (VON SUPPE) | MORNING, NOON AND NIGHT IN VIENNA (VON SUPPE) | | $1.00 | $2.00 |
| 1 | 35555 | WILLIAM S. BATTIS | PAUL REVERE'S RIDE | THE RISING OF '76 | | $1.00 | $2.00 |
| | 35556 | WILLIAM S. BATTIS | DAVID COPPERFIELD: MICAWBER | DAVID COPPERFIELD: URIAH HEEP | | $1.00 | $2.00 |
| 1 | 35558 | VICTOR MIXED CHORUS | MEDLEY: SONGS OF THE PAST, NO. 13 | MEDLEY: SONGS OF THE PAST, NO. 14 | | $1.00 | $2.00 |
| 1 | 35559 | HURTADO BROS. ROYAL MARIMBA BAND | AIDA: SELECTIONS | LUCIA DI LAMMERMOOR (DONIZETTI): SEXTET | | $1.00 | $2.00 |
| 1 | 35563 | WILLIAM S. BATTIS | TOM SAWYER: HOW TOM WHITEWASHED THE FENCE | INNOCENTS ABROAD: OUR GUIDE IN GENOA | | $1.00 | $2.00 |
| 1 | 35566 | WILLIAM S. BATTIS | DICKENS' "A CHRISTMAS CAROL": GHOST OF CHRISTMAS PAST | DICKENS' "A CHRISTMAS CAROL": MARLEY'S GHOST | | $2.00 | $4.00 |
| 1 | 35567 | WILLIAM S. BATTIS | GHOST OF CHRISTMAS PRESENT | GHOST OF CHRISTMAS TO COME | | $2.00 | $4.00 |
| 1 | 35568 | VICTOR MIXED CHORUS | MEDLEYS: SONGS OF THE PAST, NO. 15 | MEDLEYS: SONGS OF THE PAST, NO. 16 | | $1.00 | $2.00 |
| 1 | 35594 | TRINITY CHOIR | ANGELS FROM THE REALMS OF GLORY | OH, LITTLE TOWN OF BETHLEHEM | | $2.00 | $4.00 |

## VICTOR RCA VICTOR VICTOR MISCELLANEOUS DOUBLE-SIDE 10" SINGLES

| # REC | DISC # | ARTIST | A TITLE | B TITLE | YEAR | G/VG | EX/NMT |
|---|---|---|---|---|---|---|---|
| 1 | 35613 | VICTOR MIXED CHORUS | SACRED SONGS NO. 1 AND 2 | SACRED SONGS NO. 2 | 1917 | $1.00 | $2.00 |
| 1 | 35617 | ELSIE BAKER | HIAWATHA'S CHILDHOOD | HIAWATHA'S CHILDHOOD | | $2.00 | $4.00 |
| 1 | 35620 | VICTOR MIXED CHORUS | GOSPEL SONGS, NO.3 | GOSPEL SONGS, NO. 4 | | $1.00 | $2.00 |
| 1 | 35625 | VICTOR CONCERT ORCH. | MIDSUMMER-NIGHT'S DREAM: OVERTURE (MENDELSSOHN) | PRELUDE IN C SHARP MINOR (RACH-MANINOFF) | | $1.00 | $2.00 |
| 1 | 35636 | SARA CONE BRYANT | EPAMINODAS | THE LITTLE JACKAL AND THE ALLIGATOR | | $1.00 | $2.00 |
| 1 | 35642 | VICTOR CONCERT ORCH. | THE DYING POET | WHISPERING FLOWERS | | $1.00 | $2.00 |
| 1 | 35643 | SARA CONE BRYANT | THE DOG AND THE KITTY CATS, THE PIG BROTHER | THE LITTLE BUL CALF | | $1.00 | $2.00 |
| 1 | 35644 | VICTOR CONCERT ORCH. | SPANISH DANCE NO. 2, IN G MINOR | RECONCILIATION POLKA | | $1.00 | $2.00 |
| 1 | 35652 | SALLY HAMLIN | POLYANNA ARRIVES | POLYANNA AND THE BOY | | $1.00 | $2.00 |
| 1 | 35653 | WILLIAM S. BATTIS | COLUMBUS | LANDING OF THE PILGRIM FATHERS, GOD GIVE US MEN | | $1.00 | $2.00 |
| 1 | 35655 | VICTOR CONCERT ORCH. | AMOUREUSE WALTZ | VILLAGE SWALLOWS WALTZ | | $1.00 | $2.00 |
| 1 | 35656 | VICTOR CONCERT ORCH. | SUITE IN D MAJOR: GAVOTTES NOS. 1 AND 2 (BACH) | SUITE IN D MAJOR: AIR FOR G STRING (BACH) | | $1.00 | $2.00 |
| 1 | 35661 | VICTOR MIXED CHORUS | IT CAME UPON THE MIDNIGHT CLEAR | SING, O HEAVENS | | $1.00 | $2.00 |
| 1 | 35664 | SALLY HAMLIN | JACK AND THE BEANSTALK | CINDERELLA | | $1.00 | $2.00 |
| 1 | 35668 | VICTOR CONCERT ORCH. | SUITE ALGERIENNE: MARCHE MILI-TAIRE FRANÇAISE (ST. SAENS) | SUITE ALGERIENNE: RÉVERIE DU SOIR | | $1.00 | $2.00 |
| 1 | 35679 | GILBERT GIRARD | SANTA CLAUS TALKS ABOUT HIS TOY SHOP | SANTA GIVES AWAY HIS TOYS | 1918 | $5.00 | $10.00 |
| 1 | 35693 | LAURA LITTLEFIELD | AH, LOVE, BUT A DAY, THE YEAR'S AT THE SPRING | IRISH FOLK SONG | 1920 | $1.00 | $2.00 |
| 1 | 35710 | VICTOR CONCERT ORCH. | IN A MONASTERY GARDEN | ROMANCE (TCHAIKOVSKY) | 1921 | $1.00 | $2.00 |
| 1 | 35711 | GILBERT GIRARD | SANTA VISITS THE CHILDREN, PT. 1 | SANTA VISITS THE CHILDREN, PT. 2 | | $3.00 | $6.00 |
| 1 | 35712 | TRINITY CHOIR | CHRISTMAS HYMNS AND CAROLS, NOS. 1 | CHRISTMAS HYMNS AND CAROLS, NOS. 2 | | $1.00 | $2.00 |
| 1 | 35717 | VICTOR SYMPHONY ORCH. | NUTCRACKER SUITE: WALTZ OF THE FLOWERS | TRAVIATA-PRELUDE | 1922 | $1.00 | $2.00 |
| 1 | 35730 | VICTOR SYMPHONY ORCH. | FUNERAL MARCH OF A MARI-ONETTE | SPRING MORNING | 1924 | $1.00 | $2.00 |
| 1 | 35733 | VICTOR SYMPHONY ORCH. | DER FREISCHUTZ: OVERTURE (WEBER), PT. 1 | DER FREISCHUTZ: OVERTURE (WEBER), PT. 2 | | $1.00 | $2.00 |
| 1 | 35735 | VICTOR SYMPHONY ORCH. | MARTA — OVERTURE (FLOTOW), PT. 1 | MARTA — OVERTURE (FLOTOW), PT. 2 | | $1.00 | $2.00 |
| 1 | 35738 | ARTHUR PRYOR'S BAND | CHIMES OF NORMANDY | POET AND PEASANT OVERTURE | | $1.00 | $2.00 |
| 1 | 35745 | VICTOR BAND | POPULARITY MARCH (PT. 1) | POPULARITY MARCH (PT. 2) | | $1.00 | $2.00 |
| 1 | 35746 | H.M. COLDSTREAM GUARDS BAND | SPORTSMANSHIP (PRINCE OF WALES) | GOD BLESS THE PRINCE OF WALES | | $1.00 | $2.00 |
| 1 | 35749 | VICTOR CONCERT ORCH. | PRIMEVAL SUITE: DEER DANCE (SKILTON) | PRIMEVAL SUITE: GAMBLING SONG | | $1.00 | $2.00 |
| 1 | 35788 | TRINITY CHOIR | CHRISTMAS HYMNS AND CAROLS (PT. 1) | CHRISTMAS HYMNS AND CAROLS (PT. 2) | 1925 | $1.00 | $2.00 |
| 1 | 35946 | TRINITY CHOIR | CHRISTMAS HYMNS AND CAROLS (PT. 3) | CHRISTMAS HYMNS AND CAROLS (PT. 4) | | $1.00 | $2.00 |
| 1 | 36032 | ? | SONGS FOR CHILDREN (FROM THE MUSIC HOUR) | SONGS FOR CHILDREN (FROM THE MUSIC HOUR) | 1931 | $1.00 | $2.00 |
| 1 | 36033 | ? | SONGS FOR CHILDREN (FROM THE MUSIC HOUR) | SONGS FOR CHILDREN (FROM THE MUSIC HOUR) | | $1.00 | $2.00 |

## VICTOR RCA VICTOR VICTOR LABEL VARIATIONS 10" SINGLES

| # REC | DISC # | MAIN TITLE | ARTIST | G/VG | EX/NMT |
|---|---|---|---|---|---|
| 1 | 859 | MOTHER GOOSE & OTHER RHYMES | SPENCER & GIRARD | $20.00 | $40.00 |
| 1 | 87094 | A CHILD'S PRAYER | ERNESTINE SCHUMANN HEINK | $8.00 | $15.00 |

## VOCO PICTURE DISCS 6" AND 7" SINGLES AND BOXED SETS

| # REC | DISC # | ARTIST | A TITLE | B TITLE | G/VG | EX/NMT |
|---|---|---|---|---|---|---|
| 1 | X528/X628 | VOCO ORCH. WITH VOCO-LIST/VOCO ORCH.WITH VOCO-CHOIR | AWAY IN A MANGER | SILENT NIGHT | $3.00 | $6.00 |
| 1 | X529/X629 | VOCO ORCH. WITH VOCO-LIST | SANTA CLAUS COMES CALLING | O LITTLE TOWN OF BETHLEHEM | $3.00 | $6.00 |
| 1 | X530/X630 | VOCO ORCH. WITH VOCO-LIST | SANTA'S TOY SHOP | THE FIRST NOEL | $3.00 | $6.00 |
| 1 | X531/X631 | VOCO ORCH. WITH VOCO-LIST | TWAS THE NIGHT BEFORE CHRISTMAS (PT. 1) | TWAS THE NIGHT BEFORE CHRISTMAS (PT. 2) | $3.00 | $6.00 |
| 1 | X524/X624-2 | VOCO ORCH. WITH VOCO-CHOIR | HARK! THE HERALD ANGELS SING | JOY TO THE WORLD | $3.00 | $6.00 |
| 1 | X525/X625-2 | VOCO ORCH. WITH VOCO-CHOIR | DECK THE HALLS | GOD REST YOU, MERRY GENTLEMEN | $3.00 | $6.00 |
| 1 | X526/X626-2 | VOCO ORCH. WITH VOCO-LIST | A LETTER TO SANTA CLAUS | ADESTE FIDELES — COME ALL YE FAITHFUL | $3.00 | $6.00 |
| 1 | X527/X627-2 | VOCO ORCH. WITH VOCO-CHOIR | THE CHRISTMAS PUNCH AND JUDY SHOW | IT CAME UPON THE MIDNIGHT CLEAR | $5.00 | $10.00 |
| 1 | X528/X628-2 | VOCO ORCH. WITH VOCO-LIST/VOCO ORCH. WITH VOCO-CHOIR | AWAY IN A MANGER | SILENT NIGHT | $3.00 | $6.00 |
| 1 | X529/X629-2 | VOCO ORCH. WITH VOCO-LIST | SANTA CLAUS COMES CALLING | O LITTLE TOWN OF BETHLEHEM | $3.00 | $6.00 |
| 1 | X530/X630-2 | VOCO ORCH. WITH VOCO-LIST | SANTA'S TOY SHOP | THE FIRST NOEL | $3.00 | $6.00 |
| 1 | X531/X631-2 | VOCO ORCH. WITH VOCO-LIST | TWAS THE NIGHT BEFORE CHRISTMAS (PT. 1) | TWAS THE NIGHT BEFORE CHRISTMAS (PT. 2) | $3.00 | $6.00 |
| 1 | 533/633 | VOCO ORCH. WITH VOCO-LIST | WHAT WOULD YOU LIKE TO DO | HOME ON THE RANGE | $3.00 | $6.00 |
| 1 | 534/634 | VOCO RANGERS | SOURWOOD MOUNTAIN | THE LONE PRAIRIE | $3.00 | $6.00 |
| 1 | 535/635 | VOCO ORCH. WITH VOCO-LIST/VOCO RANGERS | THE SCARECROW IN THE CORNFIELD | RED RIVER VALLEY | $3.00 | $6.00 |
| 1 | 536/636 | VOCO RANGERS | THE OLD CHISHOLM TRAIL | THE BIG ROCK CANDY MOUNTAIN | $3.00 | $6.00 |
| 1 | 537/637 | VOCO RANGERS | SPUNKEY THE MONKEY | SHE'LL BE COMIN' AROUN' THE MOUNTAIN | $3.00 | $6.00 |
| 1 | 538/638 | VOCO RANGERS | BUSTER THE BRONCO BUSTER | GIT ALONG LITTLE DOGIE | $3.00 | $6.00 |
| 1 | 539/639 | VOCO ORCH. WITH VOCO-LIST/VOCO RANGERS | THE ALPHABET SONG | JACK AND JILL | $3.00 | $6.00 |
| 1 | 701/801 | BOB KENNEDY | THE RINGMASTER OF THE CIRCUS | OFF TO THE CIRCUS | $15.00 | $30.00 |
| 1 | 702/802 | BOB KENNEDY | TOM CAT THE TIGHTROPE WALKER | CIRCUS ANIMALS | $15.00 | $30.00 |
| 1 | 703/803 | BOB KENNEDY | ROVER THE STRONGMAN | SIDE SHOW | $15.00 | $30.00 |
| 1 | 704/804 | BOB KENNEDY | THE ELEPHANT CLOWN | CIRCUS SIGHTS | $15.00 | $30.00 |
| 1 | EB1/EB2 | TOBY DEANE | THE BUNNY EASTER PARTY | HAVING FUN AT THE BUNNY EASTER PARTY | $10.00 | $20.00 |
| 1 | SC1/SC1A | NOT LISTED | I WISH THAT I WERE SANTA CLAUS | JINGLE BELLS | $10.00 | $20.00 |

## VOCO NONPICTURE DISCS 7" SERIES SINGLES

| # REC | DISC # | ARTIST | A TITLE | B TITLE | YEAR | G/VG | EX/NMT |
|---|---|---|---|---|---|---|---|
| 1 | V-11 | VOCO ORCH., CHORUS AND VOCO-LIST | SKIP TO MY LOU | DID YOU EVER SEE A LASSIE? | 1949 | $1.00 | $2.00 |
| 1 | V-12 | VOCO ORCH., CHORUS AND VOCO-LIST | THE MUFFIN MAN | LITTLE BOY BLUE | | $1.00 | $2.00 |
| 1 | V-14 | VOCO ORCH., CHORUS AND VOCO-LIST | TEN LITTLE INDIANS | OH DEAR WHAT CAN THE MATTER BE? | | $1.00 | $2.00 |
| 1 | V-15 | VOCO ORCH., CHORUS AND VOCO-LIST | GOOD MORNING MARY SUNSHINE | LAZY MARY | | $1.00 | $2.00 |
| 1 | V-16 | VOCO ORCH., CHORUS AND VOCO-LIST | SIMPLE SIMON | OLD MCDONALD | | $1.00 | $2.00 |
| 1 | V-17 | VOCO ORCH., CHORUS AND VOCO-LIST | ROCKABYE BABY | BRAHMS' LULLABY | | $1.00 | $2.00 |
| 1 | V-18 | VOCO ORCH., CHORUS AND VOCO-LIST | AMERICA THE BEAUTIFUL | CAMPTOWN RACES | | $1.00 | $2.00 |
| 1 | V-19 | VOCO ORCH., CHORUS AND VOCO-LIST | ARKANSAS TRAVELER | FIDDLE DEE DEE | | $1.00 | $2.00 |
| 1 | V-20 | TOBY DEANE/KAY ARMEN | THE FARMER IN THE DELL | THE COUNTING SONG | | $1.00 | $2.00 |
| 1 | V-21 | TOBY DEANE/KAY ARMEN | THREE LITTLE KITTENS | WASH YOUR HANDS, BRUSH YOUR TEETH | | $1.00 | $2.00 |
| 1 | V-22 | TOBY DEANE/KAY ARMEN) | LONDON BRIDGE | MIND YOUR MOMMY | | $1.00 | $2.00 |
| 1 | V-23 | TOBY DEANE/BOB KENNEDY | POP GOES THE WEASEL | HIPPITY HOP BUNNY | | $1.00 | $2.00 |
| 1 | V-24 | TOBY DEANE/BOB KENNEDY | YANKEE DOODLE | LAUGH LAUGH PHONOGRAPH | | $3.00 | $6.00 |
| 1 | V-25 | TOBY DEANE | THREE BLIND MICE | WOULD YOU RATHER BE AN ELEPHANT | | $1.00 | $2.00 |
| 1 | V-26 | TOBY DEANE | DINKY THE DOGGIE | I TISKET, I TASKET | | $1.00 | $2.00 |
| 1 | V-27 | NOT LISTED/JOHNNY OLSEN | BE YOUR MOTHER'S LITTLE HELPER | BAA, BAA, BLACK SHEEP | | $1.00 | $2.00 |
| 1 | V-28 | BOB KENNEDY/GINNY GIBSON | JACK AND THE BEANSTALK | ONE TWO BUCKLE MY SHOE | 1951 | $1.00 | $2.00 |

VICTOR RECORDS
THE STORY OF PAUL BUNYAN
$4.00

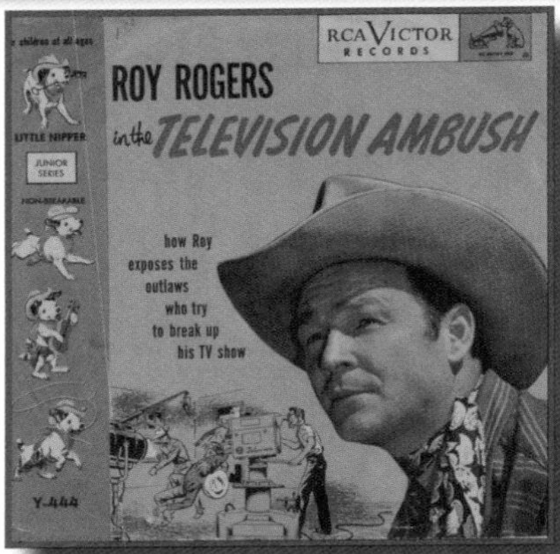


VICTOR RECORDS
THE TELEVISION AMBUSH
$30.00

VICTOR RECORDS
THE THING
$50.00

## VOCO NONPICTURE DISCS 7" SERIES SINGLES

| # REC | DISC # | ARTIST | A TITLE | B TITLE | YEAR | G/VG | EX/NMT |
|---|---|---|---|---|---|---|---|
| 1 | V-29 | BOB KENNEDY/BERNIE KNEE, GINNY GIBSON | HANSEL AND GRETEL | ROW ROW ROW YOUR BOAT, BROTHER JOHN | | $1.00 | $2.00 |
| 1 | V-30 | GINNY GIBSON/BERNIE KNEE | LOOBY LOO | LITTLE RED RIDING HOOD | | $1.00 | $2.00 |
| 1 | V-31 | BOB KENNEDY, TOBY DEANE, BOB MALLIT, VOCO ORCH. | THE THREE BEARS (PT. 1) | THE THREE BEARS (PT. 2) | | $1.00 | $2.00 |
| 1 | V-32 | TOBY DEANE, BOB MALLIT | THE THREE LITTLE PIGS (PT. 1) | THE THREE LITTLE PIGS (PT. 2) | | $1.00 | $2.00 |
| 1 | V-33 | BOB KENNEDY, GINNY GIBSON | CINDERELLA (PT. 1) | CINDERELLA (PT. 2) | | $1.00 | $2.00 |
| 1 | V-34 | TODD MANNERS, GINNY GIBSON | ALICE IN WONDERLAND (PT. 1) | ALICE IN WONDERLAND (PT. 2) | | $1.00 | $2.00 |
| 1 | V-35 | BUD ROMAN, LAURIE WAYNE, RAY BAXTER ORCH./BOB KENNEDY | TELL ME A STORY | OH SUZANNA | | $1.00 | $2.00 |
| 1 | V-36 | PAT FARWELL, DAVID BOHME & ORCH. | A TRIP IN A ROCKET SHIP (PT. 1) | A TRIP IN A ROCKET SHIP (PT. 2) | | $3.00 | $6.00 |
| 1 | V-37 | BETSY GAY | WEE WILLIE THE WHALE | WEE WILLIE THE WHALE | | $3.00 | $6.00 |
| 1 | V-38 | BETSY GAY | THE ZEBRA WHO LOST HER STRIPES (PT. 1) | THE ZEBRA WHO LOST HER STRIPES (PT. 2) | | $2.00 | $4.00 |
| 1 | V-39 | PAT FARWELL | BENNY THE HUNGRY GOAT (PT. 1) | BENNY THE HUNGRY GOAT (PT. 2) | | $1.00 | $2.00 |
| 1 | V-40 | GENE GULLIKSEN | THE HAPPY CLOCKS (PT. 1) | THE HAPPY CLOCKS (PT. 2) | | $1.00 | $2.00 |
| 1 | V-41 | MIMI MARTEL, THE HAL LOMAN ORCH./BOB KENNEDY, TOPS ORCH. | DOGGIE IN THE WINDOW | A FROG WENT WALKING | | $2.00 | $4.00 |
| 1 | VX-101 | THE MARINERS/BOB KENNEDY, VOCO ORCH. | JINGLE BELLS | I WISH I WERE SANTA CLAUS | | $2.00 | $4.00 |
| 1 | 501/601 | KAY ARMEN/TOBY DEANE | THE COUNTING SONG | THE FARMER IN THE DELL | 1950 | $3.00 | $6.00 |
| 1 | 502/602 | KAY ARMEN/TOBY DEANE | WASH YOUR HANDS, BRUSH YOUR TEETH | THREE LITTLE KITTENS | | $3.00 | $6.00 |
| 1 | 503/603 | KAY ARMEN/TOBY DEANE | MIND YOUR MOMMY | LONDON BRIDGE | | $3.00 | $6.00 |
| 1 | 504/604 | BOB KENNEDY/TOBY DEANE | ROLY POLY | OLD MACDONALD HAD A FARM | | $3.00 | $6.00 |
| 1 | 505/605 | BOB KENNEDY/TOBY DEANE | HIPPITY HOP BUNNY | POP GOES THE WEASEL | | $3.00 | $6.00 |
| 1 | 506/606 | TOBY DEANE/BOB KENNEDY | LAUGH LAUGH PHONO-GRAPH | YANKEE DOODLE | | $8.00 | $15.00 |
| 1 | 507/607 | TOBY DEANE/BOB KENNEDY | KITTY CAT | TEN LITTLE INDIANS | | $3.00 | $6.00 |
| 1 | 508/608 | TOBY DEANE | WOULD YOU RATHER BE AN ELEPHANT | THREE BLIND MICE | | $3.00 | $6.00 |
| 1 | 509/609 | TOBY DEANE | DINKY THE DOGGIE | I TISKET, I TASKET | | $3.00 | $6.00 |
| 1 | 510/610 | BOB KENNEDY/TOBY DEANE | THE LITTLE MOUNTAIN CLIMBER | ROUND AND ROUND THE VILLAGE | | $3.00 | $6.00 |
| 1 | 511/611 | JOHNNY OLSEN/NOT LISTED | BE YOUR MOTHER'S LITTLE HELPER | BAA BAA BLACK SHEEP | | $3.00 | $6.00 |
| 1 | 512/612 | NOT LISTED | EARLY TO BED, EARLY TO RISE... | HOW I WONDER WHAT YOU ARE | | $3.00 | $6.00 |
| 1 | 513/613 | NOT LISTED | NELLIE NEAT | MARY HAD A LITTLE LAMB | | $3.00 | $6.00 |

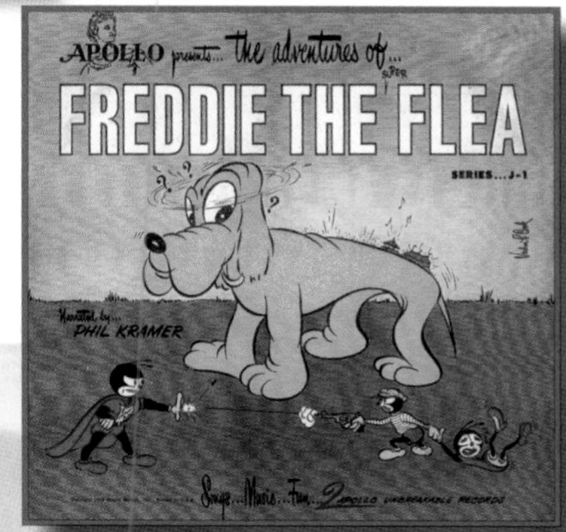


APOLLO RECORDS
FREDDIE THE FLEA
$20.00

ARROW RECORDS
JACK AND HOMER
$80.00

ATLANTIC RECORDS
THE EVER-SO-MANY AMAZING ADVENTURES OF JOHNNY
$15.00

## MISCELLANEOUS LARGE SINGLES AND DOUBLES 9", 10", AND 12"

| LABEL | SET # / DISC # | # REC | MAIN TITLE | ARTIST | YEAR | G/VG | EX/NMT | REMARKS |
|---|---|---|---|---|---|---|---|---|
| CNC PRODUCTIONS | PC 7203/4 | 1 | UNCLE JOHNNY COONS AND HIS AUTOMATIC MOUSE TRAP | UNCLE JOHNNY COONS | 195? | $4.00 | $8.00 | |
| CREST | CT-2 | 2 | AESOP'S FABLES/THE BOY WHO CRIED WOLF | STERLING HOLLOWAY | 194? | $20.00 | $40.00 | |
| CROSS | CR-1 (12") | 1 | THE ENGINE THAT LOST ITS WHISTLE | DALE CROSS | 1948 | $8.00 | $15.00 | |
| CROSS | CR-2 (12") | 1 | FLUFF & THE FIREMEN | DALE CROSS | 1948 | $8.00 | $15.00 | |
| DAIRY COUNCIL HEALTH PLATTER | R161 | 1 | BE FRIENDLY WITH THE HEALTHIES/3 SONGS FROM "HEALTH NOTES" | PUPILS OF MAYFAIR SCHOOL, PHILA, PA | 195? | $1.00 | $2.00 | |
| DALLAS | NO # | 1 | SONGS FOR SUBURBAN CHIL-DREN: YOU CAN FLY, ETC.* | DENISE FOSTER, BOB ROGERS & HIS ORCH. | 1957 | $1.00 | $2.00 | |
| DAMON | D.K. 1 (1055-6) | 2 | THE KITTEN & THE CLOCK, ETC./THE HORSE WITH THE CURLY TAIL, ETC. | MABEL MARTIN GEORGE | 1948 | $3.00 | $6.00 | |
| DAMON | D.K. 2 (?) | 2 | HAPPY LUCKY DUCK, ETC./ MENO MONKEY, ETC. | MABEL MARTIN GEORGE | 1948 | $3.00 | $6.00 | |
| DANA | 5000 | 1 | OLD KRIS KRINGLE/HAPPY NEW YEAR | JEFFREY CLAY & THE SER-ENADERS, GUS DANA | 1948 | $2.00 | $4.00 | |

*AUTOGRAPHED ON LABEL

AUDIO VISUAL MATERIAL
MUSIC FOR MOVEMENT
$4.00

BOSCO CHOCOLATE SYRUP
TOM THUMB
$10.00

BOY SCOUTS OF AMERICA
LEARN THE INTERNATIONAL MORSE CODE
$8.00

BROADWAY CHILDREN SERIES
6 MUSICAL STORIES
$2.00

BROWN SHOE CO.
MARCHING SONG
$15.00

BREMNER MULTIPLICATION RECORDS
MUSICAL MULTIPLICATION TABLES
$15.00

## MISCELLANEOUS LARGE SINGLES AND DOUBLES 9", 10", AND 12"

| LABEL | SET #/DISC # | # REC | MAIN TITLE | ARTIST | YEAR | G/VG | EX/NMT |
|---|---|---|---|---|---|---|---|
| DANA | 5001 | 1 | THREE MEN IN A TUB/LET'S DANCE TO THE ABC, THE COUNTING SONG | JEFFREY CLAY & THE SERENADERS, GUS DANA | 1948 | $2.00 | $4.00 |
| DANA | 5002 | 1 | TOM TOM THE PIPER'S SON | JEFFREY CLAY & THE SERENADERS, GUS DANA | 1948 | $2.00 | $4.00 |
| DISCOVERY | 531 | 1 | MOLASSES, MOLASSES/EV'RYBODY CLAP HANDS | LENNY CARSON & THE WHIZ KIDS | 194? | $3.00 | $6.00 |
| DIVA | 1001 | 1 | PHROOMF/SANTA'S RIDE | JOHNNIE LEE WILLS & HIS BOYS | 195? | $1.00 | $2.00 |
| DOMINION | FR 112 | 1 | KRINCHY KRONCHY/LITTLE FROGGIE, ETC. | CARL FREDRICKSON | 1951 | $3.00 | $6.00 |
| DOMINO | 0149 | 1 | KIDDIE PATROL/KIDDIE DANCE | WALTER ROGERS | 192? | $2.00 | $4.00 |
| DOT | 1240 | 1 | THE BALLAD OF DAVY CROCKETT/ DANGER! HEARTBREAK AHEAD (NON-KIDDIE) | MAC WISEMAN | 1955 | $5.00 | $10.00 |
| ERMA HAYDEN | CH 682-3 | 1 | MARCH, SAD DANCE, GAY DANCE, ETC. | ERMA HAYDEN | 196? | ¢.50 | $1.00 |
| EPIC (COLUMBIA) | 9004 | 1 | SHE WAS FIVE AND HE WAS TEN/A RIDE IN SANTA'S SLEIGH | JUDY VALENTINE | 195? | $1.00 | $2.00 |
| FANTASY | 526 | 1 | ALICE IN WONDERLAND/ALL THE THINGS YOU ARE (NON-KIDDIE) | DAVE BRUBECK QUARTET | 195? | $5.00 | $10.00 |
| FOLKWAYS | F105 | 1 | SONGS TO GROW ON: WAKE UP, CAR SONG/CLEAN-O, DANCE AROUND | WOODY GUTHRIE | 1951 | $25.00 | $50.00 |
| FUN 'N FROLIC | VOL 1: K701 - 2 | 2 | BUNNY HOP, ETC. | HENRY KNIGHT, THE MERRY MAESTROS | 195? | $1.00 | $2.00 |
| FUN 'N FROLIC | VOL 2: K703 - 4 | 2 | HOKEY POKEY, ETC. | HENRY KNIGHT, THE MERRY MAESTROS | 195? | $1.00 | $2.00 |

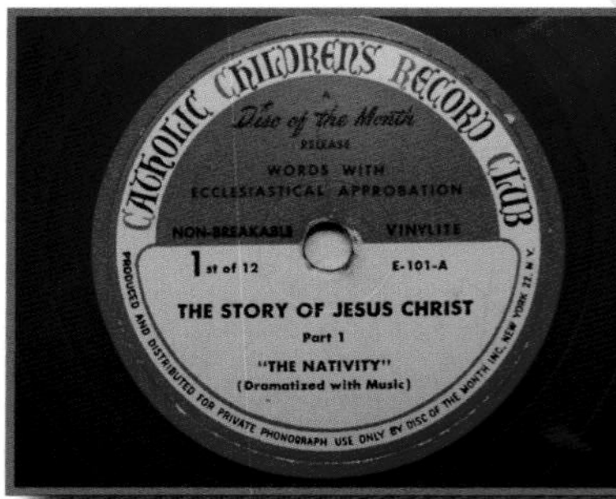


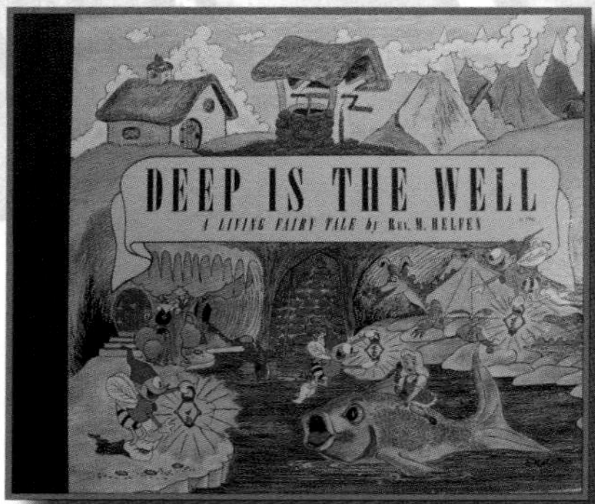


CASTLE KIDDIE RECORDS
JINGLE BELLS
$300.00

CATHOLIC CHILDREN'S RECORD CLUB
THE STORY OF JESUS CHRIST
$20.00

CDM RECORDS
DEEP IS THE WELL
$10.00

CHAPELAIRES RECORDS
THE CHRISTMAS CARILLON
$15.00

CNC PRODUCTIONS
UNCLE JOHNNY COONS
$8.00

COMMODORE RECORDS
SOD BUSTER BALLADS
$25.00

## MISCELLANEOUS LARGE SINGLES AND DOUBLES 9", 10", AND 12"

| LABEL | SET #/DISC # | # REC | MAIN TITLE | ARTIST | YEAR | G/VG | EX/NMT |
|---|---|---|---|---|---|---|---|
| GALA | 100 | 1 | CLARISSA THE FLEA/IDA, THE WAYWARD STURGEON | ? | 194? | $3.00 | $6.00 |
| GAMUT | GT 5003 (12") | 1 | RUN, RUN, ETC./RING AROUND THE ROSY, ETC. | HAZE GRIGGS | 193? | $2.00 | $4.00 |
| GENNETT | 4990 | 1 | SMALL SONGS FOR SMALL SINGERS: A BOWL OF BREAD AND MILK, ETC. | LEWIS JAMES | 1922 | $5.00 | $10.00 |
| GLORIA CHANDLER | ? | ? | ONE WORLD | GLORIA CHANDLER | 194? | $3.00 | $6.00 |
| GLORIA CHANDLER | ? | ? | NORTH AMERICAN REGIONS | GLORIA CHANDLER | 194? | $3.00 | $6.00 |
| GLORIA CHANDLER | ? | ? | NEW WORLDS A-GROWIN' | GLORIA CHANDLER | 194? | $3.00 | $6.00 |
| GOBBLY WOBBLYN | 1010 | 1 | UNDER THE LOLLY POP TREE | ARTHUR HALL, HARRY VOLTAIRE | 192? | $12.00 | $25.00 |
| GOLDMINE | NK-711 | 1 | I'M GONNA HANG UP MOMMY'S STOCKING/FUNNY LITTLE SNOW MAN | BOBBY SABATINO, CHARLES KENNY ORCH. | 195? | $1.00 | $2.00 |
| HANSEN | 102 | 1 | KING OF THE RIVER/YALLER, YALLER GOLD | GEO. BRUNS, QUINCY JONES ORCH. | 1956 | $5.00 | $10.00 |
| HANSEN | 103 | 1 | I AM NOT NOW (AND NEVER HAVE BEEN IN LOVE)/DO MI SO | TOMMY COLE, QUINCY JONES ORCH. | 1956 | $5.00 | $10.00 |
| HANSEN | 105 | 1 | HI TO YOU/HOLLY BOY | BETTY COX, QUINCY JONES ORCH. | 1956 | $5.00 | $10.00 |
| HAPPYTIMER | MI 3102/3 (12") | 1 | CHARLES LOUNSBURY'S WILL/A FATHER'S CONFESSION TO HIS SON | HUGH BARRETT DOBBS | 194? | $1.00 | $2.00 |
| HARTZ MOUNTAIN | UB 52-470 / 52-469A | 1 | HOW TO TEACH YOUR PARAKEET TO TALK | ARTHUR BARNETT | 1951 | $5.00 | $10.00 |
| ICE CAPADES OF 1950 | RR-12844/5 | 1 | TOY SHOP JAMBOREE/I FELL IN LOVE WITH A DREAM | JUD CONLON'S RHYTMAIRES | 1950 | $4.00 | $8.00 |
| INT'L MEN'S RECORDS | ? (12") | 1 | THE LITTLE UPRIGHT PIANO | HENRY SCOTT | 1954 | $2.00 | $4.00 |
| IRENE | 514 | 1 | PETER COTTON TAIL, OLD RUGGED CROSS/EASTER PARADE, EASTER BUNNY POLKA | BRANDT-MATOLA/MEADOWLARKS | 1954 | $1.00 | $2.00 |
| IRENE | 503 | 1 | SILENT NIGHT, ETC./RUDOLPH THE REDNOSE REINDEER, ETC. | NEIGHBORS/MEADLOWLARKS | 194? | $1.00 | $2.00 |
| JERI | S119 | 2 | SAY AND SING: "S"--THE SNAKE SOUND/"R"--THE ROOSTER SOUND | J.J. THOMPSON | 1955 | $2.00 | $4.00 |
| JOHN TRACY CLINIC | 14681/2 | 1 | LEARNING TO LISTEN | JUNE FORAY, ART GILMORE, VAN ALEXANDER | 195? | $3.00 | $6.00 |
| KAY ORTMAN | SET I: ? | 2 | LET'S PLAY: FARM LANDS | KAY ORTMAN | 1954 | $4.00 | $8.00 |
| KAY ORTMAN | SET II: 5407-9 | 3 | LET'S PLAY: ADVENTURES IN THE FOREST | KAY ORTMAN | 1954 | $4.00 | $8.00 |
| KAYBEE | AA-111/222 | 1 | RIGHT UNDER MY NOSE/DOWN IN OKLAHOMA | GINGER PRICE (6 YEARS OLD)T | 195? | $1.00 | $2.00 |
| KIDDIE KONCERT KARTON | K-100 (772/3) | 1 | CINDERELLA (PT. 1/2) | NOT LISTED | 192? | $10.00 | $20.00 |
| KIDDIE KONCERT KARTON | K-101 (774/5) | 1 | CINDERELLA (PT. 3/4) | NOT LISTED | 192? | $10.00 | $20.00 |

CORONET RECORDS
AL TRACE AND HIS SILLY SYMPHONISTS
$20.00

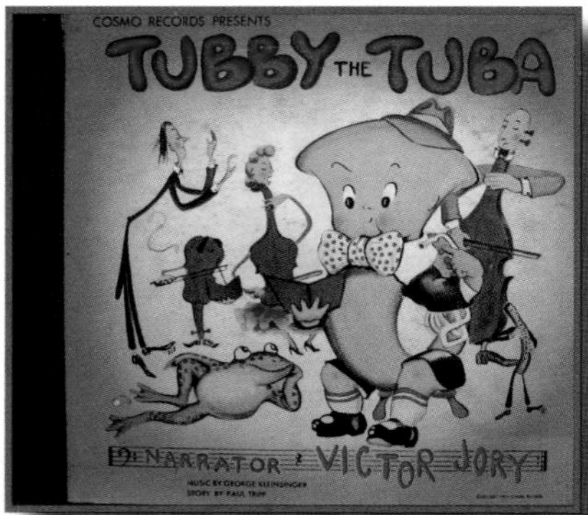


COSMO RECORDS
TUBY THE TUBA
$25.00

CREST RECORDINGS
AESOP'S FABLES
$40.00

## MISCELLANEOUS LARGE SINGLES AND DOUBLES 9", 10", AND 12"

| LABEL | SET #/DISC # | # REC | MAIN TITLE | ARTIST | YEAR | G/VG | EX/NMT | REMARKS |
|---|---|---|---|---|---|---|---|---|
| KIDISKS | ? | 1 | LONGFELLOW'S POEMS | UNCLE HENRY | 194? | $5.00 | $10.00 | |
| KIDISKS | ? | 1 | THE MISCHIEVOUS ANGEL | JOHN CRONAN | 194? | $5.00 | $10.00 | |
| KIDISKS | ? | 1 | THE WHITE LIE | UNCLE HENRY | 194? | $5.00 | $10.00 | |
| KINDER-BALLET | KB-101 | 1 | THE ZOO/POP GOES THE WEASEL, HAPPY BIRTHDAY | NOT LISTED | 196? | ¢.50 | $1.00 | |
| KINDER-LEBN | HF 1/2 - 100 A/B | 1 | YIDDISHE KINDER LIEDER | HELEN FENSTER, RAY GORDON | 194? | $3.00 | $6.00 | |
| KINDER-VELT | 2545 | 1 | SIX JEWISH NURSERY RHYMES | MASHA BENYA | 194? | $3.00 | $6.00 | |
| KING | 4854 | 1 | NUTTIN' FOR CHRISTMAS/ CHRISTMAS QUESTIONS | JOE WARD | 195? | $1.00 | $2.00 | |
| KING | 15101 | 1 | PUPPY FOR SALE/I WANT A WITTLE WABBIT | ELMER OCTOBER | 195? | $1.00 | $2.00 | |
| KINOR | K-1231 | 1 | CHANUKAH MUSIC BOX | SHIRLEY COHEN, ELY GAMLIEL | 1951 | $3.00 | $6.00 | |
| KINOR | K-1233 | 1 | PASSOVER MUSIC BOX | SHIRLEY COHEN, ELY GAMLIEL | 195? | $3.00 | $6.00 | |
| LA-NOAR | ? | 1 | KING SOLOMON AND THE BEE | ? | 195? | $1.00 | $2.00 | |
| LIGHTNING | 17 | 1 | THE BALLAD OF DAVY CROCKETT/THE GOLDEN BRACELET | GUY CHOOKOORIAN | 1955 | $2.00 | $4.00 | |
| LONE STAR | CB-502 | 1 | "BLESSED ARE YE" (BEATI-TUDES) | LUCY HUGHES | 1952 | $1.00 | $2.00 | |
| LUTHERECORDS | 1003 | 1 | JACK AND THE BEANSTALK | FRANK LUTHER | 195? | $1.00 | $2.00 | |
| LUTHERECORDS | 1004 | 1 | SLEEPING BEAUTY | FRANK LUTHER | 195? | $1.00 | $2.00 | |
| MARLOS BALLET | 4 | 1 | THE SUN & THE CHILDREN | ELLEN MARLOS, VAL WENING | 196? | ¢.50 | $1.00 | |
| MARSHALL FIELD | 2014/5 | 1 | UNCLE MISTLETOE IN WON-DERLAND | UNCLE MISTLETOE, AUNT JUDY | 1949 | $4.00 | $8.00 | |
| MARY BAKER EDDY | 8555 | 1 | O GENTLE PRESENCE/THE CHILDREN'S PRAYER, ANGELS | MARY DEAN | 195? | $5.00 | $10.00 | |
| MCNAMARA HARMONICA STUDIOS | FR-127/8 | 1 | PLAY THE HARMONICA | BETTY AND JACK | 195? | $2.00 | $4.00 | |
| MEDIA | 1011 | 1 | DANIEL BOONE: THE DADDY OF THEM ALL/MAY HEAVEN FORGIVE YOUR | KEN CARSON | 195? | $3.00 | $6.00 | |
| MELODY LANE RECORDS | MLS 101 | 1 | MOTHER GOOSE MELODIES | JULIA DAWN SALEM | 195? | $5.00 | $10.00 | |
| MEYER MUSIC BOX MU-SEUM | 18 (12") | 1 | CHRISTMAS SONGS | ? | 195? | $2.00 | $4.00 | |
| MIKE-ING HISTORY | ALB # 1 (MH 801/2 - 3/4) | 2 | SIGNING OF THE DECLARA-TION OF INDEPENDENCE, ETC. | NOT LISTED | 1946 | $5.00 | $10.00 | |
| PARAMOUNT | 20143 | 1 | PARADE OF WOODEN SOL-DIERS/NEATH SOUTH SEA MOON | NATHAN GLANTZ | 1930? | $2.00 | $4.00 | |
| PARAMOUNT | 20081 | 1 | 10 LITTLE FINGERS & 10 LIT-TLE TOES/WABASH BLUES | JULES LENZBERG'S ORCH. | 1930? | $2.00 | $4.00 | |

JOHN TRACEY CLINIC
LEARNING TO LISTEN
$6.00

JOLLY RECORDS
GAME SONGS THE CHILDREN LOVE
$15.00

KAY ORTMAN
LET'S PLAY
$8.00

## MISCELLANEOUS LARGE SINGLES AND DOUBLES 9", 10", 12"

| LABEL | SET #/ DISC # | # REC | MAIN TITLE | ARTIST | YEAR | G/VG | EX/NMT | REMARKS |
|---|---|---|---|---|---|---|---|---|
| TUNEPAC | M 521/2 (K1003) | 1 | TO MARKET, TO MARKET, ETC./PEAS PORRIDGE HOT, ETC. | VICKI STEVENS | 195? | $1.00 | $2.00 | |
| TUNES FOR TOTS | 4001 | 1 | I SAW MOMMY KISSING SANTA CLAUS/THE MOMMA DOLL SONG | EILEEN SCOTT | 195? | $1.00 | $2.00 | |
| TUTOR THAT NEVER TIRES | 4-399 | 1 | THE SINGING CLOCK | NOT LISTED | 1949 | $5.00 | $10.00 | CLOCK HANDS ON COVER — THEY MOVE. |
| TWINKLE TUNES | KD-1 | 1 | PETER PAN, ETC./THREE BLIND MICE, ETC. | NOT LISTED | 195? | $1.00 | $2.00 | |
| TWINKLE TUNES | KD-2 | 1 | BIG ROCK CANDY MOUNTAIN, ETC./THE GINGERBREAD MAN, ETC. | NOT LISTED | 195? | $1.00 | $2.00 | |
| TWINKLE TUNES | KD-3 | 1 | I SAW MOMMY KISSING SANTA CLAUS, ETC./JACK & THE BEANSTALK, ETC. | NOT LISTED | 195? | $1.00 | $2.00 | |
| UNCLE WIN'S | 2865/6 | 1 | SONG KIT NO. 2: HAPPY AL-PHABET, ETC. | UNCLE WIN, FRANK SCARDINO | 195? | $5.00 | $10.00 | |
| UNIQUE | 370 | 1 | YO-O RINTY/EVERYONE SAYS | JACK SMITH, RIN TIN TIN | 1956 | $10.00 | $20.00 | |
| VELVET TONE | 1917-9 | 3 | UNCLE DON SERIES: ETI-QUETTE IN RHYME | UNCLE DON | 192? | $10.00 | $20.00 | |
| WBAL-TV | ? | 1 | GERALD THE GIRAFFE | OFFICER HAPPY | 194? | $8.00 | $15.00 | |
| ZODIAC | Z-501 | 1 | FUN WITH FRENCH | JACQUELINE ENGLERT MARCHAL | 1955 | $3.00 | $6.00 | RECORD/BOOK COMBO |
| ZON-O-PHONE | 405 (S/S) | 1 | CHILDREN'S SONG MEDLEY | HAGER'S ORCHESTRA | 1905 | $5.00 | $10.00 | |
| ZON-O-PHONE | 868 (S/S) | 1 | JACK AND JILL | MISS ADA JONES | 1907 | $5.00 | $10.00 | |

KELLOG'S CORN FLAKES
I'M CHIQUITA BANANA
$25.00

KIDDIE KONCERT RECORDS
CINDERELLA
$20.00

KIDISKS
THE THREE BEARS
$35.00

## MISCELLANEOUS LARGE ALBUMS 10" AND 12"

| LABEL | SET # | # REC | DISC # | MAIN TITLE | ARTIST | YEAR | G/VG | EX/NMT |
|---|---|---|---|---|---|---|---|---|
| APOLLO | A-3 | 2 | 1016-7 | THE LOVE OF TWO CABBAGES | GENE HAMILTON | 194? | $40.00 | $80.00 |
| ARROW | AC-51 | 2 | 1000-1 | JACK AND HOMER | PAUL TRIPP | 1946 | $40.00 | $80.00 |
| ARROW | AC-52 | ? | ? | FERDINAND | JIM CAMPBELL | 194? | $10.00 | $20.00 |
| AUDIO VISUAL MATERIAL | VOL 1 | 2 | E1-KB-2367/8 - 9/70 | MUSIC FOR MOVEMENT | E. GOTTELEBEN | 195? | $2.00 | $4.00 |
| AUTO-PHOTO | AP-1 | 2 | ? | THE MIGHTY MAGIC MANDARIN | WENDY BARRIE | 195? | $2.00 | $4.00 |
| BANNER | B-101 | 3 | A101-2-3 | BUDDY BEAR | CECIL ROY | 193? | $15.00 | $30.00 |
| BASSETT-CHESTNUT | ? | 3 | ? | RHYTHMIC ACTIVITY | ? | 195? | $2.00 | $4.00 |
| BREMNER-DAVIS PHONICS | NO # | 4 (12") | CE2CC-5018/9-24/5 | THE SOUND WAY TO EASY READING | NOT LISTED | 1953 | $2.00 | $4.00 |
| CAMP RECORDINGS | CR-121 | 3 | ? | BUGLE CALLS | ? | 1947 | $2.00 | $4.00 |
| CAMP RECORDINGS | NO # | 2 | NO NUMBERS | GREEN MOUNTAIN BOYS' CAMP 1950 | NOT LISTED | 1950 | $5.00 | $10.00 |
| CATHOLIC CHILDREN'S RECORD CLUB | NO # | 12 | E-101 - 112 | THE STORY OF JESUS CHRIST | NOT LISTED | 195? | $10.00 | $20.00 |
| CDM | T-1 | 3 | 101-3 | DEEP IS THE WELL | REV. M. HELFEN | 1947 | $5.00 | $10.00 |
| COMMODORE | CRA-7 | 2 | ? | A DAY AT THE RINGLING BROS., BARNUM & BAILEY CIRCUS | F. BEVERLY KELLY | 194? | $4.00 | $8.00 |
| COMMODORE | CR-10 | 3 | 3002-3-4 | SOD BUSTER BALLADS | PETE SEEGER, WOODIE GUTHRIE, LEE HAYES | 1941 | $75.00 | $150.00 |
| CONCERT HALL SOCIETY | A-C | 3 | 1013/14, 15/16, 17/18 | PROKOFIEFF: MUSIC FOR CHILDREN | MS. RAY LEV | 194? | $2.00 | $4.00 |

KINDER-LEBN
SING A SONG IN YIDDISH
$6.00

KINDER-VELT
SIX JEWISH NURSERY RHYMES
$6.00

KINOR RECORDS
PASSOVER MUSIC BOX
$6.00

LA-NOAR
KING SOLOMON AND THE BEE
$2.00

LINE MATERIAL CO.
KEEPING CHRISTMAS
$6.00

LISTEN-LEARN
TINGO THE STORY OF A CLOWN
$8.00

## MISCELLANEOUS LARGE ALBUMS 10" AND 12"

| LABEL | SET # | # REC | DISC # | MAIN TITLE | ARTIST | YEAR | G/VG | EX/NMT |
|---|---|---|---|---|---|---|---|---|
| CORONET | C1 | 4 | COR 150 – 3 | KIDDIE ALBUM | AL TRACE & HIS SILLY SYMPHONISTS | 194? | $3.00 | $6.00 |
| COSMO | DMR 106 | 3 | ? | SONG OF THE SOUTH | TONY PASTOR, THE CLOONEY SISTERS | 194? | $10.00 | $20.00 |
| COSMO | DMR 101 | 2 | 6037/40-6038/9 | TUBBY THE TUBA | VICTOR JORY | 1945 | $12.00 | $25.00 |
| CREST | CT-2 | 2 | 103-4 | AESOP'S FABLES: FOX & THE GRAPES, TORTOISE & THE HARE | STERLING HOLLOWAY | 194? | $25.00 | $50.00 |
| CROWN | CR-10 | 3 | CR-138 – 40 | HAPPY THE HUMBUG FINDS HIS PARENTS | HAPPY FELTON | 194? | $25.00 | $50.00 |
| DE LUXE | 19 | 2 | 1060-1 | A CHILD'S GARDEN OF MANNERS* | TOMMY RIGGS & "BETTY LOU" | 1946 | $5.00 | $10.00 |
| DE LUXE | 21 | 2 | ? | TINGO | JERRY BARTELL | 194? | $4.00 | $8.00 |
| DISCOVERY | DC-1 | 3 | 301 - 3 | THE LITTLE BROWN DOOR MAT | PAT O'BRIEN | 1947 | $5.00 | $10.00 |
| EXERCISE | ? | 2 | ? | GROW STRAIGHT & TALL | DAISY BLAU | 195? | $1.00 | $2.00 |
| FEATHERWEIGHT | R-1-101 | 3 | SIDES 1/2 – 5/6 | NATURE MOUSE* | HARRY LANG | 1950 | $15.00 | $30.00 |
| FOLKWAYS | 51 | 3 (12") | 333-4-5 | DANCE-A-LONG | B.J.WALBERG | 1950 | $5.00 | $10.00 |
| GUARDIAN | NO # | 2 | GR 101, GR 102 | THE FLUFF BIRD | GEORGE GINGELL, ALMA CURLEY | 194? | $5.00 | $10.00 |
| HAMILTON-WHITNEY | HW 1 | 3 | SIDES 1/6, 2/5, 3/4 | SONGS ABOUT HISTORY | DONALD O'CONNOR & HIS SINGING BOOK-WORMS | 194? | $15.00 | $30.00 |

*BOXED SET **SERIES A, ALBUM C ***WITH BOOKLET

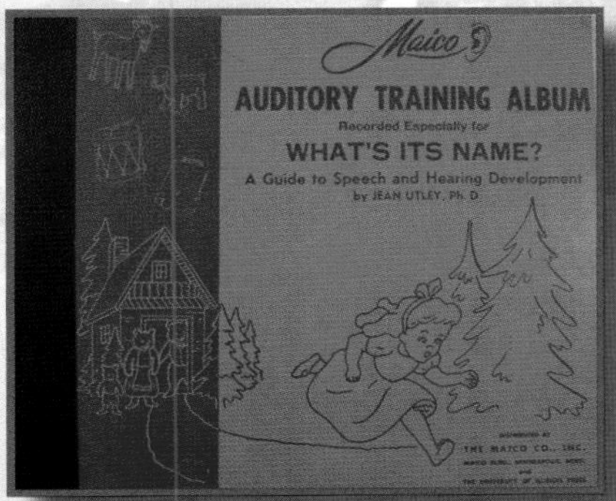


MAICO CO.
WHAT'S ITS NAME
$4.00

MINEDCO RECORDS
HEBREW SONGS
$10.00

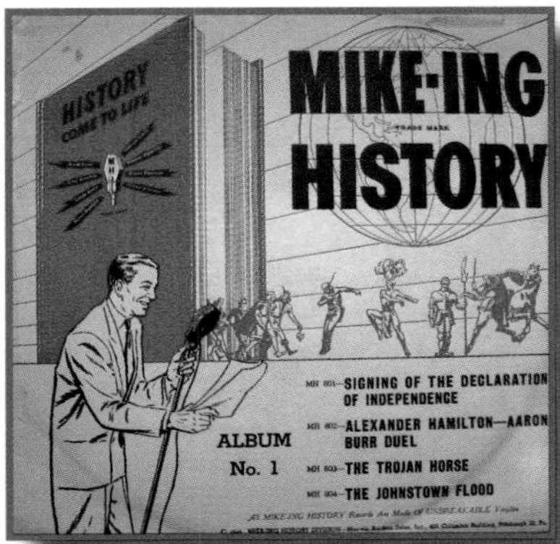


MIKE-ING HISTORY RECORDS
SIGNING OF THE DECLARATION OF INDEPENDENCE
$10.00

MINUTE MAID CORP.
HOW WE CAPTURED THE LION AT SUPER CIRCUS
$15.00

MUSICOLOR RECORDS
LISTEN AND COLOR
$8.00

NATIONAL MASK & PUPPET
PUPPET SHOW
$10.00

## MISCELLANEOUS LARGE ALBUMS 10" AND 12"

| LABEL | SET # | # REC | DISC # | MAIN TITLE | ARTIST | YEAR | G/VG | EX/NMT |
|---|---|---|---|---|---|---|---|---|
| HARGAIL | H-N705 | ? | ? | FOLK SONGS & BALLADS OF AMERICA | MARGARET DODD SINGERS | 194? | $10.00 | $20.00 |
| HOLLYWOOD VUE TONE | NO # | 1 | 71 | PETER RABBIT** | JUNE FORAY | 1947 | $12.00 | $25.00 |
| HORIZON | WM-1 | 3 | WM1/6-2/5-3/4 | BEETHOVEN FOR YOUNG PEOPLE | RICHARD JANAVER | 194? | $8.00 | $15.00 |
| LISTEN LEARN | LL-1 | 2 | ? | TINGO: THE STORY OF A CLOWN | JERRY BARTELL | 1949 | $4.00 | $8.00 |
| MAICO | NO # | 2 | M-1666478/1-2-3-4 | WHAT'S ITS NAME*** | DR. JEAN UTLEY | 1950 | $2.00 | $4.00 |
| MEDIA | 1011 | 1 | 1011 | DANIEL BOONE: THE DADDY OF THEM ALL | KEN CARSON | 195? | $5.00 | $10.00 |
| MEMO | NO # | 3 | | STORY BOOK LADY | IRMA GLEN | 194? | $2.00 | $4.00 |
| MINEDCO | ALB 1 | 2 | M-201-2 | HEBREW SONGS FOR CHILDREN | SEYMOUR SILBERMINTZ | 194? | $5.00 | $10.00 |
| MONARCH | MO1 | 2 | | FALA | DAN SEYMOUR | 194? | $5.00 | $10.00 |
| NATIONAL | C-1 | 2 | 3001-2 | LUKE THE SINGING DUCK | DAVID KURLAN | 1946 | $5.00 | $10.00 |
| NU-TONE | ? | ? | | A CHILD'S DAY | PAUL PARKS | 194? | $2.00 | $4.00 |
| PHILHARMONIC | 33 | 3 | 139-41 | SONGS AND SINGING GAMES | EARL ROGERS | 194? | $5.00 | $10.00 |
| POPULAR SCIENCE | ? | 4 | ? | SING A SONG OF FRIENDSHIP | ? | 194? | $3.00 | $6.00 |
| QUEEN | Q2 | 3 | 4147-9 | THE TWO GIANTS, ETC. | MRS. SIDNEY RAUH | 194? | $3.00 | $6.00 |
| RAINBOW | R-301 | 2 | BR 1/4-2/3 | POLLY THE PERSONALITY PARROT | CRAIG MCDONNELL, MAE QUESTEL | 194? | $15.00 | $30.00 |
| RAINBOW | R-302 | 2 | ? | SWEETY SWINGS A TALE | CECIL ROY | 194? | $15.00 | $30.00 |

*WITH SEWN IN BOOK **COMES WITH 16 SLIDES ***W/BOOK ****BOARD GAME + RECORDS

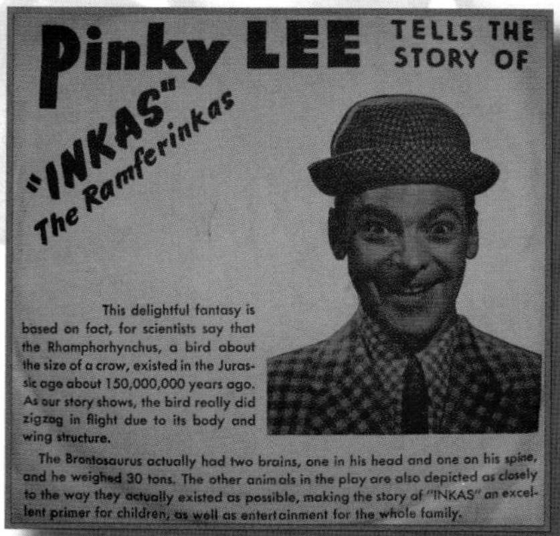


NATIONAL RECORDS
FUZZY WUZZY
$8.00

NEW HAVEN RR
TO THE ZOO
$20.00

OBERLINE RECORDS
"INKAS" THE RAMFERINKAS
$10.00

PACIFIC RECORDS
BABY BABBLE
$4.00

PEEK-O
LITTLE RED RIDING HOOD
$80.00

PETER PAN PEANUT BUTTER
THE BALLAD OF DAVY CROCKET
$20.00

## MISCELLANEOUS LARGE ALBUMS 10" AND 12"

| LABEL | SET # | # REC | DISC # | MAIN TITLE | ARTIST | YEAR | G/VG | EX/NMT |
|---|---|---|---|---|---|---|---|---|
| RAINBOW RHYTHMS FOR CHILDREN | SERIES 1 | 3 | RN-1/2-5/6 | GIANTS & FAIRIES, ETC. | NORA BELLE EMERSON | 1949 | $4.00 | $8.00 |
| RAINBOW RHYTHMS FOR CHILDREN | SERIES 2 | 3 | RN-1A/B-3A/B | THE DUCK, ETC. | NORA BELLE EMERSON | 1949 | $4.00 | $8.00 |
| RONDO | R-1004 | 3 | R-111, 124, 140 | MERRY CHRISTMAS MELODIES | COSMO TERI, SKIP BERG | 194? | $2.00 | $4.00 |
| SALLY TOBIN DIETRICH | TE-001-4 | 4 | TE-001-4 | RHYTHMIC PLAY | SALLY TOBIN DIETRICH | 195? | $2.00 | $4.00 |
| SALLY TOBIN DIETRICH | ? | 3 | ? | DANCE PLAY I | SALLY TOBIN DIETRICH | 195? | $2.00 | $4.00 |
| SALLY TOBIN DIETRICH | ? | 3 | ? | DANCE PLAY II | SALLY TOBIN DIETRICH | 195? | $2.00 | $4.00 |
| SPIRE | D1 | 3 | 21490-2 | SIX STORIES FROM THE BIBLE | SPIRE SYJPHONETTE | 195? | $2.00 | $4.00 |
| STANDARD | T-20 | ? | ? | TYPICAL FOLK DANCES | ? | 194? | $1.00 | $2.00 |
| STINSON | 345 | ? | 345-2A/B + ? | THE WAYFARING STRANGER | BURL IVES | 194? | $10.00 | $20.00 |
| STINSON | A-410 | 3 | 73/9-69/80-70/81 | FRONTIER BALLADS AND COW-BOY SONGS | BILL BENDER | 194? | $5.00 | $10.00 |
| STINSON | 101 | 3 | ? | IN THE BEGINNING | BILL NILES | 194? | $15.00 | $30.00 |
| STINSON-ASCH | A-347 | 3 | MA20/17-MA79/139-MA21/135 | SONGS BY WOODIE GUTHRIE: TALKING SAILOR, ETC. | WOODY GUTHRIE | 1947 | $75.00 | $150.00 |
| TALKING LIBRARY | ? | 2 | ? | SUGARFOOT & THE MERRY-GO-ROUND | DON MYER, JUSTINE YOUNG | 194? | $3.00 | $6.00 |
| TARZAN | T1 | 3 | TS101 – 3 | TARZAN IN THE VALLEY OF THE TALKING GORILLAS | EDWARD ARNO | 194? | $50.00 | $100.00 |
| TIFFANY | T-8-1 | 4 | B-001 – 4 | MR. BITZEL | BARRY THOMPSON, ART CARNEY | 194? | $25.00 | $50.00 |
| TIFFANY | T-A-1 | 2 | 001A/2B – 001B/-2A | THE REVOLT OF THE ALPHABET | RUTH CHATTERTON | 194? | $15.00 | $30.00 |
| TOONO | NO # | 3 | T-100 – 2 | TOONO MUSICAL GAME FOR CHIL-DREN**** | ADELE GIRARD | 1946 | $25.00 | $50.00 |
| TREASURECORDS | NO # | 3 | 1 - 2 - 3 | A CHILD'S TREASURY OF SONG | MARION ROSETTE` | 194? | $8.00 | $15.00 |
| TRU TONE | T-9 | 3 | RT 7001/2 – 5/6 | SONGS CHILDREN LOVE TO SING | RICHARD MAXWELL, LAR-KIN SISTERS | 194? | $2.00 | $4.00 |
| TUTOR THAT NEVER TIRES | ? | 6 | ? | MR. ARITHMETIC | ? | 1949 | $6.00 | $12.00 |
| UNIVERSAL | U2 | 3 | 141/2 – 45/6 | THE TOM MIX OF RADIO | CURLEY BRADLEY | 194? | $8.00 | $15.00 |
| VISUAL | CVE 3000-1 | 2 (12") | 3000-1 | SAINTS & SANCTITY | MICHAEL J. QUINN | 1948 | $2.00 | $4.00 |
| VULCAN | NO # | 3 | NO #S ON LABEL | LITTLE RED RIDING HOOD (JU-NIOR OPERETTA) | NOT LISTED | 1923 | $25.00 | $50.00 |
| YIDDISHE KINDER | 2 | 4 | MIXED NUMBERS: 102, ETC. | SONGS FOR JEWISH CHILDREN | YSAAK GLADSTONE, ETC. | 194? | $8.00 | $15.00 |

*WITH SEWN IN BOOK **COMES WITH 16 SLIDES ***W/BOOK ****BOARD GAME + RECORDS

PHONOGRAPH RECORDS
A RECORD FROM THE EASTER BUNNY
$8.00

PILOTONE RECORDS
THE FOX AND THE GRAPES
$15.00

PONY RECORDS
THE LITTLE LOST PONY
$4.00

## MISCELLANEOUS SMALL SINGLES DOUBLES AND ALBUMS 8" AND SMALLER

| LABEL | DISC # | SIZE | # REC | MAIN TITLE | ARTIST | YEAR | G/VG | EX/NMT | REMARKS |
|---|---|---|---|---|---|---|---|---|---|
| A.C. GILBERT | AF-1 | 4" | 1 | AMERICAN FLYER TALKING STATION | TRAIN SOUND EFFECTS | 194? | $8.00 | $15.00 | |
| A.C. GILBERT | 598 | 4" | 1 | AMERICAN FLYER TALKING STATION: STEAM LOCOMOTIVE/DIESEL LOCOMOTIVE | TRAIN SOUND EFFECTS | 194? | $8.00 | $15.00 | |
| AMERICAN GREETINGS (PD) S/S | 488-7 | 6" SQ | 1 | HOWDY! HAPPY BIRTHDAY! (GREETING CARD RECORD) | NOT LISTED | 195? | $4.00 | $8.00 | |
| AMERICAN GREETINGS "TUNE TOPPER" (PD) S/S | 506-HG-1 | 5" SQ | 1 | HI THERE, YOUNG FELLA, MERRY CHRISTMAS | NOT LISTED | 195? | $5.00 | $10.00 | |
| AMERICAN GREETINGS "TUNE TOPPER" (PD) S/S | 506-HG-2 | 5" SQ | 1 | A MERRY, MERRY CHRISTMAS TO YOU | NOT LISTED | 195? | $5.00 | $10.00 | |
| AARDELL | 101 | 7" | 1 | ANGELICA (WITH BOOK — PRIVATE LABEL) | PATTY ROSS, GEO. GREELEY ORCH. | 1955 | $3.00 | $6.00 | |
| BERLINER | 0441 | 8" S/S | 1 | MOTHER GOOSE RHYMES | ? | 1896 | $40.00 | $80.00 | |
| BERLINER | 1505 | 8" S/S | 1 | SLOVENLY PETER | ? | 1896 | $40.00 | $80.00 | |
| BREMNER | 1 – 5 + 5A | 7" | 6 | MUSICAL MULTIPLICATION TABLES | BILLY LEACH | 1956 | $8.00 | $15.00 | WITH INSERT CARDS |
| CAP-TONE (PD) | NO # | 7" SQ | 1 | L'IL ABNER GOES TO TOWN | NOT LISTED | 1950 | $15.00 | $30.00 | |
| CASTLE (PD) S/S | CA K-101 – 3 | 6" | 3 | JINGLE BELLS, 10 LITTLE INDIANS, WHERE HAS MY LITTLE DOG GONE | NOT LISTED | 194? | $150.00 | $300.00 | PRICE IS FOR SET OF 3 IN FOLDER, ONE-SIDED PLAYING-REVERSE FOR HOME RECORDING. |
| CHILDREN'S CLASSICS | CC 8 | 7" | 1 | CINDERELLA/ROBIN HOOD | NOT LISTED | 195? | $1.00 | $2.00 | |
| CHILDREN'S MUSIC CLUB | #1 – 8 | 6" | 8 | 46 NURSERY RHYMES: HOME ON THE RANGE, ETC. | NOT LISTED | 194? | $6.00 | $12.00 | BOXED SET |
| CLAYTON SPECIALTY MFG. (S/S) | NO # | 6" | 1 | A PERSONAL CHRISTMAS GREETING | HOME RECORDING | 195? | $3.00 | $6.00 | |
| COROTEEN TALES | E4-CT-6570/1 | 6" | 1 | THE PRETTY LITTLE GIRL | AL STILLMAN, ROBERT ALLEN | 195? | $5.00 | $10.00 | DECORATIVE BOXED RECORD |
| DAINTY MAID | PP 200 | 7" | 1 | ALL AROUND THE MULBERRY BUSH/DID YOU EVER SEE A LASSIE, ETC. | NOT LISTED | 194? | $4.00 | $8.00 | DECORATIVE BOXED RECORD WITH NECKLACE, RECORD IS MADE BY PETER PAN. |
| DOUBLE PLAY | NO # | 6" SQ | 1 | LITTLE LEAGUER | NOT LISTED | 1955 | $10.00 | $20.00 | |
| DURIUM (S/S) | NO # | 4" | 4 | OLD KING COLE'S PARTY | FRANK LUTHER | 1930 | $50.00 | $100.00 | |
| EMENEE | MNE 1/2 | 7" | 1 | MICKEY MOUSE RHYTHM BAND: INSTRUCTION RECORD | PATTY MCGOVERN, ETC. | 195? | $20.00 | $40.00 | VALUES ARE FOR BOXED RECORD W/ MUSICAL TOYS. |

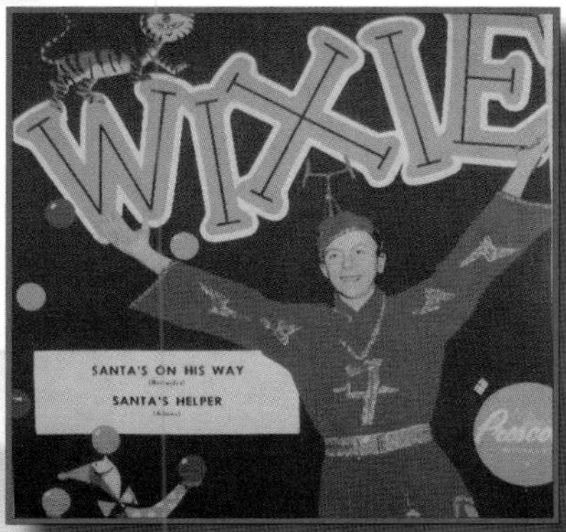


PRESCOTT RECORDS
SANTA'S ON HIS WAY
$25.00

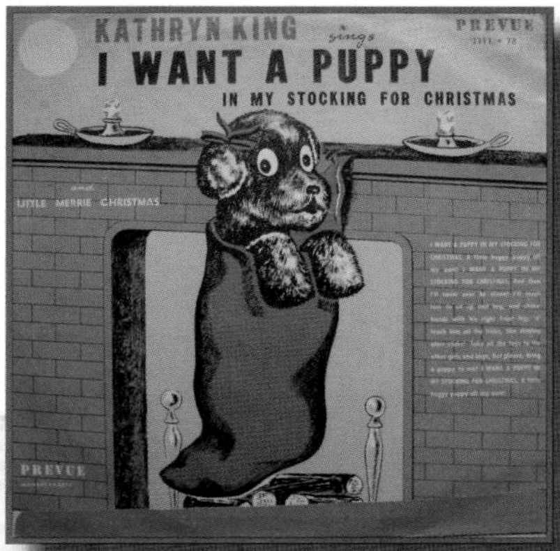


PREVUE RECORDS
I WANT A PUPPY IN MY STOCKING FOR CHRISTMAS
$20.00

PUBLIC SERVICE RECORDS
LITTLE SONGS ON BIG SUBJECTS
$20.00

## MISCELLANEOUS SMALL SINGLES DOUBLES AND ALBUMS 8" AND SMALLER

| LABEL | DISC # | SIZE | # REC | MAIN TITLE | ARTIST | YEAR | G/VG | EX/NMT | REMARKS |
|---|---|---|---|---|---|---|---|---|---|
| FELLOWSHIP | 10-A | 7" | 4 | CHILDREN'S HYMNS AND STORIES | ? | 195? | $2.00 | $4.00 | |
| FELLOWSHIP | 10-B | 7" | 4 | CHILDREN'S HYMNS AND STORIES | ? | 195? | $2.00 | $4.00 | |
| FELLOWSHIP | 10-C | 7" | 4 | CHILDREN'S HYMNS AND STORIES | ? | 195? | $2.00 | $4.00 | |
| FROLIC | K-1 | 6" | 1 | MOTHER GOOSE ALPHABET | BARRY THOMPSON, THE SMOOTHIES | 195? | $3.00 | $6.00 | |
| FROLIC | 6 | 6" | 1 | THE LITTLE TOY BAND | JERRY MARSHALL, FROLIC TOY ORCHESTRA | 195? | $3.00 | $6.00 | |
| GIBSON MUSICARD (PD) S/S | GIB-8 | 6" | 1 | HAPPY BIRTHDAY, DEAR DAUGHTER | ROSEMARY CLOONEY | 1955 | $4.00 | $8.00 | PERSONALIZED GREETING RECORD |
| GILWIN | LW 101 - 108 | 7" | 4 | SONGS FROM THE CINNAMON BEAR: FRAIDY CAT, ETC. | (BUDDY DUNCAN, ETC.) | 195? | $25.00 | $50.00 | PRICE IS FOR SET OF 4 FROM WIEBOLDT'S DEPT. STORE |
| HAWTHORNE HOUSE MELODY CARD (PD) S/S | K-4 | 7" SQ | 1 | THE FIRST NOEL (GREETING CARD RECORD) | PICKWICK CAROL GROUP | 195? | $3.00 | $6.00 | |
| HOLLYWOOD | S-8 | 8 | 1 | UNCLE ARCHIE'S CHRISTMAS STORY: BLITZEN, THE UN-HAPPY REINDEER | CAM BLAKE | 195? | $5.00 | $10.00 | |
| J.S. PUBLISHING | 40 | 7" | 1 | THE STAND-UP MOTHER GOOSE | WILLIAM ADAMS | 194? | $20.00 | $40.00 | WITH 8 STAND-UPS IN BOX |
| JOHNSON IMPROVED RECORD | A-490 | 7" | 1 | A RECORD FOR THE CHIL-DREN | WILLIAM HOOLEY | 1900 | $750.00 | $1,500.00 | FIRST TWO-SIDED RECORD MADE |
| JOLLY | 501/8 - 504/11 | 6" | 4 | GAME SONGS THE CHILDREN LOVE (HOLDER WITH 4 RE-CORDS) | JOLLY JULIA/JOLLY MIN-STRELS | 1949 | $8.00 | $15.00 | |
| JOLLY | 500/507 | 6" | 1 | ROUND THE VILLAGE/MARCH MILITAIRE | JOLLY JULIA/JOLLY MIN-STRELS | 1949 | $1.00 | $2.00 | |
| KANDY | KR-702 | 7" | 1 | WASHINGTON POST MARCH/ HAPPY MOTHER GOOSE | THE GOLDMAN BAND | 195? | $1.00 | $2.00 | |
| KAPPA | 103/4 | 7"? | 1 | THE ZOO (BEAR/GIRAFFE, ZEBRA) | NOT LISTED | 194? | $15.00 | $30.00 | |
| KAPPA | 105/8 | 7"? | 1 | THE ZOO (RHINO, HIPPO/ LION) | NOT LISTED | 194? | $15.00 | $30.00 | |
| KAPPA | 106/7 | 7"? | 1 | THE ZOO (MONKEY/EL-EPHANT) | NOT LISTED | 194? | $15.00 | $30.00 | |

## MISCELLANEOUS SMALL SINGLES DOUBLES AND ALBUMS 8" AND SMALLER

| LABEL | DISC # | SIZE | # REC | MAIN TITLE | ARTIST | YEAR | G/VG | EX/NMT | REMARKS |
|---|---|---|---|---|---|---|---|---|---|
| KAYSAM | 1 | 6" | 1 | "CURLY" THE POODLE/ "SORRY" THE HOUND | BONNIE MURRAY | 195? | $1.00 | $2.00 | RECORD CAME WITH TOY |
| KAYSAM | 2 | 6" | 1 | CAT 'N FIDDLE/OLD KING KOLE | BONNIE MURRAY | 195? | $1.00 | $2.00 | |
| KIDISKS | KD-77 | 4" | 1 | THE THREE BEARS | UNCLE HENRY | 1948 | $18.00 | $35.00 | |
| KIDDIE TUNE | ? | 7" | 1 | (NO TITLES ARE KNOWN AT THIS TIME) | ? | 193? | $5.00 | $10.00 | |
| LEAH GLEN RHODES (PD) | ? | ? | 1 | HOP HOP HOP/FUZZY FELLOW | CHRISTINE HARRISON | 194? | $8.00 | $15.00 | |
| LINE MATERIAL CO. | U-1639 | 7" | 1 | KEEPING CHRISTMAS | JIM AMECHE | 1949 | $3.00 | $6.00 | WITH INSERT BOOK: "CHRISTMAS 1949" |
| LOOK 'N LISTEN (PD) S/S | 101 | 4" | 4 | REAL BIRD CALLS AND STORIES | AUTHENTIC BIRD CALLS | 1956 | $15.00 | $30.00 | 4 PIC-DISCS ON ONE CARDBOARD SHEET, PUNCH-OUTS |
| LOOK 'N LISTEN (PD) S/S | 102 | 4" | 4 | STORIES AND REAL ANIMAL SOUNDS | AUTHENTIC BIRD CALLS | 1956 | $15.00 | $30.00 | 4 PIC-DISCS ON ONE CARDBOARD SHEET, PUNCH-OUTS |
| MARY BAKER EDDY | ZT 46871 | 7" | 1 | THE CHILDREN'S CORNER/ SHEPHARD, SHOW ME THE WAY | MARY DEAN | 195? | $2.00 | $4.00 | |
| MILLER | K502 | 7" | 1 | THE GOLDEN GOOSE | ? | 194? | $5.00 | $10.00 | |
| MILLER | K500 | 7" | 1 | THE TWELVE DANCING PRINCESSES | ? | 194? | $5.00 | $10.00 | |
| MOVIECRAFT | NO # | 6" | 1 | A MOTHER GOOSE PERSONAL BIRTHDAY RECORD (PERSONALIZED GREETING REC) | NOT LISTED | 194? | $4.00 | $8.00 | |
| MUSIC YOU ENJOY | MF 1/2 - 7/8 | 7" | 4 | ERNO RAPEE'S MELODYLAND: BILLY BEE, ETC. | MILTON CROSS | 1942 | $25.00 | $50.00 | REGULAR AND DELUXE EDITIONS |
| NORTH POLE | NO # | 3" | 1 | LISTEN TO A GREETING FROM....(PERSONALIZED GREETING RECORD) | NOT LISTED | 194? | $5.00 | $10.00 | |
| NORTH POLE | LH-102 | 7" | 1 | LITTLE HYMNS FOR LITTLE PEOPLE | BEVERLY TURNER | 194? | $2.00 | $4.00 | |
| PERSONAL RECORDS (PD) S/S | ONE | 5" SQ | 1 | MERRY CHRISTMAS FROM SANTA CLAUS (PERSONALIZED GREETING CARD) | NOT LISTED | 195? | $5.00 | $10.00 | WITH MAILER |
| PERSONNA DISC | NO # | 6" | 1 | BIRTHDAY DISC FOR... (BLANK SPACE FOR FIRST NAME) | NOT LISTED | 195? | $5.00 | $10.00 | WITH MAILER |
| PLAY ME DOLL | JP 55253/4 | 6" | 1 | WEDDING MARCH/OH PROMISE ME | NOT LISTED/DE KOVEN | 195? | $1.00 | $2.00 | ISSUED WITH DOLLS' CLOTHES? |
| PLAY ME DOLL WARDROBE | JP 55278/9 | 6" | 2 | FRERE JACQUES/AUPRES DE MA BLONDE | FRENCH CHILDREN'S CHORUS | 195? | $1.00 | $2.00 | ISSUED WITH DOLLS' CLOTHES? |
| PONY | PY 36 | 7" | 1 | LITTLE LOST PONY | ARTHUR MALVIN | 195? | $2.00 | $4.00 | RHYTHMIC ACTIVITY RECORD |
| PUNKINHEAD | TE 100/101 | 7" | 1 | PUNKINHEAD SONG/STORY | NOT LISTED | 195? | $2.00 | $4.00 | |

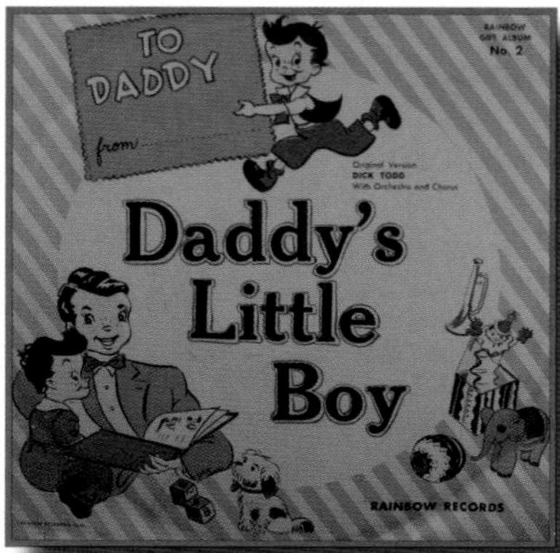


RAINBOW RECORDS
DADDY'S LITTLE BOY
$4.00

RAINBOW RECORDS
HAPPY BIRTHDAY YOUNG MAN
$8.00

RANSOM VALLEY RECORD
THE TINIEST FAIRY
$2.00

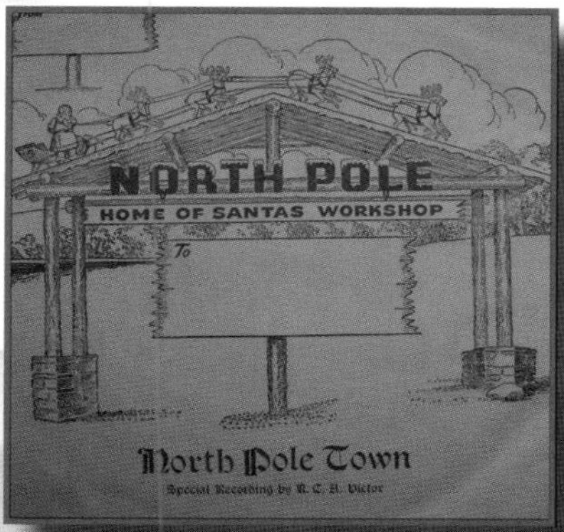


RECORDED PUBLIC RECORDS
NORTH POLE TOWN
$25.00

REDDI WIP
LITTLE JOE THE CHRISTMAS TREE
$10.00

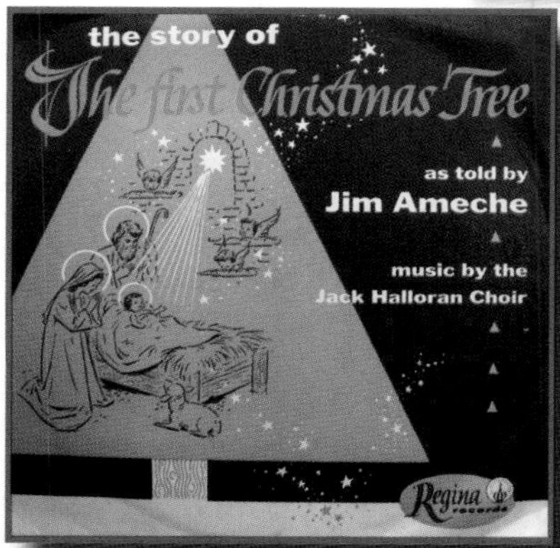


REGINA RECORDS
THE FIRST CHRISTMAS TREE
$2.00

## MISCELLANEOUS SMALL SINGLES, DOUBLES, AND ALBUMS 8" AND SMALLER

| LABEL | DISC # | SIZE | # REC | MAIN TITLE | ARTIST | YEAR | G/VG | EX/NMT | REMARKS |
|---|---|---|---|---|---|---|---|---|---|
| RECORDIO DISK (PD) | NO # | 7" SQ | 1 | (HOME RECORDING CHRISTMAS RECORD GREETING CARD | HOME RECORDING | 194? | $5.00 | $10.00 | |
| RHAPSODY (S/S) | RD-100 | 6" | 1 | JINGLE BELLS (REVERSE SIDE TO BE USED FOR HOME RECORDING) | THE ESQUIRE TRIO | 194? | $40.00 | $80.00 | |
| RHAPSODY (S/S) | RD-200 | 6" | 1 | TEN LITTLE INDIANS (REVERSE SIDE TO BE USED FOR HOME RECORDING) | THE ESQUIRE TRIO | 194? | $40.00 | $80.00 | |
| RHAPSODY (S/S) | RD-300 | 6" | 1 | WHERE OH WHERE HAS MY LITTLE DOG GONE (REVERSE SIDE TO BE USED FOR HOME RECORDING) | THE ESQUIRE TRIO | 194? | $40.00 | $80.00 | |
| SANTA SPEAKING COMPANY | NO # | 6" | 1 | SANTA SPEAKING COMPANY (HOME RECORDING TYPE) | HOME RECORDING | 194? | $2.00 | $4.00 | |
| SCRIPTURE PRESS | SP 101/2-5/6 | 6" | 3 | THE CREATION STORY | MARIE FROST | 1952 | $2.00 | $4.00 | |
| SEE-DISC | 3520 | 6" SQ | 1 | HAPPY BIRTHDAY YOUNG MAN (GREETING CARD RECORD) | NOT LISTED | 1957 | $4.00 | $8.00 | |
| SOMMERFIELD MUSICAL CARD (PD) | NO # | 7" SQ | 1 | SILENT NIGHT, HOLY NIGHT | NOT LISTED | 1948 | $4.00 | $8.00 | |
| SOUND PACKAGING (S/S) | NO # | 5" | 1 | THE BUNNY PARADE [PROBABLY A PACKAGE INSERT] | NOT LISTED | 195? | $10.00 | $20.00 | |

RHAPSODY RECORDS
WHERE OH WHERE HAS MY LITTLE DOG GONE
$80.00

RICHARD RAILTON CO.
THE BIRDCALL GAME
$15.00

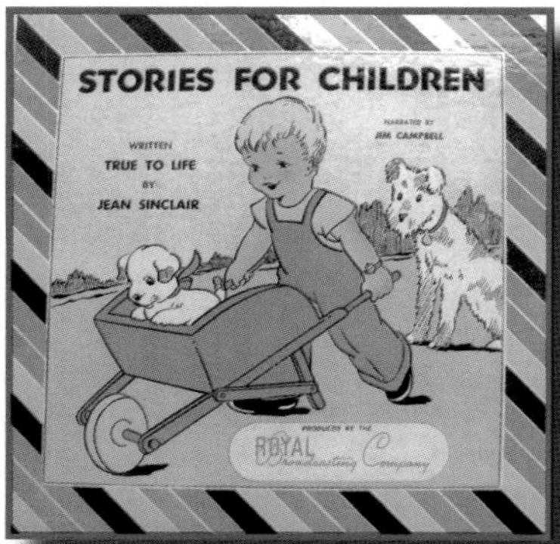


ROYAL BROADCAST CO.
STORIES FOR CHILDREN
$20.00

SALLY TOBIN DIETRICH
RHYTHMIC PLAY
$4.00

SHEERA RECORDING CO.
THE HOLIDAY OF FREEDOM
$4.00

SOUND PACKAGING CORP.
THE BUNNY PARADE
$20.00

## MISCELLANEOUS SMALL SINGLES DOUBLES AND ALBUMS 8" AND SMALLER

| LABEL | DISC # | SIZE | # REC | MAIN TITLE | ARTIST | YEAR | G/VG | EX/NMT | REMARKS |
|---|---|---|---|---|---|---|---|---|---|
| SPEC-TOYS (PD) S/S | SPEC-BUG | 4" | 1 | 101ST. CAVALRY FIGHTING BLUE DEVILS BUGLE CALLS (RIN TIN TIN) | NOT LISTED | 1956 | $10.00 | $20.00 | CARDBOARD RECORD PUNCH-OUT FROM BACKING, IN PLASTIC BAG WITH TOYS |
| SPINNER (BOXED SET) | 99-1001 - 1008 | 7" | 8 | OL MACDONALD'S CHICKEN YARD, ETC. | ARTHUR CARNEY, ETC. | 195? | $5.00 | $10.00 | BOXED SET OF AT LEAST 7, PROBABLY 8 RECORDS. |
| SUPER RECORDINGS | SR 878 (8781 - 8) | 7" | 8 | AUNT THERESA'S STORIES: JESUS BORN IN A MANGER, ETC. | THERESA WORMAN | 195? | $4.00 | $8.00 | |
| TOOTSIE TOY (DICKIE BIRD RECORD) | F1 | 7" | 1 | WILD BIRD CALLS | AUTHENTIC BIRD CALLS | 195? | $3.00 | $6.00 | |
| TWIN TUNES | 107 | 7" | 1 | PONY-BOY, RED RIVER VALLEY/HOME ON THE RANGE | JACK RUSSELL | 194? | $1.00 | $2.00 | RECORD IS FROM THE SPEAR SERIES |
| VISITONE (PD) | C 1/2 - 5/6 | 7" | 3 | A FAMILY THAT PRAYS TOGETHER STAYS TOGETHER: IMMACULATE MARY, ETC. | PAULIST CHORISTERS, BRIA SULLIVAN | 1950 | $40.00 | $80.00 | 3 RECORDS IN TRI-FOLD GATEFOLD |
| WAGNER RESEARCH GROUP (QUASI PD) | NO # | 6" | 1 | SANTA GRAM FOR...(ONE-SIDED PLAYING) (PERSONALIZED GREETING CARD) | NOT LISTED | 1952 | $10.00 | $20.00 | WITH MAILER |

SPEC-TOYS
101ST CAVALRY FIGHTING BLUE DEVILS BUGLE CALLS
$80.00

SPINNER RECORDS
OLD MACDONALD'S FARM ANIMALS
$10.00

SPIRE RECORDS
SIX STORIES FROM THE BIBLE
$4.00

THE STORY PRINCESS
ELVES AND THE SHOEMAKER
$6.00

SUSAN'S SHOW (CBS)
THE SUSAN SONG
$10.00

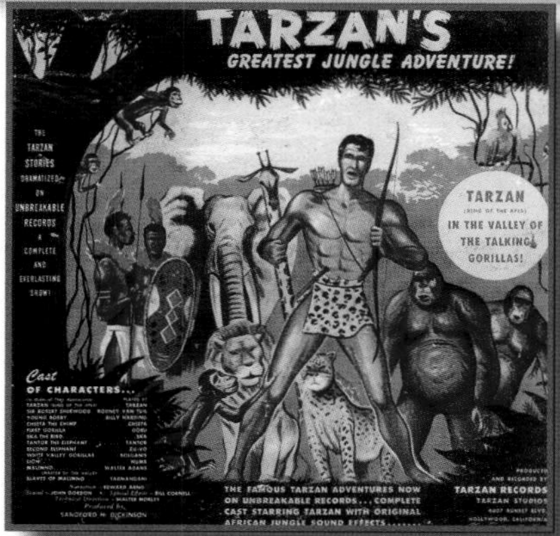


TARZAN RECORDS
TARZAN IN THE VALLEY OF THE TALKING GORILLAS
$100.00

## MISCELLANEOUS PREMIUMS, PROMOTIONS, PACKAGE DESIGN 9", 10", 12"

| LABEL | DISC # | SIZE | # REC | MAIN TITLE | ARTIST | YEAR | G/VG | EX/NMT |
|---|---|---|---|---|---|---|---|---|
| ADAMS COTTAGE CHEESE | 1 | 5" | 1 | MARY HAD A LITTLE LAMB/SING A SONG OF SIXPENCE | NOT LISTED | 195? | $1.00 | $2.00 |
| ADAMS COTTAGE CHEESE | 2 | 5" | 1 | I LOVE SIXPENCE/SIMPLE SIMON | NOT LISTED | 195? | $1.00 | $2.00 |
| BORDEN'S COTTAGE CHEESE (PD) S/S | NO # | 4" | 1 | BLUETAIL FLY, PUSSY IN THE WELL | NOT LISTED | 195? | $5.00 | $10.00 |
| BORDEN'S COTTAGE CHEESE (PD) S/S | NO # | 4" | 1 | FARMER IN THE DELL, THREE BLIND MICE | NOT LISTED | 195? | $5.00 | $10.00 |
| BORDEN'S COTTAGE CHEESE (PD) S/S | NO # | 4" | 1 | TWINKLE, TWINKLE, TEN LITTLE INDIANS | NOT LISTED | 195? | $5.00 | $10.00 |
| BOSCO CHOCOLATE SYRUP | 58-XY-225 | 7" | 1 | TOM THUMB | RUSS TAMBLYN | 1958 | $5.00 | $10.00 |
| BROWN SHOE COMPANY (S/S) | PM-5141-2J | 5" SQ | 1 | MARCHING SONG | CAPTAIN KANGAROO | 195? | $8.00 | $15.00 |
| BUTLER BROS. (PD) | NO # | 6" | 1 | WANT TO HEAR WHAT SANTA & I TALKED ABOUT AT... | NOT LISTED | 195? | $2.00 | $4.00 |
| CROSLEY APPLIANCES | 28564/5 | 7" | 1 | THE MAKE BELIEVE HOUSE: AN ADVENTURE IN NURSERY RHYME LAND | IREENE WICKER | 1950 | $5.00 | $10.00 |
| CURTISS CANDY (PD) | NO # | 3 X 5" | 1 | THE MUSICAL ALPHABET | KUKLA, FRAN AND OLLIE | 1955 | $15.00 | $30.00 |
| CURTISS CANDY (PD) | NO # | 3 X 5" | 1 | SLEEP BABY SLEEP | KUKLA, FRAN AND OLLIE | 1955 | $15.00 | $30.00 |
| CURTISS CANDY (PD) | NO # | 3 X 5" | 1 | UP ON THE HOUSETOP | KUKLA, FRAN AND OLLIE | 1955 | $15.00 | $30.00 |
| DELTA C&S AIRLINES | RR-21686/7 | 7" | 1 | LET'S PLAY PILOT ON THE SPEEDY CONVAIR 340/LET'S PLAY STEWARDESS | NOT LISTED | 195? | $12.00 | $25.00 |
| E-Z POP | F8NS-261 3" X 5" | 6" | 1 | WOMAN WHO LIVED IN A SHOE/MAN! THAT'S REAL BOPCORN! | NOT LISTED | 195? | $5.00 | $10.00 |

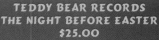

TEDDY BEAR RECORDS
THE NIGHT BEFORE EASTER
$25.00

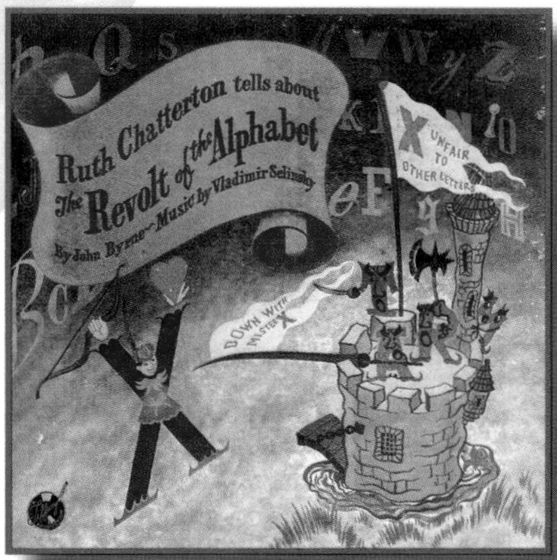


TIFFANY RECORDS
THE REVOLT OF THE ALPHABET
$30.00

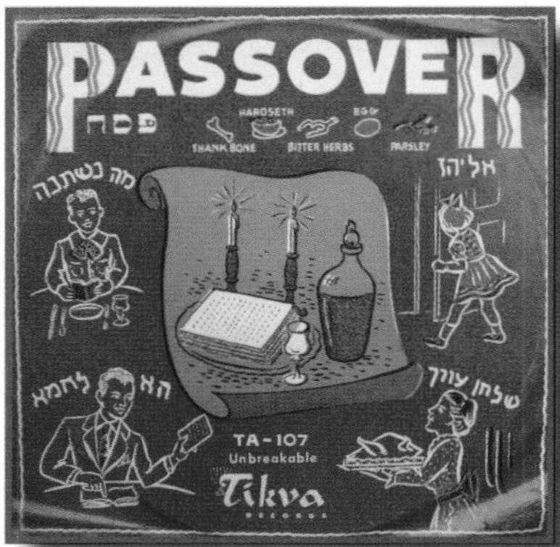


TIKVA RECORDS
PASSOVER
$8.00

TOM THUMB RECORDS
BINGO THE EASTER BUNNY
$6.00

TUTOR THAT NEVER TIRES
THE SINGING CLOCK
$25.00

TRU TONE RECORDS
SONGS CHILDREN LOVE TO SING
$4.00

## MISCELLANEOUS PREMIUMS, PROMOTIONS, PACKAGE DESIGN 9", 10", 12"

| LABEL | DISC # | SIZE | # REC | MAIN TITLE | ARTIST | YEAR | G/VG | EX/ NMT | REMARKS |
|---|---|---|---|---|---|---|---|---|---|
| FRENCH'S | 765-1475 | 6" | 1 | THE PARAKEET CIRCUS/THE PARAKEET CLOWN | FRANK KNIGHT, THE SATISFIERS | 195? | $3.00 | $6.00 | |
| GOOD LUCK CLOVER | ? | 6" | 1 | HOW TO WIN | PHIL RIZZUTO | 195? | $8.00 | $15.00 | |
| KELLOGG'S CORN FLAKES (PD) | NO # | 7" | 1 | I'M CHIQUITA BANANA.../ HERE'S CHIQUITA'S MESSAGE FOR YOU | NOT LISTED | 194? | $12.00 | $25.00 | |
| MINNESOTA VALLEY CANNING CO.(GREEN GIANT) | 12546/7 | 7" | 1 | FO FUM FI FEE, NEW HAPPY BIRTHDAY SONG/HAPPY BIRTHDAY SONG | FRED WARING & THE PENNSYLVANIANS | 1949 | $8.00 | $15.00 | WITH MAILER |
| MINUTE MAID (PD) S/S | "LINDA" | 5" | 1 | HOW WE CAPTURED THE LION AT SUPER CIRCUS (INDIVIDUALIZED PERSONAL RECORDING) | CLIFFY THE CLOWN | 195? | $7.00 | $15.00 | |
| NATIONAL MASK & PUPPET CORP. | NO # | 6" | 1 | DANNY O'DAY (VENTRILOQUIST SKETCH) | JIMMY NELSON | 195? | $5.00 | $10.00 | VALUES ARE FOR LOOSE RECORD, GIVEN AWAY AT TEXACO WITH A VENTRILOQUIST DUMMY. |
| NATIONAL MASK & PUPPET CORP. | NO # | 6" | 1 | PUPPET SHOW | DEAN MARTIN, JERRY LEWIS | 195? | $5.00 | $10.00 | |
| NEW HAVEN RR (PD POST CARD) S/S | MP-1559 | 3" X 5" | 1 | TO THE ZOO (BRONX ZOO PROMOTION) | NOT LISTED | 195? | $10.00 | $20.00 | |

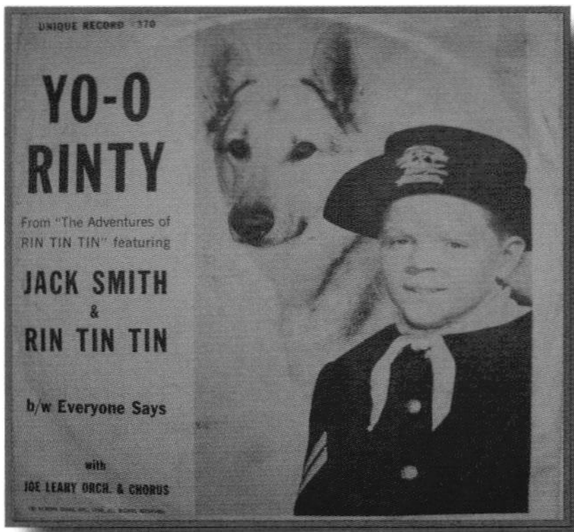


UNIQUE RECORDS
YO-O RINTY
$80.00

VISUAL RECORDS
SAINTS AND SANCTITY
$4.00

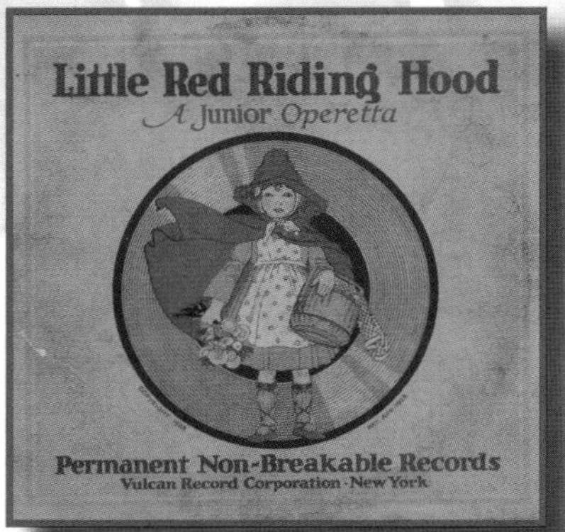


VULCAN RECORDS
LITTLE RED RIDING HOOD
$50.00

WAGNER RESEARCH GROUP
SANTA 10 RULES...
$20.00

YIDDISH KINDER RECORD CO.
SONGS FOR JEWISH CHILDREN
$15.00

ZODIAC RECORDS
FUN WITH FRENCH
$6.00

## MISCELLANEOUS PREMIUMS, PROMOTIONS, PACKAGE DESIGN 9", 10", 12"

| LABEL | DISC # | SIZE | # REC | MAIN TITLE | ARTIST | YEAR | G/VG | EX/ NMT | REMARKS |
|---|---|---|---|---|---|---|---|---|---|
| PETER PAN PEANUT BUTTER | DF100 | 7" | 1 | GREEN GROW THE LILACS/ THE BALLAD OF DAVY CROCKETT | THE SANDPIPERS, MITCH MILLER ORCH. | 1955 | $10.00 | $20.00 | WITH MAILER |
| PETERSON SCHAFER AGENCY | ? | 7" | 1 | TALES FROM THE DIAMOND K | KEN MAYNARD & TARZAN | 195? | $5.00 | $10.00 | |
| POLL PARROT SHOES | ? | 7" | 1 | LADY SKYHOOK STORIES | RICKY & THE MELON FAMILY | 195? | $5.00 | $10.00 | |
| REDDI WIP | NO # | 7" | 1 | LITTLE JOE THE CHRISTMAS TREE | JIMMY WELDON, WEBSTER WEB-FOOT | 195? | $5.00 | $10.00 | |
| SCHLITZ BREWING CO. | LST 10077/8 | 6" | 1 | MERRY CHRISTMAS: WINTER WONDERLAND/SILENT NIGHT | THE COMBINED SCHLITZ CHORUSES | 1951? | $2.00 | $4.00 | |
| SPALDING (PD) | NO # | 5" SQ | 1 | HOW TO FIELD: ALVIN DARK | ALVIN DARK | 195? | $15.00 | $30.00 | |
| SPALDING (PD) | NO # | 5" SQ | 1 | HOW TO HIT: YOGI BERRA | YOGI BERRA | 195? | $15.00 | $30.00 | |
| SPALDING (PD) | NO # | 5" SQ | 1 | HOW TO PITCH: ? | ? | 195? | $15.00 | $30.00 | |
| SUSAN'S SHOW (CBS-TV) S/S | PM 7185 | 7" SQ | 1 | THE SUSAN SONG | NOT LISTED | 195? | $5.00 | $10.00 | CAME WITH A "CINDERELLA" DRESS |
| THOMPSON'S DAIRY | NO # | 7" | 1 | TILLIE 'N DINK IN SQUARE LAND (HAPPY BIRTHDAY TO__) | ALLAN CUMMINGS, ETC. | 195? | $2.00 | $4.00 | PERSONALIZED HAPPY BIRTHDAY RECORD |
| WALL'S ICE CREAM (PD) | NO # | ? | 1 | SING A SONG OF WALL'S ICE CREAM | UNCLE ? | 194? | $8.00 | $15.00 | |
| WILLY'S MOTORS, INC. | ? | 7" SQ | 1 | MAVERICK | JAMES GARNER | 195? | $10.00 | $20.00 | |

# more great TITLES from collector books

## DOLLS

6315 **American Character Dolls**, Izen ........ $24.95
2079 **Barbie Doll** Fashion, Volume I, Eames ........ $24.95
4846 **Barbie Doll** Fashion, Volume II, Eames ........ $24.95
6319 **Barbie Doll** Fashion, Volume III, Eames ........ $29.95
6546 Collector's Ency. of **Barbie** Doll Collector's Editions, Augustyniak ........ $29.95
6546 Collector's Ency. of **Barbie** Doll Exclusives & More, 3rd Ed., Augustyniak ........ $29.95
6920 Collector's Encyclopedia of American **Composition Dolls**, Volume I, Mertz ........ $29.95
6451 Collector's Encyclopedia of American **Composition Dolls**, Volume II, Mertz ........ $29.95
6636 Collector's Encyclopedia of **Madame Alexander Dolls**, Crowsey ........ $24.95
5904 Collector's Guide to **Celebrity Dolls**, Spurgeon ........ $24.95
6456 Collector's Guide to **Dolls of the 1960s and 1970s**, Volume II, Sabulis ........ $24.95
6944 The Complete Guide to **Shirley Temple** Dolls and Collectibles, Bervaldi-Camaratta ........ $29.95
7028 **Doll Values**, Antique to Modern, 9th Edition, Edward ........ $14.95
6467 **Paper Dolls** of the 1960s, 1970s, and 1980s, Nichols ........ $24.95
6642 20th Century **Paper Dolls**, Young ........ $19.95

## TOYS & MARBLES

2333 Antique & Collectible **Marbles**, 3rd Edition, Grist ........ $9.95
6649 Big Book of **Toy Airplanes**, Miller ........ $24.95
6938 Everett Grist's Big Book of **Marbles**, 3rd Edition ........ $24.95
6633 **Hot Wheels**, The Ultimate Redline Guide, 2nd Ed., Clark/Wicker ........ $29.95
6466 **Matchbox Toys**, 1947 to 2003, 4th Edition, Johnson ........ $24.95
6840 **Schroeder's Collectible Toys**, Antique to Modern Price Guide, 10th Ed. ........ $17.95
6638 The Other **Matchbox Toys**, 1947 to 2004, Johnson ........ $19.95
6650 **Toy Car** Collector's Guide, 2nd Edition, Johnson ........ $24.95

## JEWELRY, WATCHES & PURSES

4704 Antique & Collectible **Buttons**, Wisniewski ........ $19.95
4850 Collectible **Costume Jewelry**, Simonds ........ $24.95
5675 Collectible **Silver Jewelry**, Rezazadeh ........ $24.95
6468 Collector's Ency. of Pocket & Pendant **Watches**, 1500 – 1950, Bell ........ $24.95
6554 **Coro Jewelry**, Brown ........ $29.95
6453 **Costume Jewelry** 101, Carroll ........ $24.95
7025 **Costume Jewelry** 202, Carroll ........ $24.95
4940 **Costume Jewelry**, A Practical Handbook & Value Guide, Rezazadeh ........ $24.95
6027 The **Estée Lauder** Solid Perfume Compact Collection, Gerson ........ $24.95
5812 Fifty Years of Collectible **Fashion Jewelry**, 1925 – 1975, Baker ........ $24.95
6330 **Handkerchiefs**: A Collector's Guide, Guarnaccia/Guggenheim ........ $24.95
6833 **Handkerchiefs**: A Collector's Guide, Volume II, Guarnaccia/Guggenheim ........ $24.95
6464 Inside the **Jewelry** Box, Pitman ........ $24.95
5695 **Ladies' Vintage Accessories**, Johnson ........ $24.95
1181 100 Years of Collectible **Jewelry**, 1850 – 1950, Baker ........ $9.95
6645 100 Years of **Purses**, 1880s to 1980s, Aikins ........ $24.95
6942 **Rhinestone Jewelry**: Figurals, Animals, and Whimsicals, Brown ........ $24.95
6039 Signed Beauties of **Costume Jewelry**, Brown ........ $24.95
6341 Signed Beauties of **Costume Jewelry**, Volume II, Brown ........ $24.95
6555 20th Century **Costume Jewelry**, Aikins ........ $24.95
5620 Unsigned Beauties of **Costume Jewelry**, Brown ........ $24.95
4878 Vintage & Contemporary **Purse Accessories**, Gerson ........ $24.95

## ARTIFACTS, GUNS, KNIVES, & TOOLS

1868 Antique **Tools**, Our American Heritage, McNerney ........ $9.95
6822 **Antler, Bone & Shell** Artifacts, Hothem ........ $24.95
1426 **Arrowheads & Projectile Points**, Hothem ........ $7.95
5685 **Indian Artifacts** of the Midwest, Book IV, Hothem ........ $19.95
6231 **Indian Artifacts** of the Midwest, Book V, Hothem ........ $24.95
7037 **Modern Guns**, Identification & Values, 16th Ed., Quertermous ........ $16.95
7034 **Ornamental Indian Artifacts**, Hothem ........ $34.95
6567 **Paleo-Indian Artifacts**, Hothem ........ $29.95
6569 **Remington Knives**, Past & Present, Stewart/Ritchie ........ $16.95
7035 Standard **Knife** Collector's Guide, 5th Edition, Ritchie/Stewart ........ $16.95

## PAPER COLLECTIBLES & BOOKS

6623 Collecting **American Paintings**, James ........ $29.95
7039 Collecting **Playing Cards**, Pickvet ........ $24.95
6826 Collecting Vintage **Children's Greeting Cards**, McPherson ........ $24.95
6553 Collector's Guide to **Cookbooks**, Daniels ........ $24.95
1441 Collector's Guide to **Post Cards**, Wood ........ $9.95
6627 Early 20th Century **Hand-Painted Photography**, Ivankovich ........ $24.95
6936 **Leather Bound Books**, Boutiette ........ $24.95
7036 **Old Magazine Advertisements**, 1890 – 1950, Clear ........ $24.95
6940 **Old Magazines**, 2nd Edition, Clear ........ $19.95
3973 **Sheet Music** Reference & Price Guide, 2nd Ed., Pafik/Guiheen ........ $19.95
6837 Vintage **Postcards** for the Holidays, 2nd Edition, Reed ........ $24.95

## GLASSWARE

6930 Anchor Hocking's **Fire-King** & More, 3rd Ed., Florence ........ $24.95
6821 Coll. **Glassware from the 40s, 50s & 60s**, 8th Edition, Florence ........ $19.95
6921 Collector's Encyclopedia of **American Art Glass**, 2nd Edition, Shuman ........ $29.95
6830 Collector's Encyclopedia of **Depression Glass**, 17th Ed., Florence ........ $19.95
3905 Collector's Encyclopedia of **Milk Glass**, Newbound ........ $24.95
7026 Colors in **Cambridge Glass** II, Natl. Cambridge Collectors, Inc. ........ $29.95
7029 **Elegant Glassware** of the Depression Era, 12th Edition, Florence ........ $24.95
6334 Encyclopedia of **Paden City Glass**, Domitz ........ $29.95
3981 Evers' Standard **Cut Glass** Value Guide ........ $12.95
6126 **Fenton Art Glass**, 1907 – 1939, 2nd Ed., Whitmyer ........ $29.95
6628 **Fenton Glass** Made for Other Companies, Domitz ........ $29.95
7030 **Fenton Glass** Made for Other Companies, Volume II, Domitz ........ $29.95
6462 Florences' **Glass Kitchen Shakers**, 1930 – 1950s ........ $19.95
5042 Florences' **Glassware Pattern Identification** Guide, Vol. I ........ $18.95
5615 Florences' **Glassware Pattern Identification** Guide, Vol. II ........ $19.95
6142 Florences' **Glassware Pattern Identification** Guide, Vol. III ........ $19.95
6643 Florences' **Glassware Pattern Identification** Guide, Vol. IV ........ $19.95

**1.800.626.5420** Mon. – Fri. 7 am – 5 pm CT **Fax: 1.270.898.8890**

6641 Florences' **Ovenware** from the 1920s to the Present ........ $24.95
6226 **Fostoria** Value Guide, Long/Seate ........ $19.95
6127 The **Glass Candlestick** Book, Volume 1, Akro Agate to Fenton, Felt/Stoer ... $24.95
6228 The **Glass Candlestick** Book, Volume 2, Fostoria to Jefferson, Felt/Stoer .... $24.95
6461 The **Glass Candlestick** Book, Volume 3, Kanawha to Wright, Felt/Stoer ...... $29.95
6648 Glass **Toothpick Holders**, 2nd Edition, Bredehoft/Sanford ........ $29.95
5827 **Kitchen Glassware** of the Depression Years, 6th Edition, Florence ........ $24.95
6133 **Mt. Washington Art Glass**, Sisk ........ $49.95
7027 Pocket Guide to **Depression Glass** & More, 15th Edition, Florence ........ $12.95
6925 Standard Encyclopedia of **Carnival Glass**, 10th Ed., Edwards/Carwile ........ $29.95
6926 Standard **Carnival Glass** Price Guide, 15th Ed., Edwards/Carwile ........ $9.95
6566 Standard Encyclopedia of **Opalescent Glass**, 5th Ed., Edwards/Carwile ...... $29.95
6644 Standard Encyclopedia of **Pressed Glass**, 4th Ed., Edwards/Carwile ........ $29.95
6476 **Westmoreland Glass**, The Popular Years, 1940 – 1985, Kovar ........ $29.95

## POTTERY

6922 **American Art Pottery**, 2nd Edition, Sigafoose ........ $24.95
5529 Collectible **Cups & Saucers**, Book II, Harran ........ $19.95
6326 Collectible **Cups & Saucers**, Book III, Harran ........ $24.95
6331 Collecting **Head Vases**, Barron ........ $24.95
6943 Collecting **Royal Copley**, Devine ........ $19.95
6621 Collector's Encyclopedia of **American Dinnerware**, 2nd Ed., Cunningham ... $29.95
5034 Collector's Encyclopedia of **California Pottery**, 2nd Ed., Chipman ........ $24.95
6629 Collector's Encyclopedia of **Fiesta**, 10th Ed., Huxford ........ $24.95
3431 Collector's Encyclopedia of **Homer Laughlin China**, Jasper ........ $24.95
1276 Collector's Encyclopedia of **Hull Pottery**, Roberts ........ $19.95
5609 Collector's Encyclopedia of **Limoges Porcelain**, 3rd Ed., Gaston ........ $29.95
6637 Collector's Encyclopedia of **Made in Japan Ceramics**, First Ed., White ........ $24.95
5677 Collector's Encyclopedia of **Niloak**, 2nd Edition, Gifford ........ $29.95
5841 Collector's Encyclopedia of **Roseville Pottery**, Vol. 1, Huxford/Nickel ........ $24.95
5842 Collector's Encyclopedia of **Roseville Pottery**, Vol. 2, Huxford/Nickel ........ $24.95
6646 Collector's Ency. of **Stangl Artware, Lamps, and Birds**, 2nd Ed., Runge ..... $29.95
3314 Collector's Encyclopedia of **Van Briggle Art Pottery**, Sasicki ........ $24.95
6634 Collector's Ultimate Ency. of **Hull Pottery**, Volume 1, Roberts ........ $29.95
6829 The Complete Guide to **Corning Ware & Visions Cookware**, Coroneos ........ $19.95
5918 Florences' Big Book of **Salt & Pepper Shakers** ........ $24.95
6320 Gaston's **Blue Willow**, 3rd Edition ........ $19.95
6630 Gaston's **Flow Blue China**, The Comprehensive Guide ........ $29.95
7021 Hansons' American Art Pottery Collection ........ $29.95
7032 **Head Vases**, 2nd Edition, Cole ........ $24.95
2379 Lehner's Ency. of **U.S. Marks** on Pottery, Porcelain & China ........ $24.95
4722 **McCoy Pottery** Collector's Reference & Value Guide, Hanson/Nissen ........ $19.95
5913 **McCoy Pottery**, Volume III, Hanson/Nissen ........ $24.95
6835 **Meissen** Porcelain, Harran ........ $29.95
6929 The Official **Precious Moments**® Collector's Guide to Figurines, 2nd Ed., Bomm .. $19.95
6335 Pictorial Guide to **Pottery & Porcelain Marks**, Lage ........ $29.95
1440 **Red Wing Stoneware**, DePasquale/Peck/Peterson ........ $9.95
6838 **R.S. Prussia** & More, McCaslin ........ $29.95

3738 **Shawnee Pottery**, Mangus ........ $24.95
6945 **TV Lamps** to Light the World, Shuman ........ $29.95
7043 **Uhl Pottery**, 2nd Edition, Feldmeyer/Holtzman ........ $16.95
6828 The Ultimate Collector's Encyclopedia of **Cookie Jars**, Roerig ........ $29.95
6640 Van Patten's ABC's of Collecting **Nippon Porcelain** ........ $29.95

## OTHER COLLECTIBLES

6446 Antique & Contemporary **Advertising Memorabilia**, 2nd Edition, Summers .... $29.95
6935 Antique **Golf Collectibles**, Georgiady ........ $29.95
1880 Antique **Iron**, McNerney ........ $9.95
6622 The Art of American **Game Calls**, Lewis ........ $24.95
6551 The Big Book of **Cigarette Lighters**, Flanagan ........ $29.95
7024 B.J. Summers' Guide to **Coca-Cola**, 6th Edition ........ $29.95
1128 **Bottle** Pricing Guide, 3rd Ed., Cleveland ........ $7.95
6924 Captain John's **Fishing Tackle** Price Guide, 2nd Edition, Kolbeck ........ $24.95
6342 Collectible **Soda Pop** Memorabilia, Summers ........ $24.95
6625 Collector's Encyclopedia of **Bookends**, Kuritzky/De Costa ........ $29.95
5666 Collector's Encyclopedia of **Granite Ware**, Book 2, Greguire ........ $29.95
6928 Early **American Furniture**, Obbard ........ $19.95
7042 The Ency. of Early American & Antique **Sewing Machines**, 3rd Ed., Bays ...... $29.95
6561 Field Guide to **Fishing Lures**, Lewis ........ $16.95
7031 **Fishing Lure** Collectibles, An Ency. of the Early Years, Murphy/Edmisten ..... $29.95
6932 **Flea Market Trader**, 15th Edition ........ $12.95
6458 **Fountain Pens**, Past & Present, 2nd Edition, Erano ........ $24.95
6933 **Garage Sale** & Flea Market Annual, 14th Edition ........ $19.95
3906 **Heywood-Wakefield** Modern Furniture, Rouland ........ $18.95
7033 **Hot Kitchen** & Home Collectibles of the 30s, 40s, and 50s, Zweig ........ $24.95
2216 **Kitchen Antiques**, 1790 – 1940, McNerney ........ $14.95
7038 The Marketplace Guide to **Oak Furniture**, 2nd Edition, Blundell ........ $29.95
6639 **McDonald's Drinkware**, Kelly ........ $24.95
6939 Modern Collectible **Tins**, 2nd Edition, McPherson ........ $24.95
6028 Modern **Fishing Lure** Collectibles, Volume 1, Lewis ........ $24.95
6131 Modern **Fishing Lure** Collectibles, Volume 2, Lewis ........ $24.95
6564 Modern **Fishing Lure** Collectibles, Volume 3, Lewis ........ $24.95
6832 Modern **Fishing Lure** Collectibles, Volume 4, Lewis ........ $24.95
6322 Pictorial Guide to **Christmas Ornaments** & Collectibles, Johnson ........ $29.95
6842 Raycrafts' **Americana** Price Guide & DVD ........ $19.95
7040 **Schroeder's Antiques** Price Guide, 25th Edition ........ $17.95
6038 **Sewing Tools** & Trinkets, Volume 2, Thompson ........ $24.95
5007 **Silverplated Flatware**, Revised 4th Edition, Hagan ........ $18.95
6647 **Star Wars** Super Collector's Wish Book, 3rd Edition, Carlton ........ $29.95
6827 Summers' Pocket Guide to **Coca-Cola**, 5th Edition ........ $12.95
6632 Value Guide to **Gas Station Memorabilia**, 2nd Ed., Summers/Priddy ........ $29.95
6841 Vintage **Fabrics**, Gridley/Kiplinger/McClure ........ $19.95
6036 Vintage **Quilts**, Aug/Newman/Roy ........ $24.95
6941 The Wonderful World of Collecting **Perfume Bottles**, Flanagan ........ $29.95

This is only a partial listing of the books on antiques that are available from Collector Books. All books are well illustrated and contain current values. Most of these books are available from your local bookseller, antique dealer, or public library. If you are unable to locate certain titles in your area, you may order by mail from COLLECTOR BOOKS, P.O. Box 3009, Paducah, KY 42002-3009. Customers with Visa, MasterCard, or Discover may place orders by fax, by phone, or online. Add $4.00 postage for the first book ordered and 50¢ for each additional book. Include item number, title, and price when ordering. Allow 14 to 21 days for delivery.

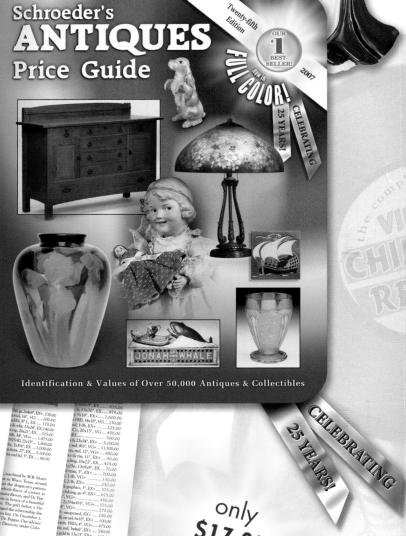

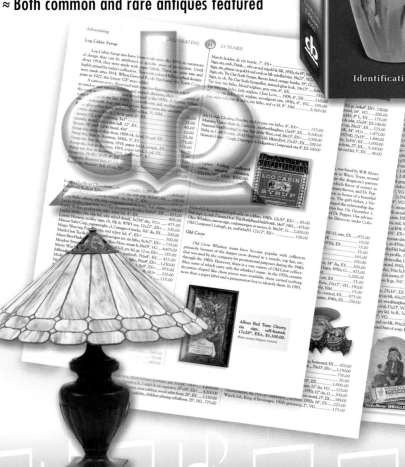